Penguin Books

The Salterton Trilogy

Robertson Davies, novelist, playwright, literary critic and essayist, was born in 1913 in Thamesville, Ontario. He was educated at Queen's University and Balliol College, Oxford. While at Oxford he became interested in the theatre and from 1938 until 1940 he was a teacher and actor at the Old Vic in London; he has subsequently written a number of plays. He returned to Canada in 1940 where he was literary editor of *Saturday Review*, an arts, politics and current affairs journal, until 1942 when he became editor and later publisher of the *Peterborough Examiner*. Several of his books including *The Diary of Samuel Marchbanks* and *The Table Talk of Samuel Marchbanks* had their origins in an editorial column. In 1962 he was appointed Professor of English at the University of Toronto, and in 1963 was appointed the first Master of the University's Massey College. He retired in 1981 but remains Master Emeritus and Professor Emeritus. He holds honorary doctorates from many Canadian universities and has received numerous awards for his work, including the Governor-General's Award for *The Manticore* in 1973. But it is as a writer of fiction that Robertson Davies has achieved international recognition with *The Deptford Trilogy* (Penguin), composed of *Fifth Business, The Manticore* and *World of Wonders*. His other books include *One Half of Robertson Davies, The Enthusiasms of Robertson Davies, Robertson Davies: The Well-Tempered Critic, High Spirits* and *The Rebel Angels* (Penguin). His latest novel, *What's Bred in the Bone*, was shortlisted for the 1986 Booker Prize.

Robertson Davies

The Salterton Trilogy

*

TEMPEST-TOST
LEAVEN OF MALICE
A MIXTURE OF FRAILTIES

Penguin Books

Penguin Books Ltd, Harmondsworth, Middlesex, England
Viking Penguin Inc., 40 West 23rd Street, New York, New York 10010, U.S.A.
Penguin Books Australia Ltd, Ringwood, Victoria, Australia
Penguin Books Canada Limited, 2801 John Street, Markham, Ontario, Canada L3R 1B4
Penguin Books (N.Z.) Ltd, 182–190 Wairau Road, Auckland 10, New Zealand

Tempest-Tost first published in Canada by Clarke, Irwin & Company Limited 1951
First published in Penguin Books 1980

Published by arrangement with Irwin Publishing Inc.

Leaven of Malice first published in Canada by Clarke, Irwin & Company Limited 1954
First published in the United States of America by Charles Scribner's Sons 1955
Published in Penguin Books 1980

Published by arrangement with Irwin Publishing Inc.

A Mixture of Frailties first published in Canada by The Macmillan Company of Canada Limited 1958
First published in the United States of America by Charles Scribner's Sons 1958
First published in Penguin Books in the United States in 1980 by arrangement with
Everest House, Publishers
Published in Penguin Books in Canada 1980

Published in one volume as *The Salterton Trilogy* 1986
Reprinted 1986, 1987

Printed and bound in Great Britain by
Cox & Wyman Ltd, Reading
Filmset in Linotron Palatino by
Rowland Phototypesetting Ltd,
Bury St Edmunds, Suffolk

[CONTENTS]

Tempest-Tost	7
Leaven of Malice	243
A Mixture of Frailties	463

Tempest-Tost

*

I'll drain him dry as hay:
Sleep shall neither night nor day
Hang upon his pent-house lid;
He shall live a man forbid.
Weary se'nnights nine times nine
Shall he dwindle, peak and pine:
Though his bark cannot be lost,
Yet it shall be tempest-tost.

MACBETH I. 3

All characters in this story are imaginary, and no reference is intended to any living person. Readers who think that they can identify the creations of the author's fancy among their own acquaintance are paying the author an extravagant compliment, which he acknowledges with gratitude.

[ONE]

'It's going to be a great nuisance for both of us,' said Freddy. 'Couldn't you make a fuss about it, Tom?'

'If your father said they could use the place, it's no good for me to make a fuss,' said Tom.

'Yes, but Daddy just said that they could use the place in a large, general way. He didn't specially say that they could use this shed. Anyway he only said it because Griselda is probably going to have a big part. It seems to me that I remember him saying that he didn't want them in the house.'

'Now Miss Freddy, you'd better be sure about that. You've got a way of remembering your Dad said just whatever you wanted him to say.'

When Tom called her Miss Freddy she knew that he had temporarily ceased to be a friend and had become that incalculable, treacherous thing, an adult. At fourteen she had no defence against such sudden shifts. People treated her as a child or an equal, whichever suited them at the moment. But she had thought that she could rely on Tom. Still, had Daddy really said that he didn't want the Little Theatre people trampling through his house? She could hear the words spoken in his voice, quite clearly, but had he really said them? Solly had once told her that she interpreted Daddy as priests interpret their gods, for her own ends. This was a moment for discretion. She would achieve little without Tom's help.

'I didn't mean that you should refuse to let them in here, or anything silly like that. I just meant that you could make it rather difficult. You don't want them snooping around in here, poking into all your drawers and using your tools, and getting everything all mixed up. That's just what Larry Pye will do. There won't be a thing left in its place by the time he gets through. You know that, Tom.'

Tom's expression showed that he knew it very well. He didn't want strangers in his workshop, messing about, dulling all his carefully sharpened edges, snarling his tidy coils of twine, using his pruning shears for cutting wire, as like as not. What might not happen if they began nosing into his special pride, the cabinet where all his seeds were kept, labelled and tucked away in tidy brown envelopes? Be just like them, to go rooting into what was none of their business. In his heart he was on Freddy's side, but he wanted to enjoy the luxury of being persuaded. Anyway, he shouldn't give way to a child too easily. Bad for the child's character.

'Maybe I don't want 'em,' he said, slyly; 'but you want 'em even less. I've got my things to keep neat. But I've got nothing to hide.'

'It's beneath you to say a mean thing like that, Tom,' said Freddy.

'Bad enough if they get larkin' around with my seed, but suppose they get hold of those bottles of yours? I don't want anybody poisoned in here, and police on the job, and you put away for anything up to forty years.' Tom guffawed, relishing his flight of fancy.

'Oh, Tom!' Freddy was disgusted. How stupid adults could be! Even a nice man like Tom.

'They'd let you off easy for murdering Larry Pye. But bootlegging! That's where they'd get you. Brewing and distilling, and thereby cheating the Government out of its taxes on alcoholic liquors! That's real crime, Freddy.'

'Tom, I'm not a bootlegger! I'm a scientist, really. I'm only a bootlegger if I offer it for sale. And I give it away. As you certainly ought to know, for I gave you a bottle of my blackberry wine last Christmas, and you drank it and said it was good.'

'And so it was good. But you put quite a bit of your Dad's brandy in that blackberry before you put it down to mature.'

'Of course. All those dessert wines have to be fortified. But it wasn't just the brandy that made it good; it was good wine, and I made it with the greatest care, and I think it's downright miserable of you to make fun of it.'

'I was just coddin' you, Freddy. It was real good wine. But I don't know what your father would say if he knew how much stuff like that you've got hidden away in here.'

'You'll know what he says in a few weeks. His birthday is coming, and I've got a dozen – a whole beautiful dozen – of champagne cider to give him. It's wonderful stuff, Tom. A year old – just right – and if he likes it, I'm going to ask him to let me study in France, and learn everything about wine, and then come back here and revolutionize the wine industry in Canada. He's got a lot of stock in a winery, and he could ask them to give me a job. Just think, Tom, maybe I'll end up as the Veuve Cliquot of Canada!'

'Can't say that I know what that is.'

'It's the name of a woman. "Veuve" means widow. Madame Cliquot's champagne is one of the most famous in the world. She's dead, of course, but her name lives.'

'Well, anything can happen,' said Tom, considering. 'Widow Webster's Wines; that's what yours would have to be called. Sounds like something you'd take for your health. But that's a long way off, Freddy. I'd give it a rest, now, if I was you.'

'I couldn't be Widow Webster if I'd married,' said Freddy, practically; 'I'd be Widow Something Else. Tom, you don't understand how serious I am. I really mean it. I'm not just playing. I really have a very professional attitude about the whole thing. I've read books about wine chemistry, and books about vintages, and everything about wine I can get my hands on. I know I'm young, but I'm not being silly, really I'm not. And if you let me down I don't know what I'll do, for there isn't another soul I can really trust. Griselda wouldn't understand; she hasn't any brains anyway, and when it comes to wine she simply hasn't a clue. And Daddy will have to be shown. Please be a sport, Tom, and don't go all grown-up on me.'

Tom was not the man to withstand such an appeal. He was fifty, he had an excellent wife, he had two sons in the Navy, he was the best gardener within fifty miles, he was a respected member of the Sergeant's Club, and he was bass soloist – unpaid, but highly regarded – in the choir of St Clement's; but age and honours could not change the fact that Freddy – Miss Fredegonde Webster, his employer's younger daughter – was a very special friend of his. As he often said to the wife, Freddy had no mother. But if he was to give in, he'd have to give some advice, as well. That was only fair; if a kid gets her way, she has to take some advice. That is part of the unwritten code which governs the dealings between generations.

'Well, Freddy,' he said, speaking her name on the low D which was so much admired at St Clement's, 'I know you're serious, right enough, but you've got to remember that you're only fourteen, and if most people knew what you was up to, they'd be shocked. They'd never believe that you could make it and not drink it. Now wait a minute; I know you just test it, because you've got to keep your palate sharp. I know you just gargle it and spit it out and smack your lips like the real wine-tasters. But they'd never believe it. They'd misunderstand. I've seen a good deal of life and a good deal of war, and I tell you, Freddy, it's a shocker how people can be misunderstood. I'll say nothing, but you be careful. You've got to keep your nose clean, as they say. If your Dad found out, and knew I knew, it'd be as good as my position is worth. And I don't want to leave this garden because you've been found tight under a lilac and I'm an accomplice. See?'

Tom was a Welshman, and the native taste for preaching was plainly strong within him this afternoon, so Freddy struck in hastily.

'Oh yes, Tom dear, I do see, and I'll be very discreet. And I do think you're being simply marvellous and big-souled about the whole thing. And I won't take to drink; I swear I won't. That isn't what interests me in wine at all. I'm really very professional. I'll say special prayers against the temptation.'

This was not a happy inspiration. Freddy had, within the last year, become rather High Church in her views; St Clement's was Broad, with a tendency to become Low under stress. Tom took breath for another lecture, but Freddy hurried on.

'It won't be a secret from Daddy after his birthday, you see. I'll give him the champagne cider, and explain everything, and I'm sure it will be all right from then on. He might even let me set up a little lab in the house – maybe even a tiny still –'

'I can see your Dad letting his daughter set up a still in his house,' said Tom, using his low D again to achieve an effect of irony. But Freddy was not to be checked. She liked to talk as well as he.

'It's sure to be a success. It's good; I can see that. Not a hint of acetification or rope to be seen in a single bottle of the dozen. I took care of sediment before I bottled. And I bottled just at the psychological moment. I bet if Veuve Cliquot had been there she would have been pleased. And now it's been ten months in bottle and should be quite fit to drink. Of course another year would do no harm, but it's ready now.'

'I shouldn't think your Dad was just the man for cider,' said Tom.

'But it isn't just old common cider. It's champagne cider. And Morgan O'Doherty says in *Life through the Neck of a Bottle* that he has tasted champagne ciders which were superior to all but the finest champagnes! And you know that ache Daddy gets in his back on cold days? Well, the doctor says it's just an ache, but I suspect it's gravel.

And do you know what's the very best thing for gravel? Cider! It says so in the *Encyclopaedia Britannica*. It says, "The malic acid of cider is regarded as a powerful diuretic which stimulates the kidneys and prevents the accumulation of uric acid within the system."'

'I told you it was medicine,' said Tom, who was not a man to let a joke perish half-savoured. 'Try the Widow Websters Wines for what ails you.'

'Tom,' said Freddy, in a cold voice, 'was your Christmas bottle of my blackberry like medicine? Your wife told me she didn't know where you got it, but that you never let it alone till it was all gone, and you sang Gounod's *Nazareth* four times without stopping and embarrassed her before company. Let's not hear quite so much about the Widow Webster.'

Tom did not receive this well. But Freddy had reached an age where she no longer felt called upon to submit without protest to the impudence of her elders, even in the case of such a valued friend and ally as Tom. There was a silence, during which Tom continued to do mysterious things with some wilted bits of green stuff which he called 'slips'. Freddy, having made her point, was willing to risk a snub by starting up the conversation again.

'Do you think we can keep them out of here?'

'We can try.'

'Daddy said they could do their play in the garden. They don't really have to come in here.'

'My experience with people who do plays is they have to go everyplace that isn't locked and they have to move everything that isn't fastened down,' said Tom, with bitterness. 'This'll be the nearest place for them to get their electric power from, and they'll have a lot of tack they'll want to store here between practices and the like. What your Dad said to me was, "Give 'em whatever help they need, and if it gets past bearing, come to me." Well, I can't go to him first off and say I don't want 'em to use the workshop and toolshed. That'd mean they have to use the garage or part of the cellar, and he won't want that. They mustn't get into the house. That is, unless we all want a row with them Laplanders.'

Tom's grammar was variable. Speaking officially to his employer, it was careful. But for emphasis he relapsed into forms which he found easier and more eloquent. He never spoke of the admirable Swedish couple who headed the indoor staff except as 'them Laplanders'.

'But we'll do our best, won't we?'

'Yes, Freddy, but I got a hunch that our best isn't going to be good enough.'

And with that Freddy had to be content.

In her daydreams Freddy sometimes fancied that her native city would be known to history chiefly as her birthplace, and this as much as anything shows the extent of her ambition. Salterton had seen more of history than most Canadian cities, and its tranquillity was not easily disturbed. Like Quebec and Halifax, it is a city which provides unusual opportunities for gush, for it has abundant superficial charm. But the real character of Salterton is beneath the surface, and beyond the powers of gush to disclose.

People who do not know Salterton repeat a number of half-truths about it. They call it dreamy and old-world; they say that it is at anchor in the stream of time. They say that it is still regretful for those few years when it appeared that Salterton would be the capital of Canada. They say that it is the place where Anglican clergymen go when they die. And, sooner or later, they speak of it as 'quaint'.

It is not hard to discover why the word 'quaint' is so often applied to Salterton by the unthinking or the imperceptive; people or cities who follow their own bent without much regard for what the world thinks are frequently so described; there is an implied patronage about the word. But the people who call Salterton 'quaint' are not the real Saltertonians, who know that there is nothing quaint – in the sense of the word which means wilfully eccentric – about the place. Salterton is itself. It seems quaint to those whose own personalities are not strongly marked and whose intellects are infrequently replenished.

Though not a large place it is truly describable as a city. That word is now used of any large settlement, and Salterton is big enough to qualify; but a city used to be the seat of a bishop, and Salterton was a city in that sense long before it became one in the latter. It is, indeed, the seat of two bishoprics, one Anglican and one Roman Catholic. As one approaches it from the water the two cathedrals, which are in appearance so strongly characteristic of the faiths they embody, seem to admonish the city. The Catholic cathedral points a vehement and ornate Gothic finger toward Heaven; the Anglican cathedral has a dome which, with offhand Anglican suavity, does the same thing. St Michael's cries, 'Look aloft and pray!'; St Nicholas' says, 'If I may trouble you, it might be as well to lift your eyes in this direction.' The manner is different; the import is the same.

In the environs of the cathedrals the things of this world are not neglected. Salterton is an excellent commercial city, and far enough from other large centres of trade to have gained, and kept, a good opinion of itself. To name all its industries here would be merely dull, but they are many and important. However, they do not completely dominate the city and engross the attention of its people, as industries are apt to do in less favoured places. One of the happy things about Salterton is that it is possible to work well and profitably there without having to carry one's work into the remotest crannies of social life. To the outsiders, who call Salterton 'quaint', this sometimes looks like snobbishness. But the Saltertonians do not care. They know that a little snobbery, like a little politeness, oils the wheels of daily life. Salterton enjoys a satisfying consciousness of past glories and, in a modest way, makes its own rules.

More than is usual in Canada, Salterton's physical appearance reveals its spirit. As well as its two cathedrals it has a handsome Court House (with a deceptive appearance of a dome but not, perhaps, a true dome) and one of His Majesty's largest and most forbidding prisons (with an unmistakable dome). And it is the seat of Waverley University. To say that the architecture of Waverley revealed its spirit would be a gross libel upon a centre of learning which has dignity and, in its high moments, nobility. The university had the misfortune to do most of its building during that long Victorian period when architects strove like Titans to reverse all laws of seemliness and probability and when what had been done in England was repeated, clumsily and a quarter of a century later, in Canada. Its buildings are of two kinds: in the first the builders have disregarded the character of the local stone and permitted themselves an orgy of campaniles, baroque staircases, Norman arches, Moorish peepholes and bits of grisly Scottish *chinoiserie* and *bondieuserie*, if such terms may be allowed; in the second kind the local stone has so intimidated the builders that they have erected durable stone warehouses, suitable perhaps for the study of the sciences but markedly unfriendly toward humanism. The sons and daughters of Waverley love their Alma Mater as the disciples of Socrates loved their master, for a beauty of wisdom which luckily transcends mere physical appearance.

At an earlier date than the establishment of Waverley four houses of real beauty were built in Salterton by the eccentric Prebendary Bedlam, one of those Englishmen who sought to build a bigger and better England in the colonies. By a lucky chance one of these, known as Old Bedlam, is upon the present university grounds, and houses the Provost of Waverley.

While upon this theme it may be as well to state that, among the good architecture of Salterton, there is much that is mediocre and some which is downright bad. The untutored fancy of evangelical religion has raised many a wart upon that fair face. Commerce, too, has blotched it. But upon the whole the effect is pleasing and, in some quarters of the town, genuinely beautiful. There are stone houses in Salterton, large and small, which show a justness of proportion, and an intelligent consideration of the material used, which are not surpassed anywhere in Canada. These houses appear to have faces – intelligent, well-bred faces; the knack of building houses which have faces, as opposed to grimaces, is retained by few builders.

It was in one of these, though not the best, that Freddy lived with her sister Griselda and her father, George Alexander Webster. The house was called St Agnes' and it was very nearly a genuine Bedlamite dwelling. But when St Agnes' was three-quarters finished Prebendary Bedlam had run out of money, and had not completed his plan. He had not died bankrupt or in poverty, for in his day it was almost impossible for a dignitary of the Church of England to descend to such vulgarities, but it had been an uncommonly narrow squeak. After his death the house had been completed, but not according to the original plans, by an owner whose taste had not been as pure as that of Bedlam, whose mania for building had been guided by a genuine knowledge of what can be done with stone and plaster. In a later stage St Agnes' had suffered a fire, and some rebuilding had been done around 1900 in the taste of that era. Since that time St Agnes' had been little altered. George Alexander Webster had made it a little more comfortable inside; the basement kitchen had been replaced by a modern one, and arrangements had been made to heat the house in winter by a system which did not combine all the draughtiness of England with the bitter cold of Canada, but otherwise he had not touched it.

His contribution to the place was made in the grounds. St Agnes' stood in ten or twelve acres of its own, and Webster's taste for gardening had brought them to a pitch which would surely have delighted Prebendary Bedlam. Under the owner's direction, and with the sure hand of Tom to assist, the gardens had become beautiful, and as always happens with beautiful things, many people wanted them.

Mr Webster did not like lending his gardens. He knew what the people thought who wanted to borrow them. They thought that a man with such gardens ought to be proud to show them off. They thought that a rich man should not be so selfish as to keep his beautiful gardens to himself. They thought that common decency positively demanded that he make his gardens available for a large variety of causes, and that he should not mind if a cause which had borrowed his gardens should thereupon charge other people admission to see them. He was, it was argued, 'in a position to entertain'; most of the people who 'gave of their time and effort' in order to advance causes 'were not in a position to entertain'; the least that he could do to minimize the offence of being better off than these good people was to assume the entertaining position upon demand. But he did not like to have other people taking their pleasure with his gardens any more than he would have liked to have other people take their pleasure with his wife, if that lady had been living.

He was ready to admit that he was well off. (Rich men never say that they are rich; they think it unlucky.) He was ready to contribute generously to good causes, even when the goodness was somewhat inexplicable. But he did not want strangers trampling through the gardens which were his personal creation, and which he liked to keep for himself. The people who wanted his gardens did not, of course, know of his opinions in this matter, nor would they have believed that any man could seriously want such large gardens all to himself. Indeed, there were people of advanced political opinions in Salterton who could not imagine that one man with two daughters could really want so large a house as St Agnes' all to himself, for any reason except to spite the workers and mock their less fortunate lot. These advanced people pointed out that a man could only be in one room at a time, sit in one chair at a time, and sleep in one bed at a time; therefore a man whose desires soared beyond one room with a chair and a bed in it was morally obliged to justify himself. An instructor at Waverley who was enjoying the delicious indignations of impecunious youth had once made a few remarks to a class in elementary philosophy on the iniquity of consuming seventy tons of coal each winter to warm one man; as Waverley had already drawn upon Mr Webster's purse and hoped to give it many a good shake in the future, the instructor was instructed to find fuel for his own fires further from Salterton. But Mr Webster, beneath the horny carapace which a rich man must grow in order to protect himself against his natural enemies, the poor, had depths of feeling undreamed of by those who talked so much about him; he dearly loved his big, rather ugly old house and his big, beautiful garden; after his daughters he loved these best of all.

It was because of his daughter Griselda that he had agreed to lend his garden to the Salterton Little Theatre for an outdoor production or, as Mrs Roscoe Forrester preferred to call it, 'a pastoral'. The particular pastoral which had been chosen was *The Tempest*, and Griselda, who had just been released from boarding-school, was named as a possible person to play Ariel. It had been Mrs Forrester's intention from the beginning that the play should be done at St Agnes', and at the meeting where the matter was discussed she began her campaign in these words:

'And now we come to the all-important question of site. There are several places in the city where a pastoral could be done. Bagot Park is just lovely, but it has been pointed out to me that there is baseball practically nightly. The Pauldrons have a lovely place, but Mrs Pauldron points out that it is right on the river, and well, if one of the boats sounded its siren right in the middle of a scene, well, it would ruin the scene, wouldn't it?' (Laughter, led by Mrs Pauldron in a manner which she later described to her husband as 'laughing the idea out of court'.) 'Anyway, it gets damp after sundown.' (Histrionic shudder by Mrs Pauldron.) 'The lawn in front of Old Bedlam is just perfect, but the Provost tells me that there are likely to be several theological conferences there this summer, and therefore he cannot be sure of anything. Mrs Bumford has kindly offered her grounds, but the committee feels regretfully that even if we put a row of chairs on the street, we could not accommodate more than sixty people in the audience. So the matter is still up in the air.'

Here a lady rose and asked if anyone had thought of approaching Mrs S. P. Solleret? Mrs Roscoe Forrester pursed her lips and closed her eyes in a manner which made it plain that she had spoken to Mrs Solleret, and that she did not wish to go into the matter of Mrs Solleret's reply.

It was at this point that Professor Vambrace, who had been primed by Mrs Forrester before the meeting, rose hesitatingly to his feet.

'Has any thought been given to St Agnes'?' said he.

Mrs Forrester's eyes flew open, and she seemed to project beams of new hope from them at the audience. 'I hadn't thought of it,' said she. 'I suppose it is because Miss Webster is likely to be a member of the cast, and we just never thought of looking among the cast for – er – um.' Mrs Forrester found these uncompleted sentences, the Greek rhetorical device of aposiopesis, very handy in her duties as president. She would drop a sentence in the middle, completing it with a speaking look, or a little laugh, thereby forcing other people to do her dirty work. Professor Vambrace, that bony and saturnine hatchet-man of the Salterton Little Theatre, obliged her now.

'May I suggest,' he said, standing in the half-squatting, jackknife position of one who wishes to address a meeting without making a formal speech, 'that Miss Griselda Webster be appointed a committee of one to approach her father regarding the performance of *The Tempest* in the gardens at St Agnes'.'

That was how it was done.

The approach which Griselda used might have surprised the meeting. It took this form.

'Daddy, have any sharks been after you for the garden this year?'

'Two or three. I said I'd think about it.'

'The Little Theatre has put me up to asking you if you'd let them do the play here. They thought I didn't see through them, but I did. They asked a few first, and pretended there was no place to go unless you kicked through. You don't have to say yes because of me.'

'Do you want to have it here?'

'Well, there's no denying that it would be nice.'

'Was that why they hinted about giving you a leading part?'

'Probably. But they wrought better than they knew. I'm really quite a good actress. And I'm not what you'd call plain. At least, not what you'd call plain when you consider that the only other possible person is Pearl Vambrace, who has rather a moustache. I'll be quite good even if we do it on Old Ma Bumford's little hanky of a weedy lawn, with half the audience sitting in the road.'

'It sounds like one of Nellie Forrester's sneaky tricks.'

'Yes. But Daddy: if you let them have your garden you have a good excuse for refusing it to everybody else for the rest of this summer. Had you thought of that?'

'Yes; I suppose so. All right. Remind me in the morning to tell Tom.'

Tom took it very well. Very well, that is to say, for a gardener. He pointed out that it was not the damage to the lawns that he minded; that could be repaired by a month or so of rolling. It was the way people got their feet into his borders that bothered him. However, he realized that his employer had to lend the garden sometimes, and from what he had heard, the Little Theatre performances did not draw very big crowds, so it might not be too bad.

Mr Webster sympathized. Nevertheless, he said, if the thing was to be done, it must be done properly. Therefore Tom was to give the Little Theatre people any help they wanted. Mr Webster did not intend to have anything to do with the business himself. It pained him to see people in his garden who did not appreciate it as much as he did, and he did not propose to give himself needless pain.

Tom accepted this direction with a mental reservation. If it was in any way possible, he meant to keep the intruders out of the part of his domain which was called The Shed. It was here that he kept his tools, neatly hung up in rows, and tidily arranged on his workbench. The sight of a rake or a hoe standing on the floor, however neatly, offended Tom's professional sense. He was the kind of gardener who sharpened hoes with a file. Mr Webster had once remarked that he had been shaved with razors which were duller than Tom's hoes. In The Shed, Tom was in the capital of his kingdom. It is a measure of his affection for Freddy that he had permitted her to store her home-made wines in a corner of The Shed, in some racks which he built for her himself. They were covered by a folded tarpaulin. Insofar as a gardener's workshop can be neat, The Shed was neat.

The Shed was a misleading name for this workshop. It was in fact a conservatory, built by the Victorian owner of St Agnes' who had bought it from Prebendary Bedlam's heirs. It was an elaborate and hideous erection; from the ground rose a stone foundation three feet high, and, above this, iron supports soared upward, to meet in an arch. Between the iron-work was glass, so that, inside and out, The Shed presented the appearance of an oblong birdcage. An elaborate system of canvas curtains had been devised to keep the sun from scorching the plants within, and these curtains were drawn up or let down by an intricate system of cording, like the rigging of a sailing-ship, which added to the birdcage a strong suggestion of a spider-web. The iron framework was ornamented at intervals with out-breaks of iron leafage and iron fruitage, which had grown rusty with time. There were no broken panes of glass in it, for Tom would not have permitted such an offence against neatness, but not all the panes matched, and some of them were discoloured by rust from the ironwork. In this conservatory Victorian lovers had doubtless flirted and whispered. And in its warmth, among displays of fern and large, opulent plants which were valued for their rarity rather than their beauty, rheumatisms long since at peace, and gouty toes which have ceased to twinge, were eagerly discussed and described by their owners. But the glory of the conservatory had fled. It was now The Shed, and the plants which served the garden and the house were grown in a modern greenhouse behind the garage. But The Shed was Tom's citadel, and he meant to defend it to the last.

As luck would have it, The Shed was the first thing to fall into the hands of the Little Theatre. It happened about a week after Griselda had spoken, as a committee of one, to her father; since then Freddy had allowed no day to pass without working upon Tom, heartening him for a vigorous resistance to any invasion of The Shed.

It was a Friday afternoon, and after a threatening morning a businesslike rain had begun to fall. Tom sat by his workbench, mixing some stuff which was related to the future welfare of begonias; Freddy sat on a pile of boxes, reading George Saintsbury's *Notes On A Cellar Book,* which was a favourite volume of hers. The door burst open without warning and Mrs Roscoe Forrester, Professor Vambrace and Griselda ran in.

'You'll be dry here,' said Griselda; 'I'll go into the house and see if I can find some umbrellas.'

She ran out into the rain again; the door which led from The Shed into the rest of the house had been locked for many years, and a heavy cupboard stood before it.

'You'll be Freddy,' said Mrs Forrester, who liked to use this Gaelic form of assertion jocosely. She was not a Scot herself, but she liked to enrich her conversation with what she believed to be Scottish and Irish idioms. 'How sweet you look, sitting there with your wee bookie!'

'I am Fredegonde Webster,' said Freddy rising. 'Good afternoon. You are from the Little Theatre. This is Mr Gwalchmai, the gardener: Tom – Mrs Forrester and Professor Vambrace.'

Tom touched his cap and said nothing. He had been a good soldier in his time – a first-rate sergeant – but he had never known what to do about surprise attacks, except to resent their sneakiness.

'We're going to be great friends, Mr – uh – but perhaps I'd better call you Tom right away,' said Mrs Forrester, reaching for his hand. Tom's hand was covered with muck, and he would have dearly liked to give it to her, but he forebore. Professor Vambrace gave what he doubtless meant to be a friendly glance, but was really a baleful glare, at both Tom and Freddy, to be shared between them.

'Wet,' said he. Classics was his subject, and he sometimes affected a classical simplicity in social conversation.

Freddy was young in years, but old in certain sorts of wisdom; she had learned from her father, for instance, that nothing is so disconcerting as silence, and she was preparing to give Mrs Forrester a lot of it. But Professor Vambrace's summing up of the weather had scarcely died upon the air before the door burst open again and Griselda rushed in with two more people under an umbrella. The first was Solly Bridgetower, a young man whom Freddy admired in a friendly sort of way; the other was an unknown woman.

'We can finish talking here,' said Griselda. 'We'll get wet if we try to make a dash for the front door.'

Griselda did not recognize The Shed as Tom's special property. She thought of it simply as an extension of her father's house. Tom was not the big figure in her world that he was in Freddy's.

'What about Larry and Mr Mackilwraith?' asked Mrs Forrester.

'We'll keep an eye out for them,' said Griselda. 'Larry wanted to finish his little sketch of the lawn. Anyway, he's hanging about to look for What's His Name – the fellow who's going to play Ferdinand.'

'Mackilwraith will not be here until after four,' said Professor Vambrace. 'School.'

'Probably not until after half-past four,' said Solly. 'If old Hector hasn't changed his ways he'll have some wretched child under his eye for at least half an hour after closing-time. One of the really great detainers and keepers-in of our time, Old Hector.'

'Mr Mackilwraith is a schoolteacher,' said Mrs Forrester to the unknown woman. 'I do hope he'll be able to take a look at the lawn; he's our business manager, and he can always tell how many it will seat, and what money that will mean, and all those things. A mathematical wizard.'

'A creaking pedant,' said Solly.

Professor Vambrace gave him a look which suggested that while irreverent remarks about schoolteachers did not necessarily affect university professors, they were in questionable taste.

'I speak, of course, in a rich, Elizabethan manner,' said Solly, with a rich, Elizabethan gesture which almost toppled a tower of small flower pots. 'He's not a bad chap really – I suppose. Freddy, I greet you. You and Miss Rich haven't met, have you? Miss Rich is from New York and she is going to direct our play. This is Fredegonde Webster; she lives here, but splendour has not corrupted her. A pard-like spirit, beautiful and swift.'

'How do you do, Miss Webster,' said Miss Rich holding out her hand.

'I am very well, thank you,' said Freddy, thinking that Miss Rich was a very well-mannered person, and nicely dressed. 'Solly is a great tease, as I suppose you have found out.'

'We only met about an hour ago,' said Miss Rich.

'Aren't we dignified, though?' said Mrs Forrester, with what she believed to be a laughing glance toward Freddy. 'When one is just growing up – oh, the dignity of it! I remember when I was that age; do you remember, Val? Wasn't I just loaded with dignity?'

'I don't really remember, Nell,' said Miss Rich.

'Well, I do.' Mrs Forrester was firm. 'We were both absolutely bursting with dignity.'

'But you got over all that, didn't you?' said Freddy, sweetly. 'I suppose that's the fun of being grown up; one has shed so many things which seem desirable to somebody of my age.'

'That will do, Freddy,' said Griselda.

Freddy was happy to leave the matter there. Griselda's rebuke carried little weight, and she was pleasantly conscious of having choked off Old Ma Forrester.

'Well, have we made up our minds?' asked Professor Vambrace. 'Will the lawn do? Will those trees give the background we want? If so, let us make our decision. What do you think, Miss Rich?'

'I think the setting is charming,' said she; 'if it is agreeable to you, I am quite happy about it. But won't Major Pye have something to say?'

'He's sure to have plenty of fault to find,' said Solly, 'but he wouldn't completely approve of any place. You know how technical men are; they love to face problems, and when there are none they create them. They're overcomers by nature; the way to please 'em is to give them lots to overcome. "To him that o'ercometh, God giveth a crown." That hymn was written especially to flatter stage managers.'

'Now don't begin antagonizing Larry at this stage,' said Mrs Forrester; 'his work will be hard enough, and we must let him get well into it before we offer any suggestions. So do be good, Solly, and jolly him along.'

'What I love about amateur theatricals,' said Solly to Miss Rich, 'is the way everything is done by jollying everybody. You must miss that dreadfully in the professional theatre. Just a dull round of people giving orders and people obeying them; no jollying.'

'You are quite mistaken,' she replied; 'there is really quite a lot of jollying to be done, though perhaps not quite so much as with amateurs.'

'Solly, if you say amateur theatricals again I shall hit you,' said Mrs Forrester; 'thank Heaven the Little Theatre left all that nonsense behind years ago. In fact, it may be said that we have a truly professional approach. Haven't we, Walter?'

'Quite,' said the economical Vambrace.

'I'm sure it may be said, but is it true?' said Solly. 'It certainly wasn't true when I went away; have two years made so much difference?'

'You're just conceited because you've been to Cambridge,' said Mrs Forrester. 'But you can't shake off the fact that you got your start with the Salterton Little Theatre, and that it has made you what you are today, theatrically speaking –'

'Oh, God,' interjected Solly.

'– if you are anything at all, theatrically speaking, which has yet to be shown. And it is a great privilege for you to be working with Miss Rich, and don't you forget it, young man.'

Mrs Forrester laughed with a little too much emphasis, to show that this lecture was intended to be friendly. She always maintained that you could say literally anything to anybody, just so long as you said it with a smile, to show that there were no hard feelings. It was going to be necessary to keep Solly in hand, she could see that.

'Mrs F., you are being grossly unfair,' said Solly. 'You want me to jolly Larry Pye, to keep him happy. Jolly Solly, that's what I'm to be. But do you jolly me? No, you jump down my throat. Why do you, if I may so express it, make flesh of Pye and fish of me?'

'You're too young to be jollied,' she replied. 'And don't you call me Mrs F.'

'Well, if you are going to badger me in that tone I certainly can't call you Nellie. If I'm too young to be jollied, you are certainly too old to be treated with friendly familiarity. What do you want to be called: Dame Nellie Forrester?'

'You can call me Nellie when you are a good boy.'

'And you shall be called Nagging Nell when you are a bad old girl.'

Mrs Forrester never lost her temper. She prided herself upon this trait and frequently mentioned it to her friends. But sometimes, as upon the present occasion, she felt a burning in the pit of her stomach which would have been anger in anyone else. How stupid it was of Solly not to be able to take a rebuke without all this bickering! She groped for something crushing which could be said in a thoroughly good-natured way, but nothing came. Luckily the door opened at this moment and Major Larry Pye came in, followed by a young man in a raincoat, but without a hat.

'Well, we can do it, but it isn't going to be easy,' said Larry, who liked to begin conversations in the middle.

'If anybody can do it, you can,' said Solly, in an artificially hearty voice.

'It'll mean a lot of new cable; that's one thing,' Larry continued, and he would have set out at once to explain the delightful difficulties he had discovered, and which he meant to overcome, if Mrs Forrester had not pounced on his companion.

'Roger,' she cried, 'how sweet of you to come in all this rain! You don't know anyone here, do you?'

'Yes; I know the Major and I've met Professor Vambrace,' said the young man.

'Twice,' said the Professor.

'This is Miss Valentine Rich, of New York, who is going to direct the play; Roger Tasset, Val, who is to be your leading man. And Griselda Webster, who will probably be our Ariel; Lieutenant Tasset. And this is Solly Bridgetower; he will sort of dogsbody and stooge for Miss Rich; he's just back from Cambridge. Oh, and I almost forgot dear little Freddy, who lives here. And Tom who is going to be our very good friend, I'm sure. Larry, have you met Tom?'

'Hullo, Tom,' said Larry.

Tom had a firm grip on the fact that Larry, at some distant time, had been a major, and was still addressed by his military title; this seemed to him to be the one truly creditable fact about the group of people who had come bursting into his Shed, tracking dirt everywhere, and talking silly. So he gave Larry something which was almost a salute.

'Good workshop you have here,' said Larry. 'Got a lathe?'

'No sir,' said Tom.

'Too bad. But we can do most of our building right here,' said the major. 'It will save a lot of cartage. We might as well have everything as convenient as possible.'

With these words Tom's last hope of saving The Shed was slain.

'The rain is growing worse,' said Professor Vambrace.

'We shan't be able to do anything else this afternoon,' said Mrs Forrester. 'I suppose we should think about ways of getting home. Now have we really decided that this is the place for the play? If there is an objection of any kind, now is the time to state it.'

'I don't understand you, Mrs F.,' said Solly spitefully. 'You know that we have had our hearts set on this place from the first. Now we've got it. Why fuss?'

'Solly!' cried Mrs Forrester, and stamped her foot. But in an instant she was smiling. 'He only does it to annoy, because he knows it teases,' she said. Solly was always quoting; she could quote too.

'It's not as cut and dried as all that,' said Larry Pye. 'Where's your heavy duty cable to come from? I'd be glad if somebody would tell me that.' He looked around at the company. All they thought about was strutting in fine clothes. But it was the old story of the grasshopper and the ant; when the practical business had to be done, they had to come to him. He knew very well where the heavy duty cable would be brought in; he had it all clear in his mind; but it would never do for them to know that.

'The lawn and the trees are quite lovely,' said Valentine Rich, 'and if you can solve your technical problems, Major Pye, I should like to use this setting very much. I've heard that you are a wonderful stage manager, and that you do miracles every year.'

'Don't know about miracles,' said Larry, looking like a little boy who has been given a six-bladed jack-knife, 'but I'll do my best. Can't say any more than that.'

'Then I haven't another worry,' said Miss Rich, smiling at him, whereupon he giggled, and decided that it really took a professional to understand what he was up against.

'Did you see the upper lawn, Roger?' asked Mrs Forrester.

'The Major showed it to me,' said Roger Tasset; 'jolly good.'

'It's wonderful of Roger to act with us,' the president continued. 'He's terribly busy, taking a course, or giving a course, or something. But I know he's going to be simply wonderful.'

'I don't guarantee it,' said Roger. 'Haven't done anything in this line since I was at school. Can't say I know the play awfully well, as a matter of fact. Is it the one where the chap turns into a donkey?'

'No, it's the one with the shipwreck,' said Solly.

'Oh? Good show!'

'We hope it will be,' Solly replied, with a courtesy which was a little overdone.

The door opened once more, and a man in a raincoat and a sober grey hat stepped inside, lowered his umbrella, and shook it carefully out of the door before bringing it in after him. Not a drop fell on Tom's floor.

'I'm sorry to be late,' said he. 'I had to oversee some detentions.'

It was Hector Mackilwraith. He brought with him an air of calm command, developed during eighteen years in the schoolroom, which had its effect even upon Solly. He did not take charge, but in his presence Mrs Forrester quickly established and ratified the already obvious fact that *The Tempest* would be performed six weeks hence on the upper lawn at St Agnes'. Major Pye agreed that the problem of the heavy-duty cable, though vexing, could be solved. From measurements supplied by Major Pye it was soon decided by Hector Mackilwraith that a sufficient audience could be accommodated to pay the costs of the production and realize a useful profit. Then a silence descended, and when it was plain that there was nothing more to be said, Griselda suggested that she should fetch the big car and drive them all home. It was Hector Mackilwraith who held his umbrella over her as they walked to the garage; and as they drove about the city, dropping the Little Theatre enthusiasts at their widely separated dwellings, it was Hector Mackilwraith who sat by her side.

When they had gone, Freddy and Tom looked at one another in glum dismay. The coming six weeks stretched before them as a period of sheer Hell.

'Well, if you won't stay with us, I suppose you won't,' said Mrs Forrester, with a pout which had been rather attractive fifteen years earlier, 'but we could have had a barrel of fun.'

'It's not that I won't, Nell; it's that I can't,' said Miss Rich patiently. They had covered this ground more than thoroughly during the evening meal. 'I shall have to be busy every day, seeing lawyers and auctioneers and so forth. I'd be a nuisance.'

'Well, then, let's not talk about it any more. We don't want to quarrel. Though I've been looking forward to having you just a little bit to myself. Haven't I, Roscoe?'

Roscoe nodded, with a smile which might have meant anything, but which probably meant goodwill, sympathy in his wife's disappointment, understanding of Valentine Rich's predicament, reluctance to let a friend of his wife's stop at a hotel, and pleasure that no guest would disturb the peaceful routine of his household. Roscoe Forrester was an admirable salesman; he made a very good income from selling insurance; one of his foremost assets in this highly competitive work was his ability to share with perfect sincerity in several opposed points of view.

They continued with their meal of spiced meat and salad from the delicatessen, ice-cream from the dairy, and cookies from the bakery. Mrs Forrester believed in what she called 'streamlining household work'.

The Forresters, as they told everyone they met, had 'neither chick nor child'. Their failure to have a chick never provoked surprise, but it was odd that they were childless; they had not sought that condition. But they were not driven apart by it, as people of more intense feelings sometimes are; if anything, Roscoe Forrester was a little more attentive toward his wife for that reason, as if he reproached himself for having failed to provide something which might have given her pleasure. He helped her in any way he could with her amusements, which she called 'activities', and he gave in to her in all matters of dispute. His attitude toward her was admiring and protective, and in his heart he believed that she was a remarkable woman.

She had, for instance, Taste. Their apartment showed it. Many people would have sworn that only an interior decorator could have produced such an effect. In the living room, he would explain, there were just two Notes of Colour; one was a picture, a print framed in natural wood, of some red horses playing rather violently in a field; the other was a large bowl, of a deep green, which stood on the pickled oak coffee table. All else in the room was cleverly arranged to be of no colour at all. The suite of two armchairs and a sofa was upholstered in a dingy shade called mushroom; the walls were distempered in a colour which recalled, if anything, vomit. The carpet, a broadloom, was mushroom too, and the hardwood floor, where visible, repeated more firmly the walls' note of delicate nausea. There was one other chair, with no arms, which sat upon a spring-like arrangement of bent wood. This was very modern indeed, and was avoided by all save the lightest guests.

An arch in one wall of the living-room gave upon the dining-room, which was smaller, but just as tasteful. Certain concessions to human frailty were permitted here; for instance, on the top of a cabinet sat an effigy in china of an old woman in a bonnet, offering for sale a bunch of rather solid-looking balloons. The furniture was of old pine, which Mrs Forrester, and Roscoe under her direction, had rubbed down with pumice, and rubbed up with oil, and shellacked until it had a permanently wet look. It was old, and the table was so low that it was rather inconvenient for large guests, but everyone assured Mrs Forrester that the effect was charming. The bedrooms, kitchen and bathroom of the flat were not carried through on this high level of Taste, but they bore many personal touches; the guest towels, for instance, were marked 'Yours' (in contrast to 'His' and 'Hers' which were used by the owners) and by the bedside in the guestroom was a cigarette box with three very dry cigarettes in it, and two packets of matches, wittily printed with the words 'Swiped from The Forresters'. Their library was accommodated in a single case in their own bedroom. The most coherent part of it was what Mrs Forrester called 'her drama library'; it comprised three anthologies of plays, a curiously unhelpful manual called *Play Direction For Theatres Great and Small* (written by a professor who had never directed a play in any theatre which might be called great), and a handful of dog-eared acting copies of plays in which Mrs Forrester had herself appeared. There was also a book about acting by Stanislavsky, which Mrs Forrester had read to the end of the first chapter and marked intelligently in red pencil, and which she recommended to amateurs who did not know what to do with their hands when on the stage. There were also several books which instructed the reader that peace of mind of the sort possessed by great saints could be achieved by five minutes of daily contemplation, and two or three complementary books which explained that worry, heart disease, hardening of the arteries, *taedium cordis* and despair could all be avoided by relaxing the muscles. There was a book which explained how one could grow slim while eating three delicious, satisfying meals a day. There was a copy of the *Rubaiyat* bound in disagreeable limp suede (a wedding gift from Mrs Forrester's aunt). And in addition there were twenty or more novels, some bound in cloth and some in paper covers.

'It's going to be a wonderful lift for our group to work with you, Val,' said Mrs Forrester as they took their coffee into the living-room; she switched on a tasteful lamp, which lit the ceiling very well, and in the increased light the red horses whinnied tastefully to the green bowl, which echoed tastefully again. 'I mean, now that you've worked with professionals for so long. You've got an awful lot to *give*. Don't you feel that?'

'I wouldn't like to say so,' replied Miss Rich; 'I feel too often that there are large tracts of the job about which I know nothing at all.'

'Ah, but that just *shows*,' said Mrs Forrester. 'He that knows not and knows not that he knows not – avoid him; he that knows not and knows that he knows not – uh, wait a minute – uh, instruct him; he that knows and knows that he knows – cleave unto him. That's the way we feel about you.'

'I don't quite see where I fit into that,' said Valentine, 'but I'll do what I can. I've done quite a few outdoor shows. They are always successful unless something absolutely awful happens. People aren't so critical outdoors.'

'Oh, but that's just where you're wrong!' Mrs Forrester caused her eyes to light up by bugging them slightly. 'There'll be people here from other Little Theatre groups everywhere within a hundred miles. And they'll have their tomahawks with them. They'll be jealous, you see. They've never done a pastoral. They've never attempted Shakespeare. They'll be on the lookout for every little flaw. Won't they, Roscoe?'

'I guess that's right, hon,' said Roscoe, smiling.

'The only thing that persuaded us to try it at all was that you would be here to give it a professional finish.'

'But Nell, you wrote me in February that it had been decided, and it was then that you asked if I would help.'

'Well, we were toying with the idea, but we would never have decided on it if you hadn't been willing. It was only decided at a full meeting of the members; the committee hadn't really made up their minds. I know that sounds undemocratic, but in these Little Theatres you have to use common sense as well as democracy, don't you?'

'One of the nicest things about the professional theatre is that it is utterly undemocratic. If you aren't any good, you go. Or maybe that's real democracy. I don't know. I'm not a bit political.'

'If you let democracy run away with you in the Salterton Little Theatre you'd end in a fine mess,' said Mrs Forrester. 'I don't mind telling you that Professor Vambrace and I have to do all the real deciding, and get it through the committee, somehow, and then the committee usually carries the meeting. Otherwise people like Larry Pye would come up with the queerest ideas; all he can talk about is doing a musical comedy, so that he can monkey with lights.'

'I hope he doesn't want to monkey too much with the lights in *The Tempest*.'

'Oh, you'll be able to deal with him. You must be used to cursing electricians.'

'No, I've never cursed one that I can remember. You see too many movies about the theatre, Nell.'

'Don't be afraid to speak your mind to our people. I've had one or two real knock-down-and-drag-out fights with Larry. Haven't I, Roscoe?'

'Sure have, hon.'

'And he respects me for it. You'll find us fully professional in that way.'

'I can usually find some other way,' said Valentine, who did not wish to appear superior, but who was not going to promise to abuse the Salterton Little Theatre's electrician merely to gratify Nellie's desire for disagreeable frankness. She was already beginning to be uncomfortable with Nellie; after all, it was fully fifteen years since they had been on intimate terms. Not that the terms were so intimate even then as Nellie appeared to think. Curious that her memory could so distort a quite ordinary friendship. Valentine's own memory was excellent.

'I'm sorry about Solly Bridgetower,' said Mrs Forrester, 'but you see how it was. When it looked as though you couldn't come to us, during that two weeks, we were desperate, and somebody thought that Solly might direct instead. He's at Cambridge, you know, only he's at home just at present because his mother has been so dreadfully ill. I was going to help him. In fact, I cast the play provisionally before we asked him to direct. Of course he accepted. Then, when you found that you could come after all, we had to ask him to step down, and told all the people who had been promised parts that the final decision would be yours. That was when he said that he would be your assistant. I was against it, but we couldn't very easily refuse. He says he'll just be your errand boy, because he wants to learn, but I'll believe that when I see it. He's conceited.'

'I thought he seemed rather nice.'

'He's a smart-alec. Education in England spoils so many Canadians – except Rhodes scholars, who come back and get Government jobs right away. There's a kind of nice simplicity about a Canadian that education abroad seems to destroy. Lots of boys go through our Canadian universities and come out with the bloom still on them, but when they go abroad they always come home spoiled. Isn't that so, Roscoe?'

'What I always say is,' said Roscoe, 'it takes all kinds to make a world. I like Solly. He's a nice boy.'

'Oh Roscoe, you like everybody,' said his wife.

'Well, that's pretty nearly true, hon.'

The interior of St Agnes' was, by Mrs Forrester's standards, lacking in Taste. The personal preference shown in the matter of furniture and decoration was that of Mr Webster, for his wife had been dead for more than ten years. He liked things that were heavy, and he liked dark wood, intricately patterned wallpaper, and an atmosphere of over-furnishing which Griselda called 'clutter'. He liked books and had a great many of them. He liked Persian and Chinese carpets, and his rooms were silent with them. He liked leather, and there was plenty of it in his house, on chairs, on fenders, on books and even on lampshades. The house was dark and somewhat oppressive in atmosphere, but it was as he desired it. Griselda had been permitted to decorate a combined bedroom and sitting-room for herself in her own taste. Freddy's bedroom was austere, for she had cleared the nursery pictures of kittens and rabbits out of it, and had added little save a bookcase which contained her favourite works on wine and the liturgy of the Church of England as it might be if the revision of the Prayer Book could be recalled. The only picture she hung in her room was a colour print of *The Feeding of the Infant Bacchus*, by Poussin; the podgy godling, swigging at his bowl, was not her ideal of a wine-taster; nevertheless, something in the picture appealed to her deeply. At the head of her bed hung a little ivory crucifix.

No, Mrs Forrester would have found St Agnes' sadly lacking in Taste, and she would have thought it a pity, for obviously a great deal of money had been spent to make it as it was.

Most of the people who thought about the matter at all imagined that the Websters dined in great state every night. But on this evening, after the successful assault upon The Shed by the Little Theatre, Mr Webster and his daughters were eating sandwiches and drinking coffee from a thermos in the large, gloomy dining-room. It was the servants' night out. Mr Webster rather enjoyed these picnics.

'The Little Theatre people were here this afternoon, Daddy,' said Griselda.

'Oh. Did they approve of my garden?'

'Mphm. They'd like to do the play on the upper lawn, against the background of big trees.'

'Well, they'll do as little harm there as anywhere. What is this bloody stuff?'

'Some kind of fish goo.'

'Aren't there any peanut butter sandwiches?'

'Yes, but I think they're meant for us. You aren't supposed to like peanut butter. It isn't a masculine taste.'

'I like it. Give me one.'

'Daddy,' said Freddy; 'don't you think you'd better say a word to Tom about keeping them out of The Shed? All the valuable tools are in there.'

'I don't suppose they'll take them,' said Mr Webster.

'No, but they might spoil them, messing about. Anyhow, you know how Tom hates people in The Shed.'

'Tom will have to get used to it.'

'Freddy was rude to Mrs Forrester this afternoon,' said Griselda.

'Good,' said her father.

'Don't encourage her, Daddy. She's above herself.'

'She was rude to me first,' said Freddy; 'I get sick of being treated like a baby. I've got just as much brains as you, Gristle, and I ought to be treated with as much respect.'

'When you are older, dear,' said Griselda, with a maddening air of maturity.

'Nuts,' retorted Freddy, rudely; 'there's only four years between us. If I had a great big bosom like yours, and a fanny like a bumble-bee, people would swarm over me just the way they do over you.'

'If you are waiting for that, I fear that you will wait indeed,' said Griselda. 'It's plain now that you are the stringy type. Your secondary sexual characteristics, if and when they come, will be poor things at best.'

'Children, don't speak so coarsely,' said Mr Webster, who had a vague notion that some supervision should be exercised over his daughters' speech, and that a line should be drawn, but never knew quite when to draw it. He had allowed his daughters to use his library without restraint, and nothing is more fatal to maidenly delicacy of speech than the run of a good library.

'The play is going to be directed by a woman,' said Griselda. 'She looks very sensible and doesn't say much, which is odd, because she seems to be a friend of Mrs Forrester's. A Miss Valentine Rich. Lived here ages ago. She's been working in professional theatre in the States. Do you know anything about her, Daddy?'

'If you ever looked inside a newspaper, Gristle,' said Freddy, 'you'd know that she is quite famous in a modest sort of way. She's a good actress. She doesn't often play leads, but she gets feature billing, if you know what that is, which I doubt. And she directs. She's directed some awfully good stuff. She did a performance of *The White Divell* two years ago, and the critics all said the direction was fine, even if the actors were rotten and it flopped.'

'If she's so good, why weren't the actors good?'

'Perhaps she can't make a silk purse out of a sow's ear; we shall see on our own upper lawn, quite soon. Anyway Americans can't act that sort of thing. They are utterly without flair.' Freddy grandly dismissed the American stage.

'I think I've heard of her,' said Mr Webster. 'Her grandfather died about six weeks ago. Old Dr Savage. He was quite a bigwig at Waverley a long time ago. He wasn't seen much during recent years.'

'She's come back to sell up his things,' said Freddy. 'She is his heir. There'll probably be an auction. Do you suppose it will bring in much, Daddy?'

'Impossible to tell. Not likely. Professors rarely have interesting furniture. She might get a few thousands, if the sale went well.'

'He probably had a lot of interesting books,' said Freddy; 'if she has an auction may I go, Daddy? I mean, may I have a little money, just in case something interesting turned up?'

'You have the instincts of a packrat, Freddy,' said Griselda. 'What do you want with dirty old books out of a dead professor's house? Aren't there enough books here already? And how do you know so much about Miss Rich?'

'My eyes are turned outward, toward the world,' said Freddy. 'Yours are turned inward, toward yourself. In the innermost chamber of your spirit, Gristle, you kneel in constant adoration before a mirror.'

Griselda smiled lazily, and threw a fish sandwich at her sister.

When this simple meal was finished, the Webster family dispersed to entertain itself. Mr Webster went to his library, and sat down to rummage through some volumes of the Champlain Society's publications. This was his favourite reading. Unlike many men of wealth in Canada he had never sought gold in the wilderness or lived an explorer's life among guides and Indians; he did not like to hunt or fish. But exploration in an armchair was his pastime, and accounts of the hardships of others were full of interest to him.

For a time Freddy shared the room with him, quietly taking down one book after another until she had gleaned all the information the library contained about the late Dr Adam Savage. It was not much; he was named in a *History of Waverley* as a professor of Greek, as a contemporary of a number of other professors who, in their turn, were named as contemporaries of his. It is a habit of the writers of such histories to list the names of dead pedagogues as Homer listed the ships, hoping for glory of sound rather than for the illumination of their audience. In the memoirs of a politician who had been a Waverley man, Dr Savage was referred to as 'grand', but this was unconvincing; to politicians any teacher whom they have subsequently surpassed in notoriety is likely to appear grand. Otherwise there was nothing. Dr Savage was dead indeed. Freddy bade her father goodnight, and went to her own room.

She removed her clothes and surveyed herself in a mirror. Griselda's remark about her figure rankled in her memory. 'I look just like a boy,' she thought. This was untrue, and if she had been more intimately acquainted with boys she would have known it. 'Gristle is right; I'm stringy,' thought she. This also was untrue. Slim she undoubtedly was, and breastless and economical in the rear, but she was not stringy, and there was promise of better things to come. But Freddy was not in a mood to be satisfied with herself, and as she put on her pyjamas and jumped into bed she wondered what Daddy would say if she suggested that in a year or two she should become a postulant in an Anglican nunnery. Somewhat illogically she broke off this train of reflection to read the large illustrated Rabelais which she had abstracted from the library. She found it very good fun, and made a mental list of several abusive terms to use in her next quarrel with Griselda.

Her older sister was likewise preparing for bed. There were four young men in Salterton all of whom were wishing, that evening, that they could take Griselda Webster out. But as none of them knew her very well, and as her beauty and her father's wealth frightened them, and as they feared that they might be rebuffed if they called her, and as they were convinced that such a girl must have all her evenings spoken for months in advance, none of them had done anything about it, and Griselda, at eight o'clock, was in the bathtub.

Long baths were one of her indulgences. She liked to lie in a scented tub, refreshing the hot water from time to time, smoking cigarettes, eating chocolates, and reading. She liked romances of two kinds; if she were not reading Anthony Trollope, whose slow, common-sense stories, and whose staid, common-sense lovers she greatly admired, she liked spicy tales of the type which usually appear in paper-bound copies, in which bishops are forced to visit nudist camps in their underwear, in which men are changed into women, in which bachelors are surprised in innocent but compromising situations with beautiful girls. Hers was a simple but somewhat ribald mind.

She shifted her hips so that the warm water swept over her stomach, which had grown a little chilly. She prodded a chocolate clinically, and as it appeared to be a soft centre she popped it into her mouth. She turned a page of *The Vicar of Bullhampton*. Peace settled upon St Agnes' for the night.

At five minutes to six o'clock Hector Mackilwraith left the YMCA and walked briskly toward the Snak Shak. This restaurant, in spite of its name, was pretentious, and appealed to the students of Waverley by a display of unnecessary electricity, unceasing popular music played by a machine which lit up like a baboon's rump with red, blue and green lights, and by quaintly scholarly touches in its decoration. One of these was a wall-painting of a goggle-eyed gnome, just identifiable as Shakespeare's Puck, which appeared over the soda fountain and food counter; from the mouth of the gnome emerged a balloon in which the words 'Lord, what foods these morsels be' were written in Old English lettering. The Snak Shak was not elegant or restful, but it was fairly clean, and it was possible to eat a three-course dinner there for sixty-five cents if you bought meal tickets by the ten dollar book. Hector was one of its most faithful supporters.

A man enters a familiar building in quite a different manner from that which he shows when going to a new place. Hector's steps took him to the door of the Snak Shak so neatly that he was able to seize the handle and enter without losing momentum. He walked to his accustomed stall, at the farthest possible distance from the baboon-rump music-box, hung up his raincoat and hat, and sat down to read his newspaper. In time his accustomed waitress – she had been with the Snak Shak for almost three months – came to him and greeted him with the friendliness which she reserved for 'regulars' who never 'tried to get fresh'.

'G'devening,' said she. 'Terrible out, eh?'

'Yes. A wet night.'

'Yeah. Terrible. Juice or soup?'

'The mixed vegetable juice, please.'

'Yeah. And then?'

'Hm. The chicken à la king?'

'I'll tell you – not so good tonight. The hamburger's good.'

'All right.'

'Heavy on the onions as usual, eh?'

'Thank you. Yes.'

'What pie?'

'The coconut chiffon.'

'I was bettin' with myself you'd say that. You got a sweet tooth, y'know that?'

'Do you think so?'

'Yeah. And why not? You're not so fat. What's your beverage?'

'Tea, please. With two teabags.'

'OK. Right away.'

Hector turned once again to his paper. He was usually a methodical reader, taking in the world news, the local news, and the editorials, in that order, and then glancing briefly at the rest. He always finished by reading all the comic strips; he did not particularly enjoy them, and persuaded himself that he read them only in order to know what his pupils were reading; but the fact was that they had become an addiction, of which he was rather ashamed.

Tonight his reading progressed slowly. He read the same report twice without realizing it, for his mind was elsewhere. Hector was debating a weighty matter within himself. He was trying to make up his mind whether he should ask for a part in *The Tempest*.

To many people, such problems are simple. If they want something they set to work to get it, and if they do not want it they leave it alone. But Hector was a schoolteacher, and a teacher of mathematics at that, and he prided himself upon the orderliness of his thinking. He was as diligent as any Jesuit at arranging the arguments in every case under *Pro* and *Contra* and examining them thoroughly. When at last he recognized what was troubling him he folded his paper neatly and laid it in the seat by him, and drew out his black notebook, a book feared by hundreds of pupils. On a clean page he wrote his headings, P and C, and drew a line down the middle. Quickly, neatly – for this was his accustomed way of making up his mind, even upon such matters as the respective merits of two Chinese laundries – he wrote as follows:

P

HM Been treasurer Little Theatre 6 yrs – served LT well – deserves well of LT

HM Probably as gd an actor as most of LT crowd

Feel need of augmented social life – all work no play, etc. have enough money to take place with best of LT

Be fun to wear costume, false whiskers, etc. – Shakes v. cultural

C

HM teacher – do nothing foolish

Couldn't take part of lover, clown or immoral person – plays full of these – Shakes often vulgar

Heavy demands on time – do nothing to forfeit respect of pupils, colleagues, etc. – not in position to entertain – Invading field of English Dept.? – remember specialist certificate in maths

He considered the page before him. The waitress brought his meal, all on one tray, and he drank his mixed vegetable juice absently, as he pondered. He was deep in his problem as he attacked his hamburger and vegetables, but he reflected momentarily that with onions he should have ordered a glass of milk, to kill the smell on his breath; still, he was not going anywhere that evening, and there was no need to consider himself; he liked the smell of onion. But he pulled himself up sharply: that was slovenly thinking and slovenly living; a gentleman, his mother had often said, was a man who used a butter knife even when alone. A slovenly action, thrice repeated, has become a habit. He called the waitress and ordered the milk. To thine own self be true, etc.; Shakes.

The problem gnawed. Usually either the *Pro* or the *Contra* column was markedly longer or weaker than the other; in this matter they were pretty evenly matched. From a folder in his inner pocket he drew a letter, and re-read it, as he had done twice before that day.

GOVERNMENT OF ONTARIO

DEPARTMENT OF EDUCATION

Dear Hec:

Just a line to let you know that you are going to be asked to be one of the Revision Board in Maths this summer – to head it up, in fact. The list has not been finalized by the Deputy, but it won't be changed now. You know what this means. You'll be Head Examiner in Maths next year, or the year after. And that means you can have a Department job if you want it, eh? Your friends here can fix it if you put up a good show on the Revision. Remember what Churchill says; Give us the tools and we'll finalize the commitment. So long Hec, old boy.

Russ

At any previous time in his life such a letter would have thrown Hector into a well-controlled ecstasy. Signal preferment was offered as an examiner in the provincial examination system, and the prospect of a job in the Department of Education, that Moslem Paradise of ambitious teachers! Here was his old friend, Russell McIlquham, himself a rising man with that most desirable of all departmental benefactions, 'the ear of the Deputy', practically assuring him that it was only a matter of time before he, Hector, would revel in departmental authority with a good chance of imposing his pet schemes upon other, reluctant teachers. But as so often happens in an unsatisfactory world, this good news came at the wrong time. His cup of professional ambition was filled at a moment when he hankered after other, strange delights. What should he do? Should he act, – a course from which his common sense told him he was unlikely to derive any benefit except his own satisfaction – or should he put out his hand and pluck this plum which had ripened in his professional life? He was somewhat astonished at himself to find that he hesitated in making his choice.

He had worked his way almost to the end of his coconut chiffon pie. He ate methodically, devouring the cardboard-like crust at the back of his segment of pie (his trained eye told him that it was a reasonable, but not an exact, sixth of a pie ten inches in diameter) but leaving one last mouthful of cream and coconut, to be chomped voluptuously when the crust was done. It was as he was about to raise this tidbit to his mouth that he lifted his eyes and saw a vaguely familiar figure standing at the counter, some distance from him.

Hector had an excellent memory for names and faces. He sometimes amused his colleagues at teachers' entertainments by reciting the nominal roll of some class which he had taught ten or twelve years before; he never hesitated over a name. He knew that this young man was Lieutenant Roger Tasset, whom he had met briefly one hour and twenty-five minutes earlier in The Shed at St Agnes'.

Tasset was talking to the waitress behind the counter. Hector could not hear what was said, but the girl leaned toward Roger, and her face was stripped of the suspicious, somewhat minatory expression which waitresses often wear when dealing with young male customers. She appeared to glow a little, and her lips parted moistly as she listened to what he said. He was, in fact, making some mention of the heavy tax on the box of cigarettes which he had bought. But to Hector's eye the girl seemed to be responding to the easy gallantry which was plain in Roger's figure and face, if not in his words.

Hector popped the gob of coconut cream into his mouth with unaccustomed haste, seized his black notebook and drew a line under the two columns. But instead of writing, as was his custom, the name of the victorious column in capitals under this line, he wrote instead: 'There are some decisions which cannot be made on a basis of reason.'

In the glare of the lamp the small but distinct bald spot on Mrs Bridgetower's head glowed dustily as she bent over her dish of oyster stew. It was an ugly lamp, but there was a solemnity, almost a grandeur, about its ugliness. Hanging from one of the false oak beams in the dining-room by an oxidized bronze chain which the passing of years had made even more rusty, it spread out like a canopy over the middle of the dining-table. The shade was of bronze strips, apparently held together by bronze rivets, and between the strips were pieces of glass so rough in texture, so shot with green and yellow and occasional flecks of red, that they seemed to be made of vitrified mucus. When she and the late Professor Bridgetower had built this house, before the First World War, it had been a beautiful lamp, for it accorded with the taste of the period. So did the rest of the room – the oak table and chairs which owed so much, but not perhaps enough, to William Morris; the 'built-in' buffet at the end of the room, with its piece of cloudy mirror and its cabinets with leaded-glass windows, in which cups and saucers and the state china were imprisoned; the blue carpet upon the floor.

It was in the manner which had been current when her house was built that Mrs Bridgetower ordered her meals and caused them to be served. The table at which she and Solly were seated was spread with a white linen cloth; she thought, quite rightly, that people who used mats did so to save washing, and she thought it unsuitable to save in that way. She did not approve of careless, quick meals, and although she did not care greatly for food herself she coursed Solly through soup, an entrée, a sweet and a savoury every night that she faced him at that table. She insisted, making a joke of it, that he wear at least a dark coat, and preferably a dark suit, to dinner. And she insisted that there be what she called 'suitable conversation' with the meal. Suitable conversation involved a good many questions.

'And what have you been doing this afternoon?'

'I had to go to St Agnes', mother, to look at the site for the play.'

'Oh, and so we are to be vouchsafed a glimpse of the gardens at St Agnes', are we? I'm sure the Little Theatre is privileged.'

'Mr Webster is lending the upper lawn.'

'As Griselda is to play a leading role, I suppose he could not very well refuse.'

'The play was provisionally cast before he was asked for the gardens, mother.'

'That does not alter the position as much as you appear to think. Not that I care whether he lends his garden or why. He is not a man I care for greatly.'

'I didn't know that you knew him.'

'I don't.'

Silence. The soup gave place to a pork tenderloin. Solly wondered what to talk about. He must keep his mother away from international politics. This had been her study – no, not her study, her preoccupation and her particular source of neurosis – for as long as he could remember. Before her marriage, as an alert college girl determined to show that women could benefit from higher education every bit as much as men, Mrs Bridgetower had been greatly alarmed, in a highly intelligent and realistic manner, of course, by the Yellow Peril. The years of the War had been devoted, patriotically, to the Prussian Menace, but she had returned to her earlier love immediately afterward. The rise of totalitarianism had kept her busy during the 'thirties, but when the Second World War began, and Japan entered it, she brought dread of the Yellow Peril to a particularly fine flowering. Since the subjugation of Japan she had developed several terrors and menaces in Latin America and South Africa, and had, of course, given the Red Menace a great deal of attention; but, by determinedly regarding Russia as an Asiatic power she was able to make the Red Menace seem no more than a magnification of the old Yellow Peril. She was growing old and set in her ways, and old perils and dreads were dearer to her than latter-day innovations.

The trouble was that when Mrs Bridgetower was talking about any subject less portentous than the Oriental plottings in the Kremlin, she was apt to be heavily ironical, and Solly did not like to expose anything in which he was truly interested to her ill-nature. However, he must say something now, or she would hint that he did not care for her company, and stage a long and humiliating scene in which he would have to protest his affection, his concern about her weak heart, and end by making it clear that so long as she lived, the outside world held no comparable charm for him. He plunged.

'I think the play may be rather good. We've got together quite a strong cast.'

'Didn't you say that Professor Vambrace was playing a leading part?'

'Yes. Prospero.'

'Hmph. He's thin enough. Who are your women?'

'Well, there's Pearl Vambrace, she will probably play Miranda, and Cora Fielding, who will be one of the goddesses.'

Mrs Bridgetower pounced. 'But that leaves only the part of Ariel free; you don't mean to tell me that you have cast Griselda Webster for that? You are confident, I must say.'

'I did not cast the play, mother; a tentative list of the cast has been drawn up, but Mrs Forrester did that before I was asked to have anything to do with it.'

'I suppose Mrs Forrester cast her because of her looks. Well, I for one have never thought much of them; she looks a regular Dolly Varden, in my view.' Just what Mrs Bridgetower meant by this condemnation was not clear. But Solly knew it of old, as a phrase used by his mother to describe any girl to whom she thought he might be attracted.

Aha, so that was it? Mother thought he admired Griselda? No wonder she was being so ugly.

At this point the tenderloin gave place to a Floating Island. Gobbets of meringue sat motionless upon a chocolate sea.

He must be cautious. He must reveal no hint of feeling for Griselda, to whom, in fact, he was reasonably indifferent, nor must he hasten to agree with his mother. She would at once suspect agreement as a form of duplicity and be more than ever convinced of this attachment.

'There are not many girls available at present who would do at all,' he said. 'I don't suppose you would prefer to see Ariel played by Pearl Vambrace?'

This was an astute move. His mother's contempt for the Vambraces was one of her lesser intellectual amusements.

'It will be six of one and half-dozen of the other, I should say. Though the Vambrace girl would probably be a little more hesitant about showing her legs. And with good reason.'

Once again Solly was compelled to admire the fire which his mother could rouse in herself by the mention of young women's legs. They were an iniquity which she attacked with the violence and vituperative strength of a Puritan divine. Not that she lacked reason in the present case; Griselda's legs were not a matter upon which anyone remained indifferent; those who did not condemn them as incitements to worldliness were lost in admiration. In her latest speech she had scored a double; she had condemned Griselda's legs because they were beautiful, and sneered at poor Pearl Vambrace's because they were not. Mrs Bridgetower had indeed benefited from higher education.

'When do you begin rehearsals?'

'At once, mother.'

'I suppose you have been busy preparing the play? A good many of your cast will find it coming quite freshly to them, I am sure.'

'I've done a good deal of work. But I shan't really be directing.'

'Oh? And why not?'

'Miss Valentine Rich has come back to Salterton for the summer, and Mrs Forrester has asked her to do it. When they asked me to step down I was glad enough to do so. After all, she's a professional. I shall work with her, and I hope to learn a good deal.'

'Valentine Rich? That granddaughter of old Professor Savage who went on the stage?'

'She has made quite a reputation.'

'So she ought. There was brains in the family. I see. And is she here now?'

'She arrived this afternoon. I think she has come home to settle up the old man's affairs.'

'I presume she was his heir. Well, she might have come back sooner. He was entirely alone at the end.'

'Not entirely, mother. He had many friends, and I heard that they were very good during his last years and his illness.'

'They were no kin. I hope I shall not have to die with only strangers at hand. However, one must take whatever Fate has in store for one.'

Solly recognized danger. When under stress of emotion it was his mother's habit to speak of herself as 'one'; somehow it made her self-pity appear more truly pathetic. But by this time the Floating Island had been consumed, and prunes wrapped in fried bacon had also come and gone. His mother rose.

'Shall we have coffee now, or will you join me later?'

This was a survival from the days when, for a few months, the late Professor Bridgetower had sat at table for precisely five minutes after his wife, drinking a glass of invalid port which had been ordered as a tonic. The notion that men lingered over their wine had taken hold, and Mrs Bridgetower still pretended that Solly might take it into his head to do so. There was no wine in the house, only the brandy kept against Mrs Bridgetower's 'spells' and Solly's own private bottle which he kept in his sitting-room cupboard. He did not trouble to answer his mother, but rose and followed her to the gloomy drawing-room, where a great many books lived in glass and leaden prisons, like the china in the dining-room. There, in the gloom, they took coffee ceremoniously and joylessly, as though it were for their health. And thus concluded what they would have been surprised to learn was the most ceremonious and ample dinner eaten that night in Salterton. It was Mrs Bridgetower's notion that everyone lived as she did, except people like the Websters, who ate much more, and took longer to do it.

'Well,' she said, as she put down her cup, 'it will be a pleasure to see *The Tempest* once again. I have seen the Ben Greet Players perform it, and also Beerbohm Tree when I was a girl. Your father and I saw it at Stratford on our memorable trip of 1934. Whatever Miss Rich and Griselda Webster concoct between them, I shall have my rich memories.'

As soon as he decently could, Solly composed his mother with a book about geopolitics, and retired to his own room in the attic, saying that he had work to do. His mother's enmity toward Griselda had produced the effect that anyone but Mrs Bridgetower could have predicted; by nine o'clock, as Griselda was reheating her bath for the third time, and wishing vaguely that she had something more interesting to do than pursue the placid love of Mary Lawther, Solly was sitting in his attic, drinking rye and tap water, and wishing that he had the courage to call her, and suggest that they meet for – what? He could not have his mother's car; he knew of no place to go. His impotence and his fear of his mother saddened him, and he poured some more rye into his glass, and put a melancholy piece of Mozart on his gramophone.

It was at this time, also, that Valentine Rich, who had escaped from the Forresters', stood in her grandfather's deserted house, holding in her hand a bundle of letters which she had written to the old man during the past twelve years. Each was dated on its envelope; all were neatly bound together with a piece of ribbon. They were the first things which she found when she had opened his old-fashioned domestic safe. She had loved and honoured him, and although she did not wish him alive again, she missed him sorely. Before she continued her search she sat in his revolving desk chair, and wept for the passing of time, and the necessary death of the well-loved, wise old man.

[TWO]

Having decided that he would ask for a part in the play, Hector Mackilwraith acted quickly, within the limits imposed by his temperament. He did nothing that Friday night. He returned to his room at the YMCA and passed a pleasant evening marking a batch of algebra tests. To this work he brought a kind of mathematical elegance, and even a degree of wit. He was not the kind of schoolmaster who scribbles on exercise papers; with a red pencil as sharp as a needle he would put a little mark at the point where a problem had gone wrong, not in such a way as to assist the erring student, but merely in order to show him where he had fallen into mathematical sin. His assessment of marks was a miracle of even-handed justice; there were pupils, of course, who brought their papers back to him with complaints that they had not been given proper credit for their work, but they did it in a perfunctory manner, as a necessary ceremonial rather than with a hope of squeezing an extra mark out of Hector.

It was in dealing with stupid pupils that his wit was shown. A dunce, who had done nothing right, would not receive a mark of Zero from him, for Hector would geld the unhappy wretch of marks not only for arriving at a wrong solution, but for arriving at it by a wrong method. It was thus possible to announce to the class that the dunce had been awarded *minus* thirty-seven out of a possible hundred marks; such announcements could not be made more than two or three times a year, but they always brought a good laugh. And that laugh, it must be said, was not vaingloriously desired by Hector as a tribute to himself, but only in order that it might spur the dunce on to greater mathematical effort. That it never did so was one of the puzzles which life brought to Hector, for he was convinced of the effectiveness of ridicule in making stupid boys and girls intelligent.

If he had dealt in ridicule wholesale, and if he had joyed in it for its own sake, he would have been a detestable schoolroom tyrant, and his classes would have hated him. But he dealt out ridicule in a selfless, almost priestly, manner, and most of his pupils admired him. Mackilwraith, they said among themselves, knew his stuff and would stand no nonsense. There is a touch of the fascist in most adolescents; they admire the strong man who stands no nonsense; they have no objection to seeing the weak trampled underfoot; mercy in its more subtle forms is outside their understanding and has no meaning for them. Hector, with his minus awards for the stupid, suited them very well, insofar as they thought about him at all.

The class upon whose work he was engaged on this particular evening lacked any remarkable dunce, any girl with a hopelessly addled brain, or a boy who was incapable of recognizing even the simplest sets of factors. But there were certain papers upon which he put a cabbalistic word which he had taken over from a teacher of his own younger days. Written always in capitals, and flaming like the Tetragrammaton on the breastplate of the High Priest, the word was TOSASM, and it was formed from the initials of a teacher's heartcry – The Old Stupid and Silly Mistake.

The following morning, however, as soon as he had taken breakfast at the Snak Shak, he went to a bookshop and bought a copy of *The Tempest*. He then made his way to the Salterton Collegiate and Vocational Institute, for although there were no classes on Saturdays it was Hector's custom to enjoy the freedom of the empty building. He let himself in, nodded to a couple of janitors who were, as school janitors so often are, mopping at something invisible in the corridors, made his way to the Men Teachers' Room, and settled down to read the play, and to make up his mind which part he would request for himself.

Hector's acquaintance with the works of Shakespeare was not extensive. When himself at school he had been required to read and answer questions about *Julius Caesar*, *The Merchant of Venice* and *Henry V*; owing to some fold or tremor in the curriculum he had been compelled to spend two years upon this latter play. In his mind these plays were lumped together with *Hiawatha*, *The Lay of the Last Minstrel* and *Sohrab and Rustum*, as 'literature' – that is to say, ambiguous and unsupported assertions by men of lax mind. But as he had grown older, he had grown more tolerant toward literature; there might be, he admitted to himself, 'something in it'. But it was not for him, and he had had no truck with it. He very rarely read a book which was not about mathematics, or about how to teach mathematics; he subscribed to *The American Mathematical Monthly*; he read newspapers and news magazines, and occasionally he relaxed with *The Reader's Digest*, for he had a taste for amateur doctoring, and liked to ponder over the miraculous drugs and therapeutic methods described there.

He found *The Tempest* somewhat baffling. He had supported the suggestion that the Little Theatre present a Shakespearean play, for he was strongly in favour of plays which were 'worth while'; it was widely admitted that Shakespeare was worth while. But in what precise union of qualities this worthwhileness lay was unknown to him. His first encounter with *The Tempest* was like that of the man who bites a peach and breaks a tooth upon the stone.

In the very first scene, for instance, there was a coarse reference to the Female Functions. He read it again and again; he consulted the notes, but they were unhelpful; in spite of a conviction held over from school days that poets were people who hid their meaning, such as it was, in word puzzles it seemed clear enough that in this case Shakespeare meant to be Smutty. Obviously this was a play to be approached with the utmost caution. He might even have to change his mind about acting.

He read on. It was toilsome work, but by mid-afternoon he had finished *The Tempest*, he understood it, he had assessed the value of every part in it, and although he would not have gone so far as to say that he liked it, he admitted to himself that there was probably 'something in it'. He had decided, also, that the part for him was Gonzalo. This person was described as 'an honest old counsellor', and he had no offensive lines to speak; he had fifty-two speeches, some of them quite long but none which would place an undue strain upon his memory; he was not required to do anything silly, and he would require a fairly impressive costume and almost certainly the desired false whiskers. This was the part for him. He would speak to Mrs Forrester about it on Monday night.

He began memorizing the part of Gonzalo that evening, and was word perfect in his first scene before he went to bed.

At twenty-five minutes past eight on Monday evening Hector was on the pavement outside the apartment building where the Forresters lived. He was a little early, for he intended to make his call at half-past eight exactly. It would not do to surprise the Forresters at their evening meal, or too soon after it. He had calculated that people in the Forresters' position ate at seven o'clock. He himself ate at the Snak Shak from six to six twenty-five precisely, every evening of his life. This evening he had returned to the YMCA, re-washed his already clean face and hands, and put on the clean shirt which he would not normally have worn until Tuesday morning. He put on a new blue tie, especially purchased, and felt as he looked in the mirror that it produced a rather rich effect under his ruddy face and somewhat heavy bluish jowl. He then waited patiently, running over Gonzalo's first scene in his head, until it was time to make his call. And, as always, he reached his destination ahead of time. So he walked to a point two blocks away, walked back again, and at eight-thirty precisely he pressed the bell of the Forresters' apartment.

Nellie opened the door. 'Good-evening, Mrs Forrester,' said Hector; 'I just happened to be passing, and I remembered something I wanted to mention to you.'

A surprise awaited him in the tasteful living-room. Vambrace, Valentine Rich, young Bridgetower and a person whom he still thought of as 'the Webster girl' were seated there. It was not until this moment that he realized how sensitive and secretive he was about his desire to act; he could not possibly blurt out his request before these people. His dismay showed in his face.

'We were just chewing over a few problems,' said Mrs Forrester. 'You sit down over there.' She pointed to an empty armchair. 'I'm sure you'll agree with me. Now listen: the first scene of the play is a storm at sea; the garden at St Agnes' runs right down to the lake; why can't we have the first scene on a real ship in the lake, and then get everybody to move their chairs to the upper lawn for the rest of the play?'

'I don't think they'd like to walk all that way, carrying chairs,' said Professor Vambrace. 'Many members of our audience are advanced in years. As a matter of fact, they may stay away from a pastoral; the damp, you know, after sundown.'

'It seems to me that Mrs Pauldron brought that up when it was suggested that we use her lawn,' said Griselda, innocently.

'It's quite a different quality of damp at her place,' said Mrs Forrester; 'and the garden at St Agnes' is on a much higher ground. The warmth of the day lingers there much longer.'

This remarkable piece of sophistry was allowed to pass without further comment.

'Larry won't like it,' said Solly; 'in fact I don't suppose he'd even talk about it. Your scheme would mean two sets of lights.'

'Not a bit of it,' said Mrs Forrester; 'the ship scene would be played before sundown. There would be a lovely natural light.'

'It isn't really practical, Nell,' said Valentine Rich. 'Audiences hate hopping up and down. And anyhow, where would your storm be on a perfectly calm bay?'

'If we are going to act outdoors, why don't we make the utmost use of Nature?' said Nellie. 'Surely that's the whole point of pastorals; to get away from all the artificiality of the theatre, and co-operate with the beauty of Nature?'

'No, Nell; I've done several outdoor plays, and my experience has been that Nature has to be kept firmly in check. Nature, you see, is very difficult to rehearse, and Nature has a bad trick of missing its cues. If I am to direct the play, I really must veto the ship on the lake.'

'All right,' said Nellie, 'but if you wish later on that you had done it, don't expect any sympathy from me.'

'I promise you that I won't,' said Valentine.

It was at this point that Roscoe Forrester came in from the kitchen with a tray of drinks. He was a man who liked to make a commotion about refreshments. When Valentine asked for a whisky and soda he was loud in his approval; that, he said, was what he liked to hear. When Griselda asked for some soda water with a slice of lemon in it he became coy and strove to persuade her to let him put 'just a little stick' in it.

'No, really,' said she; 'my father has promised me a bicycle if I don't drink until I'm fifty.'

'But you've already got a car –,' said Roscoe, and then perceiving that a mild jest was toward, he roared, and slapped his thigh, and called upon the others to enjoy it. He was the sort of man who does not expect women to make jokes.

'I don't permit Pearl to touch a drop,' said Professor Vambrace, solemnly. 'A matter of principle. And also, she is obliged to favour her stomach.'

Roscoe hastened to agree that a girl's stomach deserved every consideration. 'What about you, hon?' he asked, beaming at his wife.

'Well, just a weeny wee drinkie,' said Nellie, and as he poured it she gave little gasps and smothered shrieks as evidence of her fear that it might turn into a big drinkie.

Professor Vambrace's principle was solely for his daughter's benefit; when asked to pour for himself he was generous, though sparing with the soda which, he explained unnecessarily, was likely to cause acidity if taken in too great quantity. Hector and Solly were allowed to receive their drinks without comment.

It was then discovered that Hector had taken Roscoe's chair, and there was a polite uproar, Roscoe asserting loudly that he preferred the floor to any chair ever made, Hector saying that he could not hear of such a thing, and Professor Vambrace pointing out very sensibly that the dining-room was full of chairs, which he would be happy to move in any quantity. At last order was restored, with Roscoe on the floor smiling too happily, as people do when they seek to spread an atmosphere of ease and calm.

'There's a point which we mustn't overlook,' said Nellie, turning her wee drinkie round and round in her hands and looking solemnly. 'We'll have a lot of resistance to break down, doing a pastoral. People here haven't been educated to them, yet. Actually, you might say that we are pioneering the pastoral in this part of the world. So we'll need strong backing.'

'I don't favour advertisement,' said Professor Vambrace; 'I've never found that it paid.' This was true; in the quantities approved by Professor Vambrace, advertisement might just as well not have been attempted; he was a homeopath in the matter of public announcement.

'It isn't advertisement in the ordinary sense that I'm thinking about,' said Nellie; 'I mean, we want to get the right people behind us. I wonder if we wouldn't be wise to have a list of patrons, and put them in the programme.'

'Aha, I see what you mean,' said Professor Vambrace, glowering intelligently over his glass; 'friends, as it were, of the production. In that case, the leading name would be that of Mr G. A. Webster, the father of our charming young friend, here; he has lent his garden, and that is very real support – solid support, I may say.' He laughed, deeply and inwardly; it was as though barrels were being rolled in the cellars of the apartment house.

'It goes without saying that Mr Webster is a very important patron,' said Nellie, in what she conceived to be a tactful tone, 'and his name must be on the list along with the District Officer Commanding and both Bishops, and the Provost of Waverley and the Mayor and the president of the Chamber of Commerce. But to head the list I feel that we want a name which will mean something to everybody – the name of someone whose position is absolutely unassailable; I was rather thinking – what would you say to Mrs Caesar Augustus Conquergood?'

In such roundabout terms as these are the secret passions of the heart brought before the world. Mrs Caesar Augustus Conquergood was the god of Nellie's idolatry. This lady, whom she had rarely seen, was her social ideal; the late Conquergood had been associated in some highly honourable capacity with the Army, and he and his wife had been moderately intimate at Rideau Hall during the Governor-Generalship of the Duke of Devonshire; the widow Conquergood was reputed to be very wealthy, and doubtless the report was correct, for she enjoyed that most costly of all luxuries in the modern world, privacy; she was very rarely seen in Salterton society, and when she appeared, she might have been said to hold court. Nellie had met her but once. She did not seek to thrust herself upon her goddess; she wished only to love and serve Mrs Caesar Augustus Conquergood, to support and if such a thing were possible, increase her grandeur. If Mrs Caesar Augustus Conquergood's name might appear, alone, at the top of an otherwise double column of patrons of the Salterton Little Theatre then, in Nellie's judgement, the drama had justified its existence, Thespis had not rolled his car in vain, and Shakespeare was accorded a posthumous honour which he barely deserved.

There is a dash of pinchbeck nobility about snobbery. The true snob acknowledges the existence of something greater than himself, and it may, at some time in his life, lead him to commit a selfless act. Nellie would, under circumstances of sufficient excitement, have thrown herself in the path of runaway horses to save the life of Mrs Caesar Augustus Conquergood, and would have asked no reward – no, not even an invitation to tea – if she survived the ordeal. Such a passion is not wholly ignoble. She had schemed for four months for this moment when she would put her adored one's name at the head of a list of patrons for *The Tempest*, and nothing must go wrong now.

'I don't know that I am in complete agreement with you,' she heard tiresome Professor Vambrace saying; 'if we are to have patrons, surely they should be people who have helped our Little Theatre in some way. I cannot recall that Mrs Conquergood has attended a single performance.'

'Ah, but you see,' said Nellie, 'if we interest her, she will become a regular supporter.'

'It seems a very ostentatious method of gaining her attention,' said

Vambrace, 'and if we have to print her name in the programme to get her to come, we might perhaps be better off without her. After all, her dollar is no better than anybody else's.'

Nellie's neck flushed; sometimes she thought that Vambrace was no better than a Red. 'As though it were her dollar we were after,' she said, reprovingly; and then, with an affectation of serpent-like wisdom, 'her name would draw in a good many people of the very type who ought to be interested in the Little Theatre.'

'In that case, perhaps we ought to offer her a part,' said Solly. 'Now here, in Act Three, is my favourite stage direction in the whole play: *Enter several strange Shapes, bringing in a banquet*; she could be a Strange Shape; typecasting. I'll put it in the form of a motion if you like.'

'Solly, that isn't the least bit funny,' cried Nellie.

'I didn't mean it to be,' said Solly, 'it's cold fact.'

'If you can't do anything but sneer, the sooner you go back to England the better.'

'If you mean that you want me to retire from my job as assistant director of this play, Nellie, I'll do so gladly. You pushed me into directing, and then you pushed me into assisting, and if you want to push me out altogether you have only to say so.'

'Aw, now Solly, don't let's get sore,' said Roscoe; 'you know how Nell gets stewed up about things.'

'Roscoe, I don't,' cried Nellie, near to tears.

'There is no need for anybody to retire from anything, or to go back anywhere,' said Professor Vambrace. 'Nor, I think, is there any need for us to head our list of patrons with the name of a person who, whatever her social eminence may be – I am not qualified to speak upon such a point – has never done anything for the Little Theatre.'

'If I may offer my opinion, Professor,' said Hector, 'I think there is a good deal in what Mrs Forrester has said. There is powerful rivalry in Salterton society between town and gown, military and civil service, as everybody knows. We are not supposed to have these divisions in a democracy but somehow we have them. As an outsider – a teacher who is neither town nor precisely gown – I can see this perhaps better than you. I have heard it suggested that our Little Theatre is recruited a little more heavily from the Waverley faculty than is acceptable to some quite large groups of people. Of course we know why that is so; the faculty members are perhaps more active in their support of the arts than the military or the business people. But if we hope to offset an impression which I, as treasurer, consider an unfortunate one, we must be very careful about our list of patrons. I believe that we should have such a list, and I believe that it should be headed by some name not associated too closely with any of the principal groups which comprise the city. Mr Webster's name must come very high. But I agree with Mrs Forrester that the name of Mrs Caesar Augustus Conquergood should come first. I do not know her, but I have heard of her, and I have always heard her spoken of in the highest terms. I don't mind saying that I think it would have a marked effect at the box-office.'

His hearers were impressed. Hector had all the advantage of the man who speaks infrequently, and whose words carry special weight for that reason. Furthermore, his introduction of the word 'box-office' was masterly. Professional theatrical groups occasionally take a fling and perform some work, for sheer love, which they know will not make money; amateur groups never forget the insistency of the till. The notion that Mrs Conquergood's name might raise the takings was too much for Professor Vambrace, who gave in with an ill grace. The redness departed from Nellie's neck; she was jubilant, though she tried to conceal it. And she looked upon Hector as an oracle of wisdom.

Nellie's mind, though busy, was not complex. She had never mastered the simple principle of *quid pro quo* which was, to Hector's orderly intelligence, axiomatic. But she received a lesson in it half an hour later when Hector, with well-feigned casualness, said:

'When is the casting for the play to be completed?'

'Oh,' said Nellie, 'we are going to have auditions for all the parts later this week.'

'Surely not for all the parts? I understood some time ago that Professor Vambrace was to play Prospero, and Miss Vambrace Miranda, and that Miss Webster was to be Ariel. And I think you told me that young Tasset was to be Ferdinand. I believe that Caliban and the two funny men are also cast?'

'Well, tentatively, but of course we are going to hold a public reading before anything is decided finally.'

'But I think it unlikely that any of those parts will be allotted otherwise?'

'You know how it is,' said Professor Vambrace; 'the Little Theatre must give everyone a chance. Still, it is pretty plain that certain people will do certain parts better than anyone else who is likely to turn up.

And, frankly, there are some debts to be paid; those who have borne the burden deserve a measure of reward.'

This was an opening which Hector had not foreseen, but he took it with the skill of an experienced politician. The shyness which he felt when he first arrived had quite departed.

'I had thought of that myself,' said he. 'I have been treasurer of the Little Theatre for the past six years. When I took it over its books were in a mess; now they are in perfect order and we have a substantial sum in the bank. During the years when I have worked in the box office I have often wondered what it would be like to be with those of you who were enjoying the fun behind the footlights. And if there is a part which I could play in *The Tempest*, I should like to have it.'

'Why not wait until next year?' said Nellie. 'We're sure to be doing something which would have a part in it for you. You know, something good. A detective, or a policeman, or something.'

'I may not be here next autumn,' said Hector.

'Not here?' Nellie was horrified at the thought that a new treasurer would have to be found.

'No. I have been offered some work by the Department which would take me out of town. If I accept, it will mean beginning work at once. But of course, if I am offered a part in *The Tempest* I should turn down the Department's offer for the present, and would be here next season.'

Even Nellie could see what that meant.

'Had you a special part in mind?' she asked.

'It had occurred to me that I might try my hand at Gonzalo. The wise old counsellor,' said Hector, looking around for appreciation of this joke. But there was none. Professor Vambrace felt that in some way he had been finessed, and was trying to figure out where; Nellie was wondering if she had not been wrong, half an hour ago, to feel so warmly toward Hector; why, the man was nothing but a self-seeker and his obvious counting on her support seemed, in some inexplicable way, to dim the brightness of Mrs Caesar Augustus Conquergood. Valentine Rich and Solly had made up their minds independently that it was plain that, whoever cast the play, they were not to be allowed to do it. The gathering had a somewhat stunned and inward-looking air as it ate the sticky buns and coffee which Nellie brought forth, aided by the faithful Roscoe.

Hector ate a bun, and took one cup of coffee, and then made his departure, well pleased with his evening's work.

When he was gone, Nellie was the first to speak.

'Well, did you ever hear anything like that?' she cried. 'He simply put a pistol to our heads; he plays Gonzalo or we can get a new treasurer.'

'The way I look at it, it was a kind of a deal, hon,' said the artless Roscoe. 'He supported you about the patrons, and then you had to support him about the part he wanted. It's nothing to worry about; happens in business and politics every day.'

'This isn't business or politics, Roscoe. We've got our audiences to think about. For anything I know, this man has never acted before. Val, why didn't you step in and veto it? You could. You're director.'

'Really, Nell, the casting seems to be so much in the hands of the local committee that I saw no reason to interfere.'

'But he's so obviously unsuitable.'

'We don't know that yet. We can always change in the early rehearsals if he's too bad.'

'Val, this isn't professional theatre. You can't kick people out like that. So the only possible thing is to keep unsuitable ones from getting in.'

'When once particular personal interests begin to be consulted, artistic integrity flies out at the window,' said Professor Vambrace darkly.

'If that is meant to have any bearing on the arrangement of the patrons' list, I want to say here and now that I am acting only for the good of the Little Theatre.' Nellie confronted him, bravely but with tears in her eyes.

The Professor lolled his large, bushy head about on the back of his chair, and made gestures with his heavy eyebrows. 'In that case, there is nothing more to be said about the matter,' replied he.

'Yes, there is,' said Nellie, shaken with emotion; 'we've got to have some fairly good-sized parts to allot among all those people who are coming to the try-out reading on Thursday night. I was counting on Gonzalo as a nice little plum for somebody – something that would stop everybody saying that the casting of all the good parts is done by the committee beforehand – and now that man has just grabbed it. It's awful!'

'I still don't see what's so awful about it, hon,' said Roscoe, pacifically. 'What makes you think he'll be so much worse than the others?'

This crass comment caused Professor Vambrace to close his eyes.

'That's a very good question,' said Solly.

'Oh it's all very well for you all to sit around and sneer,' wailed Nellie, and burst into tears. Roscoe took her hand and patted it. 'Take it easy, hon,' said he; 'it'll all be the same in a hundred years.'

There was some embarrassment, but not very much, at Nellie's breakdown; most of the people present had seen her weep before, for reasons less easily understandable. But it seemed to put a period to a dull and exasperating evening, and they took their departure.

Professor Vambrace quickly swung away into the night; he was a man who genuinely liked walking, and his feet and the heavy ash walking stick which he carried seemed to spurn the ground. Valentine and Solly climbed into Griselda's car.

'Shall we drive for a while?' asked Griselda.

'I should like that more than anything,' said Valentine Rich.

It was not until they had left the city and were driving by the river that Solly spoke.

'I can't imagine what Nellie was making such a fuss about,' said he.

'You were very naughty about Mrs Conquergood,' said Griselda.

'Well, damn it, I squirm at that kind of thing. Why is it that a supposedly democratic country is so eaten up with snobbery of one sort and another?'

'Everybody has their own kind of snobbery. I suspect you of being an intellectual snob, Solly.'

'Well, what about you? You're rich – so rich, if you want to know, that I didn't dare call you a few nights ago because I didn't think I could entertain you suitably – and everybody that wants to know you and doesn't is sure that you're a shrieking snob.'

'I am the humblest of God's little ones,' said Griselda, passing another car a shade too closely.

'Anyhow, Nellie's fantod had nothing to do with me or Old Ma Conquergood. She was angry because Mackilwraith suddenly wanted to act. I don't see why he shouldn't. He's done a good job as treasurer, and I suppose he wants some of the glory of acting. He wants to be one of the gaudy folk of the theatre, weaving a tissue of enchantment for Mrs Caesar Augustus Conquergood and your father. Poor old cow, he's stage-struck. And at his age, too!'

'I rather liked him,' said Valentine. 'I thought it was sweet the way he came in pretending that he was passing by, and then popping out his bid for a part so neatly. I have a soft spot for people who are stage-struck. Next autumn I shall have been in the professional theatre for eighteen years, and I'm still stage-struck.'

'Heavens,' said Griselda, 'you must have started just when I was born. I'm sorry, that sounded rude.'

'I am thirty-six,' said Valentine; 'I was your age when I got my first job.'

'Did you have an awful struggle?' asked Griselda; 'I mean with your family, and getting a job, and all that.'

'No, I didn't. When I told my grandfather I wanted to be an actress he was most kind and sympathetic. And in those days there were some good stock companies, and I was able to get a job in one of them. And I've never really had much difficulty about jobs since, which is lucky, because it's chancy work. But I've always been willing to go outside New York, you see, and that makes a difference. And I've done some directing, which is helpful. So it has really been a very busy eighteen years. No, oddly enough, the only people who were discouraging were my friends. Nellie, for instance, was sure I'd never manage to get along.'

'If you don't mind saying,' said Solly, 'how did you get sucked in for directing *The Tempest* here? I mean, you probably don't look on it as the crown of your career. What made you say yes?'

'Well you see, I'm at that funny point in my life where I'm important enough to be asked to do favours, but not important enough to be able to refuse them without giving offence. When Nell found out that I was coming back to Salterton this summer, she wrote at once.'

'And you couldn't refuse an old friend?'

'I couldn't refuse someone whom I had once known, very easily. Of course, I hadn't seen her for ten or twelve years.'

'Really? I rather gathered from what she said that she might have given you your start.'

'No, no; we were friends as girls, though never very close.'

'That's very interesting, in the light of what we have heard.'

'It's fantastic to think of you and Mrs Forrester being about the same age,' said Griselda.

'We are, none the less. In fact, she is a few months younger.'

'I suppose the responsibility of the Salterton Little Theatre is what has worn her down,' said Solly.

'Don't be horrid,' said Griselda.

'Why not? You implied that Nellie looks years older than Miss Rich.'

'I know, but it's different, coming from a man.'

'What has got into you, Griselda?' said Solly. 'You've gone all mealy-mouthed and hypocritical.'

'I'm blossoming into womanhood,' said Griselda, 'and I have to be very careful about what I say. Daddy was mentioning it just a day or two ago. He said that people would take it amiss if I said what I really thought; he said a woman had to be at least forty-five before she dared risk an honest expression of opinion.'

When they had dropped Valentine at her hotel, Griselda said to Solly: 'Would you like to come home? What about something more to eat or drink?'

'You should never ask anyone to have anything *more*,' said Solly, 'for it implies that they have had perceptible refreshment already, which is rude. If you are going to make such a hullabaloo about your womanhood, you must be careful of these niceties.'

'Thank you for telling me,' said Griselda. 'I haven't really had a very good upbringing. You know what boarding-schools are. If some of the rough speech of the lacrosse field and the prefects' room still clings to me, I should be obliged if you would mention it.'

'What is going to happen to you?'

'Daddy hasn't made up his mind yet. There is talk of a finishing-school, but I'd like to go to Europe and be a student.'

'What of?'

'Oh, anything. It would be quite enough just to be a student. They seem to have such good times. Riots, and political action. Do you know that there is a university town in Italy where the police have not been permitted even to speak rudely to the students in centuries?'

'Don't be deceived. The university undoubtedly maintains a force of some kind which keeps the students under. Your idea of a student is about a hundred and fifty years out of date. Students today are a pretty solemn lot. One of the really notable achievements of the twentieth century has been to make the young old before their time.'

They had reached the front door of St Agnes' and Griselda opened it with her key. 'Don't tiptoe, Solly,' said she; 'it's only half-past eleven.'

'Sorry,' said he; 'I always tiptoe at home.'

They went into the library, which was dark, smoky and smelly. Mr Webster sat in a corner, reading the *Colnett Journals*.

'You know Solly Bridgetower, don't you, Daddy?'

'No,' said Mr Webster, 'who is he?'

'He's right here.'

'Oh. I'm sorry. I didn't see you in the shadow. What did you say your name was?'

'My name is Solomon Bridgetower, sir.'

'Well, well. I dare say you are some relative of Professor Solomon Bridgetower, who died a few years ago.'

'I am his son, sir.'

'I knew your father slightly. Were you aware that your father was perhaps the finest geologist this country ever produced?'

'I have heard many people say so.'

'Yes. Wasted, teaching. But he did some splendid work in his vacations.'

'Very good of you to say so, sir.'

'Mother still living?'

'She was very ill two months ago. I came home to look after things until she recovered.'

'I remember her as a girl. She was very interested in Oriental things at that time.'

'The Yellow Peril?'

'Yes, that was it. She still keeping up with it?'

'From hour to hour, sir.'

'Well, well; it is our hobbies that keep us young. Do you want anything to eat or drink?'

'We thought we'd see what there was, Daddy.'

'There isn't much of anything, I'm afraid. They left a few sandwiches but I ate them half an hour ago. It's a funny thing; there never seems to be enough food in this house. You could get Freddy up; she knows how to make sandwiches.'

'Oh, no, please don't do that,' said Solly.

'Or some breakfast food. I know for a fact that there is quite a lot of breakfast food in the pantry; several kinds. Would you like a bowl of breakfast food, Bridgetower?'

'No, really, sir.'

'What we'd really like, Daddy, is a drink, and you have a big tray of things right here.'

'Oh, certainly. Help yourself, Bridgetower. The ice has all melted, I'm afraid.'

'I like it at room temperature, sir.'

'Really? An English taste. Healthier, I suppose.'

'Shall I pour anything for you, Griselda?' asked Solly.

'No. I never drink anything. I don't think it becoming in one of my years. I expect when I'm old and hardened I'll soak. Freddy drinks.'

'What? Freddy drink? Nonsense!' said Mr Webster.

'Oh nothing serious, Daddy. She's what I'd call a nipper. A nip here and a nip there. Like health salts; as much as will lie on a ten-cent piece.'

'Rubbish. She's going through a religious spell. She can't have both a religious spell and a nipping spell at the same time.'

'Oh Daddy, don't be provincial. It's only evangelicals who can't mix drink and religion. Freddy's madly Anglo-Cat; they swig and pray like anything.'

Griselda went on chattering to Solly, and Mr Webster reflected, as he had done so many times, how wretchedly he missed his wife. She would have known what to say to young men that Griselda brought home. She would have dealt with Freddy's religious nonsense. She would have gone at once to the heart of the matter about Freddy drinking. But what can a father do? Can he confront a girl of fourteen and say, Do you drink? He cannot beat her, and he most certainly cannot reason with her. Why didn't those schoolmistresses do their job? He wished, sometimes, that as fate had decided to make him a widower, fate had done the job properly and made him a childless widower. He was very fond of Griselda and Freddy, but he confessed to himself that he really had no firm idea of how they should be brought up. If they had been boys, now –. But girls were such unpredictable creatures. He came of a generation to which any girl, before she is married, is a kind of unexploded bomb.

'I'd better go now,' said Solly, when he had finished his drink. 'My mother worries until I am home, and I don't want to distress her.'

'I hope we'll see you often, Bridgetower,' said Mr Webster.

'You will, sir.'

'Solly's helping with the play,' explained Griselda.

'Oh God,' said her father; 'do you know, for the last two or three days I have quite forgotten about that play?'

'I hope you won't find it too dreadful, sir.'

'Daddy's terribly jealous of his garden.'

'I know it sounds ridiculous, but when I am at home I can't bear the thought of strangers trampling about just outside the house. It fusses me. But it's unreasonable, of course. I recognize that. So if you see me glowering out of windows at you, pay no attention, will you?'

'I know how you feel, sir,' said Solly, and went with Griselda out of the little pool of light through the dark corridor to the door.

Instead of leading him to her car Griselda took him by the arm and headed for the garden. 'Let's walk for a few minutes,' said she. 'Your mother won't really mind, will she?'

Solly knew how very much his mother minded lateness, and how much more she would mind it if she suspected that he was walking in the moonlight with a girl who was, in her opinion, a regular Dolly Varden. But it is not easy for a young man to suggest to a girl that her charms do not outweigh his mother's displeasure, and before Solly knew quite what was happening they were approaching the upper lawn, chosen as the scene of the play.

Griselda said nothing as they walked, which alarmed Solly. The thought flashed through his mind that perhaps Griselda had been possessed by a sudden passion for him, and that she would demand something – possibly even what novelists occasionally referred to as All – from him here among the trees. Griselda was beautiful, and he was not lacking in the attributes of a man. But there is a time and a place for everything, and Solly felt that if there were to be any scenes of passion between himself and Griselda, he would like to stage manage them in his own way. The thought which was uppermost in his mind, when at last Griselda stopped and turned to him, was that his mother never went to sleep until he had come home and that her displeasure and concern, issuing from her rather as the haze of ectoplasm issues from a spiritualist medium, filled the house whenever he came home late.

'Solly,' said Griselda, looking at him solemnly, 'you said something when we were driving which worried me. You said that you wanted to take me out last week and didn't because you were afraid that you couldn't amuse me. Please, Solly, don't do that again.'

'Well, all right, I won't. But what could we do?'

'Do we have to do anything? You can come and drink Daddy's whisky and talk, if you like. Or we can go out in my car. Really, Solly, it frightened me when you said that people thought I was a snob and didn't dare ask me out unless they had lakhs of rupees and big emeralds clenched in their navels. I've been awfully lonely since I came home. I don't know many people in Salterton.'

'I wasn't really being serious.'

'I think you were.'

'Well, all right then, I was. You see how it is, Griselda. People think you expect the very best of everything –'

'Then people don't know.'

'Your father is a very rich man –'

'For Salterton. I expect really rich people sneer at him and ask him to carry their bags.'

'But it isn't just money. You look as if you expected a great deal.'

'Can I help the way I look?'

'You'd be out of your mind if you wanted to. You know that you're beautiful, don't you?'

'I'm beautiful about on the scale that Daddy's rich – for Salterton.'

'But it's more than your looks. You have the air of one who wants rather special things, and special people.'

'Of course I do. But I also want all sorts of things and all sorts of people.'

'Me among them? Thanks.'

'You're very special.'

'Oh? Well, thanks again.'

'Don't be difficult, Solly. I have to be myself. I suppose that by all the rules of what people expect I should be a loud-laughing, bug-eyed, silly little mutt at eighteen, but I'm not. I feel quite calm and collected most of the time. I'm an oddity, I suppose. Like you.'

'What's so odd about me?'

'You don't need to be told. It's not just that you have brains. It's that you seem to have a skin less than other people. People like Nellie Forrester abrade you. And when you snarl at them most people think it's superiority, but I know that it's because they sin against something you hold very dear. I've known you for years in a kind of way, Solly. I want to know you, really and truly. So promise me that if you feel like talking to me, you'll say so?'

'Of course I will, Griselda darling.' Solly was so touched by her understanding of him that he had quite forgotten about his mother. So touched indeed, that he took Griselda in his arms and kissed her, with an admirable mixture of friendliness and gallantry.

It was at this moment that a thin and watery beam of light swept across the dewy grass and fell upon them, and Freddy's voice was heard to say 'Aha!' in melodramatic accents.

'Freddy, go back to bed and stop Ahaing like Hawkshaw the Detective.'

Freddy said 'Aha!' again, with marked relish.

'Freddy, you are behaving like the comic kid sister in a cheap farce,' cried Solly. He and Griselda, hand in hand, ran across the lawn and stood under Freddy's window.

'You keep your hooks out of Solly,' said Freddy, from above. 'He's for me, if I decide not to be a nun.'

'You have entirely misunderstood the situation,' said Solly. 'I was paying a compliment to your sister's intellect and discernment, and not what you think.'

'Boloney,' cried Freddy; 'Gristle has a gob of pink goo where her brain should be, and you know it. I'm glad I had my big flashlight. You looked just like a love-scene in a cheap movie.'

'Remind me when we meet to lecture you on the proper use of coarseness in repartee,' said Solly. 'And now, I really must go home.'

Griselda drove him home, and he kissed her again before he got out of her car, and promised to see her often.

His key seemed to make a shattering noise in the lock. And when he entered the hall, which was in darkness, maternal solicitude and pique embraced him like the smell of cooking cabbage. He crept upstairs and there, as he knew it would be, was the light coming from his mother's half-open door. There was nothing else for it, so he braced himself to be a good son.

'Still awake, mother?' he said, looking in.

'Oh, there you are, lovey. I was beginning to worry. Come in.'

With her teeth out and her hair in a pigtail his mother looked much older that she did in the daytime. On the counterpane lay *The Asiatic Enigma*. Solly sat at the end of the bed, noting as he did so that she had her maternal expression on, the one which was reserved for him alone. Gone was the formality and irony of the dining-table; this was Mother, alone with her Boy.

'What kept you so long?'

'It was a long meeting. We had a lot of details to clear up.'

'At this hour? Surely not.'

'Well, afterward a few of us went for a short drive to clear our heads.'

'That must have been very pleasant. Who drove?'

'Griselda Webster.'

'I see. You weren't going too fast, I hope?'

'No, no; quite slowly.'

'Who else was with you?'

'Oh, Valentine Rich was one. She's very nice.'

'Yes, I'm sure all these girls you meet are very nice, but there's always one at home, lovey, isn't there – waiting till whatever time it may be.'

'Yes, of course, mother; you're the pick of the lot. But it's only half-past twelve, you know.'

'Really? It seemed later. But since I've been ill, I find the nights very long.'

'Then you must go to sleep at once, dear.'

Solly kissed his mother, and went to the door.

'Lovey?'

'Yes, mother?'

'There's something on your mouth, dear – something that tastes rather like scent. Something you have been eating, I suppose. Wash it off, dear.'

Hector's good sense and caution prevented him from any premature rejoicing on the strength of his tactical victory at Nellie Forrester's. He knew that Nellie and Vambrace and those who comprised the artistic element in the Little Theatre were not pleased that he should wish to act, although he was not aware how deep their opposition went or from what it sprang. There is always resentment when a beast of burden shows a desire to prance and paw the air in the company of horses trained in the *haute école*, and to Nellie and her friends Hector's ambition seemed no less pitiable than presumptuous. His superiority in the box office was freely admitted; his generalship in the annual drive to sell subscription tickets and memberships for the Little Theatre was the subject of a generously worded vote of thanks at every annual meeting; his insistence upon issuing a pink slip of authorization every time it was necessary to buy something for the plays was tolerated, because it saved a great deal of money and prevented Larry Pye from running up ruinous bills at lumber yards and electrical supply houses. He had the respect of the whole Little Theatre so long as he remained its business genius, and by applying some simple rules of business to an organization which was made up of unbusinesslike people he had achieved a reputation for fiscal wizardry. But when he expressed a desire to act, it suddenly appeared to those who admired him as a treasurer that he was a graceless dolt, intolerable in the world of high art in which they moved. Such sudden reverses of opinion are not uncommon when a man seeks to change his role in the world.

Hector knew that his battle was not quite won. Nevertheless he allowed himself to say to his colleague Mr Adams, the head of the English Department, when they met in the teachers' commonroom, 'I hope you'll be in town in late June?'

'Yes, I will,' said Adams. 'Why?'

'The Little Theatre are going to do *The Tempest*; I thought you'd be interested.'

'Yes, of course. That's very ambitious. Are they going to be able to get together a strong cast?'

'Yes, I think so. Though perhaps I shouldn't say that for it looks as though I might take a part myself. I hope I won't be the weakest link in the chain.'

'I'm sure you won't,' said Adams, who was not really sure at all, and he went on his way reflecting that wonders would never cease, and that if Old Binomial was going to appear, he would certainly not miss the play for anything, as it was sure to yield a few good unintentional laughs. Mr Adams had been an indifferent student of mathematics himself, and had a grudge against Hector because he gave too much homework to his pupils who might otherwise have been writing essays for Mr Adams. But he quickly spread the news that Hector was about to blossom forth as an actor, and the following day the Principal referred to it facetiously when he met Hector in the corridor. And all of this Hector enjoyed greatly, as an old maid might enjoy being twitted about the possession of an admirer.

But he knew very well that until he had successfully passed the test of the casting reading later in the week, where, if ever, his opponents would trip him up, the part of Gonzalo was not assured to him.

Hector's life had not been of the sort which usually brings forth actors, – even Little Theatre actors. Not, of course, that any particular circumstances can be relied upon to bring forth a particular sort of ability, but his life had been notably unfriendly toward the development of that taste for stimulating pretence which actors must possess. He had been born in a small Ontario village where his father was the

Presbyterian minister. The Reverend John Mackilwraith was a failure. The reason for his insufficiency, if it could be discovered now, probably lay in his health. He never seemed to feel as well as other men, but as he had never known good health he had no standard of comparison, and accepted his lot, almost without complaint. That is to say, he never complained of feeling unwell, and he rarely complained in an open manner about anything else, but his whole way of life was a complaint and a reproach to those who came into contact with him. He was unsatisfactory to his congregation, because when they complained to him of misfortunes they were uncomfortably conscious that he had misfortunes of greater extent and longer duration. At funerals his mien of settled woe somehow robbed the chief mourners of their proper eminence. At weddings his appearance was likely to turn the nervous tears of a bride into a waterspout of genuine apprehension. Because the church which he served demands a high standard of scholarship in its clergy it is certain that at one time he must have known a reasonable amount of Hebrew and a good deal of Latin and Greek, but these classical attainments had not wrought their supposed magic of enrichment on his mind, and nothing that could be traced to them was ever to be discerned in his sermons, which were earnest, long and incomprehensible. He pursued his career, if such a spirited word may be applied to so dispirited a life, at a time when church-going was much more a social obligation than it is now, and in communities where any lapse from conventional conduct was soon noticed and sharply censured. But, even with these advantages, he quickly reduced his congregations to a determined and inveterate rump of faithful souls who felt that without Presbyterianism, even on this level, life was not worth living. When Hector was born he was in his last, and worst, charge.

The Reverend John was no doubt to be pitied, but pity is an emotion which cannot be carried on for years. He was a gloomy and depressing parson. There are parsons who make gloom an instrument of their work. They are actively and challengingly gloomy; their gloom is from a banked-down fire of wrath against the villainies of mankind which threatens at any minute to burst into roaring flame. There are parsons who are gently melancholy, as though eternal longings had brought on a mild nausea. But John Mackilwraith's gloom had none of this professional character. Ribald fellows in the village called him Misery Mackilwraith. And yet, who knows? Professional attention to his diet, injections of a few elements missing in his physical makeup, a surgical operation, or a few hours' conversation with a psychiatrist might have made a different man of him. But none of these solutions ever occurred to him. Instead, he sent up long, miserable prayers to God, with no expectation that anything would come of them. He had grown accustomed to neglect in all quarters.

Hector's tender years were passed in an atmosphere which could not be properly described as religious, though religion played a greater part in his consciousness than would have been the case if he had been the son of a butcher or a grocer. There was no deep devotion, no consciousness of hidden sources of strength, not even a rigid puritanism in that household. But weddings and funerals, the drudgery of pastoral calls, the recurrent effort of Sunday and the consequent exhaustion of Monday were familiar to him as the accompaniments of his father's profession. And he knew from his earliest days that he was a dedicated boy; he was expected to be an example not only to all Presbyterian boys in the district but a reproach to boys of lesser faiths. He knew that much was exacted of the cloth in both the spiritual and physical senses, for when his father's black trousers were cut down into knickerbockers for him he was singled out not only by his solemnity of expression, but by the startling blackness and shininess of his lower parts. And because he had been born to this lot, he accepted it without question; as children always do, and as some adults continue to do, he invented reasons why he should be as he was, instead of seeking for means by which he might be delivered from his fate.

His mother did nothing to relieve the misery of the household, though she could not justly have been said to increase it. She took colour from her husband, for she had no strong character of her own. The Reverend John had married her in the first year of his first charge. She had been a farm girl, living with an uncle and aunt, and she had thought that it would be a fine thing to be a minister's wife. She knew nothing of men, and her suitor's glumness and lack of energy appeared to her as the attributes of a being spiritually and intellectually superior to farm boys. The latter, she knew, 'had thoughts' about girls; it was plain that the Reverend John had no thoughts of that kind about them at all. He wanted what he called 'an helpmeet'. He nominated her for this position one evening at nine o'clock in the parlour of the farmhouse; she accepted the nomination at precisely one minute after nine, and by a quarter past nine the fortunate suitor was walking back to his boarding-house, having kissed his fiancée once on the brow. They married, and she discovered that being an helpmeet to a minister was not such hard work as helping around the farm. With the man she had chosen, however, it was not enspiriting, and by the time Hector was born, twelve years later, she was as miserable and as steeped in failure as he.

She was a short, stout woman, shaped like a cottage loaf. A nubbin, with a twist of wispy hair on it, formed her head; a larger nubbin comprised her bust and upper reaches; the largest nubbin of all was formed by her spreading hips. She must have had legs, but her skirts concealed them. She had little to say, and it is doubtful if her mental processes could be called thought; they consisted of a series of dissolving views, mostly of possible disasters and misfortunes which might overtake her and her family. Because she was an unready speaker she was not able to dominate the women in the churches where her husband ministered, and because she could not dominate them she became their drudge. She always had more sewing, or baking, or money-collecting to do than any of the others, not because she did them well but because she was not alert enough to secure an organizing position whenever a bazaar or a 'drive' for funds was projected.

The birth of Hector brought to her life its one lasting passion. She loved him as dearly as her inexperienced heart would allow. He was a large and solemn baby, and he throve in spite of his mother's care. Her physician assured her that he was a splendid child, and needed nothing but food and sleep for his well-being, but Mrs Mackilwraith had lived too long with her husband to be able to believe any nonsense of that kind. She breast-fed him, and worried that he was not getting enough, or that if sufficient in quantity, her milk was deficient in quality; she could not trust herself to produce the right sustenance for her darling. She augmented his breast feedings, therefore, with patent foods, which she tried to make him drink from a cup when he was three weeks old, almost finishing him in the process. Because he was stuffed, he occasionally threw up, which convinced her that he had some malformation of his digestive fittings. She put too many frocks on him, which made him restless, and she starched them, which made him break out in rashes; she treated the restlessness by walking the floor with him, and the rashes by salves, which did no good. Kindly women tried to tell her what to do for her child, and her doctor grew almost abusive, but it was useless; she was determined that Hector was hard to raise, and with the ability to attract ill-fortune which she had caught from her husband, she made it so.

Indeed, if he had not been a sturdy child he might have succumbed to his mother's determination that he should linger close to death's door. When he grew out of babyhood she dosed him for constipation. This was a bugbear of the Reverend John's, and she was convinced that Hector had inherited it. Her husband took a large dose of castor oil every Saturday in order that his brain might be at its keenest on Sunday. But it was clear to her that such weekly dosing was not enough for a child, and Hector was plagued with syrups, pellets, suppositories and nastiness of every kind all the week through, and because his young bowels were never permitted to have a mind of their own, they behaved whimsically and he often had pains. Nor was constipation all. His mother believed that whenever a child had a white ring around its mouth, it was suffering from worms. Hector, whose inside was continually being churned with cathartics, very often had this symptom, and the worm powder was poured from its pink tissue wrapper upon his tongue, followed by a gobbet of jam which only made the dose more gritty and nauseous.

Because Hector was a growing boy, he was encouraged and indeed compelled by his mother to stuff himself, and though constipated and supposedly wormy he grew into a hearty lump of a lad, with thick, curly black hair, long eyelashes, solemn grey eyes and ruddy cheeks. When he was disturbed a dark flush crept over his face. It was this high colour, as much as anything, which made other boys dislike him. The children of Canada are not, in general, ruddy; hot summers, bitter winters and the heat of winter houses all combine to make them pale, though it is a healthy pallor. Church mothers agreed that 'that young one of Reverend Mackilwraith's looked as if he was going to have apoplexy any time', and their sons resented and bullied Hector as something different from themselves.

He bore this bullying with stoicism. He felt that he was picked on because he was better than the others. There was no snobbery in this thought; it was the way of the world that a minister's son should be better than other boys. He was even good-natured about it. But once he lost his temper.

He was being baited by a rat-faced boy, a Baptist – Hector knew the religious denomination of every child in the school, as a matter of course – who had brought a gang of his companions along to see the fun.

'Say fork,' said the Baptist, menacingly.

'Why?' asked Hector, backing against the wall of the school.

'Because I'll soak yuh if yuh don't,' said the tormentor, squinting and twisting his face menacingly. 'G'wan, say fork.'

'Oh all right; fork,' said Hector.

'Got a hole in yer pants as big as New York,' screamed the Baptist. His admirers roared with laughter, but there was no mirth in it; under the microscope the meanness in the soul of a little boy cannot be distinguished from that in the heart of an adult fascist jailer.

'Now: say spoon.'

'Spoon.'

'Yah! Suck yer mother's teat all afternoon!'

This Hector could not bear. Not for himself, but for his mother, he was suddenly possessed by anger. That this rat-face should speak of her so! He had but the dimmest notions about sex, and his mind shrank from the smutty, ignorant talk of the schoolyard, but he knew that his mother had been spoken of in a way which he could not tolerate, and live. His face turned its darkest red, and he went for Rat-face with both fists flying.

'Fight! Fight!' The schoolyard cry went up and in a few seconds there was a crowd around the two boys.

Rat-face fancied himself as a fighter. He was the sort of boy who moves from group to group in a playground, dancing and striking the air, and asking in a menacing voice if anybody wants a fight. Such boys rarely find anyone who dares to take the challenge. Hector knew nothing of fighting, but he was a heavy, powerful boy and he was angry as Highlanders are angry, with blood hissing in his head, and throbbing behind his eyes. Rat-face attempted to dance and feint, but Hector rushed in upon him, caring nothing for his blows, and hammered him until the astonished Rat-face gave up any pretence of fighting and tried to run away. But Hector seized him and swung him around with his back to the wall of the school. And there he punched and pummelled him until Rat-face, who was a puny child, fell down in a faint.

Then the cry went up! Hector Mackilwraith had killed Rat-face! Hector Mackilwraith was a brutal bully who had defied the conventions of dodging and feinting and pawing the air so dear to little boys, and had unfairly hit his opponent as hard as he could! Nobody dared to touch him, but they all screamed abuse. Shortly a teacher arrived, who shrieked when she saw blood running from Rat-face's nose and mouth, and sent a boy to fetch the principal. The principal came on the run, and Hector was sent to his office to wait, while Rat-face was restored to such limited consciousness as his heredity and his fate permitted him to enjoy.

The principal was a just and mild man, who did not want to beat Hector if he could find a way out of it; Hector had never sinned before, and it was plain that there had been some unusual reason for his fury. But when he asked Hector to explain why he had beaten Rat-face into insensibility the boy would give no answer. How could he repeat, to an adult, those shameful words about his mother? How could an adult understand them? The disgrace, the filthiness of what Rat-face had said was linked with dark mysteries of which Hector had little knowledge, but an infinity of disgusted, fascinated surmise. It was clear that adults did not want children to know of these mysteries, for they never mentioned them. How, then, could Hector mention the unmentionable to the principal? How could he ever mention it to anyone who would understand? He knew that there was no way out of his predicament, and he stubbornly held his tongue.

The principal had no alternative but to beat him. Rat-face's parents would expect it, and if he could not suggest to them that there had been fault on both sides they might complain to the school trustees. As beatings go, it was a mild affair. The principal got out the special strap authorized by the provincial Department of Education for the purpose, and gave Hector four strokes on each hand. But both the principal and Hector knew what was happening; a reputation was falling to ruin; Hector Mackilwraith, a preacher's son, was Getting The Strap, and the shadow of corporal punishment had fallen across a pulpit. In such a community as that, the preachers formed a Sanhedrin, and as they were severe towards others, they were harshly judged when disgrace touched them.

It was thus that Hector, as a boy of eleven, brought his family into disgrace which lasted for perhaps a fortnight. It was agreed in the village that it had always been plain that the boy would break out, some day; it was agreed that his parents had done a poor job of bringing-up, and that if there had been more beating at home this public disgrace might have been avoided; it was agreed that preachers' young ones were always the worst. And then a dark suspicion arose that somebody's hired girl was carrying on with a married man who worked in the woodyard, and Hector's fall from virtue was forgotten. But he did not forget it. His mother had wept over him, loving him the more in his disgrace; and he, knowing that it was because of her that he had fought, and knowing the utter impossibility of ever explaining to her why he had fought, loved her and grieved with an intensity which unobservant people would have supposed to be beyond his years.

Nobody at that school ever provoked him to fight again, and Rat-face became his toady and trumpeter. Thus Hector learned about one kind of love, and a valuable lesson about the way of the world, into the bargain.

When Hector was fourteen his father died. He wet his feet at a Spring funeral, his cold in the head became a cold in the chest, and that in turn became pneumonia. He was a disappointment to the last. It was the habit of people in that district to set great store by the last words of those who died; the last words of a Presbyterian minister would be of particular interest, for he might reasonably be supposed to tarry for a moment on the brink of eternity, and make some helpful comment upon it, before breaking finally with this world. A pious boy, dying of a ruptured appendix (diagnosed as 'inflammation of the bowels') earlier that same year, had distinguished himself by exclaiming 'I see the light' (printed in the local paper's obituary notice as 'I see The Light!') in his latter moments. It was confidently expected that a minister of the Gospel would better this. But the Reverend John lay in a coma for several hours before his death, and expired without saying anything at all.

He left his widow and son very badly off, for he had never received more than enough for bare livelihood at any time in his life. His estate amounted to about thirty-five dollars in cash, which was found in a tin box in his desk, and the furnishings of the manse. His congregation, with one of those warm impulses which restore faith in mankind, made a hasty collection, paid for the funeral and handed over two hundred and fifty dollars to his widow. They did more; after several ministers had preached for the 'call' in their church, they took care to call a young man just ordained, and unmarried, and gave him to understand that he was to have the manse, but with Mrs Mackilwraith as his housekeeper, and that this arrangement was to last for at least one year.

It seemed as though the death of the Reverend John, who attracted misfortune, released a sudden run of luck in favour of Hector and his mother. He set out at once to find a job which he could do after school hours and on Saturdays, and found one quickly at a village grocery which paid him a dollar and a half a week. And within two months an old and forgotten aunt of the Reverend John's died, leaving six hundred dollars which came to Mrs Mackilwraith. Everybody in the village knew of this, and was pleased by her good fortune. They did not even complain very much when she immediately spent one hundred and fifty dollars of it on a brass memorial plaque which was fastened to the wall of the church, to the right of the pulpit, and which declared that John Mackilwraith had been beloved not only by his wife, but by themselves. It was ironical that the topmost ornament on this plaque was the device IHS, with the letters so curiously interwoven that they looked like nothing so much as a dollar sign.

Nobody ever knew whether the young minister who consented to take on Mrs Mackilwraith as part of his manse regretted his bargain. But when the year which had been agreed upon was finished another year began without any offer to leave on the part of the widow-housekeeper. She and Hector lived on at the manse, and when the old caretaker of the church died within a year of the Reverend John, Hector asked for his job, and got it by agreeing to take less money than his predecessor. This meant that he worked hard at school, ran to the grocer's and delivered parcels and moved boxes and barrels until six o'clock, and worked hard at his lessons until nine. On Saturdays he worked at the grocer's all day. On Sundays he was in the church by seven o'clock to light the stove and sweep the building. At eleven o'clock he solemnly placed the big Bible on the pulpit cushion, and held open the door of the vestry while the young minister made his solemn march to the pulpit. He then retired and pumped the organ. During the afternoon he prepared the Sunday School room for use, and cleaned it when the school was over. At seven o'clock he repeated his morning's duties, and after evening service he closed the church. On communion Sundays he was helped by his mother in cutting bread into cubes, and in washing the two hundred little wineglasses which were used in that ceremony. If the Sunday School room was wanted during the week, which usually happened two or three times, it was his work to see that it was heated and ready. He performed all these duties well and thoroughly.

The fact is that Hector was as great a success as his father had been a failure. Not only was he strong and willing; he was also intelligent. He organized his time carefully, and if any direction was given to him which lay outside the ordinary realm of duty, he made a note of it in a little book. He was solemn and silent, and the boys and girls at the continuation school called him 'Saint Andrew', from the name of the church where he was beadle. But other people liked him because he was trustworthy and thriving, and because it was plain that he was capable of looking after his mother, who might otherwise have been a reproach to them.

It was in the third spring after his father's death that the young minister, the Reverend James McKinnon, asked Hector to come to see him in his study one evening after supper. The study was much as the Reverend John Mackilwraith had left it, except for some pipes and a tobacco jar, and a framed photograph of Mr McKinnon's graduating class. When Hector went into the study his mother slipped through the door after him, and settled herself with an air of expectancy in the only chair other than the one occupied by the minister. This meant that Hector had to sit on a low leather-covered couch, with broken springs, and placed him at a psychological disadvantage.

'Hector,' said the Reverend Mr McKinnon, 'your mother has asked me to speak to you on a matter of grave concern. In June you will complete your schooling here. What lies before you? It is your mother's wish, as it was the wish of your late father, that you should enter the service of God. As the son of a minister there are scholarships open to you at one or two universities. Your school record suggests that you might fittingly aspire to one of them.

'There is more to being a minister, however, than education, noble though the pursuit of learning is. The gown and bands may mark the teacher, but it is the working of God's spirit in the heart and mind which marks the minister. It is not too soon, now, to ask God what His will is for you. We need have no fear, I think, as to what His answer will be. It is not impossible that He has spoken to you already, in the watches of the night, though I doubt if you would have concealed the fact from your dear mother, or perhaps from myself, if that had been the case. Supposing, therefore, that you have not heard the call already, I offer myself, at your mother's request, as your guide and mentor in this all-important matter. Let us pray, therefore, for guidance.'

Mr McKinnon said all of this with great earnestness and sober kindness, and before he had quite finished Mrs Mackilwraith was on her knees, with her face in the seat of her chair. The minister rose, and as Hector did not at once follow his mother's lead, he gestured to him to kneel by the couch. But Hector remained seated, and spoke in a low, clear voice.

'Thank you sir, for your kindness,' said he, 'but I have already made up my mind that I am going to be a schoolteacher.'

'It is not for any man to say that he has made up his mind on such a matter until he has first taken some account of God's mind for him,' said Mr McKinnon.

'The call to the ministry is not the only call,' said Hector. 'I feel the call to teach.'

'It is doubtful whether at your age you have heard the call in all its plenitude,' said Mr McKinnon. 'The minister also wears the gown of the teacher, and I think that that is all of the vision that you have permitted yourself to see. The rest will come. Now let us pray.'

'No,' said Hector. 'I'm not going to be pushed into the ministry. I've no mind for it at all.'

'Are you refusing to pray with your mother and me?'

'Yes,' said Hector loudly, and the dark flush spread over his face.

Mr McKinnon sat down. He was only ten years older than Hector, and although he could keep up his ministerial dignity under most circumstances, he still, at times, suffered from a mortifying sense of insufficiency. Mrs Mackilwraith, who had been kneeling with her head twisted around toward them during this conversation, with an expression of maternal misery on her face, now climbed painfully to her feet and sat down again, weeping softly and unbecomingly. After a few false starts she found herself able to utter.

'It's a mercy your father didn't live to see this day,' she quavered. 'It was his dearest wish that you should follow him in The Work.'

'I never heard him say so,' said Hector. Because he was young and fighting for his life, he gave unnecessary vehemence to his speech; his mother took this to mean that he thought that she was lying (which she was, for the Reverend John had never made any plan or expressed any wish for Hector's future) and wept the more. For the three years past she had been romanticizing the Reverend John, and she clearly remembered his saying a good many fine things which had never, in fact, entered his mind or passed his lips.

The Reverend Mr McKinnon decided to have another try. 'Hector,' said he, 'it grieves me to see you being both cruel and foolish. Your mother knows what your father wished for you. She knows what she wishes for you. In a decision of this kind you must not think only of yourself. The sacrifices demanded by the ministry are numberless.

But its glories, too, are numberless. To be counted among the ministers of God is to be used for the highest purpose God has designed for man. The fleshpots of this world are superficially attractive; I will confess to you that there was a period of my own life when I seemed to see the beckoning finger of pharmacy luring me toward a life of worldly ease and pleasure. But I would not retrace my steps now. Nor will you wish to do so, when once you have submitted yourself to the Will of God. His yoke is easy, and His burthen light; your father found it so, and so will you.'

'You never knew my father,' said Hector. 'I don't think anything was easy for him. And I'm telling you now that I will not be a minister. I'll have to live my own life and make my own way, and it'll not be in the church. I told you I'd made up my mind.'

'Have you no consideration whatever for your mother?'

'Yes. I'm going to support her. It is my duty, and I'll do it. But I'll do it as a schoolteacher.'

'I see that it is a waste of time to argue with you while you are in this frame of mind,' said Mr McKinnon. 'I shall leave you with your mother, and if you have a spark of manhood in you, her tears, if not her arguments, will prevail with you.'

He left the room, and went to his bedroom, where he sat uncomfortably on the edge of his bed and thought the thoughts of a man who is not master in his own manse, and who has been worsted by a boy of seventeen.

Hector, left alone with his mother, made no attempt to comfort her. He sat for ten minutes, during which she cried softly and persistently. Then he went to her chair and put his hand on her shoulder.

'It's no good to cry any more, mother,' said he. 'You could have saved yourself all this if you had listened when I said I'd made up my mind. Now don't worry; I'll look after you and it'll all come out right. I've planned everything.'

No more was said on the matter until the end of June, when it appeared that Hector had matriculated with honours, and he made application for a year's training at the nearest Normal School, which was thirty miles from the village in which he had grown up.

In the autumn Hector went to the Normal School, to be trained as a teacher. He had never been away from home before but he felt no uneasiness about his situation. He had five hundred dollars, all of which he had earned himself; he had a suit for every day, which he had ordered from Eaton's catalogue; he had a best suit which the Reverend James McKinnon had given him, it being a layman's suit of blue which he had improvidently bought a bare six months before he donned black forever. These material possessions were not great, but they were all his own, and he had an immaterial possession which was of immeasurably greater value; he had a plan of what he meant to do during the next ten years. He had made up his mind.

When he left home no one would have thought that his mother had ever had any ambition for him save a teacher's life. She had an ability, invaluable in a weak person, to persuade herself that whatever was inevitable had her full approval, and was in some measure her own doing. She was eager to further his plan in any way open to her.

Hector did not want money from his mother, and he did not want her to make sacrifices for him. He felt perfectly confident that he could look after himself, and her too, as soon as his year of training was over. In the years when many boys show an indecisive and unrealistic attitude toward life, Hector had grown unusually calculating and capable. The village said that he was long-headed. He had been able to detach himself from his home atmosphere enough to see that what lay at the root of many of his father's misfortunes was a lack of foresight, of planning, of common sense. In his concerns as an errand boy and beadle, Hector found that common sense could work wonders, and that planning enabled him to get through his work with no fuss. Planning and common sense became his gods in this world.

He was too much a minister's son to be without a god in some other world, and he was lucky enough to find the god which suited him in mathematics, represented in his schooling by algebra and geometry. In these studies, it seemed to him, planning and common sense were deified. There was no problem which would not yield to application and calm consideration. He took care to do well in all his school work, but in these subjects he exulted in a solemn, self-controlled fashion. The more difficult a problem was, the more Hector would smile his dark, shy smile, and the more cautiously would he ponder it until, neatly and indeed almost elegantly, he would pop down the solution. During his last two years of school he never failed to solve a problem correctly. When Hector went to the Normal School he possessed the secrets of life – planning and common sense. He planned that within ten years he would be a specialist teacher of mathematics in a High School, and common sense told him that he could do it as he solved problems, with proper preparation, caution and calm resolve.

Normal school yielded, almost without a hitch, to Hector's system. He was quickly singled out by the teachers as a student of unusual ability. These teachers, it must be explained, were not so much engaged in teaching, as in teaching how to teach. It was their task to impart to the young men and women in their care the latest and most infallible method of cramming information into the heads of children. Recognizing that few teachers have that burning enthusiasm which makes a method of instruction unnecessary, they sought to provide methods which could be depended upon when enthusiasm waned, or when it burned out, or when it had never existed. They taught how to teach; they taught when to open the windows in a classroom and when to close them; they taught how much coal and wood it takes to heat a one-room rural school where the teacher is also the fireman; they taught methods of decorating classrooms for Easter, Thanksgiving, Hallowe'en and Christmas; they taught ways of teaching children with no talent for drawing how to draw; they taught how a school choir could be formed and trained where there was no instrument but a pitchpipe; they taught how to make a teacher's chair out of a barrel, and they taught how to make hangings, somewhat resembling batik, by drawing in wax crayon on unbleached cotton, and pressing it with a hot iron. They attempted, in fact to equip their pupils in a year with skills which it had taken them many years of practical teaching, and much poring over Department manuals, to acquire. And often, after their regular hours of duty, they would ask groups of students to their homes and there, in the course of an evening's conversation, they would drop many useful hints about how to handle rural trustees, how to deal with cranky parents, how a girl teacher of nineteen, weighing one hundred and ten pounds, might resist the amorous advances of a male pupil of seventeen, weighing one hundred and sixty pounds, how to leave a rural classroom without making it completely obvious that you were going to the privy, and how to negotiate an increase in pay at the end of your first year. Hector absorbed all these diverse pieces of information as his natural mental nutriment. There was no question about it, he was cut out for a teacher.

More clearly than in any other part of his work, this showed in his model-teaching. This was a species of practical work in which a Normal School student visited a city school, and taught a lesson to a class of living, breathing children, under the eye of an experienced teacher who made a report on the student's success to the Normal

School principal. Many students who were impeccable in the theoretical side of their work broke down badly in model-teaching. One young man in Hector's year, who had almost overcome a severe case of inherited bad English, lost his nerve and addressed his first class as 'youse'. A girl, attempting to tell a class some apocryphal stories about the early musical development of the young Handel, lost her nerve and spoke thirty-seven times of 'the harpsichord', which, as she had never seen or heard the instrument in question, was not altogether surprising. Another girl burst into tears when no child volunteered to answer the first question she asked in a classroom. But not Hector. It was plain at his first model lesson that he was the captain on his quarterdeck. He was a born disciplinarian; that is to say, he never had to mention discipline. He was a born teacher, tireless in explanation, ingenious and ready in example, enthusiastic but not flighty in his approach to his work. Teachers who sent in reports on his model lessons were unstinting in their praise, and one elderly teacher, who had seen generations of neophytes pass through these early tests, was known to have sobbed a little, in professional ecstasy of joy, when describing Hector's lesson on the Lowest Common Denominator.

His year at the Normal School was a success, qualified only by his unaccountable conduct at the Annual 'At Home' – conduct which amounted to public scandal, and for which he never offered any explanation. It was this incident which gave rise to the opinion among his fellow students that Mackilwraith was brilliant, but strange. Nevertheless it was agreed that the school which got him for a teacher would be lucky.

The lucky school was a rural establishment which appeared, to the casual observer, to be planted in the middle of a wilderness. To its pupils, and to people for two or three miles in each direction however, it was in the centre of a thriving and heavily populated area. There was one room, in which children from six to fourteen were gathered, and everything they learned was taught to them by Hector, who was now nineteen. He ruled firmly and well, and it never occurred to him at any time to be at a loss, or to doubt his authority, or to laugh at his own omniscience. He was not as popular as the teacher who had been there before him, because when she found that there was a little spare time at the end of the day, or half an hour to be got through on a Friday afternoon, she had read stories to the children;

Hector's way was to give them arithmetic to do, or to test them in 'mental arithmetic'. This amusement consisted of his firing off twenty figures or so, and then demanding the total from a pupil chosen at random. A few pupils loved this; most of them dreaded and hated it. Sometimes he would show off a little; he would permit each child in the class – there were thirty-seven of them – to toss a figure, great or small, at him, and he would add them all together in his head and write the total on the blackboard in huge figures. This was better fun than when the addition was being done by the pupils, but it was not so improving, and it did not happen often.

When his second year came around, Hector had secured his increase in salary from the trustees, and was ready to begin on a vital part of his plan. He was now sending home money regularly to his mother, who continued to live at the manse. He had begun teaching at six hundred dollars a year, and now he was getting seven. His mother received half of this, and the remainder was spent for his board. He clothed himself with money which he received for a summer job of time-keeping for a road-construction company. And in this second autumn, when he was twenty, he set to work to obtain a degree of B A from Waverley University, working extra-murally.

Getting a degree extra-murally has certain decided disadvantages. The first of these is that the student has no one to make him work, and no companionship to lighten his work. The next is that he must take in a great deal of information in circumstances which are, as a general thing, uncongenial to such exercise. The third is that he suffers from a sense of isolation from the centre of learning which he hopes to regard as his Alma Mater, and fancies that those students who are on the spot are gaining insights which are denied to him; his position is comparable to a man who is in a house where a wedding feast is going on, but who is forced to remain in the cellars and suck his portion of the cheer through a long tube. The first and second of these troubles did not bother Hector; he liked work, and could settle down to it as well in his bedroom at the farmhouse where he boarded as anywhere else. But the third concerned him greatly, for he wanted his degree in mathematics and physics, and these are not matters which can be studied alone to best advantage. Therefore Hector got rid of all the things which could be done in isolation in three years of solitary study after school hours. Each spring he would make his way to a village six miles away, where there was a clergyman who was a graduate of Waverley, and while the clergyman snored in an armchair, Hector would square himself to the dining-room table, and write an examination or two. And when he had done as well as he could by this method he gave up his rural school, and went to Waverley for two years of study in the place where study is most easily and most effectively accomplished.

Money was, as always, the problem. He had saved something from his summer jobs, but not enough to carry him through two winters of university study. It was necessary, therefore, that he should find a job which he could combine with university work. He found it, working as a waiter in a restaurant which catered particularly to students, and which used students for most of its lesser staff. There were many students who were, like himself, working their way through the university, and not merely was there no discrimination against them – they were, on the contrary, regarded as especially deserving of commendation. Their courage and determination were undeniable, but it was an unfortunate fact that much of the best that a university has to offer was denied them. When students gathered for conversation, they were working. When the weekend brought a cessation of work at the restaurant, Hector had to spend Sunday deep in his books. When a lecture or a demonstration had particularly stirred his mind he could not take time to pursue that stirring; he had to go and rush orders of coffee and doughnuts to other, less needy students. The determination of the man who works his way through the university is beyond question, but it is not likely that he will get as much from his experience as the student more fortunately placed. He has not time to be young, or to invite his soul.

Nevertheless, he achieved his end, and the glorious day came when his mother saw Hector, as one of an apparently endless line of students, receive his diploma from the Chancellor, and return to the body of Convocation Hall, an indisputable B A. He plunged at once into a summer's work which gave him the coveted specialist certificate, and with a light heart he bade farewell forever to the teaching of history, spelling, geography – all the trivial subjects which had been part of the routine of a primary school teacher. He had no trouble in finding a position in a small collegiate institute and when, four years later, the post of the head of the department of mathematics at the collegiate at Salterton fell vacant, he applied for it, and was chosen from among twenty aspirants. His cup was full. He had done all that he had meant to do, and he had done it by planning and common sense.

In his new position he received a good salary, and it was his mother's idea that she should come to Salterton and keep house for him. But Hector thought otherwise. He preferred to live at the YMCA, in a room which he had partly furnished himself and to eat at the Snak Shak. The habit of overeating which had been imposed upon him in childhood persisted, and at thirty he was already paunchy. He pointed this out to his mother as evidence that he was quite able to look after himself, far more capable of doing without her than was the Reverend James McKinnon, who had grown much older in appearance, but whether as a consequence of pastoral duties, or as the outcome of a diet of stewed beef, pie and soda crackers it was impossible to tell. Mrs Mackilwraith had saved almost every penny that Hector had ever sent her, and it never occurred to her to move out of the manse. The unfortunate McKinnon had even given up dreaming of such a thing; he lived as a lodger in his own house, the victim of other people's thoughtfulness and generosity.

Prosperity wrought slowly but surely upon Hector. After four years as a department head, he began to feel that the social side of his life needed attention, and through acquaintances who were interested in it he was drawn into the Salterton Little Theatre. He was elected to the treasurership almost at once, and he showed to advantage in that office. He was always in the background when theatre parties were given, smiling and drinking one drink. He liked to be where people were gay, but he did not permit an uncontrolled gaiety in himself. He liked to see pretty women running about in a state of excitement, and he liked the Little Theatre lingo, copied from the professional theatre, in which 'dear' and 'darling' were customary forms of address; but he never made use of such endearments himself. And it was a fact, though it was of interest to no one but Hector, that he had never known any intimacy – no, not the slightest – with a woman. There had been that terrible business at the Normal School 'At Home' – but he had driven that down into the cellarage of his mind, and had almost forgotten it.

He was forty when he decided that he would like to act, and planned and exercised his common sense to secure for himself the part of Gonzalo.

[THREE]

Roger Tasset glanced around the clubroom with the sure eye of a connoisseur, to see if there was anything there which was of interest to him. He had been in Salterton for six weeks and except for a couple of routine flirtations with waitresses he had had no association with women of the kind which he valued. If he couldn't start something soon, he told himself, he would go off his head with boredom. It was useless to deceive himself; he simply had to have women.

Roger was extremely careful not to deceive himself upon this point; indeed, it was a matter on which he offered himself constant reassurance. Most men, without being conscious of the fact, spend a great deal of time and effort in bringing about circumstances which will enable them to support an ideal portrait of themselves which they have created. Roger, from a very early age, had thought of himself as a devil with women, and in consequence he was continually obliged to seek women with whom he could be devilish. He was not of a reflective temperament, and thus it could not be said of him that he embraced libertinage as a philosophy or a way of life, as did Don Juan. But he had convinced himself that sex meant more to him than it did to most men, and that by attracting and seducing women he was being true to his nature and fulfilling a rather fine destiny.

Unlike as they were in external things, Roger shared Hector's faith in planning and common sense, and he had applied these principles to his career of seduction. And as many things respond well to planning and common sense, he had succeeded in seducing quite a number of women between his eighteenth year and his present age of twenty-five. He sincerely believed that women were all alike, and it was certainly true that those with whom he had been successful shared many characteristics in common. For one thing, they all showed an abandon which was foreign to Roger's nature; he never consummated a conquest without taking precautions which would make it impossible for a child to be attributed to him. With girls who might not understand this, he was careful to make it plain. He had a series of little talks, also, about the necessity for taking love lightly, as it came, and for relinquishing it with a smile when it was still in its fairest flower; this convenient attitude was calculated to make any girl who sought to detain him longer than he wished seem unsporting and stuffy. If anyone should think that Roger's attitude was somewhat calculating and joyless it must be said in his defence that he approached seduction professionally, or as a business; he believed success in that field to be a necessity, without which he would lose faith in his own reality and importance in the world. One does not take risks with the source of one's self-respect.

Roger was a soldier, good enough to be well thought of by his superiors and not so good as to cause them disquiet by flashes of originality. He had been sent to Salterton for a course of special training. Nellie's suggestion that he should give temporary assistance to the Little Theatre had come as a godsend to him. He cared nothing for the theatre, but he knew that it was a place where there were likely to be plenty of girls. He had arrived at the clubroom promptly at eight o'clock on the night set aside for the auditions for *The Tempest*, and found himself among the first half-dozen.

The clubroom was the top floor of an office building. It had been a public hall in the days when people did not mind climbing three flights of stairs in order to attend a political rally or a lantern-slide lecture. It was now a rather seedy place with a low platform at one end. The walls had originally been a disagreeable brown, but the Little Theatre had sought to cheer them by painting them bright yellow to a height of twelve feet; as the hall had a twenty-foot ceiling the effect was not altogether happy. The decorations consisted of pictures of theatrical interest: a programme signed by Sir John Martin Harvey on his last visit to Salterton, a similar memento of Sir Harry Lauder, a signed photograph of Robert B. Mantell as King Lear, another of Genevieve Hamper in *The Taming of the Shrew*, a telegram of congratulation from Margaret Anglin to the club on its tenth birthday, a printed postcard from Bernard Shaw refusing permission to perform *Candida* without payment of royalty, and several sets of photographs of past productions. Cupboards for costumes were built against one wall, and behind a screen was a small kitchen, where refreshments could be made. The objects most prominently displayed in the room were two framed certificates testifying that the Little Theatre had distinguished itself in the Dominion Drama Festival.

For the audition, chairs had been arranged in a semicircle with a table facing them. Three of these chairs were now occupied by women who had been mentally dismissed by Roger with the hard words 'Total Loss'. Another woman was busy behind the screen, rattling crockery. Two men were in conversation by a window; Roger knew one of them to be Larry Pye and the other was the man whom he had met briefly on that rainy day at St Agnes' – the man who knew about seats – McNabb or some such name.

Roger was bored. It looked as though a dull evening lay before him. He cheered up a few minutes later, however, when a group of girls arrived. He had little time to appraise them, for Mrs Forrester came up the stair, accompanied by Valentine Rich, and Roger gave his whole attention to them; he had always found it excellent policy to keep on good terms with older women; they always liked a fellow with a bit of dash, and their liking was worth having. The Rich woman seemed to be a silent piece; she was polite enough, but she did not glow when Roger gave her his special, intimate smile. Nellie glowed, however, most gratifyingly.

'Roger dear,' she said: 'you must meet everybody. You don't mind me calling you dear, do you dear? I'm old enough to be your mother, or an aunt, anyhow. And in this game you get into the way of calling people dear. You see?'

'If you're more than five years older than I am,' said Roger, 'my eyes are deceiving me, and they don't. Not about that sort of thing. And if you pretend to be older than you are so that you can boss me, I have to teach you a lesson, Nellie dear.'

'Five years!' Nellie gave a playful shriek in which coquetry, indignation and regret for lost youth were prettily blended. 'How old do you think I am?'

'About twenty-eight – a year or two either way.'

'My dear boy! Don't they test your eyesight in the Army any more?'

'Yes. I have perfect vision. I also have a wonderful instinct about such things.'

'Well, your instinct is wrong this time. If you want to know, Val here and I are just the same age, aren't we Val?'

Nellie meant this to be a surprise to Roger, and so it was. He had taken Valentine to be many years Nellie's junior. But he gallantly told them that he stuck to his original estimate. Valentine did not care; she thought nothing of Roger's sort of charm. But Nellie's heart was like a singing bird whose nest was in a water'd shoot. She seized upon the next couple to mount the stair. It was Professor Vambrace and his daughter.

'Pearl, dear, you haven't met Roger Tasset, have you? He's going to play Ferdinand to your Miranda.'

'Really, Nell, you must be discreet,' said Professor Vambrace; 'no parts have been officially allotted as yet. Good evening Tasset.'

Pearl Vambrace murmured inaudibly, extended her hand to Roger, and then took it back again when he seemed about to shake it. This caused her to blush. Roger eyed her professionally, reflecting that this was a little more the sort of thing he had been expecting.

'I am very happy to meet you,' he said, giving the words just a little more significance than the situation required. But Vambrace took his daughter by the arm and moved her on toward the semicircle of chairs; he seemed to choose one with special care, and place her in it, before he went to the central table, and began to unload papers and books from a large, bulgy brief-case which he carried.

'Good evening,' said a voice at Roger's shoulder, and he turned to find the treasurer of the club smiling at him, his hand extended.

'Oh, good evening, Mr McNabb,' said Roger.

'Mackilwraith,' said Hector. 'So you've come to try your luck, have you. So have I.'

Roger had not thought of his presence at the audition in quite this way. It had never occurred to him that he would not be cast as the leading juvenile of any play which he chose to act in; he was not vain, but it was unlikely that an amateur drama group would find anyone better qualified than himself for a part which demanded looks, charm and a handy way with women. But these are not thoughts which one confides to a stranger. Particularly not to a stranger who looked like this one.

Years as a successful teacher had given Hector an air of quiet authority. He was almost as tall as Roger, though he was much stouter; his hair was thick, wavy and very black; black and thick were the eyebrows above his grey eyes. His face was full – almost fat – and ruddy. He was smiling, and he had excellent teeth. His voice was low and pleasant, and three generations in Canada, and a Lowland mother, had not quite flattened all the Highland lilt out of it. But it was a quality of sincerity about the man which intimidated Roger; it was not the professional sincerity of the professional good fellow; it was the integrity of a man who has every aspect of life which is important to him under his perfect control. Roger thought it wise to be a little diffident in his reply.

'Nellie suggested that I come along and see if there was anything I could do,' said he. 'I've done a little acting at school, you know, and a bit since. Never tried Shakespeare though.'

'Ah,' said Hector, seriously, 'Shakespeare will test all of us to the uttermost.'

'I dare say,' said Roger, somewhat dismayed by this pious approach to the matter.

'Nevertheless, we are fortunate in our director. A professional, you know. She will tell us our faults. It may be severe, but we can take it.' Hector smiled darkly at the thought of the artistic travail ahead. 'There will be a great deal to be learned,' he continued, with sober satisfaction; he was still trying to convince himself that his desire to act was rooted in a passion for self-improvement, rather than in a simple wish to have fun.

Roger wondered how to get away from this fellow. Every man has his own set of minor hypocrisies and Roger's was extensive, but it did not include the trick of disguising pleasure as education. Luckily Solly was passing at the moment and he hailed him.

'Hello there, Ridgetower,' said he; 'are you going to try for a part?'

'Hello, Brasset,' said Solly; 'no, I'm not.'

'Not Brasset; Tasset.'

'How odd. Not Ridgetower; Bridgetower.'

'Sorry. I'm bad at names, I'm afraid.'

'But you never forget a face, I'll bet.'

'Well, no; as a matter of fact I don't. How did you know?'

'It is characteristic of people who forget names that they never forget faces. At least, so I have often been told. It seems a pity. Only remembering half, I mean.'

Roger had an uncomfortable feeling that he was being got at. A frowsy lot of fellows you met in clubs like this. McNabb – no, Mac-whatever-it-was – and this fellow Bridgetower, with his messy hair and his long nose. Thought himself smart, obviously; a university smart-alec. Roger squared his shoulders and looked soldierly. There was one thing he never forgot, and that was a girl's face. Neither of these fellows looked as though they had ever seen a girl at shorter range than thirty yards. He could afford to despise them.

'You have both acquainted yourselves with the play, I suppose?' said Hector, who sensed a strain in the conversation and sought dexterously to relieve it. He failed in his purpose, for Solly was affronted by the suggestion that any Shakespearean play was unfamiliar to him, and Roger, who had been in many plays and had never troubled to read more than his own part, felt that the schoolteacher was trying to be officious.

'Time enough for that when we know whether we have parts or not,' said he. And Hector, who was not as self-assured in these circumstances as he pretended, took this as a suggestion that he might be passed over in the distribution of roles, and flushed.

It was at this moment, luckily, that Nellie tapped on the table for order, and the three men parted with relief, and took chairs. Nellie told the meeting what it was for, which everybody knew, and then asked Professor Vambrace to say a few words. The Professor told the meeting, in his turn, that Shakespeare had been a playwright of genius, and that the Salterton Little Theatre, with its customary instinct for the best in everything, had chosen to present one of his finest comedies. In a rather long parenthesis he explained that a comedy need not be particularly funny. He touched upon the Comic Spirit, and quoted Meredith at some length and with remarkable accuracy. He then gave quite a full synopsis of the plot of *The Tempest* and quoted two or three passages which he especially admired, all of which, by coincidence, were from the role of Prospero. He moved himself visibly. In all, he spoke for twenty minutes, and when he sat down there was respectful applause.

Nellie rose again, and told the meeting how fortunate the Little Theatre was to have Miss Valentine Rich of New York and London to direct the play for them. She assured them that it would be a rare privilege to work with Miss Rich, and that nothing short of their utmost efforts would suffice under such circumstances. Miss Rich was a person of whom Salterton might well be proud. She was also an example to the Little Theatre of what might be achieved by sheer hard work. Miss Rich would now address them.

Valentine arose, not altogether pleased to be displayed as the result of a career of dogged persistence. She said that she was very happy to be in Salterton again, which was true, and that she looked forward to working with them, which wasn't. She hoped that they would not find her as hard a taskmistress as Mrs Forrester had suggested. She was confident that they could work together to give a very satisfactory and entertaining performance. She said this briefly, and with professional assurance and charm, and when she sat down the audience applauded in a markedly more hopeful manner than before.

With a late beginning and speeches, it was now almost nine o'clock. Nellie told the meeting that they had no time to waste, and said that they would work through the cast methodically, as it appeared in books of the play. At this point there was an audible rustling, as the meeting produced its copies of *The Tempest*, in everything from neat little single copies to large quarto volumes in which all the plays of Shakespeare, with steel engravings, were included.

The first part to be allotted, said Nellie, was that of the magician Prospero. Would those who sought this role please raise their hands?

There was no immediate response, but within five seconds Miss Eva Wildfang rose to her feet, and said that after the masterly reading which Professor Vambrace had already given of some speeches from that part she felt that many of those present would agree with her that Professor Vambrace was the man to play it. She looked about her for signs of this widespread agreement, but none were apparent. Miss Wildfang's cult for the Professor was an old story to everyone but herself and Vambrace.

The Professor closed his eyes, and rolled his head once or twice upon the back of his chair. Then he said that if it was the desire of the club that he undertake the part of Prospero, he would do so, though he would retire instantly if there were any other aspirant to it.

Nellie looked about the room expectantly, and said that if there were no comment, she would tentatively pencil in the Professor's name opposite the name of Prospero.

At this point Mr Eric Leakey rose at the back of the group, and said that he had taken literally the President's remark that the parts would be cast as listed in the book. In his copy the first name was that of Alonso, the King of Naples. He did not wish to set himself up as a rival to Professor Vambrace in matters of learning, but he had come to the meeting in order to read for the part of Prospero.

Miss Wildfang threw a glance in Mr Leakey's direction which suggested that he had in some way affronted her. Nellie smiled and knit her brows at the same time, as though Mr Leakey had created a great deal of confusion by his tardiness. It was Professor Vambrace who spoke.

'By all means,' he cried; 'by all means! Nothing is further from my mind than any desire to seize upon a role for which another man is better qualified. You must read at once, my dear sir. Come forward; come forward!'

'No, no; there is no need for that,' said Nellie, when Mr Leakey had picked his way through a maze of chairs, and was almost in front of the committee table. 'It will simply cause confusion if we all begin to move around. Just read from where you are, Mr Leakey.'

'What shall I read?' asked Mr Leakey, retreating.

'What had he better read?' asked Nellie of Vambrace.

'I suggest the greatest speech of all,' said the Professor, and in his loud bass voice he declaimed:

You do look, my son, in a mov'd sort,
As if you were dismay'd; be cheerful, sir.
Our revels now are ended. These our actors,
As I foretold you, were all spirits, and
Are melted into air, into thin air:
And, like the baseless fabric of this vision –

'Exquisite; exquisite,' he murmured, as though to himself. Then, returning to a world where such improprieties as casting-readings existed, he said, 'You'll find it in Act Four, scene one, at about line 146 if you are using the New Temple edition, Mr Leakey. Don't rush yourself. Take your time.'

This show of erudition finished Mr Leakey. He found the passage, and read it in a strangulated tone, while his bald spot grew redder and redder. He sat down amid silence, which indicated very clearly that he would not do.

'Thank you, Mr Leakey,' said Nellie, making some marks on a piece of paper. There was a general feeling that Mr Leakey had thrust himself forward; those who hoped for parts took warning by his shame.

After this things moved in an orderly fashion. As each part was announced by Nellie, a few people declared themselves aspirants, and usually took care to add that it was just a notion they had, and that they would be happy to do anything they were fit for. It was a long and weary business, and there were several parts which nobody seemed to want at all. Reading progressed in much the same diffident, flat, half-choked fashion for all the parts, as though the actors had but one voice among them, and that a bad one. But when the part of Ferdinand was in question, Roger read in a warm, attractive voice which roused the meeting from its embarrassment and torpor. He did not, perhaps, reveal the fullest meaning of the passage which was allotted to him by the demon memorizer Vambrace, but he brought to it qualities of masculine charm which are rarer in Little Theatres than female beauty, than dramatic instinct, than true comic insight, than tragic power. Even Miss Wildfang, the single-hearted, cast an appreciative look toward him as he sat down. Everyone, in fact, showed a lively interest in him, save one. That one was Griselda, who appeared to be asleep.

There are few proverbs so true as that which says that beauty lies in the eye of the beholder. As Solly looked at Griselda during the slow progress of the reading he thought that he had never seen her so beautiful before. How could he have overlooked such a miracle until this time?

Yet the beauty of girls of eighteen is rarely of a commanding sort. It is very easy to miss it unless one is in the mood for it. Griselda, at this moment of revelation, would not have seemed beautiful to Mrs Bridgetower. The white skin would have seemed to that lady to reflect bad health and late nights; the red lips were very lightly touched with colour, but they were startling in so white a face; her hair, thick, waving and the colour of honey, could have been dismissed by Miss Wildfang as stringy; Mrs Mackilwraith, observing the blue shadow on the eyelids which sheltered Griselda's cornflower-blue eyes, would have been seized with a powerful desire to give her a worm powder; and her nose, slightly more aquiline than is the present fashion, was very near to being a hook in the eyes of Nellie Forrester. If Larry Pye had been asked for his opinion of her figure he would probably have said that it would be better when she filled out. But to Solly, as he gazed, she seemed all that the world could hold of beauty and grace.

If Griselda's beauty showed to special advantage at this time it was because she was feeling a little unwell, and in consequence was relaxed and still. Quietness is a great beautifier, and in that room where there were so many tensions and expectations, so many warring ambitions and nervous cross-currents, her remoteness and her air of spiritual isolation were beautiful indeed.

Beautiful and, to Roger, irritating. He had read well; he knew it. Everybody had realized it except the pale girl. He had met her, of course. He never forgot a woman's face. But her name? Well, anyhow, her father owned that big place on the river where the play was to be done. Her indifference to his reading nettled him, and robbed him of his pleasure in the sensation he had caused. Was she asleep? Or couldn't she be bothered to open her eyes to see who was reading? There was no doubt about it, she was the best thing in the room. Those clothes meant money. Only the rich could look so elegantly underdressed. A good figure. A kid's figure, but good. Not skinny. He hated boyish figures. Sweet face. But he'd like to take that indifferent expression off it. He'd do it, too. He'd teach her not to sleep when he was doing his stuff. This was what he had come for. This, properly managed, would just about last the length of the course which he was taking. This would be a very nice little item for his collection.

Griselda was not the only girl in the room with pretensions to beauty. Valentine Rich did not pay much attention to the reading; she knew that she could, if necessary, impose an appearance of intelligence upon an actor, but she could not give a good presence to someone who lacked it; she searched the room for people who might look well in costume. Her eye was taken by Pearl Vambrace. There, she thought, was a girl with possibilities. A distinguished, rather than a pretty, face; lots of nice dark hair, rather in need of a good vinegar rinse; not a bad figure and really beautiful eyes. But it was Pearl's expression which made her face an arresting one; she had the still, expectant look of one listening to an inner voice. This was a girl, thought Valentine, who must in some way be brought upon the stage.

There was to be no difficulty about it, seemingly. When the part of Miranda was open to contest, Pearl read the test passage very well, with intonations which suggested those of her father, though not to a farcical degree. As she read Vambrace fixed her with a steady gaze, and moved his lips in time with hers; once or twice he frowned, as though to show that she had departed in some measure from the pattern he had set for her. Valentine thought this irritating and embarrassing.

When at last the reading was over the committee retired to make its decisions; as the club had no private room they were compelled to go out on the landing, shut the door behind them, and stand at the head of the stair. Those to whom this delicate task was given were Nellie, Professor Vambrace, Solly and Valentine. The other club members remained inside, where cakes and strong tea were being served.

'This shouldn't take very long,' said Nellie. 'Just as I expected, no outstanding new talent showed up. Except Roger Tasset, of course. Isn't he a dream? A wonderful Ferdinand.'

'The casting of Ferdinand must hang, to some extent, upon the casting of Miranda,' said Professor Vambrace, weightily. 'We must achieve a balance, there. Young Tasset has weight, undeniable weight. The question is, has he too much weight? We do not want him to seem – how shall I say it – too heavy for our Miranda. Whoever she may be,' he added, in a tone as though the club were alive with young women capable of playing that part.

'I don't think there's any doubt that Pearl is our choice for Miranda,' said Nellie.

'Do you really think so?' said Vambrace anxiously. 'It is very hard for me to be objective in such a decision. In fact, I shall not take part in it.'

'Your daughter read charmingly,' said Valentine. 'A little on the rhetorical side, perhaps, but that is a fault which is easily corrected. And she looks right for the part. In fact, I want her for Miranda.'

'Do you really?' said the Professor. 'You think that she has the – how can I describe it – the weight, the authority for Miranda?'

'Miranda is only fifteen,' said Valentine. 'Authority is not really so necessary as a good appearance and a nice voice. She has both.'

'You feel that her voice will suffice?' said the anxious father. 'I cannot conceal from myself that it lacks sonority, particularly in the higher tones. And you must realize that she was not at her best this evening. I warned her. I warned her repeatedly. But she would go on sucking coughdrops all evening and as a result, when it came her time to read, she was cloyed. I was quite vexed with her.'

'She will be very good,' said Valentine; 'and she will look very well with Tasset.'

'Aha,' said the Professor, rubbing his chin with a rasping sound. 'Yes; she will play chiefly with him and with whomever we may choose for Prospero. We must strive for balance, within our limitations.'

'Well, if you play Prospero,' said Valentine, 'the balance should be just about perfect.'

'The decision must be made by the remainder of the committee without reference to me,' said the Professor. 'Common decency forbids that I should have any part in it. But there is just one point – not, I think, an unimportant one – which I must make before I retire. It is this: if I play Prospero – mark you, I say *if* – the question of a convincing family resemblance between that character and Miranda is adequately dealt with.' The Professor bowed slightly, and withdrew himself to a distance of five feet from the rest of the committee, which was all the withdrawal possible on the landing. It did not occur to him to go downstairs.

'Oh do come back, Walter,' said Nellie. 'We've never seriously thought of anyone but you.' It was only in moments of the utmost emotional stress that anyone called Professor Vambrace by his first name.

'I had imagined that it was settled some time ago,' said Valentine mildly. She was wearying of the Professor's coyness.

'We did speak of it, sometimes, as a possibility; but when it comes to casting we are determined to give everyone a fair chance,' said Vambrace, whose relief and pleasure at having secured the best part for himself were wonderful to behold.

'In that case, what are we going to do with Mr Leakey?' said Valentine. 'He wanted to be Prospero, and he didn't read too badly.'

'Oh Val, he was dreadful,' said Nellie.

'Not impossibly dreadful; he was nervous, having to brave us all, poor sweet. I'd like to cast him as one of the funnies. Stephano, for instance.'

'Why not cast him for Gonzalo?' asked Nellie.

'Because I want Mr Mackilwraith for Gonzalo.'

'But Val, he's such a stodge.'

'So was Gonzalo a stodge. Anyhow Mackilwraith will look very fine with some grey in his hair and a nice beard. Shakespearean stodges must be made picturesque.'

'I'd like to be perfectly sure that Mackilwraith in that part wouldn't upset the balance of the play,' said the Professor

'May I suggest, Professor Vambrace, that I shall be able to do a good deal to give the play its proper balance?' said Valentine.

'Oh quite, quite, quite.'

'Now for Caliban, I want that rubbery-looking boy. What's his name – Shortreed.'

'But Val, he hasn't been in the club long, and he's one of the stewards in the liquor store. Will he be acceptable to the rest of the cast? We have to think of that.'

'You think of it,' said Valentine. 'I want him for Caliban.'

In this fashion the casting proceeded. Valentine got her way about everything. Faced by her determination, Nellie and Professor Vambrace were ineffective. This was the first time that Valentine had shown anything but an indifferent acquiescence to their proposals, and they wondered uneasily whether she might not prove a Tartar. The fact was that in matters relating to her work, Valentine was not a theorizer and a talker, but a worker, and this was the first occasion that she had been able to get her teeth into anything solid in connection with the play. When she saw a group of possible actors, she could do her casting rapidly and without reference to Little Theatre politics. In a remarkably short time all the male parts in the play were decided upon.

'Now,' said she, 'what about the women? We've got Miranda. Who's to be Ariel? It'll have to be a girl; you have no man with ballet training, I suppose? You said something about Griselda Webster, Nellie; is there any special reason why she should have it, aside from the fact that she is pretty?'

'Yes. She sings quite well.'

'Have you heard her?'

'Well, no; not really. But I've been told.'

'I'll hear her tomorrow. Her figure isn't precisely what I would choose for an airy spirit. However, we can't have everything. Now what about these goddesses?'

'If I may make a suggestion,' said Professor Vambrace, 'I think that Miss Wildfang should be considered for the part of Juno. She has not thrust herself forward, but she has been a very faithful worker in the Little Theatre since its foundation, and the head of the refreshment committee for the past seven years. She has, unquestionably, a classic countenance. For "ox-eyed Juno", as Homer describes her, I cannot think of a more fitting choice.'

'I can,' said Solly, speaking for the first time. 'What about Torso Tompkins?'

'Solly!' cried Nellie, in a tone of despair.

The Professor's face was bleak. 'In Shakespeare,' said he, 'a certain balance is an absolute necessity. There is a quality of modernity about Miss Tompkins which it is impossible to disguise.'

'She's widely admitted to have the finest figure in Salterton,' said Solly, stubbornly, 'and she has a large personal following. If you want to sell tickets, put The Torso in a cheesecloth shift and chase her across the stage to slow music.'

'Which was she?' asked Valentine.

'One of those girls who said they'd do anything,' replied Nellie. 'A bold-looking girl with black hair.'

'She is called The Torso for the best of reasons,' said Solly. 'She has a bosom like a girl on the dust-jacket of a historical novel, as well as other agreeable features. And when it comes to being ox-eyed, The Torso begins where Miss Wildfang leaves off.'

'I'll have a look at her,' said Valentine. 'Other goddesses?'

'I want to suggest dear little Freddy Webster for one,' said Nellie. 'She isn't here tonight, but as the play is to be done at her father's home I think it would be a very nice thing to include her.'

'Is she that dark, serious-looking child I met at St Agnes'?'

'Yes.'

'Excellent. I'll speak to her sister. Shall we go in now?'

Their reappearance in the clubroom brought an immediate silence. The hopeful readers stood about in groups, drinking the copper-coloured tea and eating the economical little cakes supplied by Miss Wildfang and her assistants. Griselda had chosen to be one of these, and was moving about with a large teapot. This made it difficult for anyone to talk to her for very long, and Roger Tasset was greatly chagrined. He was with a knot of three girls, one of whom was Miss Bonnie-Susan Tompkins, known as The Torso. She had, indeed, a splendid figure, but the beholder was rarely permitted to see its beauties at rest. If she was not swinging one foot she was tossing back her hair; she arched her neck and heaved up her rich bosom most fetchingly, but too often; from time to time she waved her hands and snapped her fingers as though to some unheard, inner dance-tune; when she laughed, which was often, her posteriors gave a just-perceptible upward leap, in sympathy. Her face was as animated as the rest of her; she was a lip-biter, an eye-roller, a sucker-in and a blower-out of breath. Her energy was delightful for five minutes, and exhausting after ten. As the committee came through the door, she laughed at a remark which Roger had made. It was a carrying laugh, and through her jersey dress her gluteals could be seen to contract suddenly, and slowly relax again. When the committee passed her on their way back to the table her eyes swivelled nimbly in their sockets. Ox-eyed doesn't begin to describe it, thought Valentine.

'We have reached several decisions,' said Nellie to the meeting, 'and I shall ask Miss Rich to announce them.'

Valentine read a cast list. No hopes were dashed, for few of those present were so vain as to think that they were certain to get parts. They were, as a group, modestly willing to act if they were thought good enough, and content to be left out if they were not. The passionate egotism of Professor Vambrace by no means represented the temper of the club.

If anyone had been watching Hector when his name was read as the choice for Gonzalo they would have noticed that he flushed a little, smiled a little, and swallowed. But no one was looking.

'A few parts have not been cast,' said Valentine, 'but I want to allot them as soon as possible. May I see Miss Webster and Miss Tompkins for a moment, please?'

Roger was indignant. Wasn't the Webster piece to be cast, after all? If so, why was he wasting his time? If the Tompkins girl was to take her place, he could reconcile himself to it, he supposed, but that was not what he wanted. He had quite forgotten about Pearl Vambrace.

Griselda and The Torso sought out Valentine in a corner, as the hubbub of conversation rose again.

'Hi, Griselda,' said Miss Tompkins. 'Long time no see.'

'Hello, Bonnie-Susan,' replied Griselda; 'what have you been doing?'

'Better ask what I haven't been doing,' replied The Torso, eyes rolling, hair tossing, bosom advancing and retreating. It was her way to pretend that she lived a life of violent erotic adventure, but this was true only in a very limited sense.

'I am told that you sing, Miss Webster,' said Valentine. 'Now I want you to tell me quite frankly: how well do you sing?'

'I've a fairly reliable soprano voice,' said Griselda, 'and I've had good lessons. Not for noise, you know, but for quality.'

'Do you sing, Miss Tompkins?'

'I was a wow in the Campus Frolic a couple of years ago,' modestly replied The Torso, 'but I don't know how I'd be on any hey-nonny stuff. But I'm a worker.' Everything about her leapt, throbbed and tossed, in token of her sincerity and eagerness.

'Suppose we say, then, that you shall play Juno,' said Valentine. 'You have a fine appearance for the part, and if your voice is suitable we'll consider it settled.'

The Torso was transported. She rushed back to her friends, hissing, 'I've got a part! Listen kids, I've got a part!'

'Does your sister sing?' said Valentine, turning to Griselda.

'Well – yes, she does. But I don't know what she would say about acting. She's an odd child.'

'Tell her I would be greatly obliged if she would consider it, will you?' said Valentine. 'We are short of singers, and the music is going to be very important.'

When Griselda had left her, Valentine felt Nellie's hand on her arm. 'Val,' said she, in a tone of gentle reproach, 'you haven't really cast Bonnie-Susan Tompkins for Juno, have you?'

'Yes, why not? The Torso is just what the part wants.'

'Oh, don't call her by that awful name. Val, darling! I don't want to interfere, but is she suitable? She's an awful one for the boys.'

'What could be better? So was Juno, in her overbearing way.'

'But in a classic, is it right?'

'Nellie darling, a lot of classics have remained classic because they have girls in them who are awful ones for the boys.'

Once in the street most of the members of the Little Theatre set off toward their homes, the lucky ones with a light step, and those who had not secured parts less blithely. And yet they were not unusually depressed; they were, most of them, people to whom defeat was an accustomed feeling. A small group remained while Nellie hunted up the janitor whose job it was to lock the door behind them.

'May I give anyone a lift?' cried Griselda, from her car.

'Me. I always want a lift,' said Solly, and climbed in beside her.

'Mr Mackilwraith, may we drop you anywhere?'

'Thanks,' said Hector, 'I'll walk. I would like fresh air. It was very stuffy in the clubroom tonight.' As he spoke he leaned through the window.

'I'm awfully glad you're going to be Gonzalo,' said Griselda, and smiled.

'It's good of you to say so,' replied Hector, and he returned the smile somewhat shyly. Then he went down the street in the determined manner of a man who is walking for air.

'Nice of you to say a kind word to Mackilwraith,' said Solly as they drove away. 'I'll bet he has a grim life, teaching wretched kids all day. That's what I face, if I can't find anything better.'

'I was glad to see him chosen when Nellie and that odious Professor Vambrace didn't want him. I thought it was horrid of them to make such a fuss when he wanted a part, just because he wasn't one of their gang.'

'Valentine Rich dealt them a few shrewd buffets in the hall when we were choosing. I like her more and more.'

'Yes. She's even holding it over my head that I may not be cast as Ariel, to Nellie's horror. Nellie thinks that a good part for me is the price for using Daddy's garden. I like Val Rich's way much better; she makes it appear that my own ability has something to do with it. Solly, would you like to come home for awhile?'

'Really, I think I'd better get back to Mother at once, Griselda.'

'I meant it quite nicely. I wasn't going to kiss you in the garden again or anything unmaidenly like that.'

'You didn't kiss me. I kissed you. But you know how Mother is.'

'No, I can't say that I do. I don't think I'd know your mother if I saw her. I believe I know her voice, though.'

'Oh? How?'

'Somebody called up a couple of days ago, and asked if you were there. I happened to answer the phone. It was a very discreet sort of voice, but something whispered to me that it was your mother.'

'"Oh great, just, good God! Miserable me!"' said Solly.

'What?'

'Browning.'

'Solly.'

'Yes?'

'Doesn't your mother want you to see me?'

'Well – I don't know.'

'Is it me particularly, or is it any girl?'

'Mother has been very ill,' said Solly. 'It makes her extremely sensitive. She's afraid that I'll forget about her. And I don't think she realizes that I'm not a child.'

'A very nice, loyal speech. Well, here we are at your home, and it's still well before midnight.'

'It's no good being huffy, Griselda. I have to take care of my mother. There's nobody else to do it.'

'I quite understand. But I'd hoped that you cared for me, a little, as well.'

'Of course I care for you. I think I'm in love with you.'

'But you can't be sure until you've asked your mother. Well, in the meantime, will you let her know where you are going when you are out? Because I don't really like having people who don't say who they are calling up to ask if you are with me.'

'Don't be silly, Griselda. You're being unfair.'

'That's what men always say.'

'How do you know what men always say? Now listen to me: while my mother is unwell my first duty is to her. If you don't like that we'd better drop this whole business right now.'

'Neatly put. Good-night.'

'Oh Griselda, darling; it's stupid to quarrel like this.'

'Yes. You'd better go now.'

'But I don't want to leave you until we've straightened this out.'

'It's perfectly straight now. I certainly don't intend to dispute your mother's claim to all your attention and love. So what more is there to say?'

'Griselda, you're indecently ready with your tongue. You can think up nasty things to say much too fast for your own good. Please don't say things that will drive us apart just for the fun of saying them.'

'I can't help it if I am not stupid enough to be good company.'

'Oh, hell!' said Solly and tried to kiss her. But she turned away her face, and he was left with his neck stretched, feeling foolish. He opened the door of the car and stepped out.

'When can we meet again and talk this over reasonably?' he asked.

'I don't see much point in talking about it at all,' said Griselda. 'Don't bang that door or your mother will want to know who brought you home.'

Solly's face was white with anger and humiliation. But he took care not to bang the door.

As Hector walked back to the YMCA he felt himself uplifted and renewed. He had done it! He had wanted a part in the play, and he was now assured that a part – the very part which he had chosen – was his. Of course, he had planned it, and he brought common sense to bear upon this, as upon all his ambitions. But until the cast was read out by Valentine Rich he had felt, far at the back of his mind, that this was conceivably a matter in which planning and common sense, those two invaluable secrets of life, might not work their accustomed magic. But they had done so! He reproached himself affectionately for his doubts. He would never doubt again. Anything he wanted could be brought about by a proper direction of his energies. Anything within reason, he reminded himself cautiously. It was not certain, for instance, that planning and common sense would make him Prime Minister of Canada. But then, he did not want that office. If he had chosen politics as a career, however, who could say? But the part of

Gonzalo was his, and what was more, he had already memorized all his words in the first two acts. He ran over a few speeches in his mind. Poetry – even such poetry as Shakespeare has given to Gonzalo – is like wine; it is not for unseasoned heads. The rhythm and the unaccustomed richness of the words worked powerfully upon Hector's sensibilities, which had until this time been teetotallers in the matter of poetry. He was in a melting mood. How very good of the casting committee, he thought, to meet his wishes in this way. He had supposed, that night at Mrs Forrester's, that there had been some unspoken opposition to his plan to act. But obviously they had thought better of it. Generous, large-hearted people! Well, they should not be disappointed in him. He had not reached beyond his capacities. If he had wished to play Prospero, now, or Caliban –. But he knew himself, and he knew what he could do. It was a great thing to know yourself.

It was a fine May night, and the moon shone brightly as Hector crossed the park. It had been nice of Miss Webster to congratulate him. He had not taken much notice of her before, but there was no doubt about it, she was an uncommonly nice girl. She had spoken so – he searched for the right word – well, so *nicely*. This was all the more meritorious in her because she had been educated in private schools. Boarding schools. He did not approve of private schools. It was a well-known fact that many of the teachers in them were not really qualified to teach; they had received no instruction in pedagogy; they merely had a knowledge – sometimes, he admitted, quite a thorough knowledge – of the subjects they taught. He was not a bigot in pedagogical matters. Still, if pedagogy were not a necessary study for a teacher, the Department would not lay so much stress upon it. Yet, in this expansive, unbuttoned mood, Hector was ready to admit that Miss Webster was a good advertisement for whatever school she had attended. Nevertheless, he chuckled to himself, he would like to throw a few quick problems in factoring at her, just to see what she made of them.

At some distance from the path, under the trees, was a bench, and upon it were a boy and girl in a close embrace. Ordinarily Hector would not have noticed them, for the eye sees only what the mind is prepared to comprehend. He saw them now; Hector the actor, rather than Hector the teacher of mathematics, took note of what they were doing. He felt indulgent. It was a fine night; why should they not seek romance?

Romance, he realized, had been a scarce ingredient in his own life. There was, of course, romance in his steady rise from a country lad to his present position, but that was not the sort of romance he meant. There had been that awful business at the Normal School 'At Home'. But had he not put that behind him? He flushed at the recollection; twenty-one years since that painful evening, but it still had power to shame him. Nevertheless, that was water under the bridge, and Millicent Maude McGuckin was a married woman in a distant city, doubtless with children near to the age that he and she had been when it all happened. Down into oblivion he thrust the dismaying memory. Just before it disappeared however, he told himself that things would be different if he had that evening to live through again. If one could have the keen appetite of youth, with the experience of age! This cliché of thought rose in his mind as fresh and rosy as Venus from the sea, and he pondered delightedly upon it.

It would be different now. He was master of himself now. If he could have his chance again! And then, so suddenly and sharply that it made him catch his breath, came the thought: Why not? But no, it was out of the question. He thrust the thought from him. But again it returned: Why not? Well, was not he the head of the mathematics department of a large school, past the time for – the expression which his mother had used, when speaking of such matters – for girling? But why not? The question returned with an insistency which made him doubt that it arose in his own mind; it was as though another voice, a clear, insistent voice, spoke to him. Why not? Why not?

Had not a girl – and not just any girl, but a pretty, well-mannered girl, a girl compared with whom Millicent Maude McGuckin in her heyday seemed clumsy and countrified – addressed him in warm and friendly terms a bare fifteen minutes before? Had she not gone out of her way to do so? Had she not offered to drive him home? Had she not smiled upon him as she spoke? Had he missed something in that smile?

Music was not an interest of Hector's, but in every mind there linger a few rags and tatters of melody, and particularly of melody heard in impressionable youth. From the deeps of memory there rose a forgotten song, a song which had been played at the Normal School 'At Home' on that fateful night:

Every little movement
Has a meaning all its own

It was an insinuating tune, a kind of harmonious dig in the ribs. Had there been a meaning in Griselda's smile which he (old sobersides that he was; he smiled at his stupidity) had overlooked? But the thing was ridiculous! She was a child; eighteen – nineteen, he did not know. He was talking himself into the idea that she was attracted to him. Still, it was not unknown for young women, and particularly young women of unusual character, to be drawn toward older men. And need he suppose that he was without attraction? He was wearing his best suit and his grey Homburg hat with the smart silk binding on the brim. A figure not utterly lacking in distinction, perhaps? Thus reflecting, and a little frightened by his thoughts, Hector arrived at the YMCA and went to bed.

Recurrently during the years his dreams had been plagued by the phantasmata, the hideous succubi, which visit the celibate male. This night, for the first time in his life he dreamed that a beautiful woman, lightly clad, leaned toward him tenderly and spoke his name; her smile was the smile which he had seen the night before. He woke in the night to the knowledge that for the second time in his life he was in love.

To keep pace with her father Pearl Vambrace had to take strides so long that her body was thrown forward, and she held her arms bent at the elbow.

'Don't slouch, Pearl,' said the Professor.

'You're going a bit too fast for me, Father.'

'No use walking unless you walk at a brisk pace. Head well up. Breathe deeply through the nose. Deep breathing refreshes the oxygen supply of the blood.'

For another hundred yards nothing was heard except the rhythmical snorting of Professor Vambrace. His nose was large and finely formed, and when he breathed for his health it made a soft whistling sound, like a phantom peanut-roaster.

'Posture is more important now than ever. In this play you will be, so to speak, on display. Acting involves severe physical discipline.'

'Yes, Father.'

'We must train like athletes. The Greeks did so. Of course there were no women on the Greek stage.'

'No, Father.'

'Nor on the Shakespearean stage, for the matter of that.'

'No, Father.'

'All the more reason why you should be in the pink of condition. Plenty of sleep. A light but sufficient diet. Lots of fruit. Keep your bowels open. Avoid draughts.'

'Yes, Father.'

'Don't suppose that there are no draughts in early summer,' said the Professor, as though Pearl had contumaciously insisted upon this absurdity. 'They are just as bad as in the winter. A summer cold is much the most difficult to shake.'

'I suppose so.'

'You may take it from me.'

'Yes, Father.'

Another hundred yards with the peanut-roaster going full blast.

'Some very odd casting done tonight.'

'What didn't you like, Father?'

'What is the sense of putting that Tompkins girl in as Juno? Where's your balance going to be with that hoyden lolloping about the stage? Eva Wildfang was the obvious person for the part. It was nothing short of perverse for Miss Rich to overlook her.'

'Maybe she thought Miss Wildfang was too old.'

'What do you mean, too old? Eva Wildfang is a woman of cultivation. She knows who Juno was. I don't suppose this Tompkins creature ever heard of Juno before tonight. And Mackilwraith! Stiff as a stick. What will become of your plasticity, your fluidity of movement, with him on the stage?'

'Maybe Bonnie-Susan will be fluid enough for two.'

'Who's Bonnie-Susan?'

'Bonnie-Susan Tompkins.'

'Bonnie-Susan! Pah!'

Another hundred yards, during which the Professor fiercely renewed the oxygen in his bloodstream. Then –

'Pearl?'

'Father?'

'That last remark of yours, about the Tompkins girl being fluid; was that intended as a jest?'

'Only a little one, Father.'

'It is not the sort of pleasantry which I like to hear from a daughter of mine. There was a smack of pertness about it.'

'Sorry, Father.'

'It had an overtone of indelicacy.'

'Oh, I didn't mean anything like that.'

'I should hope not.'

After the next spurt of walking it was Pearl who began the conversation.

'Father, who is that man who is to play Ferdinand?'

'You were introduced to him, were you not? Of course you were. He is a Lieutenant Roger Tasset.'

'Yes, but do you know anything about him beyond that?'

'He is here to do some special military course. I think that he comes from Halifax. Mrs Forrester picked him up. We lack younger men.'

'Do you think he will be good?'

'I sincerely hope so. He appears chiefly with us. Perhaps I can take him for some special coaching. I mean to give you all the help I can – not merely in the scenes which you play with me. Perhaps we might include him in some of our private rehearsals. We could work for balance.'

'Oh, I think that would be lovely.'

Pearl Vambrace lived a life which, to the casual glance, seemed unendurable. But she had grown up to it, and although she knew that it was not like the life of any other girl of her acquaintance she did not find it actively unpleasant. If the chance had been offered to her, she would not have changed her lot for that of anyone else; she would have asked, instead, that a few changes be made in the life she had.

She would have asked, for instance, that her father should not snub her so often, and so hard. She had never seen him as the casting committee had seen him, anxious and almost humble on her behalf. She saw him only as one who made constant demands on her, and was harshly displeased if those demands were not met. He insisted that she be first in all her classes during her school life, and somehow, with a few lapses from grace, she had managed it. But she was not to be a blue-stocking, he said; she was to be truly womanly, and for that reason she must have general culture, nice manners and a store of agreeable conversation. These attributes he did his best to implant in her himself, sparing no severity of tongue if she fell below the standard he had fixed. She would undoubtedly marry, he said, and she must fit herself to be the wife of the right sort of man. Neither Pearl nor her father recognized the fact, but this really meant being the sort of wife that Walter Vambrace wished he had married.

Mrs Vambrace was a devout Roman Catholic lady, and when she

had married the Professor it had been with a strong hope that he would shortly join her in her faith. It had seemed likely enough at the time. The romantic side of Catholicism had appealed to the young Vambrace, and his ravenous intellect had rapidly mastered subtleties of Catholic philosophy which were beyond her understanding. When her parents urged her to wait for his conversion before marrying, she had declined to do so, for the conversion was, in her mind, a certainty. But it had not come about. For a time the Professor stuck where he was, elegantly juggling with coloured balls of belief. But then his enthusiasm had cooled, and without anything definite being said, it became clear that he had lost interest in the project. His wife was free to do as she pleased.

What she pleased to do did not strengthen the bond between her and her husband, nor did it especially endear her to her Church. She sought mystical experience. She read, reflected, meditated, fasted, did spiritual exercises, and prayed, hoping humbly that some crumb of unmistakeable manna would be vouchsafed to her. She was gentle and kind and tried to do her best for her husband and child, but her yearning for a greater enlightenment blinded her to many of their commonplace needs. Pearl, as a child, had always been oddly dressed. She had never had a party, and was rarely asked to the parties of others. Her father, after a few disputes with his wife and one really blazing row with a monsignor who called to protest, caused Pearl to be educated in Protestant schools, but made her way difficult by insisting she be entered on the school records as an agnostic. It was the Professor's contention, after his experiment in Catholicism, that a man could lead a life of Roman virtue without any religion at all, and he harangued Pearl on this theme from her fifth year. Her mother, tentatively and ineffectually, tried to soften this chilly doctrine with some odds and ends of spiritual counsel, snippets from a store of knowledge which led her daily farther from the world in which her body had its existence, which no child was capable of understanding. If Pearl had not been a girl of more than common strength of character she would have been in danger of losing her reason in that household.

Instead she was, at eighteen, a shy, dark girl with the fine eyes which Valentine had remarked, and the look of distinction which sometimes appears on the faces of those who have had to depend very much upon their own spiritual resources. Submissive to her father, loving and helpful to her mother, she was nevertheless conscious that she had a destiny apart from these unhappy creatures, and she waited patiently for the day of her deliverance.

Had it come, had the Great Experience arrived, which would free her from the loneliness which that divided household had imposed upon her? She thought with shame of her awkwardness when he had put out his hand for hers, and she had lacked courage to give it. But what had she done to deserve such luck as to have that wonderful young man to play her lover in *The Tempest*?

> *How beauteous mankind is! O brave new world,*
> *That has such people in't!*

She murmured the words to herself as she sat on the side of her bed brushing her hair. Her father had always said that she would marry. Would she marry anyone half so thrilling as Roger Tasset? Her attempt to get new information about him on the way home had come to nothing. But her father meant to ask him to the house!

Was that anything to be thankful for? It was a neglected house, reasonably clean, but everything in it was threadbare, not from lack of money but from lack of desire for anything better. A Roman father, a mother who desired only to be alone with the Alone – what kind of household would such people maintain? She looked at her familiar room with new eyes; a white iron bedstead, a chest of drawers, a small mirror with a whorl in it, and a chair with weak back legs; her clothes hung behind a faded chintz curtain in a corner; the only picture was a framed postcard of Dürer's 'Praying Hands', put there by her mother when she was a child, as next best thing to a crucifix; but there were many bookshelves with books of childhood, and the books of a sensitive, curious lonely girl. But to Pearl, in her present mood, it looked a pitiful room for a girl who hoped to attract the notice, and perhaps the love, of a prince among men. Such a girl should have a lovely room – the kind of room which she was convinced that Griselda Webster must have – and stocks of lovely clothes. Her father had taught her to talk, as he said, intelligently, but she was not convinced that this would be allurement enough for Roger Tasset. We always undervalue what we have never been without; Pearl thought little of intelligence and the conversation that goes with it.

She peered into the cloudy depths of the mirror, expertly avoiding the worst of the distortion caused by the whorl. In her white cotton nightdress, short-sleeved and falling only to her knees, she might have been a sibyl looking for a portent in the sacred smoke; but she was only a girl with the unfashionable sort of good looks staring at herself in a bad mirror. What right had she to be thinking of that glorious Apollo, of that planner of twenty shabby seductions?

Rye and tap water; it was to this melancholy potion that Solly turned for solace after he had called in at his mother's room, and put her mind at ease for the night. He was guiltily conscious that, as he talked to her, he was comparing her age and dilapidated face, so baggy without its teeth, to Griselda's fresh beauty; when he bent to kiss her a whiff of her medicine rose unappetizingly in his face; she mumbled his cheek and called him 'lovey', a name that he detested. Then, escaping to his attic sitting-room, he was free of her.

Free? Not much more so than when he sat at her side. He sipped at his flat drink and reflected upon his condition. His loyalty to his mother was powerful. Why? Because she depended so heavily upon it. She had told him, he could not reckon how many times, that he was all that she had in the world. This was true only in an emotional sense, of course. Mrs Bridgetower had come of a family well established in an importing business in Montreal, and when her father died, well before the days of succession duties, she and a sister had shared his considerable estate. Nor had her husband left her unprovided for. Without being positively wealthy, she was a woman of means. It requires a good deal of capital for two people to live as Mrs Bridgetower and her son lived, when there has been no breadwinner in the family for ten years. Money, it is often said, does not bring happiness; it must be added, however, that it makes it possible to support unhappiness with exemplary fortitude.

If only his father had lived, he thought. But when Solly was twelve Professor Bridgetower had surprisingly tumbled from a small outcropping of rock, while with a group of students on a field expedition, and as they gaped at him in dismay and incomprehension, he had died of heart failure in two minutes. The eminent geologist, with his bald head and his surprised blue eyes and his big moustache, was suddenly no more. That night Solly had sat by his mother's bed until dawn, and in the coherent passages of her grief she made it plain to him that he was, henceforth, charged with the emotional responsibility toward her which his father had so unaccountably abdicated. The intellectual façade, the intricate understanding of the Yellow

Peril, the sardonic manner, were a shell within which dwelt the real Mrs Bridgetower, who feared to be alone in the world and who was determined that she should not be so long as there was a man from whom she could draw vitality.

It was not that she offered nothing in return. She told Solly, embarrassingly, at least once a year that if it were necessary she would gladly lay down her life for him. But in the sort of life they led nothing resembling such a sacrifice was ever likely to be required. He never made any corresponding declaration, but daily and hourly he was required not to die but to live for her. This had meant the sacrifice of much that would have made his schooldays happier, and when he had gone to Waverley it had made it impossible for him to share fully in the university life.

Escape to Cambridge had been a glorious break for freedom. A life of bondage had not unfitted Solly for freedom; it had served only to whet his appetite, and his first year at Cambridge had been the realization of many dreams. He had even managed to evade her wish that he should return to Canada for the long summer vacation, and had gone to Europe instead, living life as it can only be lived at twenty-two, dazzling his Canadian eyes with the rich wonders of Mediterranean lands. But toward the end of the Michaelmas Term a cablegram had brought him, literally, flying home: 'Your mother seriously ill. Heart. Advise immediate return. Collins.' And when he had reached Salterton three days later, Dr Collins had informed him, with a cheerful manner which seemed offensive under the circumstances, that his mother had 'turned the corner', and would be all right after six weeks in bed, if she took care of herself. By the end of the six weeks it was plain that this meant that Solly should take care of her; mention of his return to Cambridge had caused her face to fall and a gummy tear or two to creep jerkily down her cheeks; Dr Collins had informed him, on her behalf, that she should not be left alone at present.

The young are often accused of exaggerating their troubles; they do so, very often, in the hope of making some impression upon the inertia and the immovability of the selfish old. Solly's writhings in his bonds were necessarily ineffective. A sense of duty and fear of a show-down with his mother kept him in check; it was unnecessary for her to take any countermeasures against the discontent which he could not always hide, because she held the purse-strings. His allowance was still, presumably, piling up in the bank at Cambridge, but at home he had nothing except for driblets of money which his mother handed to him now and then with the words, 'You must have some little needs, lovey.'

Little needs! He needed freedom. He needed a profession at which he could support himself. He needed the love and reassurance of someone other than his mother. He needed someone to whom he could talk, without reserve, about the humiliating thralldom which she had imposed upon him since his thirteenth year. As he sat in his armchair, sipping his miserable drink, a few stinging tears of self-pity mounted to his eyes. Self-pity is commonly held to be despicable; it can also be a great comfort if it does not become chronic.

Griselda's taunts had cut him sharply. It was all very well for her to imply that he was tied to his mother's apron strings. But what did she know of his mother's illness, and of the seriousness attached to it by Dr Collins? 'Your mother must take things very gently; no upsets; you're the apple of her eye, you know; you must cheer her up – try to take her out of herself.' It was a duty, a work of filial piety which his conscience would not permit him to evade, however distasteful it might sometimes be. How unfair it was of a girl to make no attempt to understand a man's obligation to another woman whose very life might depend upon his tact and consideration! How hateful women were, and yet Griselda – how infinitely desirable! How could one who looked as she had looked tonight be as unreasonable and as wilfully cruel as she had been? He hated her, and even as he hated he was torn with love for her. There was only one thing for it; he must try to forget his wretchedness in some work.

It is a favourite notion of romantic young men that misery can be forgotten in work. If the work can be done late at night, all the better. And if the combination of misery and work can be brought together in an attic a very high degree of melancholy self-satisfaction may be achieved, for in spite of the supposed anti-romantic bias of our age the tradition of work, love, attics, drink and darkness is still powerful. The only real difficulty lies in balancing the level of the work against the level of the misery; at any moment the misery is likely to slop over into the work, and drown it.

This is what happened to Solly. He took up a copy of *The Tempest* in which he had already made a great many notes, and which was fat with bits of paper which he had thrust into it here and there, with what he believed to be good ideas for the production scribbled on them. But he could not read or think; the words blurred before his eyes, and he could see nothing but Griselda's face – not pinched and angry, as when she had turned away from his kiss, but as it had been in the clubroom, when she had seemed to sleep through Roger Tasset's reading. In a few minutes he gave up the struggle, and thought only of her. And as this palls upon even the most heart-sore lover, he went at last to bed.

[FOUR]

For two weeks after Mr Webster had told him that the Little Theatre was going to invade his garden, nothing happened, and Tom began to deceive himself that perhaps nothing ever would happen. It is thus that a man who has been told by his physician that he has a dreadful disease seeks to persuade himself that the doctor was wrong. He feels nothing; he sees nothing amiss; little by little he thinks that there has been a mistaken diagnosis. But one day it strikes, and his agony is worse because he has cajoled himself with thought of escape. And thus it was with Tom. One morning, shortly after breakfast, a large truck drove across the upper lawn at St Agnes', and with remarkable speed four men dug a great hole and planted a Hydro pole in it. When Tom rounded the house half an hour later they were busily setting up a transformer at the top of it.

'Who gave you leave to stick that thing up in my lawn?' roared Tom.

'Orders from the office, Pop,' said a young fellow at the top of the pole.

'Nobody said nothing to me about it,' shouted Tom. 'Why didn't you ask me to take up the sod before you began all this?'

'Never thought of it, Pop,' said the young man. 'Don't get your shirt in a knot. The grass'll grow again.'

'Not so much of your "Pop", my boy,' said Tom, with dignity. 'When I was in the Army I took the starch out of dozens like you.'

'That was cavalry days, Pop. Mechanized army now.'

'You come down here and get your bloody truck off my grass.'

'Who's going to make me?'

'I know how to get a monkey out of a tree,' said Tom. He had a crowbar in his hand, and with this he deftly struck the base of the pole. The young man, whose climbing irons were stuck in the pole, got the full benefit of the vibration, and did not like it.

'Hey, go easy, Pop,' he shouted.

'You get your truck off my lawn,' said Tom.

The truck was backed away to the drive, and Tom felt that honour had been preserved. But he knew also that he was fighting a rear-guard action. During the afternoon a party of soldiers arrived with another truck, which they drove on the grass, and under a corporal's direction they set up two brown tents.

'What's all this?' said Tom.

'For the Little Theayter,' said the corporal. 'One tent for lights; the other for odds and ends. Major Pye's orders, sergeant.'

Tom liked to be recognized as a sergeant in mufti, but he knew that after those tents had been up for three weeks he would never get the grass right that summer.

That evening two cars brought Mrs Forrester, Miss Rich, Professor Vambrace, Solly Bridgetower and Major Larry Pye to St Agnes'. They surveyed the pole and the tents with pleasure.

'It's always a big thrill when a show begins to shape up, isn't it Tom,' said Nellie.

Tom, who had been haunting the upper lawn in case new liberties should be taken with it, said that he didn't know, never having had any experience with shows, but if his opinion was asked he thought that the pole and the tents looked a fair eyesore.

'Of course they do,' agreed Nellie. 'But they won't when you've planted some nice shrubs and little trees around them.'

'Maybe you'd like me to camoofladge this telegraph post as a tree, ma'am,' said Tom. But his sarcasm was wasted on Nellie.

'Oh, I didn't know you could do that,' she said. 'Of course that would be wonderful.'

'We don't want to put you to extra work any more than is needful,' said Professor Vambrace, 'but it will be necessary to give us some sort of raised stage. Something about two feet high, fifty feet across and thirty feet deep will be wanted, I should think. Can you do that with sod?'

'Now, now, let's treat first things first,' said Major Pye. 'I'm going to want a pit dug right in front of the acting area – not a big thing, but a pit about four feet deep, eight feet wide and four feet across, lined with waterproof cement.'

'Oh Larry, what for?' said Nellie.

'To put my controls in,' said Larry. 'That's where I'll be all through the show. I'll have my board down there. And every change of light –

bingo! Along comes the cue and I hit it right on the nose – bingo! You can put the prompter down there with me, if she doesn't take too much room,' he added, magnanimously.

'And just when am I supposed to get all this done by?' said Tom.

'You've got the better part of five weeks,' said Nellie. 'Of course we'll be rehearsing here a great deal, and you won't be able to work while we are busy, but you'll have your mornings to yourself as a general thing.'

'Now just a minute, ma'am –' he began, but Valentine cut him short.

'I think it would be well if I made all the arrangements with Mr –?' She paused.

'Gwalchmai's the name, miss; Thomas Gwalchmai.' Rarely has the find old Welsh name of Gwalchmai sounded less accommodating to the lazy Saxon tongue than as Tom spoke it then.

'With Mr Gwalchmai,' said Valentine, smiling pleasantly and pronouncing it to perfection. 'We shan't need a raised stage, and it would be unthinkable to dig a pit in this perfect lawn. We have done quite enough damage as it is. Shall we say then, Mr Gwalchmai, that nothing need be done to the grounds until it has been discussed with me?'

'Well, I don't want to be a stumbling-block, miss,' said Tom, much softened, 'but there's a limit to what can be done, and –'

'Of course there is,' said Valentine. 'But it will be most helpful if we may rehearse here during the evenings and perhaps on a few afternoons, as well.'

'Oh, that'll be quite all right, miss,' said Tom, eager to please.

Later, when they had gone inside the house for further discussion, Professor Vambrace complimented Valentine on the skill with which she had managed Tom, whom he described as 'an obstructionist – hide-bound, like all people who live close to the soil.'

'He seems very nice,' she replied; 'we must be careful to give him his due; that's the secret of getting on with most people.'

Professor Vambrace, who had a deep conviction that he himself had never received his due, assented earnestly. Larry Pye, who considered himself a born colonel who had been kept down by jealousy in high places, nodded vigorously. The world is full of people who believe that they have never had their due, and they are the slaves of anyone who seems likely to make this deferred payment. Valentine, in a few days, had assumed this character among them, and they were all convinced that she was a woman of extraordinary penetration. She never sought or demanded anything for herself, she was ready to listen to everybody, within reason, she had no interest in humiliating or thwarting anybody, and in consequence all the keys of power in the Salterton Little Theatre had been gathered into her hands.

Always excepting, of course, those widespread powers which Nellie regarded as her own. She had, as she explained to Roscoe, grown up with Valentine Rich, and although Valentine had undoubtedly made a name for herself in the theatre she, Nellie, had gained what was perhaps an even wider experience. In the Little Theatre, she always said, you got a broader grounding; she had painted scenery, made costumes, acted, directed, dealt with matters of business, done everything, really, that could be done in a theatre. What was more, she knew Salterton as Valentine did not, and she had to see that no local apple-cart was upset. Oh, she didn't deny for a moment that Valentine knew her job, but after all, Salterton was *not* New York, and there was no good pretending that it was.

When it was time to talk about music for the play, therefore, Nellie felt obliged to make her opinions known.

'You needn't worry about it at all,' said she; 'I arranged everything with Mr Snairey last week. The Snairey Trio should sound lovely in the open air. And he's had experience, you know.'

'Surely that isn't old Snairey who used to play in the Empire for vaudeville when we were children,' said Valentine.

'I should think he played there when your grandfather was a lad,' said Solly. 'You don't seriously mean that you've asked him, Mrs F.?'

'Of course I do. He says he has some lovely music which theatre orchestras always play for Shakespeare; Sir Edward German's *Henry VIII* dances.'

'I see,' said Valentine, in a voice which suggested that she saw more than Nellie. 'And what about the songs?'

'I mentioned them, and he said he thought he could fake something. His daughter Loura can sing offstage, and the girls onstage can fill in with mime. He hasn't any music for the songs in the play, but he said he thought we could use something pretty and Old English.'

'From what I know of old Snairey, that means that they will play *William Tell* during the storm scene, and Ariel will flit across the stage to the strains of *The Farmer's Boy*. Really, Mrs F., you've done it this time.'

'Oh Solly, don't be so superior,' said Nellie; 'there are a million things to be done, and I appear to be the only one ready to do them. If you know so much, why didn't you arrange about the music?'

'Because nobody asked me to,' said Solly, bitterly.

'Well, it's settled now, for good or ill.'

'No,' said Valentine; 'Mr Snairey can be dealt with, I expect. Very likely he and his Trio can play, but someone must see that suitable music is provided. Who is the best musician in town?'

'Myrtle Swann, by long odds,' said Nellie; 'they say she has forty pupils.'

'But we don't want a piano teacher; we want someone who can direct an orchestra and some singers,' said Valentine.

'The obvious man is Humphrey Cobbler,' said Solly.

'Oh heavens, you can't have him,' said Nellie; 'he's not right in his head.'

'Who says so?' said Solly.

'Oh, lots of people at the Cathedral. And he's such an untidy dresser. And sometimes he laughs out loud at nothing. And he never gets his hair cut.'

'He has many of the superficial marks of genius,' said Valentine. 'Who is he?'

'The organist and choirmaster at St Nicholas',' said Solly. 'I assumed he would be the first man to be asked.'

'Not by me,' said Nellie. 'They say he's a Drinker.'

'That's probably just a mannerism from being an organist,' said Valentine; 'they use their feet very oddly. Go and see him, Solly, and find out what can be done.'

Nellie bit her lip, and said nothing. She thought of telling Valentine and Solly that Salterton was not New York, but decided to let them find it out for themselves.

Having decided that he was in love with Griselda, Hector reflected that he must devise some clever scheme to let her know it. He was not a reader of novels, and he very rarely went to the movies, but he felt that he knew enough about romance to carry out his plan in his accustomed efficient and successful manner. His problem was, he told himself, simple enough in essence: he loved Griselda; he would give gradually stronger hints that this was so until he was able to make an outright declaration; that done, she would love him, for he considered it impossible that a woman should be loved without loving in return; he had heard of such cases, but they did not involve young and inexperienced girls; he and Griselda would then love each other. Beyond that point he did not think. One thing at a time. Affection would beget affection; that, he assured himself, was what always happened.

The disparity in their ages was against him, in a way. And yet, had she not started the affair by that smile which she had given him? He did not attach too much meaning to it, but he did not discount it, either. Well, here was a field in which he had never tried planning and common sense before, but he would not desert those tried and true friends now. In the black notebook, over a period of a week, appeared a page filled thus:

PLAN OF CONDUCT

P	C
be dignified, friendly	*not too stiff*
make jokes	*not seem mere buffoon*
show still young, good muscles, etc.	*take off 25lb., cut pie?*
outsmart people, show trained mind	*don't overdo, seem wasteful*
spend freely	

To put his plan in action he seized a chair at the first rehearsal, and lightly threw his leg over the back of it.

'Can you fellows do that?' he asked Roger and Solly, who were talking to Griselda.

'I'd probably rupture myself if I tried,' said Solly.

Roger quickly did what Hector had done, first with his right leg and then with his left.

'Let's see you do it with both legs,' he said.

Hector tried it, and although his right leg, with which he had been practising, answered satisfactorily to the call of romance, the left leg knocked over the chair, and he stumbled.

'See what I mean?' said Solly, officiously seizing him by the arm, to prevent a fall. 'You might easily unman yourself doing a trick like that.'

What a coarse thing to say in front of a young girl, thought Hector. He would have liked to punch young Bridgetower in his loose mouth.

He was humiliated. But no one appeared to notice his humiliation. The Torso had joined them, seeing that kicking was toward, and was demonstrating how she could hold her right foot above her head with her right hand, and spin on her left leg. This showed a good deal of her drawers, which were pink and short and had lace on them. Nobody had eyes for the red-faced Hector.

As for cutting out pie, he had read in the *Reader's Digest* that slimming exercises and abstinences should not be embarked upon hastily. And so for a couple of weeks he cut out his usual piece of pie with his lunch on Tuesdays and Fridays, but did not tamper with his dinner menu.

During those two weeks he found no opportunity to address Griselda directly, but he watched her closely, and the feeling for her which he had decided to call love, a feeling in which worship and the yearning to champion and serve her were untainted by any fleshly aspiration, deepened and took hold of him as no feeling had done since he had made up his mind to get a university degree.

Solly's expedition in search of Humphrey Cobbler took him to a part of Salterton which was new to him. He walked slowly down one of those roads which are to be found in the new sections of all Canadian cities; rows of small houses lined both sides of the street, and although these little houses were alike in every important respect a miserable attempt had been made to differentiate them by a trifle of leaded glass here, a veneer of imitation stonework there, a curiously fashioned front door in another place, by all the cheap and tasteless shifts of the speculative builder. A glance at one was enough to lay bare the plan of all. Even that last modesty of a dwelling – the location of the water closet – was rudely derided by the short ventilation pipes which broke through each roof at identically the same spot. These were not houses, thought Solly, in which anyone could be greatly happy, or see a vision; no ghost would dream of haunting one of them; the pale babies being aired in their perambulators on the small verandahs did not look to him as though they had been begotten in passion; the dogs which ran from one twig-like tree (fresh from the nursery) to another, did not seem to be of any determinable breed; he could not imagine anyone at all like Griselda living in one of these dreadful boxes.

He was surprised, therefore, as he drew near the house which bore Humphrey Cobbler's number, to hear a burst of cheerful singing, accompanied with great liveliness on the piano. When he rapped at the door it was quickly answered by a red-cheeked, rather stout young woman with very black hair; her feet were bare, and her crumpled cotton frock somehow gave the impression that she wore very little beneath it. She bade Solly come in, and he found himself in a barely furnished and rather dirty room, where a shock-headed man was seated at a grand piano, and four barefoot, tousled children were singing at the tops of their pleasant voices.

'Hello!' roared the pianist. 'Sit down; we'll be with you in a minute.'

'Sweet nymph, come to thy lover,' sang the children.

'Words! Words!' shouted the man. 'Spit it out!'

Obligingly, the children spat it out, with such clarity that when they had finished their song the man cried 'Good!' and chased them away.

'We have a little workout twice a day,' he said to Solly. 'Lay the foundation of a good voice before puberty; that's the whole secret. Train them gently over the break, and then they've a voice that will last them fifty or sixty years.'

'Have you many child pupils?' Solly inquired.

'Oh, those aren't pupils; they're my own. People won't pay to have children taught to sing. What can I do for you?'

'You are Humphrey Cobbler, I suppose?'

'Yes. You're Solomon Bridgetower. I've seen you about.'

As he explained what he wanted, Solly was able to take a good look at his host. Humphrey Cobbler was the kind of Englishman who has a high complexion and black, curly hair; his nose was aquiline, his build slight. He might have been taken for a Jew, if it had not been for his bright, restless eye, like a robin's, which leaped constantly from Solly's face to his feet, from his feet to his hands, from his hands to his ears, and from his ears to something curious and amusing which apparently was hovering above his head. Cobbler, like his wife, was not overdressed; his trousers were held up by an old tie knotted around his waist, his shirt lacked most of its buttons, and his bare feet were thrust into trodden-down slippers. His hair, to which Nellie had referred, was saved from complete disorder by its curls, but there was a great deal of it, and from time to time he gave a portion of it a powerful tug, as though to brighten his wits, much as some people take pinches of snuff.

When Solly had made his suggestion Cobbler seized upon it with enthusiasm. 'Of course I'll do it,' said he; 'we can make a very complete thing of it. There's plenty of lovely music for *The Tempest*, but we'll use all Purcell, I think. I don't suppose you'd like to revise your plans and do Shadwell's version of the play, would you? A much tidier bit of playwrighting, really. No? I feared not. Wonderful music there.' Darting to the piano he burst into song:

Arise, arise, ye subterranean winds!

'Doesn't that stir you? Marvellous stuff! However, if you insist on sticking to the old Shakespeare thing we can do something very tasty. Your people can sing, I suppose?'

'They say so,' said Solly. 'I'm not sure about all of them. Perhaps you have met Miss Griselda Webster? She is to play Ariel, and she sings charmingly.'

'Let's hope so,' said Cobbler.

'I'm afraid we can't offer you any fee,' said Solly, with some hesitation.

'I didn't expect you could,' said Cobbler. 'Odd how so few really interesting jobs have any fee attached. Ah, well. You don't mind if I work Molly and the kids in for a bit of backstage singing, do you? They'd love it.'

Solly had not liked bringing up the matter of the fee, and in his relief he replied as though the presence of Molly and the little Cobblers backstage were all that was needed to make life perfect. He then brought up the matter of Mr Snairey. Cobbler opened his mouth very wide, so that Solly was able to see the pillars of his throat, and laughed in a wild and hollow manner.

'I know it's a nuisance,' said Solly, 'but Mrs Forrester has asked him, and he has accepted, and it was only with some difficulty that we persuaded her that Snairey's choice of music might be, well, undistinguished. You don't think you could get along with him, I suppose, just for the sake of peace?'

'My dear fellow,' said Cobbler, 'my whole life is moved by the principle that the one thing which is more important than peace is music. It is because I believe that that I am poor. It is because I believe that that many people suppose that I am crazy. It is because I believe that that I have just said that I will take care of the music for your play. I shall get no money out of it, and my experience of theatre groups leads me to think that I shall get little thanks for it. If, as you suggest, I get along with old Snairey for the sake of peace, it will be your peace, and not mine. I have not often heard him attack anything which I would dignify with the name of music, but when I have done so, that music has been royally – indeed imperially and even papally – bitched. I shall have nothing to do with him, in any circumstances whatever.'

'That creates rather a situation,' said Solly.

'If I'm to be captain of music I must be allowed to pick my own team.'

'Yes; I see that, of course.'

'And you also see, if I mistake not, that you will have a terrible row with Mrs Forrester, and another with old Snairey. Let me give you a piece of advice, Bridgetower; don't borrow trouble. To a surprising extent trouble is a thing one can allow other people to have, if one doesn't throw oneself in its path. You have already the harried look of a man who regards himself as the Lamb of God who takes upon him the sins of the whole world. That's silly. Now let me tell you what to do: go back to Mrs Forrester and tell her – in front of witnesses, mind – that I'll do it, but I won't have Snairey. Then let her deal with Snairey. He's senile, anyhow. Promise him a couple of seats for the play and he'll be all right. Pass the buck. It's the secret of life. You can't fight every battle and dry every tear. Whenever you're dealing with something that you don't really care about, pass the buck. You've got me to do your music; that's what you wanted, isn't it? Very well then, let Mrs Forrester clean up the mess.'

He turned again to the keyboard, and began to improvise very rapidly in the manner of Handel, singing the words 'Pass the buck' in a bewildering variety of rhythms and intonations. Solly, sensing that the interview was over, left the house, and for some distance down the street he could hear the extemporaneous cantata, for piano and solo voice, on the theme 'Pass the buck'.

Solly gave Nellie Cobbler's message, in front of witnesses as he had been told to do, at the very next rehearsal; he chose a moment when she was already distracted by other worries, said his say, and hurried off to attend to something else. He felt that he was behaving meanly, but comforted himself with the assurance that in certain complex situations perfect honour and fair dealing were out of the question. And he had, indeed, enough to worry him. Larry Pye, who had not read *The Tempest*, was discovering from the rehearsals which he occasionally overheard that there were magical devices in the play which he was expected to supply. His technique in meeting this problem was in the best Cobbler tradition of passing the buck. 'You plan 'em, and I'll make 'em,' said he, and Valentine had asked Solly, as her assistant, to see what he could do.

Solly's first move when confronted with a problem was to seek help from books. The Waverley Library, he discovered, was fairly well stocked with books about magic as anthropologists understand the word, and it could provide him with plenty of material about medieval sorcery; it also contained books by Aleister Crowley and the Rev. Montague Summers which assured him feverishly that there was plenty of magic in the world today. But of practical illusion it yielded only *The Boy's Book of Magic* and two books by Professor Louis Hoffmann, who wrote about card tricks in an intolerably facetious style and obscured his already obscure explanations still further with Latin quotations and badly drawn diagrams. After two days of poring over these works Solly reported to Valentine that Shakespeare's blithe direction 'with a quaint device the table vanishes' was still impossible of realization by any means which he could discover.

'Oh, never mind then,' said she; 'we'll just use the old pantomime tipover trick. It is really the simplest when it's well done. I merely thought you might find something better.'

So she had known a way of doing it all the time! For five minutes Solly was convinced that he hated Valentine.

He could not hate her for long, however. He was compelled, many times at each rehearsal, to admire the firmness, the good humour, the speed without haste, the practical knowledge of the stage, and the imagination which she applied to the task of training the actors of the Salterton Theatre to do what they had never done, or dreamed of doing, before in their lives. She very soon discovered what each actor might reasonably be expected to give, and then set to work to make sure that he gave it all. It was she who revealed to the world, and to Mr Leakey himself, that Mr Leakey could be quite funny if he didn't try to be his very funniest. It was she who found out that Mr Shortreed had a large bass voice, and could outroar Professor Vambrace. It was she who demonstrated that The Torso, having once been made to cry, could stand perfectly still on the stage and look unexpectedly distinguished as well as merely pretty. And it was she who allowed it to be seen, tactlessly, in Nellie's opinion, that Griselda Webster was a slacker, unwilling to make a sustained effort.

It was she, moreover, who dealt with the difficult problem created by Mrs Crundale. This lady might have been an artist of some attainment if she had not married Mr Crundale, and devoted her best efforts to furthering his career as a bank manager. The costumes which she designed for *The Tempest* were charming and imaginative. It was true that all the Reapers were expected to reveal a great deal more muscular shoulder and leg than they were likely to possess, and that costumes which she had designed for emaciated people seven feet tall had to be adapted for plump people considerably shorter after the casting had been done. But this was not the crux of the problem presented by Mrs Crundale. The crux was simply that she had designed costumes for Ariel, all the goddesses and the Nymphs which required that their bosoms be bare, not partly or fleetingly, but completely and indeed aggressively. She had shown these designs to almost everyone connected with the play and everyone had obediently admired them, while wondering what was to be done.

Mrs Crundale's position was clear, and had been clear for years. She was an Artist, and to her the human body was simply a Mass, with a variety of Planes; twelve years ago she had explained this thoroughly after a nice-looking rugby player from Waverley had spiritedly declined her invitation to pose for a portrait in the nude. Nobody connected with the Little Theatre quite liked to explain to Mrs Crundale that the breasts of several well-known young ladies of Salterton, though undoubtedly Planes, had other connotations, and could not fittingly be unveiled at a public performance. But Valentine did so.

'These dresses will look charming when they are standing still, Mrs Crundale,' said she, 'but when the girls dance your line will be completely spoiled. I suggest that you revise these slightly, giving some concealment for a strapless brassiere underneath.'

And Mrs Crundale, who had really only wanted to make the point that the human body was nothing to her but an arrangement of planes, agreed without a murmur. Devoted, tireless little Mrs Hawes, who was head of the costume-making committee, assured Valentine that because of this backing-up on the part of Mrs Crundale, she was able to breathe easily for the first time in many weeks. She had, she explained, dreaded the fittings.

Valentine showed herself no less able in her handling of intangible problems than in her swift settlement of the question of Mrs Crundale's unworldly designs. Solly was deputed, like assistant directors everywhere, to deal with a variety of matters of bothersome detail, and he revealed a genius for complicating and fantasticating all details. Instructed to look after the furnishing and decoration of the vanishing banquet table he worked busily with a group of assistants, and created a pleasant but confusing mass of gilded ewers, plates of exotic fruits, flasks of wine in colours no vintner would have recognized, and monstrous edibles which suggested that every guest was to be served with a whole wedding cake; this feast, spread upon a cloth which had been painted and gilded to the last inch, was widely admired by all except the actors who had to carry it. They were wearing fantastic masks, made by a young woman whom Solly had encouraged to do her uttermost, and they complained that they could not see. One of them, a Waverley lecturer in economics whose devotion to the drama was limited to murder plays and farces, declared that if he were expected to wear a lion mask, and carry a peacock in its pride at the same time, he would withdraw from the whole affair. Solly was aggrieved.

'But you can't achieve a big effect by niggling methods,' said he; 'of course it could all be made simpler, but this isn't a simple play.'

It was at this point that Professor Vambrace chose to explain that all works of genius were essentially simple, and were best interpreted by simple methods. In such a play as *The Tempest*, said he, it was vital that the magnificence of the words should not be lessened by too great a show of costumes and accoutrements. Simplicity, he told Solly, and the world in general, was the keynote of greatness. What was the use, he asked, of an actor like himself bringing the fullest power of his intellect to bear on the proper interpretation of his role, if the audience was to be perpetually distracted by shows of petty magnificence which had nothing to do with the play?

What followed was a full-dress row, in which wounding and bitter things were said on both sides. The Professor nobly led the forces of Simplicity, without any very useful backing, for the economics lecturer carried few guns as an aesthetic disputant, and lost his temper when Solly made an unwise reference to disgruntled accountants. Solly was not much better off, for his followers were all young women of artistic aspirations, whose idea of argument was to huff and flounce, except for the mask-maker, who wept – the difficult, lemony tears of a handicrafter whose all has been scorned. It was a moment for generalship, and Valentine acquitted herself with brilliance. Both sides, she said, were right. She hoped that they would attach some weight to her judgement, for although she did not attempt to rival them in scholarship (this went down very well with Professor

Vambrace) she had had a good deal of practical experience. What was to be sought in a Shakespearean production was a large, simple, overall plan; within that plan it was possible to elaborate many details, and to enrich anything that seemed to call for enrichment. The establishment of the basic simple plan she felt that they might safely leave to her; working with men of the intellectual stamp of Professor Vambrace she was certain that she would not go far astray. She was grateful to Solly and his assistants for the care which they had lavished upon the appurtenances of the play; such attention to detail in the professional theatre would only be obtained by spending very large sums of money. She begged them all to work together for the good of the Salterton Little Theatre. In unity there was strength. People of talent were bound to have these clashes of temperament. She had no misgivings about the production. And so on, in a gentle, but firm voice until the forces of Simplicity and the forces of Superfluity each received, in some mysterious fashion, an impression that they had slightly gotten the better of the other.

Particularly noteworthy in this instance was Valentine's use of the magical word 'temperament'. This is a quality which many people pretend to despise, but which they rather like to have attributed to themselves in a kindly fashion. Even the economist, hearing it, was mysteriously soothed; he felt that he was a good deal more highstrung than anyone supposed, and as Valentine had cleverly discovered this secret of his, he would gladly wear a lion's head mask and carry anything at all, for her sake.

The only breast which was not calmed was that of Miss Wildfang. Arriving a little late for the quarrel, and not fully understanding it, she knew only that Professor Vambrace's intellectual, moral and aesthetic authority had been challenged. She did not re-open the issue at once, but for a day or two afterward she went from group to group at rehearsal, spreading the Vambrace theory of utter simplicity. Finally the Professor himself had to ask her to desist. Theatrical people, he suggested, must be allowed their theatrical love of finery and display. A thrice-refined soul like her own needed no gaudy trappings to help it to the appreciation of a masterwork, but there were other, lesser creatures whose needs must be considered. Miss Wildfang assented, and was plunged into an even more pitiful state of mental concubinage toward Professor Vambrace than before.

It must not be supposed that rehearsals moved forward in an atmosphere of quarrelling, or that Valentine's method was always that of the oil-can. Her action in the matter of the swords was brisk. It was Roger Tasset who asked her if, when he first entered on the scene in Prospero's enchanted island, he should wear a sword. Valentine, who had not thought about the matter, said that she supposed he must, as it was wanted in the action. But then there arose a clamour among the other actors who played courtiers; they all wanted swords, and broke up the rehearsal in order to demonstrate their ideas of what they should do with them. It would be very pleasant and authentic, they thought, if they frequently drew their swords and saluted each other with them. They then began to haggle about the proper method of saluting with a sword, and Larry Pye, who was working near at hand, walked good-naturedly upon the stage and said that whatever might have been the method in the old days, this was the way it was done now. Soon half a dozen actors were stamping, frowning and brandishing imaginary swords. Valentine announced abruptly that there would be no swords in the play which were not specifically called for in the action, and that she wanted no manners from the modern parade ground; she would demonstrate the use of swords herself.

This gave offence to Roger. He felt that some slight had been made upon the profession of soldiering. He was also heard to say that he did not think that he needed to learn anything about the use of a sword from a woman. All of which was illogical and silly, but Roger's strongly masculine personality made up in emotion for anything which his words might lack in good sense.

Roger's conduct at rehearsals was unsatisfactory. An engineer by profession, he had not long been able to resist a project of Larry Pye's to put a public address system in the grounds at St Agnes'. Valentine had expressly forbidden Larry to wire the stage for sound, and to hide microphones in the bushes, which was what he wanted to do. She would make herself responsible for the audibility of the actors without any such doubtful aids, she had said. Larry had found it difficult at first to take this seriously; after all, he said, a P A system was part of the modern set-up and if it were not in evidence the audience would think that the Little Theatre was doing the thing on the cheap. But when he found that she meant what she said, he agreed to compromise on what he named a calling-system. This was an apparatus which enabled the actors who were not wanted on the stage to linger in The Shed, where a large amplifier was installed; the Stage Manager, behind the scenes, would have a microphone by means of which he might summon them to him in plenty of time for their cues. In addition, Larry said that he would rig up a talk-back between himself, in his pit in the front of the stage, the Stage Manager and Humphrey Cobbler's musicians. This arrangement, which sounded comparatively innocent to Valentine, proved to mean a great deal of wiring which Larry chose to do during rehearsal time. Roger elected to help him, which meant that he was not often ready when his cues came, that he appeared on the stage with the patronizing manner of a man who has left important work for lesser employment, and that he was sometimes to be found during scenes in which he was not concerned, crawling about the stage with a coil of wire, with the air of a man who believes himself to be invisible. It was when confronted with such situations as this that Valentine realized, more sharply than Nellie ever knew, that Salterton was not New York.

A worse thorn in her flesh than Roger, however, was Mr Shortreed. George, or as he preferred to be called, Geordie Shortreed, was a steward in the government liquor store and in that capacity was acquainted with all the gentle and simple of Salterton. He knew who drank wine, who drank imported Scotch, who drank the cheaper liquors, and who bought good stuff for themselves and what he called belly-vengeance for their guests. He had a large bass voice and a monkey-like physique which had persuaded Valentine to cast him as Caliban. Because Caliban is a large and important part, and one which was coveted by several other actors in the Little Theatre, it was thought that in casting a man who was, in essence, a bartender for it the Little Theatre had behaved in a commendably democratic way. Canadians are, of course, naturally democratic, but when they give some signal evidence of this quality in the social life they like to get full marks for it. Everybody had, therefore, been a little nicer to Geordie than was strictly required, nicer, that is to say, than they would have been to someone who was an unquestioned social equal. Geordie, however, refused to play this game according to the rules. Instead of being quietly grateful for the friendliness of professors and business men who always bought the best Scotch, he was rather noisily familiar with them, and revealed himself as a practical joker. A great patron of joke-shops, he had a large collection of ice-cubes in which a fly was imprisoned, of cigarette-cases with springing surprises in them, of rubber snakes, of cameras which squirted when they were supposed to be taking pictures. He proved to be the kind of actor whose delight it was to discompose those who were on the stage with him; to make them laugh, if possible. Valentine rebuked him for this twice and each time he allowed his great voice to drop to a rumbling whisper as he said: 'I know, Miss Rich; I oughtn't to do it, and that's a fact; don't imagine I don't realize what a privilege it is for the bunch and I to work with a real artist of the theatre like yourself; I guess it's just that it's so wonderful that makes me carry on like that; but it won't happen again, I assure you.' But it did happen again.

It could not be denied that Mr Shortreed's knowledge of the text of the play was richer and more curious than that of anyone else. Like Professor Vambrace, he knew it by heart from start to finish. But whereas the Professor showed off his knowledge only by prompting a little ahead of the official prompter, Geordie delighted in perverting lines to unexpected uses in private conversation. Like many great wits of the past, he planned his effects carefully at home, and then sprang them as impromptus at rehearsals. He was the kind of actor, too, who loved to address people offstage by the name of the character which they played on. Thus he never approached Hector Mackilwraith without roaring 'Holy Gonzalo, honourable man!' except on the day when Hector, hoping to show himself youthful in the eyes of Griselda, appeared in a new and too gay sports shirt, when Geordie struck his brow and cried 'What a pied ninny's this!'

Hector did not like this last sally, but upon the whole he admired Shortreed's wit and envied it, for it often raised a laugh. If only he could be distinguished in that way! Something deep inside him told him that Shortreed's jokes were stupid and overstrained, but his new craving to be a social success was silencing that inner voice which had kept him, for forty years, from making the more obvious kind of fool of himself. He too studied his text of the play in private, seeking lines which he might twist into a retort upon Shortreed, but his mind was ill-suited to such work, and he found little. He had to content himself with pretending to shrink from Shortreed, saying, 'Don't you come near me; you're a demi-devil,' but he knew that this was pitiful. Indeed, he became conscious for the first time of a certain thinness in his intellectual equipment which he had not noticed before.

Hector had a certain reputation as a wit, among the students of the Salterton Collegiate Institute and Vocational School. This was founded upon his occasional sarcasms and upon one joke, which he had brought to birth eight years before, and which had become a tradition in the institution. It had happened thus: one warm June afternoon Hector was supervising a gymnasium filled with students who were writing an examination; a boy had raised his hand, and said, in an offhand voice, 'Sir, do you know the time?'; Hector, with his dark smile, took out his watch, looked at it, returned it to his pocket and said, 'Yes.' What a shout of laughter there had been! And how the tale flew around the school! Young Porson, you see, had asked Mackilwraith if he knew the time; not if he'd tell him the time, you see; just if he *knew* it. And Mackilwraith had just said Yes, you see, with a perfectly straight face, because he did, you see, but he didn't say what the time was, because that wasn't what he'd been asked, you see?

In the great days of the Italian Comedy certain gifted actors prepared and polished special monologues, or acrobatic feats, or passages of mime, which became peculiarly their own, and these specialties were called *lazzi*. This witty interchange about the time became Hector's *lazzo*, and at least once a year some boy would play straight man, or stooge, to him, in order that this masterstroke of wit should be demonstrated anew. Time did not appear to wither, nor custom stale it. Thus when Hector found himself pitted against a man like Shortreed, whose jokes changed from day to day, he found himself at an unexpected disadvantage.

Geordie's career as a humorist, though meteoric, was short-lived. Like many another man before him, his fall was brought about by the sheer, inexplicable malignancy of fate.

There lived at St Agnes', under Tom's special care, an ancient horse called Old Bill, whose work it was to pull the large lawn-mower. Both Tom and Mr Webster were agreed that motor-mowers were instruments of Satan, designed to chew up and deface fine turf; the lawns, therefore, were mowed by a simple but very sharp mechanism which Old Bill dragged slowly behind him; for this work Old Bill wore a straw hat to protect his head from the sun, and curious leathern goloshes over his steel shoes, so that he would not cut the lawns. Dressed for work Old Bill was a venerable and endearing sight, and during rehearsals he became a favourite with the cast. They petted him and brought him sugar.

One afternoon Tom was cutting grass at some distance from the stage, when he became dissatisfied with the edge on one of the blades of the mower, and decided to touch it up. He left Old Bill under a tree and went off to The Shed for a file. Mr Shortreed, observing this, had a really great comic inspiration; he had a cue coming soon, and he would enter on Old Bill. Miss Rich wouldn't like it, of course, but surely when she saw what a laugh the bunch got out of it she wouldn't mind too much. Anyway, he hadn't time to worry about that, and he would chance his luck. Yes, there was old Vambrace yelling out his cue –

Thou poisonous slave, got by the devil himself
Upon thy wicked dam, come forth!

With a roar he leapt upon Old Bill, kicked the startled animal in the belly, and headed for the stage. Bill, who had never been used so in his life, bolted, and as he ran two of his leather shoes dropped off, so that he was steel-shod. As he burst through the bushes, bearing Geordie on his back, the effect was all a humorist could desire. Women shrieked; men roared; Professor Vambrace and Pearl, who were in the middle of the stage, took to their heels. It was Geordie's instant of utter triumph, the apotheosis of a practical joker. Then, bewilderingly, Old Bill gave a frightful scream, reared upon his hind legs, and dropped upon the ground. There he lay, screaming piteously for perhaps ten seconds; then he was still, his teeth bared, his eyes bulging.

Tom arrived on the run. 'Dead as a nit,' said he.

The cause of death was established by Larry Pye. 'He's gouged up the ground with his hooves, you see,' he explained. 'Here's the main cable not three inches down, in this steel conduit; Tom just put the sod over that this morning. Here's a poor join in the conduit, and he's hit the cable with his shoe. That's what did for him. Wouldn't happen once in a million years. But it happened this time. Thanks to you, you god-damned stupid bastard,' he said, regarding Geordie with an officer's eye. Geordie walked away and was noisily and copiously sick under a bush, but nobody pitied him.

Old Bill, venerable and loveable in life, was a disagreeable sight in death. His belly swelled shockingly, within a few minutes, which caused him to move a little from time to time, and to creak as though in an uneasy slumber. The actors did not want to look at him, but they could not take their eyes off him. At last Mr Leakey, moved by who can say what motives of delicacy, fetched a tweed jacket (it happened to be Larry Pye's) and draped it over Old Bill's face.

'We shan't rehearse any more this afternoon,' said Valentine. 'But I should like to see the committee for a few moments.'

It is enough to say that Mr Webster refused to allow the Little Theatre to replace Old Bill, saying without much real conviction that he supposed accidents would happen. Valentine had a frank talk with Geordie, in which she permitted herself to forget that Salterton was not New York; she was seconded by Major Larry Pye, who spoke with great restraint, all things considered. Geordie wrote a letter to Mr Webster in which the shrieking figure of Apology was hounded through a labyrinth of agonized syntax. Old Bill was hauled away to the knacker's, sincerely mourned by Tom and Freddy.

In the production of every play there comes a low point of rehearsal, after which the piece climbs to whatever climax it is destined to reach. There could be no doubt about it, the day Geordie killed the horse marked that point for *The Tempest*, as produced by the Salterton Little Theatre.

Leonardo Da Vinci asserted that the human eye not only received, but gave forth rays of light; Hector's eye, at any time before he fell in love with Griselda, might have served as a proof of this theory. But now it was dulled. In the late springtime, when he should have been deep in that exhaustive revision of the year's work which was so much a feature of his teaching, he would spend as long as five minutes at a time staring out of the window, twiddling the cord of the blind, while his pupils wondered what had come over him. His particular brand of classroom humour no longer held any charm for him. There had been a time when, during such a spring revision, he had sent two or three of the more backward pupils to the blackboard every day, to work out problems under his direct gaze; as they blundered, he had goaded them, not angrily, with a mingling of humour, pity and a little contempt. If it is true, as is so often asserted, that the greatest humour is near to pathos, Hector qualified on these occasions as a great humorist: although few of the stupid ones learned much about mathematics during these ordeals, some of them learned lessons of fortitude which were invaluable to them in later life. But this spring all the ardour of the born teacher was gone from him. He was like a sick man, but his pupils did not guess the cause of his sickness.

Spring had been his chief season for detentions. Every afternoon he had collected a group of boys and girls in his classroom after school was over, in order to make sure that they finished the work which they had not done during the lesson period. But this spring he was noticeably ill at ease for the last hour of the school day, and left as soon as the last bell had rung. He made his way at once to St Agnes' and if no rehearsal was called he would do little jobs for Larry Pye, or measure the area which had been set aside for seats, or do something to make it decent for him to linger there. Rehearsals usually began at five o'clock and ended at eight, when the light began to fail; Hector was the first to come and the last to go.

He had, in the course of a few weeks, learned much about himself. He had learned that he had no talent as a joker. But then, he was comforted to notice, Griselda did not seem to care for jokes, and never smiled at Shortreed's finest strokes, though she often laughed at young Bridgetower's nonsense, which meant nothing to Hector. He learned that his youth was gone, and that his attempts to dress youthfully made him ridiculous. Larry Pye, who was over fifty, could wear anything he liked, including very old Army shorts, and no one laughed; but when Hector wore a sports shirt he felt naked and looked foolish. He had learned that it was possible for him to throw himself in Griselda's way constantly, without her taking any notice of him. She, who had smiled so meaningly at him, did not even heed his presence now. And yet when it was necessary to the action of the play that she, as Ariel, should sing softly into his ear as he pretended to be asleep, he knew that his face reddened, that his breathing was hard and that the blood beat in his ears and eyes; he thought 'I love you, I love you,' as she knelt by him, and was hurt and dismayed that in some way the message was not plain to her. Wild schemes, as they appeared to him, kept coming into his mind by which he would make his love known. He would write a letter – but he knew his limitations as a writer. He would ask to see her privately some evening, ask for an hour uninterrupted; but would he be able to speak? No, he could not face such an ordeal; the old gods of planning and common sense had deserted him. He would wait until some lucky chance brought them together, and then, on the spur of the moment, he would speak. But chance never did bring them together. He did not know what to do.

His love for Griselda had undergone a change which frightened him. When he had awakened that morning, sure that he loved her, he had enjoyed the happiness of the sensation. For perhaps a week he had thought of his attachment chiefly as an appurtenance to himself. In his little mental drama he was the principal figure, and Griselda was a supporting player. But as time wore on the emphasis shifted, and Griselda became the chief person of the drama, and he was a minor character, a mere bit player, aching for a scene with her. For the first time in his life Hector discovered that it was possible for someone to be more important to him than himself.

He had no need now to look ruefully at the item in his Plan of Conduct which urged him to give up pie. His appetite waned, and his accustomed waitress at the Snak Shak commented on it. He did not lose any of his bulk, but he looked puffy and distressed. One day he tore the Plan of Conduct out of his book and burned it; it seemed to him to be stupid and worthless, an insult to what he felt. Indeed his whole concept of life as something which could be governed by schemes in pocketbooks appeared to him suddenly to be trivial and contemptible.

He wanted to talk to somebody about his love, but he knew no one to whom he could even hint of such a thing. He engaged Mr Adams in conversation about *The Tempest*, and led up to the character of Ariel. 'I think you'll like that in our production,' said he; 'we have a very clever girl playing Ariel, a Miss Webster.'

'She'll have to be clever,' said Adams; 'Shakespeare wrote that part for a boy, and it's always a mistake to cast a woman for it. I don't know that I care to see some great lolloping girl attempt it.' This last remark was pure spite, and Adams did not really know why he made it. But there is a spirit of Malignance which makes people say offensive things to lovers about those they love, even when that love is hidden, and Mr Adams was, for the moment, the instrument of it. Hector was wounded, but he could say nothing, for fear of revealing what might, he knew, bring him into derision.

Sexual desire played no conscious part in what he felt for Griselda. Indeed, it had never entered his life since that incident at the Normal School Conversazione. He did not long to possess her physically; he wanted to dominate her mentally. He wanted her to think of him as he thought of her, as of someone who stood high above and apart from the rest of mankind. He wanted to defend her from dangers; he wanted to bring her great gifts of courage and wisdom; he wanted to take her from the world and keep her to himself, and to know that she was blissfully happy to renounce the world for him. He thought that once he had declared his love, she might permit him to kiss her, but his imagination shrank quickly from that kiss; it would, he was sure, be a thing of such pain and joy that it might rob him of his senses. He had never, in all his forty years, kissed any woman but his mother.

Nevertheless, he was strongly conscious that Griselda was a

woman, and was subject to the disabilities which he believed to be a special and unjust burden to her sex. When, at rehearsals, she seemed to be a little out of sorts, or flung herself on the grass to rest, or wore the look of weary beauty which had worked so powerfully upon Solly at the casting meeting, Hector grieved that she might be in the throes of those 'illnesses peculiar to women' of which, as a boy, he had read in patent medicine almanacs. Thinking this, he could become quite maudlin on her account, and once remarked to the astonished Mr Leakey, out of the blue, that woman had a great deal to bear which men could only guess at.

If only he could tell someone about his love! The urge to talk about it was mastered, but only just, by his fear of making himself foolish, or of destroying the magic of his feelings by giving them a voice. Once he thought seriously of seeking an interview with Mr Webster, and telling that gentleman that he, Hector, loved his daughter and wanted her father's consent to seek her hand. This was, he realized, no longer the custom, but what he felt for Griselda demanded the fullest measure of formality. Besides, he was nearer in age to Mr Webster than to his daughter; an older man, and the father of such a girl, would surely understand the frankness and nobility which prompted such an action. Fortunately better sense prevailed, and Mr Webster was spared an interview which he would have found embarrassing and depressing.

Freddy was not so fortunate. Hector found her in the grounds at St Agnes' one afternoon when he had, as usual, arrived early for rehearsal; she lay on the grass, memorizing her words as the goddess Ceres. Hector had no fear of adolescent girls, for he had taught hundreds of them. Here, he thought, was someone he could pump about Griselda.

'I see you are getting your words by heart,' said he.

'Yes,' said Freddy.

'That's right. We won't make much progress until we are all perfect in our words.'

'I suppose not.'

'Do you find memorizing hard?'

'Not when I'm allowed to concentrate on it.'

'You should memorize each night, the last thing before you go to sleep. That is the best way to memorize formulae, or anything like that.'

'Really?'

'Why are you not at school?'

'I've been ill; I'm taking a term off.'

'Pity, pity; you shouldn't break the flow of your education until it is complete. That is, if you can afford to keep up the continuity, which not everyone is able to do.'

'The doctor told my father to keep me at home. I've nothing to say about it.'

'Ah. Pity, pity.'

A pause, during which Freddy and Hector regarded one another solemnly.

'A very fine old house you have here.'

'Thank you.'

'How old, now?'

'Oh, about a hundred and thirty years, I suppose. Prebendary Bedlam built most of it.'

'Who?'

'You aren't a native of Salterton, are you?'

'No.'

'Then it's not likely you'd have heard of him.'

'You have a lovely big room, I expect.'

'No, quite small.'

'But your sister has a lovely big room, I expect?'

'She has two rooms; a sitting-room and a bedroom with the biggest bed in it you ever saw, with a crimson silk bedspread,' said Freddy, who was getting tired of this and decided to give the pryer some well-deserved mis-information. 'She has a marvellous bathroom, with a sunken tub, and a peach basin, and a black john and a toilet roll which plays *The Lass of Richmond Hill* when you pull it,' she continued, beginning to enjoy herself.

Hector was not sure how he should take this. Long experience of girls of Freddy's age told him that she was lying. Nevertheless, she was Griselda's sister, and to that extent sacred. He decided to give her the benefit of the doubt.

'That's very interesting,' said he. 'And which would be her window, now?'

'Those big ones there,' said Freddy, pointing to her father's windows. Was he a Peeping Tom, she wondered.

'Has your sister finished school?'

'Yes.'

'Ah, she didn't lose terms like you. She'll have been very clever at school?'

'Not very,' said Freddy.

'Really? But she was a leader, I suppose? I expect she was very much admired?'

So that's it, thought Freddy. This silly old clown is stuck on Gristle. The dirty old man, chasing a girl less than half his age. Just another John Knox. With the concentrated spite of the eunuch, or the sexless, she said:

'No, she wasn't liked, really, except by a few. But she was the champion burper of the school. She can swallow an awful lot of air, you know, and belch the first few bars of *God Save the King*, while saluting. She was always begged to do it on stunt nights.'

Hector walked away, saddened. The child was a liar, and perhaps not quite right in the head, but her blasphemy had wounded him, none the less.

Hector was wrong in supposing that Griselda did not notice him. She noticed that he seemed often to be in the way, that he changed colour and breathed heavily when she sang her little piece into his ear, and that he seemed to be physically timid and fearful of accidents. This last observation was unjust, and was the outcome of Hector's solicitude for her; as Ariel she had to climb about one some platforms which Tom had put up at the back of the stage and disguised with greenery; it never entered her head to be frightened of these trivial heights, but whenever she had to get down from them, she was likely to find Hector there, with a hand outstretched, and a look of apprehension on his face; he would assist her to the ground, gingerly, and walk away, as though embarrassed. Larry Pye sometimes wanted to do the same thing, but she knew Larry; he wanted to squeeze her legs as he lifted her, and she usually jumped straight at him, causing him to skip ungallantly out of danger. But she assumed that Hector was a fusspot who thought that she could not jump six or eight feet without breaking something.

Hector, like everyone else in the company, came into the game which she played with Roger, as well. That young man had not fallen under the spell of Valentine Rich's personality, as everyone else connected with the production had done in some degree. There was between them one of those unaccountable antipathies which occasionally occur, and which nothing can be done to remedy. Roger admitted that Valentine was an unusually capable director, but he did not like her; he set her down as a Bossy Woman; perhaps this was because he knew that she could never be influenced by his sort of charm. Valentine considered Roger a godsend as a juvenile lead in an amateur play, but she did not like him; he was a type which she had met many times in the theatre, and which, except for theatrical purposes, she could not endure. And although she was fully as tactful in her dealings with him as with the rest of the company, he sensed her dislike beneath her courtesy, just as she sensed his dislike beneath his compliance. Shut out from the group which was warmed and enspirited by Valentine, he made fun of it to Griselda.

She was quickly attracted by anything which savoured of sophistication, and to the young the easy, ill-founded cynicism which finds everybody and everything just a little second-rate is a kind of fool's gold. It was flattering that Roger should make fun of the others to her; to be chosen as the confidante of a superior spirit is always flattering. Griselda was very far from being a fool; she had what Dr Johnson called 'a bottom of good sense', but she was not quite nineteen, and she had never met anyone like Roger before.

He, in his turn, was delighted that he had so quickly found a way to attract her. She was not, he recognized, like any girl upon whom he had tried his skill before. She was wealthy, which meant that he must be very careful, for one does not lightly seduce rich girls; they have too many powerful relatives, and are too much accustomed to getting the better of all things. He seriously questioned whether he could proceed to the usual conclusion of his plan with Griselda. Indeed, he marvelled dimly that gold, which could make an attractive girl so much more attractive, should also protect her so thoroughly. And as well as money, Griselda had the manners and the conversation of a well-bred girl who has read a great many books of the easier sort, and these qualities Roger mistook for worldly wisdom and unusual intelligence. For the first time in his life Roger had met a girl with whom he felt that a 'nice' – well, fairly nice – relationship was worth cultivating. Griselda was capable of giving him something which he valued even more than physical satisfaction; she could give him class. The other thing he could find elsewhere when he wanted it. Never any shortage of that.

Thus they struck up an amused conspiracy against the rest of the company. Nobody cared except Valentine, who thought it bad for the play; except Hector, who did not understand it but who saw that Griselda was too often laughing in a corner with Tasset; except Pearl

Vambrace, who had fallen as much in love with Roger as it is possible to fall in love with a man who never speaks to you except in lines written by Shakespeare, lines charged with a noble love which is nothing but play-acting.

Bad for the play – yes, Valentine thought that. But she knew that she was nettled by anything which gave Roger satisfaction, and she was angry with herself for being so petty. She could not keep up her accustomed tact one day at rehearsal when Roger repeatedly fluffed his lines in a scene with Pearl.

'Roger, it's far past the time when you should know this scene,' said she.

'Sorry,' said Roger, in a tone which suggested that he thought she was being wearisome and must be humoured.

'It's useless to say that you are sorry if you have no intention of improving,' she said; 'you have said "Sorry" in very much that tone at the last four rehearsals. I am growing tired of it.'

Pearl, moved by the desire for self-sacrifice which is one of the most dangerous characteristics of unwanted lovers, spoke:

'It's really my fault, Miss Rich,' said she; 'I make a move there which puts him off, I think.'

'No, you don't do anything of the kind,' said Valentine crossly; 'you are perfectly all right and you would be much better if you had something to act against.'

'If I am really such a nuisance, Miss Rich,' said Roger, 'perhaps it isn't too late to reconsider the casting.'

'Oh, don't talk like an idiot,' said Valentine, angrily conscious that she was growing red in the face. 'You are the best person for the part, and you know it. You can do it very well, and you will do it very well. If you drop out now you will make all sorts of difficulties for everybody. But I want you to work at rehearsals, and spend less time giggling in the background with Griselda. You are both of you behaving like children. A production like this depends on everybody's good work and good will. It simply is not fair to behave as you are doing.'

Roger was very angry. That he, a man who had got the better of so many women should be spoken to in that tone by a woman, and in front of a lot of nincompoops! He turned to leave the stage.

'Go back to your place, Roger, and finish your scene,' said Valentine in the voice which had caused two London critics to call her the best Lady Macbeth among the younger generation of actresses.

To Roger's intense astonishment, he did so, and under the stress of anger, he acted quite well. But as he looked into Pearl's eyes he saw pity and love there, and he hated her for it until the rehearsal was over, when he promptly forgot her.

At eleven o'clock that night Griselda sat at her window, studying her lines. She had been alarmed and shamed by Valentine's words; she was also angry. If that was the way Valentine thought about her, she would show that she could behave in any way she pleased, and act Ariel too. She looked out of her window at the upper lawn; there was the spot, there by that tree, where Solly had kissed her. She remembered it with pleasure. But what a mess he had turned out to be! Afraid of his mother! Griselda, who had forgotten what it was like to have a mother, and who could not know what the relationship between a man and his mother can be, was scornful. Roger wasn't such a softy. It was only since she had met Roger that she had really known how silly most people are.

Was she in love with Roger? She didn't really know, but she half suspected that she was. Anyhow, she knew who did love Roger, and that was that stupid Pearl Vambrace, whose hems were always uneven, and whose hair looked as if it needed a good wash. But Pearl wasn't going to get Roger until Griselda had quite made up her mind about him. Yes, very likely she was in love with Roger.

The fact was that Griselda's notions about love, allowing for differences of sex, were no more clear-cut than those of Hector Mackilwraith. But as she leaned out of her window and took a long breath of the warm spring night, she felt that it was a very fine thing to be eighteen and in love.

On the other side of the house Freddy crept to the window of a darkened closet and looked out. Yes; there it was; just what she had expected to see. A dark shape standing among the trees, not easy to make out, but apparently with its head thrown back and its eyes raised, undoubtedly in worship, toward the windows of her father's bedroom.

Putting half a walnut shell in her mouth she popped her head out of the window and shouted in her deepest voice: 'Who's that down there?'

There was a wild trampling of shrubbery, and a thickset figure rushed toward the road.

[FIVE]

As the time of the opening performance drew nearer there were rehearsals in the grounds of St Agnes' three or four times a week, and after many of these Griselda offered the actors what she liked to call 'a bite'. Roger said that he could not understand why she did it, and it seemed to herself that it was not in her new character as an amused observer of the human comedy. But although the flame of hospitality within her was not a bonfire, it was steady and bright, and it appeared to her to be wrong that people should come to her home and go away again without having received food or drink. Therefore she worked out a plan for giving the Little Theatre bread and cheese and fruit and coffee; she even insisted upon paying for these things herself and serving them herself, so as not to put her father to expense or to make extra work for the servants. The facts that her father did not care about such expenses and that the servants had not enough to do did not enter into the matter; she felt that the Little Theatre was at St Agnes' because of her doing and that she ought to take care of at least some of their wants. So contradictory is human nature that she could think sneeringly of her fellow-actors while taking considerable pains on their behalf. As Freddy said in her more sentimental moments, Griselda was not a half-bad old boob in her way.

The Little Theatre loved it. Acting is a great provoker of hunger and conviviality, and the bread and the cheese, the fruit and the coffee were consumed in great quantities. Professor Vambrace complimented Griselda upon the classical simplicity of this refreshment; it put him in mind of the meals in Homer, he said. Pearl and he ate heartily upon these occasions, not knowing what Spartan nastiness the preoccupied Mrs Vambrace might have left in the refrigerator for them at home. But Griselda's hospitality begot hospitality in others, and soon the actors were vying with one another to entertain the cast after a rehearsal; simplicity was forgotten, and hospitality raged unchecked. Some of these affairs were very pleasant; others were markedly less agreeable. Mrs Leakey's after-rehearsal soirée came well down in the latter category.

What Mrs Leakey felt when she discovered that Leakey was going to other people's houses to eat and drink, without her, four times a week, was simple jealousy. But it was not Mrs Leakey's way to admit to base emotions; she sublimated them. So she addressed Leakey thus:

'You can't very well go on eating everywhere and anywhere, week in and week out, without Repaying Hospitality. We don't want people to think we're cheapskates. I don't know that we're exactly in a position to entertain. Goodness knows we have little enough in the way of cups and saucers. But if other people are having the cast in after rehearsal, we'll do it too. So you'd better invite the whole tribe for next Friday night, and get it over with.'

When Mrs Leakey heard that the fare at St Agnes' was of the simplest, she smiled a superior smile. Beginning at ten o'clock in the morning on the Friday in question, she worked the greater part of the day on the food which she would serve that night. She baked a chocolate cake and a white cake; she iced the former in the difficult and lumpy Log Cabin style, and the latter she covered with a deep layer of sticky stuff resembling marshmallow. She imprisoned little sausages in pastry and baked them. She made an elaborate ice cream, and coloured it green. She made sandwiches of the utmost difficulty, possible only to a thirty-third degree sandwichmaker, in which bananas were tongued and grooved with celery; sandwiches loaded with cream cheese, or encrusted with nuts and olives; sandwiches in which lengths of chilly asparagus were entombed in two kinds of bread; sandwiches in which fish, mayonnaise and onion were forced into uneasy union. She produced pickles of her own making from the cellar cupboard, and created a jelly from which the imbedded bits of fruit stared forth, like fish from a ruby bowl. By evening she was, to use her own phrase, 'all in', and let Mr Leakey know it before he went to rehearsal.

'Don't be later than nine getting back here with them,' she said; 'we don't want them hanging around till all hours. Some of us have to get up in the morning if others don't.'

This was enough to make Mr Leakey nervous all through the rehearsal, which began at half-past six, and to put him into a state of real apprehension from half-past eight onward. But when the cast arrived in a body at the Leakey home at half-past nine, who could have been a more gracious chatelaine than Mrs Leakey?

'I'm glad you came just in whatever you stood up in,' said she, taking in Griselda, who was in slacks, the Torso, who was in shorts, and Valentine, who wore a suit but the tail of whose blouse kept popping out. Mrs Leakey wore a creation of scratchy lace which showed off her large, strong collar bones to great advantage.

She had invited a few ladies of her acquaintance to help her in serving the refreshments. Some hostesses might have felt that this was a mistake, for these ladies knew nothing about the play, were not members of the Little Theatre, and wanted to talk about other things. Now a theatrical company, however ill-assorted or however amateur, is bound together by ties which are incomprehensible to outsiders. They want to talk about their play, or if they talk of other things, they are likely to talk about them in a manner which does not readily take in strangers. Even a determined hostess like Mrs Leakey may find herself bested by this exclusiveness. She decided to make small-talk with Solly on the one topic which seemed to interest him.

'I've been hearing Eric his lines,' said she, offering him a pickle; 'I must say they don't mean much to me.'

'Oh,' said Solly, who was tired and not in a mood to encourage this line of conversation.

'I think some of Shakespeare's characters are awfully overdrawn,' said Mrs Leakey, firmly.

'Really?' said Solly, looking curiously into a sandwich.

'As a matter of fact, I've said to Eric that it seems to me that more people would like Shakespeare if he had written in prose.'

'Very likely.'

'Still, that's just one person's opinion.'

'Quite.'

The party took on a strongly Ontario character. That is to say, all the ladies gathered in the drawing room, and all the gentlemen gathered in a small room behind it, which Mr Leakey used as his 'den'. In the dining-room, enthroned behind the silver service, one of Mrs Leakey's female friends poured out coffee, and the other female friends came to the table from time to time to load up with fresh consignments of food. Roger wanted to talk to Griselda; Valentine wanted to talk to Solly; the Torso yearned in a generous and all-embracing fashion to be at the men. But the power of the hostess at such affairs is very great, and Mrs Leakey liked to run her parties on tried-and-true pioneer lines. So the sexes ate in decent segregation, and were so cowed that they obediently gobbled some of everything which was offered to them, regardless of how little they wanted it. And promptly at half-past ten the ladies rose, almost as one, and the guests departed.

'Well,' said Mrs Leakey; 'thank Heaven they didn't stay till all hours. Now we'd better get these dishes washed; I don't want them staring at me when I come down in the morning. It's been a hard day, but I don't want it to stretch over into another.'

By midnight the Leakeys had washed everything and put it away, and were in bed, having shown themselves hospitable.

It was not long before Mrs Bridgetower, who had a knack of knowing what was going on even when she was most secluded and ailing, heard about this round of hospitality.

'You know how it grieves me not to be able to do my part,' she said to Solly. 'When your Father was alive this house was a rendezvous – a regular rendezvous. But I simply couldn't see so many people at once in my present condition. I might manage a few, but I couldn't manage all.'

'Please don't worry about it, Mother,' said he. 'Nobody minds.'

'Oh, don't they?' said his mother. 'I didn't know that I'd been forgotten quite so quickly. There was a time, I can tell you, when people looked to this house for hospitality. And you know, lovey, that there is nothing I like so much as to see your friends here.'

Solly had often been assured of this by his mother, but the evidence pointed in a different direction. What his mother liked was to see his friends come to the house, fail in some direction or other to measure up to the standard which she set for companions of her only son, and depart in disgrace. It was still remembered against one miserable youth that five years before he had crumbled a piece of cake on the drawing-room carpet, and had then nervously trodden in it and tracked it into the dining-room; Mrs Bridgetower could still point out exactly where his crumby spoor had lain. Solly hoped to let the matter drop, but his mother detected this and continued:

'Perhaps the best thing would be to have them in in small groups of three or four, one group each week, for tea. If you will give me a list of their names I shall make up the groups, and telephone them as their time comes.'

'I'm afraid they wouldn't be able to come to tea, Mother,' said Solly; 'most of these affairs are rather late in the evening.'

'Oh, I could never manage that; the anxiety of waiting all evening for them to come would be too much for me.'

'Of course it would, Mother. They understand.'

'Oh, so they've been discussing it, have they? Well, I don't want them to understand anything that isn't so. I am quite capable of offering hospitality on my own terms. When I was a girl and we got up any private theatricals, we usually made rehearsals an excuse for very charming little teas, and sometimes eggnogg parties.'

'I know Mother, but this is different. Much more professional in spirit.'

'Hmph, the world seems to be advancing in everything except amenity.'

'Would you be happy if I invited a few people in, just for a chat in my room, after a rehearsal, now and again? You wouldn't need to bother with them then.'

'You could hardly invite girls to come here under those circumstances.'

'Of course not. Just a few of the men. And then we should have shown ourselves hospitable, and you wouldn't have been troubled.'

'Well, perhaps so. I shall write a note to Mrs Forrester, explaining why I have not undertaken to entertain the group as a whole, and then you shall have the men in by twos and threes.'

Mrs Bridgetower wrote the note that same day, and at the next rehearsal Nellie said:

'Oh Solly, how sweet of your mother to write to me like that! I don't know of anyone else in Salterton who would have done it. Really she's wonderful! So hospitable, and so gracious. It must be a terrible hardship to her that she can't entertain as she wants to! Of course we all understand. I'm sending her a little bouquet and a note from me and Val.'

It was not a happy inspiration which persuaded Solly to arrange the first of these masculine gatherings on a night when Miss Cora Fielding was also entertaining the company. The Fieldings were jolly people, and unlike Mrs Bridgetower they really liked to see their children's friends in their house.

Not only was there chicken and ham and potato salad and olives and anchovies and fruit salad and several sorts of sweetmeats; there was also rather a lot of liquor, and as Mr Fielding was more hospitable than discreet the party, at the end of an hour was lively and noisy. At the end of the second hour, square dances were being performed in a room which was much too small for them, and Valentine had danced a hornpipe with great success. The party broke up at midnight; several people kissed Miss Cora Fielding goodnight, and everybody assured the older Fieldings in merry shouts that they had had a wonderful time.

Solly, who was wondering what he would say to his mother if she happened to be awake, was walking purposefully toward the gate when Humphrey Cobbler hailed him:

'Not so fast, Bridgetower; let us adjourn to your select masculine gathering at a dignified pace.'

'Oh, well, really I hadn't quite realized that Cora was throwing a party tonight. Must have got my dates mixed. Probably it would be better if you came to me another time.'

'Nonsense. There is no time like the present. Procrastination is a vice I hate. Now, who's coming with us? Tasset? Hey, Roger Tasset! You're coming on to Bridgetower's party aren't you?'

'Oh yes, I remember now that I said I would,' said Roger, without enthusiasm.

'Who else? Mackilwraith? Ahoy, there, Mackilwraith; come along with us.'

'Isn't it rather late?' said Hector.

'Not a bit of it. Barely midnight. Come on. We're going to make the welkin ring at Bridgetower's.'

'The what ring?' said Hector.

'The welkin. It's a thing you make ring when you get drunk. Bridgetower has a lovely fresh welkin, just waiting to be rung. Come on!'

The half mile walk to Solly's home was not enlivened by much conversation. Why, Solly wondered, had he asked this ill-assorted group? Tasset was a man he wanted to know better, for Tasset was plainly attractive to Griselda, and Solly told himself that he wanted to study his rival. Heine, he felt, would have done so. To cast himself in the role of Heine somehow lessened the ignominy of being a rejected lover; he might be nothing to Griselda, but in his Heine role he was certainly an interesting figure to that dim, invisible, but rapt audience which, since his childhood, had watched his every move. Tasset was the crass, successful soldier – the unworthy object upon whom the Adored One chose to squander her affection: he was the scorned, melancholy poet, capable of examining and distilling his emotions even while his heart was wrung.

That explained Tasset most satisfactorily. But why Mackilwraith? Hector plodded at his side in silence, setting down his feet so hard on the pavement that his jowls gave a little quiver at every step. Why, out of all the men in the cast, had he thought of asking this dullard? He raked his mind for a romantic or even for a reasonable explanation, but he could find none.

Cobbler he had asked because he liked him. Cobbler was a man so alive, and so apparently happy, that the air for two or three feet around him seemed charged with his delight in life. But the Cobbler who was so lively a companion by daylight, in the midst of a rehearsal, seemed a little too exuberant, a little too noisy, in the stillness of the night, when one was growing nearer to Mother with every step. He had not the air of a man who would be really considerate about making a noise on the stairs. And the drinks which he had accepted from the hospitable Mr Fielding had made him noisier than usual.

As though to bear out his fears, Cobbler began to dance along the pavement and sing:

The master, the swabber, the bos'n and I,
The gunner, and his mate,
Loved Moll, Meg and Marian, and Margery,
But none of us cared for Kate.

'For God's sake, don't make such a row,' said Solly. 'You'll wake the whole neighbourhood.'

'I am full of holy joy and free booze,' said Cobbler. 'I feel moved to sing. It is very wrong to resist an impulse to sing; to hold back a natural evacuation of joy is as injurious as to hold back any other natural issue. It makes a man spiritually costive, and plugs him up with hard, caked, thwarted merriment. This, in the course of time, poisons his whole system and is likely to turn him into that most detestable of beings, a Dry Wit. God grant that I may never be a Dry Wit. Let me ever be a Wet Wit! Let me pour forth what mirth I have until I am utterly empty – a Nit Wit.' He sang again:

For she had a tongue with a tang,
Would cry to a sailor 'Go hang!'

She loved not the savour of tar nor of pitch
Yet a tailor might scratch her where'er she did itch.
Then to sea, boys, and let her go hang!

'Please be quiet,' said Solly desperately. 'We're near my home now. My mother is unwell, and she will be asleep.' (Fat chance, he thought, inwardly.) 'We'll go right up to my room; I wouldn't like to disturb her.'

'Sir, you are talking to a Fellow of the Royal College of Organists,' said Cobbler, with immense solemnity. 'You can rely utterly upon my good behaviour. *Floreat Diapason!*' He began to tiptoe exaggeratedly on the pavement, and turned to whisper Ssh! at Hector, whose feet were making a good deal of noise.

Roger thought fleetingly of excusing himself. This was going to be a miserable affair. Bridgetower was afraid of his mother, and Cobbler was playing the fool. Why had he ever allowed himself to be mixed up with such a pack?

The Bridgetower house was in darkness and the front door was locked. Solly was suddenly angry. She knew that he was bringing friends home. This was intolerable. As he rattled his key in the lock Cobbler gave another conspiratorial Ssh! Why, Solly demanded of himself, does she expose me to this kind of thing? To be shushed entering my own home! Angry, he made a good deal of noise in the hall, and led the procession upstairs. At the first landing, as he had expected, was the ray of light from his mother's door.

'Is that you lovey?'

'Yes, Mother. I've brought some friends home.'

'Oh, I did not think that you would, now that it's so late.'

'It's just a little after midnight, Mother.'

'You won't be too late, will you lovey?'

'I can't possibly tell, Mother. Did you leave some sandwiches?'

'When you didn't come home by ten I told Violet to put them away.'

'I'll find them. Good-night, Mother.'

'Good-night, lovey.'

Half an hour later they had eaten a good many sandwiches and drunk some of Solly's rye, which for the occasion he had diluted with soda water instead of the lukewarm drizzle from the tap. Humphrey Cobbler had established himself as the leader of the conversation and was holding forth on music.

'If there is one gang of nincompoops that I despise more than another,' said he, champing on a chicken sandwich, 'it is the gang which insists that you cannot reach any useful or interesting conclusion by discussing one art in terms of another. Now there is nothing I enjoy more than talking about music in terms of painting. It's nonsense, of course, and at worst it's dull nonsense. But if you get somebody who knows a lot about music and a lot about painting, it is just possible that he will have an intuition, or a stroke of superlative common sense which will put you on a good scent. If you ask me, we're too solemn about the arts nowadays. Too solemn, and not half serious enough. And who's at the root of most of the phoney solemnity? The critics. Leeches, every last one of them. Hateful parasites, feeding upon the blood of artists! Do I bore you?'

'You don't bore me,' said Hector. 'Not that I know anything about the arts. Though I have had some musical experience.' He smiled shyly. 'I used to pump the organ in my father's church.'

'Did you now?' said Cobbler. 'Do you know, that's the first really interesting thing I've heard you say. It humanizes you, somehow. Can you sing?'

'Very little. I've never had much of a chance.'

'You ought to try it. You've got quite a nice speaking voice. You ought to join the singers in the play. Now there's music that you can get your teeth into. Purcell! What a genius! And lucky, too. Nobody has ever thought to blow him up into a God-like Genius, like poor old Bach, or a Misunderstood Genius, like poor old Mozart, or a Wicked and Immoral Genius, like poor old Wagner. Purcell is just a nice, simple Genius, rollicking happily through Eternity. The boobs and the gramophone salesmen and the music hucksters haven't discovered him yet and please God they never will. Kids don't peck and mess at little scraps of Purcell for examinations. Arthritic organists don't torture Purcell in chapels and tin Bethels all over the country on Sundays, while the middle classes are pretending to be holy. Purcell is still left for people who really like music.'

'I like the music you have chosen for the play,' said Hector; 'what we heard tonight was very pretty.'

'Thank you,' said Cobbler. 'Pretty isn't just the word I would have chosen myself for Purcell's elegant numbers, but I discern that your heart is in the right place.'

'A pretty girl is like a melody,' hummed Roger.

'Excuse me,' said Cobbler, turning toward him, 'but I must contradict you. A pretty girl is nothing of the kind. A melody, if it is any good, has a discernible logic; a pretty girl can exist without the frailest vestige of sense. Do you know that that great cow of a girl they call The Torso – a pretty girl if ever there was one – came to me the other day and told me that she was musical, indeed surpassingly musical, because she often heard melodies in her head. Her proposal was that she should hum these gifts of God to me, and that I should write them down. She then hummed the scrambled fragments of two or three nugacities from last year's movies. There were two courses open to me: as a musician I could have struck her; as a man I could have dragged her into the shrubbery and worked my wicked will upon her.'

'As a matter of curiosity, which did you do?' asked Solly.

'Curiosity killed the cat,' said Hector, who was a little embarrassed by the turn the conversation had taken; nevertheless, he wanted to show himself a man's man, and something witty seemed called for.

'I deny that,' said Cobbler; 'the cat probably died a happy martyr to research. In this case I was spared the necessity for decision; Mrs Forrester called me away at the critical moment to ask if it would be necessary for the musicians to have any light, or whether they could get along with the few rays which might spill from the stage. When Nellie is in one of her efficient moods all passions are stilled in her presence.'

'She's a damned efficient woman,' said Roger. 'There wouldn't be any show without her.'

'I'd like her better if she hadn't such an insufferably cosy mind,' said Solly.

'What do you mean by that?' said Roger.

'Oh, you know; she makes everything seem so snug and homey; she wants to be a dear little Wendy-mother to us all. Not being a Peter Pan myself, I don't like it.'

'Peter Pan, the boy who never grew up,' said Hector, to show that he was following the conversation, and also that he was as keen in his appreciation of a literary reference as anybody.

'Funny, I would have thought that Peter Pan was a pretty good name for you,' said Roger.

'Would you,' said Solly; 'and just why would you think that?'

'Take my advice and don't answer that question,' said Cobbler. 'You two are bound to quarrel eventually, but if you take my advice you won't do it here.'

'And why are we bound to quarrel, may I ask?' said Roger, very much on his dignity.

'Because, as everybody knows, you are both after the Impatient Griselda. It's the talk of the company. At the moment, Tasset, you are well in the lead, but Solly may leave you behind at any moment. Your fascination – I speak merely as an impartial but keen observer, mind you, and mean nothing personal – is beginning to wane. At any moment Griselda may weary of your second-rate man-of-the-world manner, and turn toward our host's particular brand of devitalized charm.'

This was sheer mischief-making, but Cobbler liked mischief and had had enough to drink to make him indulgent toward his weakness.

'I had not realized that we were so closely watched,' said Solly. He and Roger were both caught off their guard by Cobbler's words. But they were not so startled as Hector. So intensely had he concentrated on his own passion that he had not observed anything unusual in the attentions which Roger had been paying to Griselda; nor was he acute enough to have noticed anything significant about the way in which Solly avoided her. And here he was, confronted with two unsuspected rivals, both younger and more attractive than he, whose presence had been unknown to him! He had not drunk much, but his stomach heaved, and he felt cold within. He had no time to consider his plight, however, for Roger turned to him.

'That's a lie, isn't it, Mackintosh?' said he.

'What? What's a lie?' said Hector, startled.

'A lie that everybody is watching Griselda and me. I've been giving her a mild buzz, of course. Got to pass the time somehow. But nobody's been talking about it.'

'I don't know,' said Hector.

'Of course you don't know. Nobody's been talking and nobody cares. You're lying, Cobbler.'

'Nobody says that with impunity to a Fellow of the Royal College of Organists,' said Humphrey. *'Floreat Vox Humana!'*

'And exactly what do you intend to do about it?'

'Nothing at present. But I'll embarrass you some time in public, and make you sorry.'

'I never heard such nonsense in my life,' said Solly. 'I couldn't be less interested in Griselda Webster. I've known her, man and boy, for years. She has a heart like an artichoke; one man pulls off a leaf, dips it in melted butter, and consumes it with relish; another does the same. Anybody can have a leaf, but nobody gets them all, and nobody touches the core. I've had a leaf or two; why should I grudge Tasset his turn?'

'Perhaps that's the way you talk about women in the universities,' said Roger. 'In the Army we're a little more particular.'

'In the great shrines of humanism we don't need arbitrary rules to keep our manners in order,' said Solly, bowing rather drunkenly over his glass.

'Come, come, gentlemen,' said Cobbler. 'Don't go all grand on us. You must admit, whatever you say about Miss Webster's character, that she is an unusually personable young woman.'

'Handsome is as handsome does,' said Solly owlishly. 'Griselda is attractive – damnably attractive. But it's all on the surface. If I may so express it, she is like a fraudulent bank which advertises a capital of several millions, and has perhaps five hundred dollars in actual cash. She is lovely; I repeat it, lovely. Because I am peculiarly sensitive to beauty I admit to a certain tenderness for her on that account; but her heart is cold and empty.'

'Horse feathers,' said Roger, with heat. 'She's just a kid – a damned nice kid. She has to be taught what life's all about, and what love is; just because you couldn't get to first base with her you say her heart is cold and empty. I know better.'

'Ah, I knew that we could rely upon you, Lieutenant,' said Cobbler. 'Our host is a man of theory, you, a man of action. From your remarks I deduce that you have already bruised the teats of her virginity?'

This was greeted with a moment of silence. Then –

'What the hell do you mean by that?' demanded Roger.

'Three guesses,' said Humphrey, smiling. 'It is a rather delicate phrase from the Prophet Ezekiel – one of the nicer-minded prophets. In my capacity as an organist I hear a lot of Scripture; it's an education in itself.'

'Listen, Cobbler,' said Roger, 'I've lived a rough life – a soldier's life – but I have no use for raw language, particularly when applied to women. Just be careful, will you?'

'But I was careful,' said Humphrey, smiling; 'I could have put it plainly, but I chose a Biblical phrase to suit the solemnity of the occasion. And from what I know of your past history, Lieutenant, your objection to raw language has never stood in the way of your fondness for what fussy people might consider raw conduct.'

'I've been around,' said Roger; 'and I've known a lot of girls.'

'It was said of that great and good monarch Henry VIII,' said Cobbler, 'that his eye lighted upon few women whom he did not desire, and he desired few whom he did not enjoy. Would you consider that a fair description of yourself?'

'I don't say that I haven't taken my pleasure where I found it,' said Roger, 'but it was usually a fifty-fifty deal. Girls don't get laid against their will. But don't get any wrong ideas about Griselda. She's different.'

'Aha, then you are in love!' cried Humphrey. 'There is nothing men like so much as generalizing about women; all women are alike, except the one they love. She is the exception to all rules. And there is no lover so pure and holy in his adoration as a reformed voluptuary. You love her, Tasset!'

'Very well then, I love her. I'm man enough to admit it,' said Roger and was startled and somewhat alarmed to hear himself.

'Spoken like a man!' cried Humphrey.

'I don't believe you,' said Solly, heatedly. 'Just a few minutes ago you described your attentions to her as a mild buzz.'

'Well, did you expect me to blab out my private feelings?' said Roger.

'That's what you've just pretended to do,' said Solly, 'but I don't believe you love her. How could you love her? You haven't got it in you to love anybody. The only thing that a crass, ill-conditioned yahoo like you could want with a girl like Griselda is-is-is her body.' He finished weakly, for he had wanted a strong word, and could not immediately think of one which was not also too coarse for the occasion. 'You just want to seduce her,' he said, and sat back in his chair looking hot and rumpled and somewhat wet about the eyes.

Roger stood up. 'By God, Bridgetower, there are some things I won't stand,' said he. 'Get up on your feet.'

So it was to be a fight! Solly was no fighter, but he did not lack courage; he would let Tasset hammer him to a pulp before he would take back a word of what he had said. He stood up, throwing off his coat as he did so, and confronted Roger. Humphrey Cobbler skipped nimbly behind a table, and Hector, his heart in his mouth, followed him.

The ceiling was low, and dipped at the corners of the room, for it took the shape of the roof of the house; the light was bad, for it came from a single lamp which threw a patch of brilliance on the ceiling and a poor light everywhere else. There was a small rug on the slippery floor, and a good deal of furniture everywhere. It was not an ideal battleground.

Roger was in good condition, and knew how to box. But when he took a boxing posture he found that Solly had placed himself just out of reach, and was holding his fists at waist level, and clearly intended to do nothing. Who was to strike the first blow?

They might have stood glaring at one another until good sense took hold of them if Solly had not been so frightened. But he was convinced that Roger would do him desperate harm – might indeed kill him – and he was determined to make one gesture, one final Heine-like act of defiance, before the slaughter began. So he drew up his lip in a sneer, and laughed in Roger's face.

This had the desired effect. Roger stepped lightly toward him, and hit him on the nose, twice in the ribs and once on the jaw, with such speed that it seemed to Solly that the blows all landed at once. But with a great effort he struck at Roger's diaphragm, having some dim notion that a blow there would be very telling. The treacherous rug slipped, and as he fell he jerked up his head and struck his adversary under the chin with it, causing Roger to bite his tongue painfully. They fell to the ground with a crash, and lay there, moaning from their injuries.

As the noise subsided a sound from below made itself heard; it was not loud, but it was persistent; it was the tapping of a stick.

'Oh God,' said Solly, getting up; 'it's Mother.' He hurried to the door. 'It's all right, Mother,' he called; 'something fell down; nothing wrong.' And then, foolishly inspired, he added, 'I hope we didn't wake you?'

His mother's voice came tremulously up the stairs. 'Oh, lovey, I'm so frightened. I thought the whole roof was coming down.'

'No, no, Mother; no trouble at all. You'd better go back to bed.'

Even more tremulously came the reply. 'I can't; I'm on the sofa in the hall. I feel so weak. I think I need one of my white tablets.'

'I'll have to go to her,' said Solly.

'Better clean the blood off your face, first,' said Humphrey.

It was Hector who acted. He dipped his handkerchief in the cold water in the bottom of the bowl which held ice for the drinks, and cleaned away the jammy ooze which had gathered under Solly's nostrils.

'We had better go home now,' he said.

'No, no, that would convince Mother that something dreadful had happened. Anyhow it will take me some time to get her to her room if she has one of her weak spells. Stay here and keep quiet till I come back.' Solly hurried down the stairs on tiptoe.

Roger had risen from the floor and was sitting with his tongue held between two cubes of ice, like the meat in a sandwich. Humphrey made as though to prepare him another drink, but Roger shook his head; a man who has bitten his tongue shrewdly feels a sickness all through his body which demands rest and quietness, not drinks. So Humphrey made a drink for himself and one for Hector, and sat down. Although they could not see it, all three were oppressively conscious of the pill-taking, the laboured breathing, the mute reproach, and the mordant old comedy of mother-and-son which was being played out at the foot of the stairs.

For some time nobody spoke. After perhaps five minutes Roger rose and went into Solly's bedroom, which was behind the room in which they were, and finding a washbasin there he set to work to relieve his swollen tongue by holding it under the cold tap.

Hector and Humphrey looked at each other.

'I don't like this,' said Hector.

'No. Bad business,' said Humphrey. 'But probably we'll be able to talk some sense into them when they come back.' He had had the fun of provoking a quarrel; he now looked forward with appetite to the fun of patching it up.

'I don't mean these two fellows,' said Hector; 'I mean that I don't like Miss Webster to be mixed up in a thing like this – rough talk and fighting.'

'Oh, heavens, don't worry about that. She'll probably never hear of it. Not that she would mind, I suppose; girls rather like to be fought over. Not that this was a fight a girl could take much pride in. But don't worry. Nothing will come of it.'

'How do you know that something has not come of it already?'

'Meaning –?'

'They talked – they talked quite cold-bloodedly of – well, of intimacy with her.'

'Oh well, that's just talk, you know. You know how lads are.'

'Yes, I think I do. But that sort of talk disgusts me, and makes me angry, too. I wanted to knock their heads together.'

'I don't know that I'd try that, if I were you.'

'But we are older than they are. Surely one of us should take a stand?'

'What about? I don't see what you are getting at.'

'Well,' said Hector patiently, as though explaining the binomial theorem to a pupil, 'they shouldn't talk that way about a girl's honour. A girl's honour is like a man's reputation for honesty – probably more easily destroyed. It is sacred. Men should treat it with reverence.'

'Aha, so that's your notion, is it? Well, if I recall correctly, I was the first one to suggest that Griselda's honour might have been a little blown upon. Now, in point of fact, I don't believe that. But I wanted to find out what Tasset was up to, and I thought maybe I could goad him into an admission or a display of some kind. And I did.'

'Well, then I think you ought to be ashamed of yourself.'

'I'm not, though. You're not what could be called an original moralist, are you?'

'I know the difference between right and wrong, I hope.'

'How nice for you. I don't.'

'I suppose it is nothing to you that a beautiful and innocent young girl might lose her honour?'

'Listen, Mackilwraith; do me a favour, will you; stop calling it her honour. You give me the creeps. Tasset has rather a reputation; I just wanted to find out what he was up to, if I could.'

'He leads an immoral life, does he?'

'By your standards, I suppose he does.'

'Are there any other standards for decent people?'

'That depends on the part of the world the decent people find themselves in, and the education they have had, and the place in society they occupy. Does Tasset strike you as an immoral fellow?'

'If he is loose with women I don't see that there can be any argument about it.'

'Strictly between ourselves, I don't like him either. Still, if it's his nature to chase women, should we judge him?'

'There is such a thing as self-control.'

'You certainly ought to know. You look as though you had controlled yourself, I must say.'

'Certainly. In my profession anything else would be unthinkable.'

'The unthinkable has always been rather in my line. You don't appear to have controlled yourself at the table, by the way. Quite a lad with the knife and fork, aren't you?'

'That is different. It harms nobody.'

'I see. You don't think this control business can be overdone, do you?'

'How could it be?'

'Well, you know what Galen says: If natural seed be overlong kept, it turns to poison.'

'Who was Galen?'

'Never heard of Galen? Claudius Galen? The father of medical practice?'

'Is he dead?'

'A small matter of seventeen hundred years.'

'Ah. Well I dare say his opinion has been contradicted since then. Medical opinion is always changing. Do you see *The Reader's Digest*?'

'Galen wasn't just a pill-roller. He was a first-rate psychologist. The remark I have quoted to you is really a philosophical opinion phrased as a medical maxim.'

'But it is out-dated.'

'Damn it, wisdom is never out-dated.'

'But how can the opinions of a doctor who died so long ago be any good today? In religion, of course, age is a good thing. But not in medicine.'

'All right, Mackilwraith, you win. I feel myself to be an angel, beating my ineffectual wings in vain against the granite fortress of your obtuse self-righteousness.'

'You're not an angel. I think you're rather silly. Why do you clutter your mind with what a dead doctor said?'

'Galen isn't just a dead doctor, man; he was a great spirit. Probably a lot of his ideas are fantastic now. But he had flashes of insight which we can't discount. That's what makes a man great; his flashes of insight, when he pierces through the nonsense of his time, and gets at something that really matters.'

'You are a lucky man to have room to spare in your head for truck of that sort.'

'Truck?'

'Most of us find it hard enough to keep track of the things that we really need to know.'

'Oho, now I know what you are. You are an advocate of Useful Knowledge.'

'Certainly.'

'You say that a man's first job is to earn a living, and that the first task of education is to equip him for that job?'

'Of course.'

'Well, allow me to introduce myself to you as an advocate of Ornamental Knowledge. You like the mind to be a neat machine, equipped to work efficiently, if narrowly, and with no extra bits or useless parts. I like the mind to be a dustbin of scraps of brilliant fabric, odd gems, worthless but fascinating curiosities, tinsel, quaint bits of carving, and a reasonable amount of healthy dirt. Shake the machine and it goes out of order; shake the dustbin and it adjusts itself beautifully to its new position.'

'As a mathematician I can hardly agree with you that disorder is preferable to order.'

'Mathematician my foot! Do you know anything about linear algebra? How are you on diophantine equations? Could you tell me, in a few words, what Bertrand Russell has added to modern mathematical concepts? You are a mathematician in the way that a teacher of beginners on the piano is a musician!'

'I know what I know,' said Hector, 'and it is sufficient for my needs.'

'But you don't begin to realize how much you don't know,' said Humphrey, 'and I shrewdly suspect that that is the source of your remarkable strength of character. For you are strong, you know; you talk like a fool, but you have amazing personal impact.'

It was at this moment that Roger returned, and sat heavily down in his chair.

'How's the tongue?' asked Humphrey.

'Thwobs,' said Roger.

'Aha. Swollen too, eh?'

Roger nodded. There was a gloomy silence. Humphrey slipped down into his chair and closed his eyes.

Hector looked at Roger long and closely. It was his duty, he knew, to speak to him about Griselda. He ought to tell this man to stop annoying Griselda with his dishonourable attentions. But how could he do so? It was not that he lacked moral authority; he knew what was right, and he knew what he should do about it. But how could he rebuke Roger without giving away the fact that he, Hector, loved Griselda? The shock of finding that he had two young rivals had shaken him severely. He thought deeply, and the longer he thought the harder it was to speak. But at last he found a form of words which seemed to him to meet the needs of the occasion, and he spoke, so hollowly that Roger started a little in his chair.

'Do you consider yourself a suitor for the hand of Miss Webster?'

'Eh!'

'Do you want to marry Miss Griselda Webster?'

'I don't know. I haven't thought that far.'

'Then you ought to leave her alone.'

Roger regarded him with surprise. He was not a sensitive young man, and Hector's earnest, flushed face held no message for him.

'Listen, Mackintosh, how would it be if you mind your own business?' he said, at last.

Hector could not think of a suitable reply, and silence fell again.

At last Solly returned; his face was white and drawn, except for his swollen nose and a lump on his jaw. When Hector said that it would be well for them to leave he insisted that they stay.

'No, no,' said he; 'I've given Mother a sedative, and soon she will be in a deep sleep. But if you go downstairs now you may waken her. And I'd like you to stay. I need company.'

'Listen, Bridgetower,' said Roger, 'I'm sorry about this. About disturbing your mother, I mean. And I didn't mean to hit you so hard.'

'Quite all right,' said Solly.

'You're not a type I like, if you know what I mean. But as your type goes, you're not too bad.'

'I understand you,' said Solly. 'As a matter of fact, I don't like your kind, either. Judged by any decent standard you are a pismire, an emmet, but it shouldn't be impossible for us to get along.'

'Yes, it takes all kinds to make a world, as they say. Shake hands?'

'Certainly.'

Humphrey stirred in his chair, and then started up, wide awake.

'"Deeply have I slept, as one who hath gone down into the springs of his existence, and there bathed."' said he. 'Bit of useless knowledge for you, Mackilwraith; a poet you've never heard of and wouldn't like.'

'Beddoes,' said Solly.

'Neatly spotted,' said Humphrey. 'Full marks to Master Bridgetower for identifying the quotation. A great man, Beddoes and, like Purcell, still unmauled by the mob. Did I see you fellows shaking hands? Ah, the manly press of flesh! What a wonderful device it is for bringing insoluble quarrels to an apparent end! I take it that you've slipped Mum a Mickey Finn? How wise; sedatives to the sedate. Well, well, who's got the bottle?'

'No more for me,' said Hector.

'Nonsense. You haven't got any way of providing us with some hot water, have you, Bridgetower?'

'There's an electric kettle downstairs.'

'Fetch it, like a good fellow, will you? And you might as well bring a lemon and some sugar when you come.'

When Solly had returned with the necessaries Humphrey quickly prepared four strong hot toddies.

'Now,' said he, 'while you were otherwise engaged, Mackilwraith drew it to my attention that he and I, as older men, should help you two to straighten out your affairs. This fighting over Griselda Webster won't do. If you want my frank opinion, the girl isn't worth it. A pretty little voice, but nothing out of the way. Take my advice: marry a woman with a good big mezzo range, plenty of power, and perfect pitch. Besides, neither of you really cares much about her; you just imagine that you do. "Esteem and quiet friendship oft bear love's semblance for a while." Beddoes again, Mackilwraith. Esteem and quiet friendship; that's what you feel for Griselda. So no rough stuff, with her or with each other. Agreed?'

'I'm taking her to the Ball,' said Roger.

'I shall see you there,' said Solly, who had not until that moment had any intention of going to the Ball.

An hour later two further rounds of toddy had made a great difference to Solly's party. On the floor below Mrs Bridgetower was in such a sleep as only one of her white tablets, washed down with hot milk, could give her. Upstairs in the attic sitting-room three of the four men were talking animatedly and Humphrey Cobbler was holding forth to Hector on education.

'Of formal education,' said he, 'I have had but little. When I was a lad I was sent to a choir school. I had, if I may be permitted to say so, an exceptional soprano voice. They needed me, Mackilwraith; they needed me. And if there is one thing which utterly destroys a boy's character, it is to be needed. Boys are unendurable unless they are wholly expendable.'

'Funny thing, when you flushed your closet just now,' said Roger to Solly, 'it put me in mind of a wonderful Dominion Day celebration we put on a couple of years ago when I was stationed out on the West Coast.'

'All celebrations should be wonderful,' said Solly, putting more sugar in his drink. 'And that is one of the big troubles with Canada; we have very little ceremonial sense. What have we to compare with the Mardi Gras, or the Battle of Flowers? Nothing. Not a bloody thing.'

'Because I was needed, I was impossible. I never worked at my school lessons, but I worked like a black at my music. And whenever I had to sing in Service, I put on a superb show. Well – what could they do? The Dean was headmaster of the school; was he going to boot his best soprano boy out into a cold world because he didn't do his sums? You see the situation?'

'Well, now, we had to parade on Dominion Day of course, and it was a hot day and we were all pretty well browned off. And we were worse than browned off – in fact you could pretty well say we were completely cheesed off – when an order came round that the OC wanted all the junior officers to remain in barracks that night – Dominion Day night, you see – because some bigwig from Ottawa wanted to have a look around, you see?'

'Our national dislike for doing things on a really big and spectacular scale, shows up in this play. You heard that row a couple of weeks ago when old Vambrace and Eva Wildfang were carrying on about the beauty of simplicity? They think Shakespeare can be run entirely under his own steam. He can't. You've got to have as much lavishness in costume and setting as you can, or your play will be a flop. The day of Shakespeare in cheesecloth costumes and a few tatty drapes is done.'

'Of course I knew that I had the Dean right where I wanted him. Well, suddenly some American impresario got a notion that he wanted to take part of our choir to the States for a tour. The Dean said that only boys who had achieved a scholarly record of such-and-such could go. But ha! The impresario had been to Service. "Of course I've got to have that solo boy," says he. "That boy isn't eligible to go," says the Dean. "Then I'll have to think again," says the impresario. You know, I've always thought that fellow must have been a bit of a pansy. I was good, but I couldn't have been that good.'

'There we were, you understand, cooped up in barracks, on a holiday, after a heavy afternoon in the sun. I suppose they thought we gave the damn place a lived-in look, or something. So we thought up a scheme. Or really – give the devil his due – it was a fellow named O'Carroll worked it out and when the evening came we were ready.'

'Taste is at the bottom of everything. Given taste, you can go to any lengths. For instance, you remember the row about those costumes that old Ma Crundale designed? The ones with no fronts in them? They were tossed out because the girls couldn't wear them. But given enough taste, it could be done, and it would be a knockout! In fact, if I were given a completely free hand, I think I could work a completely naked Ariel painted gold into *The Tempest* and there wouldn't be a word of complaint. Just breathless admiration! But it would all be done with taste, you see?'

'The upshot was that the Dean gave way; he didn't want to lose the publicity or the big fee, either. So away we went to the States for six months. You should have seen us, Mackilwraith! For the first part of the programme we wore our blue cassocks and our ruffs, and sang Byrd and Tallis and all that. Then for the secular stuff in Part Two we switched into evening dress, with Eton suits for us boys. Ah, Mackilwraith, if you could but once have seen me in a bumfreezer and a clean collar, singing "Love was once a little boy", it would have made a better man of you!'

'As soon as dinner was over we made our excuses and got out of the mess as fast as we could. It was easy, because the O C was dining with the bigwig. We got over to the men's quarters, which were empty; everybody was out on the town. Some of us who were engineers arranged wires on the handles of all the water closets on each floor. Then we did the same in every other building where there were any. Then we established a central control in the administration building in the dark, and waited.'

'Given taste, you can then go as far as you like with your big stage effects. Hundreds of people milling about if you like. Fill the stage with horses and dogs. Pageantry in a big way. Make it complex! Let it fill the eye! Let it be enriched, bejewelled, Byzantine! The parrot-cry that simplicity is one with good taste comes from people who cannot trust their taste in anything which is not simple. Shakespeare demands all the opulence that we can give him!'

'The man who had charge of us boys was one of the counter-tenors, a dear little chap named Thickpenny – Roland Thickpenny. You know what a counter-tenor is? No, I thought not. You've lived a dreadfully meagre life, Mackilwraith. A counter-tenor is a male alto. He is a tenor who has trained and enriched his falsetto register so that he can sing in a lovely, clear voice, and fill in the alto part in the male choir in a cathedral. You can't have women in Church choirs; they sour the Communion wine, or something. They're damned nuisances, anyhow. Well, Thickpenny was a dear – a chubby, red-faced little fellow, with a lovely voice. Women in the States went wild over him. Wanted to see what made him sing like that. Thought he was a eunuch, or something. Dear old Thickers was always being chased by some orgulous hag. But he was true to Mrs Thickpenny and all the little Thickpennies at home.'

'At last the great moment came. The OC walked out into the barrack yard with the bigwig. Every window in every building was open. We pulled all the wire controls. There was a perfect Niagara of flushing closets. We did it again. And again. It was a *feu de joie* of WCs. The OC and the bigwig scampered inside again. We never heard a word about it. That taught him to keep us in on Dominion Day.'

'Tasset, I'm going to make a life's work out of it! If it kills me I'm going to squelch this notion that there is anything meritorious about simplicity on the stage. I proclaim the Baroque, Tasset! I laud the daedal!'

'But if Thickpenny was a man of iron, Mackilwraith, I was not. For you must know that I, too, had my following. "That dear little boy," ladies would exclaim, and want to kiss me. Now, Mackilwraith, it was in a place in Montana called Butte, that a very beautiful woman, a superb creature of about thirty-five, I suppose, caught me at a party and kissed me to such purpose that my voice broke on the voyage home. And that is why I refuse to get stewed up about any woman's honour. What about my honour, such as it was at the age of eleven? Worse still, what about my voice? For once it was gone the Dean made my life a perfect misery. But you can't say my American tour wasn't educative.'

Catch as catch can, and every man for himself, the conversation spun on through the night. Only Hector was silent, nodding from time to time and allowing his glass to be filled almost without protest. At five o'clock they went home, Roger to appear at a lecture at nine, Humphrey to sleep till noon, and Hector to greet a class which found him pale, inattentive and apt to desert them while he sought the drinking fountain.

[SIX]

Eight days before the first night of *The Tempest* the following advertisement appeared in the Salterton evening paper for the last of five successive publications:

AUCTION

The complete Household Effects of the late Dr Adam Savage will be sold at auction at his former residence, 33 King Street, on Friday, June 8, beginning at 10 o'clock a.m.

All furnishings, ornaments, china and glass, carpets, bed linen, etc. will positively be sold to the highest bidder under the conditions posted on the door. No catalogue. View day Thursday, June 7.

Do not miss this sale which is the most Important to be held in Salterton so far this year.

And for this fifth appearance the following note was appended to the advertisement:

We are directed by Miss Valentine Rich, executor of the late Dr Savage, to announce that his splendid library, comprising more than 4300 volumes of Philosophy, Theology, Travel, Superior Fiction and Miscellaneous will be open to the clergy of all denominations from 10 o'clock Wednesday, June 6, and they may have gratis any volumes they choose. This is done in accordance with the wish of the late Dr Savage. Clergy must remove books personally.

ELLIOT & MAYBEE
Auctioneers and Valuers

This addition to the auction notice was printed in no larger type than the rest of the advertisement, but it caught a surprising number of eyes on the Tuesday when it appeared. Anything which concerns a subject dear to us seems to leap from a large page of print. Freddy Webster, who was no careful reader of newspapers, saw it, and snorted like a young warhorse.

'Giving away books!' said she. 'But only to preachers! Damn!'

Later that evening she met Solly, who was in the garden wondering, as all directors of outdoor performances of *The Tempest* must, whether the arrangements for the storm-tossed ship in the first scene of the play would provoke the audience to such derisive laughter that they would rise in a body and demand the return of their money at the gate.

'Yes, I saw it,' he said in answer to her question. 'Pretty rotten, confining it to the clergy. Not that I care about Philosophy, or Theology, or even Superior Fiction. But there might just be something tucked away in Miscellaneous which would be lost on the gentlemen of the cloth.'

'Whatever made Valentine do it?'

'Apparently, two or three years ago, the old chap said something, just in passing, about wanting his books dealt with that way. And they're quite unsaleable, you know. A bookseller wouldn't give five cents apiece for the lot.'

'Have you seen them, Solly?'

'No; but you know how hard it is to get rid of books. Especially Theology. Nothing changes fashion so quickly as Theology.'

'But there might just be a treasure or two among them.'

'I know.'

'Still, I don't suppose a preacher would know a really valuable book if he saw one. They'll go for the concordances and commentaries on the Gospels. Do you suppose Val would let us look through what's left?'

'Freddy, my innocent poppet, there won't be anything left. They'll strip the shelves. Anything free has an irresistible fascination. Free books to preachers will be like free booze to politicians; they'll scoop the lot, without regard for quality. You mark my words.'

Freddy recognized the truth of what he said. She herself was a victim of that lust for books which rages in the breast like a demon, and which cannot be stilled save by the frequent and plentiful acquisition of books. This passion is more common, and more powerful, than most people suppose. Book lovers are thought by unbookish people to be gentle and unworldly, and perhaps a few of them are so. But there are others who will lie and scheme and steal to get books as wildly and unconscionably as the dope-taker in pursuit of his drug. They may not want the books to read immediately, or at all; they want them to possess, to range on their shelves, to have at command. They want books as a Turk is thought to want concubines – not to be hastily deflowered, but to be kept at their master's call, and enjoyed more often in thought than in reality. Solly was in a measure a victim of this unscrupulous passion, but Freddy was wholly in the grip of it.

Still, she had her pride. She would not beg Valentine to regard her as a member of the clergy for a day; she would not even hang about the house in a hinting manner. She would just drop in, and if the conversation happened to turn upon books, as some scholarly rural dean fingered a rare volume, she would let it be known, subtly, that she was deeply interested in them, and then – well, and then she would see what happened.

With this plan in view she was at the residence of the late Dr Adam Savage at five minutes to ten on the following morning, dismayed to find that an astounding total of two hundred and seventeen clergymen were there before her, waiting impatiently on the lawn. They ranged from canons of the cathedral, in shovel hats and the grey flannels which the more worldly Anglicans affect in summer, through Presbyterians and ministers of the United Church in black coats and Roman collars, to the popes and miracle workers of backstreet sects, dressed in everything under the sun. There was a young priest, a little aloof from the others, who had been instructed by his bishop to bespeak a copy of *The Catholic Encyclopaedia* which was known to be in the house, for a school library. There were two rabbis, one with a beard and one without, chatting with the uneasy geniality of men who expect shortly to compete in a race for a shelf of books on the Pentateuch. There were High Anglicans with crosses on their watch chains, and low Anglicans with moustaches. There were sixteen Divinity students, not yet ordained, but trying to look sanctified in dark suits. There was a stout man in a hot brown suit, wearing a clerical stock with a wing collar; upon his head sat a jaunty grey hat, in the band of which was fixed a small metal aeroplane; it was impossible to say what he was, but he wore a look of confidence which bespoke an early training in salesmanship. There was a mild man with a pince-nez, who was whispered to be a Christian Science practitioner. There was no representative of the Greek Orthodox, the Syrian or Coptic Churches; otherwise Christianity in its utmost variety was assembled on that lawn.

It was never discovered how clergymen for a radius of fifty miles around Salterton got wind of Dr Savage's posthumous bounty. The local newspaper took the great assembly of holy men as a tribute to the power of its advertising columns; indeed, as Freddy approached, a press photographer was climbing into a tree to take a picture of the extraordinary sight. However, the orgulous pride of newspapers is widely understood. The gossips of Salterton decided, after several weeks of discussion, that the matter was beyond any rational explanation, but that the Christian Church must be better organized, and more at one on certain matters, than they had thought.

At five minutes past ten, when the clergy were beginning to buzz like bees, a car stopped in front of the lawn and young Mr Maybee and Valentine climbed out of it. They were a good deal surprised and discomposed to find a crowd waiting for them, and hurried to open the front door. It had been their intention to sit quietly in the library at a table, arranging some final details of the sale and welcoming the occasional clergyman who might drop in for a book. Instead they were closely followed up the steps, not rudely, but as cattle follow a farmer with a pail of hot mash. When the door was opened the clergy increased their pace, still without rudeness, but with a kind of hungry fervour, and Valentine and young Mr Maybee found that they were entering the library at a brisk trot. It was a room of moderate size, and might perhaps have held fifty people when full. Seventy rushed into it in sixty seconds, and the remainder crowded as close to the entry as they could.

One does not describe the activity of clergymen in a library as looting. They were, in the main, quiet and well-bred men, and it was in a quiet and well-bred manner that they went to work. The pushing was of a moderate order, and the phrase 'Excuse me' was often heard. Natural advantages, such as long arms, superior height, and good eyesight were given rein, but there was no actual snatching nor were the old intentionally trodden upon. No very wide choice, no thoughtful ranging of the shelves, was possible in such a crush, and with good-humoured philosophy the visitors seized whatever was nearest. There were a few friendly disagreements; a shovel hat and the brown suit had each got hold of five volumes of a nicely bound ten-volume set of the works of a Scottish metaphysician, and neither could see why the other should not yield his portion. The rabbis, pushed into a corner where there was little but New Testament material, struggled feebly to reach their Promised Land, without knowing precisely where it was to be found. The young priest found his encyclopaedia, but it was too bulky to be moved at one time, and he knew that it would be fatal to leave any part of it behind him, in the hope of making a second trip. An elderly Presbyterian fainted, and young Mr Maybee had to appeal in a loud voice for help to lift him through the window into the open air; Valentine took her chance to crawl out to the lawn, in the wake of the invalid.

'What shall we do?' she asked the auctioneer, who was a nice young man, and supposedly accustomed to dominating crowds.

'God knows,' said Mr Maybee; 'I've never seen anything like it.'

'You must cope,' said Valentine, firmly.

Mr Maybee climbed back upon the windowsill. 'Gentlemen,' he called in a loud voice, 'will those who have chosen their books please leave as quickly as possible and allow the others to come in? There is no need to crowd; the library will be open all day.'

This was no more effective than a bus-driver's request to 'Step right down to the rear, please.' The clergy at the door would not budge, and the clergy in the library would not attempt to leave until they had filled their pockets and heaped their arms impossibly high. Young Mr Maybee at last climbed down from the windowsill, and confessed defeat to Valentine.

There are times when every woman is disgusted by the bonelessness of men. Valentine had, in her time, directed outdoor pageants with as many as five hundred supernumeraries in the crowd scenes. She quickly climbed upon the windowledge herself.

'This won't do,' she cried in a loud, fierce voice. 'You must follow my directions to the letter, or I shall have to call the police. Or perhaps the Fire Department,' she added, noticing that the magical word 'police' had done its work upon these ministers of peace. 'All those in the hall go to the lawn at once.' With some muttering, the brethren in the hall did as they were bid. 'Now,' she cried, to the crowd in the library, 'you must take the books you have chosen and leave by the back door.' In three minutes the library was empty.

By half-past eleven two hundred and thirty-six clergymen had passed through the library, some of them three and four times, and the shelves were bare. Dr Savage's bequest had been somewhat liberally interpreted, for an inkwell, a pen tray, two letter files, two paperweights, a small bust of Homer, a packet of blotters and an air-cushion which had been in the swivel chair were gone, as well. The widest interpretation had been placed on the word 'library' in the advertisement, for some of the visitors had invaded the upstairs regions and made off with two or three hundred detective novels which had been in the old scholar's bedroom. Even a heap of magazines in the cellarway had been removed.

'I don't think there is a scrap of printed matter left in the house,' said young Mr Maybee.

He was mistaken. After the rehearsal that night Valentine sat on the lawn with several of the cast of the play who wanted to hear about the adventures of the morning. A picture and an account of the distribution of Dr Savage's library had appeared in the newspaper, but rumours were abroad that clergy had come to blows, that a Presbyterian had been struck down with thrombosis while taking *Calvin on the Evangelists* from a high shelf, that a book of photographs called *Nudes of All Nations*, which had appeared unexpectedly at the back of a shelf of exegesis, had been whisked away under the coat of a bachelor curate, that *Voltaire's Works* in twenty-four octavo volumes had been seized by a Baptist fundamentalist and thrown from an upstairs window to his wife, who was waiting on the lawn with a sack – the range of speculation was limited only by the fancy of the people of Salterton. Valentine was able to set their minds at rest, though in doing so she lowered the spirits of several anti-clericals and Antinomians among her hearers.

'Nothing really wild happened,' said she; 'it was all quite orderly, after the beginning, though it was amazingly quick and a bit dishevelled at times.'

'But every book went?' said Freddy.

'Not even that. Every book that could be seen went, but when Mr Maybee and I began a complete clear-out of grandfather's vault we found about ten or twelve more books. They were stored away very neatly in a wooden box; somebody had even wrapped them in brown paper. I can't imagine why; they looked like the most awful junk. Victorian novels in three volumes, and that sort of thing.'

'They sound fascinating,' said Griselda. 'I love Victorian novels.'

'These aren't really good ones,' said Valentine. 'Nothing, I mean, that anybody would want to read. I looked at one or two. We've put them in the sale, as a single lot.'

The conversation had passed to other things. But Hector had heard. If Griselda liked Victorian novels he would get these for her. It would be a distinguished gift – not expensive, but a sign of his attentiveness to her tastes. Besides, books were always a safe gift; in his journey through the world Hector had somewhere picked up the information that only books, candy and flowers might be given to a lady without seriously compromising her honour.

Freddy had heard, also. If Dr Savage thought enough of a handful of books to keep them in his vault, they were worth her investigation. Imagine Valentine putting them in the sale without so much as a thought! What ignoramuses theatre people were! Before Freddy went to bed that night she carefully counted her money. She did not expect to have to pay a big price, but she wanted to know just where she stood. Reading a favourite chapter of *Life Through the Neck of a Bottle* before she went to sleep, she was conscious of a warm glow – a book-collector's glow when he thinks he may be on the track of a good thing. Old books, old wine – how few of us there are, she reflected, who really appreciate these things.

The following day, the Thursday before the sale, was an anxious and difficult one for Hector. At lunchtime he hurried to Dr Savage's house, feeling guiltily conspicuous, as some men do when they are upon an errand connected in their minds (but in nobody else's) with love. There were few people about, and he quickly found what he was looking for; it was a box which had, long ago in the past, served for shipping of a small typewriter; the maker's name was painted on its sides. Within it were several books, neatly wrapped in brown paper; Hector lifted one out and began to unwrap it.

'Mus' ast yuh not t' handle the stuff,' said a voice behind him. It was an employee of Elliot and Maybee, a seedy man who smelled of beer.

'I merely want to see what these books are,' said Hector.

'Tha's all right. My instructions are, mus' ast yuh not t' handle the stuff.'

'But how can I tell what this is unless I look?'

'T'ain't nothing. Just books.'

'But what books?'

'Dunno. Mus' jus' ast yuh not t'handle the stuff.'

'Is there anyone in charge here?'

'Eh?'

'Who is in charge here?'

'Me. Now lookit, Joe, we don't want no trouble. You jus' slip away, see, like you was never here. Don't want yuh handlin' the stuff.'

Hector was not an expert in the management of men, but occasionally he had an inspiration. He reached into his pocket and took out a dollar.

'Let me see what these books are, and it's yours,' said he.

'Okay, Joe. But we don't want no trouble, see?'

Hector unwrapped several of the books. They were old, undoubtedly, and they had a musty smell. He had a notion that really old books were bound in leather; these were bound in dingy cloth, and the gold on their bindings was faded. Still, if Griselda wanted them, he would see that she got them. He gave the beery attendant the dollar, and an extra twenty-five cents.

'May I use the telephone?' said he. He was shown that instrument, which Dr Savage, after the custom of his generation, had kept decently out of sight in a low, dark cupboard under the stairs. The mouthpiece looked as though it had not been cleaned in the twenty years of its installation. After a long and rather complicated conversation with a girl in the office of Elliot and Maybee, he extracted a promise that she would ask old Mr Elliot not to put the box of books up for sale until at least a quarter past four on the following day; she could make no promises; she could not say exactly when Mr Elliot himself was likely to be in the office; Mr Maybee had gone to the country on business; he could try to talk to Mr Elliot after four o'clock, but she could promise nothing. Hot and annoyed and frustrated, Hector escaped from the black hole under the stairs just in time to hurry back to school for the afternoon session. His stomach was upset. He had still to make his arrangements with Pimples Buckle.

Under ordinary circumstances nothing would have persuaded Hector to visit such a person as Pimples Buckle, who was Salterton's nearest approach to a gangster. But Pimples was reputed to be able to provide what Hector, at this moment in his life, wanted more than anything else in the world – a card of admission to the June Ball.

The June Ball was the glory of Salterton's social year. Given by the cadets of the great military College which lay at the eastern entrance to the city, it had for many years been surrounded in the highest degree by that atmosphere of smartness and social distinction with which the military so cleverly invest their merry-makings. In Salterton, to be asked to it was to be a person of social consequence; not to be asked to it was to be a nobody. The invitations sent out by the cadets themselves were, of course, to young ladies who had entertained them, in one way or another, during the year; there were cadets so dead to all decent feeling that they invited girls from other cities, but the majority were properly sensible of the great cubic footage of cake and the vast gallonage of tea which they had consumed on Sunday afternoons, and they did their duty – often an extremely pleasant duty. Other guests, distinguished persons from out-of-town and the nobility and gentry of Salterton, were asked by the Commandant and his staff. There were those who said it was easy to get an invitation; there were others, and Hector was one of them, who found it the hardest thing in the world.

He wanted to go, of course, because Griselda would be there. Had not Roger declared, during that memorable night at Solly's, that he was taking her? The Ball, indeed, had split the cast of *The Tempest* into sheep and goats: most of them were going, and The Torso had received a choice of five escorts; Valentine had been asked, as a distinguished visitor to the town, and anyhow, as Dr Savage's grand-daughter, she had a prescriptive right to an invitation; all the girls in the cast had been asked, and even Miss Wildfang was to be present as the partner of a professor who liked well-matured women; even Geordie was to be there, through some miscarriage of social justice, for he announced with a wink that he had drag in a certain quarter. The Leakeys had had no invitation, and expected none; indeed, Mrs Leakey made this a point of perverse pride, telling the world that she was no high-flyer, whatever other people might be. Professor Vambrace had received an invitation for himself and his wife and daughter, and had refused it without consulting either of them, assuming that they would not wish to be present. Everybody who wanted an invitation, it appeared, had received one. Several of Hector's colleagues at the school had been invited, and it was to the head of the English department, Mr Adams, that he first turned for advice.

'Just suppose,' he said in a falsely jocular tone, 'that I wanted a bid to the Ball; where could I get one?' He thought that 'bid' was rather good; just the right note of casualness.

'Well,' said Mr Adams, who was not at all deceived; 'you might be able to get a card from somebody who had one and decided not to use it. That's sometimes done.'

'Oh? As a matter of fact, I had thought of going, just to see what it's like. You don't know anybody who has a spare card, I suppose?'

'Not a soul. There's one thing you have to be careful about, of course; if they spot you at the door with somebody else's card, they'll ask you to leave at once.'

'Oh? As stiff as that, eh?'

'Oh, very stiff. You know how these military people are. Why, I once saw a man tapped on the shoulder and asked to leave just as he was making his bow to the Commandant's wife. He turned as red as a beet, and slipped away. Several people laughed as he passed. I'd hate to put myself in that position.'

'Yes; yes indeed,' said Hector, reflecting sombrely on this disgrace, which was entirely Mr Adams' invention. If Griselda were to see, or even hear, that he had been attempting to get to the Ball on false pretences! He would never be able to explain it.

Still, there must be some way. He turned next to Geordie.

'Of course, my card is strictly legitimate,' said Geordie.

'Of course,' said Hector.

'Still, I've heard of people getting to the Ball in all sorts of funny ways. Some are smuggled in in the rumble seats of cars. I knew a fellow once who drove over in a truck, with a white coat on; said he was taking ice-cream to the caterer; drove round to the back, took off the white coat and tripped the light fantastic till three, laid a girl from Montreal in the shrubbery, and was in the group photo at five, having had a swell time. And sometimes people row across the harbour in boats; they haven't any guards along the shore, you know; just beach the boat and walk in.'

Hector did not think that any of these bold ruses would suit him.

'Of course, there are always a few invitations to be had, if you want them bad enough,' said Geordie, with the air of rectitude which becomes a man whose invitation is strictly legitimate.

'How do you get them?' said Hector.

'It's entirely a matter of money.'

'Yes; I expected that. Who has them?'

'Well, don't tell anybody I told you, but Pimples Buckle always has a few.'

Hector had not been permitted, at his first visit, to see Pimples himself. He had talked with a dark, greasy young man, who wore sidewhiskers and a dirty sweatshirt, in the office of Uneeda Taxi, which was the legitimate part of Pimples' business. Unwillingly he had revealed to the young man what he wanted, and the young man had chewed a match and looked at him with scorn.

'Ain't no use talkin' to Pimples now,' he had said. 'Come back the day before the dance.'

'You'll tell him what I want?'

'Yeah.'

'Shall I 'phone him before I come in?'

'Naw. Pimples don't like the 'phone. Don't be a dope. And bring cash.'

'How much?'

'Dunno. Better bring plenty.'

At half past four on the day before the ball Hector stood in the inner office of Uneeda Taxi, and Pimples Buckle sat with his feet on a rolltop desk.

'Well prof,' said he, 'so you want a ticket to the Big Ball.'

'Yes,' said Hector.

'What's the matter? Did yours get lost in the mail?'

'I have no invitation. That's why I'm here.'

'Oh, so that's why you're here, eh? Funny, I was wondering what brought you.'

'I supposed you knew. I left a message with your man outside.'

'Wop? Yeah, he told me you'd been in. But what I want to know is this: what makes you think I've got any tickets, eh?'

'Somebody said you usually had a few.'

'Jeeze, the stories that get around. Why, prof, don't you know I could get into a lotta trouble selling tickets to the Ball? And you'd get in trouble too; you'd be an accessory after the fact, and you'd be compounding a felony, and Jeeze knows what else.'

'Have you any tickets?'

'Not so fast, prof. You remember me, don't you?'

'Yes, I remember you.'

'Yeah, you was new at the school the last year I was there. I was in one of your classes. Algebra. And you remember what you used to tell us? Take it easy, you used to say; just take it easy. Well, prof, you take it easy now. Would you like to sit down?'

'Thank you, I would.'

'Well, you can't because there ain't no chair.' Pimples chuckled with enjoyment. 'Now, prof, why do you want to go to this Ball?'

'Is that any affair of yours?'

'I'll say it is. You don't look the type, somehow. Who's the broad?'

'The –?'

'The dame. What's a guy like you want to go to the Ball for if it ain't to take some dame? You want to romance her under the stars, prof?'

'If you will sell me a ticket, let's do it now.'

'Jeeze, you're touchy. Most fellows your age would be complimented to think somebody thought they was after a dame. Are you getting plenty of what she's got?'

'What is your price?'

'Very special to you prof. Fifty bucks. I always treat my old teachers right.'

'Fifty!'

'Sure. This ain't no two-bit belly-rub you're going to, y'know.'

Sick with humiliation and outraged prudence, Hector counted out five ten-dollar notes. Pimples reached into an inner pocket and produced an envelope, from which he drew an engraved and crested card in the upper left-hand corner of which was written, in an official hand, 'Hector Mackilwraith, Esq.'

'Make sure you get your fifty bucks worth outa the broad,' he said, winking cheerily, as Hector hurried from the room.

There was a very good crowd at the auction, which was gratifying to young Mr Maybee, for he had worked hard to persuade old Mr Elliot that the day of the Ball was a good day to hold it. Mr Elliot, product of a more leisurely age, had insisted that every woman of the sort who might be expected to attend the sale of a professor's effects would be at home on such an afternoon, lying in a darkened room with pads of cotton soaked in ice-water upon her eyes. Mr Maybee had assured his partner that, on the contrary, all of Salterton would be keyed up and eager for amusement, and what was more amusing than an auction in June? He had carried his point, and here was the crowd to prove it. The morning sale, when the bedroom furnishings and kitchen effects had been sold, had been successful; the goods had brought within fifty dollars of what he had privately estimated, and he congratulated himself on good selling and good reckoning. This afternoon he hoped to do a little better than his estimate. Like an actor, or a concert performer, he put out his feelers – his sensitive auctioneer's antennae – to receive intuitions from his audience. It was a good audience, alert, receptive to suggestion, and sufficiently excited by the thought of the approaching Ball to be ready to bid freely. After a few deep breaths to refresh his voice, Mr Maybee stepped upon his auctioneer's rostrum, and looked out over the lawn at the bidders, the curiosity seekers, the amateurs of auctions, some standing, some perched on shooting sticks. He rapped upon the table with his pencil, and promptly at two o'clock the afternoon sale began.

It was not, Mr Maybee recognized, a great sale. Old Dr Savage had owned no treasures. His furniture had been very good in its time, but like many people who live to a great age, the old scholar had become indifferent to his household belongings; Mr Maybee's trained eye told him that nothing of consequence in the house had been bought after 1925; most of the furnishing had been done about 1905. The leather chairs had scuffed, scabby surfaces; a velvet-covered sofa, upon which the Doctor had taken his afternoon nap for many years, showed all too plainly at one end that he had done so with his boots on, and at the other that he had drooled as he slept. The furniture seemed to have died with its owner; chairs which had looked well enough in the house showed weak legs when held up for sale; water-colours which had looked inoffensive on the walls seemed, on this sunny day, to be all of weak and ill-defined blues and greys, like old men's eyes. But Mr Maybee was not discouraged. He knew what people would buy.

To the surprise of everyone except Mr Maybee, the large pieces of furniture went cheap, and the trinkets went dear. A large and ugly oak dining table, with ten chairs and a hideous sideboard, went for forty-five dollars; a tea-wagon brought forty-two. A couple of lustre jugs, which Valentine could not remember seeing before, fetched the astonishing sum of thirty-six dollars for the pair. The silver sold well, for though it was ugly, it was sterling. A mantel clock, presented to Dr Savage thirty years before by the Waverley Philosophical Society, brought a staggering initial bid of fifty dollars, and went at last for eighty, though it had never been known to keep time. A kitchen clock, which Mr Maybee waggishly announced would keep either Standard or Daylight Saving Time, was sold to an Indian from a nearby reservation for six dollars, which was four dollars more than it was worth. A bundle of walking-sticks was sold to a sentimentalist who had learned a little elementary philosophy from the Doctor many years before, for five dollars. A Bechstein piano which had belonged to Valentine's grandmother was bid for briskly after Mr Maybee had played a spirited polka on it, and brought three hundred dollars. A teak workbox, described by Mr Maybee as the life's work of a life prisoner in the nearby penitentiary, brought a beggarly four dollars, which the auctioneer mentally estimated to be about ten cents for every pound of its weight.

Freddy enjoyed the sale thoroughly. She wondered, however, how long it would be before the wooden box of books would be offered.

But Hector's message had been received by Mr Elliot, who had passed it on to Mr Maybee, and it was not until half-past four that it appeared. By that time Hector was standing at the back of the crowd.

'A box of books, ladies and gentlemen. I cannot offer you a more exact description. As you know, Dr Savage's library was given away yesterday, according to his own wish, to the clergy of Salterton.' (There was some laughter here, which Mr Maybee rebuked with his eye.) 'These few remaining books were discovered in the Doctor's vault after that disposal. Anyone who wishes a sentimental souvenir of a great scholar and gentleman cannot do better than acquire this lot. What am I bid? . . . Come along, there's a spice of mystery about this box; you don't know what you'll get . . . What do I hear? Who'll say a dollar for a starter? A dollar, a dollar, a dollar – do I hear a dollar?'

'Fifty cents,' said Freddy, and blushed fiercely as people turned to look at her.

'I have fifty. Who'll say a dollar? A dollar for the mystery box. Come on, you can't lose. At least ten books here, each one worth a dollar apiece. A dollar, a dollar, a dollar. Aha, I have a dollar. Thank you sir.'

Freddy turned towards the bidder. Old Mackilwraith! What did he want books for? He didn't look as though he ever read anything but examination papers. Except menus, she thought spitefully. She caught Mr Maybee's eye, and nodded firmly.

'Two; two, two. I have two dollars for the mystery box.'

Hey, thought Freddy; I meant another fifty cents.

'Three; three; three. The gentleman at the back offers me three.'

Freddy nodded again.

Hector was quite as much annoyed as Freddy. What did she want with those books? Should he hurry to her and tell her that he was buying them for her sister? But the bidding was moving too quickly. The box was now at ten dollars, and the bid was Freddy's. He nodded again. Eleven dollars! It was ridiculous.

Mr Maybee was delighted. It was such odd contests at this time which made his life a pleasure, and picked up the sums which he could not realize from old-fashioned dining-room sets and scabrous old couches. The bidding proceeded briskly, and he knew that he had two stubborn people on his hook.

The box now stood at eighteen dollars. As Hector raised it to nineteen, Freddy made a great decision. She had only twenty dollars, but she could not be beaten; she had to have the box, now. She would simply go on, and explain to Daddy how matters had stood. Surely he would understand. He wouldn't want her to be beaten in public, like this. And even if he didn't understand he would have to pay up; he couldn't let her go to jail. People would say he had neglected her, and make a delinquent of her.

'Twenty,' said she, boldly.

'Twenty-one,' said Hector, and his face was flushed so deeply that it seemed in danger of going quite black.

On the bidding went until Freddy was at twenty-eight. She faltered. Thirty dollars was a terrible sum of money to pay for a box of – what? It might be old hymn-books for all she knew. Her eyeballs were very hot, and she was afraid that she might cry. But she wouldn't. She closed her lips firmly and looked down at the grass.

'I have twenty-nine. Twenty-nine dollars in this epic contest between two people who really know their literature! Do I hear thirty? All through at twenty-nine? Another dollar may do the trick! Am I all through at twenty-nine?'

Hector hated Freddy with the deadly hate of a man who had been made a fool of by a petty gangster, and who was now, twenty-four hours later, being made a fool of by a child. Hector was not mean, but the circumstances of his life had made him careful with money; it was the sinew of every success he had ever known. Fifty dollars to Pimples Buckle and now, twenty-nine dollars for these books! Even the children of the Webster family, it appeared, had long purses. But he had beaten her!

'Ah, I have thirty! Thank you sir. Thirty; thirty; thirty. Will you say thirty-one?'

Hector said thirty-one almost without thinking, as he sought the new bidder. There he was. A Jew! Hector became anti-Semitic in a fraction of a second.

The new bidder was, quite plainly, a Jew. A calm, bold man with a cigar, he had been unnoticed in the crowd until this moment.

The bidding rose, dollar by dollar, as Hector sweat nervous drops which seemed to draw his strength from him. The books were with the stranger, at forty. On Hector plunged, and a dreadful headache seized him. The crowd was delighted. Mr Maybee almost sang.

The books were with Hector at forty-nine. The stranger bobbed his head. Hector could bear no more. He was beset by fiends. In a blasphemous moment he permitted himself not to care whether Griselda had Victorian novels to read or not.

'Sold at fifty, to the gentleman with the cigar!'

There was a flutter of applause, mingled with some sounds of disapproval. The contest for the books had been enlivening, but a Salterton audience was not sure that it was suitable that the victory should go to a stranger. It was widely felt that the Jew, though a bold bidder, had shown himself a little too pushing. There were few things to be sold after the box of books, and by five o'clock most of the crowd had gone.

When the unknown bidder sought out the clerk after the sale, to pay his money and claim his books, he found Hector and Freddy waiting for him.

'Do you mind telling me why you wanted that box?' said Hector, more angrily than was wise.

'Surely you know why,' said the stranger, coolly.

'No, I don't.'

'Then why did you bid on it yourself?'

'I wanted those books for a special purpose.'

'And so do I,' said the stranger. It was at this moment that Valentine joined them. She too wanted to know why so much had been bid for a box to which she had given no thought.

'Oh, surely you know,' said the stranger. It took the three of them a few minutes to convince him that they knew nothing at all about it, and had not given the box more than a cursory examination. His eyelids drooped a little, and he smiled.

'You really ought to be more careful,' he said to Valentine. 'Let me show you what I mean.'

He reached into the box and pulled out a package, which he unwrapped.

'You see,' said he; '*Under Two Flags*, in three volumes, published by Chapman and Hall in 1867; in very good condition. Doesn't that mean anything to you?'

'Not a thing,' said Valentine. 'It's by Ouida, isn't it?'

'Yes. It is quite a valuable book. Now look at this: *East Lynne*, by Mrs Henry Wood; published by Tinsley in 1861. Very nice.'

'Valuable?' asked Freddy.

'Not so valuable as the other, by a long shot. But worth about a hundred and fifty dollars.'

There was a heavy silence. Young Mr Maybee had joined the group, and his nice blue eyes opened very wide at the mention of this sum.

'But you really should have been careful of this,' said the stranger, unwrapping three more volumes. 'You see: *Lady Audley's Secret*; the author's name is not given, but it was M. E. Braddon; published by Skeet in 1862. This really is a treasure.'

'How much?' It was Valentine who spoke this time.

'Hard to say. At a rough guess I would put it at about twenty-five hundred dollars. I spotted them at once when I was looking around yesterday. Pure luck, or perhaps flair; I'm here for a brief holiday, but I never take complete holidays. I am sorry about this, but if you had wanted to keep it you should not have put it up at auction, should you?'

Neither Valentine nor Mr Maybee had anything to say. The stranger transferred the books to a briefcase which he carried, and in doing so revealed an envelope which lay at the bottom of the box. It was addressed to Valentine in her grandfather's hand. She read it at once.

My dear –
As I fear that you will find little among my things that you may wish to keep, I leave you these books, which I have had by me for some time. You can easily take them back to the States with you, and if you take them to a good bookseller – a really good one – he will give you a price for them which may surprise you. Look upon this as a special bequest from me, and one upon which you will not have to pay inheritance tax.

With my fondest love
A.S.

'Well, I shall say good-bye,' said the stranger. 'If you ever happen to be in New York, and are interested in rare books, I shall be happy to show you what I have in my shop. Here is my card.'

Only Mr Maybee had the presence of mind to take it. The group broke up, and four of them went their different ways with painful and conflicting thoughts buzzing in their heads.

Long before the light began to fade on this beautiful June day the ladies of Salterton were dressing themselves for the dinner parties which came before the Ball. Already in the composing room of the local newspaper the long galleys of type were ranged in which their gowns were described, for the Society Editor had been busy on the telephone for three days past. Every lady who was to be present at the great affair had been called, and asked for a description of what she would wear; in some cases this call was inspired by courtesy rather than curiosity, for particularly among the older ladies it was not unknown for a gown to make several annual appearances, and the Society Editor could have done much of her work by simply consulting the back files. The descriptions which appeared were very brief; they conveyed nothing, to the stranger, of the real appearance of some of these remarkable garments; but to the informed reader they were rich in information. The briefest extract will suffice:

Mrs A. M. Mangin: lilac crepe, with lamé panel to tone. Miss Dymphna M'Dumphy: rust satin, with scarf in the M'Dumphy tartan, and a parure of cairngorms. Mrs Shakerley Marmion: wine velvet. Mrs M. Medbourne: écru shantung, with panels of self-coloured lace. Mrs E. P. Moubray: amethyst cut velvet. Mrs James Mylne: pleated puce crepe, with inserts of Paddy green moire . . . etc., etc.

The persistent reader, seeking information about the ladies associated with the Little Theatre's forthcoming production, might have compiled his own paragraph, thus:

Mrs Roscoe Forrester: champagne lace. Miss Valentine Rich: flame taffeta. Miss Bonnie-Susan Tompkins: a strapless peach satin, with slit skirt. Miss Pearl Vambrace: pink organdie with puff sleeves. Miss Griselda Webster: white silk jersey, with Greek drapery.

The newspaper never made any mention of what the escorts of the ladies wore; it went without saying that they wore evening dress of every cut known during the past fifty years, and that the military wore dress uniforms, some of which had been made during their slimmer days, so that the trousers had been augmented at the back with gussets which were not always a perfect match.

Since half-past five Pearl Vambrace had been in her bedroom with the door locked. At three o'clock she had taken a long and elaborate bath, in the course of which she made a violent assault upon her armpits with her father's razor. She had then composed herself for a nap, for she had read in a magazine that in order to look radiant at night, it was necessary to rest in the afternoon; such rest delayed the onset of crow's feet, the article said, and Pearl, at nineteen, was determined to show no crow's feet when she appeared at the Ball with Solly.

As she lay on her bed, trying to relax completely, she thought how astonishing it had been that Solly had asked her to go to the Ball with him. She had never, even in dreams, expected that Roger would ask her. He never seemed to pay any attention to her at all. At rehearsals he took her in his arms, and kissed her in the manner prescribed by

Valentine, and although this experience terrified and ravished her it did nothing to make Roger less of a stranger: so must some maiden of the ancient world have felt when Jove descended and absent-mindedly made her his own. Even in the two private rehearsals, in her home, which Professor Vambrace had been able to impose upon the reluctant Roger, he had paid little attention to her. No, it was beyond the range of belief that Roger would ask her to go to the Ball with him, and when Pearl heard that Griselda was to be his partner she was too miserable even to be jealous. And then, astonishingly, Solly had asked her to go to the Ball with him, and shortly afterward a note had arrived from his mother, inviting her to dinner beforehand.

Relaxing completely was hard work. Try as she might to make herself heavy, and pretend that she was sinking through the bed, as the magazine had directed, she continued to twitch and jump unexpectedly. She would look dreadful at the Ball, she was sure – a mass of wrinkles, hollows and haggard shadows. And breath! Gargle as she might before going to the Bridgetowers', how would she make sure afterward that her breath was – how did the advertisements put it? – 'free of offence'? Could she slip her toothbrush and a tube of paste into her evening bag? She must sleep! She had a long and doubtless gay evening before her, in the company of a young man whom she scarcely knew. And even before the Ball began she had a dinner party! She had never been to a dinner party in her life, and she had heard that Mrs Bridgetower was a lady who demanded a high standard of elegant behaviour from her guests. She must relax! She must! In her efforts to relax Pearl twisted herself into a ball, and closed her eyes so tightly that the red darkness behind her eyelids seemed to writhe and surge.

Her misgivings would have been greater if she had had any idea of what had been in progress at the Bridgetower home during the past week. Solly had no particular desire to go to the Ball, but his mother had accepted their joint invitation on his behalf as well as her own. He felt that, if Griselda were to be there with Roger, he might as well be there himself, to keep an eye on her. But with whom? He must have a partner. His mother, in a fit of unaccustomed perverseness, had declared that it was impossible that he should go with her alone. He must have a suitable girl, and she would accompany them in the role of dowager and chaperone. But what girl? Cora Fielding was bespoken. Any other girl whose name he suggested was for one reason or another black-balled by his mother. Finally, in a fit of rebellion, he asked Pearl, whom he hardly knew, and when she regained her powers of speech she said, very politely, that she would be delighted.

Then the fat was in the fire! His mother had risen to new and, to her, refreshing heights of satire when he told her who his partner was to be. She had then decided that, whatever impossible social situations her son might prepare for her, she would comport herself with dignity and according to the rules of etiquette which she recognized. It was out of the question that the Vambraces should invite Solly to dinner before the Ball: therefore she would give a dinner party, and invite Pearl. It would not be a large party; her health would not permit of such a thing. But she would invite young Lieutenant Swackhammer, an officer in the Royal Canadian Navy who was the son of a cousin of her husband's, and whoever he was taking to the Ball with him. This was, she later learned, a Miss Tompkins, to whom she sent a note of invitation.

Cruel things were said of Pearl Vambrace. Mrs Bridgetower insinuated that she had ugly legs, although her legs were graceful enough. Griselda had told her father that Pearl had a moustache, which was untrue, although there was a suggestion on her lip of something which might, in forty years or so, be a small and ladylike moustache. Mrs Forrester thought that her hair was greasy, but it was not uncommonly so. There was something about Pearl which attracted the malignity of most women; only Valentine Rich had seen that, under proper guidance, she had a quality which was close to beauty. Pearl herself was unconscious of anything of the kind; she had washed the offending hair the night before and rinsed it in water which contained so much lemon juice that it was now rather brittle, and flew about unaccountably. She had invested most of her small savings, painfully gleaned from the sums which her parents occasionally gave her, in some cosmetics, the first that she had ever bought. And by efforts which had been humiliating and exhausting, she had acquired a dress which she thought was suitable for the Ball.

Her parents had not been interested when she told them Solly had asked her to be his partner. Professor Vambrace, who had taken such pains to make his daughter a good talker, did not appear to show this talent. He had come to life, however, when Pearl said that she had nothing which was fit to wear on such an occasion. She had a garment of dark corduroy, with a short skirt, which had been her ceremonial garb since she was fifteen, but she had no ball gown. The Professor had announced that he himself would take this matter in hand, and Mrs Vambrace was content that it should be so. Therefore the Professor had marched Pearl into a shop, and had told a salesgirl, firmly, that he wanted a gown suitable for the Ball, and that it must be pink and of a modest design, and must not cost more than thirty-five dollars. There was only one gown answering to these specifications in the shop. Pearl tried it on. Her father stared at her long and hard.

'The straps of your chemise show,' said he.

'She'll have to wear a strapless bra,' said the salesgirl.

'A what?' asked the Professor.

'I'll fix her up with one,' said the girl.

'Don't trouble,' said the Professor; 'she can tie some ribbons on her under-garment and it will look well enough. It will look better when you are wearing the right shoes,' he said.

'These are the best ones I have, Father,' said Pearl, who was now thoroughly miserable. Unskilled in matters of dress she knew enough to see that the gown was of a very unpleasant pink, suggestive of measles, and made her dark skin look yellowish.

'Is there to be no end to expense?' asked the Professor, rhetorically. 'Have you any slippers in pink satin?'

'Nobody has worn satin slippers for about twenty years,' said the girl, who felt for Pearl. But to Pearl it seemed that the whole world of fashion had weighed the Vambrace family, and found it wanting.

At last a pair of slippers had been found which met with the Professor's approval. But they had no toes in them, and that meant a pair of new stockings. They marched home at top speed, and the Professor renewed the oxygen in his blood in a very angry manner. He had quite a lot of money, chiefly because he never spent any of it on his wife and daughter, but Pearl's outfit had run to almost fifty dollars, and he felt himself to be on the verge of bankruptcy. That evening, as they ate a rather nasty potato salad and some sour canned cherries, he had raged like a Savonarola against the vanities of female dress. Pearl, who loved her father, felt that she had ruined him, that she had behaved in a selfish and unworthy fashion, and that she was a sorrow to her parents. It was not until two days later that she could feel any pleasure in the prospect of going to the Ball.

At half-past five she began to dress. Normally she could dress herself for any occasion in three minutes, but she believed that her toilette for her first Ball should be a ceremony, and she was determined to make a ceremony of it. Her sleep had not been a success; indeed, she had never really slept at all, but had lain in a reverie compounded of all the social mishaps and miseries which could befall her in the evening to come. She was glad when it was time to dress.

Everything must be clean. She therefore put on clean underthings, and reflected that they were not very inspiring. She then put on the new stockings, in which her legs looked so well that even Mrs Bridgetower would have been hard pressed to find fault with them; it was too bad that she had to hitch these glories to a garter-belt which age and many washings had brought to a sad pass. She then put on the pink organdie dress itself, and in her excitement thought that it looked better than it had done in the shop.

It is a measure of Pearl's inexperience in such matters that she put on her dress before she began to make up her face, and set to work without protecting that garment in any way. She laid out her purchases on her chest of drawers, before the mirror with the whorl in it. What should she do first? Cream, was it? She rubbed her face with a medicated substance which she had economically purchased, and which was said to improve the complexion, keep away mosquitoes, and relieve soreness after shaving. There: her face looked shiny, but you toned that down with powder. She patted a great deal of powder into the grease; she had chosen a light shade, to relieve the darkness of her complexion, and the transformation, she felt, was remarkable. Now what? Rouge, probably. She had purchased dry rouge, and she patted a firm spot of it on each of her well-marked cheek-bones. It was surprising what this did to her eyes; they looked quite brilliant, almost wild, in fact. Now the eyes themselves. The girl in the shop had recommended a light eye-shadow, but Pearl had preferred a rich green, with flecks of gold in it; she applied this liberally to the sockets of her eyes, below as well as above. She had read somewhere that makeup, to be effective, must be put on with boldness as well as subtlety, or it was of no avail; certainly the eye-shadow made a difference, but no doubt it was designed to look its best under artificial light. Now eyebrows: the eyebrow pencil which she had was new, and it took her some time to sharpen it, for the point kept breaking; her own brows were full, though not heavy, and had never been plucked; she drew some lines over them which gave them solidity. Now lipstick, and she would be finished. She had bought a purplish lipstick, thinking that it would form a pleasant contrast with the rather chalky pink of her rouge. She had seen girls put it on; they lathered their lips generously with the colour, and then bit them. She did this, and immediately her mouth was a messy wound. With a soiled handkerchief she scrubbed it off and tried again. The very light down on her lip – so cruelly referred to by Griselda as a moustache – caught the colour, and made her look ridiculous. In all, Pearl put on five mouths before she achieved one which she decided would have to do.

Now hair. She could not dress it neatly, for washing had taken all the oil out of it, but she had a plan. She had a piece of ribbon which nearly matched her dress, and she tied this in a bow on one side of her head, and let her hair hang down behind it. This showed her ears, which were neat.

She knew now why ladies of high fashion took so long to dress. It was nearly seven o'clock, the hour when Solly had promised to call for her. Ah, there he was below, talking to Father. She seized her coat – her only coat, a much worn garment in light brown, of a vaguely sporting character – and pulled it round her shoulders, hoping that it would look as though she were the casual sort who always wore a sports coat with evening dress. She took up her bag – a rather too capacious bag of dingy red velvet, with a tassel hanging from the bottom, which had belonged to her mother – and ran downstairs. Solly seemed startled to see her, but Professor and Mrs Vambrace appeared to notice nothing amiss. Professor Vambrace was prepared to act the Fond Father, and Mrs Vambrace was not a woman who paid much attention to externals.

'Take care of her, Bridgetower; take care of our little one,' said the Professor in a voice half jocular, half tearful. 'It is the father's heart which is broken at his daughter's first ball.' This notion, he thought, was worthy of Barrie, and he was proud of it. He kissed Pearl, with his eyes shut, which may have been as well, and shortly afterward she was with Solly in his mother's car. He said very little, and seemed to Pearl to be strangely apprehensive, but as she shared this feeling she decided that he, like herself, was worried about the evening before them.

'Good evening, my dear. You look sweetly pretty,' said Mrs Bridgetower, as she greeted Pearl in the hall. But Pearl could scarcely answer; she caught sight of herself in a full-length mirror. She looked ill and slightly crazed, with a pink bow on one side of her head, and her eyes aglare. The flush of tuberculosis was on her cheeks, and her mouth looked as though she had eaten untidily of the insane root which takes the reason prisoner.

And her gown! It looked like one of the crepe paper costumes which children wear at Hallowe'en. What should she do? What could she possibly do?

'Hello, Pearl! Gosh, anything for a laugh, eh? That's the spirit!' The speaker was Bonnie-Susan Tompkins, the partner of Lieutenant Swackhammer; they had followed Mrs Bridgetower into the hall.

Pearl was stricken. When her hostess suggested that she leave her coat upstairs, she darted upward in unmistakable flight, without waiting for Ada, the elderly maid, to show her the way.

The Torso was a silly girl, and a hoyden, and unseemly in her desire for the attentions of the male. But like many silly, hoydenish, man-crazy girls, she had a great charity within her. One of her admirers had said that she had 'a heart as big as a bull', and if this special enlargement carries with it a certain sweetness and generosity of nature, the phrase may be allowed to stand. She ran up the stairs after Pearl. What she did cannot be related here, but in ten minutes they were both in the drawing-room, drinking sherry, and Pearl looked better than she had ever looked in her life; if there was any makeup on her face, it had been applied with The Torso's artful hand. And the relaxation which she had sought earlier in sleep had come now, by this great purgation through self-knowledge and terror.

Mrs Bridgetower's dinner party was an unforeseen success. She had expected nothing from it, for she disapproved strongly of Pearl Vambrace, whom she had not seen in three years, and she knew nothing of Lieutenant Swackhammer's partner, but feared the worst. And when the Lieutenant had appeared in her drawing-room with The Torso, it seemed to her that matters had gone beyond the limits even of her generous pessimism. Bonnie-Susan wore a gown of peach satin from which her beautiful shoulders emerged in startling nakedness; the creation was held in place, presumably, by some concealed armature, for it had no straps, and although it was impossible to peep down the front of it, the impression which it gave was to the contrary. And as if this were not enough, the skirt was split to the knee in such a way that very little of her left leg was visible at a time, but there was a tantalizing promise of infinite riches. It was a beautiful gown, and had cost her father a lot of money, but it was not a gown to win the approval of the anxious mother of a susceptible son. Mrs Bridgetower's first words to The Torso were to bid her to come close to the fire, lest she be cold.

The Torso, however, was a girl of a great resource. She knew that the mothers of young men rarely liked her on sight, though she was not sure why this was so, and she had developed a manner which disarmed and often won these natural enemies. She was so frank, so pleasant, that mothers usually decided that they had misjudged her; she impressed them by her common sense in agreeing with their opinions; she charmed them by taking sides with them against their sons in matters relating to the wearing of overshoes and warm scarves. She laughed at their jokes and, in her own phrase, she 'jollied' them. She jollied Mrs Bridgetower so successfully that after half an hour that lady felt that there might be some hope for the younger generation after all.

Lieutenant Swackhammer, too, was a success. He had a fund of small talk, and although he had lived inland for the first eighteen years of his life, he had subsequently developed a bluff, sailorly, salt-water manner, which went very well with his somewhat extreme deference to age and grey hairs. He laughed a good deal at nothing in particular, and had a splendid grip of whatever was obvious and indisputable.

With such guests as these, Mrs Bridgetower blossomed. The Torso laughed at all her ironies, and whenever The Torso laughed, Lieutenant Swackhammer laughed too. Pearl Vambrace, though apt to be silent, was respectful and behaved nicely, and when she did speak, she said something sensible, and said it in a neatly rounded sentence, of which her hostess approved. In the atmosphere of success, Solly brightened up, and poured out the wine with a generosity begotten of relief.

The meal was a long and heavy one, and concluded with special glasses of ice-cream, into which a spoonful of crême de menthe had been injected, like a venom; with this, chocolate peppermint patties were served and Pearl, who was unaccustomed to rich food, began to feel a little unwell and sleepy. It was at this point that Ada announced that Master Solly was wanted on the telephone.

'The telephone is the curse of the age,' said Mrs Bridgetower; 'even our after-dinner coffee is not safe from it.'

'Oh, how right you are,' said Bonnie-Susan; 'you know, Mrs Bridgetower, I often think things were really better when you were a girl. No 'phone, and no boys calling up all the time, and all those lovely horses and carriages and everything.'

'Absolutely right,' said the Lieutenant, champing a third peppermint patty.

'I do not quite ante-date the telephone,' said Mrs Bridgetower, 'but in my youth it was employed with a keener discretion than is the case today.'

Meanwhile Solly, with the receiver at his ear, was listening to Humphrey Cobbler.

'Hello there, Bridgetower, what about coming to see me tonight?'

'Can't. It's the night of the Ball, you know.'

'What Ball? Oh, that thing. Well, you don't want to go to that, do you?'

'Of course I do.'

'You amaze me. Oh, I suppose you're protecting your interests, eh?'

'I do not understand you.'

'The hell you say. She's going with Tasset, isn't she?'

'I believe so.'

'And who, if I may ask, are you escorting to this dreary brawl?'

'Miss Vambrace.'

'Who's she?'

'Miranda in the play.'

'Oh, her. Can't say I know her. She doesn't sing, does she?'

'I don't know.'

'Well, find out before you do anything silly. Remember my advice; take a woman with a good big mezzo range every time. Listen, how would it be if I came with you?'

'No.'

'I've got a dress suit.'

'You have no invitation.'

'A formality. We artists are welcome at all doors.'

'No; it wouldn't do.'

'I could carry a fiddle case; pretend I belonged to the orchestra.'

'No.'

'Don't you think you're being just a teeny-weeny tidge snobbish and class-conscious?'

'No.'

'Very well, then; sweep on in your fine carriage over the faces of the humble poor. There'll come a day . . . You don't want to reconsider?'

'No.'

'Can't you say anything but no?'

'No.'

'Very well then. Go ahead; plunge into a maelstrom of gaiety. And God forbid that, when the revel is at its height, your merriment should be dampened by thought of me, crouched over a dead fire in my sordid home, drinking gin out of a cracked cup.'

'God forbid, indeed.'

'In poverty, hunger and dirt.'

'As you say.'

'Well – good-bye.'

'Good-bye.'

The cards of invitation specified that the Ball would begin at nine o'clock. To Hector's precise mind, unattuned to elegant delay, it was therefore important that he should appear upon the stroke of nine, and he was dressed in his hired evening suit by half-past eight. He was not happy about the suit. It was not the cut or the fit that bothered him, for he was not pernickety about such things; it was, rather, the material of which the suit was made; this was a face-cloth, which time had rendered not merely smooth, but slippery. The way in which the coat cut away to the tails, and the shortness of the tails themselves, seemed to him to be not quite right, but he assumed that there were many styles in evening coats. The old man from whom he had rented the suit had assured him that it was a splendid fit, and that he looked like a prince in it. There had been no white waistcoat to go with the suit, so Hector had purchased a smart one for himself, as well as a collar, a stiff shirt and a tie which was conveniently tied already, and fastened at the back with a secret hook. The obvious newness of his linen, he hoped, would take the eye of society from the curious shininess of his suit.

By a quarter to nine he was in the hall of the YMCA, waiting for his taxi. It was prompt to the minute, and at precisely five minutes to nine he found himself at the Ball.

Nobody was on hand to receive him. Nobody asked for his card of invitation. On a dais at one end of the room the band was chatting, and a couple of orderlies in the gallery were arranging chairs. There was no one else to be seen. Turning from the hushed splendour of the empty ballroom Hector sought and found a door marked 'Gentlemen'; it was dark, quiet and comforting in there, and he settled himself to wait.

It was not a happy choice of a hiding place, for although nothing could be more natural than his presence there, and nothing less likely than that any official person, finding him, would ask to see his card of invitation, it was a retreat with humiliating associations for him. Was it not behind a similar door, similarly marked, that he had taken refuge so many years ago, at the Normal School 'At Home'?

Here, in the darkness, he could not escape that recollection. Time had somewhat blunted the edge of it, and he had got into the habit of pushing it down into the depths of his mind whenever it troubled him, but tonight he was without defence. Sweating slightly, he faced the fact that he had made a fool of himself at the 'At Home', and that it was possible that he might make a fool of himself again at the Ball, and for a similar reason.

Hector had been a prominent figure in his year at the Normal School. By the time the annual 'At Home' was due he was easily the leader among the young men of the class. Had he not been chosen by popular vote as 'Student Most Likely to Become Deputy Minister of Education'? And as such he was the obvious person to invite Millicent Maude McGuckin to be his partner at the 'At Home'. For in the atmosphere of the Normal School the cleverest boy and the cleverest girl were expected to appear together at this function; like crowned heads when a royal marriage is in prospect, they had little personal choice in the matter; their academic position determined their relationship to one another, and if either happened to have a morganatic attachment to some less brilliant member of the class, that unworthy affection had to be suppressed for the evening of the 'At Home'.

Of those girls of Hector's generation whom the chaste goddess of Primary Education called to her shrine, Millicent Maude McGuckin was the fairest and most proud. She wore glasses, it is true, but behind them her eyes were brown as the waters of a Highland stream. Her upper teeth were, perhaps, more prominent than those of the insipid stars of Hollywood, but they gave a swelling pride to her upper lip, and formed her mouth into a pout which fairly ached for kisses. Her curly hair was chestnut brown; her skin was dark and sweetly flushed over her cheeks. It was a time when the female bosom was rising again from the flatness to which the 'twenties had condemned it, and Millicent Maude McGuckin's bosom, swelling gently under the stimulus of a good mark on a test in Classroom Management, or heaving proudly in a debate on 'Resolved: That Country Children Are Culturally Handicapped In Comparison With

City Children' was a thing to make tears of ecstasy sting the eyeballs. The bosom was coming in, but the stress upon the female leg which was so characteristic of the 'twenties had not diminished, and in this department of womanly beauty, too, Millicent Maude McGuckin was richly dowered.

Is she that way,
Lovable – and sweet?

ran a song popular at the time. The answer in her case was a breathless affirmative from all the young men of her year at the Normal School.

It was never doubted that Hector would escort her to the 'At Home'. It would be his duty to call for her at her boarding house, walk her to the school, dance the first and last dances with her, squire her at supper and assist the Principal and staff in greeting the guests. But Hector boasted that he would do more. It must be remembered that he had never mixed on easy terms with boys and girls of his own age before he went to the Normal School, and his quick success there went a little to his head. He boasted to a group of other male students that in the Moonlight Waltz he would kiss Millicent Maude McGuckin. They expressed vehement and brassy doubt that he would do any such thing. He reaffirmed his intention; indeed, he took bets on it. It was the only time in his life that he bet on anything, and as it was himself, he considered it a certainty.

The night of the 'At Home' came. Hector's courage was shaky when he called for Miss McGuckin, for he scarcely knew her, and when she tripped down the stairs of her boarding house in a blue frock, looking more lovely than would be thought possible in the light of the ruby lamp which hung there, he wondered if he had not dared too much. This was not a girl to Get Fresh with, he thought. This girl was a Sweet Girl now, and the only change in her condition which was at all thinkable was the change to Wife and Mother. That he should debauch her, by so much as a single kiss, was an unnerving thought. To Hector a kiss was no trivial matter. He had never kissed anyone but his mother, and he had an unformed but insistent notion that a kiss was, among honest people, as binding as a proposal of marriage. And in his scheme of planning and common sense, marriage had as yet no place. Yet he ached to kiss her. He wanted to kiss her without being prepared to marry her. He was shocked and at the same time sneakingly proud of this voluptuousness in himself.

Millicent Maude McGuckin did nothing to allay his fears. A spirited girl, with a turn for debating, she had thoughts of a parliamentary career, and of asserting the right of women to take over everything, in a large and general way. Her attitude toward Hector, therefore, was one of mettlesome raillery. When he made as though to help her on with her coat, she said, 'Thanks, I'm still quite capable of putting on my own coat,' and when he took her arm to help her down the icy steps of the boarding house she said, 'What's the matter? Are you afraid you'll fall?' When he became silent under these witty rebuffs, she said, 'You certainly aren't very conversational tonight, are you?' And when he haltingly tried to make amends she said, airily, 'Oh don't talk if you have to make an effort; I dare say you are wishing I was some person else.' By the time they reached the Normal School, Hector was completely cowed by Miss McGuckin's bantering social manner.

Standing in the 'receiving line' was no ordeal. It was Hector's task to introduce each couple as they arrived to the Principal, who had not seen most of them since four o'clock that afternoon. The Principal then passed on these introductions to his wife, who repeated them to old Dr Moss, the principal emeritus. Miss McGuckin was on the other side of this venerable pedagogue, so that both her maddening charms and her wounding wit were spared him, for half an hour or so. But he had to join her again for the Grand Promenade which opened the 'At Home'. This ceremony probably derived from some Grand Polonaise, or other European court ceremony; nothing quite like it is traceable among the customs of the British peoples. The older guests disposed themselves in knots about the broad corridors of the Normal School, and the students, in couples, arranged themselves in processional formation in the entrance hall. Then, as the band on the third floor, where the assembly room was, played a spirited march, the pupils, arm in arm, paraded through the school and up the stairs, bowing to their guests and being bowed to in return. It was rather a pretty and pleasing custom and one which the students enjoyed, but for Hector it was a humiliation. Miss McGuckin kept whispering 'Left, left . . . you know your left foot, don't you? . . . Bow; don't just duck your head . . . Don't hold my arm so tightly.' And as she badgered him, the more he was enthralled by her, and the more eagerly he wished to dominate her, win her, hear her say 'Oh, Hector!' as he covered her full lips with kisses.

Nobody could say of Hector that he was not persistent. He danced with Millicent Maude McGuckin, as custom demanded, and made no reply to her criticism of his dancing save a sheepish smile. He endured it when she took him into a corridor to demonstrate a step. Under her direction he opened and closed windows, fetched chairs, and harried the band leader to play her favourite tunes. For although her conversation, baldly recorded here, may suggest that Miss McGuckin was censorious and demanding, it must be remembered that she was only eighteen, and the charm of youth clouded the sharp outlines of her essential character. The other girls – charming girls, destined to be capable schoolteachers and agreeable women – seemed to him insipid beside this paragon. A worshipper of planning and common sense himself, Hector adored these characteristics in Miss McGuckin, and never thought that a woman might possess more pleasant attributes. But she made him nervous, and when he was nervous his stomach, in his own phrase,' went back on him'.

This trouble was not too inconvenient until the supper interval. He felt secret stirrings in his bowels, but had no time to consider them. But a supper of eight sandwiches, two pieces of cake, six cookies, and a plate of ice cream, washed down with two cups of coffee, gave his revolting stomach something to work on.

He took supper with Miss McGuckin, of course, and also with old Dr Moss and Miss Ternan, the instructor in Art. Dr Moss described his trip to the Holy Land in considerable detail, while the others listened. The old gentleman carried in his pocket a New Testament, bound in wood from the Mount of Olives, which he showed for their admiration. Millicent Maude McGuckin was full of pretty curiosity, asking for information about the diet of the Holy Land, and demanding in particular to know whether Our Lord had subsisted chiefly on dates, pomegranates and figs; it appeared extremely probable to her that He was a vegetarian. It was not necessary for Hector to say anything, so he ate stolidly, and poured hot coffee down upon cold ice cream with the recklessness of youth. And then, all of a sudden, his stomach squealed.

The borborygmy, or rumbling of the stomach, has not received the attention from either art or science which it deserves. It is as characteristic of each individual as the tone of the voice. It can be vehement, plaintive, ejaculatory, conversational, humorous – its variety is boundless. But there are few who are prepared to give it an understanding ear; it is dismissed too often with embarrassment or low wit. When Hector's stomach squealed it was as though someone had begun to blow into a bagpipe, and had thought better of it. His neighbours pretended not to notice.

A rumbling stomach may be ignored once, but if it persists it will shake the aplomb of the most accomplished. Hector's stomach persisted, and Millicent Maude McGuckin began to raise her eyebrows and speak with special clarity, as though above the noise of a passing train. Miss Ternan flushed a little. Old Dr Moss unhooked the receiver of his hearing-aid from the front of his waistcoat and shook it and blew suspiciously into its inside, as though he feared that a scratchy biscuit crumb had lodged there. The stomach squealed loud and long, and then the squeal would drop chromatically in tone until it became a low, hollow rumble. It was as though, nearby, an avalanche of boulders was plunging down a mountainside toward a valley, in which a spring torrent raged and foamed. And then, inexplicably and in defiance of nature, the boulders would rush back up the hill, to be greeted with screams and bagpipe flourishes by the stricken mountaineers.

After an eternity of this, Hector rose. 'Got to see if the orchestra are getting any supper,' said he, and left the room, his face its darkest red.

In the men's washroom he had taken stock of himself. A fine fellow he was, to be partner to Millicent Maude McGuckin, and then carry on like that! What about the Moonlight Waltz now, and his boast that he would kiss her! Was this – the theological explanation came pat to his mind – a Judgement on him for his sinful boast that he would Take Advantage of a sweet and innocent girl, before everybody – before the Principal and his wife, before old Dr Moss, who carried a Testament bound in wood from the Mount of Olives? Like many young people, Hector was convinced that his elders were the implacable foes of Eros.

No! He had to go through with it! He had bet two dollars and fifty cents that he would do it! But the fiends in his stomach, like an offstage chorus, mocked his determination with snarling laughter. Suppose the stomach howled aloud as he danced the Moonlight Waltz? Suppose – oh, horror inconceivable! – the winds within him could not be contained as he danced! There was nothing, nothing in the world – not money, not pride, not love of Millicent Maude McGuckin – which would make him risk such shame.

So he remained where he was. Faintly he could hear the Midnight Waltz begin. For this special dance, all the lights save a few which had been covered with blue gelatine were turned off, and it was deemed to be the epitome of languorous romance, and the crowning glory of the 'At Home'. With this special dance in mind, Millicent Maude McGuckin's mother had made her a new gown of electric blue satin, wonderfully gathered so that it shimmered and crinkled as she moved, making her, as the instructor in Nature Study remarked admiringly, look just like an electric eel. Whether she danced this dance, or whether she sat it out, Hector never knew. The next day he was eyed curiously by the student body, and those with whom he had laid bets made no attempt to collect them. It was known that Mackilwraith had reached some sort of crisis at the 'At Home', but whether it was drink, or whether, as one boy suggested, he had suddenly Had the Call to the Ministry in the midst of the gaiety, no one knew, and no one liked to ask. As for Millicent Maude McGuckin, she never spoke to him again.

Nobody suspected that Hector had sat in a booth in the men's washroom through the Midnight Waltz, weeping bitterly.

Griselda was not in the best of tempers when she arrived at the Ball. Roger had called for her without a car, and had calmly said that he had supposed that they would drive in her car. He had offered to drive it for her, but she had said that she preferred to drive herself, and had hinted that he had had too much to drink. He had taken this quietly, but there was a look on his face as she parked the car, wrestling with it in a difficult place, which suggested mockery. To punish him, she kept him waiting twenty-five minutes while she left her coat and attended to her face. When they passed the receiving line and entered the ballroom, neither was in a good temper. The first couple to dance past them were Solly and Pearl.

'Good Heavens, I thought Solly was bringing his mother,' said Griselda.

'Who is that girl with him?' said Roger.

'You should know. You've kissed her at every rehearsal for the past week. That's Pearl Vambrace.'

'Really? I didn't know she could look like that.'

'She looks much as usual to me,' said Griselda, though she knew that Pearl was looking uncommonly well.

Roger danced near to Solly and touched him on the shoulder.

'May I?' said he, and danced away with Pearl, leaving Solly with the furious Griselda.

'Awfully good band,' he began.

'Don't be fatuous.'

'Dreadful band.'

'Don't try to be clever.'

'You are looking particularly lovely.'

'Thank you. So is Pearl, it seems.'

'Yes, she has brightened up, hasn't she?'

'They say that admiration is the greatest beautifier; you should feel complimented at the change you have made in her.'

'Thanks; it's nice to be appreciated.'

'Oh, she appreciates you, does she?'

'It would be immodest to reply to that one. You should ask her.'

'How does she get on with your mother?'

'Like a house on fire. Practically twin souls.'

'It looks like the hand of fate, Solly dear.'

'It does, doesn't it.'

Pearl was enjoying her first taste of social success. She did not dance well, but she followed Roger's leads adequately, and listened tremulously to his small talk. He complimented her deftly in a dozen different ways; he said what a pity it was that his work and the rehearsals had not permitted him to see more of her, and hoped that they would repair this in the future; he played his favourite trick, suggesting that they were both a little superior to the others at the Ball, and inviting her to join him in making fun of the couples who came near them. Pearl answered all that he said quietly and sensibly, but such flattery was intoxicating to her. What did it matter now that in her first attempts at making up she had dropped powder on the front of her gown, and could not get it out? The Torso had arranged her face, and dealt with the troublesome straps of her underthings by cutting them off with Mrs Bridgetower's nail scissors and doing some neat work with safety pins. She was being admired. She was dancing. She had caught the attention of the god-like Roger. As they danced past Griselda and Solly, Pearl, filled with charity toward all God's creatures, gave Griselda a beautiful smile. Griselda saw it as a smile of triumph, of mean exultation, and she ground her beautiful teeth so hard that Solly remarked upon it.

All balls are much alike. They are wonderful; they are dull. They inspire high hopes; they bring bitter regrets. The young wish that they might never end; the old fidget for the time to come when they may decently go home to bed. They are all great successes; to some of the guests they are always failures. The guests take with them to the Ball almost everything they find when they arrive there.

Hector had taken his misgivings, his sense of defeat, his fears for Griselda, his mistrust of Roger, and all the burden of a life which had never been touched by the spirit of merry-making. When he returned through the door marked 'Gentlemen' he carried with him his failure at the Normal School 'At Home', fresh and painful after twenty-one years. He mingled with the guests as a man who has no notion of where he is to go, or what he will do when he gets there.

Almost at once somebody spoke to him. To his dismay it was a member of the School Board. Now Hector, like all schoolteachers, both mocked and feared School Boards; he resented their layman's interference in the mighty mystery of education, and scoffed at it, but at the same time he dreaded their power to dismiss him. It may be said that School Boards have a similar contradiction in their attitude toward teachers: they despise them as persons who have sought a cloistered life (this being the construction which they put on daily association with noisy and demanding young barbarians) and yet they reverence them as valuable properties, not easily replaced in the case of death or resignation. This makes for some uneasiness in the relationship between Board and teacher.

This member of the Board, however, was full of affability.

'Say,' he said, buttonholing Hector, 'that was a pretty smart thing you did this afternoon.'

'What do you mean?' said Hector.

'About those books. I heard they just slipped through your fingers. Pretty smart.'

'Oh – oh yes,' said Hector, bewildered.

'Want you to meet Colonel Pascoe. Colonel, this is Mr Mackilwraith, our mathematical wizard from the Collegiate. Do you know, this afternoon he went to old Dr Savage's sale, and spotted the only valuable thing in the place. Some books. Bid up to twenty-four hundred dollars on them, and just missed them by a whisker. I'm told they're worth a cool fifteen thousand in New York.'

'Is that a fact?' said Colonel Pascoe. 'Well, well; let's have a drink on that.'

In the refreshment room Hector quickly became a hero. The Board member showed him off as a prodigy for whom he was himself indirectly responsible. The Board member explained that he hadn't had much education himself; he was, in fact, a graduate of the

University of Hard Knocks, but he respected education, particularly when it could be turned into hard cash. Hector found that he was credited with remarkable astuteness in almost having bought the books. He was introduced to the Bishop in this new character of astute bibliophile, and the Bishop invited him to drop in at the Palace some day and look at an old Prayer Book which he had; it was well over a hundred years old, and sure to be valuable, but the Bishop would like to have Hector's expert opinion on it. By the time Hector left the refreshment room he had had three drinks, and was in a happier frame of mind.

His reputation as a shrewd collector of rare books seemed to precede him wherever he went. The figures which he was reported to have bid varied from a few hundreds to a few thousands, but they were all impressive. He was represented as a knowledgeable Canadian, determined to protect his country's literary treasure from a crafty American dealer. It was said that he was trying to buy the books in order to give them to the library at Waverley. There was some suggestion that Waverley ought to give him an honorary degree, as a reward for his patriotism and knowledge of books. Wisely, Hector said nothing; he smiled and let them think as they pleased. But as he walked through the card room, and as he moved through the gallery of the ballroom, where the mothers of the dancing young people sat, he was greeted with that stir which accompanies a person of distinction, and his curious dress suit was taken as an expression of the eccentricity which is inseparable from profound knowledge. But although this unforeseen notoriety was balm to Hector, he did not lose sight of the reason which had brought him to the Ball. Griselda was never long out of his sight.

It occurred to Roger that he was being a fool. It was all very well to revenge himself upon Griselda for her slights to his masculine dignity; it was all very well to dance with Pearl Vambrace and reflect that it was possible even for an expert like himself to have a good thing under his eyes for weeks and never notice it; but these pleasures were mere self-indulgence. Griselda, in her costly gown of Greek design, gave him a cachet which was far beyond the range of Pearl, in her pink organdie; Griselda was a Webster, an heiress; Pearl was just another girl, and girls were always in plentiful supply. Therefore Roger took an early opportunity to return to Griselda, and found her repentant. That was fine, he thought. He would make capital of that repentance later on. He left Pearl with a vague suggestion that they should have another dance together later in the evening, and except when he did his duty by dancing with Nellie Forrester and with Valentine, he did not leave Griselda again.

Pearl was painfully overset by what she decided was a sudden coldness on his part. What had she done that was wrong? Was it breath, which she could amend by recourse to her toothbrush in the ladies' room, or was it dullness, or lack of sex appeal which nothing in the world could ever put right? She moped so pitifully that Solly could bear it no more, and asked her what was wrong. And then poor Pearl, who was too wretched to be anything but honest, told him that she thought that Roger disliked her, and that she wanted Roger to like her more than she wanted anything else in the world.

This sort of confession is complimentary to a man of middle age, but to a contemporary it is a dismaying bore. Solly said all the words of comfort he could think of, which were pitifully few, and leaving Pearl in the hands of his mother he sought the refreshment room, and drank whisky and soda. As he did so he found himself unaccountably wishing that Cobbler were with him; Cobbler would know what to do with a girl who had begun to moult in the middle of a party. And if anybody was to be offered medicine against the pangs of despised love, what about himself? He applied the only medicine at hand, freely.

Mrs Bridgetower was not an ideal companion for a girl in Pearl's position. She did her best to be entertaining, telling of Balls which she had attended in her youth, and deploring the fact that few men wore white gloves any more. Of modern dancing she held a low opinion. Of modern dance music she could not trust herself to speak. She approved of the wisdom of Pearl's mother in keeping her daughter Sweet; so many modern girls, she said, ceased to be Sweet almost before they began to think about Balls. She was pleased that Pearl was ready to leave the dancing and sit for a while with a boring old woman like herself. No, no, Pearl must not protest; she was fully aware that she had little to say which could be of interest to a young girl.

Suitable replies to such conversation as this demand the utmost ingenuity, even in one trained by Professor Vambrace. Pearl was glad when The Torso and Lieutenant Swackhammer came along, and asked her to join them.

'Honey, you look like a poisoned pup,' said Bonnie-Susan, frankly, when Mrs Bridgetower was out of earshot. 'You'd better come into the john with me and let down your hair.'

In a quiet corner of the ladies' lounge, Pearl told her story to The Torso's sympathetic ear, and received that experienced young woman's advice.

'Listen, Pearl, you're just wasting your time. Roger hasn't got anything that you want. I get around, and I know. He's just a heel – a smooth, good-looking heel.'

'But for a few minutes he seemed really interested in me.'

'Yes, but Roger plays for keeps. And you haven't got anything that he wants. Griselda has.'

'I know she's prettier than I am.'

'And richer, and classier.'

'Well, why don't you tell her what you think of him?'

'Because she doesn't need advice and you do. Griselda can look after herself – I think. And if she can't her Daddy can get the smartest lawyers in the country to look after her.'

'Oh, Bonnie-Susan, don't you believe there's anything at all in love?'

'I certainly do, honey, but there's no love where Roger is for anybody but Roger.'

It was after the supper interval that Roger took Griselda outside, and across the barrack square toward the lake. On the shore was an old stone redoubt, built to defend Canada against the assaults of the USA, and it was on the outworks of this redoubt that he spread his coat, and they sat down.

'I'm sorry if I annoyed you earlier this evening,' said he.

'It was nothing,' said Griselda; 'I was in a bad temper anyhow.'

'Why? Or may I know?'

'Oh, Freddy kept nattering all the time I was getting dressed about some old books that were sold this afternoon.'

'Ah, yes. The purchase of the great Mackilwraith.'

'No, he didn't get them.'

'Why did that make you angry?'

'Oh I don't really know. But it did. I wished I had gone to the sale, and I wished I knew a lot about old books – or anything else. Just discontentment, I suppose.'

'Boredom, probably.'

'Probably.'

'You want something to wake you up.'

'Yes, and I know what you think it is.'

'What?'

'A love affair with you. You've said so before.'

'Well – don't you think I'm right?'

'How do I know? One can't love somebody in cold blood.'

'I wasn't thinking of it in terms of cold blood.'

'I think I'd rather get a job.'

'Why?'

'Why not?'

'Jobs are for people who need them. You don't need one. You'd be taking it from somebody else who did.'

'Well, maybe I'd like to go on a long journey.'

'You couldn't go alone. But you could go on a honeymoon tour.'

'That would mean that I would have to marry a very rich man, doesn't it?'

'I don't think I like that remark.'

'Why not?'

'Are you suggesting that I'm interested in you because of your money?'

'I've had money dinned into me ever since I can remember. Not at home, but by other people. When some people look at me I can see dollar signs forming in their eyes. Girls of well-to-do families become rather touchy about such things.'

'I've never talked to you about money.'

'No, but whenever you talk about a possible future for us, you always talk in terms that mean money. And you have your Army pay. Would you be surprised to know that I have looked it up, and know how much it is?'

'You've inherited your father's business sense, haven't you?'

'Perhaps.'

'I didn't know you were so money-minded.'

'Under the circumstances, that's rather funny.'

'You know, you're a damned insulting girl.'

'You were advising me a few weeks ago to see people clearly – as they really are. What have you to complain of?'

'I don't know whether to kiss you or slap you.'

'I have always been a lover of comfort. Perhaps you'd better kiss me.'

Roger kissed her, and staked a possible future as a rich woman's husband on that kiss. It was a miracle of technique. The way in which he took Griselda in his arms, and kissed her warmly upon the lips; the way in which he followed this with a tighter embrace, as though passion raged in him like a fire, and pressed his mouth upon hers until the pressure was pain; the way in which, with a quick intake of breath he laid his hand upon her breast, and kissed her throat again and again, her ears, her hair, and at last her lips; the way in which his tongue met hers, and caressed it within her mouth – these things could not have been bettered for neatness of timing and execution. It would be useless to pretend that Griselda was not moved; such address in the art of love would have stirred an anchoress. But when at last he released her she drew away from him, and pulling her coat about her, sat silent for awhile, looking out at the lake.

'Well?' said Roger, at last.

'Well what?'

'Is that to be all? Suppose we do it again?'

'No, suppose we don't,' said Griselda, moving a little farther away.

'Was it unpleasant?'

'Not in the least.'

'Well then – why not?'

'Just because I think not.'

'You're not going to give me a talk about chastity, are you?'

'Well, Roger, since you bring it up, I suppose I might. Do you know what chastity is? Not the denial of passion, surely. Somebody wise – I forget who it was – said that chastity meant to have the body in the soul's keeping.'

Roger pondered upon this for a while.

'I get it,' he said at last; 'I don't measure up to the demands of your soul, is that it?'

'I know it couldn't possibly sound more priggish and foul, but that's it.'

'Well God damn it, I've been given the bird for some funny reasons, but that's the funniest.'

'I know. Shall I take you home now?'

'Take me –?'

'It's my car, you know.'

'Then you can damn well take yourself home. I'll walk.'

Furiously Roger leapt up and rushed back to the refreshment room, where he caused comment by demanding and drinking a tumbler of neat Scotch.

Neither Griselda nor Roger had noticed a bulky figure following them down to the redoubt. It was Hector. Beneath the earthworks, as a communication between the trench around the tower and the lakeshore, was a passage lined with stone, damp, chilly and unwelcoming. It was in this that he stationed himself, for here he could see the two figures, but was in no danger of being seen. He could not hear their soft conversation. But he saw the kiss. It was such a kiss as he had never conceived possible. It pierced his bowels like a spear, and a historic disquiet began therein. His stomach gave a warning squeal, and then the avalanche-like roar. There, in the passage, it seemed to him that it must be audible to the couple on the lakeshore, although they were twenty feet away. With tears in his eyes, and a sick horror in his heart, and with forty wildcats shrieking their rage in his entrails, Hector turned and ran back toward the military college.

He did not return to the ball, but neither had he the power of will to go home. Instead he paced a long avenue of trees, flanked on one side by the lake and on the other by the gardens of the college, until dawn. His head was bursting; he had, he was certain, seen the first horrible move in the seduction of the girl he loved, and what had he done? He had run away. Was this because he too, long ago, had boasted that he would smirch a girl's honour at another, humbler Ball? His agony was incoherent and fearsome. But when the sun was already high he realized that he must get his coat and go home, so he returned to the square in the centre of the college.

There was a crowd there, and his appearance was greeted with a shout. This was the undefeated army of merrymakers who had remained until the very end of the Ball, while poorer spirits had driven home along the very avenue where Hector had walked away the weary night. Nothing would satisfy them except that Hector, now known as the hero of the greatest near-miss in the history of book-buying in Canada, should pose with them in a group photograph. And that was why, in the newspaper which appeared later that day, Hector was to be seen in the centre of the merry throng, between two girls with their arms around his neck, and a third saucily perched upon his knee. It was a splendid likeness, and the fact that he was described in the caption as Professor MacElroy did nothing to diminish the prestige which his pupils accorded him as a result of this publicity.

[SEVEN]

The dress rehearsal was over, and Valentine was near the end of her director's harangue to the cast. The actors sat around her in their costumes, some upon the lawn and some on the properties of the play. Larry Pye had given them the light from a single large flood, and far above the moon rode proudly.

'I think that's everything,' said Valentine. 'Oh, no; I have a few personal notes on this page. Mr Leakey, you must not wear your Masonic ring on the stage. And Mr Shortreed, I know you took off your wrist-watch before your second entrance, but be very careful about that, won't you? Will you two men check on each other tomorrow night five minutes before curtain time? And Professor Vambrace –'

'Mea culpa, mea culpa!' cried the Professor, with scholarly waggishness, burying his face in his hands.

'Yes; your spectacles in the vision scene. It's very easy to forget. Can you find someone to keep an eye on you about that?'

'I'll be very happy to,' cried Miss Wildfang.

'There are one or two of you whom I should like to see privately for a moment before you go home. Mr – hm, no; Miss Vambrace is the only one, I think. Oh, yes, here's a note I'd overlooked: there was some awfully odd makeup, particularly on you girls in the dance of Nymphs and Reapers. What have you been doing to yourselves?'

There was an uneasy silence.

'Who put that stuff on your faces?'

'Auntie Puss,' said a Nymph, faintly.

'Who?'

Valentine was conscious of someone tugging her skirt from behind. It was Mrs Forrester. 'Shut up, Val,' she whispered.

'See me about it later,' said Valentine. 'Now I want you all to feel happy and confident. It was a very good dress rehearsal. Nothing was seriously wrong and everything that was out of order can be corrected before tomorrow night. Don't believe that old nonsense about a good dress rehearsal making a bad first night. Get some rest tomorrow if you can, and please be here by seven o'clock; if you are late you worry the Stage Manager, and that is inexcusable. Thank you all very much. Now your President wants to say something to you.'

Nellie rose, and her face was drawn into what she believed to be an expression of whimsical concern.

'Well,' she said; 'I'm sure you'll all agree with me that Miss Rich has done marvels, simply marvels, with the material she had. I've never seen you do better, in an experience of this club which goes back more years than I care to count. And I sincerely hope she's right about a good dress rehearsal not meaning a bad first night. Some of us can remember occasions when the old saying was only too true. There's a lot in some of these old beliefs. But we'll hope for the best. It's a pity that three names have been left off the programme, and that Mr Smith's initials are wrong; there are two thousand programmes, and if we can get enough volunteer help the corrections can be made by hand tomorrow. Will anyone offer to help with corrections? I'd do it myself, but my day will be a very full one.'

There were no volunteers, except Mr Smith, one of Larry Pye's assistants, who was determined that he should appear before the world as J. K. Smith and not A. K. Smith, as had wrongly been printed. Nellie continued.

'As you all know this is our first attempt at a Pastoral. It's an experiment, and we are breaking new ground. Whether the public will like it remains to be seen. What the critics will say we simply won't know until we see the papers. But whatever happens, we can say that we pioneered the Pastoral in Salterton, and when you try something new you have to take the rough with the smooth. And now I have a surprise for you; our good friend Mr Webster, to whom we owe so much for the use of his beautiful grounds, invites you to supper before you go home.'

This speech was greeted with great applause, for nothing appeals so strongly to the heart of the amateur actor as a thoroughly depressing estimate of his work, followed by a promise of food. As the group in the floodlight broke up, it was agreed that Miss Rich, though she undoubtedly knew her business, was too optimistic; after all, they knew enough about Theatre to be certain of one thing only, and that was that you could Never Tell. Even Professor Vambrace, so ardent a rationalist in the other affairs of life, clung to the superstition that a good dress rehearsal made a bad performance; everybody likes to be superstitious about something, and the stage provided the Professor with a holiday from the gritty scepticism which scoured the gloss off everything else he did. They moved away to take off their costumes somewhat disappointed that Valentine had not scarified them, told them that they were the worst actors in the world, regretted that she had ever consented to work with them. Nellie's speech, though a good try, was not sufficiently gloomy to slake their masochistic thirst.

A few remained in the area of lawn which formed the stage, waiting to catch Valentine's eye. But Nellie was lecturing her.

'Val, you'll have to be terribly tactful about makeup. Dear old Auntie Puss just loves to do it, and if you criticize it you'll break her heart.'

At this moment they were joined by the artist in question. Miss Puss Pottinger was very small, very old, but nimble in a rickety fashion, and when she moved she jiggled all over, like a mechanical toy. For a woman considerably over eighty she was smartly dressed.

'I believe you had some criticism of the makeup on the girls, Miss Rich,' said she, and her voice, like her walk, was brisk but quavery, as though it proceeded from a gramophone which was being dragged over rough ground. 'If you will tell me what the matter is, I shall be very happy to correct it, very happy indeed.'

'I think it was a little over-bold, Miss Pottinger,' said Valentine.

'Aha, yes, but I don't think you make allowance for the lights, my dear. Stage light, you see, is much brighter than ordinary light. I try to make full allowance for that, and of course the effect looks overdone when you stand near it.'

'I quite understand that, Miss Pottinger, but I watched the girls from considerable distance away, and they looked very strange.'

'Aha, yes, but I gave them what I call a Ballet Makeup. Don't worry, when the lights are fully turned on, you will see the effect I intend.'

'But my dear Miss Pottinger, we had all the lights on tonight that we are ever going to use.'

'Aha, yes, but Shakespeare requires an exaggeration which you are probably not accustomed to. I have been doing this sort of work – as an amateur, of course – for a great many years. Indeed, when they used to have regular amateur theatricals at Rideau Hall, in the Earl of Minto's time, I always looked after the makeup. His Excellency was once kind enough to say that I was a real artist at the job, and as you know, he painted china beautifully himself. Am I to understand that my ability is being called into question?'

'Oh no, dear Auntie Puss, of course not,' said Nellie, bending over and speaking sweetly into the fierce old face. 'You know that we just couldn't get along without you. Auntie Puss has made up at least somebody in every play our group has ever done,' she said to Valentine, in a voice which warned that respect for the aged must come before every other consideration. 'We'd be just broken-hearted without her.'

'I can't be expected to do everybody, as I used to,' said Auntie Puss, somewhat mollified. 'And of course I don't see quite as well as I did. I have to use this, now.' She hauled in the slack of a black silk ribbon which hung around her neck, and held up a large and powerful magnifying glass. 'I don't need anything for ordinary use, but for reading and makeup I find now that I need this.'

Feeling, apparently, that she had won the day, Auntie Puss rattled nimbly away, stumbling over a root as she left the lighted area.

'Gallant, gallant,' sighed Nellie watching her.

'Her makeup's bloody, and that's all that matters,' began Valentine, but Professor Vambrace moved forward from the group which lurked, ready to pounce upon her.

'I don't want to cause any extra trouble,' said he, in the voice of a man who is going to do precisely that, 'but could the stage management contrive to give me a stem of grapes with exactly seven grapes on it; to have it concealed, I mean, in the basket on the banquet table, so that I can get it before my Big Speech? I mean

The cloud-capp'd towers, the gorgeous palaces –

of course. Then I could eat seven grapes, during that speech, and at the end –

We are such stuff
As dreams are made on, and our little life
Is rounded with a sleep. –

I could toss away the stem. You take me? Rather fine, eh?'

'I'm afraid I don't fully grasp the point, Professor,' said Valentine.

'Oh, come, Miss Rich. Surely? Seven grapes – what does that put you in mind of? The Seven Ages of Man, eh? From *As You Like It*. It is pretty clearly understood that the Melancholy Jaques is an early study for the character of Prospero. Now here we have a chance to make a synthesis – to draw Jaques and Prospero together, with this piece of business with the grapes. That's why I came on the stage with my glasses on; I had been scanning *As You Like It* in the wings. As a matter of fact, I have felt some big thing moving within me all day, but it wasn't until half-past nine that I knew what it was. Will you speak to the stage management, or shall I?'

'I do not think that we should introduce anything new into the production at this point,' said Valentine. The Professor was astonished, but as the palaver appeared to be at an end, he moved away, giving place to Geordie Shortreed, who was next in line. Geordie spoke in a low voice, as though ashamed and fearful of being overheard.

'Miss Rich,' said he; 'will it be all right if I slip a hot-water bottle under my costume for that scene where I have to lie on the ground so long? I got awful trouble with my kidneys, and if I get a chill they'll seize right up. I got a pension for sixty per cent disability.'

'You may have your hot-water bottle if you give me a solemn promise that you won't play any tricks during the run of the show,' said Valentine, severely. She had received private information that Geordie had been seen in the joke shop the day before, buying a large squirt and several feet of rubber tubing.

'Cross my heart and hope to spit myself to death,' said Geordie, and went away smiling.

The last to approach was Pearl Vambrace.

'Falsies for you, my girl,' said Valentine.

'I don't understand you, Miss Rich.'

'Pads for the bosom. Ask Bonnie-Susan; she probably has some she would lend you. Though what she would need them for,' Valentine reflected, 'is beyond me.'

'Oh, but won't I look terribly big? I mean, I shouldn't be gross, should I?'

'You're a long way from grossness now. And you must make allowance for stage light; it's brighter than ordinary light,' said Valentine, borrowing a leaf from Auntie Puss's book.

The refreshment provided by the domestic staff of St Agnes' consisted chiefly of a very large supply of chicken chow mein. A June night in Salterton is chilly enough to make a hot dish grateful to tired pioneers of the Pastoral. They gathered in knots upon the lawn and champed and worried about the play with great satisfaction.

'I'd be happy if I could just get enough light to kill those shadows,' said Larry Pye; 'but do what I will, everywhere an actor goes, he casts a shadow.'

'And why not?' said Solly. 'What could be more natural? Here we are in bright moonlight, and every one of us has a shadow. Larry wants us all to be like Peter Schlemihl, who sold his shadow to the Devil. I never knew a stage manager yet who didn't believe that people cast no shadows.'

'It's not one shadow I complain of,' said Larry. 'It's four or five, mostly on other people's faces.'

'Never mind, Larry,' said Valentine; 'your light is charming. But I do wish you could tone down that intercommunication system; every time you speak backstage, we hear your voice from The Shed, roaring behind the audience. It's confusing and often blasphemous.'

'Got to keep it sharp,' said Larry. 'Suppose you want somebody in a hurry?'

'Do the best you can,' said Valentine.

'Oh Miss Rich,' sighed Miss Wildfang, who was prompter, 'you have the patience of a saint! Too much patience, perhaps, if such a thing is possible. Tonight we were braced for really severe criticism; we expected it, and I may almost say that we wanted it. We cannot improve if we are not told about our faults.'

'I told you about your faults,' said Valentine. 'All those, that's to say, about which anything can be done. I really don't believe that people thrive on harsh criticism. I've had a good deal of experience, and I've always found that you get the best out of people by being decent to them.'

'Ah, yes – professionals,' said Professor Vambrace. 'But we are spirits of another sort – if I may quote another of the Immortal's works. Most of us are university people, or professional people. We can accept criticism of a type which would be unacceptable to the more – how shall I put it – the more – well, the more elementary intelligences of professional players.'

Valentine was a little nettled. 'Sir Henry Irving said that the best of amateurs were but children in art; one must teach children by kindness, and not expect everything from them which one might demand from adults. Irving also said that the hardest thing for an amateur to do was to get over the habit of stressing personal pronouns. I refuse to minister to the perverse desire of any amateur actor to be abused in public.'

This was hard hitting, for the matter of personal pronouns had been mentioned before, and to the Professor himself. He turned away, and was heard to say to Miss Wildfang that the limitations of the professional stage were easily understood, in the light of his recent experience. A small matter of seven grapes, which could, nevertheless, awaken an echo of *As You Like It*, had been denied to him. Was a really evocative theatre possible if such lack of perception were to prevail? Yes, he agreed with Miss Wildfang that the sooner a university theatre was established, the better. Then, with long rehearsal and ripe scholarship – not all of it from the Department of English, of course – the essential oneness, the great overall unity of Shakespeare's plays could be revealed.

Much as they might wish to be abused by Valentine at a dress rehearsal, it was plain that the actors were distressed at the thought of being criticized in print.

'Whatever the papers say,' said Nellie, 'I shall always think that we have done the right thing. But I can't answer for the others. A bad press may hit them very hard.'

'What press will there be?' asked Valentine.

'The local paper, of course, and probably something in the *Waverley Review*, when it next appears, sometime in November,' said Solly.

'No out-of-town papers?'

'One or two, perhaps. Your name will draw them.'

'Well, what have you to worry about?'

'I'm worried about the out-of-towners; there might even be one of those radio critics, and they are so patronizing, even when they're favourable. And if other drama groups hear that we've been panned, they'll gloat so.'

'I think you are just worrying because you think you should, Nell,' said Valentine. 'Criticism can't possibly hurt the show; you've sold enough tickets already to assure success. Stop fussing.'

'Spoken like a professional,' said Cobbler, who had joined them. 'I never pay any attention to criticism. Most critics of anything are frauds. Worse, most of them are bachelors or spinsters. Their opinions of what other people create are firmly hitched to their own sexual cycle. Show me a bachelor critic in whom desire burns like a furnace, and I'll show you a fellow who will boost your show to the skies or damn it to the pit, according to the way the leading lady strikes his fancy. Show me the same critic at the bottom of his twenty-eight day round, and I'll show you a fellow who will give you faint praise. Every critic carries a twenty-eight day clock in his gizzard, and what he says about you depends on whether he is ready to strike twelve or one. Rule out the few critics who truly love the arts, and who would be critics even if they weren't paid for it, and the rest are needy riffraff, laughed at by all serious artists.'

'What is a spinster director supposed to make of that?' said Valentine.

'If you refer to yourself,' said Cobbler, 'I am forced to reveal that I do not consider it possible that a lady of your charm can be a spinster in anything except the most technical sense. Furthermore, you are a true artist – a creator. Such people are not twenty-eight day clocks; they are towers in which the carillon peals whenever God chooses to stir it with his mighty breath.'

'Thank you,' said Valentine, who possessed the rarest of female graces, in that she knew how to receive a compliment. She blushed delightfully.

'Don't thank me; thank God,' said Humphrey. 'I said that you spoke like a professional. You and I are two of the three professionals involved with this show. We must stand together.'

'Who is the other?' asked Larry Pye, hoping for a compliment.

'That gardener,' said Humphrey. 'I don't think any of you realize what a wonderful job he has done for you in making his garden look like an enchanted island.'

'Oh, yes; Gawky,' said Larry. 'That reminds me, I want a word with him. Hey, Gawky!' He shouted at Tom, who was walking around the lawn with a pointed stick and a bag, picking up bits of paper.

'Not Gawky. The man's name is Golky,' said Professor Vambrace, who stood nearby, eating a third dish of chow mein in an abstracted manner. He despised food, but he always ate a great deal at affairs of this kind where it was good and plentiful.

Tom, however, was ready to answer to almost any Saxon assault upon his name, and he came near.

'We've worn away some grass on the stage already,' said Larry. 'Can you do anything about that?'

'I'll cut the lower lawn tomorrow, sir,' said Tom, 'and sprinkle the cuttings about seven o'clock. I'll do that every night, just to keep the place looking fresh.'

'That's very kind of you, Mr Gwalchmai,' said Valentine.

'Not at all miss. It's my show, too, in a way. And the cuttings will do no harm. I believe in returning everything to nature that comes from nature. But,' he said, angrily spearing the glass-paper casing of a cigarette box which Larry had just thrown down, 'nobody'll ever convince me that this-here cellophane ever came from nature, and nature'll never absorb it again. So I'll thank you, sir, not to throw it on my grass, unless you want your enchanted island to look like a rubbish-tip.' He moved away.

'Let me get you another plate of that stuff,' said Solly to Valentine.

'I'll come with you,' said she, and they broke away from their group.

'I wanted to get away,' said she; 'everybody wants to plague and worry me about nothing. They'll all be all right tomorrow. What's worrying them?'

'They are sacrificing to our Canadian God,' said Solly. 'We all believe that if we fret and abuse ourselves sufficiently, Providence will take pity and smile upon anything we attempt. A light heart, or a consciousness of desert, attracts ill luck. You have been away from your native land too long. You have forgotten our folkways. Listen to that gang over there; they are scanning the heavens and hoping aloud that it won't rain tomorrow. That is to placate the Mean Old Man in the Sky, and persuade him to be kind to us. We are devil-worshippers, we Canadians, half in love with easeful Death. We flog ourselves endlessly, as a kind of spiritual purification. Now, what about some chow mein?'

They replenished their plates, and withdrew to a quiet spot where bushes half-screened them from the others.

'There's one man I must speak to before tomorrow,' said Valentine. 'And that's Mackilwraith. I didn't want to shame him before the others, but he was quite dreadful. He was never very good, but during this past week he's been impossible. He comes as near to fading completely into the background, leaving a gaping hole where Gonzalo should be, as any actor I've ever seen. His lines mean nothing; if I didn't know them I doubt if I'd ever distinguish them.'

'Shocking,' agreed Solly. 'I wondered what you would do.'

'I suppose I'd better get it over. Will you hunt him up and tell him I'd like to see him here? This is private enough; I'll just keep out of the way of the others.'

Sated with food, the actors showed no signs of going home. Cobbler and his wife and children were sitting on the lawn, singing for a large audience. The treble voices and the one bass were sweet upon the moonlit air.

Come again,
Sweet love doth now invite –

they sang, and other voices were stilled to hear them.

Not all voices, however. Mr Webster, who had been somewhat shyly circulating among his guests, most of whom were strangers to him, found that he was being shadowed by a small, monkey-like man, whose face bore traces still of the elaborate makeup of Caliban. What the devil does he want, thought Mr Webster. Perhaps he is worshipping me because I am rich; there are such people. Maybe he hates me because I am rich; that's far more likely. I wish he wouldn't dart behind trees like that. But now he was confronted by the creature, and it was necessary to speak.

'I suppose you've had something to eat?'

'Yes, indeed, Mr Webster; as a matter of fact, yes.'

'Enough?'

'Oh yes, indeed. An ample sufficiency, as the fellow says. Ha ha.'

'What fellow?'

'Eh? Oh, I guess it was some fellow in a story. Or maybe a movie.'

'I see. I'm very interested in history. I like to find out what fellow said everything, whenever I can.'

'Ha ha. Yes, I guess that's right.'

'Coffee?'

'Uh? No, no, I've had lots of coffee, thank you very much.'

'Cigarette?'

'Oh, thanks very much. But here, you have one of mine.'

'No, thank you. I always smoke cigars.'

'Very wise. A more wholesome smoke, as you might say.'

'I've never heard anybody say that.'

'Oh, yes. It's a well-known thing. Unless somebody happens to give you an exploding cigar. Ha ha.'

'Why would anybody give me an exploding cigar?'

'Oh, just as a joke.'

'I don't think I've even seen an exploding cigar.'

'Oh, haven't you? Well I've got one in my pocket. Here.'

'But I don't want an exploding cigar.'

'Oh not for yourself, of course. Give it to somebody for a joke.'

'No, no, you keep it.'

'All right. And I certainly wouldn't offer one to you, Mr Webster. Not after what's passed between us, I mean.'

'What's that? Has anything passed between us?'

'Well, there was that matter of the horse.'

'What horse?'

'Well, of course a horse wouldn't mean much to a man in your position, but a horse could be a very serious item to me. I mean, with my sixty per cent disability because of my kidneys, you see. Frankly, Mr Webster, I wanted to say it to your face; you were white about the horse.'

'What the hell are you talking about? I haven't got a horse.'

'I know. And I take the full blame. You were a prince about it. I hope my letter cleared it all up?'

'Oh! You're the fellow who killed Old Bill?'

'I did, and I tell you frankly, it shook me up as nothing has shaken me up since the Battle of the Bulge.'

'You're the fellow who wrote that extraordinary letter?'

'I'm not much of a man with the pen, but I put everything I had into that letter.'

'Oh. Well – you won't have any more coffee?'

'No sir. Permit me to shake you by the hand.'

'Oh – ah.'

'You're a white man, G A.'

'Uh.'

'Maybe some day I'll be able to do as much for you.'

'Ah.'

'The lion and the mouse, you know.'

'Mf.'

His conscience freed of its burden, Geordie walked away toward the group who were listening to the music, and his host scuttled inside to the privacy of his library. To be perfectly sure that no one else could find him and tell him that he was white, he locked the door.

'Well, have you made a new man of him?' Solly had been watching from a distance, and when Hector came from behind the shrubbery where Valentine was, he joined her.

'I doubt it very much,' said she. 'He was sorry, and all that, but he didn't really seem to be listening to me. He said something about private trouble, and a weight on his mind, but all actors do that when they've been making a mess of a part.'

'You do him too much honour when you describe him as an actor.'

'No, poor sweet, he'll never be an actor if he lives to be a thousand. I've done my best for him, but only a new heart and a new soul could make an actor of him.'

'You might as well add a new body to the list of requirements. Did you ever see such legs?'

'I know. Beef to the heels. I wanted the costume people to give him a long gown, but they insisted on tights. Long experience has taught me to judge pretty accurately what men are hiding under their trousers.'

'You fill me with apprehension. But I know what you mean. The male leg is rarely a thing of beauty.'

'Yes. I wonder why.'

'It's very simple. Just an example of evolution, or natural selection, or something. In the periods when women wore long skirts they had awful legs; look at the nudes painted during those periods if you don't believe me. But when they had to show their legs, they willed fine legs into existence. And when men wore tights they had fine legs too, because they needed them. But modern man conceals his legs, and what have they become? Stovepipes.'

'Or, as in your own case, toothpicks.'

'That X-ray eye of yours makes me uncomfortable. As a matter of fact I possess what I like to define as the Scholarly, or Intellectual Leg. Vambrace has toothpicks, if you talk of toothpicks. I popped into the men's dressing-room just now to call Mackilwraith, and Vambrace was changing. Do you know that he wears a species of bone-coloured long underwear, even in weather like this? A shocking sight. I felt like the sons of Noah when they had uncovered their father's nakedness.'

'It's a mistake to see people dressing. One should see them either dressed or naked; those are the only two decent states. All else is shame and disillusion.'

'Just for curiosity's sake, why did you refer to Mackilwraith as "poor sweet", just now?'

'He is rather sweet, don't you think? So serious, and at heart such a really decent, nice man.'

'His pupils don't think so. He's a classroom tyrant.'

'Yes, that seems very probable.'

'Then why sweet?'

'Well, he just seems that way to me. I hated to speak hardly to him. What do you care about whether he's sweet or not?'

'Jealousy, really. I bet you don't think I'm sweet. Not, upon reflection, that I would care to be so described.'

'Oh, Solly, you've far too much intelligence for anything like that, but you're a darling, all the same, and I do thank you for the help you've given me with this show.'

'Val, I love you.'

'What?'

'Oh, don't be alarmed. I don't want to marry you, or tag around after you, or monopolize you. I just mean that I love you. You're a wonderful person and so much like a woman. That sounds silly, of course, but you know what I mean. So many women, even the young and pretty ones, aren't like women at all. They haven't got that wonderful, magical quality that real women have – like you. What you are explains what all the really first-rate poets are talking about. You're the first one I've known well who has it, and I love you, and I'll go on loving you. But it's nothing for you to worry about – just something for me to enjoy. Do you know what I mean?'

'Yes, Solly dear, I do. And I'm very grateful. At my age, you see, it's very flattering to hear that sort of talk from somebody as young as you. But you mustn't be foolish about me; you should look for someone younger than yourself.'

'Oh, I certainly will. But I'll try to find somebody as much as possible like you. And that won't be easy. Shall we join the others?'

'Yes. And don't think I shall forget what you have said.'

Solly took Valentine in his arms and kissed her. Then they joined the company on the lawn.

Ever since she had parted with Roger at the Ball, Griselda had been ill at ease. She had wanted to be rid of him. Of that she was perfectly sure. But she had not wanted to lecture him on morality. She had not wanted to pop out that pious little saw about the body being in the soul's keeping. That was what she meant, of course, but she wished that she had expressed it differently. Still, if she had not done so, what would have happened? Roger had made it plain enough that he wanted her to be his mistress. What a silly expression that was! She didn't want to be a mistress, and especially not the mistress of somebody like Roger. He hinted too much about his prowess with women. What was it he had said? That a woman's body should be played upon and made to sing like a musical instrument. He had got that out of Balzac. She had read Balzac on that subject herself, and thought it nonsense. If anybody was going to make her sing like a musical instrument it would have to be somebody who had first of all made her happy as a human being, and Roger had never done that. He was flattering, and amusing, but somehow not very likeable.

Still, she wished that she had not spoken to him like that. He would think she was just a Pill. He would probably tell other people that she was a Pill. Not that she cared what other people thought. Daddy always said that you could never be happy so long as you gave a damn what other people thought. But of course Daddy wasn't a girl, and besides, he was always worrying about what somebody thought himself, so it didn't count.

She was, she decided with some shame, much simpler than she had imagined. She was like the girls in Trollope; she wanted to be loved, and to love, and when these conditions were met, there was nothing she would not do. But she did not want to mess around with Roger, even though it might be fun while it was going on. She was, she decided after a depressing session with herself, inclined to be Pure. But she wanted it to be quite clear that she was Pure without being a Pill.

And imagine saying that she had looked up his income! Of course she had done so. He talked so much about money that she wanted to know how much he really had. It was the kind of thing girls did that girls should never admit to. But he had talked about marriage, and who wants to marry a girl of eighteen, unless she has money? Griselda was as sensitive on the subject of money as her father.

She was glad to be rid of Roger, but sorry that she had been nasty to him. Well, if that was the case, she would find an opportunity to show him that she was ready to be friendly, but not too friendly. Definitely not a mistress. On the contrary, a Trollope. Not a bad joke that. She would tell it to Freddy if the kid were not so utterly idiotic and likely to blab everything she knew out of sheer childish irresponsibility.

The opportunity came at the party after the dress rehearsal. Griselda was standing by the serving-table on the lawn, eating a plate of chow mein, while most of the company were at some distance, listening to the Cobbler family sing. Roger approached.

'Hello, Roger,' said she. 'Have some of this. It's good.'

'Thanks, I've eaten,' said he, in a tone which he believed to be one of distant politeness, but which was really rather surly. 'I want a cup of coffee for The Torso. You're still stuffing, I see.'

'Not still. Just. I've been hostessing. Roger?'

'Yes?'

'Don't be cross about the Ball. I didn't mean to be horrid.'

'I don't understand you.'

'Oh yes you do! I was a pig, and I'm sorry.'

'You mean you've changed your mind?'

'No, I don't mean that. But I was a pious pig. Will you let me explain?'

'Certainly.'

'Let's walk.'

'All right.'

'What about The Torso's coffee?'

'Oh she's probably forgotten she wanted it by now. Anyway, too much coffee isn't good for her. I'll drink it.'

They set off toward the lower lawn. Hector, watching from a distance, saw them pass into shadow, then into a patch of moonlight, and then into shadow again. How should he know that Griselda was industriously eating chow mein as she explained herself, somewhat incoherently, to Roger? He saw only that Roger had put his arm around her shoulders, and then they disappeared into shadow again, and he turned away, heartsick, toward the shrubbery. It was there that he narrowly escaped walking into Solly and Valentine, who at that moment were in each other's arms. It was a bad night for Hector.

A bad night, and the latest of many such nights. Since the Ball he could think of nothing but Griselda, and of what he supposed to be her intrigue with Roger. He could not sleep. During the daytime he was supposed to be watching over pupils who were writing summer examinations, but he brought no vigilance to this task, in which he had once delighted. In former years he had kept up an incessant prowling in the examination room. Soft-footed, he had paced slowly up and down between the rows of desks, his eyes alert for talkers, peepers, cheats. But this year he had sat slumped at his desk, his eyes fixed on space, and examinees who wanted extra paper or ink were sometimes forced to snap their fingers three times before he took it to them.

His appetite had deserted him. Only habit took him to the Snak Shak at regular intervals; once there he ordered food, but he ate little of it. His skin sagged, and it seemed to him that his hair was turning white. In strict fact, grey hairs had been appearing at his temples for five years, but he had not noticed them or paid heed to them before. In these terrible days they appeared to him to be symbols of the conflict which was going on in his heart.

He loved Griselda, and it seemed to him that in that love there was no room for thought of himself. His longing for her was a pain which filled his whole body. And she was, he felt certain, the creature of that vile thing Tasset; he had persuaded her, by his villainous arts, to give her body to him. She was ruined. A soul so delicate as hers, once in contact with sin, would most certainly be shattered beyond any recovery.

At night he lay in his bed, his body rigid under the stress of the painful thoughts which would not be banished from his mind. She was a harlot. No, no! Not a harlot; not that lovely child, so new to the world and so fresh in her womanhood! She might still be reclaimed, and oh! how grateful she would be to the one who drew her back from the abyss of shame and threw the mantle of a great, understanding, world-defying love around her! After one of these bouts of self-torture, Hector would weep, and his YMCA bed creaked under the violence of his sobs. His mother's early attempts to purge him had given him a horror of drugs, but under this stress he began to take aspirin tablets, sometimes two at a time, so reckless was he, and they helped him to get a little sleep.

It was curious that during this dreadful week, when Hector's sufferings were real and intense, he found time to regret that he had not had a more literary education. His passions were too big for his vocabulary, and he could not put all that he felt into words, even to himself. As for planning and common sense, he saw them for the extremely limited servants that they were, and the foundations of his whole scheme of life were shaken.

He knew that he was wretchedly insufficient in the part of Gonzalo. He accepted the rather mild rebuke which Valentine gave him without rancour, and almost without hearing it. He was numbed by his pain, and all that he could do was to stand as much out of sight as possible, and watch Griselda. The sight of her eased his heart. But when she went off to the lower lawn with Roger, he turned into the shrubbery like a sick animal, to be alone. The sight of Solly and Valentine was bitter to him, but only as a blow on the back hurts a man who has been stabbed to the heart. He thought of the chow mein, or a cup of coffee, but suddenly all food was repugnant to him. He found a bench hidden among the fragrantly flowering shrubs, and sat upon it. From the lawn came the song of the Cobbler family, light and free on the summer air:

Gentle Love,
Draw forth thy wounding dart;
Thou canst not pierce her heart;
For I, that do approve,
By sighs and tears
More hot than are thy shafts,
Did tempt, while she
For triumph laughs.

He broke into a cold sweat and a horrible nausea seized him. Not far away was Griselda, and Roger with her. What were they doing? He clung to the back of the bench, his eyes shut, retching horribly.

Hector slept not at all that night. As a general thing, when that expression is used, people mean that they slept five hours instead of their accustomed eight. But Hector went to bed at one o'clock and lay awake until seven, when he rose and tried to rouse himself with a shower. The pelting of cold water on his weary flesh brought him some refreshment of body, but none of mind. In his room he tried to beguile the time with a batch of examination papers. Mechanically he spotted errors; mechanically he wrote TOSASM when that comment was justified, but he was like a man with a mortal sickness, and no temporary distraction could make him forget Griselda. At last he rose and went to the Snak Shak, where he could take nothing but a glass of orange juice – a small glass, not the Mammoth Jumbo Special.

He had no school work that morning, for examinations were nearly over, and he intended to correct papers in the Men Teachers' Room for the greater part of the day. He was free, therefore, to go to a florist's, where he ordered a large bunch of flowers.

'To whom shall we send it?' asked the clerk.

He could not speak her name. A flush spread over his face and his head ached.

'I'll write the address for you,' said he.

'You'll find a nice selection of cards on the desk.'

A nice selection of cards. The first one he saw said 'In deepest Sympathy'; the next, 'For a Joyous Occasion'; a third, bearing the picture of what might have been a baboon, but was perhaps intended for an Irishman, said 'May good luck go wid ye. And throuble forgit ye'. He chose a plain white card, and pondered long over his message. Dared he make a declaration of love in this way? No, no; the florist's men might read it, and know what was for her eye alone. But could he not say something which would mean nothing to the idly curious, but which would carry his meaning to her? He wrote:

Whatever you may have been, you can count on me for anything, even Death itself.

HECTOR MACKILWRAITH

He read it several times. He could not put his finger on what was wrong with it, but somehow it would not do. When he tried to crush the immensities of his emotions into words, he could not get his meaning clear. At last he wrote:

You can count on me for anything.

HECTOR MACKILWRAITH

He addressed the envelope and hurried out of the shop before the florist should learn his secret.

'Half an hour. This is your half hour call. You will receive a call at the quarter hour, and another at five minutes before curtain time. The beginners will then assemble backstage.' Larry Pye's voice, vastly amplified, rang through The Shed. He spoke solemnly, as befitted a man using a public address system of his own devising, and his enunciation was pedantically clear.

Roger Tasset leapt from the chair in which he was being made up, and seized a small microphone which hung near the loud-speaker.

'Stage Management? Stage Management? Message received. Wilco.'

Larry's voice was heard again, excited and quite normal in tone.

'How's it coming in, Rodge?'

'Fine, Larry; couldn't be better.'

Delighted, Roger submitted himself again to the hands of the makeup artist.

What babies men are, thought Valentine. All this fuss about messages that could be much better done by a call-girl.

The Shed was filled with people. Tom had cleared it for the use of the Little Theatre, and tables and chairs for makeup had been brought in. Several experienced hands were at work on the faces of the actors, under Valentine's watchful eye, and in a corner Auntie

Puss laboured over Hector Mackilwraith. She treated his face as though it were a blackboard; if an effect did not please her, she roughly scrubbed it off with a towel and tried another. She would examine him intently through her magnifying glass, and then go to work without its aid.

'A little white at the temples, I think,' said she. 'What we call a Distinguished Grey. Very becoming.'

'Miss Pottinger, why are you putting yellow in Mr Mackilwraith's hair?' said Valentine.

'Dear dear; I must have picked up the wrong stick in error. Ah, well; a little powder will mend that; it's a very neutral sort of yellow.'

'Perhaps one of the others will put on Mr Mackilwraith's beard, Miss Pottinger. You must not tire yourself.'

'Please do not worry about me, Miss Rich. I understand all about beards.'

'I am sure you do. But I do not want to impose on your good nature.'

'Miss Rich, the Earl of Minto once told me that he considered me to be a real artist at this work. And as you know, he painted china beautifully. Give me time, and I shall finish Mr Mackilwraith and put touches on all the others.'

Not if I know it, thought Valentine. She had contrived to have all the girls made up elsewhere, in a room which Griselda had offered inside the house, and she felt that she could protect the men against Auntie Puss. Great God! Look at her! With a black lining-stick she was drawing what appeared to be comic spectacles around Mackilwraith's eyes. Oh well, he's so bad anyway that it doesn't matter too much what he looks like. We'll just have to write him off as a total loss; every amateur show has at least one.

The door opened and Freddy bounced in, dressed as the goddess Ceres.

'Miss Rich,' said she, 'Mr Cobbler wants to know whether you want *God Save the King* played at the beginning or end of the performance.'

'At the beginning,' said Valentine; 'we decided that days ago.'

'He said you had, but Mrs Forrester told him to play it at the end.'

'I'll talk to them about it,' said Valentine, and hurried out.

'You're quite a cute kid, painted up like that,' said Roger to Freddy.

'I object very much to being called a cute kid,' she replied. 'If it is God's will that I should be pretty, I'll be pretty; if I am to be plain, I shall be plain without complaint. But come what will, I shall never be vulgar. Only vulgar people are cute kids.'

'You're going to be pretty, like your sister,' said Geordie Shortreed, hideously made up as Caliban.

'Griselda is very pretty,' said Freddy. 'It's a shame she has no brains. If brains ever came back into fashion for girls, it would be a bad day for her. The Torso's a bit squiffed. I can't stand people who don't know how to hold their drink.'

'The old Torso squiffed?' said Roger. 'Why?'

'She says she took just a nip to give her courage for the performance. That nip went to her head, so she had another to straighten her out, and they both went to her legs.'

'As who wouldn't?' said Geordie, and was crushed by an austere look from Professor Vambrace, who now had a beard two feet long.

'She's been nipping at intervals ever since,' Freddy continued. 'She has a flask in the girls' dressing-room. She may have to be put down with a strong hand.'

Solly had come in. 'Talking about The Torso?' said he. 'Juno has certainly been hitting the jug. When I last saw her Griselda was holding an ice-bag on her head, and Cora Fielding was laying hot-water bottles to her feet. A gay girl, lovable and undependable.'

The door opened and an elderly man with two teeth, carrying a violin case, entered The Shed, followed by a colourless thin woman, and a dark and greasy man with a piano accordion hanging around his neck on a leather strap.

'This where we come?' asked the old man. He then caught sight of Solly.

'Oh, hello there,' said he. 'Glad to see you, Mr Bridgetower. Can we just have a little run over the play before we start? You tell me where you want the music to come, and we'll fit it in somehow.'

Solly turned white. 'Good evening, Mr Snairey,' said he, and fled through the door.

'It is useless to appeal to me in this matter,' said Humphrey Cobbler when, a few minutes later, he, Valentine, Mrs Forrester, Solly and the Snairey Trio gathered on the lawn outside The Shed. 'I am a musician, and as such I have come here to provide music for this play. I have devoted approximately twenty hours of rehearsal to it. I have assembled a choir of ten and an orchestra of eight, and they are all in readiness at this moment. We have rehearsed the music with the full company six times. Now, if you want me to go away, I shall do so. If you want me to stay, I shall be delighted. But what I positively will not do is wrangle with Mr Snairey.'

'Solly, I told you to tell Mr Snairey that we had changed our plans,' said Nellie, close to tears.

'You told me to get Mr Cobbler, which I did,' said Solly. 'You distinctly said that you would see Mr Snairey yourself.'

'You were the fella come to see me first,' said Mr Snairey. 'I'm a reasonable man, but I got my living to make, same's anybody else. Joe here coulda had two other jobs tonight, but he come here to oblige me. Either we play or we sit out, and we get paid either way. Don't know's I ever seen you before, young fella,' he said, turning toward Cobbler with what he probably intended as a look of menace.

'I don't suppose you have,' said Humphrey; 'I've only been in Salterton about five years.'

'Oh, what shall we do?' moaned Nellie. 'Val, do something.'

'I don't altogether see why I should,' said Valentine. 'You and Solly have created this situation. I suppose you must pay Mr Snairey; I don't imagine his rates can be very high.'

'Union scale,' said Joe the accordionist. 'You got a big show here. Musicals come high.'

'It's not the money so much as my feelings,' said Mr Snairey. 'Fella my age doesn't like to get pushed around like he was some young punk. We come here to play, and I guess we better play.'

From inside The Shed Larry's voice boomed through the loudspeaker, announcing that it was five minutes till curtain time.

'Oh, what shall we do?' cried Nellie, weeping openly. 'I must get to Larry. We can't possibly begin till all the people are in their seats. He may want to start before some really important people have come. Oh, I wish we'd never attempted this damned play!'

'What's the trouble, hon?' said a bland voice behind them. It was Roscoe Forrester. In a rush, Nellie explained, assisted by Valentine and Solly.

'I'll handle this,' said Roscoe. 'The rest of you just get on with what you have to do. Now, Snairey, you listen to me.'

Oh, sweet relief! Oh, miraculous lightening of hearts! How they thanked God for Roscoe, the man of business, accustomed to dealing with difficult situations. Valentine could subdue a group of hostile actors or dominate an unfriendly audience, but the Snaireys of this world, the pushing incompetents, daunted her. Solly and Nellie hurried away, blaming each other in their hearts. And after three brisk minutes with Roscoe the Snairey Trio climbed into its Ford and struggled down the drive of St Agnes', against the steady stream of cars bringing people to the play.

Behind the scenes Nellie bustled up to Larry. 'It's all right,' she said. 'We can begin at once. They're all here. Mrs Caesar Augustus Conquergood has just taken her seat.'

Larry pressed a button. In the shrubbery where Humphrey Cobbler was established a red light flashed on his music desk, and then a green. The National Anthem burst forth, somewhat blurred by the sound of eight hundred people rising to their feet. *The Tempest* had begun.

Sending flowers to Griselda in June was carrying coals to Newcastle indeed. The gardens at St Agnes' were filled with flowers, and Hector's two dozen roses could add nothing to the splendour of the arrangements which Mr Webster's housekeeper placed at every advantageous spot in the house. Further, Hector's card disturbed Griselda. So she could count on him for anything, could she? But she didn't want to count on him. He was a bore, and he had a dreadful habit of staring at her. Griselda knew that she was well worth looking at, but she hated to be followed by what appeared to her to be a fixed and baleful glare. After a moment of brief annoyance at his card, she decided to put Hector's roses in the girls' dressing room, and if necessary to explain that they were a tribute from Mr Mackilwraith to the female members of the cast.

It was from the window of that dressing-room that she leaned out as the actors trooped along a garden path from The Shed to the back of the stage, immediately after Larry's five-minutes call. Roger looked up and caught sight of her.

'You'd better hurry up,' he called, 'or Larry will be in a stew.' He looked more intently at her, and blew a kiss. 'You look like the Blessed Damozel, leaning down from the golden bar of Heaven,' he said.

How nice he looks as Ferdinand, thought Griselda. And he's obviously not angry any more. I must have made myself quite clear last night. He doesn't think I'm a Pill. From the dressing-table nearby she took one of Hector's roses from its vase, kissed it, and tossed it down to Roger, who fielded it expertly, fastened it to his doublet and hurried on toward the stage.

'Who was that for?' asked The Torso, who was sitting miserably in a chair, with her head almost between her knees. Pearl Vambrace was putting cold compresses on the back of her neck.

'For Roger,' said Griselda.

'Pearl, honey,' said Bonnie-Susan in a controlled voice. 'Don't squeeze that damned cold water down my back.'

'I'm sorry, Bonnie-Susan,' said Pearl. 'My hand jerked.'

'A likely story,' said The Torso. 'Just leave me alone and run down there and fascinate the open-mouthed throng. With that makeup and my falsies you should get yourself a beau or two. They just dote on us painted creatures of the theayter.'

Exhausted by this flight of irony she dropped her head between her knees again, and moaned softly. Moaning seemed to ease her pain.

Hector had seen the rose thrown from the window; there were roses everywhere, but he was sure that it was one of his. However, he had no time to brood deeply about it, for he was needed in the first scene. To simulate the rolling and pitching of a ship at sea Larry Pye had devised an ingenious contraption upon which the actors stood, partly screened by shrubbery, while they were tossed and heaved hither and thither by the tempest, the sound of which was simulated by Cobbler's orchestra and a variety of wind-machines and thunder-strips backstage. It was a taxing scene and Hector, who had never been good at doing two things at once, had to exert all his wits in order to keep his balance and recognize his cues when they came. When this ordeal was over, and the audience was applauding heartily (as audiences always do when they see actors being put to great inconvenience and indignity) Hector was just able to roll seasickly to a bench and close his eyes, trying to calm his queasy stomach; he had had virtually nothing to eat for the past forty-eight hours, and the world swam giddily about him while the great voice of Professor Vambrace was heard from the stage, in Prospero's seemingly interminable narrative of misfortune.

It was a long wait until Act Two, when he appeared again, and Hector sat lonely on his bench, with bustle all about him. Griselda, lovely in the costume of Ariel, seemed once about to approach him, and he raised his eyes to hers, but then she knit her brows and turned away. Wherever she was, he was conscious of her. He was by no means sensitive to music, but when she sang 'Come unto these yellow sands' and 'Full fathom five' his soul was ravished because it was Griselda who was singing. When she stood ready to run onto the stage in the costume of a water-nymph, which Mrs Crundale conceived as the merest wisp of sea-green gauze, his bowels yearned at her beauty, and his heart ached because so much of it was to be seen by any member of the audience who had paid his dollar for a seat. But most of all he grieved because the rose which she had thrown to Roger – one of his own roses – was conclusive proof to him that she was frail, that she was no better than those hired girls, taken in sin, whom it had been the Reverend John Mackilwraith's duty to scold, exhort and pray over in the manse parlour in the days of his childhood.

At the beginning of Act Two of *The Tempest* Gonzalo is required to appear as a rather jolly and witty old gentleman. Hector had never fully succeeded in rising to the demands of this scene, though he never failed in it with such thoroughgoing dismalness as on the first night. But one thing happened which puzzled sharp-sighted members of the audience: when Ariel bent over the form of the sleeping Gonzalo and sang in his ear

While you here do snoring lie,
Open-eyed conspiracy
His time doth take.
If of life you keep a care,
Shake off slumber and beware:
Awake, awake!

it was observable that Gonzalo stirred in his rest like a tortured man, and a single, unmistakable tear crept down his left cheek. Fortunately he had little to do in the Third Act, for what he said was inaudible and when he moved he seemed to stumble more often than a simulation of old age could excuse.

She had seen him, of course. The throwing of that rose to Roger was coldly calculated; it was a sign to him that she had received his message, understood it, and scorned it. Well, let it be so. He had had no solid food that day; his head ached and buzzed, and often dizziness overcame him so that he stumbled. But it would not be for long.

The single interval which Valentine had decreed for the play was over, and Act Four was about to begin. Gonzalo was not wanted in Act Four. Gonzalo was not wanted anywhere, it appeared. Very well. When you weren't wanted there was only one thing to do, and that was to get out.

Hector hurried quietly along the path to The Shed. Good, it was empty. He did not need long. No necessity to rule his black book into *Pro* and *Contra*. He knew exactly what he wanted to do, and it would not take much time to do it.

Would she be sorry? Would she ever know? There were his roses, and their message, to speak for him. Perhaps she would be sorry that she had not accepted the help which he had offered. Would she ever know that behind that offer of help there lay a great love, everything that a man of forty, who had made his own way in the world and risen in a difficult profession, could offer? Surely she would realize it. And, realizing it, would she not sicken of the hateful Roger, reject him and live a good life – a life beautiful and sad – ever after? Or might it not be that in the course of time she would meet some kind and understanding man whom she would marry, and with whom she would bring up a family in which the name of Hector Mackilwraith would be honoured? Undoubtedly that would be it. Indeed, in this terrible hour he was certainly gifted with prophecy; that *was* what would happen. But as every good thing must spring from sacrifice and atonement, he must not falter now.

Plenty of cord here; good, heavy stuff; a superior sort of sashcord. He unfastened one of the many ropes which controlled the glasswork in the roof of The Shed, and sought to tie a noose in it. But one cannot tie a good noose without some training and previous experience, and after ten minutes all that Hector had achieved was a loop, contrived with clumsy granny-knots. The knot which his purpose demanded had, he had been told, thirteen turns in it; however, this would serve. He was ready. After a few unsuccessful throws he managed to get the noose over one of the iron supports in the ceiling, and it hung above some boxes which were hidden behind a screen. Good. He estimated the drop at about eight feet; in that, at least, he could be sure of accuracy.

Before climbing on the boxes he looked at himself in one of the make-up mirrors. His face was hideous with Auntie Puss's handiwork, and his hair was streaked with yellow paint. He tore off the false beard, and mopped his face with a towel. He was calm now, though he felt deathly ill.

With the aid of a chair he climbed upon the boxes, and settled the noose about his neck.

Well, this was it. But before he left the world forever, should he not say some word of committal? It was many years since he had prayed, but he had always thought of himself as a religious sort of man, and he believed firmly in God. Would God understand this sudden abandonment of a decreed existence? Yes, undoubtedly Hector's God would understand Hector; there would be no TOSASM scribbled across his final record. God would know that it was an atonement, a sacrifice that another might be cleansed, indeed the only way to save the soul of Griselda Webster. God would know why he had done it.

Nevertheless, something seemed to be called for. He groped in his mind for prayer, but nothing came. A favourite phrase of his father's, used often when the Reverend John was gravelled for lack of matter in an extemporary prayer, came back to him. 'O Lord, take Thou a live coal from off Thine altar and touch our lips.' Yes. Then what? By now Hector was weeping desperately, and all that he could think of was 'O God, here I come!' It seemed unworthy of the moment, but it was the best he could do.

Sobbing, hardly conscious, Hector leaped from his platform into the unknown. There was a jerk, a crash, a sound of artillery fire, and oblivion.

[EIGHT]

Into Hector's consciousness swam a fearful eye, a blue iris rolling upon what might have been a mound of bloodshot blancmange. Sometimes it was horribly clear; sometimes it retreated into nauseating deliquescence. A huge, accusing eye, set, no doubt, in the Head of the Supreme Being. The eye seemed to melt, growing larger as it did so; then it suddenly became very clear again, and from far away he heard a voice.

'Whatever made you do such a wicked thing?'

At the sound he experienced that sensation of falling swiftly which is so common after the first few minutes of sleep. Sensations rushed upon him. He was wet and miserable; his head ached dreadfully; he had a pain in his neck; he was cold. And there, kneeling beside him on the floor of The Shed, was Auntie Puss, staring intently into his face through her magnifying glass.

'You poor, wretched, sinful man,' she said. 'Are you all right?'

'My head aches,' he said. And immediately: 'My throat hurts.'

'You may think yourself lucky that your head is still on your shoulders,' said Auntie Puss. 'Can you get up?'

Hector tried to raise himself, but sank back dizzily, squelching in a pool of whatever it was he was lying in.

'Is it blood?' he asked, his eyes closed.

'No; I presume it is whatever you were drinking before you attempted this rash act. You appear to have had plenty of it, I must say.'

Under this unjust accusation Hector stirred a little, and the liquid foamed and seethed all about him.

'I must get help,' said Auntie Puss, and added unnecessarily, 'you stay where you are.'

She went out, locked the door of The Shed and carried away the key in her pocket. Backstage she found Valentine, and plucked her by the sleeve. Then she whispered in her ear.

'You must come with me at once. Most important.'

But Valentine was in an extremely bad temper. Professor Vambrace, disregarding her opinion in the matter, had sneaked a stem of seven grapes upon the stage, and had attempted to eat them during the most famous speech in the play. It is not simple to eat seven grapes while speaking thirteen lines. Three grapes had undone him, and five made him sound like a man talking under water; he had desperately gulped his mouthful, and pushed in the last two grapes, but he was badly rattled by his experience, and as he tossed away the empty stem – the crown of his ingenious bit of byplay – a loud and prolonged belch had burst from the depths of his beard. There had been laughter and some ironical applause. Valentine was waiting for the Professor to come off the stage. She had something to say to him.

Auntie Puss tugged at her sleeve again, and drew Valentine down so that she might whisper in her ear. A moment later they were hurrying toward The Shed.

Valentine was, as Cobbler had said, a thorough professional, and her first remarks to Hector proved it.

'What the hell do you mean by trying to kill yourself in the middle of a performance?' said she. 'Before a performance, perhaps: after a performance, possibly. But what in the name of common sense possessed you to do it while you still have an entrance to make? Do you realize that there are eight hundred and thirty-two people out there, of whom seven hundred and ninety have paid admission, whose pleasure you have imperilled? Do you realize that you have very nearly ruined the effect of seven weeks' rehearsal? Get up at once, and pull yourself together.'

Hector was startled by this display of heartlessness and bad temper, and he tried to do as he was told. But he could not rise beyond a kneeling posture, and fell down again. Valentine was contrite at once.

'I'm sorry, Mr Mackilwraith, but I'm terribly angry at that fool of a Vambrace, and I'm taking it out on you. What's the matter? Do you feel very dreadful? What can I get for you?'

The kindness in her voice was too much for Hector, and he sobbed.

'What made you do it? Can you tell me? I'll help you if I can.'

He tried to speak, but the only word he could say was 'Griselda', and then he wept again, hiding his face in his arm.

That was enough for Valentine, however. So the poor, silly man loved Griselda Webster, and it had brought him to this! There he lay, in a pale frothing liquid which she had, for a dreadful moment, believed to be some eccentric vital fluid of his own, but which issued from a case of broken bottles which lay near him. He was drenched, his face was smeared with makeup, and there was yellow paint in his hair. All pity for him, she dragged him to drier ground, and sat upon the floor, with his head in her lap. She wiped his face with a handkerchief.

'Poor Hector,' said she; 'was it very bad?'

He nodded, and she could feel his body relax a little. Her comfort had started him back on the road to self-possession. It was for the best part wordless comfort – the warm, cherishing, unquestioning feminine sympathy which he had not known (and then, how meagrely) since his childhood – which Valentine gave him, but it drew him gently back from Death and the longing for Death. And so they sat for perhaps ten minutes, during which she said little, and he said nothing, but his face, which had been shapeless and hideous with grief, began to take on a more human look. His spirit was returning.

Larry's voice boomed from the loud-speaker: 'Everybody for Act Five please. Act Five in three minutes. Has anybody seen Gonzalo? Act Five.'

All the healing stillness left Valentine in an instant. 'Oh, God!' she cried; 'what do I do now?'

But almost as she spoke she had leaped to her feet. Hector's beard was upon the table; she quickly dabbed her face with spirit gum and fastened it on. He had removed his cloak and cap before he had climbed upon the boxes. She put them upon herself. 'If Sybil Thorndike could play Lear, I don't see why I can't play Gonzalo,' she said to Hector, and in her voice the actress had wholly supplanted the divinely tender creature who had seemed to coax him back from the realm of the dead. 'Stay here; I'll be back as soon as I can.'

Transformed into a somewhat odd old gentleman, she rushed through the door. Auntie Puss was keeping faithful guard there.

'Is he all right?'

'He will be, Miss Pottinger. Don't let anybody in.'

'You may rely on me.'

'I'm sure I may.'

'Did he say anything to you about why he tried it?'

'Yes. To you, too?'

'He was unconscious, but he mentioned a name, more than once.'

'We'd better keep that quiet, don't you think?'

'Miss Rich, nothing could make me divulge it.'

Auntie Puss had need of all the resolution which an old-fashioned upbringing had given her, in order to keep her word. As soon as Valentine appeared upon the stage as Gonzalo, the whole cast seemed to know, magically, that Mackilwraith was ill, that there was some mystery about his illness, and that Auntie Puss had the key to the mystery. The audience suspected nothing, for they had paid little heed to Gonzalo before, and idly noted that he appeared to have come to life in the last act, although he played most of it with his back to them. But the audience did know that Roscoe Forrester had beckoned Dr Bliss from his seat, and that Dr Bliss had tiptoed out with that stealth peculiar to doctors, which is so much more noticeable than a frank exit. The play came to its end, and the cast was recalled for six bows, but Valentine did not remain with them. She ran at once to The Shed and was locked within with Hector and the doctor, while Auntie Puss stood guard at the door, and refused to say anything to anybody.

The general opinion was that Hector had had a fit. Some said it was apoplexy; others said it was heart. Geordie Shortreed, for no reason that anybody could discover, thought that it was a scandal of some kind; those quiet ones were the worst, he said with relish; perhaps it was something about a boy. The cast would not go to their dressing-rooms and change; they stood about behind the stage, chattering and gossiping and speculating, big with the mystery of The Shed. There are those, however, who had other concerns. Nellie Forrester, near to tears, rushed to Professor Vambrace.

'Oh Walter, wasn't it awful?'

'Distressing, certainly, but it will be all right tomorrow night.'

'But how can it be?'

'I shall rehearse it all day tomorrow.'

'What are you talking about?'

'My business with the seven grapes: I shouldn't have called it "awful", myself. I'm sure the audience didn't notice. It just needs touching up.'

'I don't know what you mean.'

'Indeed? I suppose you are engrossed in this nonsense about Mackilwraith.'

'I don't know anything about him. But didn't you see her go?'

'Who?'

'Mrs Caesar Augustus Conquergood. She left before the beginning of the fifth act. I felt so humiliated.'

'Probably she found the night air a little chilly. But don't be distressed; there are still four performances. I'll buy a pound of grapes tomorrow and make Pearl work with me all afternoon. I shall have my business with the grapes perfect by tomorrow night.'

'I don't think it was cold at all. She left because she was bored. I just knew it. Do you suppose we ought to have put her name on the programme in bigger type? She was as big as Val and bigger than Shakespeare. It was a mistake ever to do this play out of doors. I'll never have anything to do with a Pastoral again.'

It was impossible to keep everyone in the dark. When Dr Bliss had assured himself that there was nothing wrong with Hector except shock, hunger, and a wetting, he suggested that he be moved to a place where he might rest, and that meant that Mr Webster had to be let into part of the secret. Both guestrooms at St Agnes' were occupied, one by the Nymphs and the other by the girls who had speaking parts in the play, for at the last minute Griselda had decided that it would be inhospitable to make the girls use makeshift dressing rooms. Mr Webster was a humane man, but something within him powerfully resisted the idea that an unsuccessful suicide should curl up in his bed, and therefore he led the way to his daughter Griselda's pretty room, and Roscoe and Dr Bliss helped the feeble Hector to slip off his wet clothes, put on a pair of Mr Webster's pyjamas, and crawl into the bed there. As they passed the Nymphs' dressing room the door was opened a crack, and a bright eye appeared for a moment, and within a few minutes the Nymphs, and the girls in the other dressing room, and all their friends, knew that Hector Mackilwraith had attempted to drown himself, and had been taken upstairs in St Agnes', soaking wet.

Fortunately The Shed had not been used as a dressing room for the men of the cast, but only as a makeup room and a greenroom. But even so, there were a variety of personal articles in it which had to be restored to their owners, and it was not Valentine's wish to have everyone snooping around The Shed, guessing at what happened. Therefore she sought out Solly and Cobbler, told them that she wanted to keep The Shed closed, and asked them to see that the men's property was taken back to the men's dressing room, which was in the basement of the house. They went to The Shed and found the way barred by Auntie Puss.

'No one may go in here at present,' said she.

'But Miss Pottinger,' said Solly, 'we have special orders from Miss Rich.'

'Perhaps, then, Miss Rich will be good enough to come here and tell me so.'

'My dear lady,' said Cobbler; 'it is needless to dissemble; we are privy to the dark secret of The Shed. We are going in to mop up the blood.'

'I don't understand what you are talking about,' said Auntie Puss.

'It's really quite all right,' said Solly; 'we know what happened.'

'If that is so, you have no right to speak of it in that flippant tone.'

'And why not, if I may ask?' said Cobbler, argumentatively. 'Why should we go all solemn because Mackilwraith has hashed up his attempt at suicide?'

'Hush!' said Auntie Puss, fiercely. 'Don't you dare to use that word.'

'It's the right word, isn't it?'

'It will provoke a scandal if it gets around. Do you want to ruin the man's life?'

'He's just done his best to ruin it himself.'

'That has nothing to do with it. He has been spared, doubtless for some purpose beyond our understanding. If you so much as hint at it again, Mr Cobbler, I'll speak to the Dean about you, and you will have to find yourself another position.'

'Blackmail!' said Cobbler.

'Call it what you like,' said Auntie Puss. 'This man deserves his chance, and I shall do whatever I can to see that he gets it. I do not approve of the modern custom of babbling disgraceful secrets to anybody and everybody. I do not know Mr Mackilwraith well, and what I do know about him I do not care for, but I will not be a party to his ruin. Do you understand me, Mr Cobbler?'

'I hear you, Miss Pottinger, but I shall never understand you. The world is full of people who have tried to kill themselves, or who have at least thought about it. It's as natural as falling in love or getting one's heart broken. I don't see what's so disgraceful about it. It's the first interesting thing Mackilwraith has ever done, so far as I know.'

Valentine appeared around the corner of the house.

'Thank you so much, Miss Pottinger,' said she. 'Will you let me have the key now? Mr Webster is offering some refreshment in his library. Perhaps you had better have a hot drink. You've been wonderful, keeping watch for so long.'

'I am glad to do whatever I can,' said Auntie Puss, who had been shivering a little in the night air. 'And I advise you to remember, Mr Cobbler, that I can do more.' She rattled off toward the house, her head erect.

'My respect for Mackilwraith was never very high, and it is dropping every minute,' said Solly, as they went into The Shed. 'Can you imagine a man of any gumption at all thinking that he could hang himself with a rotten old rope like that? I'll bet it's fifty years old. What a boob.'

'I don't suppose he thought about it very clearly,' said Valentine.

'Oh yes he did,' said Cobbler. 'He probably imagined he was wrapped up in his sorrows, but we all have keener perception than we know. The superficial Mackilwraith, the despairing lover, thought the rope would do, but the true, essential, deep-down Mackilwraith knew damn well that it wouldn't. You don't play safe for forty years and then cut loose. Our Hector was looking for pity, not death.'

'Why do you call him the despairing lover?' asked Valentine, who had thought that this was a secret between herself and Auntie Puss.

'Because it's obvious that's why he did it. He's been mooning after the Impatient Griselda for weeks. Surely you noticed? Anyway, he told me so – or as good as admitted it – at that awful brawl of yours, Bridgetower. I had a notion that he'd do something silly, though I never thought it would be anything as silly as this.'

'Well, do keep it quiet, won't you, Humphrey,' said Valentine. 'We don't want to make trouble for him – more trouble than he has now, that's to say.'

'I don't know why everybody imagines that I am going to run around town blatting everything I know. That old poll-parrot at the door said exactly the same thing to me, though much less nicely. I'm not going to blab. On the honour of a Fellow of the Royal College of Organists. But I don't see why I can't discuss it with you two; you know all about it anyway.'

'It would be rather hard on Griselda. People might think she had driven him to it.'

'That would merely enhance her reputation as a charmer. But really I don't suppose she had anything to do with it.'

'What, then?' asked Solly.

'She was just a hook on which Mackilwraith hung a middle-aged man's nerve-storm. Do you know what I think ails Mackilwraith? Male menopause. This is his last fling at romance before he goes out of business entirely as a male creature.'

'He can't be much over forty,' said Valentine.

'Spiritually – if one may use the word of Hector – he's been seventy for years. No, it's the male climacteric. The last gutterings of the candle – the gurgle of the last pint of suds in the drain.'

'Well, I don't agree,' said Solly. 'I think it's the logical outcome of his education and the sort of life he has led. He's vulgar. I don't mean just that he wears awful suits and probably eats awful food: I mean that he has a crass soul. He thinks that when his belly is full and his job safe, he's got the world by the tail. He has never found out anything about himself, so how can he ever know anything about other people? The condition of a vulgarian is that he never expects anything good or bad that happens to him to be the result of his own personality; he always thinks it's Fate, especially if it's bad. The only people who make any sense in the world are those who know that whatever happens to them has its roots in what they are.'

'I think you are both hard on him,' said Valentine. 'When I found him he was really very touching. You're both away off the track.'

'Dear Val,' said Solly; 'if I were in a mess like that I would pray to be found by somebody like you. Somebody that pities, and doesn't natter and theorize.'

'I'm happy to theorize,' said Cobbler; 'I keep my feelings for musical purposes.'

'I'm going to see if I can get Griselda to talk to him for a little,' said Valentine.

'That's brilliant,' said Solly; 'maybe that will put him on his feet.'

'A wonderful idea, but do you think they should be alone together?' said Cobbler. 'I mean, there ought to be somebody there, just to see that he doesn't get maudlin and embarrass the girl. I'd be happy to do it, if nobody else wants to.'

'You're aching to snoop,' said Valentine.

'Of course I am. Curiosity is the mainspring of my life. If I weren't curious I'd probably be an egocentric pinhead like Mackilwraith.'

The door of The Shed opened, and Freddy came in, dressed in slacks and a shirt, followed by Tom.

'We came to clean up,' said Freddy. 'I suppose you'll want this room again tomorrow night?'

'Tomorrow afternoon,' said Valentine. 'Hadn't you heard that we are doing a special matinee for school children?'

'A brutish auditory, at half-price, but we artists must bear it in the sacred name of education,' interjected Cobbler.

'No; I hadn't heard a thing about it,' said Freddy.

'Heavens, I thought I had told all the cast. It was a last-minute decision of Nellie's; it appears that a few hundred kids are still confined to school, and they can all be roped in at fifty cents a head. I must go at once and make sure everybody knows,' said Valentine, and ran out of The Shed.

'We'll help you clear things away,' said Solly.

'Oh don't bother. Daddy's giving drinks to a few favoured souls in the library. I'm sure you would count as favoured souls if you went along.'

'We'll go when we've helped you,' said Cobbler. 'I'm anxious to know what this stuff is that Mackilwraith knocked over. It has a vinous smell. In fact, Roscoe told me that Mackilwraith smelt like a big pickle as he was hoisting him up your stairs.'

'That's my champagne cider,' said Freddy, sadly. 'Tom hid it away so nicely. It looks as though the old fool had contrived to break every bottle, and even at that he couldn't finish himself off.'

'Not every bottle,' said Cobbler. 'Here are a couple with the corks in under this table. Shall we try it?'

'Please do,' said Freddy. 'There's not much point in keeping two. But we'll have to drink out of the necks, turn about.' Two corks popped merrily, and they sat down to sample Freddy's vintage.

'Not bad,' said Tom.

'Thanks, Tom, you're a big encouragement to me,' said Freddy. 'You know, Tom and I have figured out why Mackilwraith tried to kill himself.'

'How did you learn that?'

'Oh, everybody knows it, except Nellie and Walter Vambrace and a few of the stupider sort.'

'Well, why did he do it?' said Cobbler.

'Cheap religion,' said Freddy.

'The way we see it, sir,' said Tom, after taking a second long draught of the champagne cider, 'is like this. Too many people today are like this fellow Mackilwraith. They don't believe, and they haven't got the strength of mind to disbelieve. They won't get rid of religion, and they won't go after a religion that means anything. They just mess with religion. Now if this fellow Mackilwraith had been a believer – and I don't mind saying that I'm thinking of the C. of E. – he would have known that suicide is a sin, and his belief would have held him up in his trouble. And if he'd been an unbeliever he'd either have had too much guts to do it, or guts enough to finish it off proper. See?'

'If he'd been a strong believer or a strong unbeliever he wouldn't have been pushed off his trolley just because he couldn't get to first base with Gristle,' said Freddy. 'Do you know, Tom, this isn't bad at all; just as soon as the apples come in, I'm going to get busy on a bigger and better batch.'

'Not bad,' said Cobbler, 'but not champagne. Just good cider with ideas above its station.'

'I know,' said Freddy, a little sadly, 'but you can't make something wonderful unless you start with the right stuff.'

'Like making a romantic lover out of Hector Mackilwraith,' said Solly.

The second bottle clutched in his hand, Cobbler launched into a lecture on religion, speaking as one who had been in the service of Holy Church since his ninth year.

Hector was not quite asleep. He lay happily in the bed, the softest he had ever known, with a hot-water bottle at his feet, and a cup of beef-tea and brandy working magically in his stomach. He had no thoughts beyond the moment, and a general thankfulness that he was not dead.

Outside the door someone seemed to be moving, very quietly, as though standing first upon one foot and then the other. The room was wonderfully peaceful in the light of a single lamp, and Hector could not summon up enough interest even to wonder who it might be. But at last the door opened, and Griselda came in, wearing her dressing gown.

'Are you asleep?'

'No.'

'Valentine said she thought I'd better come and say good-night.'

She stood by the foot of the bed, saying nothing, looking lovelier than Hector had ever seen her. Now, mysteriously, he was no longer afraid of her.

'I'm glad you came.'

'Thanks. Sorry you're feeling mouldy.'

'I'm all right.'

'The doctor says you can't go home tonight, of course.'

'I hope I'm not putting anyone out of this bed.'

'Oh that's all right; I can sleep in one of the other rooms.'

'It's yours?'

A dark flush spread over Hector's face. He was in Griselda's bed! But he was too tired, too blissfully at rest, to be deeply embarrassed. Griselda seemed to be trying to say something; she was blushing, and dug into the carpet with one foot. For the first time Hector saw that she was not much more than a child. At last she spoke.

'You shouldn't have done it, you know.'

'No, I shouldn't.'

'You must promise not to do it again.'

'I won't.'

Another pause, and Griselda was now very red. She suddenly sat down on the bed and took his hand.

'I'd feel dreadful if you did, you know. Because of me.'

So she knew. Well, he didn't care. He was too happy.

'What made you think it would help?'

'I can't really remember, now.'

She said no more. He felt that he must say something.

'Griselda.'

'Yes?'

'You're too good for Tasset. Don't let him spoil you.'

'I don't care for him at all. Did you think I did?'

'Yes.'

'And it was because of that?'

'Yes.'

'I never knew that you cared about me at all.'

'I did.'

'But you don't any more?'

'Not the same way; now that I know you're safe.'

'What are you going to do?'

'I'm going away from Salterton. I've had an offer of a job in the Department. A very good job, really; quite a step up.'

'How wonderful.'

Another pause. At last Griselda spoke.

'I'd better go now. But I don't want you to think I don't know what a lot of trouble I've made for you.'

'It was nothing.'

'But I couldn't know, you see.'

'Of course not. You couldn't know.'

'And it wouldn't really have done, would it?'

'No: I see that now. It wouldn't have done at all.'

'Well, good-night, Mr Mackilwraith.'

Hector looked up into her serious face, and for the first time in weeks, he laughed. After a puzzled moment, Griselda smiled.

'Good-night, Hector.'

She leaned forward as she had done in that first dream, and kissed him. Then she turned out the lamp, and closed the door behind her.

Hector slept.

Leaven of Malice

*

Grant us to put away the
leaven of malice and wickedness
that we may alway serve Thee
in pureness of living and truth

THE PRAYER BOOK

[ONE]

It was on the 31st of October that the following announcement appeared under 'Engagements', in the Salterton *Evening Bellman*:

Professor and Mrs Walter Vambrace are pleased to announce the engagement of their daughter, Pearl Veronica, to Solomon Bridgetower, Esq., son of Mrs Bridgetower and the late Professor Solomon Bridgetower of this city. Marriage to take place in St Nicholas' Cathedral at eleven o'clock a.m., November 31st.

Few of the newspaper's readers found anything extraordinary about this intimation, or attached any significance to the fact that it was made on Hallowe'en.

When fortune decides to afflict a good man and rob him of his peace, she often chooses a fine day to begin.

The 1st of November was a beautiful day, and the sun shone with a noble autumn glory as Gloster Ridley, editor of *The Bellman*, walked through the park to his morning's work. The leaves rustled about his feet and he kicked them with pleasure. It was like tramping through some flaky breakfast food, he thought, and smiled at the unromantic fancy. That was not in the least what his colleague Mr Shillito would think about autumn leaves. He recalled what Mr Shillito had written yesterday on the subject of Hallowe'en – which Mr Shillito had managed five times to call All Hallows' Eve and twice 'this unhallowed Eve' – and his face darkened; the Old Mess had been at his most flowery and most drivelling. But Ridley quickly banished Mr Shillito from his mind; that was a problem to be dealt with later in the day. Meanwhile, his walk to his office was his own, for his own agreeable musings. His day had begun well; Constant Reader had prepared an excellent breakfast for him, and the hateful Blubadub, though faintly audible in the kitchen, had kept out his sight. He sniffed the delightfully cool and smoky autumn air. The day stretched before him, full of promise.

In less than a week he would be fifty. Middle-aged, unquestionably, but how much better he felt than ever in his youth! From his seventeenth year until quite recently, Anxiety had ridden him with whip and spur, and only when well past forty had he gained any hope of unseating her. But today . . . ! His bosom's lord, he told himself, sat lightly in his throne. Who said that? Romeo. Pooh, Romeo knew nothing about the quiet, well-controlled self-satisfaction of a man who might well, before he was fifty-one, be a Doctor of Civil Law.

To be Doctor Ridley! He would not, of course, insist upon the title, but it would be his, and if he should ever chance to be introduced to a new acquaintance as Mister, there would almost certainly be someone at hand to say, probably with a pleasant laugh, 'I think it should be Doctor Ridley, shouldn't it?' Not that he attached undue importance to such distinctions; he knew precisely how matters stood. After what he had done for Waverley University they must reward him with a substantial fee or give him an honorary doctorate. Waverley, like all Canadian universities, was perpetually short of money, whereas its store of doctorates was inexhaustible. They would not even have to give him a gown, for that glorious adornment would be returnable immediately after the degree ceremony. It would be a doctorate, certainly, and he would value it. It was a symbol of security and success, and it would be another weapon with which to set his old enemy, Anxiety, at bay. He would feel himself well rewarded when he was Doctor Ridley.

He had fairly earned it. When it had occurred to some of the Governors of the University two years ago that Waverley ought to establish a course in journalism, it had been to him that they turned for advice. When the decision was taken to make plans for such a course, he had been the only person not directly associated with the University to sit upon the committee; tactfully and unobtrusively, he had guided it. He had listened, without visible emotion, to the opinions of professors upon the Press and upon the duty which some of them believed they owed to society to reform the Press. He had discussed without mirth or irony their notions of the training which would produce a good newspaperman. He had counselled against foolish spending, and he had fought tirelessly for spending which he believed to be necessary. Little by little his academic colleagues on the committee had recognized that he knew what he was talking about.

He had triumphed in persuading them that their course should occupy three years instead of two. His had been the principal voice in planning the course, and his would certainly be the principal voice in hiring the staff. Next autumn the course would be included in the Waverley syllabus, and now his work was almost done.

One task still lay before him, and it was a pleasant one. He was to deliver the first of the Wadsworth Lectures for the current academic year. These public lectures, founded twenty years before to inform the university opinion on matters of public importance, were to be devoted this year to 'The Press and The People'. A Cabinet Minister would speak, and the United Kingdom High Commissioner; a celebrated philosopher and an almost equally celebrated psychologist were also to give their views. But the first of the five lectures would be given by himself, Gloster Ridley, editor of the Salterton *Evening Bellman*, and he was determined that it should be the best of the lot. For, after all, he knew at first hand what a newspaper was, and the other lecturers did not. And it was widely admitted that under his guidance *The Bellman* was a very good paper.

Yes, he thought, he had a shrewd idea what the Press was. Not a cheap Press, nor yet the pipedream Press that the university reformers had talked about at those early meetings. And he knew about the People, too, for he was one of them. He had had no university education. That was one of the reasons why it would fall so sweetly upon his ear to be spoken of as Doctor Ridley.

Oh, yes, he would tell them about the Press and the People. The Press, he would explain, belonged to the People – to all of the People, whether their tastes and needs were common or uncommon. He would speak amusingly, but there would be plenty in his lecture for them to chew on. He would begin with a quotation from Shakespeare, from *All's Well that Ends Well*; a majority of his listeners, even in a university audience, would not have read the play, but he would remind them that people outside university halls could be well-read. Of a newspaper he would quote, 'It is like a barber's chair that fits all buttocks; the pin-buttock, the quatch-buttock, the brawn buttock, or any buttock'. And then he would develop his theme, which was that in any issue of a good daily paper every reader, gentle or simple, liberally educated or barely able to read, should find not only the news of the day but something which was, in a broad sense, of special concern to himself.

It would be a good lecture. Possibly his publisher would have it reprinted in pamphlet form, and distribute it widely to other papers. Without vulgar hinting, he thought he could insinuate that idea into his publisher's mind.

Musing pleasantly on these things, he reached the newspaper building.

He climbed the stairs to his second-floor office somewhat furtively, for he did not want to meet Mr Shillito and exchange greetings with him. He was determined to do nothing which might appear two-faced, and Mr Shillito's greetings were of so courtly and old-world a nature that he was often enticed into a geniality of which he was afterward ashamed. He must not feed the Old Mess sugar from his hand, while concealing the sword behind his back. But his path was clear, and he slipped into his office unseen by anyone but Miss Green, his secretary. She followed him through the door.

'No personal mail this morning, Mr Ridley. Just the usual. And the switchboard says somebody called you before nine, but wouldn't leave their name.'

The usual was neatly marshalled on his desk. Miss Green had been solicitous about the morning's letters since the day, more than three days ago, when somebody had sent him a dead rat, wrapped as a gift, with a card explaining that this was a comment upon *The Bellman*'s stand on a matter of public controversy. She had failed, since then, to intercept an envelope filled with used toilet paper (a political innuendo) but in general her monitorship was good. There were ten Letters to the Editor, and he took them up without curiosity, and with a thick black pencil ready in his hand.

Two, from 'Fair Play' and 'Indignant', took the Salterton City Council to task, the former for failing to re-surface the street on which he lived, and the latter for proposing to pave a street on which he owned property, thereby raising the rates. Both writers had allowed anonymity to go to their heads, and both had added personal notes requesting that their true names be withheld, as they feared reprisals of an unspecified nature. From 'Fair Play's' letter Ridley deleted several sentences, and changed the word 'shabby' to 'ill-advised'. 'Indignant' required more time, as the writer had not used enough verbs to make his meaning clear, and had apparently punctuated his letter after writing it, on some generous but poorly conceived principle of his own.

The third letter was so badly written that even his accustomed eye could make very little of it, but it appeared to be from an aggrieved citizen whose neighbour spitefully threw garbage into his back yard. Other iniquities of the neighbour were rehearsed, but Ridley marked the letter for Miss Green's attention; she would return it with the usual note declining to publish libellous material.

The next three letters were legible, grammatical and reasonable, and dealt with a scheme to create a traffic circle at a principal intersection of the city. They were quickly given headings and marked for the printer.

The seventh letter urged that a hockey coach who had trained some little boys the winter before be prevented, by force if necessary, from training them in the winter to come. He was, it appeared, a monster and a heretic whose influence would prove the ruin of hockey tactics and the downfall of that sport in Canada. It was signed with a bold signature and a street address, but the editor's eye was not deceived. He consulted the Salterton *City Directory* and found, as he had suspected, that there was no such number as 183 Maple Street, and no such person as Arthur C. Brown. With a sigh for the duplicity of mankind, he threw the letter into the wastepaper basket. He was a little pleased, also, that the intuition which suggested to him that a signature was a fake was in good working order.

The eighth letter was from a farmer who charged the Salterton Exhibition Committee with great unfairness and some measure of dishonesty in the matter of awarding prizes in the Pullet sub-section of the Poultry Division of the Livestock Competition at the fall fair. He was aware, he said, that the fair had taken place seven weeks ago, but it had taken him a little time to get around to writing his letter. It went into the waste basket.

The ninth letter caused Ridley both surprise and annoyance. It read:

Sir:

Warm congratulations on the editorial headed 'Whither The Toothpick' which appeared in your edition of 28/x. It is such delightful bits of whimsy as this which raise the tone of *The Bellman* above that of any other paper which comes to my notice and give it a literary grace which is doubly distinguished in a world where style is rapidly becoming a thing of the past. This little gem joins many another in my scrapbook. Happy the city which can boast a *Bellman*! Happy the *Bellman* which boasts a writer who can produce the felicitous 'Toothpick'.

Yours, etc.

ELDON BUMFORD

No error about that signature; old Bumford, at eighty-four, was reversing the usual tendency of old men to damn everything, and was loud in his praise of virtually everything. No reason not to publish it. Dead certainty that if it did not appear within a day or two old Bumford would be on the telephone, or worse still, in the chair opposite his desk, asking why. And yet it was out of the question that the thing should be published. Ridley laid it aside for later consideration.

The tenth letter was in a well-known hand, in green ink. Letters in that hand, and in that ink, appeared on Ridley's desk every two weeks, and their message was always the same: the world had forgotten God. Sometimes it showed this forgetfulness by permitting children to read the comic strips; sometimes drink – invariably referred to as 'beverage alcohol' – was the villain; sometimes it was the decline in church attendance which especially afflicted the writer; in winter the iniquity of ski-trains, which travelled during church hours and bore young people beyond the sound of church bells, was complained of; in summer it was the whoredom of two-piece bathing suits, and shorts which revealed girls' legs, which was consuming society. The writer was able to support all her arguments by copious quotations from Holy Writ, and she did so; now and then she related a modern enormity to one of the monsters in Revelation. The letter at hand urged that the Prime Minister be advised to declare November 11th a National Day of Prayer, in which, by an act of mass repentance, Canada might be cleansed of her wrong-doings, and at the end of which her iniquity might be pardoned. The letter was marked 'Urgent – Print this At Once'. Wearily, Ridley laid it aside. This was, perhaps, the voice of the people, and the voice of the people, no editor is ever permitted to forget, is the voice of God. It was a pity, he reflected, that God's utterances needed such a lot of editorial revision.

Disposing of the remainder of the morning's mail was easy. Ridley ran his fingers quickly through it: propaganda, some of it expert and much of it amateurish, from a dozen bureaux maintained by a dozen foreign Governments. *The Bellman* was invited to espouse two opposed causes in India; it was offered a ringing denunciation of the partition of Ireland; it was urged to celebrate the 250th anniversary of a French poet whom Ridley could not recall having heard of; it was reminded of seven quaint celebrations which would take place in Britain during November.

There were four long mimeographed statements from four trades unions, setting forth extremely complex grievances which the Government was admonished to settle at once. There was a pamphlet from a society which wanted to reform the calendar and had received the permission of Ecuador, Liberia, Iceland and the Latvian Government-in-exile to go ahead and do it. There was a mass of material from United Nations. There were five printed communications of varying length from religious and charitable societies. There was something stamped 'Newsflash' in red ink, advertising a new oil well in terms which were not intended to sound like advertisement. A bluebook, to which was attached the visiting card of a Cabinet Minister, presented a mass of valuable statistics, eighteen months out of date. Four packages offered *The Bellman* new comic strips of unparalleled funniness, which Ridley read through with undisturbed gravity.

He threw the whole lot into the waste basket, filling it almost to the brim.

There was a rich, rumbling sound outside his door, a voice which said, 'Ah, Miss Green, as charming as ever, I see. Nobody with the Chief, I presume?' and the door opened, admitting Mr Swithin Shillito.

Mr Shillito was seventy-eight years old, and frequently put people into a position where they had to tell him that he did not look it. His white hair, parted in the middle, swept back in two thick waves. His white moustache was enormous, and was shaped like the horns of a ram. Lesser moustaches, equally white, thick and sweeping, served him for eyebrows. His very large, handsome head appeared to be attached to his small, meagre body by a high stiff collar and a carefully knotted tie, in which a nugget of gold served as a pin. On his waistcoat hung a watch-chain with huge links, from one of which depended an elk's tooth, mounted in gold. Other interesting elements in his dress were brightly shined high boots, an alpaca working coat, and wicker cuffguards on his sleeves. Gold pince-nez hung from a little reel on his waistcoat, ready to be hauled out and nipped on his large nose when needed. He carried some papers in his hand.

'Nothing strange or startling this morning, Chief,' said he, advancing with a jaunty step. 'I thought I'd do my stint a little early. Nothing heavy: just one or two odds and ends that may prove amusing, and fill up a corner here and there. I wanted to get my day clear, in order to do some digging. I tell these young chaps in the news room, "Dig, dig, it's the secret of the Newspaper Game. I'm seventy-eight and still digging," I say. Some of them won't believe it. You'll do the leader yourself, I suppose?'

'Yes Mr Shillito,' said Ridley. 'I have two or three things I want to write about today.'

'And I dare swear you have them written in your head at this moment,' said Mr Shillito, wagging his own head in histrionic admiration. 'Plan, plan; it's the only way to get anything done on a newspaper. They won't believe it, the young chaps won't, but it's the gospel truth.'

'I have been reading one or two reports on the seaway scheme which suggested some ideas to me.'

'Ah, that's it! Read, read. Dig, dig. Plan, plan. That's what takes a journalist to the top. But the young chaps won't listen. Time will weed 'em out. The readers, the diggers, the planners will shoot to the top and the rest – well, we know what happens to them. Do you want to cast your eye over those things while I wait?'

I'm damned if I do, thought Ridley. Mr Shillito loved to watch people reading what he had written, and as he did so he would smile, grunt appreciatively, nod and in other ways indicate enjoyment and admiration until all but the strongest were forced by a kind of spiritual pressure to follow his lead. In his way, the old fellow was a bully; he was so keen in his appreciation of himself and his work that not to join him became a form of discourtesy.

'I am rather busy, at present,' said Ridley. 'I'll read them later.'

'Ah, you don't have to tell me how busy you are,' said Mr Shillito; 'I know, perhaps better than anyone, what the pressure is in your job. But if I may I'll drop in again later in the morning, when you've had time to read those. I've noticed that a few of my things haven't appeared in print yet, though you've had them in hand for a fortnight or more. Now, Chief, you know me. I'm the oldest man on the staff, perhaps the oldest working journalist in the country. If there's any falling-off, any hint of weariness in my stuff, you've only to tell me. I know I'm not immortal. The old clock must run down some day, though I must say I feel in wonderful form at present. But be frank. Am I getting too old for my job?'

Oh God, thought Ridley, he's beating me to it! He's making me say it the meanest, dirtiest way. He's putting me in the position of the Cruel Boss who throws the Faithful Old Employee into the street! I must seize the helm of this conversation from Mr Shillito's skilled hand or all will be lost.

'You mustn't think in those terms, Mr Shillito,' he said. 'Your work seems to me to be on the same level as always. But it is not my wish or that of the publisher to rob you of the ease to which your seniority entitles you, and in the course of a few days I want to have a talk with you about the future. Meanwhile, I have some pressing matters to attend to, and if you will excuse me –'

'Of course, of course,' said Mr Shillito, in a voice which suggested movement, though he remained firmly in his chair. 'But you understand how matters are with me. I don't wish to be sentimental. Indeed, you know that any display of feeling is repugnant to me. An Englishman, and what I suppose must now be called an Englishman of the Old School, I will submit to anything rather than make a display of my feelings. But you know, Chief, that the Newspaper Game is all in all to me. When the Game becomes too rough for me, I don't want to watch it from the sidelines. If I have a wish, it's that I may drop in harness. I'm not a conventionally religious man; my creed, so far as I've had one, has been simple Decency. But I've prayed to whatever gods there be, many and many a time, "Let me drop in harness; let the old blade wear out, but not rust out!"'

Mr Shillito delivered this prayer in a voice which must have been audible in the news room, even though the presses had begun the morning's run, and Ridley was sweating with embarrassment. This was becoming worse and worse. To his immense relief, Miss Green came in.

'An important long-distance call, if you can take it, Mr Ridley,' said she.

'Aha!' he cried. 'You'll excuse me, Mr Shillito? Confidential.' He hissed the last word, as though matters on the highest government level were involved. The lover of the Newspaper Game raised his great eyebrows conspiratorially, and tip-toed from the room.

'What is it, Miss Green?' asked Ridley, mopping his bald brow.

'Nothing, really, Mr Ridley,' said Miss Green. 'I just thought you might like a change of atmosphere. There was a call a few minutes ago. Professor Vambrace wants to see you at eleven.'

'What about?'

'Wouldn't say, but he was rather abrupt on the line. He said he had called earlier.'

'Professor Vambrace is always abrupt,' said Ridley. 'Thank you,

Miss Green. And I am always busy if Mr Shillito wants to see me, for the next few days.'

Miss Green nodded. She was too good a secretary to do more, but there was that in her nod which promised that even the gate-crashing talents of Mr Shillito would be unavailing against her in future.

Sighing, Ridley turned to his next task, which was a consideration of the editorial pages of thirty-eight contemporaries of *The Bellman*, which had been cut out and stacked ready to hand. He would have liked to take ten minutes to think about Mr Swithin Shillito and the problem which he presented, but he had not ten minutes to spare. People who form their opinions of what goes on in a daily newspaper office upon what they see at the movies imagine that the life of a journalist is one of exciting and unforeseen events; but as Ridley intended to say in his Wadsworth lecture, it was rooted deep in a stern routine; let the heavens fall and the earth consume in flames, the presses must not be late; if the reading public was to enjoy the riotous excess of the world's news, the newspaperman must bend that excess to the demands of a mechanical routine and a staff of union workers. Before one o'clock he must read all that lay on his desk, talk to the news editor, plan and write at least one leading article, and see any visitors who could win past Miss Green. He could spare no ten minutes for pondering about Mr Shillito. He must read, read, dig, dig, and plan, plan as the Old Mess himself advised.

Upon the right-hand drawboard of his desk was his typewriter; he slipped a piece of paper under the roller and typed a heading: *Notes and Comment*. It was an ancient custom of the paper to end the editorial columns with a few paragraphs of brief observation, pithy and, if possible, amusing, and Ridley wrote most of them. It was not that he fancied himself as a wit, but the job must be done by somebody, and better his wit than Shillito's; the Old Mess had a turn for puns and what he called 'witty *aperçus*'. He picked up the first of the editorial pages, and ran his eye quickly over it: a leader complaining of high taxation, and two subsidiary editorials, one sharply rebuking a South American republic for some wickedness connected with coffee and another explaining that the great cause of traffic accidents was not drunkenness or mechanical defects in cars, but elementary bad manners on the part of drivers. There were no paragraphs which he might steal, or use as priming for the pump of his own wit, and only one joke. It read:

WAS LIKE HIM

OFFICE BOY: Man waiting to see you, sir.
BOSS: I'm too busy for time-wasters. Does he look important?
OFFICE BOY: Well, not too much so, sir. About like yourself.

Ridley sighed, and put the sheet in the waste basket. The next three yielded nothing that he could use. The fourth contained a note which looked promising. It was:

An American doctor says that hairs in the ears help hearing. Barber, hold those shears!

Surely a witty *aperçu* could be wrought from that? He pondered for a moment, and then typed:

A Montreal physician asserts that hairs in the ears are aids to hearing. In future, it appears, we must choose between hearing and shearing.

When it was on paper he eyed it glumly, changed 'asserts' to 'says' and picked up the next sheet. It was from a prairie paper, whose editor was of the opinion that the chief cause of motor accidents was faulty brakes. None of its notes were worth stealing, but tucked in a corner was:

ONE FOR THE BOSS

BOSS: You say there is a man at the door wishes to see me. Does he look like a gentleman?
OFFICE BOY: Well, not exactly like a gentleman, sir. Just something like yourself!

The next three papers brought him no inspiration, but among the *Notes* in the fourth appeared the following:

A local merchant is still reeling from the answer he received when he asked his secretary to describe a visitor. 'Nobody important,' replied the fair one, 'pretty much like yourself.'

Ridley hurried on. The next page which came to hand carried a sharp warning to the Government that continued high taxation would beget a dreadful vengeance at the next general election, and a lesser piece which said that modern children would be less prone to delinquency if they read fewer comic books devoted to the doings of criminals and fixed their admiration upon some notable hero of the past, such as Robin Hood. This paper also carried an editorial which took issue with some opinions *The Bellman* had expressed a few days before, on prison reform; the editor of *The Bellman*, it was implied, lacked a kind and understanding heart. Ridley made a note to write a counterblast, pointing out that Robin Hood was a criminal and a practical communist, and that no one but a numbskull would hold him up as a hero to children.

Thus he worked through the pile of contemporary opinion. He paused to read what a medical columnist in one paper had to say about gallstones. They could, it appeared, 'sleep' for years, causing little or no distress beyond an occasional sense of uneasiness. Ridley wondered if he had sleeping gallstones; he certainly had a sense of uneasiness, though it was nothing to what it had been a few years ago. To sit in an editor's chair, even reading epidemic jokes and groping for witty *aperçus*, was a good life; better, certainly, than his days as a reporter and, later, as a news editor. He read on, plunging deep into the pool of Canadian editorial opinion: the wickedness of the Government, the wickedness of the nation in spending several times as much on liquor as it gave to charity, the wickedness of the U S A in not sufficiently recognizing Canada's greatness, the wickedness of Britain in not spending more money in Canada: he scanned these familiar topics without emotion, thinking only that the newspapers, like the churches, would be in a poor way if there were no wickedness in the world. Indeed, a good many editors seemed to think of themselves, primarily, as preachers, crying aloud to a godless world to repent of its manifold sins. Some, who did not regard themselves as preachers, appeared to think of themselves as simple, shrewd old farmers; they wrote nostalgically of a bygone, Arcadian era, when everybody was near enough to the farm to have a little manure on his boots, and they appeared to think that farmers were, as a class, more honest and less given to gaudy vice than city folk. Ridley, who had lived in a rural community for a few years when a child, had never been able to find out where this opinion had its root. Other editors, who were disguised neither as preachers nor farmers, donned newsprint togas and appeared as modern Catos, ready to shed the last drop of their ink in defence of those virtues which they believed to be the exclusive property of the party not in power; these were also exceedingly hard upon the rising generation, whom they lumped together under the name of 'teen-agers'. To be an editor was to be a geyser of opinion; every day, without fail, Old Faithful must shoot up his jet of comment, neither so provocative as to drive subscribers from his paper, nor yet so inane as to be utterly contemptible. The editor must not affront the intelligence of the better sort among his readers, and yet he must try to say something acceptable to those who really took the paper for the comics and the daily astrology feature. Truly, a barber's chair, that fits all buttocks.

While musing, Ridley had drawn moustaches and spectacles on pictures of four statesmen which appeared in a paper under his hand. He sketched a wig of curly hair on a bald man. With two deft dots of his pencil, he crossed the eyes of a huge-breasted girl under whose picture appeared the caption: 'Miss Sweater Girl for this month is lovely Dinah Ball, acclaimed by outstanding artists for her outstanding physique'. If a new Sweater Girl every month, why not an Udders Day, for the suitable honouring of all mammals? Could a witty *aperçu* be made of that? Probably not for a family journal.

But this was idleness. He must work. The editor of an evening daily has no time for profitless musing until after three o'clock. He tore up the defaced pictures, so that Miss Green should not find them, and turned once again to his task.

When another twenty minutes had passed he had perused the editorial outpourings of his thirty-eight contemporaries and had produced four more paragraphs of *Notes and Comment*. It was possible, he knew, to buy syndicated material of this sort, but he rather liked writing his own; the technique had its special fascination. It was possible, when desperate for material, to make an editorial note about virtually anything, or out of nothing at all. Consider, for instance, his startling success of the previous June: a mosquito in his office had annoyed him, and when he mentioned it to Miss Green she borrowed an atomizer filled with some sort of spray from the janitor, sought out the monster, and stifled it. 'There's a spray for every kind of bug now, Mr Ridley,' she had said. 'Except the humbug, Miss Green,' he had replied, thinking of Mr Shillito. And there had been a Note, ready to hand. He had typed it at once:

An eminent scientist asserts that there is now a spray for the control of every form of bug. Excluding, of course, the humbug.

One always attributed any foolish remark upon which one intended to pun either to an eminent scientist, a prominent physician, or a political commentator; it gave authenticity and flourish to the witty *aperçu* which followed. This gem, so quickly conceived and executed, had been copied by eighteen other newspapers, with appropriate credit to *The Bellman*, stolen by several more, and had appeared a month afterward in the magazine section of the New York *Times*, attributed to the late Will Rogers.

It was now time for him to settle down to work on the leader for the day, his editorial on the St Lawrence seaway. This was a nervous moment, for he hated to make a beginning at any piece of writing. As the Old Mess had told him, it was already written in his head, but what is written in the head is always so much more cogent and firmly expressed than what at last appears upon the page. He longed for a discretion, something that would postpone beginning for a few more minutes. His wish was gratified; Miss Green came in, carrying three books.

'Shall I put these with the other review books, Mr Ridley?'

'No, let's have a look at them, Miss Green.'

Books for review always gave him a moment of excitement. There was the chance, faint, but still possible, that among them there would be something which he himself would like to read. But not this time. The first was a volume of pious reflections by a well-known Canadian divine; just the thing for Shillito. Next was a slim volume of verse by a Canadian poetess. Why are such volumes always 'slim', he wondered; why not 'scrawny', which would be so much nearer the truth? Miss Green could polish off the poetess. Next – ah, yes, the choice of an American book club, a volume somewhat larger and heavier than a brick, with a startling jacket printed upon paper so slick as to be somewhat sticky to the touch. *Plonk* was its title, and the inside flap of the jacket declared that 'it lays bare the soul of a man and woman caught up in the maelstrom of modern metropolitan life. Rusty Maloney fights his way from Boston's Irishtown to success as an advertising executive, only to fall under the spell of Siva McNulty, lovely, alluring but already addicted to Plonk, the insidious mixture of stout, brandy and coarse-ground poppyheads which brings surcease to screaming nerves and abraded passions. An Odyssey of the spirit on a scale rarely attempted, this novel is redolent of . . .' No use giving that to Shillito; his usual reviewer of novels which were redolent of something was in hospital, having a baby, and he did not want the Old Mess being offensively moral through four inches in the review column. Who, then? Ah, Rumball!

He rang the bell and asked Miss Green to find Mr Rumball and send him in. Meanwhile he made a bet with himself that the first sex scene in *Plonk* would be found between pages 15 and 30. He won his bet. It was by no means a certainty. Sometimes this important scene came between pages 1 and 15.

Henry Rumball was a tall, untidy young man on the reportorial staff; his daily round included visits to the docks, the university and the undertakers. He presented himself wordlessly before the editor's desk.

'I thought you might like to review *Plonk*,' said Ridley. 'I know you take an interest in the modern novel. This is rather special, I believe. Stark stuff. Say what you think, but don't frighten any old ladies'

'Thanks, Mr Ridley. Gosh, *Plonk*,' said Rumball, seizing the volume and seeming to caress it.

'You know something about it?'

'I've seen the American reviews. They say it moves the novel on to an entirely different plateau of achievement. The *Saturday Review* man said when he'd finished it he felt exactly as if he had been drinking plonk all night himself. It's kind of tactile, I guess.'

'Well, say so in your piece. Tactile is a handy word; tends to make a sentence quotable.'

Rumball rocked his weight from foot to foot, breathed heavily, and then said, 'I don't know that I really ought to do it.'

'Why not? I thought you liked that kind of thing?'

'Yes, Mr Ridley, but I'm trying to keep my head clear, you see. I'm avoiding outside influences, to keep my stream unpolluted, if you know what I mean.'

'I don't know in the least what you mean. What stream are you talking about?'

'My stream of inspiration. For *The Plain*. My book, you know.'

'Are you writing a book?'

'Yes. Don't you remember? I told you all about it nearly a year ago.'

'I can't recall anything about it. When did you tell me?'

'Well, I came in to ask you about a raise –'

'Oh yes, I remember that. I told you to talk to Mr Weir. I never interfere with his staff.'

'Yes, well, I told you then I was writing a novel. And now I'm working on my first draft. And I'm not reading anything, for fear it may influence me. That's the big danger, you know. Influences. Above all, you have to be yourself.'

'Aha, well if you don't want *Plonk* I'll find someone else. Will you ask Mr Weir to see me when he has a free moment?'

'Could I just talk to you for a minute, about the novel? I'd appreciate your help, Mr Ridley.'

'This is rather a busy time.'

But Rumball had already seated himself, and his shyness had fallen from him. His eyes gleamed.

'It's going to be a big thing. I know that. It's not conceit; I feel it just as if the book was somebody else's. It's something nobody has ever tried to do in Canada before. It's about the West –'

'I recall quite a few novels about the West.'

'Yes, but they were all about man's conquest of the prairie. This is just the opposite. It's the prairie's conquest of man. See? A big concept. A huge panorama. I only hope I can handle it. You remember that film *The Plough that Broke the Plain*? I'm calling my book *The Plain that Broke the Plough*. I open with a tremendous description of the Prairie; vast, elemental, brooding, slumbrous; I reckon on at least fifteen thousand words of that. Then Man comes. Not the Red Man; he understands the prairie; he croons to it. No, this is the White Man; he doesn't understand the prairie; he rips up its belly with a blade; he ravishes it. "Take it easy," says the Red Man. "Aw, drop dead," says the White Man. You see? There's your conflict. But the real conflict is between the White Man and the prairie. The struggle goes on for three generations, and at last the prairie breaks the White Man. Just throws him off.'

'Very interesting,' said Ridley, picking up some papers from his desk. 'We must have a talk about it some time. Perhaps when you have finished it.'

'Oh, but that may not be for another five years,' said Rumball. 'I'm giving myself to this, utterly.'

'Not to the neglect of your daily work, I hope?'

'I do that almost mechanically, Mr Ridley. But my creative depths are busy all the time with my book.'

'Aha; will you ask Mr Weir if I may see him?'

'Certainly, sir. But there's just one thing I'd like your advice about. Names. Names are so important in a book. Now the big force in my book is the prairie itself, and I just call it the Prairie. But my people who are struggling against it are two families; one is English, from the North, and I thought of calling them the Chimneyholes, only they pronounce it Chumnel. The other is Scandinavian and I want to call them the Ruokatavarakauppas. I'm worried that the vowel sounds in the two names may not be sufficiently differentiated. Because, you see, I want to get a big poetic sweep into the writing, and if the main words in the novel aren't right, the whole thing may bog down, do you see?'

'I want to see Mr Weir at once,' said Ridley, in a loud, compelling voice.

'I'll tell him right away,' said Rumball, moving toward the door, 'but if you should happen to think of a name that has the same rhythm as Ruokatavarakauppas but has a slightly darker vowel shading I'd be grateful if you would tell me. It's really going to be a kind of big saga, and I want people to read it aloud as much as possible, and the names are terribly important.'

Reluctantly, he left the office, and shortly afterward Edward Weir, the managing editor, came in and sat in the chair from which Rumball had been driven with such difficulty.

'Anything out of the ordinary last night?' asked Ridley.

'Just the usual Hallowe'en stuff, except for one story we can't track down. Some sort of trouble at the Cathedral. The Dean won't say anything, but he didn't deny that something had happened. Archie was going home a little after midnight and he met Miss Pottinger coming from the West Door of the Cathedral. He asked her if anything was wrong and she said, "You'll get nothing out of me," and hurried off across the street. But she had no stockings on, and bedroom slippers; he spotted them under her coat. Now what was she doing in the Cathedral at midnight on Hallowe'en with no stockings on?'

'At her age lack of stockings suggests great perturbation of mind, but nothing really interesting. Did Archie try to get into the church?'

'Yes, but the door was locked. He could see light through the keyhole, but there was nothing to be heard.'

'Probably nothing at all happening, really.'

'I don't know. When I called Knapp this morning he was very short, and when I asked him if it was true that someone had tried to rob the Cathedral last night he said. "Where did you hear about that?" and then tried to tell me he meant nothing by it.'

'Why don't you try the organist? You know, that fellow – what's his name? – Cobbler. He never stops talking.'

'Called him. He said, "My lips are sealed." You know what a jackass he is.'

'We'd better keep after it. Tell me, is that fellow Rumball any good?'

'Fair. He was better when he first came on the staff. He moons a good deal now. Maybe he's in love.'

'Perhaps Mr Shillito could give him one of his talks on the virtue of digging in the Newspaper Game.'

'God forbid. Are you going to do anything about that matter?'

'I'm moving as fast as I can. It's very difficult. You have no heart, Ned. How would you like to be thrown out of your job at seventy-eight?'

'If I had a pension, and a house all paid for, and a nice little private income, and probably a good chunk of savings, like Old Shillito, I would like nothing better.'

'Has he all that?'

'You know it as well as I do. He just likes to prowl around this office and waste everybody's time.'

'He says he prays to whatever gods there be that he may drop in harness. He's not a conventionally religious man, but that is his prayer.'

'The old faker! When he caught on to this Cathedral story this morning he was in my office like a shot out of a gun. "Ned, my boy," he said, "take an old newspaperman's advice and let this thing drop; I've been a staunch churchman all my life, and there's nothing I would not do to shield the church against a breath of slander." Of course I tried to find out if he knew anything, but he shut up like a clam. Gloster, why don't you give him the axe? He's just a pest.'

'I inherited him. And he was editor himself for a few months before I was appointed. I don't want anybody to be able to say that I was unfair to him.'

'It's your funeral. But he's a devil of a nuisance. Always in the news room, keeping somebody from work. The boys are sick of him. They aren't even civil to him any more, but he doesn't notice.'

'I'm going to do something very soon. I just want to be able to do it the right way. If we could ease him out gloriously, somehow it would be best. I had a notion involving an illuminated address which might work. But leave it with me for a few days more. Nothing else out of the way?'

But the day's news was barren of anything else which the managing editor thought Mr Ridley should know, and he went back to his own office leaving the editor once more with the task of writing his leader. To postpone the dread moment a little longer he picked up the few typewritten sheets which Mr Shillito called 'his stint', and read that which was uppermost.

A VANISHING AMENITY

That the walking-stick is disappearing from our streets – nay even from our hall-stands – is a fact not to be gainsaid by the boldest. Where once:

Sir Plume, of amber snuffbox justly vain
And the nice conduct of a clouded cane,

took pride in possessing half-a-score different sticks for every occasion – for dress, for church, for the town stroll and the rural ramble – your modern man, hastening from business to home and from home to club in his comfortable car, needs none and, be it said, desires none. Macaulay's schoolboy, young model of erudition, might be excused today for failing to distinguish between rattan and ebony, between cherished blackthorn and familiar ashplant. Beyond question the walking-stick has – *hinc illae lacrimae* – gone where the woodbine twineth.

Ridley sighed and then, slowly and painfully, was possessed by rage. His weakness in failing to get rid of the Old Mess condemned him to publish this sort of hogwash in the paper of which he was known to be the editor. The mantle of the eighteenth-century essayist – old, frowsy, tattered, greasy and patched with Addison's gout-rags and the seat of the gentle Elia's pants – had fallen upon Swithin Shillito, and he strutted and postured in it, every day, in the columns of *The Bellman*. And why? Because he, Gloster Ridley, lacked the guts to tell the Old Mess that he was fired. He hated himself. He despised his weakness. And yet – a pious regard for old age and a sincere desire to be just and to use his power wisely restrained him from acting as he would have done if the offender had been, for instance, Henry Rumball. And, who could say, might not many readers of *The Bellman* – even a majority of them – share the opinion of Eldon Bumford, who revelled in Mr Shillito's essay on the fate of the toothpick and exulted in his discussions of the importation of snuff and birdseed? To what extent was he, Gloster Ridley, justified in imposing his taste upon the newspaper's subscribers? Still, was it not for doing so that he drew his excellent salary and his annual bonus reckoned upon the profits? What about the barber's chair; might there not be a few buttocks for Shillito? But he could go on in this Hamlet-like strain all day. There was only one thing for it. He rang for Miss Green.

'Please call Mr Warboys and ask if I may see him for half an hour this afternoon,' said he.

'Yes, Mr Ridley. And Professor Vambrace called again and said he couldn't come at eleven and insists on seeing you at two.'

'Very well, Miss Green. But what is all this about Professor Vambrace? What does he want to see me about?'

'I don't know sir, because he wouldn't give me any hint on the phone. But he was very crusty. He kept repeating "Two, sharp," in a way I didn't like.'

'He did, did he? Well, whenever he comes, keep him waiting five minutes. And I don't want to be disturbed until lunch.'

'Yes, sir. Here are a few letters which came with the second mail.'

These were quickly dealt with. A temperance league called for 'renewed efforts', and Moral Re-Armament asserted in three paragraphs that if everybody would try to be decent to everybody else, all problems between management and labour would disappear. A young Nigerian wrote, 'I am African boy but always wear American shoes,' and wanted a Canadian pen-friend, preferably a girl between 14 and 16. Another, deeply critical of *The Bellman*, was so eccentric in grammar and spelling that it took five minutes of Ridley's time to prepare it for the printer; there is nothing that makes an editor feel more like St Francis – a loving brother to the ass – than this sort of remedial work on a letter which accuses him of unfairness or stupidity. At last Ridley was ready to write his leader.

After all his fussing it came out quite smoothly, and by mid-day he had everything prepared for the printers and was ready to think about his luncheon.

Considering that he prepared and ate it in strict privacy, Gloster Ridley's lunch was a matter of extraordinary interest to a great many people in Salterton. There are some ways in which a man may be eccentric, and nobody will think anything of it; there are others in which eccentricity becomes almost a moral issue. Having no wife to return to at the middle of the day, the obvious thing was for him to eat at an hotel or a restaurant. But instead he preferred to prepare his own luncheon and eat it in his office. This oddity might have been overlooked if he had uncomfortably devoured a sandwich at his desk, and washed it down with milk; such a course might have won him a reputation as a keen newspaperman, unwilling to relax for an instant in his contemplation of the day's horrors; it might have brought him those stigmata of the conscientious and ambitious executive, a couple of ulcers. But he was known to prepare and eat a hot dish, and follow it with some cheese or a bit of fruit, and make himself black coffee in a special percolator. It was even suspected that he sometimes took a glass of sherry with his meal.

These enormities might have been forgiven if he had made a joke of them, or had asked other men of business to come and share his repast. But he obstinately considered his lunch to be nobody's business but his own. Consequently spiteful things were said of him, and it was hinted that he wore a blue apron with white frills while preparing his meal, and more than one Letter to the Editor had suggested that if he knew as much about politics, or economics, or world affairs or whatever it might be, as he did about cooking, *The Bellman* would be a better paper.

Cooking, however, was his hobby, and he saw no reason why he should not do as he pleased. He would probably have admitted – indeed, often did admit to his particular friend Mrs Fielding – that he was a bit of an old woman, and fussed about his food. He hated to eat in public, and he hated the kind of food which the restaurants of Salterton offered. In a modest way he was a gourmet. He cooked his own dinners in his apartment, and often asked his friends to dine with him. They agreed that his cooking was excellent. He permitted his housekeeper (whom he always thought of as Constant Reader because she devoured *The Bellman* nightly and gave him unsought advice about it daily) to cook his breakfast, but otherwise he took care of himself in this respect. He did not realize that his daily luncheon was taken almost as a personal affront by several ladies in Salterton who regarded all unattached men with suspicion, and if he knew that other men laughed at him he did not care.

Perhaps the most irritating part of the whole business to those who disapproved of his custom was his extreme thinness. A man who makes so much fuss about his food ought, by all laws of morality and justice, to be fat. He should bear about with him burdensome evidence of his shameful and unmanly preoccupation. But Ridley was tall and thin and bald, and was referred to by the staff of *The Bellman*, when he was out of earshot, as Bony.

He liked his lunch-time, because it gave him an opportunity to think. On this first of November he moved the little hot-plate out of his cupboard as usual, took two eggs and other necessaries from his brief case, and made himself an excellent omelette. He sat down at a small table near his window and ate it, looking down at the Salterton market, which was one of the last of the open-air markets in that part of Canada, and a very pretty sight.

He was thinking, of course, about Mr Shillito. When he saw his publisher that afternoon, he would explain that Mr Shillito must go, and he would ask Mr Warboys to help him to ease the blow. Execrable as Mr Shillito might be as a writer, and detestable as he might be about the office, he was an old man with somewhat more than his fair share of self-esteem, and Ridley could not bring himself to wound him. But there must be no half-measures. Shillito must have an illuminated address, presented if possible by Mr Warboys himself. The whole staff must be assembled, and Mr Shillito must be allowed to make a speech. Perhaps the Mayor could be bamboozled into coming. And a picture of the affair must appear in *The Bellman*, with a caption which would make it clear that Mr Shillito was retiring of his own volition. It would all be done in the finest style. Why, if Mr Warboys were in a good mood, he might even suggest a little dinner for Mr Shillito, instead of a staff meeting. Ridley found that his eyes had moistened as he contemplated the golden light in which Mr Shillito would depart from *The Bellman*.

But why do I worry about him? he asked himself. Does he ever give a thought to my convenience? Doesn't he use me shamelessly whenever he can? What was that incident only a week ago? Shillito had burst into his office with some dreadful freak in tow, a grinning little fellow called Bevill Higgin – how tiresome he had been about the lack of a final 's' on his name – who wanted Ridley to publish half-a-dozen articles by himself on some method of singing that he taught. Print them and pay for them, if you please! Ridley had been furious, but when really angry he did not show it. Instead he gave them both what he thought of as the Silent Treatment. He had allowed little Higgin to chatter on and on, making silly jokes and paying him monstrous compliments, while he sat in his chair, saying nothing and only now and then gnashing the scissors which he held in his hand. The Silent Treatment never failed, and at last Shillito had said, 'But we mustn't detain you, Chief; shall I make arrangements with Mr Higgin for the articles?' And he had replied, 'No, Mr Shillito, I don't think we need trouble you to do that.' Higgin had blushed and grinned, and even the Old Mess knew that he had been snubbed. But if people invaded his office unasked and tried to force upon him things which he did not want, did they deserve any better treatment? One of Shillito's worst characteristics was that he looked upon *The*

Bellman as a sort of relief centre and soup kitchen for all the lame ducks he picked up in a social life which yielded an unusual number of lame ducks. A lunatic, lean-witted fool, presuming on an ague's privilege, he quoted to himself, and at once felt sorry for the Old Mess. But he really must stop thinking of him as the Old Mess. It was one of his worst mental faults, that trick of having private and usually inadmissible names for people. Some day a few of them were sure to pop out. When he was on the operating-table, under anaesthetic, for instance.

Thus, rocking between anger against Mr Shillito and pity for him, Ridley ate his biscuits and cheese, drank his excellent coffee, put his dishes on Miss Green's desk to be washed, and composed himself for his invariable twenty-minute after-lunch sleep in his armchair.

Miss Green coughed discreetly. 'Professor Vambrace is waiting,' she said.

Ridley leaped from his chair. He hated being caught thus; he had an uneasy conviction that he was unsightly when asleep. And he had overslept by ten minutes. 'Keep him till I ring,' he said.

When Miss Green had gone he combed his hair and rinsed his removable bridge in his tiny washroom. Sitting at his desk, he fussed with some papers, but he could not calm himself. He was disproportionately ashamed of having been found asleep. His nap, like his lunch, was no guilty secret, but he hated to be caught unprepared. How long had Miss Green watched him, perhaps listened to his snores, considered the dry and iridescent matter, like the sheen on a butterfly's wing, which formed on his lower lip when he slept? To escape this uncomfortable train of thought he rang his bell, and Professor Vambrace stalked from the door to the space before his desk, and glared down upon him.

'Well,' he said, and his deep voice vibrated with anger, 'have you decided what you are going to do?'

'As I have no idea what you are talking about, Professor,' said Ridley, 'I can't say that I have. Won't you sit down?'

The Professor sat, majestically. 'I do not believe you, but I'll soon tell you what I'm talking about,' said he, 'and I'll tell you what you're going to do, as well.'

Walter Vambrace was a tall, gaunt man who looked like a tragedian of the old school; his large, dark eyes glowed balefully under his demonic eyebrows. From an inner pocket he produced a wallet, and drew a clipping from it with great care. Ridley, to whom the faces of newspapers were as familiar as the faces of his friends, saw at once that the clipping was from *The Bellman*, and prepared himself for trouble.

'In the next three issues of your paper you will publish this, and the retraction and apology which I shall also give you, in large type at the top of your front page,' said Professor Vambrace.

'Aha,' said Ridley, in a noncommital tone. 'May I see the clipping, please?'

'Do you mean to tell me that you are not aware of its contents?' said the Professor, working his eyebrows menacingly.

'I have no idea what you are talking about.'

'Good God, don't you read your own newspaper?'

'Of course I do, but I still don't know what has offended you.'

'Refresh your recollection, then,' said the Professor, with a rich assumption of irony, and handed Ridley the scrap of newsprint upon which was printed the engagement notice with which the reader has already been made familiar.

The editor read it carefully. 'This seems quite in order,' said he.

'In order! There is not one word of truth in it from beginning to end. It is a vile calumny!'

'You mean that your daughter is not engaged to Mr Bridgetower?'

'Is not, and never will be, and this damnable libel exposes me and my wife and my daughter to the ridicule of the entire community.'

Ridley's heart sank within him. Physicians say that this cannot happen, but editors know a sensation which may not be described in any other phrase.

'That is most regrettable. I shall do everything possible to find out how this notice came to appear in print. But I can assure you now that we have a system which provides every possible safeguard against this sort of thing, and I cannot understand how it could have failed.'

Professor Vambrace's expression, which had been one of anger, now deepened to a horrible grimace in which rage and scorn were mingled. 'You have a system!' he roared. 'Read it again, you fool, and then tell me, if you dare, that you have a system, or anything except the mischievous incompetence of your disgusting trade to explain the insult!'

Ridley was thoroughly angry himself, now, but caution was ingrained in his nature, and he turned his eyes once again to the clipping.

'To take place November 31st,' hissed the Professor. 'And when, you jackanapes, is November 31st? Is that date provided for in your system? Hey?' he was shouting, now.

All Ridley's anger was drained out of him, and a great but not unfamiliar weariness took its place. He was a good editor, and when praise came to *The Bellman* he took it on behalf of the staff; when blame came to it, he took that alone. He was, in law and in his own philosophy of journalism, personally responsible for every word which appeared in every issue of his paper. He looked into the eyes of his visitor and spoke the speech which was obligatory on him on such occasions.

'I cannot tell you how much I regret this,' he said; 'however, it has happened, and although this is my first knowledge of it, I accept the full blame. Someone has played a tasteless joke on the paper, and, of course, upon you and your family as well. I am deeply sorry that it has happened, and I will join you in doing everything that can be done to find the joker.'

'Pah!' said Professor Vambrace, with such violence that quite a lot of spittle shot across Ridley's desk and settled upon the papers there. 'What kind of newspaper do you call this, where nobody knows how many days there are in November? That alone should have been enough to warn any intelligent person, even a newspaper editor, that the thing was a vile hoax. Quite apart from the ludicrous implication in the notice itself; whatever made you think that my daughter would marry that nincompoop?'

'As I have explained, I have not seen this notice until this moment. And how should I know whom your daughter might or might not marry?'

'Don't you see what goes in your own paper?'

'I see very little of it, and certainly not the engagement notices. These matters are left in the hands of our staff.'

'A fine staff it must be! The thing is preposterous on the face of it. Do you know this Bridgetower?'

'I have met him two or three times.'

'Well? An idiot, nothing better. What would my daughter be doing with such a fellow?'

'I do not know your daughter.'

'Do you imply that she would take up with any simpleton who came along?'

'Professor Vambrace, this is beside the point.'

'It is not beside the point. It is the whole point. You have linked my daughter with this fellow Bridgetower. You have coupled them in the public mouth.'

'I have done nothing of the sort. *The Bellman* has been the victim of a practical joke; so have you. We must do what we can to set matters right.'

'Exactly. Therefore you will publish this notice on your front page, along with the apology which I have here, for the next three days, beginning today.'

'We shall publish a correction . . .'

'Not a correction, an apology.'

'A correction, but not on the front page, and not for three days.'

'For three days, beginning today.'

'Impossible. The paper has gone to press.'

'The front page.'

'The page on which these announcements appear. For you must understand that our correction will appear for one day only, in the same place that the erroneous notice appeared.'

'That is what you will publish.' The Professor pushed a piece of paper at Ridley. It began rather in the rhythm of a Papal Encyclical: *With the uttermost apology and regret we make unqualified retraction;* Ridley read no more.

'Look here, Professor,' said he, 'we've both been made to look like fools, and we don't want to make matters worse. Leave this matter in my hands, and I'll deal with it in a way that will make an adequate correction and attract no unnecessary attention.'

'This will be settled in my way, or I'll take it to court,' said Professor Vambrace.

'All right, then, take it to court and be damned,' said Ridley.

The Professor glared horribly, but it was the glare of a man who was wondering what to say next. Ridley saw that he had the advantage for the moment and followed up his lead.

'And spare me your histrionics,' said he; 'I am not intimidated by them.'

This was a shrewd thrust, but tactically it was a mistake. The Professor was a keen amateur actor, and fancied himself as the 'heavy' of the Salterton Little Theatre; Ridley's remark disconcerted him, but deepened his anger. However, the editor had at last secured the upper hand, and he continued.

'You must understand that I have had more experience in these matters than you have.'

'That is a confession of incompetence rather than a reassurance,' said Vambrace.

'Kindly allow me to say what I have to say. *The Bellman* will not apologize, because it has acted in good faith, and is just as much a victim of this hoax as yourself. But we will correct the notice, printing the correction in the same place and in the same size of type as the original; we shall do this once only, for the notice appeared only once. If you will think about the matter calmly, you will see that this is best; you do not want an undignified fuss, and you do not want people to hear about this false engagement notice who have not heard of it already. Comparatively few people will have seen it –'

'My family is not utterly obscure,' said the Professor dryly, 'and the Personal Notices are one of the few parts of your paper which are widely read. Scores of people have been asking me about this already –'

'Scores, Professor Vambrace? Did I understand you to say scores?'

'Yes, sir, scores was the word I used.'

'Now, now, precisely how many people have spoken to you about it?'

'Don't take that tone with me, if you please.'

'My experience has been that when angry men talk about scores of people they mean perhaps half-a-dozen.'

'Do you doubt my word?'

'I think that your annoyance has led you to exaggerate.'

'A man in your trade is hardly in a position to accuse anyone of exaggeration.'

'Now let us be reasonable. Of course we shall do everything in our power to find out who perpetrated this joke –'

'I don't call it a joke.'

'Nor do I. This outrage, then.'

'That is a better word. And what do you propose to do?'

It was here that Mr Ridley lost the advantage he had gained. He had no idea what he proposed to do. Therefore he looked as wise as he could, and said, 'That will take careful consideration. I shall have to have a talk with some of the other men on the paper.'

'Let us do so at once, then.'

'I shall talk to them later this afternoon.'

'Let me make it plain to you that at this moment my daughter and my whole family rest under a vile imputation of which this newspaper is the source. Anything that is to be done must be done at once. So get your men in here now, and I will talk to them just long enough to find out whether you really mean to do anything or whether you are stalling me off. And unless you have an immediate plan of action I shall go straight from this office to my lawyer.'

The Professor had the upper hand again, and this time he did not mean to lose it. Ridley rang for Miss Green. 'Will you find Mr Marryat and ask him if he will join us here,' said he; 'it is urgent.' When the secretary had gone he and the Professor sat in painful silence for perhaps three minutes until the door opened again, and the general manager of *The Bellman* appeared.

Mr A. J. Marryat's principal interest was in advertising, and he had the advertising man's optimism and self-assurance. He came in smiling and greeted the Professor warmly. He told him that he was looking well. 'And how is Mrs Vambrace?' said he.

'My wife is in bed, under strong sedatives, because of what you have done here,' replied Vambrace, and breathed noticeably and audibly through his nostrils.

Ridley took the general manager by the arm, guided him to a chair, and explained the trouble as briefly as he could.

Mr Marryat's rule was never to display perturbation. He continued to smile. 'That's bad,' he said, 'but we'll find out who did it, and then we'll show him a joke or two.' He laughed comfortably at the prospect; but under cover of his bonhomie he was taking stock of the situation. Ridley, obviously, was in a tight spot or he would not be discussing a matter of this kind with himself in front of the injured party. Well, A. J. Marryat knew all there was to know about tight spots, and one of his most valuable pieces of knowledge was that the sharpest anger can be blunted by good humour, courtesy and a relaxed manner, all of which could be combined with a refusal to do anything you did not want to do. He turned to Ridley. 'Let's hear the details,' said he.

When he heard the details concerning November 31st, Mr Marryat was disturbed, but his outer appearance of calm was maintained without a ruffle.

'That was inexcusable stupidity,' he said, 'but I'm sure you know, Professor, how hard it is to get people to pay attention to things of that kind.'

'It is your work to do so, not mine,' said the Professor. 'I am only concerned with the fact that your paper has involved my family in a scandal. My professional dignity and my family honour make it imperative that this announcement be denied, and a full apology made, with the least possible waste of time. I want that done in today's paper.'

'That's a mechanical impossibility,' said Mr Marryat. 'The presses will begin rolling in about fifteen minutes.'

'Presses can be stopped, can they not?'

'They can be stopped at very great expense.'

'Probably less than it will cost you if I take this matter to court.'

'Now just a minute, Professor. Let's not be fantastic. Who's talking about court?'

'Your associate, Mr Ridley, told me to take my case to court and be damned.'

'I apologize,' said Ridley, 'but you were very provocative. You called me a fool and a jackanapes, you know.'

'I did, and I see no reason to retract either term.'

'Oh, come now, Professor,' said Mr Marryat, with his genial and ready laugh; 'let's not lose our perspective on this thing.'

'Mr Marryat,' said the Professor, rising, 'I have not come here to be cajoled or lectured. I came to tell you what you must do, and it is plain to me that you will twist and squirm all day to avoid doing it. I have no time to waste and this atmosphere is repugnant to me. You will shortly hear from my lawyers.' The Professor walked rapidly out of the room.

'Well, how do you like that?' said Mr Marryat.

Mr Ridley moaned, and wiped his brow.

'The gall of that guy,' said Mr Marryat. 'Professional dignity! Family honour! You'd think we did it on purpose. And what's all this scandal he talks about? Do you know this fellow Bridgetower?'

'Yes. He's a junior professor.'

'Well? Has he got two heads, or a common-law wife, or something?'

'So far as I know there's nothing against him except that he is the son of old Mrs Bridgetower.'

'That's plenty, mind you. And Vambrace's daughter, what about her?'

'I haven't seen her for two or three years. I think she's in the Waverley Library, somewhere, but I never meet her there. So far as I know she's just a girl.'

'Probably she's engaged to somebody else. That notice was somebody's half-baked joke. Well, I'll trace it. I'll get busy on it right now, and if we hear anything from Vambrace's lawyers, we can explain to them. They'll soon put a stop to that talk about scandal.'

'I'd be grateful if you'd let me know anything you find out as soon as possible, A.J.,' said Ridley.

'At once,' said Marryat, smiling the smile of a man who knows that he has an office system which cannot go wrong.

It was an hour and a half later when Mr Marryat returned. 'Well,' he said, sitting down opposite Ridley's desk, 'this isn't going to be as easy as I thought.'

'What's wrong?' said Ridley.

'If I've told them once, I've told them a million times that we have to have a record of every personal notice and classified ad that goes in the paper,' said Mr Marryat. 'When the yellow form is written out for the composing room a carbon copy is made on the blue form that goes into the files; the customer gets a pink form with all this on it, as a receipt. All three forms have to be initialled by the girl who takes the order, and the advertiser. You'd think it was foolproof. But look at this.' He handed Ridley a blue form.

It bore the text of the offending engagement notice and some marks which meant nothing to the editor, but Mr Marryat was already explaining them.

'Number of insertions: one. Payment: cash with order, $3.25. Date received: October 30th. Date of insertion: October 31st. Order received by: L E Advertiser: blank. Now what do you think of that?'

'It doesn't give the name of the advertiser,' said Ridley, who knew that this was a foolish answer, but obviously the one expected of him. When playing straight-man to Mr Marryat or anyone else with a load of grief, these steps must not be omitted.

'Exactly. And do you know why?'

'No. Why?'

'It's the kind of thing that sickens you; you think you've got a staff trained so that this kind of thing won't happen; you think you can trust everybody; then it happens.'

'Yes. But how?'

'Lucy takes all these classified ads. A dandy girl. Comes from a fine family. But she's young, and by God, sometimes I swear I won't have another woman in the office that isn't over fifty. Whenever she leaves the desk she's supposed to tell Miss Ellis; she's allowed fifteen minutes every morning and afternoon for coffee and a rest, and for ordinary purposes besides. But if Miss Ellis is out of the office, Lucy likes to slip off to the girls' room for a smoke. This ad was taken at 11.42 on October 30th. Miss Ellis was in my office, going over some figures for the monthly statement. Lucy was downstairs for a cigarette and Miss Porter took the ad, and Lucy initialled the form when she came back.'

'I see.'

'It took me over an hour to get that story out of them. Tears! The more these damned girls are in the wrong, the more they cry.'

'Hadn't Miss Porter enough sense to make whoever-it-was sign in the space for the advertiser's name?'

'She swears she did. And she swears he signed. My guess is that he signed the customer's own pink receipt slip and put it in his pocket and she didn't notice.'

'Aha, then she knows it was a man?'

'Yes, at least she remembers that. And he gave her the copy, typewritten, and she clipped it to the order for the composing room. Here it is. But it doesn't tell us anything.'

'Except that the writer was not used to a typewriter; and it is done on a piece of cheap linen correspondence paper; and the ribbon was in poor condition. What does she remember about the man's appearance?'

'She thinks he wore a blue suit. It might have been a dark grey.'

'Useless. What else?'

'Not a thing. Believe it or not, she can't remember whether he was young or old, dark or fair, wore glasses or not. She does remember that he had what she calls a funny voice.'

'What kind of funny voice?'

'Just funny. I asked her to imitate it, and she opened her mouth and let it hang open; then she cried again. Would you believe anybody could be so dumb and not be in an institution?'

'Most people are very unobservant.'

'You can say that again. Well, you can see what this does to us.'

'We haven't a leg to stand on.'

'Not a leg.'

'Still,' said Ridley, 'the advertisement isn't libel, and Vambrace's lawyers won't advise him to go ahead on that line.'

'Of course not,' said Mr Marryat, 'but if they ever find out that there was any carelessness here they'll make our lives miserable. So I'm taking these papers out of the files and putting them in the safe till we know what's going to happen.'

'I've got to see Mr Warboys this afternoon about another matter. Should I mention this to him, do you think?'

'What for? It won't come to anything. I wouldn't bother him.' And after a few more reflections upon the untrustworthiness and tearfulness of girls Mr Marryat withdrew.

It was half-past three, and Mr Ridley was to see his publisher at half-past four. At four o'clock he received a call from the legal firm of Snelgrove, Martin and Fitzalan, asking that he see Mr Snelgrove at ten o'clock the following morning on a matter of urgent importance.

Clerebold Warboys was not primarily interested in the publication of the Salterton *Evening Bellman*; he had been born wealthy, and in the process of becoming much wealthier he had acquired several properties, of which *The Bellman* was one. It had come upon the market as an ancient and almost bankrupt newspaper, and he had bought it because he did not want to see an institution which was so much a part of his native city disappear from that city's life; he also thought that the application of business acumen to the newspaper might improve its fortunes. He was right, as he usually was about such matters, and Mr Marryat and Mr Ridley had made *The Bellman* not only a very much better paper than it had been before, but a profitable business, as well.

Mr Warboys never interfered with the paper, and this was a source of disagreement between himself and his daughter-in-law, Mrs Roger Warboys, who lived with him and was his housekeeper and hostess. Mrs Roger Warboys, who had been widowed before she was forty, had a great store of energy which was not fully absorbed by her stewardship for Mr Warboys and the many women's causes into which she threw herself. Her dearest dream was to 'take over' *The Bellman* and to give it a policy more in line with her own opinions. She had a passion for crusading, and she felt that with a newspaper at her command she could do tremendous things to defeat juvenile delinquency, the drug traffic, comic books, immodest bathing suits and other evils which were gnawing at the foundations of society; she would also be able to do much to improve the status of women which, in her view, was unsatisfactory. But her father-in-law, who had passed the greater part of his life in public affairs and had acquired a considerable store of worldly wisdom, refused to pay any attention to her wishes. He was wont to say, 'Nesta, you have what most of the world wants: leisure and the money to enjoy it; why don't you relax?' But for Mrs Roger Warboys there could be no happiness which was not also turmoil and the imposition of her will upon other people. Perhaps twice a year she renewed her attack upon her obdurate father-in-law, and the rest of the time she seized what opportunities she could to call his attention to what she believed were fatal weaknesses in the editorship of Gloster Ridley.

It was with no quickening of the spirit, therefore, that Ridley found Mrs Roger Warboys in the publisher's study, pouring tea.

'Ridley,' said his employer, 'I've got the title for my book, at last.'

'Splendid!' said Ridley, with false enthusiasm.

'Yes. *Politics: The Great Game*. What do you think of that?'

'Absolutely first-rate!'

'Really? Don't give a snap decision. Do you really think it's what I want?'

'It's very original,' said Ridley.

'It sounds well. But of course most people won't hear it. They'll read it. How do you think it would look? Nesta, give me that dummy.'

His daughter-in-law handed him a book from the desk. Upon it Mr Warboys had put a piece of white paper, to resemble a dust jacket, and had crudely lettered *Politics: The Great Game*, by CLEREBOLD WARBOYS, across it.

'Very fine,' said Ridley: 'it has a kind of ring about it, even in print.'

Conversation as they drank their tea was all about Mr Warboys' book. This work had been *in utero*, so to speak, for eight years, but even at the age of seventy he could not find time to write it. Instead, he made copious notes for it, which he revised whenever a political contemporary died; when they were all dead, and the decks cleared, he might actually write it. Meanwhile he sustained the enthusiasm of an author at a remarkably high level, year in and year out, and Ridley rarely visited him without being asked for advice on some point relative to the great work. But at last the moment came when Ridley was able to raise the question of Mr Shillito.

'It is by no means easy,' he explained, 'because Mr Shillito is in a sense a legacy from the former management. He is a link with the past of the paper. But the sort of thing he writes no longer has a place in *The*

Bellman, and I feel that it is not in the best interest of the paper to postpone his retirement.'

'There's no doubt about it that he's a bloody old nuisance and not worth his keep,' said Mr Warboys, who was only eight years younger than Mr Shillito and felt no need to beat about the bush. 'Well; we've got a pension scheme. What's it for? We'll bounce him with all honours, as you suggest.'

'Mr Shillito never subscribed to the pension scheme,' said Mrs Roger Warboys, unexpectedly.

'How do you know?' asked her father-in-law.

'He asked me to tea on Sunday last. The poor old man is getting very frail, Father, and he has some nice things he wants to see in good hands before he dies. He was really very touching about it. He gave me the loveliest little bronze bowl – Chinese, and very good; I have it in my sitting-room. He hasn't much in the way of money, he says, but he has a few treasures, and he doesn't want them to go to just anybody when he dies. He told me that he had never felt able to contribute to the pension scheme.'

'I don't know how that could be,' said Ridley. 'Miss Ellis has always been very good about arranging payment plans for anybody who needed special help.'

'Perhaps you don't understand Mr Shillito's way of looking at things, Mr Ridley,' said Mrs Roger Warboys, quietly censorious. 'He's one of those proud old Englishmen who would rather die than ask anybody for help.'

'Then why didn't he take advantage of the pension scheme?' asked Mr Warboys.

'Because he didn't think he would ever live to enjoy it,' said his daughter-in-law. 'He told me that he worked himself so hard in the last few years before you took over *The Bellman* that he never expected to reach his present age. He has always expected that he would drop in harness.'

'Well, let him have the good sense to get out of harness,' said Mr Warboys, 'and he needn't drop so soon.'

'I know I have no right to interfere,' said Mrs Roger Warboys, in the tone she always used when she meant to do so. 'I think Mr Shillito should have every consideration. His judgement alone should be worth something. Even if he simply stays at *The Bellman* to keep an eye on things in general, he would be valuable. His knowledge of the city and its people is surely the most extensive of anyone now on the staff. For instance, I'm sure he would never have passed that ridiculous engagement notice about Pearl Vambrace and young Bridgetower.'

'That matter is in hand,' said Ridley, turning white.

'That's just as well,' said Mrs Roger Warboys, smiling unpleasantly. 'For Professor Vambrace phoned me about it this afternoon, just to make it clear that if he has to take it to law, there is nothing personal intended toward myself. I have worked very closely with him for years,' she explained, 'on the Board of the University Alumni.'

It was then necessary for Mr Ridley to explain to Mr Warboys what the dispute was between *The Bellman* and Professor Vambrace. Mr Warboys was not inclined to pay too much attention to it. 'These things soon blow over,' said he.

'Nevertheless, I think my point about Mr Shillito is well taken,' said Mrs Roger Warboys. 'The Professor was hardly off the phone before Mr Shillito called about it. He said that the minute he saw it he knew there had been some dreadful blunder, for the feud between the Vambraces and the Bridgetowers dates from when Professor Bridgetower was alive. He just wanted me to know that he would never have permitted such a thing to appear in print, but of course his power on the paper is very limited – at present.' These last words were directed with a special smile to Ridley.

'The damned old double-crosser,' said Mr Warboys, who understood these matters very well.

Ridley could think of no comment save lewd and blasphemous variations on that of his publisher, so he held his peace, and soon returned to his office.

It was after six o'clock when he reached it. He stopped in Miss Green's office, and after some rummaging, he drew a sheet of paper from a file and took it to his desk. It was an obituary, prepared some years before and kept up to date, for use when it should be needed. It read:

VAMBRACE, WALTER BENEDICT, b. Cork, Eire, March 5, 1899 only son Rev. Benedict V. and Cynthia Grattan V., a second cousin to the Marquis of Mourne and Derry; Educ. at home and Trinity Coll. Dublin. (MA.) Emigrated to Canada 1922 joined classics dept. Waverley as junior professor. Married Elizabeth Anne Fitzalan dr. Wolfe Tone Fitzalan, June 18, 1925, one daughter Pearl Veronica b. 1933. Full professor 1935; head classics dept. 1938. Supported for

Dean of Arts 1939 but defeated by one vote by the late Dean Solomon Bridgetower. Did not stand again after Dean Btwr's death in 1940. Author: *Contra Celsum with Notes and Commentary* 1924; *Enneads of Plotinus Newly Considered* 1929 (*Times Lit. Supp.* says 'valuable though controversial' in review which might have been by Dean Inge); *Student's Book of Latin Verse* 1938 (sold 150,000).

Professor Vambrace was no austere scholar, but a man who gave richly of himself to a variety of worthy causes. Always accessible to his students, he opened to them the stores of scholarship which he brought from famed Trinity College, Dublin. Graduates of Waverley will long remember the rich and thrilling voice in which he read Latin poetry aloud, seeming to – as one graduate put it – 'call Horace smiling from his tomb and Vergil from the realm of the shades.' This same noble organ was for years to be heard in performances given by the Salterton Little Theatre, of which Professor Vambrace was at one time Vice-President. His most notable performance by far was as Prospero in *The Tempest*, of which *The Bellman* critic of that time, Mr Swithin Shillito, wrote: 'It was said of Kean's Shylock, "This was the Jew, That Shakespeare drew"; still borne aloft upon the wave of poetry evoked by Walter Vambrace (away with all Misters and Professors in the presence of Genius) your annalist can but murmur, "This is the Mage, From Shakespeare's page."'

After fifteen minutes' careful work Ridley had revised this paragraph to read thus:

Professor Vambrace, an austere scholar, was associated with many causes. To his students he brought a store of scholarship from famed Trinity College, Dublin. Graduates of Waverley will long remember the voice in which he read Latin poetry aloud, seeming, as one graduate has put it, to call Horace from his tomb and Vergil from Hades. The late Professor Vambrace had a strong histrionic bent and was for some years an amateur performer with the Salterton Little Theatre.

It was not much, and it might be years before it bore fruit, but it made him feel a little better.

[TWO]

It was not for Gloster Ridley only that November 1st was embittered by the incident of the fraudulent engagement notice. The first person, who was in any way concerned with that notice, to read it in *The Bellman* was Dean Jevon Knapp, of St Nicholas' Cathedral. Returning to the Deanery at half-past five on October 31st he picked up his copy of the evening paper, and having prudently brought his handsome wrought-iron footscraper indoors so that naughty boys would not run off with it in celebration of Hallowe'en, he went into his study to read the news. It was his professional habit to turn first to the column of Births, Marriages and Deaths – Hatch, Match and Dispatch as he called it when he was being funny – to see if there was anything there which called for his attention. He read of the engagement of Pearl Vambrace and Solomon Bridgetower with annoyance; if people proposed to be married in his church it was the least they could do to tell him before announcing it to the world. He spoke to his wife about it during dinner.

'I resent the casual assumption that I shall be on call, and the Cathedral ready, whenever anyone chooses to be married,' said he. 'And how stupid to announce a marriage for November 31st; everybody knows that there is no such day.'

'The Vambraces are very odd people,' said Mrs Knapp. 'Mrs Vambrace is a Catholic, I believe; I never knew that he was anything. Of course it is Mrs Bridgetower who wants the marriage to be in the Cathedral.'

'Then why has not Mrs Bridgetower said so to me?' asked the Dean. 'I called on her only last week, and she did nothing but moan about Russia and her heart. She gave me to understand that unless the Russians change their tune at UN she will have a heart attack, presumably to spite them. She never breathed a word about her son's marriage. And nobody has booked the Cathedral for the last day of

November, which is presumably the day they mean. I will not be taken for granted in this irritating way.'

'Well, Jevon,' said his wife, 'why don't you call up Professor Vambrace and say so?'

'I shall call him after dinner,' said the Dean, though he did not relish the idea. He hated wrangles. But at eight o'clock precisely he was on the telephone.

'Good evening, Professor Vambrace, this is Dean Knapp of St Nicholas' speaking. I hope you are well?'

'Good evening, Mr Knapp.'

'I saw the notice of your daughter's engagement in *The Bellman* this evening, and I wished to speak to you about it.'

'You are under some misapprehension, Mr Knapp; my daughter is not engaged.'

'But her engagement is announced in this evening's paper, and her wedding is said to be at St Nicholas'.'

At this point the Dean's telephone clicked, and a steady buzzing told him that his communication with the Professor had been cut. So he patiently dialled the number again, and heard Vambrace's voice.

'Who is it?'

'This is Dean Knapp of St Nicholas' speaking. We were cut off.'

'Listen to me, whoever you are, I consider your joke to be in the worst of taste.'

'This is not a joke, Professor Vambrace. I am Dean Knapp –'

'Dean Humbug!' roared the Professor's voice. 'Do you suppose I am not aware, whoever you are, that this is Hallowe'en?' And the line began to buzz again.

The Dean was angry, but he was not one of those lucky men who are refreshed and stimulated by anger; it shook his self-confidence and upset his digestion and put him at a disadvantage with the world. He was ill-prepared, therefore, when the telephone rang a few minutes later and Professor Vambrace's angry voice roared at him.

'So there was a notice of my daughter's engagement in the paper!'

'Yes, of course, Professor Vambrace, that was what I called you about.'

'And what do you know about this outrage, eh?'

'I know nothing about it. I wished to know more.'

'What? Explain yourself.'

'That is what I intended to do, but you rudely rang off.'

'Never mind that. What do you know of this?'

'I saw the notice. I had heard nothing of any such wedding, and I called to make inquiries.'

'What about?'

'Well, I am Dean of St Nicholas' and when a wedding is announced there I feel that I should be informed first.'

'The whole thing is an outrage!'

'To what do you refer, Professor Vambrace?'

'My daughter is not engaged to anyone. Least of all is she engaged to that yahoo of a Bridgetower.'

'Indeed. Then how do you explain the notice?'

'I don't explain it! How do you explain it?'

'What have I to do with it?'

'Isn't your church mentioned?'

'Yes, and that is what I called you about in the first place.'

'I have nothing to do with it, I tell you!'

'You need not shout, Professor.'

'I do well to shout. What do you know about this? Answer me! What do you know?'

'I only know that if you did not authorize the announcement, and it is dated for an impossible date, it looks as though the whole thing were a practical joke.'

'Joke? Joke! You dare to call this dastardly action a joke?'

'Professor, I must ask you to moderate your tone in speaking to me.'

There was an angry howl from the other end of the line, and the communication was cut for the third time, presumably because the Professor had slammed his telephone down in its cradle. Dean Knapp's evening was ruined; for an hour he expostulated with his wife, whom he tried to cast in the role of Professor Vambrace, but she sustained it so poorly that he sank into silence and pretended to read a book. But all the while he was thinking up crushing retorts which he should have made when the opportunity served. There is nothing worse for the digestion than this, and before he went to bed the Dean took a glass of hot milk and two bismuth tablets.

He was in his first sleep when the telephone bell rang, and after a little prodding from his wife the Dean trudged downstairs to answer it, sleepily counting over in his mind those among his parishioners who were so near death that they might need him at this hour. But the voice on the telephone was tremulous with life and excitement.

'Mr Dean! Mr Dean!'

'Dean Knapp speaking. Who is it?'

'It is I, Mr Dean. Laura Pottinger.'

'What is the matter, Miss Pottinger?'

'Something terribly wrong is going on at the Cathedral, I know it. Lights are flashing on and off. And I am sure that I can hear the organ.'

'The organ, Miss Pottinger? Surely not.'

'Yes, the organ; I went out on my steps, and I am sure I heard it. And shouting. A dreadful, unholy sound.'

'Not from the Cathedral, Miss Pottinger. You must have been mistaken.'

'Indeed I am not mistaken. And I have called you so that you may take proper action at once.'

'What do you expect me to do, Miss Pottinger?'

'Do, Mr Dean? It is not for me to tell you what you should do. But if something is wrong at the Cathedral, do you not know what you should do?'

'But I am sure that you must have been deluded in some way, Miss Pottinger.'

'Deluded, Mr Dean? Do you suppose that because I am no longer young I do not know what I hear with my own ears? Do you mean to disregard this matter? Who knows what it may be – sacrilege of some sort, or robbery. There is a lot of fine plate in the Cathedral, Mr Dean, and it is not in the safe, as you know.'

This was a telling thrust. The Dean liked to have the Communion plate laid out at night, ready for the morning, and many of his parishioners, of whom Miss Pottinger was one, felt that it should be kept in the safe until it was needed. If anything were stolen, this quirk of the Dean's would not be forgotten, so he said, 'Very well, Miss Pottinger. I shall go over and see that everything is all right.'

'I shall meet you at the West Door.'

'No, no; you must not think of venturing out.'

'Yes, I shall. I want to know what is happening.'

'If there is anything amiss there might be trouble, and you must not be in any danger.'

'I am a soldier's daughter, Mr Dean.'

'Miss Pottinger, as your priest, I forbid you to come to the Cathedral. Now please go back to bed and do not worry any more.' And with that the Dean hung up his telephone, hoping that he had quelled her. Miss Pottinger, who was over eighty, and very High in her religious opinions, rather liked to be ordered about by clergymen, and was always impressed by the word 'priest'.

By this time the Dean was thoroughly awake, and cold and miserable. His stomach was churning within him and he wanted to go back to bed. But unless he went to the Cathedral he would never hear the end of it. The chances were that Miss Pottinger was mistaken, and his journey would be for nothing: but on the other hand there might be something wrong, and he would face – what? The Dean had been through the 1914–18 war and he felt that his brave days were over. All he wanted now was a quiet life. But the service of the Church was terribly unquiet, sometimes. So he went back to his bedroom, and put on a pullover, and his socks and shoes, and drew on his cassock over his pyjamas. His wife, who was accustomed to night calls, did not stir. He found the large cloak which he wore for winter funerals in the coat-cupboard in the hall, and set forth.

It was only a block from the Deanery to the Cathedral, and the night was bright with moonlight, and mysterious with a film of mist. As the Dean drew near to the Cathedral his heart sank, for unmistakably there was music on the air, a loud and merry tune played upon the organ, mingled with singing voices and an occasional shout of laughter. And unquestionably there was light in the large church, not much, but some. As he approached the West Door the Dean thought that he saw a lurking figure, but when he drew near it had vanished. St Nicholas' Cathedral in Salterton is not one of your common Canadian cathedrals, in sham Gothic; it is a reproduction, on a much smaller scale, of St Paul's, and it has a periwigged dignity of its own. The West Door was under a columned portico, darkly shadowed at this time of night.

The Dean took out his key, and listened. The music and the laughter were not so plainly to be heard here as in the street, but they were plain enough, and eerie. The Dean admitted to himself that he was frightened. He was a devout man, and while devotion undoubtedly brings its spiritual rewards it brings its spiritual terrors too. This was All Hallow's Eve, and if he truly believed in All Saints on the morrow, why should he not believe in the Powers of Darkness tonight? He had never been the sort of Christian who wants to have things all his own way – to preach the love of God and to deny the existence of the Devil. Well, if he had to meet the Devil in the line of duty, he would do so like a man. He muttered a prayer, unlocked the door and tiptoed into the vast shadows of the church.

At first it seemed to him that the chancel was filled with people, but when his astonishment subsided he judged the number to be six or seven. In his own stall – the Dean's stall! – a man was standing on his cushion, waving his arms in time to the music of the organ and the voice of the organist. It was a good tenor voice, and it was singing:

Man, Man, Man,
Is for the woman made,
And the woman for the man!

On the chancel steps a group of people, hand in hand, were circling in a dance, a sort of reel, and now and then one of them would cry 'Heigh!' in the high voice used by Highland dancers.

As the spur is for the jade
As the scabbard for the blade,
As for digging is the spade
As for liquor is the can,
So Man, Man, Man,
Is for the woman made.

The voice was full and joyous and the accompaniment skirled and whistled from the reed pipes of the organ. The Dean stood amazed for a time – it could not have been long, but he was so astonished that he was unable to make any estimate of it – and then wondered what he should do. These were no devils, and as people they did not look very frightening. Indeed, he realized with astonishment at himself that he had been looking at their antics with admiration, thinking what a pretty sight they made, dancing there, and how beautiful his Cathedral looked in this light, with this music and with these inhabitants. Such thoughts would never do. He strode forward and shouted in a loud voice: 'What is the meaning of this?'

The effect was everything that he could have desired, except that the music did not stop. The men roared, and scurried for cover behind the choir stalls; the women – or girls, he judged them to be – shrieked and hid themselves; one leapt into the Bishop's throne and slammed the little door behind her, and another dived into a pew where, on the principle supposed to be favoured by ostriches, she hid her head, but left a great deal of silk-stockinged leg and some inches of thigh in clear view.

Be she widow, wife or maid,
Be she wanton, be she staid
Be she well or ill array'd
Whore, bawd or harridan,
So Man, Man, Man,
Is for the woman made,
And the woman for the man!

The voice concluded triumphantly. Then as the notes of the organ seemed to fly away into the shadows at the roof of the chancel it cried again: 'How was that?'

'Mr Cobbler, what is the meaning of this?' called the Dean sternly.

'Oh, my God!' said the voice, dismayed, and from the organ console emerged the figure of Humphrey Cobbler, the Cathedral organist, dishevelled and ill-dressed, badly in want of a haircut, plainly drunk, but with an air of invincible cheerfulness which shone through even his present discomfiture.

'Mr Dean,' he said, fatuously, 'this is an unexpected pleasure.'

'Mr Cobbler,' said the Dean, now fully in command of the situation, 'answer my question: What is going on here?'

'Well, Mr Dean, it isn't altogether easy to explain. Very odd, on the face of it. As I shall be the first to admit. But when taken in the light of everything that has gone before, and viewed historically, if I may so express myself, quite inevitable and defensible and not in the least reprehensible, if I make myself clear.'

Cobbler delivered this speech with a fine rhetorical air, and there was an appreciative snigger from one of the hidden figures.

'Who are these people?' said the Dean, gesturing broadly. When he had entered the Cathedral he had suffered from the sense of insufficiency which afflicts a man who is wearing no trousers under his cassock: now he was free of that disability, and had indeed acquired the spacious and authoritative manner of a man who is wearing, and has a right to wear, a handsome cloak. 'Come out, all of you, at once,' he cried.

'If you please, Mr Dean,' said Cobbler, 'don't ask that. This is entirely my fault, and I accept the full responsibility. Don't ask them to come out. Not fair to them. My fault.'

'Be silent, Mr Cobbler,' said the Dean sternly. 'Come out, all of you, and be quick.'

Shuffling and scraping, they came out. And the Dean was amazed to see, not a pack of middle-aged roisterers, but four boys and three girls of university age, plainly students at Waverley, and all looking shame-faced enough to melt a harder heart than his.

'Students, I see,' said the Dean, because he could think of nothing better to say.

'My students, Mr Dean, and here entirely because of me,' said Cobbler. 'I hope that you will allow me to send them away, now, for they are really not to blame for what has happened.'

'You must all go away, at once,' said the Dean. 'And I shall see you, Mr Cobbler, at the Deanery at half-past ten tomorrow morning. Now go.' And he herded them toward the West Door.

But as they drew near to it, he had a sudden thought, and pushing past the boys and girls he opened the door a crack and peeped out. Yes, there was a figure, lurking, which could only be Miss Pottinger. The Dean was annoyed. He wanted time to make up his mind about this matter, and he did not want any interference. He was angry with Miss Pottinger for snooping around the Cathedral when he had told her to stay at home. Perhaps unreasonably, he was angrier with her than with the sheepish students who had been making merry in his Cathedral. So he turned, and without explanation, drove them before him to a door which communicated with the Church House and Sunday School annex of the Cathedral, and from there he dismissed them into a street far from where Miss Pottinger kept her vigil. When they had been gone a few minutes he followed them, and went back to the Deanery wrapped in thought.

Miss Pottinger, shivering with cold and disappointed curiosity, hung about the West Door until Archie Blaine, *The Bellman* reporter, returning late from the office, approached her and asked if anything was wrong. And, as often happens when something is wrong, Miss Pottinger denied it vehemently and scampered across the street to her own house.

It would probably be unjust to Miss Laura Pottinger to describe her as a busybody; she preferred to think of herself as one who possessed a strong sense of her responsibility toward others. She was a soldier's daughter, as she had told the Dean; her father had for many years been a colonel of militia, and if he had not been somewhat too busy for service when the first Boer War broke out, and somewhat too old for it when the second Boer War came along, he would undoubtedly have distinguished himself in the field. He was a very successful wholesale grocer, and his business yielded the means to support his military dignity on the highest level; indeed, in his household it was possible to maintain the most idealistic concepts of military honour, of good breeding and of Victorian Anglicanism, without ever being troubled about such base considerations as money. Miss Pottinger, in her advanced years, had yielded nothing to the spirit of the times; two world wars had beaten vainly against her sense of propriety, and the reduction of her means (though she was very comfortably off) had only served to increase her devotion to what she believed to be the public good.

She was aggrieved, but not surprised, that Dean Knapp had behaved so oddly in the matter of the midnight disturbance in the Cathedral. She had long ago decided that the Dean lacked those qualities of decison, censoriousness and command which she included under the general heading of 'gimp'. But she was devoted to the Cathedral, and was ready to put all her own boundless stock of gimp at its service. Therefore she made her way to early Communion on All Saints' Day in a martial spirit, and as soon as the service was over she buttonholed Mr Matthew Snelgrove, the lawyer, as he made his way toward the door.

'You are not locking up the Communion plate, Mr Snelgrove?'

'Surely that is not necessary, Miss Pottinger? There will be another service at eleven.' Mr Snelgrove was chancellor of the diocese, and although it was not strictly his duty to do so, he usually locked the church valuables in the vault, and made himself responsible for their safe keeping.

'I hope that there was nothing missing this morning?'

'Not that I know of. Why would there be?'

'There was something very odd going on in the Cathedral last night, at midnight and after. A dreadful clamour, as though the place were full of rowdy people. I called the Dean, and I believe he took some action, though of course I don't know. Naturally I was anxious. After all, there were many fine pieces on the altar all night, including the chalice which father gave to St Nicholas' on the successful conclusion of the South African War. I was concerned. And of course I concluded that you, as chancellor, would have news which would be some time in getting down to those of us who are merely parishioners.'

Simple though this speech appears, it contained many of those qualities of hidden meaning and implication which made Miss

Pottinger a remarkable, if unrecognized, rhetorician. It aroused suspicion in the mind of Mr Snelgrove, and warmed up his well-developed animosity against the Dean; it suggested sacrilege, which to his lawyer-like mind was deeply repugnant; it brought into the open the old quarrel about whether the altar should be decked with Communion plate at night (which was convenient) or in the morning (which was safe); it reminded Mr Snelgrove that the Pottingers had been an influential and generous family in Cathedral life for almost a century, and that when Miss Pottinger died her small fortune might come to the Cathedral if she got her way in some Cathedral affairs; its mock humility flattered the chancellor, while goading him, and gave him an excuse to harry the Dean. Mr Snelgrove's keen legal mind grasped all these points at once, and after a few more words with Miss Pottinger he hurried off to the vestry, like a ruffled old stork, to tackle the Dean about it.

It must not be supposed, because Dean Knapp was not in every respect satisfactory to Miss Pottinger, Mr Snelgrove and some others among his parishioners, that he was less than capable as a clergyman. He was, on the contrary, a man of more than ordinary ability in his profession. But in every church there are people who, for reasons which seem sufficient to them, do not approve of their pastor and who seek to harry him and bully him into some condition more pleasing to themselves. The democracy which the Reformation brought into the Christian Church rages in their bosoms like a fire; they would deny that they regard their clergyman as their spiritual hired hand, whom they boss and oversee for his own good, but that is certainly the impression they give to observers. Dean Knapp attracted this sort of bullying, for he had his share of personal vanity, and it was his desire to be considered urbane. Although he lived in Canada, in the middle of the twentieth century, his clerical ideals were those nineteenth-century clergymen in England who were witty men of the world, as well as men of God. His aptitude for this sort of masquerading was not great, but he tried hard, and often committed innocent follies in pursuit of his urbane goal. He made little literary jokes which people did not understand; he sometimes suggested that certain minor sins were unimportant and rather funny, instead of ignoring them completely as a really tactful Canadian clergyman should; he lacked zeal for the more uproarious sorts of boys' work, and when it was necessary to raise money for good causes he did not show that wholehearted reverence for money which is so reassuring to a flock composed predominantly of business people. And, worst of all, he sometimes refused to be serious when dealing with people who were angry. It was this characteristic of the Dean's which especially annoyed Mr Matthew Snelgrove, who was often angry and who liked people to share his anger or tremble at it. A surprising amount of Mr Snelgrove's time was spent in trying to make the Dean be serious when the Dean wanted to be urbane.

Mr Snelgrove entered the vestry, with the most cursory of knocks, just as the Dean had removed his cassock and was about to put on his waistcoat and coat. It is not as easy to be urbane in shirtsleeves as when fully dressed.

'What's this I hear about trouble in the church last night?' asked Mr Snelgrove.

But Dean Knapp was not to be caught that way, and he replied: 'Well, what do you hear about it, Mr Snelgrove?' He then smiled, as though to say that Mr Snelgrove was making a fuss about nothing.

'Miss Pottinger thought that there might be some danger to the plate which was on the altar. It is of considerable value, you know.'

'It is certainly more valuable than one might think, without being as valuable as the donors suppose,' said the Dean, and laughed urbanely. Not bad, thought he, for a man who has not yet had his breakfast. But Mr Snelgrove was not pleased.

'We should have our work cut out to replace it, if any of it were stolen,' said he.

'Then perhaps we should increase the insurance,' said the Dean.

'The insurance is all right as it is,' said Mr Snelgrove. 'But associations, and sentiment, and the devotion to the Cathedral which those pieces represent can't be replaced with insurance.'

'No, of course not,' said the Dean, pulling in his horns. He rarely had the temerity to be urbane straight through even the shortest conversation.

'What was happening here last night?'

'What was not happening last night? Hallowe'en, you know. The first thing to happen was that someone made an impudent use of the Cathedral's name in connection with a practical joke.' And then the Dean told Mr Snelgrove about the false engagement notice, and the unreasonable treatment to which he had been subjected by Professor Vambrace. But that was not enough to assuage the curiosity of the lawyer.

'And what was happening at the Cathedral? Miss Pottinger spoke of some rowdiness here.'

'Some people got in and were skylarking, but they meant no harm. I quickly cleared them out.'

'If they got in someone must have let them in. There are not so many keys. Who admitted them?'

'I did not ask.'

'Didn't ask, Mr Dean! And why didn't you ask? Is it nothing that people should break in here and skylark, as you call it? Did Smart let them in?'

'Smart is the most discreet of caretakers, Mr Snelgrove.'

'Who, then? Was it Cobbler?'

'I assure you, Mr Snelgrove, I have the matter in hand and will take steps to prevent it happening again.'

'Then it was Cobbler. I have said many times, Mr Dean, that we ought to get rid of that man.'

'Mr Cobbler has his faults, but he is an excellent musician. It would be easier to get rid of him than it would be to replace him.'

'I know little about music, Mr Dean, and frankly I care little. But Cobbler's character is such that it will one day bring disgrace upon this church, and if you insist upon defending him you may be seriously implicated.'

'That is not a risk which worries me, Mr Snelgrove. And as Mr Cobbler comes directly under my authority I think that the matter of disciplining him may safely be left to me. And I must remind you, by the way, that it is you, and not I, who associate him with the trifling disturbance here last night.'

'And you have not denied that he was responsible. I must remind you, Mr Dean, that as a lawyer I am not unaccustomed to evasiveness.'

'That is very frankly stated, Mr Snelgrove,' said the Dean, and the two men parted, each feeling that he had been called evasive by the other, and resenting it.

Although it seemed to Mr Snelgrove that he had made no impression upon the Dean and had been rebuffed by him with something approaching impertinence, he had in fact worried the Dean considerably. In a life spent in church work, the Dean had never become accustomed to the vigilance of parishioners in observing his every movement, or to the rapidity with which rumour and surmise circulated among them. If their zeal for their salvation, he thought, began to equal their zeal for minding his business, the New Jerusalem would quickly be at hand. He wanted to pass off the affair of the students in the Cathedral as quietly as possible; he hated rebuking people, partly from timidity and partly from genuine kindness, and he valued the Cathedral organist highly. Working with Cobbler he had been able to raise the aesthetic standard of the Cathedral services to a level in which he took pride; he was continually astonished by the slight effect which this work of his appeared to have upon his congregation. Indeed, the better Cobbler's music was, the more the organist's personality seemed to grate upon a number of influential Cathedral parishioners. As the Dean looked at Cobbler when the latter appeared in his study at half-past ten on All Saints' Day, he wondered if these disapproving parishioners were not, perhaps, in the right.

The organist had assumed what was, for him, ceremonial garb for this solemn occasion. That is to say, he wore an ill-fitting and rather dirty blue serge suit, the trousers of which were so short that no one could miss seeing that he wore no socks, and that of the laces in his scuffed black shoes, one was black and one was brown. His shirt was clean but ragged, and his tie had ridden toward his left ear. His hair, which was black, thick and very curly, stood out from his head like a Hottentot's; he had cut himself several times while shaving, and had staunched the blood with tufts of cotton wool. But it was not the man's poverty or untidiness which made him a disturbing object; it was the smiling concentration of his lean, swarthy face, and the nervous rolling of his large, black, bird-like eyes. He looked like a gypsy. His appearance was of the sort which causes housewives to lock up their spoons and their daughters.

'This is a serious matter, Mr Cobbler,' said the Dean, who found it hard to begin.

'Serious, indeed,' said Cobbler agreeably.

'I had hoped that your escapade of last night would not become widely known, but already the Press has been plaguing me with questions about what has been happening in the Cathedral.'

'Tck, tck.' Cobbler clucked his tongue sympathetically.

'The Press,' said the Dean, finding himself suddenly incensed against *The Bellman*, 'is a powerful and often a mischievous agency.'

'Dreadful,' said Cobbler, with feeling.

'I cannot guarantee that the story of your escapade may not become known,' said the Dean. And indeed he could not tell whether Miss Pottinger or Mr Snelgrove might not babble something which a reporter might pick up. 'You realize what a juicy morsel it would make?'

Cobbler closed his eyes, giving an unconvincing imitation of a man whose thoughts lie too deep for utterance. The Dean knew that he was not achieving the effect he sought. He decided to try another line.

'Mr Cobbler, have I not always tried to be fair with you in all matters relating to your duties at the Cathedral?'

'Mr Dean, your sympathetic co-operation makes my work a pleasure, as the gynaecologist said to the lady contortionist,' said Cobbler, earnestly. The Dean blinked, but decided to ignore the similitude.

'Then why are you not fair to me?' he asked. 'You must know that it is not always easy for me to defend you against people in the Cathedral who disapprove of you. Why do you provoke trouble in this wanton fashion?'

'The move into the Cathedral was unpremeditated,' said Cobbler. 'I never expected that there would be any trouble.'

'Rowdy singing! And dancing! And you say you did not expect any trouble!'

'It happened very simply. I had been talking to a group of students about music. Walking home, I had another idea, and as I happened to have my key with me, we popped into the Cathedral for a brief illustration.'

'You were singing what sounded to me like a bawdy song.'

'The words are misleading. The tune is a roundelay, and true roundelays are not easy to find. Poets use the word, but you know what loose thinkers poets are. The words are insignificant.'

'Those young people were dancing. And three of them were girls. Young, attractive girls,' added the Dean, severely, for as every moralist knows, youth and charm in a woman makes any deviation from ordinary conduct doubly reprehensible.

'Stirring about rhythmically, perhaps. You know how musical people are.'

'Dancing. Unquestionably they were dancing. I saw a lot of leg.'

Cobbler said nothing, but his eyes rolled in a way the Dean did not like.

'If it was all so innocent, why did they hide when I came upon them?'

'Frightened, I suppose. After all, it was Hallowe'en.'

'What is that, Mr Cobbler?'

'I only meant that you are an awe-inspiring figure in your cloak, Mr Dean.'

'You had been drinking, Mr Cobbler.'

'Not really. I mean, I've usually been drinking. But only a sip here and a sup there. Nothing, really. I might have had a beer, early in the evening.'

'Mr Cobbler, let us be plain. You had been drinking, and you brought a rowdy group into the Cathedral. You played secular music, very loudly, and you sang a song of obscene implication. Because of the excellence of your work in general, I might overlook such conduct once, but how am I to defend you against parishioners who feel themselves affronted by your conduct?'

'You mean Auntie Puss?'

'You should not speak so disrespectfully of Miss Pottinger.'

'No disrespect whatever, Mr Dean. All her dearest friends call her that.'

'You are not one of her dearest friends.'

'Through no fault of mine, I assure you.'

'You annoy her, and others.'

'In what way, Mr Dean? Apart from last night, I mean.'

'It's something about you. You don't look like a Cathedral organist.'

'That's lucky for me. Funny chaps, a lot of them. Seem to have no faces. But what can I do about it?'

'You might dress more neatly. You look too Bohemian for your position.'

'Oh, not that, surely. Bohemian is a word we use of the bad habits of our friends. I'm sure Auntie Puss doesn't say I look Bohemian.'

'If you wish to know, she says you look like a gypsy golliwog.'

Cobbler opened his mouth very wide, and laughed a loud, long laugh, which made several ornaments on the mantelpiece ring sympathetically. 'I wouldn't have thought the old faggot could think up anything so lively,' he said when he had done.

'You must not call Miss Pottinger an old faggot.'

'Why not, if she can call me a gypsy golliwog?'

The Dean was greatly troubled now. 'You will not be serious,' he said.

'Oh come, Mr Dean. That's what Auntie Puss says about *you*. We mustn't get our characters mixed.'

'I mean that you will not look at your situation in a proper way.'

'I know. That's what one of my teachers used to say. "Er ist nicht ernst," he would mumble, because I wouldn't get all sweaty about Brahms.'

'You must be serious. You have a wife and children to support. That is serious, I suppose?'

'Not really.'

'What is serious then?'

'Music, I suppose, in a hilarious sort of way,' said Cobbler, ruffling his hair and grinning.

'The Cathedral is not serious?'

'Perhaps the Cathedral is too serious,' said Cobbler. 'It is the House of God, isn't it? How do we know that God likes His house to be damned dull? Nobody seems to think that God might like a good time, now and then.'

'We are achieving nothing by this conversation,' said the Dean wearily. He felt the old weakness coming over him. He agreed with half of what Cobbler said, and in order to keep from being completely won over he was driven into a puritanical position which he did not enjoy, and in which he had little belief. Before they parted, he had won something resembling an apology from the organist, and a promise that the outrage of the previous night would never be repeated. When they parted, Cobbler's step was light, and the Dean was sitting hunched up in his chair, greatly troubled. Anyone coming upon them suddenly would not have known that the Dean had been rebuking and disciplining his organist; it looked as though the reverse had been the case.

Professor Vambrace was not a man to utter an empty threat. When he left the office of *The Bellman* after his unsatisfactory talk with Mr Ridley and Mr Marryat, he went at once to the chambers of his lawyers, Snelgrove, Martin and Fitzalan.

Chambers is the only possible word to describe the place in which this old-established firm discharged their affairs. Offices they were not, for an office suggests a place touched by modern order and efficiency. Nor were they simply rooms, for they had lofty architectural pretensions, and enclosed a dim light and a nineteenth-century frowst which distinguished them from common apartments. They partook largely of that special architectural picturesqueness which is only to be found in Canada, and which is more easily found in Salterton than in newer Canadian cities. Now the peculiar quality of this picturesqueness does not lie in a superficial resemblance to the old world; it is, rather, a compound of colonialism, romanticism and sturdy defiance of taste; it is a fascinating and distinguished ugliness which is best observed in the light of Canadian November and December afternoons. This picturesqueness is not widely admired, and examples of it are continually being destroyed, without one voice being raised in their defence. But where they exist, and are appreciated, they suggest a quality which is rather that of Northern Europe – of Scandinavia and pre-revolutionary Russia – than of England or the USA. It is in such houses as these that the characters in the plays of Ibsen had their being; it was in this light, and against these backgrounds of stained wood and etched glass that the people of Tchekov talked away their lives. And, if the Canadian building be old enough, the perceptive eye may see faint ghosts from Pushkin and Lermontov moving through the halls. This is the architecture of a Northern people, upon which the comfort of England and the luxury of the United States have fallen short of their full effect.

To reach the offices of Snelgrove, Martin and Fitzalan the Professor had to climb a long flight of stairs, which had a marked list to the right, and an elaborate balustrade which seemed to have no purpose but to keep the climber from pitching into the wall which rose directly beside it. The central room of the law chambers was lofty, and suggested a Victorian railway station and a vestry, without precisely resembling either. In it, at a number of tables and desks, sat several stenographers working at typewriters, and as these instruments tapped, the milky opaque glass which composed the partitions which shut off the private rooms of the partners rang and jingled protestingly. Mr Fitzalan was not engaged, and the Professor was shown at once to his private room.

This was a small apartment, much too tall for its floor area, and consequently rather like a well. Its single window looked out on the street, but as the exposure was a northeasterly one it was dark in November. The partition which separated it from the main office was composed of Gothic groining in wood, and the varnish on this wood had, through the years, acquired the rough and scaly surface of an old lizard. In the arches of the partition was a frosted glass, in which an elaborate floral scrollwork had been cut. In such a setting, Ronnie Fitzalan looked oddly frivolous and out of place. He was in his early forties, and on close inspection he looked it, but a first glance did not take in his bald spot, the mottled red of his cheeks, and his dull and drooping eye; it was the jaunty twist of his moustache and the elegance of his tie which held the gaze. He was a cousin of Vambrace's wife, and he greeted the Professor with cordiality.

Vambrace told his story, displayed the offending clipping from *The Bellman*, and demanded to know how quickly he could bring an action for libel. But Fitzalan gave him little comfort.

'You'd better forget all about it, Wally,' said he. 'Libel's the very devil even when you've got a good case, and you've got no case at all. Who put the thing in the paper? You don't know. You want to sue *The Bellman*. Right? Well, they'll fight just as hard as you will. You'll get all kinds of publicity you don't want. That'll do you no good and *The Bellman* no harm. Suppose you win; what've you got? Suppose you lose – and you could lose, you know, just as easy as dammit – you've got a big bill for costs and you've been made to look a fool. You'd better take *The Bellman*'s offer of an apology.'

'But they will not apologize,' said Vambrace.

'Not the way you want them to,' said Fitzalan. 'How can you expect anybody to eat dirt like that? But they've made you an offer, and it's the best one for you. It'll save face for you, and save face for them, and it won't attract a hell of a lot of attention, which is what you seem to want. Damn it all, Wally, do you want to make little Pearlie look like a fool? Do you want to spoil her chances of ever nabbing a husband, poor kid? If you do, just go ahead and shout her name around the court for a few days, or get it on the front page of *The Bellman*, suggesting that some poor chap has had his head knocked off for pretending he was engaged to her.'

'You are far away from the facts,' said Vambrace.

'I know that, Wally, but not half as far as the general public will be after you've had your fun. They'll get all the details jumbled up, and rumours will be everywhere that Pearl threw down some chap in a nasty way, or that you are such a jealous father that nobody dares come near your girl. You've got to give some thought to Pearlie, Wally. And this fellow Bridgetower; you've got to give him some consideration.'

'Why?' said the Professor.

'Why? Well, for decency's sake, that's why. He's at the University, isn't he? So are you. Do you want to kick a colleague around? Maybe you do, but it wouldn't look well.'

'Decency has never troubled the Bridgetower family in their relations with me,' said Vambrace.

'Oh, I know all about that old quarrel with this fellow's father. But it was never as bad as you pretended.'

'I think I am the best judge of that. And this young man has offered me insults which I cannot brook.'

'Listen, Wally, stop talking like a novel by Sir Walter Scott. You should have some thought for Liz and Pearlie.'

'I have. That is why I intend to see this thing through to a finish. It shall not be said that I allowed any reflection to be cast upon them.'

'Wally, you're crackers. Libel is the slipperiest charge you can take into court. Most libel cases are not worth a damn to anybody but the lawyers. And before you've finished with this one, some smart cross-examiner will make you look like a monkey, and then you'll be worse off than ever.'

Although he despised his cousin-in-law's vocabulary, and detested being called Wally, and hearing his wife and daughter called Liz and Pearlie, the Professor respected Fitzalan's ability as a lawyer, and in spite of his protests he was beginning to think that he might forgo the excitements of a law case, and accept *The Bellman*'s limited apology. But it was at this moment that the senior partner of the firm, Mr Matthew Snelgrove, put his head in at the door.

'I'm very sorry,' said he, 'I didn't realize there was anyone with you, Fitzalan. I was looking for a book.' He made as though to withdraw, but did not do so, for the fact was that he had learned from the office girls that Professor Vambrace was with his junior partner, and after his chat with the Dean that morning, he thought that he could guess why. So after some symbolic shuffling, intended to signify polite withdrawal, he said to the Professor, 'I hope that it is nothing unpleasant that brings you to us, Professor Vambrace.'

'Something most unpleasant,' said the Professor, falling into the trap.

'Really?' said Snelgrove, feigning surprise and concern. 'If I had suspected that anything was really wrong I would not have inquired. Please overlook my poor attempt at jocularity. Of course any advice that we can give you is at your disposal.'

'My cousin has been giving me what I presume is good advice; he urges me not to go to law.'

'A libel action, Mr Snelgrove,' said Fitzalan. 'I've been telling Wally how tricky they can be. Never like to advise anyone to start a libel case – unless it's something really rough, and when you have a chance of winning.'

'Now what do you think of that?' said Mr Snelgrove, smiling at the Professor with an urbanity which Dean Knapp might have envied. 'Imagine a lawyer advising a client not to go to law! Still, Fitzalan has a very level head about these things. Libel is very strange; very strange indeed. But if you think two heads are better than one, I'd be happy to hear the facts – at no extra charge, of course.' And again he laughed in a manner which was supposed to convey his knowledge that Fitzalan would not charge a relative for advice, and that he concurred in such generosity. And in another minute Mr Snelgrove was sitting down, the door was closed and the Professor was rehearsing his grievance against *The Bellman* once more, just as Mr Snelgrove intended.

Matthew Snelgrove presented, in himself, one of those interesting and not infrequent cases in which Nature imitates Art. In the nineteenth century it appears that many lawyers were dry and fusty men, of formal manner and formal dress, who carried much of the deportment of the courtroom into private life. Novelists and playwrights, observing this fact, put many such lawyers into their books and upon the stage. Actors deficient in observation and resource adopted this stock character of the Lawyer, and he was to be seen in hundreds of plays. And Matthew Snelgrove, whose professional and personal character was being formed about the turn of the century, seized upon this lawyer-like shell eagerly, and made it his own. Through the years he perfected his impersonation until, as he confronted Professor Vambrace, he was not only a lawyer in reality, but also a lawyer in a score of stagey mannerisms; a lawyer who joined the tips of his fingers while listening to a client; a lawyer who closed his eyes and smacked his lips disconcertingly while others talked; a lawyer who tugged and polished at his long nose with a very large handkerchief; a lawyer who coughed dryly before speaking; a lawyer who used his eyeglasses not so much as aids to vision as for peeping over, snatching from the nose, rubbing on the lapel, and wagging in his listener's face. He was a master of legal grimace – the smile of disbelief, the smile of I-pity-your-ignorance, the smile of that-may-safely-be-left-in-my-hands, as well as a number of effective frowns, signifying disapproval, impatience and disgust. Like many another professional man, Mr Snelgrove had become the prisoner of a professional manner, and as his legal skill was by no means extraordinary it was often impossible to tell whether he was really a lawyer or an indifferent character actor playing the part of a lawyer. Whatever the truth of the matter, his life-long performance had brought him great respect and no small measure of wealth.

For the practice of the law he had no particular intellectual endowment except an enthusiasm for the *status quo* and a regret that most of the democratic legislation of the last century could not be removed from the statute books. If Dean Knapp's ideal was the urbane cleric of the nineteenth century, Mr Snelgrove's was the lawyer-squire of the eighteenth; he was a snob, ready to play the dignified toady to anyone whom he considered his superior, and heavily patronizing to those beneath him; it was with people who might be considered his equals that he was uneasy and contentious. But as no client can be considered the full equal of his lawyer during a professional consultation he was quite at ease with Professor Vambrace.

As he listened to Vambrace's story he realized that this was a case peculiarly fitted to his own talents and temperament. Fitzalan could not be expected to understand it. The law firm of Snelgrove, Martin and Fitzalan was composed on a familiar principle; Mr Martin was particularly adept at corporation law and did all the firm's business in that line; Fitzalan was a Catholic and a Liberal in politics, and brought a good deal of business into the office from those quarters; Mr Snelgrove was a Conservative who liked to be called a Tory, and he attracted Tory business in wills and estates. But he also considered himself the firm's expert on what he called 'the niceties' – meaning matters of offended honour, as opposed to vulgar rape and breach of promise. Obviously the matter of the false engagement notice was a 'nicety', and he would pronounce upon it himself. When the Professor had finished, Mr Snelgrove fitted the tips of his fingers together, smacked his lips, raised his eyebrows and peeped over his pince-nez, and feeling that this was enough of what actors call 'business' for the moment, gave utterance.

'I see what Fitzalan means, of course. It would not be easy to determine whether the publication of this distasteful notice constitutes libel. Libel, as you are probably not aware, is that which brings a man into hatred, contempt or ridicule, or which lowers a man in the estimation of his fellows; where there is a defamatory imputation which can be plainly shown to the court, it is not necessary to prove special damage – loss of money, or some actual loss of that sort. If this is a case at all, it is a border-line case. Judges as a rule do not like border-line cases, and if you were to go to court on this matter you might be badly disappointed.'

'Just what I mean,' said Mr Fitzalan, who had not been with Mr Snelgrove long enough to know when to keep his mouth shut. When Mr Snelgrove was rolling the sweet morsels of the law under his tongue, he did not care to be interrupted, and he put on the face of one who thinks he detects an escape of sewer gas, but is not quite sure. But Fitzalan went on: 'You see, Wally, you've got to decide who would be the plaintiff in a case you brought. How old is Pearlie?'

'My daughter Pearl is twenty-two,' said the Professor.

'Well, you see, she's not a minor. Is she to be the plaintiff? Who has suffered the libel, you or her? Does she want to bring a case?'

'I have naturally not discussed such a painful and distasteful matter with her.'

'Well, you'd better do it before you go any farther. If Pearlie doesn't put a good face on it in court, and act like a girl who is wronged the judge will think you've forced her into the action, and the defence lawyers will get it out of her, and you'll look like a tyrant and a fool as well. You'd better watch your step, Wally.'

'My wife and daughter and I have all suffered more than you can suppose, Ronald, from this iniquitous thing,' said the Professor. 'It is not inconceivable that we might appear as joint plaintiffs.'

'Oh, now, hold on, Wally,' said Fitzalan. 'You know what a mess Liz would make of it in the box; anybody could make her swear that black was white. You're making a mountain out of a molehill. Anyhow, what have you to gain by an action?'

'I have this to gain: I should make those idiots on *The Bellman* feel something of the pain that I have felt. I should make them smart.'

'Oh, Wally, never go to law for simple vengeance; that's not what law is for. Redress, yes; vengeance, no. You talk as if *The Bellman* did it to spite you. Of course it was damn silly of them to take an ad with a date like November 31st in it, but wrong dates are common enough. You'd be surprised how many law cases hang on a wrong date. But they were just as much the victims of this practical joker as you.'

'Precisely,' said Mr Snelgrove, snatching the conversation to himself. 'Now my advice, Professor Vambrace, is this: to threaten an action for libel is not necessarily to go to court and fight it. You think *The Bellman* has been negligent, and I agree with you. A sharp lesson will do them no harm. I have no special affection for the Press; indeed, in a long career in the courts, I have despaired of teaching the Press manners. Rather than face an action, *The Bellman* would probably consider some reparation out of court. But it would not be good strategy to let them think that we would do so. If you care to leave the matter in our hands, I should like to think it over, and advise you.'

Thus Professor Vambrace experienced that sensation of bereavement which so often comes to a man who seeks professional assistance with a grievance, and shortly finds that his grievance is no longer his own personal property, and that much of the flavour has gone out of it.

When the Professor had left the office, Mr Snelgrove sat silent, his finger-tips together, peering over his spectacles, until Fitzalan spoke.

'Do you want to see the people at *The Bellman* or shall I?' said he.

'Perhaps I had better attend to it,' said Mr Snelgrove. 'You are a relative of Professor Vambrace, are you not?'

'I'm his wife's cousin. I thought you knew that.'

'I wasn't sure just where the kinship lay. I think there might be some indelicacy about your appearing too openly in such a matter. I'll be glad to deal with it.'

'As a matter of fact, Mr Snelgrove, I'm not at all sure that anything should be done. I told Wally to forget about it, or take *The Bellman*'s apology.'

'I don't agree with you. The Vambrace family has undoubtedly sustained some injury of reputation. They have a right to expect some reparation.'

'I always think it's better to swallow a little hurt to a family reputation than to get tangled in a lawsuit, or a law wrangle in private. It always comes out, and sounds worse. Wally's cracked on his family reputation. Doesn't amount to a damn. Who cares, anyhow?'

'Isn't Vambrace related to a noble family in Ireland?'

'Second cousin to the Marquis of Mourne and Derry. He brings it up fairly often, in order to say that such things mean nothing to him.'

'Aha; and isn't his wife's family, and yours, rather a distinguished one, among the Irish families in this part of Canada?'

'Well, we didn't emigrate during either of the Potato Famines. I suppose that's something. Liz's father, old Wolfe Tone Fitzalan, drank a bottle of whisky a day for thirty years and was never drunk. That's distinction, of course.'

'You make light of it, but these things have their significance. Fine old families should not suffer affront in silence.'

'Don't you worry that Wally will be silent. He'll bellyache about this till the day he dies. I just hope he doesn't scare all the boys away from Pearlie because of it. Her chances aren't first rate, anyhow, working in Waverley Library; there's a graveyard of matrimonial hopes, let me tell you!'

'I'll undertake it, and let you know what happens.'

'If you insist, sir, there's nothing I can say. But I'm against it. You're fighting *The Bellman*, but they're as much a victim of this joke as Wally and his family, and they may dig in their heels and refuse to pay up.'

'Ah, yes, the anonymous practical joker should come in for his share of the punishment, of course, or the matter cannot be considered closed.'

'Exactly. And how do you think you'll find him?'

'As a matter of fact,' said Mr Snelgrove, pausing at the door before making a well-timed exit, 'I have a shrewd idea that I know who he is.'

And with this remark he went, leaving his junior impressed against his will.

Who reads a newspaper? In a very large city, where newspapers are many, the question is of real concern to publishers, to editors, to circulation managers. But in such a city as Salterton, though it is no mean city, there is little question as to who reads *The Bellman*; it is no great exaggeration to say that everybody reads it. But with what a range of individual differences they read it!

Even in our time, when there is supposed to be so much rush and bustle, there are people who read a newspaper solemnly through, taking all evening to do so, missing nothing; international news, district correspondence, local affairs, editorials, special articles and advertisements even down to the humblest adjuration to 'End Pile Torture Quickly', all are grist to their mill. What it means to them is never easy to discover; they are usually aged and uncommunicative people, and they rarely make themselves known to the staff of the paper which affords them so much entertainment, unless it is to confess to a reporter on a ninetieth birthday that they are still able to read *The Bellman* without glasses. How different are they from those others, usually women, who confess under questioning that they have 'skimmed through' the paper, but who appear to have missed the chief news of the day. It was to this class of skimmers, perhaps, that the lady belonged who was discovered in London in 1944, and who admitted that she had never heard of Hitler. The vagaries of female readers, however, are beyond all reason; the simplest group for study is that which reads the paper from back to front, dropping its central portions to the floor early in the proceedings, and reassembling the whole on a principle which makes it intolerable to those who attempt to read it later.

Inevitably the literacy and comprehension of a newspaper's readers ranges over the widest scope. *The Bellman* had readers who read the column headed 'City and Vicinity' every night of their lives, and never failed to speak of it as 'City and Vinicity'. At the opposite pole to these were some members of the Waverley faculty who affected a fine superiority to the paper, spoke of it as 'the local rag' and were alternately amused by it or angry with it; indeed, they were almost ashamed to be seen ordering half a dozen extra copies when some references to themselves or their work appeared in it. But there were others at Waverley who thought differently, and who knew something of the part which the old paper had played in the history of its country. Of course there were readers who asserted that *The Bellman* was not nearly so good as it had been when they were younger; they found that this stricture applied to much else in life as well.

Gloster Ridley's editorials were read by people who were interested to know what *The Bellman* thought about current affairs, as well as by people who wanted to know what the paper thought in order that they might, as a matter of principle, disagree with it. Of these readers, only a very few bore in mind that each editorial was simply an expression of opinion by one man, who had made up his mind after some consultation with perhaps two or three other men; the majority thought of newspaper editorials as the opinions of a group of remote beings, like the Cabinet, or the justices of the Supreme Court, but with this difference: it was a mark of grace to dissent from them, if only in some slight particular. Thus it was that many people who met Ridley for the first time said, 'I always read your editorials; of course I don't agree with all of them' – as though this revealed a special independence of spirit in them, and put the editor in his place. Many people feel it necessary to be especially belligerent when talking to an editor, to show that they are not afraid of him; for however foolish an editor may be in private life, when he puts on his editorial 'We' he is like a judge who has put on his wig, and has added a cubit to his stature. And the readers who least resembled these editor-quellers were those who read the paper chiefly for its comic strips. Not that these were frivolous; the solemn devotion with which they followed the snail-like progress of those serial adventures was as great as that of the devout who read the syndicated Bible comment which was published every Saturday.

Devout also, but rarely edified, were the readers of the sports pages. It is a tested axiom of newspaper work that the sporting fraternity are never content. Although the proportion of most newspapers which is devoted to sport is far greater than the proportion of the population which is seriously interested in sport, sports lovers usually feel that a niggardly allowance of space has been given to their hobby. They tend to be zealots, and they believe their kind to be more numerous than is really the case; and because they are frequently superstitious, and possess a strong mythopoeic faculty, they attribute to newspaper sports reporters grudges and malign intentions toward their favourites of which those hard-working men are innocent. It sometimes seems to harassed sports editors that sports enthusiasts read the papers only to find food for their vast disgruntlement.

The Bellman was closely perused by countless specialists, and by none more keenly than the specialists in morality; the reports from the police court were their special meat, and they acquired and retained a wide knowledge of who had been before the magistrate, and upon what charge; reckless driving, drunkenness, non-support of wives, all the common offences were docketed in their minds, enlivened now and again by a lively fist-fight or tasty bit of indecent exposure. Everybody looks at a police court report now and then, but the specialists never missed one; wherever a report might be printed, separated by some mechanical necessity from others of its kind, they would sniff it out, make it part of their mental fabric, never forget it, and recall it when the offender died, or when his daughter married, or when some distinction or piece of good fortune brought him once again into the news. They were good people, these moralists, who rarely offended against the law themselves; but if by chance one of their kind were found, say, drunk and in charge of a car, they knew at once all the details – that his wife was pregnant, or his aged mother trembling upon the threshold of death (for these are the two commonest afflictions of wrongdoers, as every newspaperman knows) and bemoaned his fall with an intensity which might almost have been mistaken for relish.

To set down all the special interests to which a paper like *The Bellman* ministers every night would be a gigantic task and weary reading. For who, in his heart, really wants to give much of his time to another man's concerns? Most people will sympathize with the schoolchildren who search the columns of the paper for items about 'Current Events' to take to school to appease a teacher who approaches history by that path. But who except a physician searches the columns of accident news, to see what other physicians may be mentioned; and who but a lawyer gives special attention to the lawyers who are named in the reports of court cases? Professional etiquette forbids the gentlemen of the short and the long robes to advertise their skill, but they do not like to be overlooked in the news columns; as Mr Marryat sometimes bitterly remarked, they were fond enough of advertising when they did not have to pay for it. Even the clergy are not above this human weakness; they may personally choose to do good by stealth, but their congregations like themselves and their pastors to be frequently and favourably mentioned. The page of social news was read with eagerness by those who hoped to be included, or who admired or envied those who were named, for even in democratic Canada the fire of social ambition burns with a hard, gem-like flame in many bosoms. There were thousands among *The Bellman*'s readers who apparently never wearied of reading that 'lovely flower arrangements and tapers in dainty silver holders graced the table'; they always wanted to know who had 'poured', at afternoon teas, for to 'pour' is for many ladies the pinnacle of social achievement. And the wedding photographs were keenly scanned by all the photographers, of course, to see whose work had been printed and what could be found wrong with it.

Specialists of all sorts find the daily newspaper a mine of treasures for their delight. Sometimes this delight lies in indignation, and here both labour and management can be accommodated by a single item of news, for both are convinced that newspapers never use them with complete fairness. Indignation, also, was sought by the old lady who nightly scanned *The Bellman* for pictures of girls in bathing-suits; upon finding such a picture, she never failed to write to Gloster Ridley, threatening to cancel her subscription if the offence were repeated. The advent of the two-piece suit, with its inevitable concomitant of a few exposed navels, was an unlooked-for source of delicious indignation to her. There were the people who read everything about royalty, and pasted it in a scrap-book, and the people who did the same with all news about movie stars. There were the people who always worked the simple crossword puzzle, or who read the article on bridge. There were the people who read the advice to the lovelorn, sometimes for laughter but usually in deep earnest. There were the people who read the nightly article of the medical columnist, seeking always a new name to apply to the sense of insufficiency, of dissatisfaction, of heart-hunger which gnawed at them. And of course everyone who had written a letter to the editor sought early for it until it was printed, or until hope died and resentment came to fill its place.

As well as these specialists there were of course the professional newspapermen who read the paper closely for their own reasons. Mr Rumball read all that he himself had written to see whether the city editor (who was, of course, jealous) had cut that splendid paragraph of 'colour' in his report of a street accident. Archie Blaine looked to see whether, as he suspected, he had not written considerably more news reporting than anyone else; he was not jealous, but he sometimes wondered whether the fellows who had taken journalist courses at universities would ever write as much, as fast, as well, as he did. Mr Swithin Shillito invariably read all that he had written aloud to Mrs Shillito, and then pondered aloud on possible reasons why some of his witty *aperçus* ('Quite good enough for *Punch*, though I say it myself, my dear') had not been printed. Jealousy, he feared; yes, it was a pity that poor Ridley could not rise above jealousy. Nevertheless, his brilliant couple of paragraphs about the decline in the quality of shoelaces had been used, and certainly Mr Eldon Bumford would comment on it when next they met.

Matthew Snelgrove read his evening copy of *The Bellman* with a special gloomy relish, for it never failed to yield several instances in which rampant democracy had been guilty of some foolishness which could never, he was convinced, have happened under the old squirearchy – particularly if a sufficient number of squires happened also to be lawyers. Life, as he conceived of it, was a long decline from a glorious past, and if a reader approaches a newspaper in that spirit, he can find much to confirm him in his belief, particularly if he has never examined any short period of the past in day-to-day detail. Bleak also in her approach to *The Bellman* was Mrs Solomon Bridgetower, the mother of that Solomon Bridgetower whose name had been unwarrantably linked with that of Pearl Vambrace. She was a lady whose life had been devoted in great part to the study of world politics; when she was a young and keen-witted undergraduate of Waverley she had explored and dreaded the Yellow Peril with an intensity which was beyond her years, and won the admiration of her professors. As a young wife during the First World War she had been a great expert on German atrocities; she had successively foreseen and dreaded the Jazz Age, the Depression, the Rise of Fascism and the Second World War, but she had always had a soft spot for her first dread, the Yellow Peril, and insisted on regarding the rise of Russia to world power as an aspect of it. Higher education and a naturally acute mind had enabled her to dread all these things much more comprehensively and learnedly than most ladies of her acquaintance, and had won her a local reputation as a woman of capacious intellect. She read her *Bellman* with a special pair of scissors at her side, so that she might cut out and keep any particularly significant and doom-filled piece of news.

The only other reader of the Salterton paper who used scissors was the secretary to the archbishop of the Roman Catholic diocese which had its cathedral there. Unknown to each other as they were, Monsignor Caffrey and Mrs Bridgetower had both read and been impressed by a book written in the 'twenties by a French abbé, who recommended the clipping of newspapers as a method of clarifying and understanding what appeared in them. But while he did not use scissors, Gloster Ridley made it his nightly duty to read *The Bellman*, using a blue pencil to mark every error of spelling, punctuation, proof-reading and grammar; from time to time he confronted his staff with these marked papers, as a means of urging them toward the perfection which danced before him, an ever-fleeting goal.

There was one other paper-marker in Salterton, and that was Mrs Edith Little, Ridley's housekeeper, and it was this habit of hers which made him think of her as Constant Reader.

'Come on there, Ede, come on! Let some of the rest of us have a look at the paper!' It was Mrs Little's brother-in-law, George Morphew, who spoke, and he playfully punched the November 1st issue of *The Bellman* from behind, as he did so, startling her from her absorption.

'You can have it in a few minutes,' she said, with dignity. 'Just be patient.'

'Patient, hell! I got to check up on my investments.' George laughed loudly.

'Oh, your investments! You're more of a baby than Earl. And speaking of Earl, just mind your language, George.'

'He's in bed.'

'But not asleep. He can hear everything. And he just picks up everything he hears. So just let's have a little less of H and D, please.'

George's reply was to belch, long and pleasurably. His sister-in-law gave him a sharp glance, and although his face was solemn, she knew that he was kidding her. George thought of himself as a great kidder. Pity there was such a coarse streak in George. Still, that was how it was with most men; swear or burp or even worse, and think themselves funny. She went on with her painstaking reading of the paper; from time to time she wetted her pencil and marked a typographical error. It was not long until her sister came in. George caught his wife by the wrist and drew her down into his lap. He kissed her with relish, while she struggled and giggled in his arms.

'Cut it out, Georgie,' she cried.

'A fine thing!' said George, feigning dismay. 'A fellow comes home after five days on the road, and he can't even get a little smooch!'

'Not in front of Ede,' said his wife.

'Cripes! Can't swear because of Earl; can't give you a smooching because of Ede! What the heck kind of house is this anyway?'

'Don't mind me,' said Edith, but she was blushing.

'Lookit, Ede's blushing!' cried George, delighted. 'Come on, Kitten, let's show her a real burner, and she'll go up in smoke!' He seized his wife again, and kissed her in what he believed to be a Hollywood manner.

'George, that's enough!' said Kitten. 'You got to remember that Ede's living a single life, and that kind of thing isn't fair to her. She's got her feelings, you know.'

'OK, OK,' said George, with assumed docility, and as his wife sat on his lap rearranging her hair, he whistled *When I Get You Alone Tonight*, rolling his eyes in rapture. This caused Kitten to give him a playful punch in the chest, to which he responded by slipping his hand under her skirt and snapping her garter against her thigh. Edith sniffed and glowered at the paper. These nights when George came home from 'the road' were always difficult. She wondered how Kitten could stand for it. Funny how some people seemed to lose all the refinement they'd been brought up with, after marriage. These thoughts of hers were well understood by her sister, who thought that what Ede needed, maybe, was a little cheering up. Nothing raw, like George wanted to pull, but some fun.

'Ede's marking up the paper for her fella,' said she, winking at her husband.

'Oh, that's it, eh?' said George. 'Say, how's the big romance coming along, Ede?'

'I haven't the slightest idea what you're talking about,' said Mrs Little, blushing again.

'Go on! Sure you have. You and Mr Shakespeare Ridley. Have you named the day?'

'Things between Mr Ridley and I are just exactly what they've always been, to wit, strictly formal as between employer and daily homemaker.'

'Strictly formal, eh? Like the time he was sick and asked you to give him a bed-bath?' said George.

'George Morphew, you made that up out of whole cloth, and I'd just like you to understand I don't like it!'

'Well, cripes, Ede, keep your shirt on! Cripes, it's nothing to me if you give him a bath. For all of me you can get into the tub together,' said George, who delighted in this subtle baiting of his sister-in-law and was prepared to continue on these lines for an hour. But Mrs Little's cheeks were very red, and there were tears in her eyes.

'I'd just like you to know, George, that I'm a part owner in this house and I don't have to put up with that kind of talk,' said she. 'And if there's any more of it, I'll march right out of here with Earl, and you can carry the whole thing, mortgage and all.'

'Now you've made her sore, George,' said Kitten. 'Why do you always have to go so far? Can't you ever kid without getting raw? Lookit, now you've got her bawling.' She went to her sister and set about those shoulder squeezings, proffering of bits of partly-used Kleenex, and murmurings, with which women comfort one another.

'OK, OK, you don't have to take that line with me,' said George who, like many great kidders, quickly became aggrieved. 'I know we've got a mortgage just as well as anybody else in this house, and if you don't want Earl to know it too, you better not shout so loud. You don't have to throw the mortgage up in my face, just when I get home from five days on the road.'

'When you get back from the road, all you want to think about is One Thing,' said Mrs Little, with an air of injured virtue.

'Yeah? Well, just because you're not getting any of it yourself you don't have to pick on me,' said her brother-in-law, who now firmly believed himself to be the injured party.

'Georgie! You just take that right back!' It was his wife who spoke. 'Just because Ede's had hard luck and is left to fend for herself and her kiddie you got no right to taunt her because she's living the life of a single girl and it gets her all nervous and stewed up –'

'I'm not stewed up,' shrieked Mrs Little, and hid her face in the sofa cushions, sobbing.

'Now look what you done!' roared George, happy to blame his wife for something.

'Mo-o-ommie!' The child's voice floated down the stairs.

'Oh, God, you've wakened up Earl,' said Mrs Little, hastily mopping her eyes. 'Coming, Lover! Mommie's coming to you right away!' She hurried from the room.

'Well, now you've made a fine mess of it,' said Kitten.

'Aw, hell, Kitten, she's not the only one that's nervous. I've been five days on the road and I'm nervous as a cat. You know how I get.'

'I certainly do,' said Kitten, in what she meant to be a disapproving voice, but there was a strong hint of self-satisfaction in her tone.

'Well, all right; you wouldn't like it if I didn't come home that way, would you? Best compliment a wife can have. You don't have to jump on me, just because I kid Ede a little bit. I tell you how Ede is: you got to kid her to keep yourself from taking a punch at her.'

'Now, Georgie, that's my sister you're talking about.'

'Sure, sure, I know. But she gives me a heartburn the wrong end of my digestive track, like the fella says. We ought to have a place of our own, Kitten.'

'We've been over all that lots of times, Georgie. We can share this big house with Ede a lot cheaper than we can live separate. We share the mortgage, and there's what we get from the boarder, don't forget.'

'I don't like having a boarder.'

'It's all money, and Mr Higgin is no trouble. With you on the road most of every week, it doesn't bother you much. You wouldn't want a room to stand empty, would you?'

'I guess not. But in this house everything's for the boarder, or for Ede, or for that kid.'

'Aw now, honey-bunch, don't be sore. There's one thing in this house that's all for Georgie.'

'Yeah? What?'

'Me,' said Kitten, and gave her husband a long and passionate kiss. She was a pretty little woman, and because she loved and was loved in return, she was rounded and attractive. Edith, though she had a child, looked sharp and unfruitful compared with her childless sister.

George was an unromantic figure, a travelling salesman for a food company, whose hair was thinning in front, and whose slack paunch slid down into the front of his trousers when he stood up. But so far as his nature allowed, he loved Kitten, and would have fought tigers for her. He kissed her now, greedily, and slipped his hand expertly into the bosom of her dress. And thus they remained, for perhaps a minute, until a key turned in the front door and the boarder came in.

'I hope I don't intrude,' said he, popping his head around the corner from the hallway.

'Oh, not a bit. Come in, Mr Higgin,' said Kitten, jumping up and tidying her hair and frock.

'Jeez, Kitten, you don't have to jump like that. I guess it's legal, after six years married,' said George. 'Take a chair, Mr Higgin.'

Bevill Higgin was a small, very neat man, so small and neat that the shininess of his suit and the oldness of his shoes did not at once attract attention. Although he was not eccentrically dressed, there was something old-fashioned in his appearance. His face was of a fresh, salmon pink, and his eyes were of a light and shiny blue. Although the top of his head was shiny and bald, the rusty hair which fringed it was long, and was brushed upward in an attempt to minimize his baldness, and this gave him a look of surprise. He had a long, inquisitive nose, and his little mouth was usually drawn into a bow, but from time to time it expanded in a smile which showed very white, very shiny false teeth. He was a teacher of elocution by profession, and, unlike many of his kind, he spoke in a pleasant voice with no particular accent, though an expert in such matters would have detected him as an Irishman. He perched himself neatly on a chair, and twinkled his eyes and his teeth at George and Kitten.

'I shan't stay long,' said he. 'I see that you are – busy, shall I say?' And he laughed; his laugh was of a kind infrequently heard, which can only be suggested by the syllables tee-hee, tee-hee. 'I wanted to ask a favour. I am acquiring a few pupils now, quite a number, really, and it is not always convenient for me to teach them in their homes. Many of them are business young men and women, who live in lodgings. I hoped that I might beg the use of this room for a couple of nights a week – when you are from home, naturally, Mr Morphew – for two or three hours' teaching?'

'Well, I'd have to give that some thought, Mr Higgin,' said Kitten.

'Naturally, I should wish to pay extra for the extra accommodation. But perhaps we could leave the matter of fixing a sum until I found out just how many hours I would need the room,' said Mr Higgin.

'Well –' Kitten was always open to suggestions which would bring more money into the house. There was that mortgage.

'Perhaps we might make some reciprocal arrangement,' said Mr Higgin. 'I would be very happy to make the extra payment in lessons. You yourself, Mrs Morphew, have a delightful voice; a little training, and who can say what might not come of it? Or the little boy – a charming child, but think how his opportunities in life would be increased if, from infancy, he learned to speak with – shall I say? – an accent which would at once make him *persona grata* among persons of cultivation?'

'Yeah, that'd be great,' said George, the kidder rising triumphant above the frustrated lover in him. He put one hand on his hip, and patted at his back hair with the other, speaking in what he believed to be the accent of a person of cultivation: 'Good mawning, mothaw deah. Did I heah Uncle Georgie come in pie-eyed lawst night? Disgusting, yaws? Haw!' After this flight of fancy he could contain himself no longer, and burst into a guffaw.

'Georgie, that's not funny,' said Kitten. Like many women, she had a superstitious reverence for teachers of all sorts, and she did not like to see Mr Higgin affronted. But Mr Higgin was tee-heeing happily.

'Oh, it's easy to see where the talent lies in this house,' said he. 'You have a real gift for comedy, Mr Morphew. I'd give a great deal to do some work with you, but I know you men of affairs. You'd be too busy.'

'Eh?' said George. 'Well, some of the boys think I'm pretty good. Stunt night at the club, and that kind of thing.'

'Indeed, I know it,' said Mr Higgin. 'I've had a wide experience of club smokers myself. Not for ladies, of course,' he cried, tee-heeing at Kitten, 'but very good, oh, very good. It's a pity so much talent is lost to business, but I don't suppose anything can be done about it. Still, it would be a pleasure to help you.'

'You mean, give me a few lessons?' said George. 'Well, I don't see why not. Maybe I could work up a little new material, eh. For club night?'

'Do you know a song called *The Stub of Me Old Cigar*?' Mr Higgin's eyes twinkled wickedly. 'Or, *If You Don't Want The Goods, Don't Maul 'Em*?' His eyes fleetingly sought Kitten. 'Both delightful songs. I know *all* the verses.'

'It's a deal,' said George, excitedly, and he would have closed with Mr Higgin then and there, but his sister-in-law came downstairs at that moment, greeted Mr Higgin formally, and sat down again to her paper, pencil in hand.

'What do you think, Ede,' said George. 'Mr Higgin is going to give me a little training in a few little take-offs and sketches. Get a little new material.'

'Your brother-in-law and sister have talent, I feel,' said Mr Higgin. 'One develops an instinct for such things. And you, too, Mrs Little; I feel that you are by no means the least talented of this gifted family. But your flair is for the serious rather than the comic. You and your sister might pose for a study of Comedy and Tragedy. You know the famous portrait of Garrick between Comedy and Tragedy? What a tableau you might make, with you, Mr Morphew, as Garrick, of course.'

'Never heard of Garrick, but I'm strong on garlic,' roared George. He was one of those men to whom onions, in all forms, were exquisitely comic.

'Oh, Mr Morphew, what an impromptu!' cried Mr Higgin, tee-heeing until his face was a deep carrot colour. 'What a radio MC you might make! Or television!' Mr Higgin waved a tiny hand, as though indicating boundless vistas of achievement before George. But George was not the only one who had fallen under his spell.

'Funny you should compare Kitten and I with Comedy and Tragedy,' said Edith, 'because that's the way our lives have always worked out. Hers is a great big joke, all the time, but I've always seemed to get the dirty end of the stick.'

'Aw now, Ede, it's not as bad as that,' said Kitten.

'That's how it seems to you,' said Edith, 'but you haven't gone through what I've gone through.'

'Husband ran out on her,' said George, who had no sense of artistic form and did not understand that such a revelation as this should have come after much preliminary hinting. 'Left her with the kid.'

'Left her before the baby came,' said Kitten. 'What I said at the time was, how big of a stinker can a fella get?'

Mr Higgin said nothing, but he looked at Edith very seriously, his mouth so pursed as to be completely circular. At last he said, 'Perhaps you were well rid of him.'

'I was,' said Edith, who was enjoying the situation. 'But if there's one thing means more to me than anything else, it's duty, and he's got a duty to little Earl, and the dearest wish of my life is to see that duty done.'

'Yes?' said Mr Higgin, for that seemed to be what was wanted of him. But once again George clumsily robbed Edith of her moment.

'Wants to catch up with him,' said he, 'to dig money out of him for the kid's education. But no luck, so far.'

'Your boy will bless you for it,' said Mr Higgin, turning his eyes solemnly upon Edith. 'A parent cannot give a child anything finer than an education to fit it for life. As I was suggesting a few moments ago to Mrs Morphew, I might perhaps undertake the little lad's speech-training; a really well-trained voice, from his earliest years, would put him far beyond ordinary children, who speak very carelessly in Canada, I must say. And in such a talented family –'

'No, Ede, don't you do anything that'll make the kid talk different from other kids,' said George. 'A kid's got to be regular. Other kids hate a stuck-up kid. If a kid isn't just like other kids it keeps him from getting to be outstanding, and going ahead in the world. Nope, I won't go for any teaching the kid to speak like a sissy.'

'And what's it got to do with you?' said Edith coldly.

'The kid's got no father and I feel a kind of a duty to give the advice a father'd give. You want the kid to grow up regular, don't you?'

'I'm not sure I want him to grow up to travel in canned goods,' said Edith.

'Oh, and what's wrong with travelling in canned goods? Just as good as being a house-painter, I'd say.'

'Earl's father was a sign-painter and letterer,' said Edith haughtily.

'And you have found no trace of him?' said Mr Higgin, who wanted to steer the conversation into calmer waters.

'Not hide nor hair,' said Kitten, and added portentously, 'and from that day to this Ede has lived without men. Bob Little was the first and the last.'

'Oh, not the last, I'm sure,' said Mr Higgin gallantly. 'He will be presumed dead, after a time, and then I am sure that you will have suitors galore. Galore,' he repeated, savouring this fine word.

'A widda with a kid isn't going to draw much of a crowd,' said George, with more gloom than seemed really necessary.

'Oh, I must contradict you,' said Mr Higgin, tee-heeing. 'A widow is a very attractive creature,' and he began to sing softly:

Have you heard of the widow Malone?
Ochone!
Who was bred in the town of Athlone?
Alone!
Och, she bothered the hearts
Of the swains in them parts,
So lovely the Widow Malone
Ochone!
So lovely the widow Malone!

This outburst was so surprising that no one offered to speak immediately after it, and Mr Higgin followed up his advantage.

'Not only a rare melancholy beauty, but also literary taste and intellect, Mrs Little,' and with his hand he indicated the newspaper and the pencil which she was holding.

'Oh, that,' said Edith, blushing for no reason that she could think of. 'Oh, that's just a hobby of mine; every night I go through and mark the mistakes.'

'Ede keeps house for the editor,' said George. 'Fella by the name of Ridley.'

'Mr Gloster Ridley,' said Edith primly. 'I oblige him as a daily homemaker.'

'Washes the dishes after he cooks,' sniggered George. 'Cooks all his own meals. Wears an apron, too, I bet. That's what happens to kids that aren't regular.'

'Mr Gloster Ridley?' said Mr Higgin. 'And you mark errors in the paper for him. Do you find many?'

'Not really for him,' said Edith. 'But I feel I ought to help all I can. I can't say he's very grateful. In fact, I don't mention it very often; I just take my marked paper and leave it where he'll see it. Usually he doesn't look.'

'How interesting. What kind of errors do you find?'

'All kinds. Names reversed under pictures, and misprints, and that kind of thing. Like this –' She pointed to a mark she had made on the social page. 'See here, in this report of the Catholic Women's League tea, it says: "The table was centred with a mass of dwarf nuns." Of course, that ought to read "dwarf mums".'

'Mums? Mothers, do you mean?'

'No. Chrysanthemums. He'll be sore when he sees that. But I won't be the one to point it out. Sometimes he's as good as hinted that he'd as soon I didn't mark the paper.'

'Ah, touchy?'

'Very touchy. Yesterday there was a wrong date in an engagement notice. Said a marriage would take place on November 31st. What do you think of that?'

'I think some poor guy is probably making the mistake of his life,' said George, winking at Kitten, who punched him affectionately.

'I wouldn't mention it to him. He marks a paper himself, and I just happened to see it this morning, before he went to work, and he hadn't caught it. There'll be trouble about that.'

'I should think so,' said Mr Higgin, his eyes wide. 'Was it the engagement of anyone you knew?'

'Not to say I actually know them,' said Edith. 'One was the daughter of a professor at the University and the other was Solly Bridgetower. I guess everybody knows about him; a while ago he was chasing after that Griselda Webster, but you wouldn't catch a rich girl like that marrying a poor wet like him. They said his mother broke it up.'

'Well, wouldn't it be interesting to know what happened about that,' said Mr Higgin, laughing his little laugh. 'If you know this young Bridgetower, you will probably hear all about it.'

'Oh, it isn't as if we actually *know* him,' said Kitten. 'But you know how it is; we've lived in Salterton all our lives, and we get to know about a lot of people we don't actually know to *speak* to, if you understand me.'

'I must speak to my friend Mr Shillito about it,' said Mr Higgin. 'He is very highly placed on *The Bellman*, and he has been most kind to me since I came to town. Indeed, it was he who sent me to see Mr Bridgetower at the University.'

The conversation moved to more immediately interesting matters, such as the latent talent of the Morphews and Mrs Little, the striking cleverness of little Earl, the nobility and fortitude of a grass-widow of thirty-two who brought up her fatherless child single-handed, the desirability of daily home-making as a career over factory work (in that it allowed a refined person to keep herself to herself), the vagaries of life on the road, the art of salesmanship and the toll it took of the salesman, and kindred topics. So congenial did Mr Higgin prove that they sat until twelve o'clock, drinking some beer and eating cheese and crackers. They were greatly surprised to find how late it was, and when Mr Higgin sang as much as one man could of the Midnight Quartet from Flotow's *Martha* (an opera in which, he said, he had once toured in Southern Ireland) the Morphews were lifted to such a romantic pitch that they did not observe that Mr Higgin had taken Edith's hand and was pressing it tenderly to the breast pocket of his shiny blue suit. As Edith undressed in her own room – dark, so that Earl might not wake – she could hear his light tenor voice singing in the boarder's room, and she reflected that however distant Mr Ridley might be, not all men of cultivation were unmoved by her presence.

[THREE]

In the music room of Waverley University Library, Pearl Vambrace had abandoned herself to a deplorable form of self-indulgence. If Mr Kelso, the lecturer on music, were to find her he would certainly be angry. If Dr Forgie, the Librarian, were to find her he would be angry too, for although he had no ear for music he knew an idle assistant when he saw one. But the chances were good that nobody would find her, for Mr Kelso had cancelled his Music Appreciation Hour for that afternoon, and everybody knew it but Dr Forgie. So Pearl had seized her chance. It had been a hateful day, and it would undoubtedly go on being hateful. She sprawled in a large armchair, her head resting on one arm and her legs dangling over the other, and gave herself up to illicit, healing pleasure.

The phonograph in the Music Room was of the largest and most expensive kind; it would play a great many records without being touched. But it was temperamental, like so many great artists, and only Mr Kelso and Pearl, who acted as his helper during music lectures, were permitted to go near it. Under Mr Kelso's extremely critical eye Pearl had learned to pick up recordings by their edges only, to wipe them with a chamois, and to place them on the spindle of the costly, fretful machine. She was permitted to act as Mr Kelso's handmaiden, and as nursemaid to the phonograph, because she had, in her own undergraduate years, been a particularly apt pupil in Music Appreciation; she could appreciate anything, and satisfy Mr Kelso that her appreciation was akin to, though naturally of a lesser intensity than, his own. Play her a Gregorian chant, and she would appreciate it; play her a Bartok quartet and she would appreciate that. And what brought a frosty and unwilling smile to Mr Kelso's lips was that her appreciation, like his own, was untainted by sentimentalism; she did not rhapsodize foolishly about music, as so many of his students did; she really seemed to understand what music was, and to understand what he said about it in his singularly unmusical voice. When Pearl, the autumn after her graduation, was taken on the Library staff, Mr Kelso had asked that she be allowed to help him in the Music Room, when he lectured there.

It would never occur to Mr Kelso that Pearl was a hypocrite, or that Music Appreciation, as taught by him, was something which a stone-deaf student could learn and pass examinations in. But such was the case, and her post as bottle-washer to Mr Kelso and the machine gave Pearl occasional chances for indulging what she fully knew to be a base side of her nature.

Among the very large collection of phonograph records which the Library maintained were perhaps a hundred which Mr Kelso called his Horrible Examples. These were pieces of music which he despised, sung or played by people whose manner of interpretation he despised. Now and then Mr Kelso would play one of these, in order to warn his students against some damnable musical heresy. It had taken Pearl a long time to recognize and admit to herself that just as there were times when she had to buy and eat a dozen doughnuts in one great sensual burst, there were also times when the Horrible Examples, and nothing else, were the music she wanted to hear.

As she lay in the chair on the afternoon of November 1st, a bag in which there were still ten delicious greasy doughnuts was on the floor at her side, and on the turntable of the phonograph was what she called, to herself, a Vambrace Mixed Concert. At present, in the concert hall of her mind, the world-renowned pianist, Pearl Vambrace, was playing Sinding's *Rustle of Spring*; as the cascades of sound gushed and burbled from the instrument the audience asked itself how it was that this frail girl could produce a body of tone which might have been (and in plain fact *was*) that of two players with a piano each: and the only reply that the audience could give itself was that this was the mastery vouchsafed to an artist who lived wholly for her art . . . Spring ceased to rustle, the gramophone gave a discreet, expensive cough, and at once broke into the rather thin strains of *I'll Sing Thee Songs of Araby*. Pearl Vambrace, the contralto marvel of the age, stood by the piano, singing the sweet ballad with a melancholy beauty which suggested very strongly the voice of a once-great Welsh tenor . . . To cheat thee of a sigh, or charm thee to a tear . . . With heartbreaking loveliness, with ineffable, romantic silliness, the exquisite voice mounted to the last note, and Pearl's eyes were wet as her hand stole down into the bag for another doughnut . . . This lot of records was nearly done. Only one more to be played. It was Sibelius' *Valse Triste*, which Mr Kelso was accustomed to call an aberration of genius, but which Pearl thought of in quite different terms. This time she appeared upon the stage of her imagination as Pearl Vambrace, the great ballerina, floating with pathetic grace through a dance of love and death. It was unbearably beautiful, and yet, somehow, it made life much more bearable. It made it possible, for instance, to think with some composure about Father.

Sherlock Holmes was accustomed to think of a difficult case as a three-pipe problem. In Pearl's life, Father was becoming more and more a dozen-doughnut problem. Without the greasy, bulky comfort of a dozen doughnuts distributed at various points through her digestive tract the Professor's daughter found it hard to think about him at all. His behaviour last night, for instance; his terrible rage, his rhetorical ravings after he had finished talking on the telephone with Dean Knapp; it was all that she could do to bring herself to think of them. He had not been so much angry as amazed, to begin with, but gradually, over an hour's time, he had worked himself up to a pitch of shouting fury. And what a personal fury! Great as his rage was, it was only big enough for himself. She and Mummy might have been the culprits, rather than the sharers in any disgrace or scandal that there was.

Mummy had taken it, as always when there was trouble, incoherently and in tears, and finally in agonized prayer. That Mummy loved Father there was no shadow of doubt, and that Mummy loved God was equally apparent. But she seemed always to be so frightened and guilty before them both. Perhaps if Father had not forbidden Mummy to bring Pearl up a Catholic things would have been easier at home. Pearl knew, of course, that when they had married, Father had promised (but 'as good as promised' was the exact phrase that Mummy used on the rare occasions when she spoke of it to Pearl) to join his wife in her faith, but he had refused to do so (or as Mummy always said, 'had been unable to do so'). He had insisted that Pearl be brought up an agnostic, like himself. Nor was this done by neglect of religion, or silence about it; long before she could understand what he was talking about Father had lectured her on the nature of faith, of which he had a poor opinion. And as Mummy became more and more devout, and gave more and more of her time to meditation and spiritual exercises, Father's unbelief grew rawer and more aggressive.

Home was not easy. But Pearl was a loyal daughter and it never occurred to her that home was, in many ways, a hell.

Last night Mummy had spent at least two hours at the *prie-dieu* in her bedroom, weeping softly and praying. Pearl had no such refuge. Father had paced the floor, his eyes glaring, and at one time foam, unmistakable foam, had appeared at the corners of his mouth. He had talked of a plot, on the part of a considerable number of unknown persons, to bring him into disrepute and mockery. He had been darkly conscious of this plot for some time; indeed, it had begun before he had been done out of his rightful dignity as Dean of Arts. That was when the late Professor Bridgetower had been voted into the dean's chair. Bridgetower! A scientist, a geologist if you please, who would not even have been in the Arts faculty if the composition of the Waverley syllabus had not been ridiculously out of date! What if the man was called Professor of Natural Philosophy; in the present day such terminology was as ludicrous as calling a man Professor of Phrenology. They had been out to defeat him and they had done so. But, not content with that shabby triumph, they now sought to disgrace him through his family. Through his only child – a daughter! What would they have contrived, the Professor demanded of the world at large, if he had had a son?

The first part of the Vambrace Mixed Concert had come to an end, and Pearl rose to put a new pile of records on the turntable. But that which was uppermost in the group she had chosen was a violin rendition of *The Londonderry Air*, and she felt suddenly that she could not bear anything Irish, however good it might be. So she put on Tchaikovsky's Symphony Number Six, and in no time, in that vast imaginary concert hall, the great woman conductor, Pearl Vambrace, was letting an enchanted audience hear how unbearably pathetic the *Pathétique* could be.

No, decidedly nothing Irish. Pearl was pleased, in a vague way, to be of Irish blood on both sides of her family, but she had had enough of Ireland last night. Professor Vambrace was strongly conscious of his own Irish heritage, and in periods of stress it provided him with two character roles which appealed deeply to his histrionic temperament. The first of these was the Well-Born Celt, proud, ironical and aristocratic of manner; was he not a cousin of the Marquis of Mourne and Derry? The other was the Wild and Romantic Celt, untrammelled by pretty Saxon considerations of reason, expediency, or indeed of fact. When this intellectual disguise was on him he assumed a manner of talking which was not quite a brogue, but which was racy, extravagant and punctuated by angry snorts and hollow laughter. His mode of expression owed a good deal to the plays of Dion Boucicault, which the Professor had seen in his boyhood. It was a hammy performance, but Pearl and her mother were too near to it to be critical; they feared the Professor in this mood, for he could say very bitter things.

Last night the Professor had given one of his most prolonged and elaborate impersonations in this vein. He was, he said, being persecuted, hounded, mocked by those who were jealous of his intellectual attainments, of his integrity, of his personal dignity. People who hated him because he was different from themselves had found a new means by which they hoped to bring him low. Ha, ha! How little they knew their man! He was unpopular. He needed no one to tell him that. His letters to the City Council about garbage disposal had won him no friends; he knew it. His wrangle with the Board of Education, when he had refused to have Pearl vaccinated at their request, still rankled; no one needed to tell him that. He had spoken out at meetings of the faculty of the University; no man who attacked incompetent colleagues – in public, mind you, and not like a sneaking, night-walking jackeen – need hope for popularity, let alone preferment. His success as an amateur actor was bound to create jealousy; his performance as Prospero had been something of a triumph, in its small way, and every triumph created detractors. He had fought in the open, like a man, against stupidity, and Bumbledom, and mediocrity, and he knew the world well enough to expect a bitter return.

But that he should be attacked through his daughter! Even his realism had not foreseen that! A false announcement of an engagement when they all knew that no suitor had ever so much as darkened the door of his house! That was cruelty. That was catching a man in a place where he could hardly be expected to defend himself. He was, ha ha, surprised that they could rise to cruelty, for cruelty on that level demanded a touch of imagination, and that was the last thing he had expected. If they could accuse his daughter of being engaged, they would next be spreading a report that his wife was a witch.

Tchaikovsky, filtered through the splendid machine, was dying by inches; his groans, his self-reproaches filled the room with Slavic misery. Pearl's eyes were full of tears, and she reached for the second-to-last doughnut.

It had been Mummy who broke first, and went weeping to her room. Pearl knew that Mummy's unhappiness was for her, as well as for her husband. Of course Daddy didn't realize that it was painful to have it said so many times, and in so many different ways, that no young man had ever been interested in her. She didn't care for herself, but she supposed a girl had a duty to her family in such a matter; nobody likes it to be thought that their daughter lacks charm.

Once, by an odd chance, this same Solomon Bridgetower had taken her to the Military Ball, the great event of Salterton's social year. But that was when they were both in a play, and he hadn't meant anything by it. Anyway, it was four years ago and she had not spoken a dozen words to him since. And he was the recognized property, though low on her list, of the local heiress and beauty, Griselda Webster. It was queer that anyone should think of playing a trick in which her name was linked with his. Anyway, no young man had asked her to go anywhere with him since then.

No; that was not quite true. No young man with whom she could be bothered had approached her. She had been conscious, recently, that Henry Rumball, a reporter on *The Bellman* who came every day to the University, seeking news, was persistently attentive to her. But he was a joke among all the girls in the Library.

Solomon Bridgetower, however, was not. That morning she had been aware as soon as she put her coat in her locker in the staff-room that something was in the air, and that it concerned her. The first to congratulate her had been her great enemy, Miss Ritson in Cataloguing.

'Well,' said she, 'aren't you the sly one? Carrying him off right from under Tessie's nose! No ring yet, I see. Or don't you choose to wear it at the daily toil? Congratulations, dear.'

Miss Ritson moved away, humming. It was an ironical hum, but it was lost on Pearl, whose father had been so determined that she must be an agnostic. For Miss Ritson was humming *God moves in a mysterious way, His wonders to perform*.

Tessie was Miss Teresa Forgie, daughter and principal secretary to the Librarian. She was of classic features (that is to say, horse-faced) and formidable learning. It was obvious that she would make a wonderful wife for any ambitious young professor, and it was well known among her associates in the Library that she had chosen Solly Bridgetower as the recipient of this rich dower. But Miss Forgie was as high-minded as she was learned, and when she greeted Pearl no one would have guessed that she had cried herself to sleep the night before.

'I am so deeply happy for you, Pearl,' she said. 'There is so much that a man in academic life needs – so much of simple femininity, as well as understanding of his work.' She glanced around, and continued in a lower tone. 'So many needs of Body, as well as of Mind. I hope that I may continue to be a dear, dear friend to you both.'

Pearl understood the import of this very well. She was in charge of Reference, and that included a locked section of the book-stacks called Permanently Reserved, where books were kept which could only be read on the spot, upon presentation of a permit signed by the Librarian. Tessie plainly thought that Pearl had won Solly by subtle arts learned from the Hindu Books of Love, and from Havelock Ellis' *Studies in the Psychology of Sex*.

All of the girls had congratulated her, in one way or another, within an hour of opening time. Some of them seemed genuinely glad that she was to make her escape from the Library. And Pearl had said nothing to arouse further curiosity. Was this wise? But with Daddy talking about lawyers and suits she did not know what else to do; there would be trouble enough in time. She had trembled, when she overheard some of the girls talking in whispers about arranging a shower for her.

A shower! She had intimate knowledge of these affairs, at which the friends of an engaged girl lavished everything from handkerchiefs to kitchenware upon her. What would she do if she suddenly found herself the recipient of twenty handkerchiefs, or a collection of candy-thermometers, lemon-squeezers and carrot-dicers? As Tchaikovsky moaned his last, Pearl cowered in the armchair, licking the sugar from the last doughnut off her fingers, and sweated with fright.

Suddenly the light flashed on in the dark room. It was old Mr Garnett, the Library janitor, with his trolley of cleaning materials.

'Sorry. Didn't know anybody was here.'

'It's all right, Mr Garnett. I'll just put away these records, and then I'll be through. Please go ahead with your work.'

'OK, Miss Vambrace. Looks pretty clean in here anyways.'

'There wasn't any class this afternoon. I was listening to some music alone. You won't tell anybody, will you?'

'I never tell what ain't my business. You got a right to be alone, I guess. Won't be alone much longer, I hear.'

'I'll put these records away at once.'

'That's what they say about marriage. Never alone again. Well, that can be good, and it can be pure hell, too. Ever think of it that way?'

'I'll just throw this bag right into your wastepaper box, shall I?'

'What's the fella's name?'

'I beg your pardon?'

'The fella. The fella you're engaged to? Somebody mentioned it, but I forget, now. One of our fellas, isn't it?'

'Oh, you know how people talk, Mr Garnett.'

'It was in the paper. That's not talk. When it's in the paper, you mean business. What's the fella's name?'

'Oh. I forget.'

'What? How can you forget?'

'Oh – well – the name in the paper was Mr Solomon Bridgetower.'

'Yeah. Yeah. Young Bridgetower. Well, I knew his father. I've seen worse.'

Pearl had replaced the records, and she fled. Oh, what despicable weakness! She had named him, as her fiancé, to someone outside the family! What would father say? How would she ever get out of this hateful, hateful mess?

In twenty-five years of marriage Professor Vambrace and his wife had never reached any satisfactory arrangement about food; she was preoccupied, and thought food a fleshly indulgence; he liked food, but disliked paying for it. In consequence they lived mainly on scraps and bits. Now and then Mrs Vambrace would parch, or burn, or underdo a large piece of meat, and the recollection of it would last them for two or three weeks. They never had sweets, because the Professor did not like them, but they ate a good deal of indifferent cheese. They never had fruit, because the Professor considered it a dangerous loosener of the bowels, though he made an exception in favour of stewed prunes which he thought of as regulators, or gastric policemen. Their refrigerator, which seemed to be in permanent need of de-frosting, and smelled, was always full of little saucers of things which had not been quite finished at previous meals, and they always seemed to be catching up with small arrears of past dishes. They were great keepers of bowls of grease in which, now and again, things were fried. They tended also to fall behind with their dish-washing.

Nevertheless the Professor, as became a cousin of Mourne and

Derry, firmly believed that there was a formal programme which governed their eating, but which they had temporarily agreed to set aside. The most substantial meal of their day was always eaten at one o'clock, give an hour or so either way, but he would not permit it to be called dinner, for only common people ate dinner then. It was luncheon. Not lunch; luncheon. If he chanced to be at home during the afternoon he always suggested that they skip tea. They had never actually had tea in years. Supper, he maintained, was a meal which one ate before going to bed, and as the food they ate between six and eight could not possibly be called dinner, it was usually referred to as 'the evening meal.'

When Pearl came home after her music-and-doughnut orgy at the Library it was well after six o'clock, but nothing had yet been done about the evening meal, so she prepared it. As she had acquired her notions of housekeeping from her mother, and as the cloth and such things as salt and pepper and sugar were never removed from the dining-table, this did not take long. She called her mother, who had been having a nap on her bed, and tapped at the door of her father's study, and the evening meal began.

For a time no one spoke. Pearl, glutted with doughnuts, worried a plate of stewed prunes and some bread. Mrs Vambrace ate a kind of cardboard which her doctor had recommended to her years before, as a bread substitute during a brief illness, and took a little jelly which had been left from luncheon two days ago, and which had withered and taken on a taste of onion in the refrigerator. The Professor, as became a man, was a heavier eater, and he had a saucer of cold macaroni and cheese, upon which he poured a little milk, to liven it; he followed this with the remains of a custard, the component parts of which had never really assembled, but which had a splendidly firm skin. Hunger partly satisfied, he was ready to talk.

'I have struck the first blow in my campaign, today,' he announced.

'Yes, dear?' Mrs Vambrace had a calm and sorrowful face, which belied her character, for she was inclined toward hysteria. She had also a low and pretty voice.

'It is a good policy to carry the war into the enemy's camp. I have instigated a suit against *The Bellman*.'

'Oh, Walter! A lawsuit?'

'Of course a lawsuit. What other kind of suit could I possibly mean?'

'But Walter! A lawsuit can be such a dreadful thing.'

'You should know, Elizabeth. Your family have been lawyers for long enough.'

'Did you talk to Ronny?'

'Yes, and little good it did me. Ronny shares your opinion, Elizabeth. He too thinks that a lawsuit is a dreadful thing. I would think that with his objection to suits he would get out of the law and find some other profession.'

'But Walter, I am sure that if Ronny advised against a suit he meant to spare you pain. Father always said that Ronny was a very good lawyer, for all his flippant way.'

'Your father himself enjoyed a great reputation as a lawyer, Elizabeth, and much of it was founded on his habit of persuading people not to go to law. He was a sentimentalist, I fear. It is the curse of a certain type of Irishman. Ronny would naturally appeal to him.'

'If you don't consider Ronny competent, Walter, why did you go to him?'

'That is a ridiculous question, Elizabeth. He is one of the family. Of your family, that is to say. Family means something. Not much, but something. My own family is not entirely inconsiderable, though I do not attribute a pennyworth of my own success in my chosen career to that. Still, there is the connection with Mourne and Derry. There is what I suppose may be called the aristocratic tradition, which is chiefly a tradition of not allowing oneself to be trampled over by a pack of louts and cheapjacks. So far as family gives one courage to resist what is vulgar and intrusive and impertinent, family is a very good thing. Ronny may not understand that, but his senior partner certainly does so.'

'Mr Snelgrove?'

'Yes.'

'Oh dear, Walter.'

'What about him?'

'Father always disliked him so.'

'Very possibly. Your father disliked many people.'

'Only superficially, Walter. But he really disliked Mr Snelgrove. He said he was one of those men who gravitate to the law because they delight in mischief.'

'Your father was quick to find some fanciful reason for discrediting a man who had defeated him in court.'

'That is unkind, Walter. And Mr Snelgrove never defeated Father anywhere. Father was a great advocate.'

'Everyone says so, Elizabeth. It is generally admitted that if it had not been for his weakness he could have done anything he chose.'

'He had a very large heart, Walter. We had such a happy home.'

'I dare say.'

The thought of that home made Mrs Vambrace weep a few tears, perhaps because of the contrast between those laden tables and her loving, witty, drunk-every-night father, and the stewed prunes which she shared with the invincibly sober Vambrace. Pearl, who had not wanted to speak until she had heard more of her father's campaign, cleared away the dishes and set in place the inevitable *pièce de résistance* of a Vambrace evening meal, a large plate of soda crackers and a pot of very strong tea.

'I also visited the editor of *The Bellman*,' said the Professor, when he had buttered a biscuit very thickly and sprinkled it generously with salt.

'Yes?' said his wife. Her resistance, such as it was, had been broken for the evening.

'There's a fool, if you happen to be in search of a fool,' said the Professor, while crumbs flew out of his mouth. 'Family is little enough, as I said. But there's a fellow with no family. A self-made fellow. And what a thing he has made of himself! He crumpled up at once, when I told him what I intended to do. I despised him. First of all, he has no character. That's where family comes in. Then he has no real education. That's where the university comes in. To think that a mind of that quality should be in charge of a newspaper! Is it any wonder that the Press is the engine of mischief that it is! When I told him I meant to sue he went as white as a sheet.'

'Did you go to him first?' said Mrs Vambrace.

'Of course.'

'You threatened a suit before you had seen your lawyers? Oh Walter!'

'Elizabeth, you really have the most curious notion of the place of a lawyer in a man's life. I decide to sue, and I tell my lawyer to go ahead with it. I do not ask his advice; I give him my instructions.'

'Father.' Pearl spoke now for the first time. 'What will the suit mean?'

'It will mean justice, I trust. Retribution. An absolute retraction of this foul attack, and substantial damages. The private citizen has some redress in cases of this sort, I hope. The Press is powerful, but it has not quite got us all under its thumb.'

'Will I have to appear in court?'

'I don't suppose so. Why should you?'

'If I don't, who will?'

'Don't be absurd, Pearl. I shall appear, of course.'

'Are you bringing the suit?'

'And who else would bring it?'

'But in my name?'

'Not at all. Why in your name, of all things?'

'Because if anyone has been wronged, it's me.'

'It's I. How often have I –'

'Listen, Father. I won't go.'

'What do you mean? Won't go where?'

'To court. I couldn't bear it.'

'What makes you think you would appear in court? I am defending you. You are my daughter. Why should you appear anywhere?'

'Father, I'm over twenty-one. You can't defend me that way. If I have been offended, I must at least appear and say so.'

'Nonsense. You don't know anything about law.'

'I know that much. Father, please don't go on with it.'

'Of course I shall go on with it. How can you speak so ungratefully, Pearl? I know what must be done. You are still very much a child.'

'In law I'm not a child. I'm a grown woman. And I won't go to court and be made a fool of. I'll talk to Cousin Ronny.'

The Professor pushed his teacup aside and brushed some crumbs into a heap on the cloth.

'I refuse to continue any such discussion as this at the table,' said he. As a cousin of Mourne and Derry he kept up a strong pretence that there are certain things which cannot be discussed while eating. As he was an inveterate quarreller-at-the-table himself it was never easy for his family to know what these things were.

The Professor and his wife went into the living-room and sat in their accustomed chairs on either side of the fireplace. Pearl gathered up the dirty dishes, took them to the kitchen, held them briefly under the cold water tap and stacked them up, to be washed at some indefinite future time. It was a received belief of Vambrace housewifery that dishes might be left thus if they had been rinsed. She then went and stood between her parents, waiting to be recognized, but as neither of them would look at her she screwed up her courage and spoke.

'Father, please don't have a lawsuit.'

'I beg your pardon?'

'Please don't have a lawsuit.'

'I shall do what I think best.'

'Yes, but think what it will mean for me.'

'And what, precisely, will it mean for you?'

'I'll have to go into court and say it was all a mistake, or a joke, or whatever it was. They'll ask me questions. I'll be a laughing stock.'

'Your honour will be vindicated.'

'It'll make me look silly.'

'And how, pray, do you suppose you will look if this foul lie is not exposed for what it is?'

'But what's foul about it?'

'What? How can you ask such a question? Haven't you realized that this is a blow at me? A public statement that my daughter is to marry the son of a family which has always sought to push me aside and belittle me – is that nothing at all?'

'I thought you had given up all that about the Bridgetowers?'

'And what made you think that, may I ask?'

'You've been in the Little Theatre with Solly for quite a while.'

'Solly? I had not known that you were on terms of familiarity with him.'

'Everybody calls him Solly.'

'Do you do so to his face?'

'No. Not exactly. But I don't see him often.'

'That is as well.'

'But Father –'

'Yes?'

'Well –'

'Yes, yes, yes. If you have something to say, say it.'

'I – well, I –'

'Come along, Pearl. What is it?'

'It's hard to put it in words.'

'Then you are not ready to speak. What is clearly apprehended is capable of being clearly expressed. Think again. And I venture to say that when you have thought this matter over you will be in agreement with me.'

Pearl went to her bedroom, changed into a better frock, and made herself tidy. She was not skilled in presenting herself, and when she had made her best efforts she still looked somewhat tousled and distracted in her dress. As she dabbed at her face in front of her small mirror (which had a whorl in it) she worried about her failure to impress her father. How could she possibly tell him what she really felt? How could she tell him that such a lawsuit as he contemplated would harm, and perhaps ruin, her chances of ever marrying?

Because she had never been able to look at her parents from any distance, Pearl was unable to guess why they were as they were, but she knew that they would take in very bad part any suggestion from her that she was interested in marriage, or regarded her chances of marriage as an important factor in her life. She was certainly not clear on the subject herself. She had done nothing to attract any man, and men had shown little enough interest in her. She had no clear notion of what marriage would be like, or the kind of husband she wanted. But she had, deeply rooted in her nature, a feeling that she wanted a husband, and that if she did not get one, of some kind, at some time, her life would be incomplete. She was humble. She did not expect a Prince Charming, and she did not think that it would be easy to marry anybody. But she did not see any reason why, when girls no more attractive than herself were able to marry, she should not manage to do so.

She also knew that if there were a lawsuit, and her father said that she must appear in court, and look like a fool, that she would do so. She would protest, of course, but it was unthinkable that he should be disobeyed.

She would dearly have liked to go out without saying anything to her parents, but she knew that such a course was quite impossible. So when she had put on her coat she went to them.

'I don't expect to be very late.'

'You are not going out?' The Professor looked at her with histrionic amazement.

'The Yarrows are having a party. They've asked me.'

'When did they ask you?'

'At least a week ago.'

'And, in the light of what has happened, you are going?'

'Well – why not, Father?'

'Why not? Pearl, are you utterly out of your mind? Here we are, facing a law action because your name has been publicly linked with that of the one man in Salterton, above all others, whom you should avoid, and you ask me why you should not appear in society! Have you no sense of fitness?'

'But Father, are we to keep ourselves locked up until the case is over? It will be months, probably.'

'Surely, the very night after this false notice appeared, you wish to keep out of sight?'

'Well, it isn't my fault, really.'

'Has anyone questioned you about this matter?'

'Some of the girls at the Library congratulated me today.'

'And you told them the truth?'

'I didn't say anything. I didn't know what to do. I thought I should wait until you had thought it over. Father –'

'Well?'

'Couldn't the newspaper just publish a retraction, or an apology, or something?'

'They utterly refuse to do so.'

'You asked them?'

'I gave them a written form of apology. They refused it. With insolence.'

'I think I'll have to go. It will look awfully funny if I don't.'

'You are determined?'

'Well – you see how it is, Father.'

'I see that you are determined not to be guided by me in this matter. You are your own mistress, I suppose.'

'Please don't feel badly.'

'You are over twenty-one.'

'I really think I ought to go. I promised.'

'This is the spirit of the age, and of the New World, I suppose. I had hoped that as a family we would see one another through this.'

'Well, of course I'll stay at home if you feel like that, Father.'

'No, no. Go. You want to go. Don't stay at home and look at me reproachfully all night.'

And so, after a few more interchanges, Pearl went, feeling thoroughly ashamed of herself.

Waverley was a staid university. The establishment of a School of Journalism was being undertaken only after long debate and a considerable measure of opposition; as Professor Vambrace complained, there was still a Professor of Natural Philosophy attached to the Faculty of Arts who was also, in effect, the Dean of Science. But the University had a very active Chaplain, and as his work had become so heavy that he needed an assistant, his department had been enlarged in September by the inclusion of Norman Yarrow, PhD, whose first academic appointment it was.

Norman Yarrow was in his early thirties, and for two years after receiving his doctorate he had worked in the social service department of a large Canadian city. When he was invited to join the staff at Waverley he had been able to marry Yolande Spreewald, a young woman who was also in social service, as an assistant director of recreation.

It was agreed in the circle in which they moved that Norm Yarrow and Dutchy Spreewald were made for each other, and that they would be an invincible team. Norm was not, the social workers agreed, one of those nut psychologists. He did not appear to belong to any special school of psychology. He frankly admitted that he relied upon his own commonsense, rather than theory, to guide him in dealing with people who seemed to need psychological assistance. Confronted with somebody whose mental hygiene appeared to be defective, he first asked himself, 'How does this guy deviate from what's normal?' Having found that out, he knew how to proceed. He just had to jolly the fellow into a normal attitude, and that was that.

If anyone asked him how he knew what was normal, he would smile his slow, boyish smile, and explain that he was pretty normal himself – just an ordinary guy, really – and he took that as his guide. He was tall and well-built, and if his eyes were small, they were kindly and bright. If his hair had not become thin in his twenties, he might have been considered handsome. Worried women, and boys in their 'teens, were attracted by him and found him reassuring. He put great faith in what he called The Personal Influence in Guidance. He was very popular with his colleagues on his own level, and it was unfortunate that he had attracted the jealousy of his immediate superior. It must have been jealousy, for why else would his superior have suggested that he seek another position? Jealousy of that kind is not normal, and Norm had lost no time in handing in his resignation and seeking an academic post at Waverley. After some sifting of applicants, and some disappointments, the Chaplain had given Norm a contract for a probationary year. Whereupon Norm had married Dutchy.

Dutchy was every bit as normal as he. She was a girl of abounding and restless energy, physically attractive in a muscular way, of whom it was said that 'she made things go'. She was well suited to her work as a recreation director, for she was convinced that any sort of inactivity was evil, and that people who had worked all day needed to be guided into some sort of activity at night. She was immensely popular with people who agreed with this belief, and who acknowledged her superiority as a leader. She worked wonders with most children, and with amiable and submissive adults. Like everyone in her line of work she met with the occasional screwball who refused to be assimilated into the group; she directed such screwballs at once to Norm, who did what he could to jolly them into a more normal attitude. But her failures were few. Her work lay chiefly among people who were poor, without being in poverty, and among such people resistance to recreational programming and creative activities can usually be overcome.

She loved Norm in a normal, healthy way. That is to say, she was determined to do everything that lay in her power to advance him in the world, without herself being swallowed up in marriage. For marriage, as she told a great many people, was an equal partnership, with nobody on top.

Norm loved her, as was to be expected, normally. Which meant, as he explained to Dutchy while their romance was ripening, that as long as their marriage proceeded in a perfectly normal way, he was for her one hundred per cent.

Their many friends said, many times, that they made a swell couple. They received many wedding presents, including a set of twelve table mats, of spongeable glacé leather, made and given by the Sixth Ward Women's Leather-working Class, which was Dutchy's first achievement in organized recreation. And after their wedding they had a wonderful party, which Dutchy had organized, at which, for once, everybody knew all the figures of every square-dance that was performed.

The party for which Pearl was bound was the first that Norm and Dutchy had given in Salterton; indeed, their wedding party was the only one that they had given before it. But they had made friends quickly. Norm was a success with the students, with some of the younger faculty members, with the administrative and Library staff, and he was already on terms of apparent intimacy with a great many people. There was something about him which attracted confidence. Perhaps it was the frankness and ease of his manner; perhaps it was his title of Doctor, which is enough in itself to break down the reserve of many people; perhaps it was the widespread notion that a psychologist is a fountain of good counsel. Whatever it was, Norm had managed in six weeks to become the confessor of a surprising number of people who had never felt moved to confide in any of the members of the official staff of the Psychology Department. He wanted to entertain these trusting souls, and some others who, for one reason or another, might repay cultivation. And Dutchy was only too happy to organize a party; after all, that was her business. Though she told Norm several times that she was scared to death to make her first appearance at a party as a prof's wife.

'I mean,' she said, as they were cleaning their teeth together in the small bathroom of their apartment one night, 'in the ordinary way in a new town you'd get things rolling even before they came in the door by hanging up a sign "Please Remove Your Shoes Before Entering". Get people with their shoes off right away, and the ice is broken. But at a university – Gee, I don't know how far this dignity stuff has to go.'

'Just carry on as you would anywhere, Dutchy,' advised her husband. 'These people are all regular. All nice and normal, really. Some of them have talked to me pretty freely, and I think they could do with some shaking up. They need what you've got to give.'

'OK,' said Dutchy, and later, as they lay together in bed, she told Norm that the wonderful thing about him was his insight, and the way he sensed that practically everybody is really a great big kid at heart.

Pearl was one of those who had succumbed to Norman Yarrow's charm. She had first met him in the stacks at the Library, when she was checking a reference for Dr Forgie in Locke's *Essay on Human Understanding*. 'Can I help you?' the strange man had said. 'I doubt it; I'm looking for *Understanding*,' she had replied. Norman Yarrow was not a man to miss such an opening; 'Aren't we all?' he said, and when Pearl blushed he did not laugh or pursue the conversation. But two days later he had appeared in Dr Forgie's outer office with some questions about books for his students, and since then they had had two or three conversations in which Pearl, who was not used to a sympathetic male listener, had said a good deal more than she meant to say about her life. And thus the invitation for this evening came about.

When Pearl heard the rumble of a party through the apartment door she realized that she had not expected a big gathering, and had been secretly hoping for a very small one, perhaps a simple evening with understanding Dr Yarrow and his wife, who was certain to be equally understanding. But she had already rung the bell, and when the door opened the noise of the party seemed to jump out at her, like a big dog. And there was a young woman who must be Mrs Yarrow, radiating vitality like an electric heater, who seized her hand in a painfully muscular grasp.

'You're Pearl,' she shouted, in a voice pitched for the noise within; 'I'm Dutchy. Come on in, we're just warming up and you're a couple of drinks behind. Here's the bedroom, throw your coat on the bed. Yeah, it's a double bed and it's legal; ain't that wonderful!' Dutchy laughed the loud and shameless laugh of the enthusiastic bride. 'The john's in there; if you don't want it now, you sure will later. Now don't waste time primping, kid; they're waiting for you inside.'

Dutchy had lost any misgivings she might have had about being a prof's wife. Gin had banished it. Neither she nor Norman had been what they called 'drinkers' when in social service work. But as people rise in the world their social habits change. Dutchy knew that as a prof's wife she ought to make some advances in what she was unselfconscious enough to call 'gracious living' and Alcohol, though bad for the poor, was probably expected in academic life. Norm was, after all, a Ph D and she herself was a trained social worker, and had written an unusually good thesis, at the age of nineteen, on *Preparing the Parent for the Profession of Parenthood*; they were not the kind of people who were brought to ruin by drink, and so they had made a few experiments.

Gin had come to Dutchy like fire from heaven. At the first swallow she was conscious of that shock of recognition with which psychologists and literary critics are so familiar. It was as though, all her life, she had been dimly aware of the existence of some miraculous essence, some powerful liberating force, some enlightening catalyst, and here it was! It was gin! Why be nervous about being a prof's wife, why worry about a party going well, when gin could make the crooked straight and the rough places plain? Dutchy, as Norm laughingly said, had taken to gin as a duck takes to water.

Pearl was hauled into the combined living and dining-room of the apartment by the hand, while Dutchy cried, 'Gangway! Here's a poor erring sister who's a couple of drinks behind!' She was conscious of some familiar faces, but she saw no people whom she knew well. On the dining-table was a large glass jug, containing a purple liquid, and from this Dutchy poured a tumblerful, slopping a good deal on the table, and forced it upon her. 'Drink up!' she ordered. Pearl sipped suspiciously. It was gin; unquestionably it was a great deal of gin, to which some grape juice and ice water had been added.

Dutchy subdued the conversation by shouting 'Hold it! Hold it!' and when she had comparative silence she harangued her guests thus: 'Now, gals and guys, we've come to the second part of the party. Maybe you didn't know a party had a second part? Sure it has. There's the Hello; that's the beginning, when you meet everybody. You've had that. The second part's the What Now? That's where we've got to. This is the crossroads of a party. You can either go on to the Ho Hum, when everybody wishes it was time to go home, or you can go on to the Whee! What's it to be? The Ho Hum, or the Whee?'

The guests, who were unfamiliar with up-to-date techniques of recreational programming, looked somewhat astonished, and made no reply. But Dutchy was used to carrying crowds on her own enthusiasm, and she immediately made enough noise for all.

'The Whee! The Whee! Come on, let's hear it! Whee!'

A few guests politely said Whee, in rather low voices.

'OKAY!' shouted Dutchy, in a clarion voice, and in no time at all the Whee was in progress.

Pearl was not quite able to see how the Whee worked, it was so rapid and so noisy. A bowl containing scraps of paper was shaken under her nose, and she chose one. All the people in the room seemed to be engaged in some very rough game. In her surprise and dismay she hastily gulped some of the sickly gin drink, and as someone jostled her she spilled it on her front. She was dabbing at herself with her handkerchief when a man seized her slip of paper, gave a yell, and darted away, to return at once dragging a protesting young man who had been lurking at the far end of the room. Before Pearl knew what was happening another man pressed a large piece of adhesive plaster over her lips, she was forced back to back with the protesting young man, who was similarly gagged, and they were tied, by the wrists and ankles with grocer's string. This had been happening all over the room, and only Dutchy and two or three of her muscular lieutenants were free. Dutchy addressed her trussed-up guests.

'Now folksies, this is just the start of the Whee! You chose your partners by lot, and now you've got 'em. I'm going to time you, and the first couple to get untied without breaking the string, and to pull off the adhesive tape without using your hands, gets the Grand Prize. Ready? Go!' She discharged a cap pistol which she held in her hand.

Pearl had heard of people wishing to die, in books, but she had never experienced that feeling herself until now. For the young man with whom she was bound and gagged was Solomon Bridgetower.

Professor Vambrace did not sit long in his chair after Pearl had gone. A plan was working in his mind, like yeast. That is to say, part of a plan was there, and he was sure that the remainder of it would follow soon. But he did not want to wait until the plan had completed itself. He wanted to be up and doing. He was still smarting from the feeling that his grievance and his lawsuit had been taken from him and had become the property of Mr Snelgrove. Pearl's unwillingness to play the role of a submissive, wronged daughter with perfect trust in his power to win justice for her had nettled him. Nobody, it appeared, saw this matter in the proper light. But he was not a man without resource, and he would uncover the whole plot – for a plot it surely was.

'I shall be out for a time,' he said to his wife, and added mysteriously, 'on this business. If anyone should call, say that I'm in but cannot be disturbed. You understand?'

'Oh Walter!' said she; 'you are not going to do anything rash, are you?'

The Professor laughed, for it pleased him to be accused of rashness.

'You need not worry about me, Elizabeth,' he said, almost kindly. 'I know what I am doing.'

This latter claim was perhaps an exaggeration.

The Professor went to the coat cupboard, and put on, first, a thick cardigan under his jacket, and then a heavy, long scarf which was a relic of his university days. Next he brought out, from the back of the cupboard, a very long, very heavy tweed overcoat, belted across the back, which he had not worn for years. He put this on, and a pair of heavy gloves, and from the depths of the hall-seat he recovered a tweed cap, which he had not worn since the days when they were fashionable wear for golfers. He took a blackthorn walking-stick from the umbrella vase, and surveyed himself in the small, dim mirror in the back of the hall-seat. No question about it, he was effectively disguised, ready for rough weather and rough exploits, a man not to be trifled with. In fact – he finally admitted the word into his conscious thoughts – he looked like a detective. He left the house and strode briskly up the street.

Disguised the Professor was, in the sense that he was unusually dressed. He was not, however, unobtrusive, looking as he did like a fugitive from some Irish racecourse. A tall, gaunt man, nothing could disguise his characteristic long, swift stride, nor the thin, whistling sound which he made with his nostrils as he walked. But faith is a great gift and, atheist as the Professor was in matters of religion, he was not troubled by even the slightest agnosticism concerning himself and his abilities. In his own opinion, he was wrapped in a cloak of invisibility.

He was not sure where he was going, nor what he meant to do when he arrived, but he thought that a general reconnaissance would be a good beginning to his detective work. Therefore he made his way to the house in which Gloster Ridley's apartment was. This was a Victorian mansion toward the middle of the city, and when the Professor reached it, there were lights on all three floors.

It is well known to readers of detective stories – and Professor Vambrace liked to relax his mind in that way – that detection must be conducted according to the School of Force, or the School of Intellect; the detective can either burst into rooms and fight whomever he may find there, or he can collect infinitely tiny pieces of information, fit them together into a mosaic, and astonish the simple by his deductions. The Professor was unhesitating in his adherence to the latter school. Looking carefully in all directions to make sure that no one was watching, he hastened to the back of the Victorian mansion and literally stumbled upon valuable evidence in the form of a collection of garbage cans. They made a clatter, and almost at once the back door on the ground floor opened and a female voice said, fiercely, 'Get out of that, you filthy brute!'

The Professor, in detective parlance, 'froze'. That is to say, he crushed himself flat against the wall, ducked his head, and stopped breathing. Unfortunately, in this manoeuvre, he dropped his heavy stick among the garbage cans and made another clatter.

The unseen woman came further out of the house, and said, 'Scat!'

There was an inaudible question from within.

'It's those damned dogs again,' said the woman. She heaved half a brick among the garbage cans, frightening the Professor, and hurting him when the brick bounced and hit him on the shin. But she then went inside, and after a few rigid moments he carefully extricated himself from the cans, and observed them closely. Upon one was roughly lettered RIDLEY. Aha! Well, he had known that Ridley lived in this house, but there was satisfaction in proving it in this thoroughly detective-like way. Here was another can with the same mark. Tut! He had heard that Ridley was unnaturally interested in food; a glutton, it was said, for all his thinness. Still – two garbage cans for a single man! It was effete.

As this part of the house yielded no further evidence the Professor crept around to the front, and went into the main entrance, which was in a square Victorian tower which ran up the façade of the house. Three cards were enclosed in three brass frames. George Shakerly Marmion; yes, it had been Mrs Shakerly Marmion who had mistaken him for a dog. Gloster Ridley; the second floor apartment. Mrs Phillip West; top floor. Well, he now knew *precisely* where Ridley lived; he had seen lights on the second floor; Ridley was within. No car was parked near the house; Ridley was probably alone. Deduction was going smoothly, and bit by bit was being added to the mosaic. True, there was nothing absolutely new in any of this, but Rome was not built in a day.

Then, all of a sudden, there was a sound on the stairs within the door which was marked with Ridley's card! The detective was nonplussed, and in his confusion he did what he knew at once was a silly thing. He tried the door of the Shakerly Marmions' apartment, and when it would not yield, he rang the bell. The footsteps in Ridley's entrance grew louder, and the Professor was conscious that the hair on his head was stirring. He pressed his face against the Marmions' door, to conceal it, and thus he could not tell who it was that came out of Ridley's door and stood so near to him. Why didn't the man go outside, and let him make his escape before the Marmions' door was opened! But no; there were mail boxes in the hall, and whoever it was put a key in one of them, and stood by it, presumably examining some letters. The door of the Marmions' apartment opened, and there was Mrs Shakerly Marmion, whom he knew slightly, and who might be expected to recognize him, looking him in the face. It was a moment of ingenuity, and the Professor rose to it.

'Would yez like to subscribe to *The War Cry*?' he asked, disguising his voice as completely as he could, and assuming what he later realized was the broadest possible Cork accent, recollected from childhood. To give colour to his performance, he winked confidentially at Mrs Shakerly Marmion, who immediately slammed the door in his face.

The man in the hall had gone. The Professor hurried into the street, and – yes, there he was, just turning the corner. After him!

It was Ridley, and Vambrace set out to – detective parlance – tail him. After a block or so, however, he became conscious that his quarry was hurrying in a nervous fashion. Aha, Ridley knew that he was being tailed! But the Professor was equal to that; he halted for a moment, and then changed his step to a limp – a good, audible limp, such as a man with a club foot might own. That was disguise! In his exertion to maintain his limp and a high rate of speed, the Professor's nasal whistling became positively uproarious, and cut through the November night air with astonishing clarity.

Ridley, almost on the run, turned into a house, rushed up the steps and entered without knocking. Vambrace knew it. It was the home of the Fieldings. Well, it had been an exciting chase. Now he would, in the best detective fashion, lounge unobtrusively at some little distance, ready to follow his man when he came out again.

Pearl's first coherent thought after her chaotic dismay at finding herself bound and gagged with Solly Bridgetower, was that this was what came of disobliging her father. He had not wanted her to come to this party; she had insisted on coming; this was the shameful result. It was so often like this! Whenever she tried to assert herself, and to prove to Father that she was an adult, she got into some dreadful scrape. It was as though Father were in league with God. In spite of her atheistic upbringing Pearl still had, at the back of her mind, a notion of God as a vindictive old party who was determined to keep her humble and uncertain. God and Father were not mocked. Mock them, and what happened? Some kind of unpredictable, farcical hell, like the Whee.

There was little time for painful reflection. Having briefly enjoyed the spectacle of her guests in bonds, Dutchy was moving around the room, giving advice.

'It's a technique,' she said; 'best thing is to get the plaster off your mouths first. Then you can work out of the string. Come on, folksies, don't be shy!'

Norm, who had been tied to a lady in middle life who was secretary to the University registrar, showed the way. It involved rubbing the face against the face of the partner, until the sticking-plaster could be rolled off. The middle-aged lady, who had a bad breath and a short temper, was not fully co-operative, but this only added to the fun of the thing, for Dutchy. Couple by couple the guests, realizing that this was the price of freedom, set about a sheepish rubbing of face upon face. For men who had not shaved since morning, for women who wore heavy makeup, it was a painful and messy business. Their necks were twisted; the string bit into their wrists and ankles; some stockings were torn and a good deal of dust was picked up from the floor. Most of the guests weakly pretended to think their predicament funny; a few were inwardly raging but still, borne down by Dutchy's overwhelming gaiety and a weight of painfully acquired politeness, they did not break into open rebellion.

Pearl knew Solly Bridgetower well enough by sight. She had once acted in a play – that same performance of *The Tempest* in which Mr Swithin Shillito had so admired her father – of which he was assistant director. She had met him a few times at social gatherings; she had seen him from time to time in the Library. But these were scarcely preparations for rubbing her face repeatedly against his, while their eyes watered, and they breathed stertorously. Her hair fell forward, and when she tried to throw it back with a jerk of her head she bumped Solly sharply on the nose with her chin. His nose was long and apparently very sensitive, for from beneath his sticking-plaster came a sound which might have been a cry of pain, or an oath.

Dutchy, who was running about the room, encouraging and exhorting, stopped beside them.

'Say, I only just heard about you two,' said she, excitedly. 'Congratulations, kids! But this ought to be duck soup for you two. Come on! Do it like you meant it! Say, I'll bet this was a plant. I bet you fixed it so's you'd get his name, Pearl!'

'No, I arranged that,' said one of her assistants, a large, dark, genial dentist. 'I didn't even look at her piece of paper; just grabbed Solly and tied them up.' He laughed the self-approving laugh of one who knows that he has done a good deed.

Pearl's mouth was free at last. 'I want to get out of this,' she said.

'Sure you do,' said Dutchy. 'And seeing it's you, I'll give you a hint; the way the string's tied, you can get loose at once if he lies down flat and you crawl right up over his head; then the string drops off without untying the knots. 'Bye now.' And she was off to encourage other strugglers, who lay in Laocoön groups about the floor.

Solly made a noise which sounded like entreaty. Pearl, maddened by the arch looks of the dark dentist, leaned forward, seized a loose corner of his sticking-plaster in her mouth, and jerked her head backward savagely. Solly howled.

'I think you've killed me,' he said when he could speak.

'I wish I had,' said Pearl, venomously.

'It's not my fault. I didn't ask to be tied to you.'

'Oh, shut up!'

'No use shutting up, when we're tied together like this. Let's get out. What's the trick? I lie down and you crawl over me, or something.'

'I won't.'

'You must.'

'Don't you dare tell me I must.'

'You're being a fool. If we don't get out of this mess we'll be the last, and you'll have to do it with everybody looking. Come on; I'm lying down.' And he did lie down, and Pearl had no choice but to lie down also. Solly was on his face on the floor, and she lay flat on his back.

Inch by inch she hitched herself upward along his spine and at every move Solly groaned. But as she moved the strings became looser, and at last, as she hunched her bottom over his head, they were free enough to permit her to shake them off, and stand up. In a moment Solly, much ruffled, stood beside her.

They were one of the last couples to escape, but they were not observed by the others, who were too much occupied in trying to straighten and dust their clothes to pay close attention to anything else. Nor did Dutchy leave them time for embarrassment; swift passage from one delightful experience to another was part of the technique of party-giving, as she professed it. Very rapidly she herded her guests into a circle of alternate men and women.

'Now this one's easy, kids,' she said. 'Here's an orange, see? You stick it under your chin, Jimmy, see?' Jimmy, the dark, zealous dentist, did so. 'Now you just pass it to the lady on your right, not either of you using his hands, see, and she gets it under her chin, and so you pass it all around the circle back to me. Anybody drops it, they have to fall out of the game.'

This last remark, as Dutchy quickly realized, was an error. The more reticent and more selfish people made haste to drop the orange as soon as it reached them, sometimes without any pretence at gripping it. There were, however, eight or nine people who either feared Dutchy's disapproval, or felt some necessity to do as their hostess wished, or who positively liked passing oranges from neck to neck, and they remained in the middle of the room, while Dutchy spurred them on the finer flights. After the orange they passed a grapefruit in the same way; after the grapefruit came a melon. And after the melon appeared a watermelon, which Dutchy and Jimmy the dentist passed merrily between them a few times, just to show that it could be done. The watermelon had been borrowed from the freezing locker of a neighbour in the apartment building, and its coldness was the matter for much mirth. But the secretary to the registrar was not amused.

'When I was a girl I always hated the kissing games at parties,' said she, 'and until tonight I thought that they had gone out of fashion.' Her tone was low, but a surprising number of the guests heard her, and the dissatisfied faction gained heart. So much so, indeed, that Dutchy sensed a change of atmosphere, and decided that she would not continue with her programme as she had planned it. Dutchy was not stupid, but she had not had much previous experience with people whom she could not dominate – who did not, indeed, welcome domination. She passed the purple drink, and became conciliatory. She asked her guests what game they would like to play next.

It is as dangerous, in its way, to ask a group of people associated with a university to choose their own games as it is to leave the choice in the hands of a trained director of recreation, like Dutchy. The secretary to the registrar immediately set out to explain a kind of charades which she called The Braingame; it was, she declared, a barrel of fun.

'It's just like the old kind of charades we played as children,' said she, 'except that a letter must be dropped from each syllable as it is guessed, in order to get the right answer, and when the group acts out the full word, it must express both the full word, and the word which is left when the superfluous letters are dropped. Is that clear?'

It was not clear.

'Let me give you an example. Suppose, for instance, that your real word – the word the others must guess – is "landscape". Well, the word which the group acts is "blandscrape". They pretend to be eating a pudding, and putting more salt in it; that gives the word, "bland". Then "scrape" is easy; you simply act somebody in a scrape.'

'As it were, crawling backward over a complete stranger?' asked a masculine young woman from the Dean's office, who had had to do this not long before with a young man from the classics department, who had playfully pinched her bottom. The registrar's secretary laughed lightly, and went on.

'Now, recall that your word was "landscape"; you must now act the whole word, or rather, both words. So you act "blandscrape". One of the group is being given a smooth shave, while the others peer admiringly at an imaginary view. You see? Blandscrape and landscape at once. Of course after a round or two we can have some really hard ones.'

The party seemed depressed by this notion. The masculine young woman seized her chance to make the cunning suggestion that they play a game in which they could all sit down. This was greeted with such eagerness that she launched at once into an explanation.

'Simple as A B C. Just Twenty Questions, really, but with knobs on. Somebody's It. They go outside and make up their minds that they are somebody – movie star, games champ, person in history – anybody at all. Then they sit in the middle of the room and we ask them questions to find out who they are. But – this is what makes it fun – if we ask them who they are we do it indirectly or by definition only, and they must show they know what we're talking about, or they're out of the game. I mean, I'm It. You question me. You find out I'm a famous literary woman who lived long ago. So you say, "Did you live on the Isle of Lesbos?" And I say, "No, I'm not Sappho" –'

'And we all laugh,' said the registrar's secretary in a voice which was not quite low enough.

Dutchy had not met with tensions of quite this kind in her career of recreation planning. But she was learning rapidly the arts of a faculty wife, and she intervened at this juncture in time to prevent a lively exchange between the two ladies, who were enemies of several years' standing. Such games, she said, would be wonderful for the clever university people, but there were a few dopes like herself and Jimmy present, whose minds did not work that way. Therefore they would play The Game.

As always, there were a few people present who did not know what The Game was, but they were told that it was a form of accelerated charades, and after sides had been chosen they played it quite peaceably and even with enjoyment.

Pearl and Solly were on the same side, and although she could act quite well, and make her ideas clear to the others, he was without skill in this direction. He became confused when it was his turn to act; he scowled and beat his brow; he pawed the air meaninglessly with his hands. He could not remember the rule that everything must be done in silence, and made despairing and inarticulate sounds. Pearl watched him with contempt; it was to this idiot that an unknown practical joker had linked her. She understood better what her father meant when he raved about the insult of it.

If there is anyone who has not played The Game, it may be explained that two teams are chosen, and that each team gets its chance to present the other team with a number of pieces of paper, upon which proverbs, quotations, catchwords and the like are written; each player is given one of these, and his task is to convey its meaning to his team by means of pantomime. If they guess what he is trying to tell them, they score a point. The other team, knowing the secret, watch the struggle with enjoyment.

In the fifth round of The Game, Solly was handed his paper by Norm, as captain of the opposing team, and when he read it he moaned, and muttered 'O God!' and gave every sign of despair. Norm and his team were delighted. Solly turned toward his own team in misery, and stood with his mouth hanging open, sweating visibly.

'How many words?' asked the Registrar's secretary, who had a very businesslike approach to The Game.

With his fingers Solly indicated that there were thirty-five words.

There was a roar of dismay from his team. Protests were made that this was impossible. Norm's team merely laughed in mockery.

'Is it a verse?' demanded the Registrar's secretary.

Solly shook his head.

'A saying?'

Solly looked confused, nodded, shook his head, and nodded again. Then he contorted himself violently to signify his despair.

'A quotation?' went on the Registrar's secretary, who had the phlegm of a Scotland Yard detective.

Solly nodded violently.

'Quotation from a writer?'

Solly thought for a moment, made a few meaningless gestures, then took up a rhetorical stance, and pointed toward the wall. Becoming frantic, he walked toward the Registrar's secretary and waved his hands before her face; he repeated this manoeuvre with a man, then seemed to lose heart, and stood once more at a loss, shaking his head.

Pearl's voice was heard, low and calm: 'You can fool some of the people all of the time, and you can fool all of the people some of the time, but you can't fool all of the people all of the time.'

There was an instant of silence, and then a roar from the opposing team. Solly gaped, and, forgetting that he was now privileged to speak, pantomimed extravagant delight.

'Is that right?' demanded the Registrar's secretary.

'Sure it's right,' said Norm; 'how did you guess it, Pearlie?'

Pearl was abashed. 'I don't know,' said she; 'but he somehow looked a little bit like Lincoln, and then he pointed south, toward the States, and I just said it.'

This brilliant stroke won the game, and it was time for refreshments. Consequently the company had plenty of time to talk about what Pearl had done. Although such uncanny guesses are by no means uncommon in The Game they always arouse excitement when they happen. Solly, upon being questioned, said that he did not know that the saying was attributed to Lincoln, nor had he been aware that he was pointing south; he had merely tried to behave like a man who was fooling some of the people some of the time – obviously a politician. This made Pearl's feat even more remarkable. It was Norm who, as a psychologist, offered the explanation which the company liked best.

'When people are very close, they often have the power of communicating without words,' said he. 'For instance, sometimes in the morning when I don't want an egg for breakfast, it will occur to me while I'm shaving, and then, when I get to the table, I'll find that Dutchy hasn't cooked me an egg; maybe it will turn out that there isn't even an egg in the house. It doesn't always work, of course. But obviously there's a Thing between Pearlie and Solly right now – at this stage of their relationship, I mean. It certainly looks as if they were made for each other.'

This remark naturally brought inquiry, for only Norm and Dutchy, and their friend Jimmy, appeared to have read of their engagement. Professor Vambrace would undoubtedly have been astonished that ten of the people present were utterly ignorant of the shame and insult which had been forced upon him. But when Norm had finished his explanation they knew all about it, and offered their congratulations in the shy and affectedly casual manner in which people felicitate acquaintances. Dutchy, however, insisted that a toast be drunk in the purple fluid, and hurried about, filling glasses.

'Oh no, please don't!' cried Pearl.

'Oh, don't be so modest,' shouted Dutchy.

'I'd really much rather you didn't!'

'Now Pearlie, you've got to conquer that shyness,' said Norm, in a fatherly manner.

Pearl turned a look of desperate appeal upon Solly, but he was sitting with his head down, in a condition of abjection. She was furious with him. What a fool! Oh, Daddy was so right! What a nincompoop!

Norm rose to his feet, his glass held at eye-level in that curious gesture which people never use except when they are about to propose toasts.

'Friends,' said he, making his voice full and thrilling, 'let's drink to Pearlie and Solly. Dutchy and I can't claim to be old friends of either of them, but we know what married happiness is, and I think that gives us a kind of claim to speak now. Pearlie we know a good deal better than Solly. I do, that is to say, because we've had some talks. I guess you all know that Pearlie is one hell of a swell kid, but life hasn't been much fun for her. A shy kid, brainy, not the aggressive type, she's had the idea that she's a failure in life – that she isn't attractive. A religious problem, too, which I won't touch on now, but I guess all of us who have a sincere but modern and scientific Faith know that it's pretty lonely if you haven't got that and are wandering around in the dark, so to speak. I don't want to introduce a solemn note now but as a psychologist and as a professional in guidance I know what can happen in a life which lacks what I call the Faith Focus, and there's nobody more pleased than I – and I know here that I speak for Dutchy too – that Pearlie has found herself, and that all those doubts and fears and misgivings are sublimated in that vast Power the happiness of which is something upon which Dutchy and I feel ourselves peculiarly qualified to speak. I mean getting engaged, of course. So I ask you to drink to Pearlie and Solly, and if I can remember it I'll just recite a little verse that seems to fit the occasion. Now let's see – ah. "Hurrah for the little god with wings" – no, that's not it. Oh, yes –

Hurrah for the little god of Love,
May he never moult a feather,
When his big boots and her little shoes
Are under the bed together.'

This speech was granted a mixed reception. Some of the guests appeared to be stunned. Others took it in the spirit in which it was offered, and, led by Jimmy, broke feebly into 'For they are jolly good fellows'. Pearl was miserable, but angry enough to keep back her tears; Solly looked very weary. When the song died down, he said 'Thanks', and his tone was such that even Norm and Dutchy did not press him for more.

The Fieldings' comfortable drawing-room rang with the brilliant arpeggio passages of the *Mink Schottische,* which Humphrey Cobbler was playing on the piano. As far as possible from the instrument, Gloster Ridley sat with Mrs Fielding on a sofa. He disliked music, and wished that the noise would stop. In a nearby chair sat Miss Vyner, Mrs Fielding's sister; she was a soldierly lady, at the last of youth but not yet begun upon middle age, and she was working her way through a box of fifty cigarettes, helped by occasional swigs at a whisky-and-soda. She too disliked music, and thought Cobbler a bore and a fool; these were the only two opinions she shared with Ridley, and as neither had given voice to them, this agreement could do nothing to lessen the hatred which had sprung up between them on sight. Mr Fielding, however, was enjoying himself greatly, and as he sat in his deep chair he wagged one finger, bobbed one foot, and occasionally made little noises in his throat, appreciative of the music. His wife, also, appeared to be perfectly content, which maddened Ridley, for he wanted to talk to her.

It could not be said of Ridley that he coveted his neighbour's wife. He was more than happy that Richard Fielding should live with Elspeth Fielding, sleep with her, be the father of her children and be first in her heart so long as he, Gloster Ridley, was free to call on her whenever he pleased, talk to her, confide in her, and enjoy the solace of her presence. He kissed her on her birthday, on Christmas, and on New Year's Eve, and was never ambitious to do more. Yet he loved her more truly than many men love their wives, and she and her husband both knew it. He loved her because she was beautiful, wise and kind; he also loved her because she was married, safe and would never want him to do anything about it. Such affairs are by no means uncommon nor, whatever the young may think, are they despicable.

'Wonderful stuff, Humphrey, wonderful!' said Mr Fielding, as the schottische came to a rousing finish. 'You ought to make a collection of things like that.'

'Nobody wants them,' said Cobbler. 'Music is a serious business. You may publish collections of literary oddities, but nobody wants musical oddities.'

'Then why not a concert? That's the idea! You could tour, playing a programme of forgotten Victorian music.'

'Not enough people want to hear it. And rightly so, I suppose. It's trash, though fascinating trash. It's the trashy art of an age which gives us its real flavour, far more than its handful of masterpieces. Don't you agree?' He turned his black eyes suddenly on Miss Vyner.

'Haven't a clue,' said that lady, morosely.

'But this is authentic Canadiana,' said Cobbler. 'A suite of dances, composed in this very city in 1879 and dedicated to the Marchioness of Lorne. Title: *The Fur Suite*. I've played the *Mink Schottische*. I can give you the *Beaver Mazurka*, the *Lynx Lancers*, the *Chinchilla Polka* or the *Ermine Redowa*. Every one of them re-creates the loyal gaiety of Victorian Canada. You name it; I've got it. What'll it be?'

Miss Vyner said nothing, but gave him the look of bleak, uncomprehending boredom which the unmusical wear when they are trapped among musicians. Mr Fielding elected for the *Ermine Redowa*, and quickly its solemn but scarcely sensuous strains filled the room. Ridley sighed audibly.

'Why don't you talk, if you want to?' said Mrs Fielding.

Ridley muttered and made a gesture toward the piano.

'Oh, that's not the kind of music you have to be quiet for. Dick and Humphrey will be at it all night. What's bothering you?'

'I was followed here tonight by Professor Vambrace. I really think he's off his head. He was lurking near my door, pretending to be a solicitor for the Salvation Army,' said Ridley. And at some length, and with the sort of anguished exaggeration which he could use when talking to Mrs Fielding, but which was denied him otherwise, he told the story of his afternoon. Mrs Fielding was sympathetic, asked a great many questions, and they became so absorbed in their talk that they did not notice that the *Ermine Redowa* had finished, and that they had the full attention of the others until Miss Vyner spoke.

'Well, I suppose you have to expect that kind of thing with newspapers,' said she. 'I'm not a socialist, thank God, but I'd like to see the newspapers taken over by the Government. Or a strong control put on them, anyhow. They need some responsibility knocked into them.'

Miss Vyner was looking for a fight. She was a lady with a large stock of discontent and disapproval always on hand, which she could apply to any question which presented itself. She had been a guest in the Fieldings' house for three days, and its atmosphere of easy-going happiness grated on her. She knew that Ridley was a special friend of her sister and brother-in-law and she felt that for the good of everyone she should insult him. But Ridley was not in a mood for further insult that day.

'Quite possibly you are right,' said he. 'But what you would get then would not be newspapers free of error, or newspapers edited according to some splendid principle, but gazettes of fact, probably no better authenticated than the facts in newspapers at present. You see, newspapers are written and edited by journalists, and journalists are rather special people. Drive them out of the newspaper offices, and send in civil servants to replace them, and I do not think you would like the result.'

'I haven't noticed anything very special about the journalists I've met,' said Miss Vyner.

'Perhaps not, but why should you? Nevertheless, a journalist is not something which just happens. Like poets, they are born. They are marked by a kind of altruistic nosiness.'

'That's what I don't like about them,' said Miss Vyner. 'They're always poking their noses into what doesn't concern them.'

'Certainly. But they also poke their noses into what concerns everybody. This nose-poking isn't something you can turn on and off like electricity. If you want the benefit of what journalists do, you must put up with some of the annoyance of what they do, as well.'

'Of course you have to stick up for them, I suppose. That's how you get your bread-and-butter.'

'Yes, and I like getting my bread-and-butter that way. I like being a journalist and a nose-poker. I like it not only because I am made that way, but because journalism is one of the few jobs which has been able to retain most of its original honesty about itself.'

'Don't let Pat bother you,' said Mrs Fielding, who thought that her sister was being surly. 'We all know that journalism is a very honourable profession.'

'Excuse me, Elspeth,' said Ridley, 'but I don't like to hear it called a profession. That word has been worked to death. There are people in the newspaper business who like to call it a profession, but in general we try not to cant about ourselves. We try not to join the modern rush to ennoble our ordinary, necessary work. We see too much of that in our job. Banking and insurance have managed to raise themselves almost to the level of religions; medicine and the law are priesthoods, against which no whisper must be heard; teachers insist that they do their jobs for the good of mankind, without any thought of getting a living. And all this self-praise, all this dense fog of respectability which has been created around ordinary, necessary work, is choking our honesty about ourselves. It is the dash of old-time roguery which is still found in journalism – the slightly raffish, *déclassé* air of it – which is its fascination. We still live by our wits. We haven't bullied and public-relations-agented the public to the point where they think that we are gods walking the earth, and beyond all criticism. We are among the last people who are not completely, utterly and damnably respectable. There is a little of the Old Adam even in the dullest of us, and it keeps us young.'

'That's what I like to hear,' said Cobbler, and played an Amen on the piano. 'That's what's wrong with my job, too, you know. Too much talk about the nobility of it, and how the public ought to get down on its knees before the artist simply because he has the infernal gall to say that he *is* an artist, and not enough honest admission that he does what he does because that is the way he is made. My life,' he declared, rolling his eyes at Miss Vyner, 'is a headlong flight from respectability. If I tarted up in a nice new suit and a clean collar, I could spend hours and hours every week jawing to Rotary Clubs about what a fine thing music is and how I am just as good as they are. I'm *not* as good as they are, praise be to God! As a good citizen, I am not fit to black their boots. As a child of God, I sometimes think I have a considerable bulge on them, but I'm probably wrong. Sometimes I have a nightmare in which I dream that I have gone to heaven, and as I creep toward the Awful Throne I am blinded by the array of service-club buttons shining on the robe of the Ancient of Days. And then I know that my life has been wasted, and that I am in for an eternity of Social Disapproval. Wouldn't it be an awful sell for a lot of us – all the artists, and jokers, and strivers-after-better-things – if God turned out to be the Prime Mover of capitalist respectability?'

His eye was still upon Miss Vyner, who was uncomfortable. She never thought about God, herself, but she had a sleeping regard for Him, as a Being who thought very much as she herself did, though more potently. Dragging God into a conversation embarrassed her deeply. The organist continued.

'Your story fascinates me. Particularly the part about Vambrace playing sleuth. That explains what he was doing out in the street when I came here, dolled up like a racetrack tout. It never struck me that he was avoiding notice. Quite the most eye-taking figure in town tonight, I would have said.'

'It's the engagement that interests me,' said Mrs Fielding. 'Of course I saw the piece in the paper; I never miss them. I thought it a splendid match. Solly needs a wife dreadfully, if only to get away from his mother, and Pearl is a dear child, and a great beauty as well.'

This comment made Ridley and Fielding start.

'A great what?' said her husband. 'Why, the girl looks as if she had been dragged backward through a hedge.'

'I haven't seen her in some time,' said Ridley, 'but it certainly never occurred to me that she had any looks.'

'That's because you are both getting a little old,' said Mrs Fielding. 'When a man doesn't notice that a girl under thirty has any looks, just because she is a little rumpled and doesn't know how to present herself, he is far gone in middle age. That's why men like you take up with obvious, brassy little blondes, when you take up with anything at all. You can't see real beauty any more. Give me Pearl Vambrace and five hundred dollars, for a week, and I will show you a beauty that will make even your eyes pop. She's quite lovely.'

'Elspeth and I never agree about looks,' said Mr Fielding. 'She's always pretending to see beauty that I can't see. Now my idea of a real beauty is Griselda Webster.'

'Very nice, I grant you,' said Cobbler, 'but I agree with your wife. The Vambrace girl has something very special. Mind you, I don't mind 'em a bit tousled,' said he, and grinned raffishly at Miss Vyner, who was, above all things, clean and neat, though she tended to smell rather like a neglected ash-tray, because of smoking so much. 'This business of good grooming can be carried too far. For real attraction, a girl's clothes should have that lived-in look.'

'I suppose you really like them dirty,' said Miss Vyner.

'That's it. Dirty and full of divine mystery,' said Cobbler, rolling his eyes and kissing his fingers. 'Sheer connoisseurship, I confess, but I've always preferred a bit of ripened cheese to a scientifically packaged breakfast food.'

Miss Vyner found herself without a reply. She felt, though no socialist, that a man who talked like Cobbler ought to be taken over by the Government, and taught responsibility.

'Unfortunately, there appears to be no question of this suitable match coming off, Elspeth,' said Ridley; 'and meanwhile I am in very hot water, and I am not even sure that I can leave this house without having trouble with Vambrace. I had to run the last few yards in order to get here at all.'

'I thought that was what you liked,' said Miss Vyner. 'From what you said just now I thought you wanted to go back to the days when editors were horsewhipped by people they had injured.'

'But as you doubtless overheard me saying to Elspeth, I have not injured the Professor. Somebody else has injured him, using my paper. If I am to be horsewhipped, I at least want to have my fun first.'

'I have to go now,' said Cobbler. 'I'll lure the Professor away.'

Ridley protested, for he did not like Cobbler, and certainly did not want to be under an obligation to him. The editor was ready to play the raffish journalist in order to annoy Miss Vyner, but the genuine raffishness of Humphrey Cobbler disturbed him. But it was impossible to shake the organist's determination, and when at last he left the house even Miss Vyner joined the other three in peeping through the window curtains, to see what he would do.

Professor Vambrace, cold and cross, was leaning against a tree in the park which was on the other side of the street from the Fieldings' house. To be fair to him, he would not have been noticed by anyone who was not on the lookout for him. He saw Cobbler hurry down the walk, cross the street until he was standing at the edge of the park directly in line with himself. And the Cobbler began to dance, and to sing in a very loud voice:

This is the way to the Zoo, the Zoo,
The Zoo, the Zoo, the Zoo;
The monkey cage is nearly full
But I think there's room for you;
And I'll be there on Saturday night
With a bloody big bag o' nuts –
NUTS you bastard!
NUTS you bastard!
Bloody big bag o' nuts!

The Professor attempted to creep away unseen among the trees, but even he could not deceive himself that the song was not an aggressive act of derision, aimed at himself. And all his detective enthusiasm melted from him, leaving him naked to his own scorn. For the Professor, who was immoderate in self-esteem, was similarly immoderate in his condemnation of himself, and as he strode swiftly toward his home he hated himself as a buffoon who had spent an evening, ridiculously dressed, stumbling among garbage cans, skulking among trees, and spying on people who had, unquestionably, spent the whole evening comfortably indoors, laughing at him. Not only was it bitter to be mocked; it was worse still to feel that he was worthy of mockery.

Dutchy and Norm were a little surprised that their party ended so soon. But immediately after refreshments had been served the guests showed a restless eagerness to leave, excepting Jimmy the dentist and one or two others whose thirst for organized Whee was not fully slaked. Solly and Pearl spoke in undertones over their coffee.

'Come on. I'll take you home.'

'You will not.'

'Don't argue. Get your things.'

'Don't speak to me like that. I'll go by myself.'

'And chance what Dutchy will have to say about it? You come with me. I've got to talk to you.'

'I don't want to talk to you.'

'Yes you do. Don't be a fool. We've got to get together about this thing or we'll never hear the end of it.'

'I can't go with you. I don't want to see you, ever again.'

'I know all that. But we've got to leave this place together. Please.'

And so they left the party as quickly and unobtrusively as they could, and Solly helped Pearl into his tiny Morris quite as though they wanted to be together.

'Now,' said Solly, when they had gone a short distance, 'I suppose you don't know anything about all this?'

'Of course I don't,' said Pearl. 'How would I?'

'I didn't suppose you did. But before I can do anything about it myself I have to be quite sure.'

'Before you do anything about it?'

'Yes. Didn't it occur to you that I might want to contradict that notice?'

'Surely I am the one to do any contradicting that is done.'

'Why, precisely?'

'Well – because I'm the one that's been dragged into this mess.'

'Why you more than me?'

'Because –' Pearl was about to say 'because I'm a girl,' but she felt that such a reason would not do for the twentieth century. There was a short silence.

'I think that you had better get things straight,' said Solly. 'You haven't been dragged into the mess any more than I have. And I am every bit as anxious to contradict this story as you are.'

Pearl was surprised to feel herself becoming angry. It is one thing not to want to marry a young man; it is quite another thing to find that the young man is offended that people should think he wants to marry you. She sat up very straight and breathed deeply through her nose.

'There's no sense snorting about it,' said Solly. 'And you needn't expect me to be gallant about it, either. This damned thing has put me in a very queer position, and God only knows what will be the upshot of it. It could very easily ruin everything for me.' He frowned over the wheel at the dark street.

'You mean when Griselda Webster hears about it?' said Pearl, in a well-simulated tone of polite interest.

'Yes. That's what I mean,' said Solly. 'Though what you know about it, or how it concerns you, I don't understand.'

'I only know what everybody knows. Which is that you have been hounding Griselda for the past three years; and that on her long list of suitors you rank about fifteenth; and that now she is in England you write to her all the time, and even take her little sister Freddy for drives to get the news of Griselda that she doesn't trouble to write to you. And as for how it concerns me, well – I am sure Griselda will hear it from somebody, by air-mail, probably the day after tomorrow, and she will be glad because it will relieve her of the nuisance of thinking she has blighted your life. However, if it will relieve your mind, I will write to her myself, and tell her that you are still her faithful slave, and that contrary to public report, I haven't stolen you away from her.'

'You!' said Solly, with so much scorn and horror and – worst of all – amazement, that Pearl was goaded beyond bearing.

'Yes – me!' she shouted.

By this time they had reached the Vambrace home, and by unlucky chance Solly stopped his car just as the Professor was about to open his front gate. Her father heard Pearl's indignant shout, and in an instant he had pulled open the door of the Morris and, bending more than double from his great height, thrust his head into it.

'What does this mean?' he demanded.

Solly was weary of feminine illogicality, and was delighted to see a fellow man, with whom he could argue in a reasonable manner.

'Professor Vambrace,' said he, 'I've been wanting to see you. Pearl seems to have some very queer ideas about this mix-up – you know, this newspaper nonsense – and I think we ought to get together and straighten matters out.'

'Do you so!' roared the Professor, in such a voice that the whole body of the tiny car hummed with the sound. 'Is it get together with you, you sneaking little cur? There's been too much getting together with you, I see! Get out o' that contraption!'

This last remark was addressed to his daughter.

'Daddy,' said she, 'there's been a mistake –'

'Get out of it!' roared the Professor. 'Get out of it or I'll pick you out of it like a maggot out of a nut!' And with these words he brought his stick down on the roof of the Morris with such force that he dented it badly and smashed his treasured blackthorn to splinters.

'Daddy,' said Pearl, 'please try to understand and be a little bit quiet. Everybody will hear you.'

'What do I care who hears me? I understand that you sneaked out of my house tonight, like a kitchen maid, to meet this whelp, to whom you have got yourself clandestinely engaged.'

'We're not engaged,' shouted Solly. He was badly frightened by the Professor, but a shout was the only possible tone in which this conversation could be carried on.

'You're coupled in the public mouth,' roared Vambrace.

'We're not coupled anywhere, and never intend to be!'

'Do you dare to say that to my face?'

'Yes, I do. And stop banging on my car.'

The Professor was now quite beyond reason. 'I'll bang on what I choose,' cried he, and began a loud pummelling on the roof. Whereupon Solly, who was not without resource, leaned on the horn and delivered such a blast that even the Professor was startled. He seized Pearl by the shoulder.

'Get out,' said he. And he pulled at her coat so sharply that she fell sideways out of the car on to the pavement. Solly leaned forward.

'Have you hurt yourself?' said he. 'Can I help you?'

It was involuntary courtesy, but it was like gasoline on the flame of the Professor's wrath. Gallantry before his very eyes! The product of who knew what shameless familiarity! He stooped and jerked Pearl to her feet.

'You dirty little scut!' he cried. 'Roaring drunk in the car of the one man you should be ashamed to see! God!'

And he pushed Pearl toward the gate, and as she fumbled with the latch, he cuffed her shrewdly on the ear.

The quietest, but most terrible sound in this hurly-burly was Pearl's sobbing as she ran up the path. Solly started his car with a roar.

Half an hour later, the Professor sat in his study, white with anger. In the circumstances he should have been drinking whisky, but there was never any whisky in the house, and he had made himself some wretched cocoa, that being the only drink he could find. His thoughts were incoherent, but very painful. He had played the fool all night; he had been bested. Yet unquestionably he was right – the only person connected with this villainous business who was right. He hated Pearl who, he was now convinced, was no longer pure, perhaps – O torturing thought! – no longer a virgin; certainly no longer his little girl. He had struck her! Struck her, like any bog-trotting peasant beating his slut of a daughter. And it was all for love of her.

The Professor was suddenly, noisily sick, and then, in the silence of his ugly house, he wept.

Solly crept quietly into his mother's house, removed his shoes, and crept past his mother's bedroom door to the attic where his living-room and bedroom were. Quickly he made himself ready for bed, and then, from inside a folio copy of Bacon's *Works*, where he fondly hoped that his mother would never think of looking, he brought out his photograph of Griselda Webster. It was of her as she had appeared as Ariel in *The Tempest*. Stealthily he mixed himself a drink of rye and tap-water, and sat down in his armchair for his nightly act of worship. But as he gazed at Griselda, the sound of Pearl Vambrace, weeping, persisted in his ears. He thought it the ugliest sound he had ever heard, but none the less disturbing. He should have done something about that.

Pearl was still weeping, but silently, when dawn came through her window. She felt herself to be utterly alone and forsaken, for she knew that she had lost her father, more certainly than if he had died that night.

[FOUR]

There are not many people now who keep up the custom of At Home days, but Mrs Solomon Bridgetower had retained her First Thursdays from that period, just before the First World War, when she had been a bride. Without being wealthy, she had a solid fortune, and it had protected her against changing customs; this made her a captain among those forces in Salterton which sought to resist social change, and every First Thursday a few distinguished members of this brave rearguard were to be found in her drawing-room, taking tea. At half-past three on the First Thursday in November tea had not yet appeared, but Miss Pottinger and Mrs Knapp, the Dean's wife, were seated on a little sofa at one side of the fire, and Mrs Bridgetower, regally gowned in prune silk, with écru lace, sat in her armchair on the other. The atmosphere, though polite, was not easy.

'It seems perfectly clear to me,' Miss Pottinger was saying, 'that the two events are linked. Both happened on Hallowe'en, and both concern the Cathedral. Then why should we not assume that both spring from the same brain?'

'But as we do not know what brain it was, what good can it do us to assume anything of the sort?' said Mrs Bridgetower, who had been highly educated, and would undoubtedly have had a career of some kind if she had not relinquished it to be all in all to the late Professor; the consciousness of this education and this possible career led her, in all but the most intimate circumstances, to talk in a measured, ironical tone, as though her hearers were half-witted.

'If everyone told everything they knew, we wouldn't be in doubt for long,' said Miss Pottinger. This dark comment was directed at Mrs Knapp, a small, rather tremulous lady who tried to follow her husband along the perilous tightrope of urbanity.

'I'm quite sure you're right,' said she, 'and I am sure that the Dean would dearly love to know who put that false engagement notice in the paper. He was dreadfully angry about it. But he has never suggested that Mr Cobbler had anything to do with it.'

This was not pedantically true, for the Dean had said to her many times that he hoped to heaven Cobbler had nothing to do with it, for it would mean firing him, and the Dean wanted to keep his excellent organist as long as Cathedral opinion would permit. But Mrs Knapp was on thin ice, and she knew it.

'I happen to know that Mr Snelgrove has told the Dean that he thinks it was Cobbler,' said Miss Pottinger sharply, for she thought it ill became a Dean's wife to palter with the truth, and she suspected, quite rightly, that the Dean told his wife everything. Loyalty between husbands and wives appeared to Miss Pottinger only as a shabby betrayal of the female sex.

'If Mr Snelgrove has interested himself in the matter,' said Mrs Bridgetower, 'I am sure that we can leave it in his capable hands.'

'You mean that you don't intend to take any action yourself, Louisa,' said Miss Pottinger.

'I have not yet decided what I shall do,' said Mrs Bridgetower, with a reserved smile.

'You don't intend to take this lying down, I suppose?'

'I think you know that it is not my way to pass over a slight, Puss dear.'

'Well, it is now three days since that piece appeared, and your friends are wondering when you are going to declare yourself.'

'My friends need not be concerned; my real friends know, I am sure, that I am not one to take hasty or ill-advised action in any matter. I have not the robust health which would permit me to scamper about the town, making useless mischief. Even if I had a temperament which took pleasure in it.'

In Mrs Bridgetower's circle, this was tough talk, and Miss Pottinger ground her false teeth angrily. But Mrs Knapp, who had known these ladies for a mere ten years or so, and was thus a virtual newcomer to Salterton society, interjected an unfortunate attempt to make peace.

'Oh, I am quite certain dear Auntie Puss has no such desire,' said she. 'We all know that her intentions are of the very best.' Then, catching the lightning from Miss Pottinger's eye, she subsided with an exhalation which was meant to be a social laugh, and sounded like fright.

'I suppose I am old-fashioned,' said Miss Pottinger, 'but I still do not see why sacrilege and assaults on people's good names should be passed over without a thing being done. You have a phlegmatic temperament, Louisa, and are perhaps too ill to care what goes on, but I would have thought that Solly would have had something to say for himself by this time.'

'My son has faith in my judgement,' said Mrs Bridgetower.

'Of course, but a man with any real gimp in him would have done something before he had had time to talk to you.'

This was insufferable! Mrs Bridgetower moved into action, which, in her case meant that she relaxed in her chair, allowed her heavy lids to drop a little farther over her eyes, and smiled.

'And what would he have done, Puss, pray? Would he have rushed to Mr Cobbler, and struck him in the face? To have suspected Mr Cobbler in this matter he would have had to take guidance from you, for you seem to be the one who wants to hang Mr Cobbler's hide on the fence, as the boys used to say when we were young. And I do not think that it has ever occurred to Solomon to consult you in any matter, particularly. And a certain gallantry which you, dear, might not appreciate, forbids a man to deny in the open market-place that he is engaged to a girl after such a report, without knowing precisely what he is doing. There are still gentlemen in the world, Puss, whatever our experience may have been.'

This was dirty fighting indeed, and referred to the sudden disappearance, many years before, of a man who, without being actually engaged to Auntie Puss, had put that lady into a mood to accept him if asked. Pouring salt into wounds was a specialty of Mrs Bridgetower's, and the older the wound was the better she liked it.

Auntie Puss took refuge in hurt feelings. Her chin quivered and she spoke in a tremulous voice. 'If you don't take care, Louisa, that is all there is to be said about it. My concern was for you, and for the good name of the Cathedral. A soldier's daughter probably sees these things differently from most people.'

'I think that even a soldier's daughter should know who the enemy is before she fires,' said Mrs Bridgetower who, as a woman herself, set little store by wobbling chins and tearful voices in others. She might have gone on to demolish Auntie Puss completely if, at this moment, reinforcements had not arrived in the person of Mrs Roger Warboys. Because of her connection with *The Bellman* it was impossible to say at once if she were friend or foe, and all the time which was occupied by bringing in the tea, and pouring it out, and passing thin bread and butter, was needed before it became perfectly clear that Mrs Warboys had come expressly to talk about the great scandal, and that she was on the side of those whose privacy and inmost feelings had been so grossly violated.

Mrs Warboys' position was a peculiar one, distinguished by many interesting shades of feeling, and she enjoyed it very much in a solemn, stricken way. She felt a family loyalty to *The Bellman*, of course. She thought a newspaper a powerful influence in a community and a great trust; she yearned to see *The Bellman* conducted according to the highest standards of journalism, as she conceived them. She had repeatedly impressed these views of hers upon her father-in-law, Mr Clerebold Warboys, who – although she was the last one to say a word against the late Roger's father – paid no attention to them. If she could, only for a month, have a free hand at *The Bellman*, it would be a very different paper thereafter. Some heads would roll, and although she named no names, certain powerful editorial influences would be removed. She was humiliated by the incident of the false engagement notice, and had come to Mrs Bridgetower's First Thursday most unsure of her welcome. She appreciated perfectly how she would feel herself, if she were in Mrs Bridgetower's position, but she did not wish to lose friends over a matter which she had been powerless to prevent, but which she might be able to amend.

She permitted all of these admissions to be wormed out of her, as it were unwillingly, with Auntie Puss as chief inquisitor, and gained immense moral prestige by fouling her own nest, which was a situation especially congenial to her temperament. She might have been some noble-minded Russian who had, at immense personal risk, escaped to give aid to the democracies.

As Mrs Warboys was basking in her glory, the doorbell rang, and the elderly maid admitted Mrs Swithin Shillito, who was accompanied by Mr Bevill Higgin.

'Dear Louisa,' said the old lady, 'I hoped that I might introduce Mr Higgin to you, for I know you have so much in common, and as he is still a stranger in Salterton –'

'But of course,' said Mrs Bridgetower. 'It is rarely nowadays that I see gentlemen at my Thursdays, and so Mr Higgins is doubly welcome.'

'I am honoured,' said Mr Higgin, bowing, 'to meet a lady of whom I have heard so much. The name is Higgin, *without* the "s". Yes.' And Mr Higgin was introduced to everyone and was very much at ease, rather like an indifferent but experienced actor in a comedy by Pinero. At last he seated himself on a low pouffe next to his hostess, and looked rather like a pixie on a toadstool.

'And where are you living in Salterton, Mr Higgin?' said Mrs Bridgetower, after some general conversation.

'For the time being I have taken rooms, rather in the north of town,' said he.

'With some people called Morphew,' said Mrs Shillito.

'I don't know anyone called Morphew,' said Mrs Bridgetower.

'I'm sure you don't,' said Mr Higgin. 'They are a very good sort of people in their way, and I am very comfortable there, but it is not the sort of place in which one would wish to stay indefinitely. But until I have acquired some pupils, and have had an opportunity to look round for a bachelor flat, with a studio, it will do very nicely.'

And then, without much prompting, he told the company that he taught singing and elocution, and Mrs Shillito said all the complimentary things about his abilities which he wanted said, but which he could not suitably say himself.

'Connection is everything, of course, for an artist like Mr Higgin,' said that lady, 'but it takes time to meet the right people.'

'Less so, perhaps, in a university town than elsewhere,' said Mr Higgin, with a bow which included all the ladies. 'And in a young country, so avid for culture as Canada, I hope that it will not take me too long to make my way.'

'I have been urging Mr Higgin to seek some connection with the Cathedral,' said Mrs Shillito. 'Perhaps, Mrs Knapp, you can tell us if there is any part of the musical service in which Mr Higgin's talents could be of use?'

Mrs Knapp said that Mr Cobbler looked after everything of that kind.

'Oh, my dear, you are too modest,' said Mrs Shillito, who was a rosy, round little old lady, got up in grey and purple and, like her husband, English with the peculiar intensity of English people abroad. 'We all know how musical Mr Dean is, and I am sure that Mr Cobbler does nothing except on his advice.'

'I have been trying to see Mr Cobbler,' said Higgin, 'but he is a very elusive man.'

'He may soon be downright missing, if I am any judge,' said Miss Pottinger, who had been seething for some time. Mrs Bridgetower's opposition to her conviction that Cobbler was at the root of the great scandal had served only to intensify her certainty of his guilt.

This pregnant remark brought the conversation back to the great theme again, and as Mr Higgin was acquainted with it, having heard much about it from the Shillitos, he was able to enter into it with some spirit, though modestly, as befitted a newcomer. He listened with wide-open blue eyes, and said 'Oh!' and 'Ah!' with the right amount of horror at the right places.

'If I may venture to say so,' said he, smiling at all the ladies in turn, 'I think that it will not be at all easy to get satisfaction from Mr Ridley. I have only met him once, of course, but he seemed to me to be a very saturnine kind of man.' And he told the tale of his visit to Ridley, under the wing of Mr Shillito; and, as he told it, it appeared that Ridley had shown a strongly Philistine attitude toward the cultural advancement of Canada, and the improvement of *The Bellman*. He told his story so well, and imitated Ridley so drolly, that it made the ladies laugh very much, and gave particular satisfaction to Mrs Warboys.

'When I think of him sitting there, without a word to say for himself, and snapping at the air with those scissors,' said Higgin, 'I really can't help smiling, though I assure you it was rather embarrassing at the time.'

This led to further discussion of Ridley, whose eccentricities, habits of cooking, and single state were all thoroughly rehearsed.

'Perhaps it is as well that he never married, if he is so disagreeable,' said gentle little Mrs Knapp.

'Is it widely believed that he is unmarried?' said Higgin, with a very knowing look.

'Why, whatever do you mean by that, Mr Higgin?' said Mrs Knapp.

'Perhaps I'd better say no more – at present,' said Higgin, leaving Mrs Knapp most unsatisfied, and the other ladies even more incensed against Ridley for daring to have a secret, though they admired Mr Higgin for his discretion in not explaining it, to the only one of their number who did not know it.

'And that is the man,' said Auntie Puss, 'to whom Waverley thinks of giving an honorary degree! Strange days we live in.'

'Because of Swithin's association with him – his strictly professional association, I should say – it would ill become me to comment on *that* matter,' said Mrs Shillito. 'But I would have thought that the University would have wanted its new course in journalism to be formed by those with a – shall I say? – more literary approach to the matter?

Writing – the light touch – the formation of a style – you know the sort of thing I mean.'

They all knew. It meant Mr Shillito, and whimsical little essays about birdseed and toothpicks.

'The degree has not been conferred yet, or even formally approved,' said Mrs Warboys, in a marked manner. And as everyone present knew, or thought they knew, that she had several members of the University Board of Governors in her pocket, this was a great stroke, and brought forth a good deal of murmuring and head-nodding.

The tea, and the thin bread and butter, and the little cakes, and the big cake, having been pretty well disposed of by this time, it was a pleasant diversion when Mrs Shillito begged Mrs Bridgetower, as a personal favour to herself, to permit Mr Higgin to try her piano. This instrument, which was an aged Chickering, was a great ornament of the drawing-room, for its case was beautifully polished, and its top was covered with photographs in silver frames, and the late Professor Bridgetower's military medals, exhibited on a piece of blue velvet. Mrs Bridgetower graciously gave her consent.

'I hope that an artist like yourself will not be too critical, Mr Higgin,' said she. 'I do not play so much now as once I did, and it may not be completely in tune.'

With appropriate demurral, Mr Higgin sat down at the piano and struck a chord. It was not so much out of tune as out of voice. The sound board had split under the rigours of winter heating, and the old wires gave forth that nasal, twangling sound peculiar to senile pianos and Siamese cats. Some of the photographs jingled as well. But Mr Higgin dashed off a few brilliant arpeggio passages, and smiled delight at his hostess.

'May I give myself the pleasure?' said he. 'Oh, do say that I may.' And without waiting for further permission he began to play and sing.

It might be said of Mr Higgin that he brought a great deal to the music he performed – so much, indeed, that some composers would have had trouble in recognizing their works as he performed them. He had a surprisingly large voice for a small man, and he phrased with immense grandeur and feeling, beginning each musical statement loudly, and tailing off at the end of it as though ecstasy had robbed him of consciousness. He enriched the English language with vowels of an Italian fruitiness, so that 'hand' became 'hond', and

'God' 'Goad'. It was plain that he had had a lot of training, for nobody ever sang so by the light of Nature.

His first song, which was *Because* by Guy d'Hardelot, he sang with his eyes opening and closing rapturously in the direction of Mrs Bridgetower, in acknowledgement of her ownership of the piano. But when he was bidden to sing again he directed his beams at Auntie Puss.

'I should like to sing a little thing of Roger Quilter's,' said he, 'some lines of Tennyson.' And he launched into *Now Sleeps the Crimson Petal*. It is doubtful if, at any time in her life, anyone had sung directly at Miss Pottinger, and she was flustered in a region of her being from which she had had no messages for many years.

So fold thyself, my dearest one, and slip –
Slip into my bosom, and be lost in me.

Thus sang Mr Higgin, and in that instant Miss Pottinger knew that here was the man who must succeed Humphrey Cobbler on the organ bench at St Nicholas'.

'Sorry to be late, Mother,' said Solly, coming into the room. He caught sight of Mr Higgin, who was still at the piano, and frowned.

'My son, Mr Higgin, my great, grown-up boy,' said Mrs Bridgetower fondly.

'We have had the pleasure before,' said Mr Higgin, with what Solly thought an impudent grin.

Solly was always late for his mother's First Thursdays, and they kept up the pretence between them that it was pressure of university work which made him so. Very soon after his arrival the guests went home, well pleased with their afternoon's work. For they all thought that Mrs Warboys would see that the insufferable Gloster Ridley lost his job, and received no doctorate from Waverley. Miss Pottinger thought that she had done much to undermine Cobbler with Mrs Knapp and thus with the Dean. Mrs Knapp thought she had made it clear that the Dean exonerated Cobbler, and that this would divert the wrath of Miss Pottinger. Mrs Shillito thought that she had further ingratiated herself with Mrs Warboys, thus securing her husband's position. And they all felt that the matter of the great scandal had been brought somewhat nearer to the boil.

When her guests had gone a dramatic change came over Mrs Bridgetower. Solly had seen them to the door, and he returned to the drawing-room to find his mother, as he knew she would be, slumped from her splendidly relaxed but commanding position in her armchair, with her eyes closed, and her face sagging with fatigue.

'Do you want to go upstairs at once, Mother?'

'No, dearie, give me a moment. Perhaps I'd better have one of my white tablets.'

As he climbed the stairs her voice reached him again faintly. 'Bring me one of my little yellow pills too, from the table by my bed.'

'Don't you think it would be better to leave that until you are in bed? What about a dose of your medicine instead?'

'If you think so, dearie.'

In time Solly returned, and when the tablet and then the dose of medicine were taken with much histrionic disrelish, he took off his mother's shoes and put on her slippers, and covered her knees with a small tartan rug. She opened her eyes and smiled fondly upon him.

'Bad, bad little boy! Late again!'

'I had a lot of papers to mark, Mother, and I simply had to get them done. Anyway, I knew you'd want to talk to your friends alone.'

'Friends, dear? What are friends compared with you? And I so much need someone to help me now, passing things and so forth. I wonder how much longer I shall be able to keep up my First Thursdays. They take so much out of me now.'

'No, no; you mustn't give them up. You must see people, you know. The doctor said you must keep up your interests.'

'You are my only real interest now, dear. If your father had lived – but it is useless to talk of what might have been. But I need you to help me. There was a gentleman here today. You should have been here to help entertain him.'

'It looked to me as though he were doing the entertaining.'

'Yes, dear, but suppose he had wanted to wash his hands? Who would have taken him?'

'If he needs to wash his hands in the course of an hour's visit he ought to stay at home. Or wear one of those things.'

'What things do you mean, dearie?'

'Those things soldiers wear when they're on sentry duty.'

'Don't be coarse, dear. I can't bear it.'

'Sorry, Mother.'

'So nice to have someone sing at one's Afternoon. It's been years since it happened. Such nice songs, too. Your father loved *Because* –

Because God made thee mine
I'll cherish thee –

I was terribly moved. Lovey –'

'Yes, Mother?'

'I think I could take a glass of sherry. Perhaps with a little something in it.'

Solly obediently brought a tray and gave his mother a glass of dry sherry, in which he had put a generous dollop of gin.

'Thank you, dear. It takes away the taste of that horrid medicine.'

'Mother, how did that fellow Higgins get here?'

'Higgin, dear. No "s". Maude Shillito brought him.'

'Do you think he is the sort of person you ought to have in the house?'

'Whatever do you mean, dearie? Maude Shillito brought him.'

'I know, but the Shillitos know all kinds of terrible people. I've met Higgin before, and I thought he was an awful little squirt.'

'Please, lovey; you know how I dislike rough talk. Where did you meet him?'

'He hunted me up at the University. Wanted me to let him talk to my classes about how to speak English.'

'Well, lovey, from what you tell me about them, I think your classes might well have some instruction in how to speak.'

'That's not what the classes are for. And I can't bring in odd visitors just as I please. Anyway, he was terribly patronizing about it, and obviously thought I'd jump at the chance. I was a bit short with him.'

'Really, dear? Was that wise?'

'He rubbed me the wrong way. Talked as if we were a lot of barbarians out here.'

'We must learn all that we can from Older Civilizations, lovey.'

'Just what Older Civilization does Higgin represent? Second-rateness comes out of his pores like a fog. There's something disgusting about him.'

'Dearie, you are speaking of a gentleman who was introduced into our home by an old and valued friend. I don't know why you are so severe on English people, dear.'

'I'm not severe on English people, Mother, but I hate fourflushers, wherever they come from, and if Higgin isn't a fourflusher, I don't know one.'

'Let us not discuss it, dearie. When you are vehement you weary me, and I can't stand much more today. I think I could take another glass of sherry.'

Strengthened by two heavily spiked sherries, Mrs Bridgetower was able to go upstairs – 'to tackle the stairs' as she gamely put it – moving upward very slowly, with Solly half-boosting, half-pulling, and with a rest at the landing. When at last they reached her room, he helped her to undress, for it was understood that the elderly maid had all she could do to clear up after the At Home.

There was no unseemliness in this assistance. Seated on her bed, Mrs Bridgetower undid various mysterious fastenings through her gown, and Solly was able to pull off her stockings and put on her bedsocks. Then she toiled to a hiding-place behind a screen, and herself struggled out of the remainder of her garments, returning at last in a voluminous bedgown. Solly gently boosted her into bed, in which he had already put a hot-water bottle, and propped her up on her pillows. When he had picked up the discarded clothing from behind the screen and put it away, Mrs Bridgetower was ready for her tray.

It was understood that there could be no proper dinner on First Thursdays, as the servant had burnt herself out in preparing dainties for tea. But from the kitchen Solly fetched two trays, upon which suppers consisting chiefly of tea debris had been arranged, and he sat in a chair with one, while his mother took the other in bed. With the sherry and two kinds of medicine mingling uneasily inside her, her appetite was capricious, and to use her own expression, she picked at her food. But her spirit appeared to be refreshed, for she attacked Solly on the subject which had been uppermost in her mind for three days.

'We must make some decision, dearie, about what we are going to do.'

'I suppose all those women talked about it all afternoon.'

'It is no good being resentful and childish. This is a serious matter, and we cannot dilly-dally any longer.'

'I think the best thing is to ignore it.'

'Your father certainly would not have thought so.'

'How can we tell what Father would have thought?'

'The enmity between us and Professor Vambrace was not of your father's choosing, but he never permitted Vambrace to get the better of him. We owe something to your father's memory.'

'Oh, Mother, let's talk sense. About three years ago I took Pearl Vambrace to the Military Ball. You had her here to dinner beforehand. You were very decent to her.'

'There was a very good reason why you took her. I don't entirely recall what it was, but there was something to do with that play – that one in which the Webster girl showed so much of her legs. I have no quarrel with Pearl Vambrace, poor creature. But her father is a very different matter. I will not have people thinking that we have knuckled under in that affair.'

'Oh, Mother, we can't go on fighting forever.'

'Who said anything about fighting? It has been publicly announced that you are engaged to Pearl Vambrace. You are nothing of the kind. Someone has done this for spite. And I think I know who it was.'

'Who?'

'Professor Vambrace himself. It's just the kind of crazy thing he would do. To make us look ridiculous.'

'You can't be serious. He couldn't do that to his own daughter.'

'Pooh, he could. She's completely under his thumb. And that poor Elizabeth Fitzalan that married him – utterly crushed. The man's insane. He did it. Within six months they'll have to put him away, you mark my words.'

'Mother, do you realize that Vambrace is threatening to sue *The Bellman*? He's telling it all over the campus, as a great secret. Everybody's talking about it. He says it's a plot to bring him into disrepute by associating his name with ours.'

'More madness! A great many people are very peculiar. Puss Pottinger is absolutely insane about that organist at the Cathedral – what's-his-name. She won't rest until she has taken his position from him. She thinks *he* put that piece in the paper.'

'Good God! Cobbler! What makes her think that?'

'Because there was some skylarking in the Cathedral on Hallowe'en and she is sure Cobbler was at the bottom of it. And if he was at the bottom of that, why shouldn't he have made other mischief the same day?'

'And does she call that logic?'

'Puss Pottinger doesn't know what logic is. But that's the kind of thinking that gets big rewards for detectives, whatever the mystery-writers may say about clues and deduction and all that rubbish. But I think she's wrong. Vambrace did it. I have more insight in my little finger than Puss Pottinger has in her whole body.'

Solly chewed wretchedly on a dry sandwich. He was thinking, as he had been thinking all day, of Pearl Vambrace running into her house, pursued by her father.

'Well, what do you think we ought to do?' he said at last.

'The dignified and sensible thing is for you to go to *The Bellman* and see this man Ridley. You must give him an announcement which he will insert, denying the report of the engagement and apologizing for having printed it. You must speak to him very firmly.'

'No good. Vambrace did that on Tuesday and Ridley flatly refused. So there's going to be a court action. That's the talk on the campus.'

'And what are the grounds of this court action to be?'

'Libel.'

'Libel? And where does the libel lie?'

'In suggesting that I am going to marry his daughter. Now, Mother, there's no use looking like that. That's what he says.'

'Libel! Libellous to suggest that you –'

Solly was very much alarmed, for it seemed that his mother might have a seizure. But anger is a powerful stimulant, and Mrs Bridgetower's wrath did her good. She seemed to drop twenty years before his eyes, and for ten minutes she called up the past iniquities of Professor Vambrace and uttered violent judgements on his present conduct. Her peroration was delivered in trumpet tones.

'Let him bring such a suit if he dare! We'll bring a counter-action! Libellous to suggest that you should marry his daughter! Calculated to bring him into shame and disrepute? We'll fight! We'll spend money like water! We'll break him, the old hound! Libellous to suggest that a Bridgetower would so lower himself! If there is any libel it is against us! But we'll fight, my boy, we'll fight!'

'Mother, please be calm. What's the good of saying we'll fight? We'll all look like fools, that's what we'll do.'

'How can you talk so? Puss Pottinger was right. You haven't any gimp!'

'All right, then, I haven't any gimp. But it seems to me that you and Vambrace have no thought for Pearl or me; you'd make us look like a couple of children in leading-strings.'

'You have a lot of consideration for Pearl Vambrace, I must say. More than you have for me, it seems. Nasty, scheming little thing!'

'Very well, then, leave Pearl out of it. What will I look like if you go to court to fight a counter-action against Vambrace's libel suit?'

'No, we will not leave Pearl out of it. It seems to me that you are very ready to fly to Pearl's rescue. Solly, tell me honestly, is there any crumb of truth in this report about you and Pearl?'

'If you aren't going to listen to my advice I don't think you can expect me to answer that question,' said Solly, and was quite as surprised as his mother to hear himself say so.

The dispute went on, without anything new being added to it, for another half-hour. It ended with Solly fetching five volumes of the *Encyclopaedia Britannica* to his mother's bedroom, so that she might read all that pertained to the law of libel. He also gave her her pink medicine, and arranged her reading light. Later details of washing and removing her teeth would be attended to by the elderly maid. In spite of these filial acts there was a barrier between them, for Solly had created an uncertainty, and an uncertainty about Solly was something which his mother found frightening and intolerable. But she was so stimulated by hatred and the love of combat that she was able to retain some composure, and contented herself by saying that she hoped that in the morning he would be in a more reasonable frame of mind, and see things as she saw them. Thus he left her, and went upstairs to his attic study.

Solly's first act when he was in his own room was to take down Bacon's *Works* in order that he might refresh himself with a look at his photograph of Griselda Webster. It was not a particularly good photograph, but the eye of adoration could see much in it, and it had been his solace in every dark hour since Griselda herself, several months before, had gone to Europe to travel for an indefinite period. In the picture she appeared as Ariel, in *The Tempest*, an unquestionably beautiful girl, even in the tabby-cat greys of a poor photograph. He had other photographs of the Salterton Little Theatre's grand assault upon Shakespeare, hidden in other chapters of Bacon, but he did not look at them often, for his interest was in Griselda alone. But tonight he hunted them down in the large folio, supposing that in this way he was putting off the moment when he must settle down to his work. They looked like the photographs of almost any Little Theatre production; the cast had been taken in groups, some of the players self-conscious in costume and grinning at the camera, others keeping 'in character' with great ferocity, and acting very hard, though without movement. Griselda was in two or three of these, and the one for which he was looking showed her standing on a grassy mound, obedient to the command of Prospero, who was Professor Vambrace.

At Prospero's side, but apparently unconscious of Ariel, stood Pearl Vambrace as Miranda.

She had looked well as Miranda, thought Solly. He had to give her that. She stood well, and had dignity, and the dark stillness of her face suited the part. She was not to be compared with the wonderful Griselda, of course, for Griselda was a goddess. But as mortal women went, Pearl had good gifts. A pity they didn't show more in the costume of every day. And when he had last seen her, white with anger and nervous irritability, at the Yarrows, and then stumbling toward the Vambrace house, she had looked awful. As he thought about it, the sound of her miserable cries came into his ears again, and to rid himself of that memory he closed Bacon, and went to his desk to work.

A pile of fifty-two essays lay before him, in which First Year Science men had expressed their opinions on 'The Canterbury Pilgrims and their Modern Counterparts' or 'The Allegory of the Faerie Queene in Terms of Today'. Imposing as these titles were, and productive of large and learned books as they might be, First Year Science was expected to say what it had to say in not more than a thousand words, and to base its opinions on a small red book called *Magic Casements, Vol. 1: Beowulf to the Elizabethans*; nobody supposed for a moment that Science students had time or inclination to read and ponder Chaucer and Spenser at first hand: indeed, it went against the grain with Science students to bother with English at all.

Solly picked up the first essay, which was by Igor Kaczabowski, and read the first sentence: 'The poems of Geoffrey Chaucer are among the richest jewels of our British heritage. He was called the Father of English Poetry because everybody who came after him sprang from him. In an age of unbridled licence he was an honest civil servant and wrote many poems in his spare time of which the best known are *The Canterbury Tales*, *Troilus and Criseyde* and *The Treatise on the Astrolabe*. Couched as they are in what is to the modern reader virtually a foreign tongue we will go a long ways before we improve on his ability to size up our fellow man.'

Sighing, Solly tucked Kaczabowski into the middle of the pile, to come upon him as a surprise later on. Picking up another, from Jean Thorsen, he found another reference in the first paragraph to our British heritage, and a further hunt revealed that two more Scandinavians, a Pole and three Russian Jews had claimed Chaucer as their own. He was annoyed; lifting from *Magic Casements* was legitimate enough, all things considered, but he wished that they would read what they lifted with greater care and introduce a little artistry, some hint of individuality, into it. Nobody seemed to have tackled the problem of allegory in modern life, and he didn't blame them; *The Faerie Queene* had little to say to First Year Science.

He had lost the battle, he knew, the minute that he faltered with Kaczabowski; in marking essays the great thing is to go straight ahead, without deviation or consideration of personal taste. To admit that one paper might be more pleasing than another was to allow his critical powers to work on the wrong level; his job was to correct the grammar of First Year Science, and to untangle the more baffling syntactical messes; to begin thinking about Chaucer, or even common sense, was fatal. He pushed the heap of essays aside; if the worst came to the worst he could always award marks between B minus and C plus arbitrarily, and not give back the papers at all.

Our British heritage; what a lot was said about it in Canada, one way and another, and it always meant people like Chaucer and Spenser; it never seemed to mean people like Bevill Higgin who were, after all, more frequent ambassadors from the Old Country. He wished that he had not mentioned Higgin to his mother. But to find the little pip-squeak in the house, mooing Tennyson to all those old trouts in the drawing-room! He had thought himself rid of Higgin.

It was – how long? – three weeks at least since last he had seen him. Solly had been having a difficult morning; he had talked to First Year Science at eight o'clock, and at ten o'clock he had met another group who were getting a quick run through Our British Heritage; these were students of mature years, who had already taught in primary schools for some time and were getting university degrees in order that they might teach in high schools, and most of them were older than Solly. After his lecture one of these men, who was perhaps thirty-five, and had glasses and a bald spot, had approached him and said: 'Professor Bridgetower, I'm not getting anything out of your course; I don't mean anything personal, you understand, but frankly I don't think you have any pedagogical method; in our work, you know, pedagogical method is everything, and if you'd give me a little extra time on some of this Milton, why I'd be glad to give you some pointers on pedagogical method; as you explained to me, I could point out to you where you weren't doing it right, do you see?' Solly had rejected this kindly offer with abruptness, and had told the well-meaning fellow that a university was not an infant class, and that he was welcome to exercise his pedagogical method upon himself. But the student's words had hurt him; he knew that he was a bad teacher; he hated teaching; he shrank from eager minds, and was repelled by dull ones. It was with a sharp increase in his haunting sense of failure that he mounted the stairs to his office.

And there, in his office, where he had hoped to sit down and mope quietly about his failure, had been Bevill Higgin, who had introduced himself with the most ridiculous affectation of what he considered to be a university manner, and who had proposed that he, Solly, should permit Higgin to give readings from English poetry to his classes, in order, as Higgin put it, to give them the sonorous roll of the verse and to illuminate what had, it was implied, been presented to them in a dull and lifeless manner. To make his meaning perfectly clear he had declaimed a few lines of Satan's Address to the Sun, in an embarrassing, elocutionary manner, like a man trying out his voice in a bathroom.

It was a bad moment to approach Solly with such a scheme. He was conscious that he left much to be desired as a teacher of English; this point had just been rubbed into him by one of his own students who had – a final insult – meant it with sincere kindness. It was obvious that Higgin had approached him because he was the most junior member of the English staff, and thus, presumably, the easiest mark. He had sulked, and said that the thing was impossible.

And then, to his astonishment, Higgin had said, very confidentially, that he was on the lookout for pupils, and that if he drew any pupils from Solly's classes, he would be willing to remit to Solly one-half of their first month's payment for lessons.

Of course, Solly knew now, he should not have done what he did. But, in a mysterious way, the man offended his sense of propriety. It was not the offer of the kick-back on lessons – no, no, it was something that he had felt before Higgin got that far. It was, he supposed, a snobbish feeling. The little man was such a second-rater, such a squirt, such a base little creature. And so he had risen, and pushed Higgin toward the door, not hard or roughly, but just a good firm, directing push. He had said, he remembered, 'No soap!' which was a sadly unacademic remark, but the best that he could think of at the moment. And when Higgin was in the corridor he had slammed the door.

Undignified. Silly. But he was too disgusted with himself to think of what he was doing, and since that time he had thought little about the incident. But when he had met Higgin at Mother's At Home, there was no mistaking the look of malicious triumph on Higgin's face.

Solly tried to banish thoughts of Higgin by further work. Not intimate communion with the finer thoughts of First Year Science, but with his Grand Project, his Passport to Academic Preferment. From a shelf above his desk he took down a book bound in dingy brown cloth, upon the front of which, inside a border of ornamental stamping, was printed the title, *Saul*. Inside, on the title page was:

SAUL
A DRAMA
IN THREE PARTS

Montreal
Henry Rose, Great St James Street
MDCCCLVII

This was it, the principal work of Canada's earliest, and in the opinion of many people, greatest dramatist, Charles Heavysege. Had not Longfellow, moved by we know not what impulse, declared that Heavysege was the greatest dramatist since Shakespeare?

Solly had not been drawn toward Heavysege by any kinship of spirit. Heavysege had been given to him, with overwhelming academic generosity, by the head of the English Faculty, Dr Darcy Sengreen. He remembered the occasion vividly when, a few months before, Dr Sengreen had asked him to lunch. And, when they had eaten, and were sitting at the table from which everything had been removed but a bouquet of paper roses, Dr Sengreen had said: 'Now, Bridgetower, you've got to get down to work. What are you going to do?'

Solly had muttered something about having a lot to learn about lecturing and the preparation of his courses.

'Ah, yes,' Dr Sengreen had said, 'but that isn't enough, you know. You've got to get to work on something that will make your name known in scholastic circles. You've got to publish. Unless you publish, you'll never be heard of. You've nothing in mind?'

Solly had nothing in mind save apprehension as to what Dr Sengreen might say next.

'Well, if I were a young fellow in your position, I wouldn't hesitate for an instant. I'd jump right into Amcan.'

Solly knew that Dr Sengreen meant the scholarly disembowelling of whatever seemed durable in American-Canadian literature.

'Amcan's the coming thing, and particularly the Canadian end of it. But there isn't much to be done, and the field is being filled up very quickly. Now, I'll tell you what I'm going to do. I'm going to give you Heavysege.'

And half an hour later Solly had left Dr Sengreen's house carrying first editions of the two plays, the three long narrative poems, and the single novel of Charles Heavysege, which Dr Sengreen had let him have at the prices which they had cost him. And, within a week, he had written to several learned papers asking for information about Heavysege, to be used in connection with a critical edition of that author upon which he was at work. Not, of course, that he expected any information, but this was a recognized way of warning other eager delvers in the dustheaps of Amcan that he had put his brand on Heavysege, had staked out a claim on him, so to speak, and that anybody trespassing on his property was committing an offence against the powerful, though unwritten, rules of academic research.

And here he was, landed with Heavysege. Within a year at most Dr Sengreen would expect a learned and provocative article on Heavysege, from his pen, in some journal or quarterly of recognized academic standing.

Amcan. A new field in literary study, particularly the Can half. In twenty years they would be saying, 'Dr Bridgetower? The big man in the Heavysege field; yes, the collected edition is pretty much all his own work, you know, though he let X and Y do the bibliography, and Z did a lot of the digging on Heavysege's newspaper writings; yes, a monument in Canadian scholarship; wonderful tribute to old Darcy Sengreen in the general introduction, but the dedication is "To my Mother, who first taught me to love Amcan, *Si Monumentem requiris, circumspice*"; yes, one of the very biggest things in Canadian literary studies.' Holding the brown book in his hand, a sudden nausea swept over Solly, and he gagged.

Why do countries have to have literatures? Why does a country like Canada, so late upon the international scene, feel that it must rapidly acquire the trappings of older countries – music of its own, pictures of its own, books of its own – and why does it fuss and stew, and storm the heavens with its outcries when it does not have them? Solly pondered bitterly upon these problems, knowing full well how firmly he was caught in the strong, close mesh of his country's cultural ambitions. Already he was being asked for advice by hopeful creators of culture. Who was that fellow, that reporter on *The Bellman*, who had been at him only a few days ago? Bumble, was that his name? No; Rumball; that was it. Poor Rumball, toiling every spare minute of his time at what he was certain would be the great Canadian prose epic, *The Plain That Broke the Plough*.

Rumball had approached him with great humility, explaining that he had no education, and wanted to find out a few things about epics. Solly, capriciously, had said that he had more education than he could comfortably hold, and he was damned if *he* could write an epic. He had advised Rumball to model himself on Homer, who had no education either. He had expressed admiration for Rumball's theme. God knows it had sounded dreary enough, but Solly felt humble in the presence of Rumball. Here, at least, was a man who was trying to create something, to spin something out of his own guts and his own experience. He was not a scholarly werewolf, digging up the corpse of poor Charles Heavysege, hoping to make a few meals on the putrefying flesh of the dead poet.

But this was not getting anything done. He looked at his watch. Nine o'clock. He put *Saul* back on the shelf, removed his shoes and crept downstairs with them in his hand. Outside his mother's door he listened; though the light was still on, thin, tremulous snores assured him that she was asleep and would probably remain so for many hours. He stole down to the ground floor, shut himself into the telephone cupboard and dialled a number.

'Yes?'

'Is that you, Molly? It's Solly. Is Humphrey at home?'

'Yes.'

'May I come over? I need you.'

'Righto, ducks.'

In the dimness of *The Bellman*'s news room a cone of light shone from above Henry Rumball's desk, illuminating his typewriter; Rumball, balancing on the back legs of his chair, gazed fixedly into the works of his machine, as though seeking inspiration. He was alone, having returned early from an entertainment given by a class of backward boys before a Home and School Club. He should have been thinking about the backward boys, but he was thinking about *The Plain That Broke the Plough*.

It was an epic, there could be no doubt about that. It seemed to become more epic every day. It swept on and on, including more and more aspects of life in the great Canadian West, until he was thoroughly astonished by it. He had read about this business of books getting away from their writers, taking their own heads, so to speak, but he was astonished to experience it himself. He was happily amazed at the wilfulness of his own creative mind; this ability to go on and on, without much effort or conscious control, certainly made him feel that he was, well, in the grip of a power greater than himself. It was humbling to feel so . . . Now, about those backward boys –

But at this moment the footsteps and the rumblings of which he had been conscious at the back of his mind became fully audible, demanding attention, and Mr Shillito walked into the news room.

'Ah, good evening,' said he. 'Just out for a breather and thought I'd look in to see if anything was doing.'

He went to the city desk, rummaged among the papers on it, and looked at one or two copy-hooks, and then walked over to Rumball's desk and sat down familiarly on one corner of it.

'Knocking out your stint, I see,' he said. 'Good. Good. Always write your story while it's fresh in your mind; never leave it till tomorrow. What is it?'

'Backward boys, gym and handicraft display,' said Rumball.

'Hmph, yes; even that – do it while it's hot. Well, well; I'll push on. Always walk a mile or two every evening. Find some of my best ideas come to me then. I still carry a notebook, you know,' said Mr Shillito, with the arch manner of one confiding a surprising secret. 'A good phrase comes into my head while I'm walking, out comes the notebook, under a street lamp, and I pop it down. Then, in the morning, I look at the book and sometimes I find something already written in my head, ready to pop out when the right phrase calls it up. Strange how the writer's mind works.'

Rumball grunted. He did not like to think that Mr Shillito's mind worked along lines so closely resembling his own.

'Yes, it's all part of the romance of the craft. You're young in the craft, and I'm old in it – the greatest game in the world.' Mr Shillito's voice trembled with emotion. Then his mood became conspiratorial. 'Nothing new about the great mystery, I suppose?'

'Nothing that I've heard.'

'Wish that could be cleared up. It isn't good to have a thing like that hanging over a paper.'

'Oh, I don't know. It'll all come out in the wash.'

'I wouldn't say that, lad. No, I wouldn't say that.'

'Sure. A libel threat isn't anything. The lawyers will probably fix it up between them.'

'You think so?'

'Even suppose they don't, it couldn't cost the paper much. It's not serious libel, if it's libel at all. No court would give much in the way of damages on a thing like that.'

'It isn't the public result I'm thinking of. It's the secondary results. Here in the office, for instance. Some pretty big apples could be shaken from some pretty high branches.'

'You mean Boney?'

'Don't say I said so.'

'No, of course not. But Gee, Mr Shillito, what would bring it to that?'

'Towns like this, my boy, are very close-knit – at the heart, I mean. You may tread on some people's toes, and nothing will happen to you. But if you trouble the waters in the wrong quarter, you wish you hadn't. Divide families, turn father against daughter – that kind of thing – no good comes of it.'

'Father against daughter? You mean Vambrace and his daughter?'

'I shouldn't speak of it. Still – I saw what I saw. I'm an old man, and I've seen a good deal of life, but I'm still shocked, thank God, when I see a woman beaten.'

'Beaten! You mean Vambrace has been lighting into Pearl?'

'Did I say so? Well – off the record, mind – he was dragging, positively dragging her into the house. I was out in the garden calling Blue Mist, our Persian, and I saw most of it. And when I went out into the street, do you know what I found, Rumball?'

'What?'

'A blackthorn stick, broken right across. Right across, mind you. When you bring a white man to that pass, Rumball, you've got to answer for it.'

With his usual dramatic sense Mr Shillito rose from the desk, and went to the door, thoughtfully sweeping aside his ramshorn moustaches. Before leaving he fixed Rumball with a stern glance, and flourished his walking stick at him.

'Off the record, mind you,' he said, and was gone.

Once again Rumball was alone, peering into his typewriter. Was it up to him to do anything? He knew Pearl. Indeed, he admired her. He had first met her when he sought some information for TPTBTP (which was the cabbalistic way in which he thought of his book) in the Waverley Library. She had been very helpful and nice, and he had told her about the book. She had seemed interested. Lonely as he was, he had two or three times asked her if she would like to have a meal with him at the Snak Shak, and talk about TPTBTP, but she had always refused, though nicely. And so he had put her out of his mind. After all, he had to save himself for the book. But – beaten with a blackthorn stick! Should he do anything? And if so, what? Should he go to her in the morning, and offer himself for any service she might command? Pearl, in distress, seemed much more desirable and important than before.

But then, what about his duty to TPTBTP?

Professor Bridgetower ought to be considered, too. He was involved in the mess. And he was the first professor who had ever been human to Rumball. Usually, when Rumball was on the University beat, he called on a few professors who said 'Nothing today' as soon as he approached them. But when he had wanted to talk to Bridgetower about his novel, Bridgetower had asked him to sit down, and had taken him seriously. A nice fellow. For his sake, as well as for Pearl's, something ought to be done. But what?

Much troubled, Rumball began to type: 'An audience which almost filled the gallery of the gymnasium of Queen Elizabeth School witnessed the annual display by the Opportunity Class on Thursday evening . . .'

Norm and Dutchy Yarrow lay happily in bed. Her head was snuggled on his breast, and his left arm held her close to him. A bedside lamp with a pink shade threw a rosy glow over the scene. They were deeply content, and almost asleep, until Dutchy spoke.

'Gee, it's wonderful to be so happy.'

'That's right, honey-bunch.'

'It just makes you sorry for everybody in the world that isn't as happy as we are.'

'That's a sweet thought, sugar.'

'It just breaks my heart, thinking about those two poor kids.'

'Certainly is tough for them.'

'D'you s'pose they'll ever have anything like this? D'you s'pose they'll ever be as happy and as close as we are, right this minute?'

Norm thought about it. He tried to imagine Pearl, lying beside Solly in the connubial bliss which enfolded Dutchy and himself. Somehow the vision did not seem quite right. Happy lovers very often feel the generous wish that others may be as happy as they, but it is only human to think that one has gone a little farther in this sort of happiness than others are likely to follow.

'Well, I don't know, sweetie. Happiness is a kind of a talent. And the physical relationship is a talent, too. Solly and Pearlie are both kind of nervous. I don't think their background is right for it. I mean, they could be happy, but as for being as happy as we are – well, that's expecting a lot.'

'I'll say so. I don't suppose anybody was ever as happy as I am right this minute.'

Far down in the bed, Norm tickled her with his toes. She tickled him with hers. They scuffled and giggled and kissed.

'See?' said Dutchy. 'Can you imagine Solly and Pearlie playing toesies? I just can't.'

'I don't know about that,' said Norm. 'There's a touch of the gammon in Pearlie.'

'The what?'

'The gammon; it's a French expression for a delinquent girl. Still, you can't tell. There are people,' said Norm portentously, 'who never get any fun out of sex at all.'

'Oh sure, I know. Case histories. But you don't think they'll end up as a couple of case histories, do you?'

'Could happen. I mean, if it's true about Pearlie and her father.'

'Oh, Norm, don't you think there's been some mistake about that?'

'You ought to know. It was you that Jimmy phoned about it.'

'Yes. I just hate to believe it, but he phoned just as soon as Mrs Shillito was out of his office. She's the Vambraces' next-door neighbour, and she practically saw everything. And Jimmy told it to me just as she told it to him. She was in getting her lower plate tightened up a little bit, so she was able to talk all the time he was working on it. And she swears it's true.'

'She actually saw Vambrace break the stick over Pearlie's head?'

'Not over her head, her back.'

'Ah, well, psychologically that makes all the difference. I mean, even where on her back makes a difference. I mean, if he hit her over the shoulders it might have been just rage, but if he hit her over the fanny it was definitely sex.'

'You mean there's sex between Pearlie and her father?'

'Honey, you're a trained recreationist; you know that there's a lot of sex everywhere.'

'Oh, Norm, how awful. I mean, imagine!'

'Jimmy said Mrs Shillito actually saw it, did he?'

'No, her husband saw it. At least, he heard an awful noise, and went to his front door, and there was Vambrace walloping Pearlie with the stick. And a car was dashing away which must have been Solly's car, because he drove her home from here, remember? And old Mr Shillito ran out and found the stick, and it was one of those blackthorn sticks, smashed in two over Pearl's body. And you know what awful thorns those sticks have, and she was wearing just a thin dress and a short coat, so the lacerations must be something awful.'

'It makes you think, doesn't it? I mean, right here in Salterton, among university people – that kind of thing, that you only associate with case histories.'

'Norm, after a thing like that, do you suppose they could ever be really happy?'

'Well, I couldn't say, honey-bunch. But I'll go this far: it doesn't look too good.'

There was silence for a time, until Norm felt a wetness on his shoulder.

'Lambie-pie! What's the matter?'

'I just can't bear to think of those two having such a tough time, when we're so lucky!' And the good-hearted Dutchy sobbed loudly.

'Oh, honey, that's wonderful of you! Gee, that's just wonderful. Come on, now, cheer up. Give daddy a smile. Come on, just a little, teentsy-weentsy smile.'

'How can I smile when there's so much unhappiness in the world?'

'Well, take that attitude, peachie, and everybody would commit suicide. It's not normal to take other people's troubles so hard.'

'Yes, but Norm, these are people we *know*.'

'Well, now, you cheer up, honey, and we'll see what we can do.'

'Aw, Norm, do you really mean you can *do* something?'

'Well, for heaven's sake, isn't that our whole life? Isn't that what we're trained for?'

'You mean you think we could do some social engineering, and make everything jake for those two poor kids?'

'We can certainly try. Now it's plain that the place to relieve the pressure is with Professor Vambrace himself. His attitude simply isn't normal. I don't like to butt into a man's private life, but this thing is bigger than our personal feelings. I'll just have to go to him and explain to him what's biting him.'

'Oh, Norm! I think you're wonderful!'

'Yes, I'm going to have to explain to the Professor about the Oedipus Complex.'

'What's that?'

'It's rather a complicated concept. And, honey, I don't want to talk about it right now.'

'Gee, Norm, I think you're just the most wonderful person!'

'Don't wriggle around like that.'

'I'm going to get up and get us some coffee and stuff.'

'No, you're not.'

'You mean you don't want to eat?'

'Later.'

'Oh, Norm!'

The Cobblers lived in a row of small, impermanent-looking houses, all exactly alike and all – though not more than a few years old – with an air of weariness, like children who have never been strong from birth, and have a poor chance of reaching maturity. Molly Cobbler opened the door to Solly's knock, and in her usual silent fashion nodded to him to follow her upstairs.

When they entered the bedroom Humphrey Cobbler was invisible, but in the old-fashioned bed, shaped rather like an elegant sleigh, a heap of bedclothes showed that he was sitting up and bending forward, and a strong smell, and some very loud sniffings and exhalations, made it clear that he was inhaling the fumes of Friar's Balsam.

'Come along, now; you've had enough of that,' said his wife, unveiling him. His mop of black curls was more untidy than ever, and the steam had given his face a boiled look.

'Bridgetower, you find me very low,' said he.

Solly said that he was sorry.

'I have a cold. It would be nothing in another man, but in me it is an affliction of the utmost seriousness. I cannot sing. Suppose I lose my voice entirely? I am not one of your fraudulent choirmasters who *tells* people how to sing; I *show* 'em. I'm at a very low ebb. Don't come near me, or you may catch it. You wouldn't like a precautionary sniff of this, I suppose?' He held out the steaming jug of balsam.

'I've brought you the only reliable cold cure,' said Solly, producing a bottle of rye from his pocket.

'Bridgetower, this is an act of positively Roman nobility. This is unquestionably the kind of thing that Brutus used to do for Marc Antony when *he* had a cold. God bless you, my dear fellow. We'll have it hot, for our colds. Molly, let's have hot water and lemon and sugar. Would you believe it, Bridgetower, I have been so improvident as to fall ill without a drop of anything in the house?'

The invalid looked very much better already, and was now sitting up in bed in a ragged dressing-gown, wrapping up his head in a silk square which obviously belonged to his wife.

'Have a chair, my dear fellow. Just throw that stuff on the floor. I can't tell you how much I appreciate this visit.' He fetched a large and unpleasant-looking rag from under his pillow and blew his nose loud and long. 'E flat,' said he, when he had finished. 'Funny, I never seem to blow twice on the same note. You'd think that the nose, under equal pressure, and all that, would behave predictably, but it doesn't. See this?' He held out the rag. 'Piece of an old bedsheet; never blow your nose on paper, Bridgetower. Save old bedsheets for when you have a cold. They're the only comfort in a really bad cold, and the only way of reckoning its virulence. I consider this to be a two-sheet cold.'

By this time his wife had returned, with glasses, lemon and sugar, and an electric kettle which she plugged into an outlet in the floor. Solly chatted to her, and Cobbler plied the bedsheet, until the water was hot and the toddies mixed.

'Aha,' roared the invalid, who seemed to grow more cheerful every minute. 'This calls for a toast! What'll it be?'

'It had better be to Solly's engagement,' said Molly. 'After all, it's his whisky.'

'Engagement? What engagement? Oh, yes, I remember. I heard about it last night, but this pestilent rheum knocked it right out of my head. Who are you supposed to be engaged to, Bridgetower?'

'Pearl Vambrace was the name given in the paper,' said Solly, watching Cobbler very closely.

'That's nonsense,' said Cobbler. 'I simply don't believe it.'

'Nor do I,' said Solly. 'But why don't you?'

'It's psychologically improbable, that's why. You are, as everybody within a fifty-mile radius knows, an ardent but unsuccessful suitor for the hand of Miss Griselda Webster. Very well. Suppose you *do* get some sense? Suppose you *do* get it into your head that she will never marry you if you both live to be a hundred? Very well. You bounce. On the rebound you get engaged to somebody else. But would that somebody else be Pearl Vambrace? Most certainly not! Intuition and reason alike are outraged by such a supposition.' And here Cobbler took a very big drink of his boiling toddy, and for the next few minutes Molly and Solly were busy patting his back, fanning his face and assuring him that he would survive.

'What I mean to say,' he continued in a whisper, mopping his eyes with his piece of sheeting, 'is that Pearl Vambrace is not the kind of girl to catch any man on the rebound. Such girls are either the soft, squeezy kind, who secrete sympathy as a cow secretes milk, or scheming old mantraps who will accept a man when he's not himself.'

'Well, I'm glad to hear you say so,' said Solly, 'for somebody put a notice in the paper that I am engaged to her, and there is a very strong body of opinion which thinks that that person was you.'

Once again Cobbler got himself into trouble with his hot drink, and when he had been put to rights again Solly told him of all the dark suspicions of Auntie Puss, and Cobbler told Solly of the Hallowe'en party in the Cathedral, and of his serenading Professor Vambrace in the park, which he said that he had been unable to resist.

'Well, there you are,' said Solly. 'Everybody knows you can't resist any lunatic notion that comes into your head. And so, when something like this happens, your name is bound to crop up.'

'Only in such a diseased fancy as that of Auntie Puss Pottinger. I am many reprehensible things, in the eyes of the bourgeoisie, because I am unlike them. But therein lies my defence. Can you conceive of any practical joke more tiresomely bourgeois, more quintessentially and ineluctably lower middle class, than shoving a fake engagement notice in the paper? Is Cobbler, the running sore of Salterton society, the man to do such a thing? Never! What's more, this trick required careful planning, deft execution, and prolonged secrecy to assure its success. Is Cobbler, the man of impulse, Cobbler the Blabbermouth, the man to bring it off? Once again I cry – Never! And to conclude, this has been done by someone who knows you, some false friend who is privy to your bosom, yet ready to exhibit you as a Merry Andrew to the jeers of the mob. Could this be Cobbler the True, Cobbler who has eaten your bread and salt, and drunk your rye toddy, Cobbler who is to you as secret and as dear as Anna to the Queen of Carthage was? No! The echoing air repeats it –' And Cobbler was about to shout 'No' again, in a very loud voice, but he was seized with a terrible fit of coughing. 'God,' he said, when he could speak again, 'I'm going to fetch up the callouses off the soles of my feet in one of those spells.'

'Well, that's what I thought myself,' said Solly. 'It just didn't seem like you.'

'Your simple eloquence touches my heart,' said Cobbler. 'Molly, my pet, I need another length of old sheeting.'

Molly took the sodden rag from his hand and left the room.

'What would you do if you were me?' said Solly.

'What would I do in your place?'

'No, no; you'd do something fantastic and get farther into the soup. I want to know what you would do if you were intelligent but prudent. What would you do if you were me?'

Cobbler pondered for a moment. 'Well,' he said, 'I suppose if I were you – that's to say a somewhat inert chap, half content to be the football of fate – I'd go right on doing whatever I was doing at the moment, and hope the whole thing would blow over.'

'Yes, but I can't do that. I'm absolutely fed up with what I'm doing. I'm a bad teacher; I loathe teaching; I'm expected to teach English literature to people who don't want to know about it; I'm expected to make a name for myself in Amcan; damn it, sometimes I think seriously about suicide.'

'Lots of people do,' said Cobbler, 'But don't delude yourself. You're not the suicidal type.'

'Why not?'

'You're too gabby. People who talk a lot about their troubles never commit suicide; talk's the greatest safety-valve there is. I always laugh at that bit in *Hamlet* where he pretends to despise himself because he unpacks his heart with words, and falls a-scolding like a very drab; that's why the soliloquy about suicide is just Hamlet putting on intellectual airs. A chatterbox like that would never pop himself off with a bare bodkin. No, the suicides are the quiet ones, who can't find the words to fit their misery. We talkers will never take that way out. Anyway, you wouldn't dare commit suicide, because it would upset your mother; she'd need more than six kinds of medicine to get her out of that.'

Molly came back into the room. She had put on her nightdress in the bathroom, and her black hair hung loose about her shoulders. Solly had never seen her look so striking.

'You look like one of those wonderful Cretan women,' said he, in honest admiration.

'Thanks. I'm going to go to bed, if you don't mind. The furnace is out. But don't think that means you have to go. We'll be very jolly like this.'

And with a flash of legs she was in bed with Cobbler, and settled back against her pillows with a basket of socks to mend.

'Solly is thinking of suicide,' said her husband, making a beginning on his new piece of sheeting.

'Solly needs a wife,' said Molly.

'But not Pearl Vambrace,' said Cobbler, with great decision. 'She's too much like him in temperament. Married couples should complement each other, and not merely double their losses. There's much to be said for the square peg in the round hole, as the Cubist told the Vorticist.'

'I don't want a wife,' said Solly, passionately. 'I've got a mother, and that, God knows, is enough to warn me off the female sex for life. I don't want a wife, and I don't want my job, and I don't want Charles Heavysege.'

'You want to run away to sea,' said Cobbler. 'But you wouldn't like it, you know.'

'I suppose not,' said Solly. 'Don't pay attention to anything I say tonight. I'm utterly fed up.' He looked into his glass, which was empty.

'Perhaps you are beflustered by the blabsome wine,' said Molly Cobbler.

'Impossible. I've only had one. But where did you get that business about being beflustered by the blabsome etcetera?'

'You used it last time you were here.'

'That was weeks ago.'

'Yes. But it stuck in my mind.'

'Molly, do you realize that you have been quoting from the great Charles Heavysege?'

'Oh? Never heard of him. Yes I have, too. You've mentioned him.'

'I've mentioned him! What an understatement! He obsesses me. He is my incubus – my succubus. He is becoming part of the fabric of my being. I expect that within ten years there will be more of Heavysege in me than of the original material. Do you realize what Heavysege is? He is my path to fame, my immortality and the tomb of my youth. I wish I'd never heard of him.'

'Mix us some more toddies, like a dear,' said Molly. 'If he's so important to you, why do you wish you'd never heard of him?'

Solly busied himself with the glasses. 'Do you really want to know why?' said he.

'If it's not too long, and not a bore,' said Molly.

'It is very long, and it is a bore, but I'll tell you anyhow. You can go to sleep if you like. Fortunately you are in a position to do so. It's getting cold in here.' And Solly lifted a red eiderdown from the bed and draped himself in it.

'I am now gowned as Dr Bridgetower, the eminent authority on the works of Heavysege,' said he. 'The great scholar in the Heavysege field will now address you.

'It was on May 2nd, 1816, that Charles Heavysege first saw the light of day in Liverpool. When I write my introduction to his *Collected Works* I shall embellish that statement by pointing out that the shadow of the Corsican Ogre had but lately faded from the chancelleries of Europe, that the Industrial Revolution was in full flower in England, that Byron had been accused of incest by his wife, that Russia's millions still groaned under the knout, and that in Portland, Maine, the nine-year-old Longfellow had not, so far, written a line. I'll make it appear that little Heavysege hopped right into the middle of a very interesting time, which is a lie, but absolutely vital to any scholarly biography.

'What happened between 1816 and 1853, when Heavysege came to Canada, I don't know, but I'll fake up something. He was a wood-carver by trade, which is good for a few hundred words of hokum about craftsmanship, but he soon became a reporter on the Montreal *Witness*.'

'That was the trumpet-call of the Muse,' said Cobbler, and blew his nose triumphantly.

'Exactly. From there on it's plain sailing, as scholarship goes. Heavysege's major work was his great triple-drama, *Saul*. Now *Saul*, ladies and gentlemen, presents the scholar with the widest possible variety of those literary problems which scholars seize upon as dogs seize upon bones. The first of these, of course, is: What is *Saul*? It is in three parts, and fills 315 closely-printed pages. Therefore we may fittingly describe it as "epic in scope" – meaning damned long. It is brilliantly unactable, but is it fair to call it a "closet drama"? Is it not, rather, a vast philosophical poem, like *Faust*? We dismiss with contempt any suggestion that it is just a plain mess; once scholarship has its grappling-hooks on a writer's work there is no room for doubt.'

'Nobody has ever written a great play on a Biblical theme,' said

Cobbler. 'Milton couldn't pull it off. Even Ibsen steered clear of Holy Writ. There's something about it that defies dramatization.'

'Please do not interrupt the lecturer,' said Solly. 'Heavysege did not write a mere Biblical drama; he wrote a vast, cosmic poem, like a fruit-cake with three layers. Only the middle layer concerns Saul and mankind; the top layer is all about angels, and like everything that has ever been written about angels, it is of a deadly dreariness; the bottom layer, which is thicker than the others, is about devils, and much the best of the three. Heavysege was awed by angels, sobered by Saul, but right in his element with the devils. He makes them comic, in a jaunty, slangy, nineteenth-century way; he provides love-affairs for them. In fact, he is at his best with his devils. This obviously suggests a parallel with Milton; in scholarly work of this kind, you've got to have plenty of parallels, and Heavysege provides them by the bushel. Heavysege reveals traces of every influence that even the greediest scholar could require.

'But in your eyes I see a question of the greatest import. Was Heavysege, in the truest sense, a Canadian writer? I hear you ask. Set your minds at rest. Who but a Canadian could have written Saul's speech:

If Prompted, follow me and be the ball
Tiny at first, that shall, like one of snow,
Gather in rolling.

Does not Jehoiadah behave like a Canadian when he refuses to cheer when his neighbours are watching him? Is it not typically Canadian of Heavysege's Hebrews that they take exception to Saul's "raging in a public place"? Is it not Canadian self-control that David displays when, instead of making a noisy fuss, he "lets his spittle fall upon his beard, and scrabbles on the door-post"? Friends, these are the first evidences of the action of our climate and our temperament upon the native drama.

'I could go on at some length about the beauties of Heavysege, as they appear to the scholar. *Saul* is full of misprints. Correcting misprints is the scholar's delight. On page 17 we find the word "returinag". Did Heavysege mean "returning"? That's good for a footnote. On page 19 we find the word "clods" where we might expect "clouds". But can Heavysege have meant something deeply poetic by "clods"? That's good for a paragraph of speculation, for we must be true to the printed text at all costs, and avoid any mischievous emendations. Does the poet allow anything of his own life to colour his drama? Well, at one point Saul speaks of "poignant emerods", and the adjective opens up an alluring avenue of speculation; we must find out all we can about Heavysege's state of health in 1857, when *Saul* was published. Had Heavysege a personal philosophy? What else can we call the four lines which he gives to an Israelite Peasant? (Incidentally, this peasant makes his appearance smoking a pipe; Heavysege has not even denied the editor the luxury of a nice, juicy anachronism.) This Peasant says:

Man is a pipe that life doth smoke
As saunters it the earth about;
And when 'tis wearied of the joke,
Death comes and knocks the ashes out.

Can we hear that unmoved?'

'I can hear it totally unmoved,' said Cobbler.

'Then you have no soul, and do not deserve the intellectual feast that I am spreading before you,' said Solly. 'But there, in a nutshell, is Heavysege. I spare you his other play, his two long poems and his newspaper writings, which it will be my duty to find and sift. There, my friends, is the ash-heap upon which I must lavish my efforts and thought, in order that I may loom large in the firmament of Amcan. It's devilish cold.'

'Poor Solly, you look miserable,' said Molly Cobbler. 'You'd better get in with us.'

Solly looked at the bed dubiously. 'But how?' said he.

'Give us all nice hot drinks again. Then loosen the covers at the foot, take off your shoes and hop in. You can put your legs up between us. We'll warm you. And I'll spare you one of my pillows.'

Solly did as he was bidden, and a few minutes later was surprised to find himself snugly tucked in, facing the Cobblers, and with his feet in the remarkable warmth which they had created.

'I feel like the sword which Lancelot laid between him and whoever it was,' said he. Molly Cobbler said nothing, but laughed and tickled one of his feet, which made him blush.

'You know, you tell a very pathetic story,' said Cobbler, who had been blowing his nose and pondering, 'but it doesn't hold water. You want us to be sorry for you because you're tied to Heavysege and teaching people who don't want to learn. But you're not tied, you know. Nobody has to teach if they don't want to. I remember my own fiasco as a teacher of music appreciation at Waverley. That repulsive Tessie Forgie came to me one day and said, "Mr Cobbler, do I understand that I am responsible for all the operas of Mozart?" I said, "Miss Forgie, if you were responsible even for one of Mozart's overtures I should clasp you to my bosom, but you aren't; if you mean, do you need to have a knowledge of Mozart's work to appreciate music, the answer is yes." That finished me as a teacher. I expected my students to know something, instead of being examination passers. That's why I only see a few of the university brats privately now, as on that memorable Hallowe'en. If you don't like teaching, get out of it.'

'But what else can I do?'

'How do I know? But you won't find out while you are hugging your miserable job. And why do you bother with Heavysege? Why don't you write something yourself?'

'Me? What could I write?'

'How should I know? Write a novel.'

'There's no money in novels.'

'Is there any money in Heavysege?'

'No, but there are jobs in Heavysege. Get a solid piece of scholarship under your belt and some diploma-mill will always want you. Don't think I haven't considered writing something original. But what? Everything's been written. There aren't any plots that haven't been worked to death.'

'You've read too much, that's what ails you. All the originality has been educated out of you. The world is full of plots. I'll give you one. In a town like Salterton lives a wealthy, talented and physically beautiful couple who have two beautiful and talented children. Arthur is a boy of twenty-one and Alice is a girl of eighteen. Although they live in wealthy seclusion the news leaks out that Alice has had a child, and that Arthur is the father. There is a scandal, but nobody can do anything because no charge has been laid. Then Alice and Arthur enter their child in an international baby contest sponsored by UN, and it sweeps off all the first prizes. They explain that this is because incest strengthens the predominating strains in stock, and as their physical and mental predominating strains are all good, they have produced a model child. Their parents reveal that they also are brother and sister, and that the family has six generations of calculated incest, practised on the highest moral and eugenic grounds, behind it. UN takes up the scheme and the free world has a race with

Russia as to which can produce the most superior beings in the shortest time. Amusingly written, it would sell like hot-cakes.'

'You don't think it a little lacking in love-interest, do you?' said Molly.

'Oh, that could be taken care of, somehow. What I am saying is that it is an original plot. If every story has to be a love-story, you'll never have any originality, for a less original creature than a human being in love cannot be found. But I get sick of hearing people crying for originality, and rejecting it when it turns up.'

'Your plot is utterly impossible,' said Solly; 'it would offend against the high moral tone of Canadian letters, for it is at once frivolous and indecent.'

'Oh, very well,' said Cobbler. 'Go on ransacking the cupboards of oblivion for such musty left-overs as Heavysege; that is all you are good for. I have a horrible feeling that in two or three more years I shall despise you. Quite without prejudice, mind.'

The hot toddy and the bed were working strongly upon Solly's spirit. 'I have a strong sense of being ill-used,' said he murmurously. 'I am in seven kinds of a mess. I am trapped in a profession I hate, and I am saddled with a professional task I hate. I am the victim of a practical joke which puts me into a very delicate relationship with a girl I hardly know and whom I don't think I like. I ask advice of the one man I know who seems to be free of petty considerations, and all he does is mock me. Very well. Loaded as I am with indignity I can bear this also.'

'Hogwash!' said Cobbler, groping under his pillow for his piece of bedsheet. 'Don't come the noble sufferer over me, Bridgetower. You are in a richly varied mess, true enough. But, much as I like you, I am clear-eyed enough to see that it is the outward and visible reflection of the inward and invisible mess which is your soul. You think life has trapped you, do you? Well, my friend, everybody is trapped, more or less. The best thing you can hope for is to understand your trap and make terms with it, tooth by tooth. If this seems hard, reflect that I speak from what may well be my deathbed.' He blew his nose resoundingly. 'B natural,' said he; 'my cold drops more than a full tone every hour. Obviously I am dying. Well, accept these hard words as a parting gift. You are the prisoner of circumstance, Bridgetower, and it is my considered view that you are not one of the tiny minority of mankind that can grapple with circumstance and give it a fall.'

Solly pondered. 'We'll see about that,' he said, after a time, but his host and hostess were both asleep.

Much later Solly woke, and found that Molly Cobbler was kicking him, gently but persistently. 'It's time you went home, ducks,' said she. 'It's long after three.'

'Good God,' cried Solly, sitting up. 'What'll Mother say?'

'Tell her you were in bed with a married woman, and didn't think it polite to hurry away,' said Molly. And then, surprisingly, she kissed him. 'Don't pay any attention to what Humphrey said; he was ill and cross. You'll find a way out.'

Her kindness went right to Solly's heart, and he felt a sudden warmth there.

'Thanks,' he said, and kissed her in return. 'I know I will.'

From force of habit he began to tiptoe down the stairs, then, recollecting where he was, he clumped noisily to the bottom, and thence out into the cool night. At least his mind was made up about one thing: he should have tried to protect Pearl from her father.

[FIVE]

Gloster Ridley sat at his breakfast. From the kitchen came the voice of Mrs Edith Little, his housekeeper, raised in song. It was a high voice, wiry, small and tremulous, a carefully modulated snarl. When she had finished *Just A-Wearyin' For You* she addressed her son Earl.

'Like that, lover?'

'Goog.'

'Good? Aw, you're a flatterer. Are you going to be a flatterer when you grow up?'

'Blub.'

'You going to be a flatterer like Ugga Bev?'

'Ugga Bev.'

'Aw, you're crazy about Ugga Bev, aren't you? Eh? You're just crazy about him.'

'Gaw.'

'Well, you just grow up half as smooth as Ugga Bev and you'll be all right. Ugga Bev is certainly a smoothie. You going to be a smoothie, lover?'

'Smoo.'

'You are? Say, you're just too smart, that's what you are. Just too smart for your old Mommie. But you'll always be Mommie's fella, won't you?'

'Blub.'

'Yes, sir. Mommie'll always be your best girl, eh? Tell Mommie she'll always be your best girl.'

'Blaw.'

'Aw, you're a flatterer.'

Ridley sighed as he spooned up the last juice from his grapefruit. This was, he knew, a carefully staged scene, intended to impress him with the beauty of mother love, and the delightful cleverness of little Earl. He was not a vain man, and it had never occurred to him that his housekeeper sought to ensnare him with her charms, but he knew that she was, for some mysterious purpose, intent upon calling his attention to her son. She frequently told him stories of the child's brilliance and whimsical humour, and she had once asked him if he had never longed for a child of his own? He was both too weak and too kind to tell her the truth, which was that he feared and mistrusted virtually all children, and he had temporized somehow. But when Christmas came, a few weeks later, he had bought a large and expensive toy panda for Earl, and after that Mrs Little had begun to bring the child to work with her occasionally, and to stage these dialogues within his hearing. And he had, though somewhat ashamed of the emotion, begun to hate Earl intently.

Was it ever permissible, he wondered, to describe a child as a slob? Surely slob was the only accurate word for little Earl. Though the child was not much more than three, he already had a hulking, stooping walk, his round abdomen suggested the prolapsed belly of middle age, and in the corner of his mouth was a damp hole, as though provided by nature for the soggy butt of a cigar. If ever a child were a slob, Earl was a slob. Not that he thought of him as Earl; he had some weeks ago christened the child Blubadub in the secret baptistery of his mind. The name had come out of the deep past, when, as a child, he had seen a picture in a bound volume of some English magazine (was it *Punch*?) of a pretty young mother talking with just such a surly brat: 'And what does Mama call her darling?' 'Blub-a-dub,' the brat replied. 'That's right,' said Mama, 'Beloved Dove!' Blubadub, the son of Constant Reader.

Mrs Little brought him his egg and a rack of toast. 'I hope I don't bother you with my singing,' said she.

'Not at all,' said Ridley. It would have been true, but churlish, to say that he would prefer silence; bachelors pay a high price for any sort of female care.

'I'm a regular lark these days,' said Mrs Little, 'singing all the time. I'm taking voice.'

'Indeed.'

'From the gentleman who boards at our place. Mr Bevill Higgin. He's a wonderful teacher; he just seems to get it out of you, kind of. I often tell him he could get music out of anything. We're all taking, me and my sister and her husband and even Earl.'

'The little boy too?'

'Oh yes. Mr Higgin says you can't start a kiddy too young. He could sing himself before he could talk. Would you like to hear Earl?'

'Some day, yes.'

'Oh, but he's right here. I sometimes bring him with me, while I'm working here mornings. He just sits as good as gold, while I'm working. I'll bring him in.'

Ridley felt a wave of despondency sweep over him, as she hurried to the kitchen. I should be a happy man, thought he. The sun is shining on my breakfast table; I have a very nice apartment; my housekeeper is clean and capable. But I feel wretched, and now I shall have to listen to Blubadub sing. Well, I'm not going to let my egg get cold anyhow.

Mrs Little returned, leading Earl by the hand. The child was nicely dressed in a yellow jumper and brown corduroy overalls, but in Ridley's eye he was a slob. He hulked, and in his dimple a ghostly cigar butt seemed to nestle.

'Now, lover,' said Mrs Little, kneeling, 'sing for Mr Ridley. Just like you sing for Ugga Bev. That's what he calls Mr Higgin. He means Uncle Bev, of course. Come on, lover – Jack and Jill went up the hill –'

'Faw down, bo cown,' mumbled Blubadub.

'Ah now, lover, you know that comes later,' said Mrs Little, playing the loving mother with many an arch glance toward her employer and quarry. 'Come on, lover; Jack and Jill,' she prompted in her own tiny, wiry voice.

'He got baw head,' said Earl, fixing Ridley with a surly stare.

'Now, lover, that's bold,' said Mrs Little, blushing very much. 'You sing for nice Mr Ridley.'

'Not nice,' said Earl, and struck at the air in Ridley's direction. 'Stinky. Got baw head.'

Ridley saw no reason why he should help Mrs Little out of her difficulty, and went on eating his egg, after casting a malevolent look at Blubadub. The child well understood its meaning, and stamped and struck at the air again. Mrs Little thought that the time had come to show that she could be firm, as well as sweet, in the motherly role, so she took Earl's fat fist in her hands and shook it mildly.

'Now, lover, Mommy wants you to sing for Mr Ridley just like you sing for Ugga Bev. Now, come on.'

'Ugga Bev bastard!' said Earl, with greater clarity than he had given to any previous speech. 'Baw head bastard!'

With a smothered cry Mrs Little seized her child in her arms and fled to the kitchen.

Ridley was much cheered. He hoped that Earl was in serious

trouble. He ate his egg with better appetite, and positively enjoyed his toast and coffee. After all, he thought, the day which lay before him might not be so painful as he feared. He had slept badly. The thought of a difficult day to come always gave him a restless night. But looking out of the window at the autumn sunshine it seemed that things might not be quite so laborious as he supposed. He must see Balmer this morning. He must see Mr Warboys, and in all likelihood his enemy Mrs Warboys, late in the afternoon. Well, it must be lived through, somehow.

Fighting down anxiety he changed from his dressing-gown into his jacket, gave a final brush to what remained of his hair, collected some papers into his briefcase and sought out his hat and coat. As he was about to leave the apartment, Mrs Little appeared again from the kitchen, with swollen eyes, from which tears still welled.

'I just don't know what to say,' she said. 'What you must think of Earl's language I don't know. I don't know where he picks up that kind of talk.'

'Don't give it a thought,' said Ridley, seeking to make his escape.

'Oh, but I do! I never think of anything else. That child's all I've got, and really, well – I guess I just live for him. You'll never know what it is to try to bring up a boy single-handed. Sometimes it just gets to be too much.' And Mrs Little wept again.

'Please don't distress yourself. He'll probably be much like other boys.'

'That's what I'm afraid of. I just dread that he'll end up just such another as his father was before him. In front of you, of all people! And when you're so worried about the paper and everything.'

'Eh?' said Ridley, who thought, like many another worrier, that he showed no outward sign of his distress.

'Of course you're worried. *I* can tell. I guess I see you the way nobody else sees you. It's that piece about Professor Bridgetower and Professor Vambrace's daughter, isn't it?'

'What makes you think that?'

'There's a lot of talk about it, and I hear a good deal. Of course everybody knows I'm connected with *The Bellman*, sort of. I know how you've been worrying. I can see how your bed is all screwed up these mornings, and how you've been taking soda, and everything. Oh, I wish there was something I could do!'

This was a cry from the heart, and though she stood perfectly still before him, Ridley had a dreadful sense that in a moment Constant

Reader might throw herself into his arms. He was alarmed, and without a word he rushed out of his apartment and down the stairs. He had a sense that even his home had become menacing.

Mrs Little, overwhelmed by the thought that she had been bold, sat down in Ridley's armchair and wept.

'The root of the matter is the malice of X, and the party to the action which can find X first will win it,' said Gordon Balmer.

'I see,' said Ridley.

'The whole business is ridiculous,' Balmer continued, 'but it would make a very pretty case, for all that.'

'I don't see that it's ridiculous,' said Ridley. 'You tell me that it could cost *The Bellman* a heavy sum in damages. That wouldn't be ridiculous.'

'It depends what you call a heavy sum. *The Bellman* could stand a few thousands. But what the judge would advise a jury to grant the other side, if you lost, mightn't amount to very much, especially if Vambrace and Snelgrove asked for something very big. A judge often takes a poor view of a big claim. No, it's precedent you have to avoid. If they got a judgement, even for a thousand dollars, on a thing of this kind, people all over the country would be trying to shake down newspapers because of all kinds of trivial errors, and getting settlements out of court. That's where it could cost you a lot of money. Anyhow, I said it *could* cost you money; I didn't say it *would*. It's my job to see that it doesn't. That's why I want to get my hands on X.'

Mr Balmer poured a glass of water out of a vacuum jug on his side-table and drank it with relish. His office was very different in atmosphere from that of Snelgrove, Martin and Fitzalan; indeed, it could hardly be said to have anything so needless as an atmosphere at all. Mr Balmer sat behind a steel desk, in a scientifically-sprung chair; Ridley sat in a chair which matched it exactly. There was nothing on the desk but a blotter, nothing on the floor but expensive linoleum, and nothing on the walls save some framed evidences that Mr Balmer was a lawyer, and a QC. Mr Balmer himself, though a stout, bald man, managed to suggest that his flesh was merely some scientific modern substance, as it might be foam rubber, over a steel frame. The glass of water set some lawyer-like and explanatory machinery at work inside him, and he continued.

'They will charge libel. Snelgrove was in to see me yesterday, and that is what they have in mind. It will be a difficult charge to prove, but it could be done. However, it is one thing to prove libel, and another to get anything substantial in the way of damages for it. The judge might very well take the line that the libel didn't amount to much. Still, you published the libel, and you're guilty. If the judge didn't like newspapers – and judges don't, as a usual thing – he could be ugly about it. Now, our defence should be that you are a victim of malice. Malice is a vague term in law, but though it's hard to define it isn't hard to understand. You are the victim, along with Miss Vambrace and Mr Bridgetower, of the malice of X. Give me X, and I'll put him in the stand and pretty soon the whole issue will be fogged over, because you, and Vambrace, will both be anxious to get at him. The judge probably won't be able to do anything to X, unless a charge is brought against him – a charge of malice. Whether that could amount to anything will depend on who he is. I wouldn't advise such a charge, unless the circumstances are exceptional; malice is even slipperier than libel.'

'And what happens if they get X?' asked Ridley.

'Ah, then they would probably keep him under wraps until they had got what they could out of you, and bring another case against him. Or they might even bring him in late in the case, as a surprise, and question him in such a way as to further discredit you. X is the key to the case. Give me X, and the whole thing will be sewed up.'

'But I can't give you X. I'm trying to find him; Marryat's trying to find him; Weir is looking for him. But we haven't a thing to go on. We'll never find him.'

'Don't say that. Snelgrove is looking for him, and so is Ronny Fitzalan. Vambrace is hunting him, and I hear some very queer rumours about that. When a lot of people are looking for a thing, it usually turns up. Not many people can cover their tracks, and even fewer can keep from telling a secret if they know one. I'm sure X will be found. I just want our side to find him first.'

'I suppose compromise is quite out of the question?' said Ridley.

'No, not by any means. Ronny Fitzalan has been to see me, without Snelgrove knowing. He's a cousin of the Vambrace girl, and he wants to keep the thing quiet for her sake. But to shut Vambrace up you'll have to eat a lot of dirt and do it in public, what's more. I'd advise against it. Technically, you're in the wrong; morally, you're in the clear. Give in on this, and God knows what demands you won't face next. You've got a good case, and I think you should fight it. Next time you might not have such a good case; the time for a show of strength is when you're strong.'

'I see. Well, can you suggest anything? Should we hire detectives, or anything?'

'I've been in the law for twenty-five years, and I've yet to see a detective who could work effectively in anything except a very big city. In a place like this you can smell 'em. Anyway, they do a lot of their work through the underworld, and the underworld of Salterton is just one man, Pimples Buckle. He controls everything crooked in a fifty-mile radius. Leave it to me. I'll establish diplomatic contact with Pimples. Meanwhile keep up the search.'

And with this Ridley had to be content.

It was on Monday morning, at the same hour when Gloster Ridley was in consultation with *The Bellman*'s solicitor, that Solly at last found Pearl in the music room of the Waverley Library. Since the previous Friday, following his visit to the Cobblers, he had been in search of her, for he was now convinced that if they could talk over their difficulty they could find a way out of it. At least, that is what he told himself when he sought Pearl at the Library on Friday morning, and that was his certainty when he sought her again on Friday afternoon. At both times she had been busy and he felt a shyness about asking for her at the main desk, so he had mooned about the reading room hoping that she might come into view and, unsuspected by himself, attracting a good deal of attention among the other librarians, who assumed that he had come for a sight of his fiancée, or a word with her. By Friday night his need to talk to Pearl had become a source of discomfort to him, but he dared not call her on the telephone, and he knew of no place where he might find her.

On Saturday morning he had visited the Library again, but without better success. The Library closed at one o'clock, and he had hung about in the street outside, thinking that he might see her as she left to go home. Had he known it, Pearl was watching him from a window, and did not leave until he had gone. Lunchtime in the Bridgetower house was a fixed appointment; the Vambraces did not care when they ate. Pearl told herself that she could not imagine what he wanted to say to her; by a not uncommon trick of the mind she resented and even hated Solly because he had been a witness to the disgraceful scene between herself and her father. If he chose to hang about on a wet day, hoping to speak to her, he was free to do so. She rather wished he might catch cold.

This was a harsh thought, and harsh thoughts were a new and luxurious experience for Pearl. Since that dreadful Wednesday night, when she had lain awake weeping for the loss of her father, she had thought many harsh things about a wide variety of people. And although uncharitableness is widely believed to be an enemy of beauty, and may be so if continued for many years, a few days of it improved Pearl's appearance remarkably. Feeling herself now to be alone in the world, she stood straighter, her eyes were brighter, and she moved with brisk determination. As she was no longer burdened by a sense of family, and felt free for the first time in her life from the Vambrace tradition of despising all worldly things which cost money, she drew a substantial sum from her savings account and bought herself two new outfits, smarter than she had thought proper before. She went farther. She had grown up under the shadow of her father's belief that short hair for women was a fad, which would quickly pass, and her own black hair was long and indifferently dressed. But on Saturday afternoon she went to a hairdresser and had her hair cut to within three inches of her head, and curled. It was an act of defiance, and at the evening meal that night, as her parents consumed a trifle composed of left-over blancmange and jelly-roll, she was powerfully conscious of their eyes upon her. But they said not a word.

The fact was that Professor Vambrace was cowed, for the first time in his relationship with his daughter. He was bitterly ashamed of the scene that he had made in the street, ashamed because he had behaved in an undignified fashion in front of young Bridgetower; ashamed because he had clouted his daughter over the ear, like some peasant and not like a cousin of Mourne and Derry, ashamed because he had allowed his daughter to see how deeply he was hurt by the failure of his attempts as a detective. His mind refused to admit that he was ashamed to have hurt the feelings of his child, who had worshipped him; but his heart's pain was the worse for this refusal. Yet it was not in the Professor to ask forgiveness, to explain, to make any move toward reconciliation with his daughter; he desperately desired to be forgiven, but in his hard way of thinking it was out of the question for a parent to ask forgiveness of a child. A child was, through the very fact of being a child, always in the wrong in any dispute. He told himself that he would wait until Pearl was in a proper frame of mind, and then he would allow her to creep back into his good graces. This was his attitude until Saturday morning, and Thursday and Friday were dark days in the Vambrace home.

The Professor had no lecture to deliver on Saturday morning, but he went to the University all the same, and he was sitting in his office, reading a quarterly devoted to classical studies, when there was a knock on the door and a tall, heavily good-looking young man entered without waiting for an invitation.

'Professor Vambrace,' said he, 'I'm Norm Yarrow.'

'Indeed?' said the Professor, without expression.

'We haven't met, but I'm a new boy on the student guidance staff. A friend of Pearlie's.'

'Of –?'

'Pearlie. Your daughter.'

'So? I am not accustomed to hear her called that. Hypocorisms are not employed in my household.' The Professor was very much the cousin of Mourne and Derry that morning.

'Professor, let's get down to brass tacks. I'm only here because I want to help. I want you to understand right now that my job is simply to understand, not to accuse. Now, you're an intelligent man, so I don't have to beat about the bush with you. We can take the gloves off right at the start. I take it that you've heard of the Oedipus Complex?'

'I am familiar with all forms of the Oedipus legend.'

'Yes, but have you understood it? I mean, as we moderns understand it? Have you got the psychological slant on it?'

'Mr Yarrow, I should hardly be head of the department of Classics at this University if I were not thoroughly acquainted with all that concerns Oedipus.'

'But the Complex? You know about the Complex?'

'What Complex are you talking about? All art is complex.'

'No, no; I mean do you recognize what the story of Oedipus really is? I mean about every man's childhood desire to kill his father and marry his mother? You've heard about that?'

'I have naturally heard something of such trash. Now may I ask the purpose of your visit, Mr Yarrow? I am engaged, as you see, in reading.'

'I'll put it in a nutshell. Has it ever struck you that there's a kind of an Oedipus thing between you and Pearlie?'

Professor Vambrace was not a merry man, but he was not without his own sort of humour. After a long look at Norm, he replied.

'An extremely interesting suggestion, my dear sir. Perhaps you would like to expand it?'

Norm beamed. As he always said to Dutchy, they were easier to deal with when they had some brains, and didn't weep, or shout at you.

'I'm glad you're taking it like that, Professor. Now about Pearlie; there's been talk. And particularly about that scene in the street a night or two ago. They say you were walloping her with a pretty big stick –'

'They say? Yes, much has been said about me, Mr Yarrow. I can guess who your informants were. They have been saying such things for many years. And now they say that I have been chastising my daughter in public, do they? With a stick? I am not in the least surprised. And how does the legend of Oedipus bear upon this accusation?'

'Professor, you love Pearlie.'

'Do I, Mr Yarrow? An extraordinary idea. That a man should love his daughter is understandable, but surely my detractors deny me any such natural feeling?'

'I mean, you love Pearlie too much.'

'And so I chastise her in public with a stick?'

'Exactly. You're jealous, you see. You're jealous of her normal love-object, young Solly Bridgetower.'

'Oh, you believe her to be in love with Bridgetower, do you?'

'Well, isn't she engaged to him?'

'What makes you think so?'

'Well – wasn't it in the paper?'

'Aha, so you believe what you see in the papers? A strange confession for a psychologist. No, Mr Yarrow, she is not engaged to him, nor has the idea of being engaged to him ever entered her head. Now, to return to your opinions about Oedipus, which I find refreshingly novel, what has Oedipus to do with all this?'

Norm had a feeling that he had lost the upper hand in this interview; it was not normal for the interviewee to be so icy calm, so impersonal, as this.

'From the piece in the paper it was natural to assume that she was engaged to him. You'll admit that. Now Oedipus is a kind of symbol of a particular kind of love, you see, and . . .'

'Oedipus might be taken as a symbol of many things. In accordance with the prophecy, he slew his father Laius, and married Epikaste, the widow of Laius, to discover later that she was his mother. A strange love, certainly. But my dear mother died when I was a child of two, Mr Yarrow, and I have no recollection of her. I fail to see the resemblance between Oedipus and myself.'

'Perhaps you don't know yourself as thoroughly as you should. Not that I mean to blame you, of course. It takes training to know yourself in the way I am talking about. But if you turn the Oedipus legend around, you get a daughter who kills her mother and is in love with her father. Do you follow me?'

'Inverted legends are no novelty to a classicist, my dear sir. Let me help you out; it is your idea that my daughter loves me to excess, and that in order to correct this undesirable condition I beat her publicly with a stick? Is that it?'

'No, not exactly. You're being too literal. What I'm trying to get at is that your desire to keep Pearlie from her natural love-object, to keep her all to yourself, is – well, let's not say unnatural; let's just say it isn't usual. Go on that way, and you may be headed for a crack-up. Maybe I shouldn't have brought Oedipus into this. All that Freudian stuff is pretty complicated, and anyway I'm sure things haven't got that far yet with you and Pearlie – if I make myself clear.'

'But you do not make yourself clear. And I am anxious that you should do so before you leave this room. After all, it is not every day that a man of my age, and of my quiet and retired mode of life, is confronted with a stranger who suggests that he lives in an unnatural relationship with his daughter. I should like to hear more.'

'Now, Professor, let's not get extreme. When I was talking about Oedipus I was talking symbolically, you understand.'

'I do not profess to understand psychological symbolism, Mr Yarrow, but it does not require much training to realize that Oedipus is a symbol for incest. Isn't that what you imply?'

'Oh, now just a minute. That's pretty rough talk. Not incest, of course. Just a kind of mental incest, maybe. Nothing really serious.'

'Fool!' said the Professor, who had been growing very hot, and was now at the boil. 'Do you imply that the sins of the mind are trivial and the sins of the flesh important? What kind of an idiot are you?'

'Now, Professor, let's keep this objective. You must understand that I'm talking on the guidance level, not personally at all. I just want to help you to self-understanding. If you understand yourself, you can meet your problem, you see, and I'm here, in all friendliness, to try to help you to understand yourself, and to help Pearlie, and so forth, do you see?'

'But you have not yet told me what all this has to do with Oedipus.'

Norm was by this time sick of the name of Oedipus. A horrible suspicion was rising in his mind that the Oedipus Complex, which he had for some time used as a convenient and limitless bin into which he dumped any problem involving possessive parents and dependent children, was a somewhat more restricted term than he had imagined. The chapter on Freudian psychology in his general textbook had not, after all, equipped him to deal with a tiresomely literal professor of classics who knew Oedipus at first hand, so to speak. Norm had received his training chiefly through general courses and from some interesting work which proved fairly conclusively that rats were unable to distinguish between squares, circles and triangles.

'Let's forget about Oedipus,' he said, and smiled a smile which had never failed him in all his career in social work.

'Not at all,' said the Professor, grinning wolfishly. 'I am increasingly reminded of Oedipus. Do you not recall that in that tragic history, Oedipus met a Sphinx? The Sphinx spoke in riddles – very terrible riddles, for those who could not guess them died. But Oedipus guessed the riddle, and the chagrin of the Sphinx was so great that it destroyed itself. I am but a poor shadow of Oedipus, I fear, and you, Mr Yarrow, but a puny kitten of a Sphinx. But you are, like many another Sphinx of our modern world, an under-educated, brassy young pup, who thinks that gall can take the place of the authority of wisdom, and that a professional lingo can disguise his lack of thought. You aspire to be a Sphinx, without first putting yourself to the labour of acquiring a secret.'

'Aw, now, Professor, let's not be bitter –'

'Bitter? Have I not a right to be bitter? You intrude upon me with your obscene accusation, and your muddle of old wives' tales about me beating my daughter in the streets, and you tell me not to be bitter! No, you listen to me: I shall inform your superior of this, and if you dare to repeat any of this filthy nonsense to anyone else, I shall not only drive you out of this University in disgrace, but I shall take you to court and strip you of everything you possess. Get out of here! Get out! Get out!'

The Professor had worked himself up into a rage by this time; flecks of white bubbled from his lips, and his eyes rolled horribly. He seized his walking stick – not a blackthorn, for that was broken, but a knobbly ashplant – and he might have struck Norm with it if the expert in guidance had not darted into the corridor, to escape down the iron staircase so rapidly that it rumbled like thunder.

But when he was in safety he felt a certain comfort coursing warmly through him. The Professor's rage, though alarming, was the normal response to what Norm had said; when a man was shown to himself he invariably wept or raged. It had been the Professor's period of quiet, controlled watchfulness which had worried Norm. That was definitely abnormal, and hard to figure out. In fact, the more he thought about it, the less he understood it. And all that talk about Sphinxes – that didn't sound too good. Simply made no sense at all. The Professor would bear watching.

The more Norm reflected on the interview, the more he was convinced that he had understood it all thoroughly. Which, as he was the expert on human behaviour, was perfectly normal.

Although nothing would have made him admit it, Norm's visit had had some effect on the Professor; it made him yearn toward his daughter more painfully than at any time since that Wednesday night when he had wept alone in his study. But this also he could not admit. If only she would show signs of wishing forgiveness, how quickly, how magnanimously he would forgive her! But there she sat across the table from him, in clothes which he had not seen before, and which even his unpractised eye could recognize as better than her usual garb, and with her hair cut short and dressed in a strange new fashion. His spirit was nearly broken, and he decided to make the first move toward reconciliation.

'I received a visit from a friend of yours today,' he said to her, 'a young man from the chaplain's department, who called himself Yarrow.'

'He is not a particular friend of mine.'

'Indeed? He appeared to know a good deal about our family affairs.'

Pearl said nothing.

'Tell me, Pearl, is it your custom to discuss family matters with outsiders?'

'No, Father.'

'But you have discussed your home with this man Yarrow?'

Pearl's first instinct was to lie. Before that dreadful, emancipating

Wednesday night she would certainly have done so. But three days of bitterness had changed her.

'Yes, Father.'

'I see. And may I ask why you did so?'

'I must talk to someone occasionally.'

The Professor said no more, and his heart was very heavy. He did not suppose, of course, that Pearl had told Yarrow that he had beaten her with a stick, or that he had an incestuous passion for her. That was plainly the spiteful talk of the cabal which had so long been at work against him. But he knew that Pearl had shut him out of her life because of that night.

Sunday was a black, silent day in the Vambrace home.

Sunday was not much better for Solly than it was for Professor Vambrace. He was possessed by the seemingly contradictory convictions that Pearl was a wretched, inconsiderable, bungling creature who had introduced a last intolerable complication into his already complicated life, and by the feeling that he must talk to her as soon as possible. In his mind's eye he could see her – dark, dowdy and withdrawn. Therefore it was with surprise that he encountered the reality in the music room in the Library on Monday morning; it was as though a picture, previously much out of focus, had been made clear to him.

'Ah – can I have a minute? I mean, I've simply got to talk to you. It's desperately important.'

'I'm very busy.'

'I can't help that. You must listen; it's as much your business as mine.'

'Please go away.'

'I won't go away. I've been chasing you for days. We've got to have a talk. How can we get out of this bloody mess if we don't discuss it?'

'I don't know. And I don't think you are likely to find a way.'

'Oh, I know; you're angry with me because I didn't do anything the other night. Well, what could I do? How would it have been if I'd knocked your father down when he was cuffing you? Or called a policeman? Damn it, I'm sorry. I'd have done something if it could have made any difference or settled anything. But I couldn't think of anything, so I got out of the way. Look: I'm terribly sorry. And don't think I came here for fun. I'm not enjoying this a bit more than you.'

'That's a very charming remark.'

'Well, how charming have you been, since I came? Can't we behave like sensible creatures and talk this thing out? I hear your father is suing *The Bellman*.'

'Yes. What's that to you? All you have to do is get up in the witness box and swear that you never had any intention of marrying me, and you will be as white as driven snow. The judge will probably offer you the pity of the court in your wronged condition.'

'Well if that isn't the most nauseating feminine attitude I've ever heard! Do you suppose I want anything of the kind? I don't want anything to do with a court action. Do you?'

'Oh don't talk like a fool! Of course I don't. How do you suppose it will make me look?'

'Well, then, why don't you repudiate the action?'

'How?'

'Simple. You hire a lawyer. When the case comes up he gets on his feet and says, "Your Honour, my client, Miss Pearl Vambrace, wishes me to say that she does not consider herself libelled, and wants it understood that she has nothing to do with bringing this action, and that it's all a pipedream of her father's, who has got into a fantod about nothing very much." Or however lawyers phrase these things. It'd blow the case sky-high.'

Pearl gazed at Solly with reluctant admiration. She had been agonizing about her situation for several days, and had seen no ray of light. But here was a man who cut through the complications with easy brilliance.

'If it was known you were going to do that, I doubt if the case would ever come to court,' Solly went on. 'It'd just be a waste of money. Do you know a lawyer?'

'My cousin Ronnie is a lawyer.'

'Fitzalan? No good. He's old Snelgrove's partner, and Snelgrove has been telling half the town, in strict confidence, that he is going to take the hide off *The Bellman*.'

'Well, and so he should. It's libelled me. And you too.'

'Don't be silly. If it's libel to say I'm engaged to you, and if it's libel to say you're engaged to me, surely we are both such lepers that the two libels cancel out. It's a mistake, a damn silly mistake, but still a mistake.'

Once again Pearl was dazzled by Solly's grasp of the fundamentals of her problem. His law might be shaky, but his reasoning was sound.

'You mean you don't care about that engagement notice appearing?'

'Of course I care. It can make a hell of a mess of things for me. But it isn't the end of the world, you know.'

'You mean it would be awful for you if Griselda Webster came to hear of it?'

'Well, it certainly wouldn't make things any simpler.'

'I'm sorry I was so nasty about Griselda and you the other night.'

'Forget about all that. You were upset, understandably. So was I. All that crawling about on the floor, and hitting me on the nose, and playing those blood-soaked games. Very unnerving.' Solly caught her eye, and Pearl smiled. And she was so surprised to find herself smiling after four bitter days that she laughed and he laughed with her. They were so delighted and relieved to be laughing that they did not notice that the door had opened, and that the Librarian, Dr Forgie, stood beside them. A chronic sufferer from asthma, he spoke bubblingly, like a man under water.

'Well,' said he, looking up at them from his five foot three of scholarly obesity, 'I have surprised you, I see. Now I really must protest, Bridgetower, against these, ah – tender assignations during Library hours. Miss Vambrace has her work to do, and I must beg you to confine your meetings to leisure time, which is ample – ample. We shall not quarrel about this single transgression of rules. Cupid plays strange tricks upon us all. Permit me to congratulate you both!' And here Dr Forgie seized Solly's hand and wrung it powerfully. He then reached up to Pearl's shoulders and dragged her down to a level with his own face, and kissed her with a smack. 'I must beg that there will be no repetition of this incident,' said he, and strutted out of the room.

'Unless you want to be kissed again by Dr Forgie, we'd better part,' said Solly.

'How do you suppose he knew we were here?'

'His daughter Tessie told me where to find you. With many tender and insinuating sighs and glances, I may say. Cupid has a firm friend in Tessie. Then I suppose she regretted her kind action, and blatted to Pa.'

'How like Tessie. You must go.'

'When do I see you again?'

'Eh? What for?'

'We haven't half settled things. I keep telling you that we must talk.

Unless we have a united plan of action, this is going to be bad for both of us. Can I see you tonight?'

'I suppose so.'

'Where shall I call for you?'

'At home.'

'What? Won't your father mind?'

'I haven't any notion. Come about half-past eight. I'll be watching for you. No – just blow your horn, will you?'

It was Solly's turn to admire. Casually blown motor horns, he was sure, would not soothe the breast of Pearl's father. And yet she did not seem to care. Clearly Pearl was a girl of greater spirit than he had supposed.

Punctually at half-past four Ridley arrived at the home of his employer, and as concisely as possible he reported to him the conversation which had passed between him and Gordon Balmer, *The Bellman*'s solicitor, earlier in the day.

'So he's going to Pimples Buckle?' said Mr Clerebold Warboys.

'Yes. I didn't tell him that Weir went to Buckle last week; we know just as much about Buckle's influence as he does. But it's no good. Buckle knows nothing about the affair, and isn't interested. He has his pride, you know. He says this isn't crime – merely kid stuff – and he's only interested in crime. He wouldn't budge unless we would promise him a good deal of newspaper protection next time he comes into court, and of course we can't do that.'

'So we're still up in the air about X.'

'Yes. Worse than up in the air, I'm afraid. Snelgrove has nabbed X.'

'What!'

'I had a call from Balmer just as I was leaving the office. Snelgrove had called him not long before; they say they've got X, but of course they won't tell us who it is. Balmer's guess is that it is a woman. Anyhow, Snelgrove wanted us to meet him tomorrow, for a show-down, in his office. Balmer fought that, because he wanted the meeting to be in his office. But after a lot of wrangling I've arranged that the lawyers, and Vambrace, and X, should all meet in my office. We have to keep some sort of face.'

'Quite right. If we have to climb down and make terms, we'd better do it on our own ground.'

'You think we should climb down?'

'I don't know. And I'm not going to be there. You must handle this.

Let them think they have winkled me out of my house and down to the office, and they'll imagine we are worried. Which, of course, we are. But we mustn't show it. That's why you must deal with it yourself.'

'Very well; if you think that best.'

'I do. Fight to the last ditch. We mustn't climb down if we can possibly avoid it.'

'I'm glad you feel that way.'

'I certainly do feel that way. There is nothing lawyers like better than to score off a newspaper. In fact, you might say there is nothing most people like better than to score off a newspaper. And it's understandable that they should feel that way. There have been times in my political life when I would have been glad to silence every newspaper in the country. Newspapers, as you very well know, can be damned nuisances.'

Ridley smiled. 'There have been two or three times in my life when I would have done anything to keep something out of a paper,' said he; 'anything, that is, except give the order for a story to be killed.'

'I know what you're talking about,' said Clerebold Warboys. 'But in spite of all the hogwash that is talked about the freedom of the Press, and in spite of the nauseating slop which the newspapers sometimes write about it, the freedom of the Press is a damned important thing. Not that this pin-prick has much to do with it. At worst it will cost us some money. But what I don't like is being pushed around by people who hate the paper and want to make it look foolish. God knows we can make ourselves look silly enough, without any outside help. We've got a case of some sort. We are as much abused as Vambrace. So we'll fight, just to show that a newspaper doesn't have to look like a fool to please a few cranks. We'll get Pettypiece to fight the case for us, if it goes to court. He's forgotten more about newspapers and libel than old Snelgrove will ever know. We won't climb down unless they can show that we have really been careless and haven't a leg to stand on.'

'I'm afraid we have been careless,' said Ridley.

'It could happen to anybody. Anyway, they don't know we've been careless yet. And they won't, unless this comes to court. Don't let this thing worry you, Ridley. A pin-prick.'

'I'm afraid it is a little more than a pin-prick for me, sir,' said Ridley. 'This is not easy to explain, because it makes me look vain and probably a little foolish. You know I've done a great deal to arrange the new journalism course at Waverley. In fact, I might say that I've done all the real work. It's meant a great deal of time for several months. There has never been any talk of reward, and I don't want money. I can say quite honestly that I haven't done it for money. But it has crossed my mind, once or twice, that I might be named for an honorary degree.'

Thus modestly he brought out the ambition which had been his constant, lively companion for many weeks.

'Well, what about it? Vambrace has no say in such things. He isn't a Governor.'

'He is very close to several Governors.'

'Which ones?'

'This is rather embarrassing, but I think he carries a great deal of influence with your daughter-in-law.'

'With Nesta? Oh, I don't think she sees much of him.'

'Mrs Roger Warboys has been interesting herself in this matter to a greater degree than you apparently know. And you are aware that she has a poor opinion of me as an editor. She is a friend of Mrs Bridgetower's as well.'

'Well, God bless my soul! You think she's out to sink you, for this honorary degree, or whatever it is?'

'I'm afraid so.'

'Well, what do you expect me to do about it?'

'I have not mentioned it to you before because I do not expect you to do anything about it. I have too much pride to appeal to you in a thing of this kind.'

'I'm glad of that,' said Mr Warboys who, like many people, had a keen sense of the triviality of ambition in others. 'I couldn't interfere, you know. Most of the Governors are friends of mine, but I couldn't go hat in hand to them and ask them to do something for somebody who was working for me. They might take it amiss. But you can leave it to me to put Nesta straight. It would be a fine thing for you to have a doctorate. A very nice crown to your career. A good thing for *The Bellman*. But if it doesn't work out, don't worry. These things are pretty chancy. Anyhow, you don't care much about it, do you?'

Ridley longed to say that he cared passionately about it. But life had not encouraged that sort of boldness in him, and he muttered something which suggested that he cared little for worldly gauds. Mr Warboys was plainly relieved, and after a few further remarks, Ridley rose to go. As he was about to leave the room Mrs Roger Warboys entered.

'There's a taxi at the door,' said she to Ridley. 'I thought, it must be yours. You always come and go in taxis; why don't you get yourself a car?'

'I prefer taxis,' said he. 'I find them much more convenient.'

'Not a bit convenient, really,' said Mrs Warboys, contradicting absent-mindedly and without interest. Then something seemed to strike her, and she looked at Ridley keenly. 'What news of Mrs Ridley?' said she.

Ridley turned very white, and the bony structure of his brow stood out in stronger relief. But when he spoke it was quietly and with self-possession. 'The news does not change very much, and never for the better, Mrs Warboys,' said he, and hurried out of the room.

'You shouldn't have asked him that, Nesta,' said Clerebold Warboys. 'Anyhow, you're not supposed to know.'

'Nobody's supposed to know,' said his daughter-in-law, 'but somehow everybody does.'

Drawing up outside the Vambrace house at about half-past eight o'clock, Solly sounded his horn in a discreet, rather than a challenging blast. He did not wish to see Pearl come through the door pursued by an angry father. A light in an upper window went out at once, and immediately afterward Pearl came down the walk, perfectly self-possessed, and stepped into his car as though this were the most ordinary thing in the world. Solly could not refrain from admiring comment.

'You made it all right?'

'Of course. What did you expect?'

When he had hunted down Pearl that morning in the music room she had been too surprised to assume her new role of woman of the world, which she had not yet been able to make fully her own. Thinking about their conversation afterward, Pearl had decided that she had been too friendly; the truth was that she had been so amazed by the common sense which Solly had brought to their common predicament that she had been pleasanter than she intended; he had even made her laugh. But he had referred tactlessly to her father's treatment of her; he had let her know, quite needlessly, that he had seen that cuff on the ear, had heard those sobs. Therefore she was determined to give him a double dose of the woman of the world tonight.

Solly was properly intimidated. He had thought, that morning, that Pearl would be easy to deal with; she had laughed with him, and he set great store by laughter. So he drove in silence along a country road until he came to a point where it ran directly beside the bay upon which Salterton faces, and there he brought the car to a stop.

There was a silence, which Solly and Pearl both found embarrassing, but after a very long time – perhaps two or three minutes – he broke it.

'Well?' said he.

'Well?' countered Pearl. She did not mean to be difficult, but she could not think of anything better to say.

'Well, here we are. The meeting is now open. Ladies first; what do you want to say?'

A woman of the world should always be able to say something, and Pearl felt herself to be at least as much a woman of the world as the Old Woman in *Candide*, so she plunged into speech.

'We must look at this reasonably,' said she. 'There's no use getting excited; there's been quite enough of that. We've been reported engaged. We're not engaged and aren't going to be. We want the report contradicted. It isn't really so dreadful. Of course Father thinks it is. He hates your family.'

'He doesn't,' said Solly. 'Only a couple of years ago when we were all working on *The Tempest* he was easy enough to get on with. And not so many years ago he and my mother appeared together on some sort of public committee about some current affairs thing, and they got on like a house afire. What's all this about hating my family? It's a good fifteen years since my father nosed him out as Dean.'

'Father's hates ebb and flow,' said Pearl. 'He hates you now and that's all there is to it.'

'He's as mad as a hornet at the thought of your marrying anybody. That's what it is.'

'Please. We aren't here to discuss my father.'

'Very well, Madam Chairman. But I'll bet we can't keep off him for long. Go ahead.'

'As I was saying, this report is a nuisance, and it will take some living down, but there is no very great harm done, provided there is no legal action.'

'No very great harm done?'

'Father thinks so. I don't. After all, you're a human being. It is within the range of possibility that I might have been engaged to you. There are people who aspire to that condition, in case you don't know it; and in the case you do know it and are conceited about it, I may tell you that Tessie Forgie is the most avid of them all. But the fact is that I'm not engaged to you, and while I am annoyed at the report that I am, I do not consider it to be libellous or insulting.'

'You overwhelm me.'

'Please don't be sarcastic. I'm simply trying to be objective.'

'You are succeeding magnificently. I hardly feel as if I were present in the flesh at all.'

'Unfortunately, my father takes a very serious view of this whole affair. He thinks it is part of a plot to make him appear ridiculous.'

'Please! You're turning my head with all this subtle flattery.'

'He wants to bring an action against the newspaper. The editor is behaving abominably. Do you know this man Ridley?'

'I've met him once or twice –

A poor, unfruitful, prying, windy scribe,
Who scratches down hell's witsome sprits, that he
May show them to her vulgar, gaping crowds,
Extended on his tablets.'

'What?'

'I am amazed that you, a librarian, cannot place the quotation instantly. From the great Charles Heavysege, Canada's earliest and foremost dramatist. I presume that when your father formed his opinion of me he did not know that I was the coming big man in the Heavysege field.'

'The what field?'

'It's a rich new vein of Amcan. We scholars are pegging out our claims in this new Yukon.'

'Please be serious. Ridley has behaved with dreadful discourtesy to Father. So far as I can see there's only one way to appease Father, and that's to find whoever put that notice in the paper.'

'And how are we going to do that?'

'Well, surely you have some ideas? Am I expected to do everything? All I can think of is that it must be somebody who knows us both.'

'Quite a wide field.'

'Not too wide when you think it must be somebody who knows us both and hates us both.'

'Oh, come, surely whoever it is only hates you. I'm just an insulting accessory to this business. Still, you're right. Who can it be? What goblin of ignoble mind?'

'Heavysege again?'

'Quite right.'

'I think Father knows already.'

'Really?'

'He was being extremely mysterious and hinting a lot this evening.'

'Well, why didn't you ask him?'

Pearl hesitated for a moment. 'At present it isn't very easy to ask him questions,' said she.

Solly thought he knew why, but this time he had tact enough not to refer to the happening of Wednesday night.

'If we could find out who it was,' said Pearl, 'without asking Father, naturally, we might be able to do something. Perhaps even go to see the person.'

'Have you thought of calling your cousin Ronnie?'

'I did. I went out to a public phone, and called him. All he would say was that Mr Snelgrove knew, but wouldn't tell him. He thinks there's to be some kind of big pow-wow tomorrow at Snelgrove's office at three.'

'If we're to catch whoever it is first, we'll have to be quick. Frankly, I don't think we have much of a chance.'

'Oh, don't be so defeatist! Don't you want to get this settled?'

'Pearl, have you said your say?'

'Why yes, I suppose so. For the present, anyhow.'

'Well, then, it's my turn. So far as I'm concerned this affair is settled, in its most important aspect, already.'

'How?'

'You mentioned Griselda this morning. I got this cable this afternoon.'

Solly brought a yellow cable form from his breast inside pocket, and gave it to Pearl, turning on the light on the dashboard of the car. She read:

DARLING DELIGHTED NEWS PEARL DEAR GIRL JUST RIGHT FOR YOU HAPPY FOR YOU BOTH GIVE PEARL KISS FOR ME MUCH LOVE WRITING GRISELDA

'Oh, Solly,' said Pearl, in a stricken voice.

'Yes,' said Solly. 'That's the end of an old song.' And he switched off the light.

In the half-darkness Pearl stared at him. She had ceased to be a woman of the world. Her eyes filled with tears, and very slowly they brimmed over and ran down her cheeks.

Solly was wretched, for he thought his heart was broken. Very probably it was so, in the meaning which is usually attached to the phrase. Most hearts of any quality are broken on two or three occasions in a lifetime. They mend, of course, and are often stronger than before, but something of the essence of life is lost at every break. Still, hurt as he was, he could not see Pearl weep unmoved. He took her in his arms, and comforted her as well as he could, and for a time they were miserable together.

'I wouldn't blame you if you threw me into that bay,' said Pearl, when she felt a little better, and had been accommodated with a clean handkerchief out of Solly's breast pocket. 'I've been a self-centred fool. I talked endlessly about myself and what this meant to me, and now you've lost Griselda. Everybody knows how much you loved her.'

'Yes,' said Solly, 'I'm afraid I have been rather obvious for a couple of years. Well, I don't care. I suppose it's better to feel something and look a fool than to take damned good care to feel nothing, and *be* a fool.'

'Would it help if I wrote to her? I could explain everything.'

'No you couldn't. This doesn't really concern you. I knew some good friend would be quick to tell Griselda. They even went to the expense of a cable. I'm sure it was a relief to her. She never cared much about me, really. I'm certain that cable means every word it says, quite literally. She'd be happy to think I had stopped crying for the moon, and had taken up with somebody else. Sorry, I didn't mean that the way it sounded.'

'Please don't feel guilty,' said Pearl. 'I said dreadful things to you. You must loathe me.'

'I don't loathe anybody,' said Solly, 'except myself.'

But Pearl was not to be denied self-abasement. 'I'm not very good about other people's feelings,' said she. And then, much more fully than she had ever been able to confide in Norman Yarrow, she told Solly about her life at home. About the division which her mother's religiosity and her father's agnosticism had made there. About the hard egotism, rising sometimes almost to the point of madness, which possessed him. About the life she led between them, torn this way and that, and cut off from young people, from ordinary pleasures, and with little before her save a continuance of this weary course, ending undoubtedly in the bitter role of the unmarried daughter who nurses both parents into the grave. She spoke without self-pity, but she spoke with point.

Solly was horrified. 'My God,' said he. 'It's monstrous. Of course everybody knows you have a grim time in that house, but everybody's always thought of it as a kind of joke. They're horrible.'

Pearl shook her head. 'No,' said she, 'that isn't it at all. They have done everything they have done out of love. They loved each other very much, and I think they still do, if they could hear one another, in their private worlds. And they loved me as much as they were able. They did the best for me that they could – the best they knew. Don't try to persuade me to think differently now. It's all I can bear at home now – more than I can bear for long, I know. But in spite of it all I love them very much.'

Solly's heart, which had contracted and grown hard that afternoon, when he received Griselda's cable, seemed to melt and beat freely now for the first time.

'I know what you mean,' said he. 'It's much the same with my mother. I'm tied to her apron strings. I'm a joke, I know. Griselda was very bitter about it once. But filial piety isn't simply a foolish phrase. It's a hard reality. Some people never seem to feel it. In happy families it is never put to any real test. But duty to parents is an obligation that some of us must recognize. However hellish parents may be, the duty is as real as the duty that exists in marriage. God, what a lot we hear about unhappy marriages, and how little we hear about unhappy sons and daughters. There's no divorce for them. You've told me about your parents. Well – you know my mother. And that reminds me that it's half-past ten, and she won't go to sleep till I come home, and she needs sleep.'

Saying no more, he started the car and drove Pearl back to her door.

'Good night,' said she, and held out her hand to him.

Solly turned toward her. His face was set and white. But as their eyes met his expression softened, until he smiled.

'"Ah, lovely hellsnake, wilt thou stare at me?"' he whispered.

'Heavysege?' said Pearl.

He nodded, and for the second time that day they laughed

together. Solly suddenly seized Pearl, and kissed her again and again. Then, once more he seemed to be angry.

'Damn it all,' said he, 'haven't you any name but Pearl?'

'I've got a saint's name,' she said. 'Veronica.'

'That's a little better,' said Solly, and kissed her again.

'I must go in,' she said, struggling free.

'Yes,' said he, and this time the shadow of Wednesday night did not divide but united them.

Solly tiptoed up the stairs, but the light under his mother's door was shining, as he knew it would be. He tapped and went in.

'You're late, lovey,' said Mrs Bridgetower. Without her teeth, and with her thin long hair in a braid, she was both pitiable and terrible.

'Not really, Mother. It's a little after eleven.'

'It always seems late when you're out, dear.'

'Sorry. Now you must go to sleep.'

'Where were you, dear?'

'Just out, Mother.'

'Dearie, it hurts me so to be shut out of your confidence.'

'Oh, you know I haven't been up to anything very terrible.'

'Dearie, I'm worried.'

'What about, Mother?'

'I'm worried that I'm going to lose my little boy.'

Oh God, thought Solly, here we go. She's coming the pitiable over me. There ought to be rules for these encounters – an inter-generation agreement about hitting below the belt.

'Well, and how do you expect to lose him this time?'

Mrs Bridgetower had had a sedative pill, and was groggy, but Solly knew her well enough to know that she could be most dangerous when at her groggiest. She spoke lispingly from her toothless mouth.

'Dearie, there's nothing in it about this girl, is there?'

'What girl?'

'This horrid Vambrace girl.'

'She's not horrid, Mother. You know her.'

'The whole family is horrid. Dearie, say there's nothing in it.'

'But, Mother, you know the whole thing began as a practical joke.'

The old eyes filled with tears; the old chin quivered a little.

'Then say it, lovey. Mother wants to hear you say it. There's nothing in it, is there?'

'Now, Mother dearest, you must get off to sleep, or you won't be able to get up tomorrow.'

Solly kissed his mother and turned off her bedside lamp. A night-light glowed from the floor. As he reached the door his mother's voice came to him, lisping still, but sharp and without assumed infantile charm.

'I wouldn't like it to be said that *my* marriage had begun as the result of a practical joke.'

He closed the door and hastened to his attic. What a demon she was! It was impossible to conceal anything from her. She could smell a change of emotion in him!

Yet what Pearl had confided to him about her family life had strengthened him, and as he lay in his bed he pitied his mother. And the more he pitied his mother, the more he thought of Pearl, until he could think of nothing else.

Veronica; as Veronica she seemed to be someone quite new.

Mrs Bridgetower also lay awake, and her heart yearned toward her son. He was all that she had in life. All – save a large house and nearly half a million dollars very shrewdly invested. Her heart longed toward him.

How easy, how utterly simple, for Solly to turn back to Mother – to drive away the powerful but still strange vision of Veronica, and to give himself to Mother forever! Should he run down the stairs and into her room *now*, to kiss her, and tell her that he would be her little boy forever? Thus life and death warred in Solly's bosom in the night, and in her bedroom his mother lay, yearning for him, willing him to come to her.

Of course, sensible modern people, though they believe a variety of strange things, do not believe in any such communion in emotion as this which seemed to be at work between Solly and his mother in the darkness of their house. That is why such things are never mentioned by those who have experienced them.

Gloster Ridley had fled for comfort to Mrs Fielding as soon as he felt that he could decently do so, and he arrived in her house precisely at half-past eight, but it was ten o'clock before he had a chance to speak to her intimately. No man should ever assume that he will be able to get the immediate and undivided attention of a woman who has children. Miss Cora Fielding was going to a dance, and needed her mother's help in certain fine details of dressing. Even Ridley was called into service, Mr Fielding being out, to help with a stuck zipper; the women had a pitiful faith in the ability of a man to meet such a problem, and Ridley broke two fingernails, and pinched Cora severely, in order to sustain the credit of his sex. Young George Fielding, who was seventeen, was encountering the Crimean War for the first time in his history lessons and, although he did not say so, he clearly had a feeling that Ridley remembered this encounter as a personal experience, and repeatedly came into the living-room to ask him questions about it. Ridley finally found it quicker to dictate an essay on Balaclava than to help George to find the facts himself. But at last the essay was done, and at last Cora's escort called for her, and at last Ridley was alone with Mrs Fielding.

'Now, Gloss, tell me all about it,' said she, leaning back in her chair and turning her level gaze upon him.

This was exactly what Ridley was aching to do, but he could never get used to the way in which Elspeth Fielding cut corners. He had expected at least a quarter of an hour of preliminaries before he got to his theme, and without them he was not completely sure that he knew what that theme was.

'All about what?' he said, to gain time.

'All about what's worrying you half to death. Dear old Gloss, you come here white as a sheet, you smoke without a stop, your hands shake, you pinch poor Cora, you lecture Georgie as if he were a public meeting, and then you try to pretend that everything is all right. Richard will be home in about an hour, and unless you tell me quickly, you may not tell me at all. Is it about this lawsuit with Professor Vambrace?'

'How did you guess?'

'It comes out of you in strong rays. Now let me get you a drink, and then you can tell me all about it.'

Ridley told her all that he thought was relevant. And because he was a good journalist, and was used to getting a story straight, he told it briefly and with all the points in the proper order. But Mrs Fielding was not to be fooled.

'But you don't really care about an honorary degree. Don't tell me that. Of course it would be very nice, but you don't need it and you don't want it – not as much as you're pretending.'

'How do you know, Elspeth? I'm not a university man. An honorary degree to me means the degree I might have earned years ago. I've earned it a different way. I've always missed a university training. I didn't have an easy time when I was young. I thought you understood all that.'

'Of course I understand it. But you're not a vain man. An honour of that sort wouldn't mean all this to you. You wouldn't shake and look sick at the thought of missing it.'

'I'm not a very self-assured man. I need things to bolster me up. Comfort, for instance. People think me a fussy old bachelor to take so much thought for my own comfort, though I really don't think I live any more comfortably than most married men I know. And the position I've made for myself. I'm really very well thought of as an editor, you know. And money. Of course I haven't a lot of money; my expenses have been heavy. But what I've got is rather carefully placed. All these things are necessary to me in a way that I don't suppose they are to most people. I've got to be secure.'

'Yes, that's an obsession of yours. But what has this particular trouble got to do with your security? How can it shake you, even if you do have a lawsuit, and lose it? Even if you lose your piddling degree. You'll still be you, won't you?'

'Don't hector me, Elspeth. I don't feel up to it.'

'Gloss dear, I'm not trying to hector, only to find out. Tell me truly – I'll never breathe it to a soul – do you terribly want that red gown? I'd understand, if you said you did. Nearly everybody has some hankering like that. Please tell me? Does it mean something very special?'

'It would be one more thing between me and –'

'Between you and what?'

'And – it sounds strange, but it's the only phrase that fits – between me and being found out.'

'Found out in what?'

'You know very well. Of course you do.'

'You mean about your wife?'

'Yes.'

'But, Gloss, everybody knows about that!'

Ridley's face was more white and drawn than ever. He looked at Mrs Fielding coldly, almost with dislike.

'Precisely what do you mean, "Everybody knows about that"?' said he.

'Not everybody, of course, but dozens of people. I suppose that several hundred people in Salterton know that your wife has been in an asylum for nearly twenty years. Really, Gloss, for a newspaperman you are very stupid about secrets. How many Salterton secrets do you know? It must be hundreds. Scandals about money; adulteries; suicides; even murders. And you know how all those secrets came to your ears, and how many people know them beside yourself. Did you really, truly suppose, that your little secret could be kept when so many others were known? I have never mentioned it, because I knew you wouldn't want me to do so. But Dick knows, and somebody told him. And I've heard it mentioned several times. Gloster Ridley's wife is in an asylum near Halifax. Nobody thinks about it, but all kinds of people know it. Gloss, is all this passion for security an attempt to rise above that? You poor darling, what a lot of unnecessary agony! Why didn't you tell me about that years ago? When you told me about your wife?'

'I have never really told you about my wife.'

'No? Is there more to it? But it can't really be very dreadful.'

'Can't it? Elspeth, I visit my wife twice a year. I make myself do it. She hasn't recognized me once in the past fifteen years, and now I don't even see her. They let me look into her room. She lies there all day, curled up on a mattress in a corner, with a blanket pulled over her head. She has to be fed artificially.'

'Poor Gloss! How dreadful! But really, my dear, wouldn't it be better not to go? If you can't do anything, I mean?'

'No. I must go. It is absolutely necessary for me to go.'

'But why?'

'Because she is there through my fault. And – this is what shakes me, Elspeth – there is still a chance, remote, but a chance, that she might recover. Might be well enough to return to me, the doctors say. Can you imagine that? The murderer's victim to rise from the dead, to live with him and share his daily life! Do you think murder a strong word to use? Do you? I use it, in my thoughts; often I can't escape it. Murder! She is in a living death, and I cannot stifle the feeling that I murdered her.'

'Oh, Gloss! I'm sure you didn't.'

'I wish I were sure, one way or the other. But I'll never know. However, as Salterton knows so much about my affairs, I suppose this is all stale news to you?'

'Oh, darling, don't be bitter. Of course I want to know everything about it, if you'll tell me. But I won't pry.'

'It isn't as though there were much to tell. You'll find this hard to believe, Elspeth, but when I was young I was very romantic. I was always falling in love – not lightly, but deeply and painfully. When I was twenty-one I met a girl who seemed to me to be the most beautiful and desirable creature that I could conceive of. I wanted to devote my life to her. She had no very strong feeling for me; she had no strong feeling about anything; but I talked her into marrying me. That happens oftener than people suppose. Love is a great force, and because I was a stronger character than she, I was able to persuade her. I was sure that she would grow to love me after we were married. She didn't. Perhaps she couldn't have loved anyone. I suppose I was an impossible fool. I know that I reproached her. She was stupid, and she was a wretched housekeeper. I know that sounds petty, in a love story, but we lived a pig's life, for I had a job with a very poor salary, and it was all intolerable. I thought I couldn't bear it. I considered running away from her, and do you know why I didn't? Because of my mother; I didn't want her to think ill of me. I didn't know what to do. But one day my wife and I were driving in a borrowed car; I was going, I remember clearly, to report a small country fair for my paper. We quarrelled for several miles. Suddenly the car went out of control, and we turned over in the ditch. That is the phrase the papers always use – "the car went out of control" – you see, it accuses nobody. It is for the court to make accusations. But in this case there was no court. I wasn't very much hurt, but my wife was badly shaken. It was shock, the doctors said, and after shock came pneumonia. And within a year, a serious breakdown. Schizophrenia, hallucinations, thinking she was somebody else, all that kind of thing. No need to go into detail about it. That meant the hospital, and that's where she has been ever since. Now she is as near to being dead, to being nothing at all, as a living human creature can be. And what I have never been able to decide is whether that accident was really an accident, or whether I created it.'

'But of course you didn't create it! You mustn't think such a thing! I'm sorry, Gloss; I know that was a silly and useless thing to say.'

'It's very sweet of you to have such belief in me. Of course I, as I exist at this moment, didn't create it. But I was a very different person then. I wished her dead, or myself dead, time and time again. And you see, so much of my life has been devoted to making myself into a person who couldn't possibly have created that accident, who couldn't possibly have done that murder. And if you think the red gown of a Doctor of Laws wouldn't be a help in that, you haven't understood what a very inferior creature I am, and how much apparently small things can mean to me.'

'But, my dear, a red gown can't change your own opinion of yourself. The man you live with, and feed and wash and dress and go to bed with doesn't wear a red gown. He's the man that counts. Oh, Gloss darling, you must stop torturing yourself. What's the good of winning honours and the good opinion of the world if you can't live on good terms with yourself?'

'Do you know anybody who isn't a fool who really lives on good terms with himself?'

'Yes, of course I do.'

'I shouldn't have married her, but I did. Very well. Having married her, I should have borne it better, shown more restraint, and more kindness. But I didn't. Can I forget that, or forgive myself?'

'But it's done and past repair. Now, Gloss, you must listen to me.'

It would be of little avail to set down in detail what Mrs Fielding said to Ridley. None of it was extraordinarily wise, or uncommonly deep, but it was all rooted fast in love and womanly tenderness. Nor would it be truthful to say that Ridley was set free from his bugbear forever. But his burden was so much lightened, and confession had so cleansed him, that he was very much changed, very much cheered, and when at last Mr Fielding came home Ridley greeted him with a warmth of affection that surprised that gentleman, old friends as they were.

When at last Ridley set out for home, his step was light, and he felt free and vigorous. If only, he thought, I had had the good luck to marry somebody like Elspeth. But that was fruitless speculation, and he had learned that night how profitless, how diminishing, fruitless speculation can be. At fifty he was perhaps rather old to be coming to such conclusions, but we all subscribe thoughtlessly to many beliefs, the truth of which does not strike home to us until experience gives them reality. Wisdom may be rented, so to speak, on the experience of other people, but we buy it at an inordinate price before we make it our own forever.

'If I could hold fast to this state of mind I am in now, I might at last be free,' thought Ridley exultantly.

When he went into the vestibule of the old mansion in which his apartment was, he found a figure huddled on the floor, partly asleep. It started up, and revealed itself as Henry Rumball.

'I've been waiting for you sir,' said he. 'I've found X.'

He held out his hand. In it was a pink slip for a *Bellman* classified advertisement.

Mrs Edith Little had completed her self-imposed nightly task of marking the typographical errors in *The Bellman* and was knitting on a sweater for little Earl. It was a complicated pattern, designed to make the finished garment look as though it had been made from heavy cable, and she was often compelled to consult her pattern book, from the page of which smiled the photograph of an offensively neat and handsome little boy, wearing the sweater in question. The Morphews' living-room presented a peaceful domestic scene. Mrs Morphew was painting her toenails coral pink, having spent an agreeable hour rubbing the hair from her legs with a pad of fine emery paper. The radio had been discoursing music, comic repartee, news and advertising all evening but neither Ede nor Kitten had paid any attention to it. They were lost in their thoughts. But when an announcer said that it was, at that very instant, eleven o'clock, Ede spoke to her sister censoriously.

'You'd better stop that. The boys'll be home soon.'

'What of it? I got a whole 'nother foot still to do.'

'D'you want them to catch you at it?'

'Why not? Georgie knows I do it. Georgie likes it.'

'What about Bev?'

'Bev's an old sport. He'd like it.'

'It isn't right for men to know what women do.'

'If you'd let Bob Little know a little more what you did, maybe he wouldn't've run out on you.'

'That is one hell of a thing to say.'

'Yeah, ain't it though!'

'Yes, it is! If I wanted to throw my legs around I could get men to look at me too. The way George looks at you sometimes, it makes me creep!'

'I'll bet it does.'

'All right, if you're proud of that kind of thing.'

'George is still living right here with me, and glad to, in case you hadn't noticed.'

'And so he ought. You're a wonderful housekeeper. I give you that.'

'That's only part of what I am.'

'Oh, you both of you make so much of that! Still, it hasn't brought you any children.'

'Ede, that's a dirty, lousy thing to say, even between sisters!'

'Well, who threw Bob Little up to me a minute ago? I may not have a husband, but I've got my child, and I'd a lot sooner it was that way than the other way.' And Ede knitted ostentatiously.

'You're a liar but I forgive you,' said Kitten good-naturedly. 'Listen, why don't you start looking around?'

'I'm not interested, thank you very much.'

'Well then, get interested. Earl's going to need a daddy. If you don't think much of George, get a man of your own to bring up the boy.'

'I can manage Earl without any man.'

'All right. Go on wishing old Baldy Ridley would take a tumble to you. And I'll bet you wouldn't wait for any ring if he did either.'

'That's a fine thing to say about your own flesh and blood.'

'Ede, you got more refinement than sense; that's what's wrong with you.'

'I've got a child to think of; I can't just let myself go.'

'Oh, so I've let myself go, have I? I can get into clothes you can't even touch.'

'I meant mentally. Living with George you've just sunk to his level. You've just become George's Thing, if you want to know what I really think! Just his Thing!'

Kitten was unable to reply to this, for she had thrown herself backward in her chair and was kicking her feet vigorously in the air in order to dry her nail-varnish. It was at this moment that the front door opened and George and Mr Higgin walked in, followed by a stranger.

'Looka there!' shouted George, and seizing one of his wife's feet he nipped her playfully on the big toe with his front teeth. 'What I always say, kid, you're good enough to eat!'

'Georgie, lemme down! Georgie!' squealed Kitten, and after a great deal of bare leg and frilly panties had been displayed, and after George had pretended to strum on her leg as upon a guitar, he did let her down, and she made a great show of modesty, tucking her feet up under her.

'What a pleasant homecoming,' said Mr Higgin, laughing delightedly, his bright eyes missing nothing of Kitten's display. 'You would have been proud of George, Kitten, indeed you would. He was quite the hit of the smoker, wasn't he, Mr Rumball?'

'Uh-huh,' said Rumball, without much enthusiasm.

'Meet m'friend Henry Rumball,' said George; 'Hank, meet the wife. Meet Ede. Siddown. Getcha drink.'

'Don't bother, Mr Morphew,' said Rumball. 'I'll have to go in just a minute, anyway.'

'Hank's a reporter,' said George. 'Gonna write us all up in *The Bellman*, aintcha, Henry?'

'I can't promise anything,' said Rumball. 'I only dropped in to see Mr Higgin; Mr Shillito insisted that I should. It wasn't a regular assignment, you know. I only came to see if there was anything about Mr Higgin I might work up into a feature story. There won't be any report of the smoker.'

'No report of the smoker?' said George, greatly indignant. 'And why not? Ain't we boys at the club subscribers? Ain't we got any rights? Listen, son, just tell me one thing; you've heard about the freedom of the Press?'

'Sure, sure,' said Rumball uneasily.

'O K then, why don't the smoker get a write-up?'

'Well, it was a private performance, Mr Morphew.'

'You're damn right it was private. So what were you doing there, sticking your nose into it?'

'Well, as I said, Mr Shillito asked me to go to see what Mr Higgin was doing, and to see if I could write something about it.'

'Now lookit,' said George pugnaciously, 'about this freedom of the Press. That means the club has as much right to a plug in the paper as anybody, don't it? And if not, just kindly tell me why not, will ya? Just explain.'

'Don't get excited, George,' said Higgin. 'It was a private show. And a very good thing too. Oh, if you could have seen George!' He giggled rapturously.

'I was good, wasn't I?' said George, restored to good humour. He was not entirely drunk, but he was in a variable mood, and there were traces of greasepaint on his face.

'You were sensational,' said Mr Higgin, giggling again.

'What'd you sing, Georgie?' asked Kitten, who had surveyed all of this with complacency.

'The ones I practised,' said George, then winked at Higgin and went off into a fit of laughter so great that he fell into his wife's chair. When they had sorted themselves out, he was sitting in the chair and Kitten was in his lap, her coral toes hanging over the arm.

'Oh, but it was the encores,' said Mr Higgin, bubbling with mirth. 'That was where he really had them, eh, Mr Rumball?'

'Yes, I guess it was,' said Rumball.

'"I'll be up 'er flue next week,"' sang George, loudly, and collapsed in laughter.

'What?' cried Kitten, who had caught the infection and was laughing herself, without knowing why.

'It's his song,' said Higgin, wiping his eyes. 'He sings it in the character of a chimney-sweep. It's all about his work, you see, and that's the refrain – "I'll be up 'er flue next week" – and the meanings people seem to see in it, you'd never think! What we in the profession call the *double entendre*,' he said to Edith, feeling that she should be included in the gaiety, if possible on a higher level of culture than the others. But Ede merely snorted.

'I'd like to get along now, if that's all right?' said Rumball.

'Yes, of course. You wanted to see my press-cutting book. I'll get it at once,' said Higgin, and trotted up the stairs.

'I'll expect to see something in the paper about the show tonight,' said George, in a loud, bantering tone. 'We got some influence, you know. Ede here's got influence on *The Bellman*, ain't that right, Ede?'

'George, that'll do,' said Edith, with dignity.

'"I'll be up 'er flue next week,"' sang George, *sotto voce*, and pinched Kitten from below. She slapped him playfully and they scuffled under the embarrassed eyes of Mr Rumball until Bevill Higgin came downstairs, carrying a large press-cutting book.

'Here it is,' said he. 'A complete record of my career, with photographs, clippings, programmes – all dated and arranged in proper order. You will be very careful with it, won't you? All my life I have been methodical. I cannot bear to part with any of my little clippings from the past. A few may be loose in the book. When you have done with it, if you will give me a call, I'll pick it up at *The Bellman* offices myself. Please, please be careful. This is my life,' he said, patting the volume with a wistful charm which no one but Edith fully appreciated.

'Yes, I'll be careful,' said Rumball, and then, nervously to the others, 'well, good night, everybody.'

'Remember, we got influence!' shouted George, as the door closed behind the reporter.

'Do you really think you'll get a write-up?' asked Edith very seriously when, a little later, they had all been accommodated with glasses of rye from the bottle which Georgie produced from his bundle of costumes. 'It would be wonderful publicity, Bev – bring you all kinds of pupils.'

'I have hopes,' said Mr Higgin demurely. 'My friend Mr Shillito is, so to speak, editor *emeritus* of the newspaper; I have been given to understand that he carries very great influence – very great. He thinks something should be done. Of course, that young man will write his *critique* on what he finds in my cuttings-book. Tonight's work was not my best line, of course.'

'Oh yes it was,' said George, 'that's the stuff the public wants. You got to give the public what it wants. And it wants the heart stuff and the funny stuff. This arty stuff is all baloney.'

'Listen to who's talking,' said Edith.

'Yeah? Well, if you'd heard how I went over tonight you'd change your tune, Ede. Bev says I got talent and I guess tonight I proved it, eh, Bev?'

'Oh, no doubt about it,' said Mr Higgin, and giggled again. 'You ladies should have heard him. Or no – perhaps you shouldn't have heard him. But for a male audience it was a treat, really it was.'

'Well, I kind of half hope you don't get a write-up in the old *Bellman*,' said Kitten. 'Because if you do you'll get so many pupils and be so famous we'll lose you from here, and I'd certainly hate that.'

'Oh, you dear creature,' said Mr Higgin, tittering.

'Yes, and what would Earl do without his Ugga Bev?' said Edith, throwing him a glance heavy with solicitous motherhood.

'Oh, my dears, you must never believe that I would leave you,' said Mr Higgin, and though he looked tenderly toward Kitten, it was Edith's hand that he patted. 'I've come to look upon this as my own family. I have indeed. And you can never know what that means to a weary, wayworn wanderer such as myself.' There was a tear in his eye.

'Well, Bev, I guess we all understand that, and I know I speak for the girls as well as me when I say that we feel the same in regards to you,' said George, whose tipsiness had suddenly taken a formal turn.

'Sure, Bev, we know how tough it is to make your way in a new country and all that,' said Kitten.

'Yes, we have to remember that everybody was new in Canada once,' said Edith, and then, suddenly, the gathering rose from this solemn and somewhat literary note to a higher plane of enjoyment. The rye went round again, and for a third time, and then Mr Higgin sang *Believe Me, If All Those Endearing Young Charms*, and the Morphews and Edith, as befitted his pupils, provided harmonies of uncertain character but of rich intent. By the time they went to bed all their hearts were high and full.

Edith hummed the lovely Irish air as she undressed, and returning from the bathroom she heard its strains from the door of the Morphews' bedroom. She hummed it still as she stood before her mirror, and arranged her hair in metal curlers, which stood out like a *chevaux-de-frise* around her face. It was a caressing air, and its gentle melancholy aroused agreeably painful feelings in her breast. The way Kitten was always at her about men! But she wasn't the sort to throw herself at anybody that came along, or settle for a big loudmouth like George. Love, if she were ever to feel it (for she had long since decided that her feeling for Robert Little had not been the Real Thing) would be something fine, gentle and wistful. She couldn't bear a man to whom she was nothing but a Body as, quite unjustly, she supposed that her sister was to George. Her love, if and when it came, would be a thing of Mind, of Soul.

There was a very gentle tap at her door. Supposing it to be Kitten she opened it, and Mr Higgin slipped quickly into the room. He was in his pyjamas and a dressing-gown, and with his pink face and small stature he looked like a small boy.

'Shh!' said he, with his finger on his lips. 'After such an evening of true friendship I simply couldn't go to sleep without saying good night to my little pupil.'

He tiptoed to the cot in which Earl lay asleep, and looked tenderly down at him. His thoughts seemed to be too fine for utterance, but he smiled and sighed. Edith, who was somewhat alarmed at being caught in her nightdress, felt reassured, but reached for a kimono.

'Don't trouble,' said Higgin, 'I'm just going.' He looked back at the child. 'Your treasure,' said he. 'What would I not give to have the right to call him mine as well. Still, it is no small thing to be his "Ugga Bev". I want you to know, Edith, how much I cherish that.'

Ede felt that this demanded something equally fine from her, but she was not ready with phrases. 'Well, I want you to understand, Bev, how much it means to Earl, and to me too,' she said at last. 'I mean, your influence, and everything.'

Mr Higgin looked at her and his face filled with tender admiration.

'Thank you,' he said, with a more than ordinary simplicity. 'You can never know what that means to me. Oh, Edith, to see you standing there, in simple loveliness! It's a picture; that's the only expression I can use; a picture!'

Edith was suddenly conscious that she was standing in front of the only light in the room and that her nightdress was thin. She hastily moved toward her kimono again, where it lay on the bed.

'No, no, dear child,' said Mr Higgin, very tenderly, but laughing a little in a disembodied manner. 'Don't misunderstand me. And please don't put on your gown. Your loveliness, Edith, has not been revealed to any profane gaze. Just slip into your bed, and let me tuck you up.'

Obediently Edith got into bed, and Mr Higgin drew the covers up to her chin, and smoothed them.

'The little mother tucks up her babe, but who is to tuck up the little mother, eh?' said he, tenderly. And then, absent-mindedly, he sat down on the bed. 'You know,' he continued, 'my life has been a wandering one, and not easy, but I have always cherished the domestic virtues.' He seemed to turn the expression over in his mouth, savouring its fine flavour. 'Yes, the domestic virtues. An artist seeks his inspiration where he finds it, but I have always felt that, for me, the richest soil of inspiration was a family and a home. But that was denied me.'

Mr Higgin was speaking now in a rich, actorly manner, and the sigh with which he followed his words would have carried to the topmost gallery of a good-sized theatre.

'I have known love,' he continued. 'Love as the artist knows it, fleeting, turbulent, sweet. Love of the sort which life has denied to you, sweet child, though you are framed for it as few women are. But that is past. I find myself now at the age when all that is a lovely memory. I don't suppose that you have any notion of my age. I am forty-eight.'

Edith said nothing. She would have taken him for considerably over fifty, and she was ashamed to have misjudged a man whose suffering had plainly been so deep.

'Forty-eight,' said Bevill Higgin. 'Yet the heart is young. The heart, I may say, feels as young as that of that blessed child yonder. It is, truly, a child's heart. "In the heart of age, a child lies weeping." Do you know that lovely poem? Ah, so true, so true of me. In my heart is a child, a child who seeks the mother.'

Edith was awed by the beauty of Mr Higgin's talk. There was a grandeur and a sweep about it for which she had longed all her life, and now that she actually heard it, addressed solely to herself, she was entranced. Softly but quickly Mr Higgin turned out the lamp, and slipped under the covers beside her. He lay at some distance, and she was not strongly aware of his presence, but only of his voice.

'And where is the mother to be found,' asked Mr Higgin, 'but in every loving, understanding heart? Edith, life has not been kind to me. When Fortune frowns on a man, every hand is against him. Misfortune in the Old Country drove me abroad. I could have fought it out there, with small-minded detractors. But there is such a thing as pride. And so I came here, and though I found a haven in this house, my path was not smooth abroad. No, no; not smooth. I found friends' (here his hand stole under the sheet and clasped hers) 'and I must say I found enemies as well. Shall I name those enemies? I fear that if I do so I shall wound a heart which has become very dear to me.'

Here Mr Higgin moved himself nearer to Edith, and in a deft and practised manner slipped one arm under her head, so that she lay partly on his bosom. He smelled strongly of rye, and his manner suddenly became jocular.

'What a trusting little heart it is,' he murmured. 'Working loyally every day to bring comfort to a man who is unworthy of such gifts. What a dear, trusting, silly little heart.' He giggled.

'Who are you talking about?' said Edith. Her voice came tremulously.

'Can't you guess? About your Mr Ridley, of course.'

'What's wrong with him, Bev?'

'He has been very harsh to me, dear one. Very harsh and scornful. So have some others. But I think they regret it now.'

'Who do you mean, Bev?'

'The young man at the University. I wasn't worth his consideration, though I could have helped him. Snotty young pup! And the girl in the Library. I couldn't use the Library without an introduction. Oh no, I wasn't good enough. And your Mr Ridley, snapping his scissors at me. I'm not spiteful. I don't bear a grudge. But I've had my little game with them, just the same.'

'Bev, did you! –'

'Aha, what a sharp little thing it is! And you are the only one that knows! Because I think I'm on the upward path now. I think I've broken the ice. And when I'm established here, they'll all feel the weight of my hand, and not in little jokes either.'

He was giggling a great deal now. Edith was much puzzled. Here she was, in possession of the secret which had so much troubled her idol, Mr Ridley, and yet now that she was able to be of use to him, he was no longer her idol. This pink, sweet-talking little man seemed suddenly to have filled her whole being with warmth and comfort and wonder.

'You'd never tell, would you?' said he teasingly.

'Oh, Bev, no – never, never,' she whispered.

Bevill Higgin leaned forward and kissed her, very softly, but for a long, long time. A delicious warmth suffused her. She seemed to melt, to move toward him without any will of her own. Gently, very gently, his hand stole in the front of her nightdress and caressed her breast. She shuddered with pleasure as he slipped the straps from her shoulders, and, pushing the nightdress downward, stroked first her stomach and then her thighs with a touch as light as a feather. She heaved gently on a warm, smooth sea.

'Mommie.' It was Earl's voice, sleepy but loud. 'Mommie, I wanna go to the bathroom.'

Edith came to herself with a start. She pushed Higgin roughly from her. 'Get away!' she whispered roughly, 'get away from me, you nasty old thing.'

'Edith,' said he, in a very low voice, 'don't be frightened. It's me! It's Bev! Be calm!'

Hampered as she was by her downthrust nightdress she nevertheless managed to scramble quickly over him to the floor. Seizing a hairbrush in one hand, and screening her naked breasts with the other, she struck at him, and as he guarded his head from the blows she beat furiously at his hands.

'Get out of here,' she whispered. Earl, concerned only with his own mounting need, wailed from the cot. 'Get out,' she whispered, over and over, until Higgin, scrambling from the bed, rushed from the room. She threw his slippers after him.

Later, she sat up in her bed, marvelling at herself. She had as near as a toucher been seduced! She had always thought of seduction as something that happened in fine hotels, or in the backs of very expensive cars. And right here, in her house and the Morphews', in this little room, with her hair in curlers, and little Earlie asleep not three feet away! It was staggering. It was shattering.

Yet she could not weep. The experience had been immeasurably stimulating. She felt no shame, only triumphant virtue. She wasn't anybody that could be had by any slick old fellow with a line of smooth talk! It had been a narrow escape, but the more she thought about it, the more she knew that she would never have let him go the limit.

And she had the secret! How Ridley would thank her! How he'd be grateful to her! For he wasn't one of the kind that always looked at a woman with one thing in mind. He was above all that. She'd be there extra early in the morning. She'd wake him up with her news.

Her ideal was triumphantly restored to his throne.

[SIX]

At half-past two on Tuesday, November 7th, Gloster Ridley was arranging his office for the meeting with the lawyers. Miss Green had done all the necessary work well beforehand, but still he fussed nervously with the chairs, rearranged heaps of paper on his side-table, laid pencils conveniently on his blotter, tinkered with anything and with everything. How different was the demeanour of Mr A. J. Marryat, who stood calmly by the window, smiling out at the beauty of the late autumn. But the difference between the two men was superficial; though the one fussed and the other was at ease, both had an air of confidence.

Mr Marryat turned to Ridley. 'Gordon Balmer has just come in the front door,' said he. 'Now, remember, the important thing is never to lose face. They'll talk a lot about court, but *this* is the trial. We've got to maintain face.'

Ridley smiled, and concealing his nervousness for the first time, he stood behind his desk in an attitude which was almost debonair. It was not long until Miss Green opened the door to admit *The Bellman*'s lawyer.

'I'm a little late,' said Mr Balmer. 'I wanted to get over earlier in order to do some arranging; there's a lot in the way these situations are handled.' He made his way directly behind Ridley's desk, and put his briefcase upon it. 'I'll sit here, if you don't mind,' said he. 'I have a good many papers and I'll need somewhere to put them.'

'I've thought of that already,' said Ridley, 'and I've arranged a place for you here.' He indicated a chair on the other side of the desk. 'You see, I've cleared a place for all your papers.'

'Of course I had no intention of taking your chair,' said Mr Balmer, though that was what he had just been prevented from doing. 'But as I suppose I shall be in charge of the meeting I more or less unconsciously made for this place. You see,' he said, lowering his voice confidentially, 'there's a certain psychological advantage about dominating the room, on these occasions. And the man who sits behind the desk always dominates the men whose legs can be seen. It's a funny thing; not one in a thousand thinks of it.'

'Extraordinary!' said Ridley, but he did not budge from his position, which made it impossible for Mr Balmer to get the dominating chair without forcibly pushing him aside. 'As a matter of fact, I've tried to give you a psychological advantage of another sort; I've put you with your back to the window, and Mr Snelgrove will sit facing full into the light. I think that's rather good, don't you?'

Mr Balmer muttered something which might have been assent. Certainly he did not seem to think that any advantage of lighting could make up for the loss of the dominating chair, the chair which, by his attitude, he had put in the position of the Bench. With an ill grace he moved to the less desirable chair indicated by Ridley, and began to take some things out of his brief-case.

Ridley looked toward Mr Marryat, who was behind Balmer. Though his expression did not change, his eyes signalled 'Face?', and equally without expression Mr Marryat signalled back 'Face, indeed!'

Again there came a tap at the door, and Miss Green ushered in Mr Snelgrove and Professor Vambrace.

'Good afternoon, gentlemen,' said Ridley. 'I had expected three in your party. I hope that X has not disappointed you?'

'You may be sure that X will appear at the proper time,' said Mr Snelgrove. 'As we are to have this meeting under circumstances which I must say I consider to be very irregular, I must ask for certain necessary accommodations. I have many papers, and I shall want a desk. I presume that there will be no objection if I sit here?' And he also made for Ridley's chair, but the editor stood his ground.

'I am sure that you will find everything you want here, opposite Mr Balmer,' said he. 'Blotting paper, pens, ink, pencils – we have tried to anticipate your wants, but if anything is lacking my secretary will get it for you at once.'

'I would greatly have preferred to hold this encounter in my own chambers,' said Mr Snelgrove, in a voice which temper was already causing to tremble. 'I consider it most unusual and undesirable to meet a colleague who may become an opponent in his client's office.' And he glared at Gordon Balmer in a manner which was intended to make Ridley, as a non-legal person, feel superfluous and intrusive.

'I am not on my home ground, either, Mr Snelgrove,' said Balmer, and went on ostentatiously arranging some papers. It was to be a source of astonishment to Ridley and Marryat, during the ensuing hour, that both the lawyers had brief-cases containing a great many papers which could not possibly have had any bearing on the matter in hand, but which peeped importantly from their satchels as though they might, at any moment, leap forth to prove or disprove something of the utmost importance.

Professor Vambrace said nothing, but took a chair somewhat to the rear of Mr Snelgrove. He had, for the occasion, put on a suit of dark, heavy tweed, and a black tie, and looked more than ever like a tragedian of the old school.

Once again the door opened, and Miss Green showed in Dean Jevon Knapp.

'Sorry to be late, if indeed I am late,' said he, smiling urbanely at everyone. He fixed upon Mr Marryat, as the most amiable-looking person present, and shook him by the hand with great cordiality, to his astonishment.

'I find it difficult to ask the question,' said Ridley, 'but I cannot hold it back. Are we to understand that Dean Knapp is X, Mr Snelgrove?'

'I am not in a mood for facetious questions, sir,' said the lawyer.

'I assure you that I have no wish to seem facetious. But you have promised to produce X, and the only unknown quantity here is the Dean. I think my question a very natural one.'

'Quite natural,' said Mr Balmer, who felt that, as a lawyer, he ought to say something as soon as possible, and who was himself puzzled.

'I asked Mr Dean to join me here,' said Mr Snelgrove, 'in order that he may be a witness to what I intend to disclose. I have a particular reason for doing so and it is of direct concern to him. I repeat, X will be forthcoming in due season.'

'Very well,' said Mr Balmer. 'Now, I think we have wasted quite enough time, and if you have no objection, I should like to clarify one or two points which are still in doubt.'

As he spoke, Ridley sat down behind his desk, and Mr Marryat, moving a chair from a corner, sat down almost beside him. It was a well-timed move, for both the representatives of *The Bellman* were behind the desk, with their legs concealed; they were on the Bench and the two lawyers were, so to speak, in court. The Dean seated himself in an armchair at some distance, and immediately detracted from the dignity of the proceedings by producing a small and evil-smelling pipe, which he lit with a great deal of noise and sucking. He was the only person present who seemed to have no sense of the importance of face.

'May I ask at once,' said Mr Balmer, 'whether you intend to proceed against *The Bellman* for libel?'

'I shall advise my client on that point when this meeting is over,' said Mr Snelgrove. 'I need not explain to you that the law of libel exists as a safeguard of private reputation. I do not think that there is any doubt whatever that the publication of this false notice of engagement places Miss Pearl Vambrace in an exceedingly uncomfortable position, and will tend to make her avoided and shunned by young men of her acquaintance. A young woman's good name is her most precious possession; not in a legal, but in a moral sense, it is a major portion of her dower. This affair will unquestionably expose her to a certain amount of ridicule, perhaps to a great deal of ridicule and distress of mind. The refusal of *The Bellman* to do anything whatever to mitigate the wrong it has done her can only increase the unpleasantness of the situation in which she has been put. If this is not a civil libel, I should very much like to know what you would call it?'

'I should hesitate to call it libel,' said Mr Balmer, very blandly. 'After all, it is an everyday occurrence for a young woman to be reported engaged to a young man. Many young women take it as a compliment to be so reported, and laugh it off if the report has no truth.'

'A formal notice of engagement, printed in a newspaper, is something very different from social gossip,' said Mr Snelgrove, raising his eyebrows very high, and tapping his front teeth with his eyeglasses. 'It is a deliberate and premeditated untruth, designed to wound and surround the victim with an atmosphere of ridicule.'

'The common description of libel is that which exposes the victim not only to ridicule, but also to hatred and contempt,' said Mr Balmer. 'You will not pretend that anything remotely resembling hatred or contempt could spring from this prank?'

Professor Vambrace, whose face had grown dark during the foregoing, now spoke in his deepest tones. 'I consider that hatred and contempt have been engendered against me,' he said. 'Rumours of the most foul and obscene order are being spread against me. They have been thrown in my face by complete strangers. I can call witnesses to prove it.'

'Will you be good enough to leave this to me?' said Mr Snelgrove to his client. 'I shall bring up these matters at the proper time.'

'Frankly, I am happy that Professor Vambrace has spoken,' said Mr Balmer. 'I should like to know who has been libelled, the Professor, or Miss Vambrace? The lady is not here; that suggests to me that she does not choose to associate herself with this dispute.'

'My daughter is not here because I would not bring her into a discussion of this kind,' said the Professor. 'I do not consider this a proper place for a young girl.'

'Ah, I had not understood that Miss Vambrace was a minor,' said Mr Balmer. 'That, of course, puts quite a different complexion on the case.'

'She is not a minor,' said the Professor. 'She is a lady, and entitled to be guarded against disagreeable experiences and associations.' He scowled deeply at Marryat and Ridley, who looked as though they did not understand what he meant.

'Not a minor?' said Balmer, with a show of surprise. 'In that case then, Professor, may I ask a pointed question: if she is not a minor, is she still subject to corporal punishment in her home?'

'Do you see?' roared Vambrace at Snelgrove, starting up from his chair. 'These damnable rumours pursue me everywhere! How dare you ask me such a question?' he shouted at Balmer.

'Only because it is a question I should be obliged to ask you in court if this matter were to come to trial,' said the lawyer, blandly. 'Very disagreeable questions may be asked in court, and they cannot be avoided there as easily as here.'

'Sit down, sir, at once,' said Mr Snelgrove. 'Sit down and be silent, or, I warn you, I shall throw up your case here and now. I only took up this matter to help you; I shall not put up with any interference.'

'If Miss Vambrace is the injured party, I really think she should be here, however repugnant the proceedings might be to her,' said Balmer. 'If it is Professor Vambrace who fancies himself injured, we must change our ground. I don't quite see the damage to him in this affair.'

'In libel it is not necessary to prove damage,' said Mr Snelgrove, playing the wily lawyer to the hilt. 'Damage is presumed, as you well know.'

'Damage would be presumed when the jury had decided whether the engagement notice was capable of a defamatory meaning,' said Balmer. 'You can't tell what a jury might make of a thing like this. They might think it was a huge joke. One outburst from your client in court and they would be very likely to do so.'

'Don't tell me what a jury is likely to do, sir,' said Mr Snelgrove. 'I know just as much about juries as you do. The standard in such matters is what the Reasonable Man might think.'

'Are you putting forward your client as the Reasonable Man?' asked Mr Balmer. The Professor growled, but was hushed by Mr Snelgrove. Mr Balmer pressed his advantage.

'My own opinion is that the Reasonable Man would say that my clients have been ill-used, and are, in fact, innocent victims of a hoax. No jury of business men would find against them for an honest mistake. Everybody makes mistakes and nearly everybody at some time is victim of a hoax. They are, I assure you, just as anxious to find the real perpetrator of this hoax as you are.'

'I think the jury's sympathy for your clients would be a good deal cooled when it was explained how negligent they had been,' said Mr Snelgrove. 'They claim to have a system of records which tells them who inserts all such advertisements as this. Why have those records not been brought forward? I think the answer must be because they cannot produce any such record. The matter of a completely impossible date in the advertising copy would take a good deal of explaining to the Reasonable Man.'

'A small matter,' said Mr Balmer.

'Perhaps, but taken in conjunction with the fact that they have no record of who inserted the advertisement it is not a small matter. If they have any records, and are not, in fact, irresponsible, why do they not themselves know who X is?'

'That is something which we shall make known at the proper time – in court, if need be,' said Mr Balmer. 'But I have another question I wish to ask your client.'

'I forbid you to answer, Professor Vambrace,' said Mr Snelgrove.

'Oh, very well,' said Balmer. 'If you have it all cooked up between you, so that he speaks only when you give him leave, I don't mind. But it suggests even more strongly what I have suspected for some time, that Professor Vambrace is in this thing simply in the hope of getting a big money settlement. You and he are in this together; it's a shakedown.'

'My honour has never been called in question,' shouted the Professor, starting up. 'That is a lie, a damned, malicious lie, and I demand that you apologize immediately.'

'I'll apologize,' said Balmer, 'if you will give me your word of honour that anything you get out of your libel suit – after you have paid your lawyers their very considerable fees will be given to a charity.'

'Say nothing!' commanded Mr Snelgrove. 'Don't imagine that I don't see what you are up to! You are trying dirty, underhanded tricks to make my client discredit himself or frighten him off suit. Your conduct, sir, is a disgrace to the Bar, and don't suppose that I won't bring it up at the next meeting of the Bar Association!'

The atmosphere of the room had become very hot. The Dean's pipe had gone out, and he tittered occasionally, from nervous tension. Marryat and Ridley were, to tell the truth, a little ashamed of their lawyer, whom they had never seen in action in quite this spirit before.

'Please yourself about that,' said Balmer. 'I'm tired of this discussion, which is not leading us anywhere. You say that there is libel, and that my clients were negligent. All right. Prove it. Let's have X. Where have you got him hidden?'

With great dignity Mr Snelgrove rose and walked to the window. Having trained his eyeglasses upon something in the street below, he took out his pocket-handkerchief, and solemnly waved it three times. He then returned to his chair, and glared at Mr Balmer in silence, which was broken only by a furious nasal whistling from Professor Vambrace.

Some time passed, uncomfortably for the six men in Ridley's office, until Miss Green's knock was heard, and she opened the door to admit Humphrey Cobbler, followed by Ronnie Fitzalan. No one seemed to have anything to say, and no word was spoken until Mr Snelgrove had waved Cobbler into a chair which Ronnie, rather apologetically, placed very much in the centre of the room.

'Well, Mr Cobbler,' said Mr Snelgrove, now the stage lawyer to the life, 'I daresay you are wondering why you have been asked to come here?'

Cobbler produced a very large wad of torn sheeting from his jacket pocket and blew his nose resoundingly. 'I'm sure it's something pleasant,' said he, 'and I love the suspense. Whenever lawyers want me for anything, I always assume that it is because somebody has left me a fortune. Just let me have the details slowly, saving up the actual glorious figures for the last.' He spoke in a thickened voice, and his face was pale. Closing his eyes, he relaxed as much as he could in the straight, armless chair which he had been given.

'I'd advise you not to take that tone,' said Mr Snelgrove. 'This may be an extremely serious affair for you.'

'You needn't worry about what tone I take; I have perfect pitch,' said Cobbler. 'As for seriousness, I have risen virtually from my death-bed to be here, chiefly because Mr Fitzalan is a very persuasive fellow. My one thought now is to get back to bed.'

'My dear fellow,' said the Dean, solicitously. 'Are you worse since Sunday?'

Cobbler made no reply, but blew his nose as though painfully expelling his soul from his nostrils.

'Gentlemen,' said Mr Snelgrove. 'Behold X.'

The moment fell short of great drama. Ridley and Marryat seemed unmoved, and Balmer glanced momentarily at Cobbler, only to return to a paper which he held in his hand. The Dean, who did not know what X meant, except that it was something vaguely discreditable, merely looked confused. Only Professor Vambrace scowled upon Cobbler, and as the organist had his eyes shut, this was not particularly effective.

'I shall be brief,' continued Mr Snelgrove. 'Cobbler, I put it to you that on October 31st, on Tuesday last to be precise, you and a gang of hoodlums invaded the premises of St Nicholas' Cathedral, taking liquor with you. There you created a disturbance, the details of which I shall not specify; it was, however, sufficient to arouse the attention of some of the Cathedral neighbours, and even of the Dean, who arrived after some lapse of time and drove you forth. Is this true?'

'Guilty, m'lord,' said Cobbler, without opening his eyes.

'It was on the following night,' said Mr Snelgrove, 'that you sought out Professor Vambrace in a public place, and there sang a ribald song, directed at him personally, while indulging in drunken and derisive antics. What do you say?'

'Guilty as hell,' said Cobbler, indifferently.

'Oh come,' said Ridley, 'Mr Cobbler was not drunk on that occasion. I was with him shortly beforehand, and I know.'

'Oh, you do, do you?' said Mr Snelgrove, rounding on him. 'I was not aware that there was an association between you two. Where were you and what part did you play in this disgraceful and libellous action toward my client, may I ask?'

'You may not ask,' said Mr Balmer. 'Please do not interfere, Mr Ridley. You interrupt my friend's train of reason.'

'If you do not answer me now, I do not greatly care,' said Mr Snelgrove. 'There will come a time, and a place, where I shall question you under circumstances where you will be compelled to answer, and then we shall uncover whatever link there is between you and this shameless rowdy. You're thick enough, I dare say.'

'I object to the suggestion that I am *thick* with anyone,' said Cobbler, as though half asleep. 'It's an expression I particularly dislike.'

'Go on, sir, go on!' said Mr Snelgrove, who had worked himself up into a fine forensic fit. 'Be as impertinent as you please! Now, I put it to you that before you insulted Professor Vambrace in the park, and on the same day that you so grossly abused your position as cathedral organist, you caused this to be inserted in the paper edited by your friend, here.' And with a flourish Mr Snelgrove produced from among his papers a very large sheet in the exact middle of which the tiny clipping of the engagement notice had been pasted, and upon which a secretary had made a notation in a very small hand, in red ink.

Cobbler opened his eyes, and took the paper. 'Aha,' said he, showing little interest, 'so that's what it looked like. I missed it when it came out.' And, handing it back to the lawyer, he closed his eyes again.

'Well, sir,' said Mr Snelgrove. 'What have you to say for yourself?'

'Nothing,' said Cobbler.

'You will now understand, Mr Dean,' said Mr Snelgrove, 'why I asked you to come here. You have, for several years, obstinately defended this man against those of us who understood his nature and his pernicious influence in the Cathedral. You hear him now confess that he has nothing whatever to say in extenuation of this exceedingly mischievous and, I fully believe, libellous action. It has caused great inconvenience to you, to Professor Vambrace and his daughter and, I fully expect, to Mrs Bridgetower and her son, though I am not empowered to speak for them. I hope, sir. that your eyes are open at last. I must say, also, that I hope that in future you will look upon your Cathedral Chancellor as something more than a man of straw. I am sorry to have involved you in a disagreeable scene, but there seemed to be no other equally powerful way of carrying conviction to you. Now, Mr Ridley, will you be good enough to inform me if *The Bellman* intends to take action against this man?'

'No,' said Ridley.

'Then I shall advise my client to take action for libel against *The Bellman* and against Cobbler, and because of his conduct toward my client in the park, I shall prove that libel in the full meaning of the term was intended. Further, I shall bring forward your refusal to prosecute, after what you said earlier, as an indication that you knew of his guilt and tried to shield him.'

'But I don't know of his guilt,' said Ridley. 'Indeed, I know that he is not guilty. I have proof of it here.' And, reaching into a drawer of his desk he drew out a pink receipt for a classified advertisement.

'But he has admitted guilt,' said Mr Snelgrove.

'No I didn't,' said Cobbler. 'I simply didn't deny it. Never deny; never explain. That's my guiding rule of life.'

'Oh, come, that will never do,' said Mr Snelgrove, with elaborate contempt. 'You permitted me to put the question to you, backed by extremely strong circumstantial evidence, and you did not utter a word of denial. That will require a great deal of explanation.'

'Not really,' said Cobbler, still with his eyes closed. 'I was curious to hear what you would say. And a pretty poor show you made of it, I must say, for a lawyer. Circumstantial evidence! Guess-work and spite; nothing more.'

Mr Snelgrove was very angry now. His face was extremely red, and as he had not blushed for many years the unaccustomed feeling bereft him momentarily of the power to speak. The Dean seized his opportunity.

'Mr Cobbler,' said he, 'will you give me your word of honour that you had nothing to do with this engagement notice?'

The accused man sat up smartly in his chair and turned toward his questioner. 'Honour bright, Mr Dean,' said he. 'It's a simple matter of psychology; I do a lot of damn silly things on the spur of the moment, but I'm not a calculating practical joker. Unless you call letting Mr Snelgrove make a jackass of himself a calculated practical joke. Anyhow, Bridgetower's a friend of mine. And I'm sorry I made Professor Vambrace feel cheap; I didn't mean it very seriously. But he looked so funny hiding behind trees, playing I-spy. And I've paid dearly for that; look at the cold I caught, dancing and getting heated. I'll gladly admit that I'm a fool, if it will make anybody happy, but I really don't think I'm malicious or underhand.'

The Dean smiled and nodded several times, and applied himself again to his smelly little pipe. As for Mr Snelgrove, it appeared that he might have a stroke. His face was contorted, and he made gasping noises so alarming that Ronnie Fitzalan hastened to pour a glass of water from Ridley's thermos jug, which he offered to his senior partner.

Ridley's eyes moved to meet those of Mr Marryat. Face? they

seemed to ask, and the reply beamed back, Indubitably Face. The editor spoke.

'I feel sure that everyone present would be glad to meet the real X,' said he. 'And as I think he is in the building at this moment, it can easily be managed.' He pressed a bell. 'Miss Green, will you ask Mr Shillito to bring his visitor in here?'

There was another short wait. Cobbler, who seemed much recovered, sang very softly, under his breath,

The charge is prepared,
The lawyers are met,
The judges all ranged –
A terrible show!

– but he caught the cold eye of Mr Balmer upon him, and desisted. Mr Snelgrove appeared to recapture something of his self-possession, and was giving a powerful impersonation of a man who had something very telling up his sleeve. Professor Vambrace was sunk even deeper than before in his melancholy; his face was as grey and forbidding as a rock. Ridley, though he wore a bland and hopeful look upon his face, was kicking one leg furiously under his desk. Would his scheme come off? It was 3.30, and everything should be in readiness, but so often people were unpunctual and – But before his nerves got the better of him Miss Green opened the door again, and this time it was Mr Swithin Shillito who entered, ushering before him Mr Bevill Higgin.

Mr Shillito was about to embark on an elaborate round of greetings, but something in the atmosphere of the room stopped him just as he made a move toward the Dean. Mr Balmer spoke.

'I don't intend to make a stage-play of this,' said he, with a look at Mr Snelgrove, 'and I shall content myself with asking a very few questions. Your name is Bevill Higgin, is it not?'

'That's right,' said Mr Higgin, smirking nervously. The sight of the assembly had put him palpably upon his guard, and his voice shook a little.

'Mr Higgin, did you, or did you not, on the thirty-first of October, at some time in the morning, insert and pay for an engagement notice in this newspaper? This notice, to be precise?' and Mr Balmer produced a sheet of paper, very much like Mr Snelgrove's, on which the tiny piece of newsprint was pasted, with a notation in blue.

Bevill Higgin did not reply at once, and the nervous smirk did not leave his face. But his eyes flickered quickly from Balmer to Ridley, and from him to Snelgrove. 'What makes you think I did?' said he.

'Because the receipt for payment was found in that scrapbook, which is your property, and which you are now carrying under your arm,' said Mr Balmer.

'And how do you connect that with me?' said Higgin. 'Is my name on it?'

'The whole text of the notice is written on it in what is demonstrably your handwriting.'

'I deny any knowledge of it. I write like a great many other people. I should like to know why I have been asked here to be questioned in this way?'

'Because you did it.'

'Prove that. I suppose you're a lawyer. You know that what you're saying is libellous. You haven't one scrap of real evidence to connect me with what you're talking about. If it's the text of an advertisement somebody must have signed it. What is the name on the receipt?'

'You signed it with a false name.'

'Oh yes! Very likely! Anything to get a scapegoat! You don't catch me like that! I bet you haven't got any receipt.'

Ridley lifted the pink slip from his blotter, where it had been concealed and waved it gently in the air. 'We have it, and we have you, Mr Higgin,' said he. 'Also, I have a witness – I need hardly tell you her name – who will testify, if necessary, that you confessed to her that this advertisement was your doing. There's no point in keeping up a pretence. We've got you. Mr Snelgrove, Professor Vambrace, allow me to present X.'

This, too, should have been a satisfactorily dramatic moment, but it failed. For, as every eye turned upon him, Bevill Higgin's face changed from its usual bright pink to a deep red, crinkled into a mask of misery, and with embarrassing noise and openness, the little man cried. Cried so that tears ran down his cheeks and dropped upon his threadbare blue serge jacket. Cried so that Mr Marryat and Ronnie Fitzalan looked away from him in deep embarrassment. Cried for what seemed an age, but what was perhaps ninety seconds. Cried until a clear ball of mucus formed at the end of his nose, then swung by a thin string in mid-air. He did not raise his hands to his face, nor did he close his eyes. He wept with the abandon of a guilty child, but his whole figure spoke of failure, of genteel poverty, of hopeless middle age. The sound worked horribly upon Ridley's nerves, and just as he was about to shout at the man, to shout that all would be forgiven him if only he would stop that dreadful weeping, Mr Swithin Shillito drew a very large, very clean white handkerchief from his breast pocket, and handed it to Higgin, deftly fielding the pendulous nose-drop as he did so. At the same moment Fitzalan, taking the water glass from Mr Snelgrove, who still nursed it, offered it to the stricken man. By less than two minutes of weeping Higgin had washed all the starch out of his judges.

Mr Snelgrove was the first to act; his quick legal mind saw in this a chance to recover the prestige which he had lost in the matter of Cobbler. He pounced.

'You admit your guilt?'

Higgin, mopping his eyes, nodded, but said nothing.

'Well, then we have X at last,' said Mr Snelgrove, looking round the room with the air of a man who has at last triumphed over the stupidity and obscurantism of others. He continued, with heavy irony: 'Now, Mr Higgin, perhaps you will have no objection to explaining your motive for inserting that advertisement?'

Higgin mumbled something, in a voice still thick with tears.

'Hey?' said Mr Snelgrove, cupping his hand to his ear. 'I can't hear you. Speak up. Let us all hear what you have to say.'

Again Higgin spoke, somewhat more loudly, but again Mr Snelgrove shook his head.

'He says it was only a joke, sir,' said Ronnie Fitzalan.

'A joke!' said Mr Snelgrove in what was almost a whisper of horror. 'Have you any conception, man, of the mischief you have made? Of the trouble you have brought into the life of my client, Professor Vambrace? Have you any notion of this?'

'Never meant any harm to Professor Vambrace,' said Higgin, his voice tripping over a sob as he spoke. 'Haven't the pleasure of his acquaintance.'

'God bless my soul!' said the Professor. It was a strange comment from a professed agnostic, and it rose to his lips unbidden.

'And if your joke, as you choose to call it, was not directed at my client, just what did you expect to gain by it?' asked Mr Snelgrove.

'Permit me to point out that I also represent injured parties in this matter,' said Mr Balmer. 'On behalf of *The Bellman*, Mr Higgin, I put this question to you: Did you realize when you inserted that advertisement, that you were involving this newspaper in a fraud, and a possible action for libel? Did you think of that?'

Higgin shook his head.

'Do you realize that at this moment you stand on the brink of suit both by my client and this newspaper?' asked Mr Snelgrove. 'Well, man? Say something! And don't attempt to impose upon us by any more tears. They will have no effect upon me. None whatever. I can assure you of that.'

Higgin raised his head, and spoke with more self-possession than before. 'It was only my little joke,' said he. 'I never thought it would cause any real trouble. I just wanted to play a little joke on Professor Bridgetower. No real harm meant.'

'And what moved you to involve my daughter in your joke?' said Professor Vambrace, menacingly.

Higgin giggled weakly, and blushed. 'I really do assure you, sir, I meant no harm,' said he.

'Do you know my daughter?'

'I only had the pleasure of meeting Miss Vambrace once. In the Waverley Library. A charming young lady.'

'You meant this to be a joke on Mr Bridgetower and Miss Vambrace?' said Balmer.

'Yes, sir.'

'No one else involved? No reference to Professor Vambrace at all?'

'Oh, none, I assure you.'

'I think you also meant it to be a joke on me,' said Gloster Ridley. 'And I think I know why. It was because I refused to publish and pay you for articles about yourself, which you wanted to write for this newspapeı. Wasn't that it?'

'Oh, no, Mr Ridley.'

'Oh, *yes*, Mr Higgin. I recall your visit here very clearly. You got Mr Shillito to introduce you. This advertisement was to make trouble for me because I ignored you. Isn't that right?'

'Oh, no, Mr Ridley.'

'Oh *yes*, Mr Higgin. You did it to spite me, didn't you?'

Higgin was silent, but a nervous grin flitted across his face, and disappeared.

'If it was spite against me, was it spite against Mr Bridgetower and Miss Vambrace? Was it spite against Professor Vambrace?'

'No indeed. I have never met Professor Vambrace until now.'

'Then it was spite against my daughter,' said the Professor. 'And what reason had you to play this vile trick upon her, you scoundrel?'

Again Higgin was silent, but again he smiled, the imploring, sick smile of one who strives to avert another stroke of the lash.

'Had she ignored you at some time?' said Ridley. 'Had Mr Bridgetower ignored you?'

Still Higgin said nothing, but looked from face to face, still with his imploring smile, a figure of cringing abjection.

'Are we to understand that this whole matter was prompted by malice?' asked the editor.

There was a longer pause, and at last the sickly smile faded from Higgin's face, and he nodded.

No one spoke for a time, and it was Mr Marryat who first broke the silence. 'Well, what are we going to do about that?' said he.

'Malice is a very ugly charge,' said Mr Snelgrove. 'A rare charge in law, but a horrible one. The law brings us face to face with some detestable things – things from which the minds of decent men withdraw in loathing – but few more detestable than the charge of malice.'

'But is it a possible charge at all?' The question came, to the surprise of everyone, from Dean Jevon Knapp, who had been forgotten in his corner.

'Rather an obscure offence,' said Mr Balmer. 'You recall what I told you about malice, Mr Ridley. I've never met with it, as an isolated charge, before.'

'And may that not be because it is an offence more in my realm than in yours?' said the Dean. 'I don't find malice so horrible as you, Mr Snelgrove; perhaps because I see more of it; or perhaps I should say because I recognize it more readily than you do. But it is horrible enough, certainly. In the Prayer Book you will find a special plea to be preserved from it, appointed for the first Sunday after Easter: "Grant us so to put away the leaven of malice and wickedness that we may always serve Thee in pureness of living and truth". The writer of that prayer understood malice. It works like a leaven; it stirs, and swells, and changes all that surrounds it. If you seek to pin it down in law, it may well elude you. Who can separate the leaven from the lump when once it has been mixed? But if you learn to know it by its smell, you find it very easily. You find it, for instance, in unfounded charges brought against people that we dislike. It may cause the greatest misery and distress in many unexpected quarters. I have even known it to have quite unforeseen good results. But those things which it invades will never be quite the same again. I assure you that you will always have the greatest difficulty in isolating the leaven, once it has set to work. I do not wish to preach out of my pulpit, but I doubt if any of us here can truthfully say that he has not been touched by the leaven of malice, either in the remoter past, or during the past week.'

What might have been said in reply to the Dean must always remain a matter of conjecture, for as he finished speaking, there was another tap at the door, and this time Miss Green admitted Solly and Pearl. Professor Vambrace started to his feet at once.

'Pearl,' said he, pointing at Higgin, 'do you know this man?'

Pearl was taken aback, but after a moment she spoke. 'No, Father,' said she, 'I have never seen him before.'

'And what have you to say to that?' demanded the Professor of Higgin.

'Some mistake,' said he. 'I thought Miss Vambrace was a short, stout lady with reddish hair.'

'My God,' said Solly, 'he's got you mixed up with Tessie Forgie!' And to the astonishment of the others, he and Pearl began to laugh.

'Though I would ordinarily be pleased to see you,' said Ridley, 'I must ask if you can wait for a few minutes. As you see, I have rather an important conference here at the moment, and if you have not come to join it, I hope that you will not be offended if I ask you to retire.'

'We have come to join the conference,' said Solly. 'We know what it's all about, of course. We've come to ask you not to do anything about a law case, or a retraction of that engagement notice, for at least a week. We want time to discuss several important matters.'

'And what, precisely, do you mean by that?' said the Professor.

'Surely it's plain enough,' said Mr Marryat. 'They mean that they may become engaged after all. I can tell by looking at them.'

Pearl went to her father. 'Please don't say anything now,' she said; 'let us talk to you tonight.'

It was a critical moment. The Professor looked black, but for the first time in a week his daughter was talking to him with earnest affection. Her hands were on the lapels of his coat. Suddenly, moved by some deep wisdom, she stood on tiptoe and kissed him on the mouth, a thing she had not done in several years.

The Professor's face did not seem to relax greatly, but a look of nobility and almost of peace came over it. His eye was bright, and he said, 'Of course I shall do nothing further until my daughter and I have talked the matter over thoroughly.'

'Well, that blows the whole case sky-high,' said Mr Balmer, rising and putting papers back into his brief-case.

'How so?' asked Mr Snelgrove, whose emotional apprehensions had never been keen, and who was still chewing over the Dean's lecture on malice, and wondering if any of it could possibly have been directed at him.

'Because if these two young people are engaged, or become engaged, there is no libel in that advertisement. Justification is a perfect defence. Not that I think that there would be much sense in suing this man,' said Mr Balmer, looking at Higgin.

'I have exactly nine dollars and twenty-five cents in the world,' said Bevill Higgin, and for the first time that afternoon he had a touch of dignity.

'Let me warn you, my friend, that poverty is a poor protection, if you choose to make a hobby of public mischief. You've had a very narrow escape, and you'll never be so lucky again.' With these minatory words, Mr Balmer nodded to Ridley and Marryat, and left the room.

'May I go now?' asked Higgin.

Ridley nodded. The little man, some of his usual jauntiness restored, looked about him, as though to take his leave. No one would meet his eye. At last he turned to Swithin Shillito, and put out his hand. 'Shall I give you a call in a few days?' said he.

'No, Mr Higgin,' said the old gentleman; 'in future neither I nor Mrs Shillito will be at home to you.'

Bevill Higgin drew on his thin, mended cloth gloves, and went.

Professor Vambrace and Mr Snelgrove walked down the stairs a few steps behind the Dean.

'May I offer you a lift, Professor?' said the lawyer. 'Fitzalan will be happy to drop you anywhere you want to go.'

'I prefer to walk, thank you.'

'An extraordinary business, that. I could have sworn Cobbler was the guilty party. It was on the tip of my tongue to accuse him directly. But of course, one learns to be cautious in our profession; I merely put it to him as a possibility. As for that other fellow – Beneath contempt. However, I am deeply indignant, Professor, on your behalf. Deeply indignant.'

They were on the pavement by this time. The Professor faced Mr Snelgrove, very much the cousin of Mourne and Derry.

'Your indignation, sir, is a purchasable commodity; it will be healed by tomorrow. Mine, I assure you, is made of more lasting stuff. Be good enough to send me your statement at your earliest convenience.'

The Professor walked away, leaving Mr Snelgrove gaping. But though the Professor had spoken of indignation, his head was high, and there was even a proud smile on his face. His daughter had been restored to him. He would talk to Pearl that evening. Yes – perhaps he would even talk to young Bridgetower. He had never really had anything personal against the boy.

As he overtook and passed the Dean, he raised his hat with a sweeping gesture. 'An uncommonly fine day, Mr Dean,' said he; 'we are having a wonderful autumn.'

Outside the offices of *The Bellman* Solly and Pearl were tucking themselves into the little English car when Cobbler hurried up to them.

'Let me come with you,' said he.

'We're going for a drive in the country. We'll be glad to drop you at your house.'

'No, no; I don't want to be dropped. I'll go with you on your drive.'

'But we have several things to talk about.'

'I know you have. I'll help you.'

'They're private.'

'Not from me, surely? Not from your old friend? I'll be a great help. Let me come along.'

'You won't be a great help at all. Anyhow, you've got a cold. You want to go right back to bed.'

'Not a bit of it. I found that meeting most refreshing. You missed the cream of it, when old Snelgrove tried to put the finger on me; he thought I put that piece in the paper. The desire to think ill of me completely submerged his judgement. I led him on, I'm afraid. Very wrong of me, but utterly irresistible. I'll have no trouble with him, for a while.'

'Cobbler, Miss Vambrace and I want to be alone. Can you understand that?'

'Worst thing in the world for you. You'll brood, and upset each other. I'll just hop in the back seat.'

He did so.

'I'm taking you straight home,' said Solly, pulling away from the curb.

'If you do, I'll lean right out of the window and shout "Solly Bridgetower loves Pearl Vambrace" over and over again, and the whole place will know. I warn you.'

'By God, I believe you would.'

'Of course I would. I want to go for a drive. My cold has reached that stage where it absolutely demands a drive. Let's go out across the bridge.'

Solly turned a corner. They were passing the Deanery, and at that instant Miss Puss Pottinger was hastening up the steps. Thrusting all of the upper half of his body out of the window, Cobbler waved to her.

'Yoo-hoo, Miss Pottinger, looking for news? I'm free! Free! Not a stain on my character! Bye-bye!' He pulled himself back into the car. 'I'd like to be a fly on the wall when the Dean talks to her,' said he. 'The old boy is very hot on malice this afternoon; she won't enjoy her sandwich and bit of seed-cake, I'll bet.'

Until they were out of the city, Cobbler sat quietly in his place, and no one spoke. But as soon as they had crossed the river he hitched himself forward on the back seat, and thrust his smiling face between Solly and Pearl.

'Now,' he said, 'let's get down to business. When are you going to announce your engagement? Perhaps I should say, when are you going to confirm Higgin's premature announcement? Listen, Bridgetower, what has he got his knife into you for?'

Briefly, Solly told him of his first encounter with Bevill Higgin.

'Well, well,' said the organist. 'And he thought Miss Vambrace was Tessie Forgie. Now why, I wonder?'

'I think that she must have been sitting at my desk on my day off, and refused him library privileges, or something like that,' said Pearl. 'She has a very short way with people she thinks don't matter.'

'Remarkable! Obviously a very impetuous fellow. And full of conceit, I suppose. Thought he'd show you all that you couldn't slight him. Poor bleeder! I'm sorry for him.'

'I could cheerfully kill him,' said Solly.

'Oh no! You'll be grateful to him in a little while. And years from now, as you sit at the door of your rose-entwined cottage, with your grandchildren tumbling on the grass before you, you'll be saying, "I wonder whatever became of Bevill Higgin, that fragrant old soul who brought us together."'

'Listen, Cobbler,' said Solly; 'get this through your head. We're not even engaged. It seems remotely possible that we may be, but we're not yet. We have a great deal to discuss, before we can contemplate any such step. So will you please stop your nonsense? It's embarrassing.'

'My dear children, I'm only trying to be helpful. Most couples who are going to get engaged think that they have a lot to talk over before they really do it. Utter waste of time. Forget all I said to you the other night about Miss Vambrace not being suitable, Solly. I was wrong. Now the scales have fallen from my eyes. Not only is the hand of Fate discernible in this affair; Fate has been leaving fingerprints all around the place ever since Higgin got his bright idea. Miss Vambrace – or may I call you Pearl? –'

'I'd rather you called me Veronica,' said she.

'How very wise. Much, much better. Well, Veronica, help me to bring this fellow to his senses. I'm sure that you, with your infinitely superior emotional grasp, see that this marriage is fated. Believe me, I've seen a lot of couples get engaged, and they could cut down their time by three-quarters if they would just stop talking and creating absolutely artificial difficulties once the thing was in the bag. You'll enjoy being married, you know. You can help Solly with Heavysege.'

'Ah, but that's one of the difficulties,' said Solly. 'I've given Heavysege the heave-ho. I met Dr Sengreen this morning, quite by chance, and entirely on the spur of the moment I told him that I was putting Heavysege aside because I had something of my own, something original, that I wanted to write. I told him I wanted to be a creator of Amcan, not one of its embalmers. I should have been more careful, I suppose, but Oh hell –. But I can't get married – not in fairness to Veronica – until I've written it, and it has proved either a success or a failure.'

'Nitwit!' said Cobbler. 'Your first book won't be a success. Don't make marriage conditional on the success of a book, or your mother dying, or anything unlikely of that sort. Put first things first. Get married, and plunge into all the uproar of baby-raising, and loading yourself up with insurance and furniture and all the frowsy appurtenances of domestic life, as soon as you can. You'll survive. Millions do. And deep down under all the trash-heap of duty and respectability and routine you may, if you're among the lucky ones, find a jewel of happiness. I know all about it, and I assure you on my sacred honour that it's worth a try. Come on! You know how all this will end up. You'll act on instinct anyhow; everybody does in the really important decisions of life. Why not get some fun out of it, and forget all the twaddle you'll have to talk in order to make it seem reasonable, and prudent, and dull.'

They drove in silence for a time, and then Pearl turned her head toward Cobbler.

'I think you're right,' said she. 'And I hope you'll always be our friend.'

For once, Cobbler said nothing, but for the rest of the drive he leaned back in his seat and sang very pleasantly, in an undertone.

When the conference broke up, Gloster Ridley was left alone with Mr Marryat.

'Well,' said the general manager, 'I hope we've heard the last of that. The trouble you can get into in this business! And mostly because so many people take themselves so seriously. Still, we kept up face, eh?'

'Yes, we did that,' said Ridley. 'In fact, I think we've even gained a little, in some quarters. Vambrace was positively human when he said good-bye. He had the decency to say that a misunderstanding might happen to anyone.'

'So he might,' said Marryat. 'When I think how he carried on in here just a week ago –!'

'Yes, but it was more than old Snelgrove saw fit to do.'

'A fine monkey *he* made of himself! Well, I've got some things to do.' And Mr Marryat went.

But as he left the room another figure, who had been lurking outside the door, slipped into the editor's office. It was Mr Swithin Shillito.

'Chief,' said he, 'what can I say?'

'I really don't know, Mr Shillito. Perhaps it would be best to say nothing.'

'No, no; I feel that much of what has happened is my fault. After all, I introduced Higgin to you. Had it not been for that, all this trouble might have been spared. I've many faults; I don't have to be told that. Perhaps when I am gone it will be said that a foolish generosity was one of them. I wanted to do the poor chap a bit of good. Loyalty to a fellow Britisher, you know. But I realize that in the Craft there can only be one loyalty – to one's paper, and of course to its Chief. I'm in the wrong. I admit it, freely and even gladly. At my age I can still admit that I am often foolish. But not small, I think. No, not small.'

'Please do not feel it necessary to accuse yourself,' said Ridley. 'Anybody can make a mistake, and yours was undoubtedly a generous one. But as we are together, Mr Shillito, I shall take this chance of telling you that the publisher has raised the matter of your retirement. No, please do not protest; Mr Warboys will not hear of you being tied to the daily routine any longer, and I am in complete agreement with him. Confidentially he is organizing a banquet in your honour, and you are too old a hand at these things not to realize that such a tribute will involve a presentation, as well. I understand that it is to be a full-dress affair, with the Mayor present, and some representative journalists from other cities. It will take place between Christmas and the New Year. You will want to prepare a speech, I am sure, and I suggest that a valedictory article, in your own characteristic style, would be welcome.'

It was the sack. But it was a silken sack, lined with ermine, and the Old Mess knew it, and responded accordingly. He spoke of generosity, of long ties, of his hope that *The Bellman* would call upon him whenever he could be of use, of his high regard for Mr Warboys, and his admiration for the Chief.

'I had hoped,' said he, in conclusion, 'that I might remain in harness until next Convocation. It would have been a keen pleasure to me to write an editorial on the occasion of your honorary degree.'

'To be quite frank,' said Ridley, 'I'd rather not have a degree. For a working editor it might prove an embarrassment. When the time comes for me to retire – well, the University might like to do something for me then. But I've thought this matter over very carefully, and if I'm offered one now, I shall decline, with thanks. I'd be grateful if you would pass that information on to people who might be interested – to Mrs Roger Warboys, for instance.'

'You may depend on me,' said Mr Shillito, and turned to go.

'And Swithin,' said Ridley, recalling him. It was the first time in their years of association that he had used the old man's first name, and he was somewhat surprised to find how gently it came off his tongue. 'I didn't want to show that receipt slip to the lawyers, for a reason that will interest you. It was signed, you know, with a false name.' He handed the slip to the old man. The name written, very clearly across the bottom, was Swithin Shillito. There was a pause while the old man took it in, and then, 'I should have known that fellow wasn't a sahib,' said Mr Shillito, with dignity, and walked out of the office.

Ridley sat down at his desk. The afternoon was almost gone, and he did not feel in the mood for work, but it was too early for him to go home. What would he do at home? He would call Mrs Fielding later and angle for an invitation to dinner. Meanwhile, he savoured the poignant sweetness of renunciation. How painfully, how exhaustingly, he had desired a doctorate. Now, for the past eighteen hours, he had known that he did not need this honour to silence the voice of his inner guilt. He was a man released from bondage.

Silently Miss Green entered, and laid a copy of the afternoon's edition of *The Bellman* on his desk. The editor picked it up and idly leafed through it. Truly, *It is a barber's chair, that fits all buttocks . . .* Now that this hubbub was over he might find a few hours in which to prepare his Wadsworth Lecture; he was more determined than ever to make it a distinguished piece of work . . . *The pin buttock* . . . Poor Mrs Little, poor Constant Reader, who had come to him that morning even before he was out of bed, trembling with her great news about Bevill Higgin, destroying her idol, and Blubadub's Ugga Bev, in order that *The Bellman* might be vindicated. Indeed, for a moment he had almost suspected that she had some personal feeling toward himself . . . *The quatch buttock* . . . That boy Rumball must be given a rise. He had shown a lot of gumption by discovering that receipt. Loyalty was a great quality in a reporter – but no, he was thinking like the Old Mess . . . *The brawn buttock* . . . Professor Vambrace was not a man that he could ever like but, as an editor cannot allow himself the luxury of many friends, so he must also be careful not to use his power unjustly, and pursue enmities beyond the grave. Quickly, Ridley opened a locked drawer of his desk and took out the emended obituary of Walter Vambrace which he had prepared in anger the week before. To restore it to its original form was confidential work, too confidential even for the close-mouthed Miss Green; he would do it himself before he left his office. As he slipped a piece of paper into his typewriter to do so, his telephone rang. Was Miss Green not there, to take the call? After three rings, he lifted the receiver himself.

'Yes? . . . Yes, I see . . . Yes, of course I shall be very happy to do so . . . But may I ask if you are quite certain that there will be no objection from either family? . . . You can guarantee that? By tomorrow morning? . . . And you will speak to the Dean at once? . . . Well, in that case, would you both be able to come to my office some time tomorrow in order to sign the order? You will understand my caution, I am sure . . . And may I offer my congratulations? . . . Oh, very kind of you to say so . . . Good-bye.'

Turning back to his machine he typed, slowly and precisely:

Professor and Mrs Walter Vambrace are pleased to announce the engagement of their daughter, Pearl Veronica, to Solomon Bridgetower, Esq., son of Mrs Bridgetower and the late Professor Solomon Bridgetower of this city. Marriage to take place in St Nicholas' Cathedral at a date to be announced later.

In red pencil he wrote beneath this: *To be set, but not inserted until I O K the copy.*

He looked at it for some time, and then he wrote again: *Debit the cost of this advertisement to me personally.*

Face? No, no; he felt that it was the least that he could do.

A Mixture of Frailties

*

Nothing softeneth the Arrogance of our Nature like a Mixture of some Frailties. It is by them that we are best told, that we must not strike too hard upon others because we ourselves do so often deserve blows. They pull our Rage by the sleeve and whisper Gentleness to us in our censures.

HALIFAX

[ONE]

It was appropriate that Mrs Bridgetower's funeral fell on a Thursday, for that had always been her At Home day. As she had dominated her drawing-room, so she dominated St Nicholas' Cathedral on this frosty 23rd of December. She had planned her funeral, as she had planned all her social duties and observances, with care.

Of course the Prayer Book sets the form of an Anglican funeral, and Mrs Bridgetower had no quarrel with that. Every social occasion has its framework; it is in enriching that framework with detail that the exceptional hostess rises above the mediocrity. Not two hours after her physician had pronounced her dead, her lawyer, Mr Matthew Snelgrove, had put a fat letter in the hands of her son Solomon, on the envelope of which was written in her firm, large hand, *Directions for My Funeral*.

Poor Solly, thought her daughter-in-law Veronica, what a time he has had! The most difficult job of all had been getting, at short notice, a coffin which was as nearly as possible a mate to that in which the late Professor Bridgetower had been buried sixteen years before. Mrs Bridgetower had supplied the number and specifications of that model, but styles in coffins change, so it was only by great exertions that a similar one had been found in time. And as Mrs Bridgetower had said that she did not wish to lie in a vault, and as the frost was already in the ground, arrangements had to be made to dig her grave with the aid of blow-torches and pneumatic drills. There had been no difficulty in persuading her oldest friend, Miss Laura Pottinger, to arrange the flowers in the church – 'dear Puss has always had unexceptionable taste in such matters' – but Miss Pottinger had been so swollen with grief and self-importance that she had quarrelled with everyone and struck at an undertaker's assistant with her walking-stick. Luckily Veronica had been able to spare Solly most of the dealings with Miss Puss. And Veronica had addressed the two hundred cards of invitation herself, for Mrs Bridgetower, while insisting on a private funeral, had left a long list of those whom she wished to be present at it. She had also specified the gown in which she was to be buried, and as it would no longer go over her great bulk at the time of her death, Veronica had personally altered it and put it on the corpse – a task which she had not relished. Veronica also had dressed Mrs Bridgetower's hair and delicately painted her face, for the *Directions* had said that this should be done, but were firm that no male undertaker should do it; Miss Puss had stood at her elbow during that macabre hour, offering advice and fretful comment. Veronica had done everything possible to spare her husband, who now sat beside her, pale and worried, not with grief but with fear that something might yet go wrong.

It was not the service which was troubling him. That was under way and out of his hands. It was the funeral tea which was to follow the return from the graveyard which was on his mind. That was certain to be an ordeal, for all the funeral guests were bidden, and most of them were certain to come. He had attempted, that morning, to remove his mother's accustomed chair from the drawing-room, fearing that the sight of it might distress some of her old friends. But the oldest of these, Miss Puss Pottinger, had caught him in the act, and berated him for heartlessness. Louisa's chair, she said through angry tears, must stay where it had always been; she, Miss Puss, would not permit this relic of a great and fragrant spirit to be banished to an upstairs room on the very day of the funeral. And to make sure that no one committed unwitting sacrilege by sitting in it, she would herself lay one of the funeral wreaths – the cushion of white roses from the Imperial Order, Daughters of the Empire – on the seat. So the chair remained, a shrine and, for Solly, a portent of the ordeal which was yet to come.

The service was running according to schedule. A full choir had been specified in the *Directions*, and as full a choir as could be mustered on a weekday was present. Because the schools had closed for the Christmas holidays, eighteen of the Cathedral's twenty boys had been secured; eight of the singing-men had been able to come. Forty dollars for the men and thirty-six for the boys; well, Mother had wanted it. They had sung Samuel Sebastian Wesley's *Man That Is Born* and had followed it with Purcell's *Thou Knowest, Lord*. Luckily in these two selections Mother's taste had agreed with that of the Cathedral organist, Humphrey Cobbler. The hazard was yet to come.

This hazard was Mrs Bridgetower's personal contribution to the funeral service. She had attended many funerals in her time, and had been unfavourably impressed by the fact that what the Prayer Book had to say about death seemed to apply chiefly to men. A feminist of a dignified sort all her life, she felt that the funeral service lacked the feminine touch, and she had arranged for this to be supplied at her own burial. She had specified that a certain piece of music be sung, and that it be sung by a female voice. She admired, she said in her last letter to her son, the fine choir of men and boys which Mr Cobbler had made so great an adornment of St Nicholas', but at her funeral she wanted a woman to sing *My Task*, E. L. Ashford's lovely setting of Maude Louise Ray's dear and inspiring poem.

The Dean had not liked the idea, but he did not go so far as to forbid it. He knew that he would have to brave Miss Puss if he did so. But Humphrey Cobbler had hooted. Cobbler was a personal friend of Solly's and he had spoken with great freedom. 'Music is like wine, Bridgetower,' he had said; 'the less people know about it, the sweeter they like it. You can't have that sickening musical bonbon at your Mum's funeral. It'll disgrace us all.' But after prolonged argument he had succumbed. He had even undertaken to find a woman to sing.

She was about to sing now. The Dean, rather sneakily in Solly's opinion, was uttering a disclaimer.

'At this point,' he said, 'there will be sung some verses which were dear to our deceased sister, and which she specifically requested should be given utterance at this service.' Then he seated himself in his stall, looking as much as possible as if he were someone else, somewhere else, and deaf.

It's not really the poem that's biting him, thought Solly, angrily. It's the idea of the poem applied to Mother. Well, she wanted it, and here it is. To hell with them all.

The singer was by the organ console, with Cobbler, and thus could not be seen by the mourners in the nave. Pure, sweet and clear, her voice made itself heard.

To love someone more dearly ev'ry day;
To help a wand'ring child to find his way;
To ponder o'er a noble thought, and pray;
And smile when ev'ning falls –
This is my task.

That was how she thought of herself, mused Veronica. Probably it didn't seem as sticky to her as it does to us. And Oh, that last six months! Was that what she called smiling when evening falls? But I tried; I really did try. I slaved for her as I never slaved for my own mother. I did all I could to make her feel our marriage was a good thing for Solly. Did I ever pierce through to her heart? I hope so. I pray so. I want to think kindly of her.

A very little wintry sun struck through one of the Cathedral windows. The calm, silvery voice, somewhat hollow and echoing under the dome, continued.

To follow truth as blind men long for light – Veronica cast a sidelong glance at her husband. Silently, he was weeping. He truly loved his mother, in spite of everything, she thought. How I wish I thought that his mother had loved him.

[TWO]

The funeral tea was even more of an ordeal than Solly had foreseen. Such a function is not easily managed, and his mother's two old servants had been quick to declare that they were unable to attempt it. They were too broken up, they said. They were not so broken up, however, that they were incapable of giving a lot of trouble to the caterer who had been engaged for the work. They thought poorly of his suggestion that three kinds of sandwiches and three kinds of little cakes, supplemented by fruitcake, would be enough. The relatives from Montreal, the Hansens, would expect cold meat, they said; and as it was so near Christmas ordinary fruitcake would not suffice; Christmas cake would be looked for. Madam had never been one to skimp. When old Ethel, the cook, remembered that Thursday had always been Madam's At Home day, she had a fresh bout of grief, and declared that she would, after all, prepare the funeral tea herself, if it killed her. Solly had been unable to meet this situation and it was Veronica who, at last, made an uneasy peace between Ethel the cook, Doris the housemaid, and the caterer.

The caterer had his own, highly professional attitude toward funeral teas. What about drinks? he said. Sherry would be wanted for the women who never drank anything except at funerals, and there were always a few Old Country people who expected port – especially if there was cold meat. But most of the mourners would want hard liquor, and they would want it as soon as they got into the house.

These winter funerals were murder; everybody was half perished by the time they got back from the graveyard. Solly would have to get the liquor himself; the caterer's banquet licence did not cover funerals. He would, of course, supply all the glasses and mixings. He advised Solly to get a good friend to act as barman; it wouldn't do to have a professional barman at such an affair. Looked too calculated. Similarly, the icing which said Merry Christmas would have to be removed from the tops of the fruitcakes. Looked too cheerful.

Obediently, Solly procured and hauled a hundred and fifty dollars' worth of assorted liquors from the Government purveyor on the day before the funeral. But his acquaintance among skilled mixers of drinks was small, and in the end he had to ask the Cathedral organist, Humphrey Cobbler, to help him.

Was Solly grieving for his mother, when he wept during the singing of *My Task*? Yes, he was. But he was also grieving because Veronica had had such a rotten time of it during the past three days. He was worrying that there would not be enough to eat at the funeral tea. He was worrying for fear there would be too much to eat, and that the funeral baked-meats would coldly furnish forth his own table for days to come. He was worrying that Cobbler, triumphant behind the drinks-table, would fail to behave himself. He was worrying for fear the Hansen relatives would hang around all evening, discussing family affairs, as is the custom of families at funerals, instead of decently taking the seven o'clock train back to Montreal. He was hoping that he could live through the next few hours, get one decent drink for himself, and go to bed.

[THREE]

Solly and Veronica rode to the graveyard in an undertaker's limousine with Uncle George Hansen, Mrs Bridgetower's brother, and Uncle George's American wife. But as soon as the burial was over they hurried to where Solly had left their small car earlier in the day, and rushed with irreverent haste back to the house, to be on hand to greet the mourners when they came ravening for liquor, food and warm fires.

'Do you think they'll all come?' said Veronica, as they rounded the graveyard gate.

'Very likely. Did you ever see such a mob? I didn't think more than a hundred would go to the cemetery, but it looks as if they all went. Have we got enough stuff, do you suppose?'

'I can't tell. I've never had anything to do with one of these things before.'

'Nor have I. Ronny, in case I go out of my head before this tea thing is over, I want to tell you now that you've been wonderful about it all. In a week or so we'll go for a holiday, and forget about it.'

[FOUR]

When they entered the house it looked cheerful, even festive. Fires burned in the drawing-room, dining-room and in the library, where Cobbler stood ready behind an improvised bar. There was some giggling and scurrying as Solly and his wife came in, and Ethel and Doris were seen making for the kitchen.

'Just been putting the girls right with a strong sherry-and-gin,' said Cobbler. 'They're badly shaken up. Needed bracing. Now, what can I give you?'

'Small ryes,' said Solly. 'And for heaven's sake use discretion, Humphrey.'

'You know me,' said Cobbler, slopping out the rye with a generous hand.

'I do,' said Solly. 'That's why I'm worried. Don't play the fool for the next couple of hours. That's all I ask.'

'You wound me,' said the organist, and made an attempt to look dignified. But his blue suit was too small, his collar was frayed, and his tie was working toward his left ear. His curly black hair stood out from his head in a mop, and his black eyes gleamed unnervingly. 'You suggest that I lack a sense of propriety. I make no protest; I desire only to be left to My Task.' He winked raffishly at Veronica.

He's our oldest friend as a married couple, thought she, and a heart of gold. If only he were not so utterly impossible! She smiled at him.

'Please, Humphrey,' said she.

He winked again, tossed a lump of sugar in the air and caught it in his mouth. 'Trust me,' he said.

What else can we do? thought Veronica.

The mourners had begun to arrive, and Solly went to greet them. There was congestion at the door, for most of the guests paused to take off their overshoes and rubbers, and those who had none were scraping the graveyard clay from their feet. It was half an hour before the last had climbed the stairs, left wraps, taken a turn at the water-closet, descended the stairs and received a drink from Cobbler.

They had the air, festive but subdued, which is common to funeral teas. The grim business at the graveside done, they were prepared to make new, tentative contact with life. They greeted Solly with half-smiles, inviting him to smile in return. Beyond his orbit conversation buzzed, and there was a little subdued laughter. They had all, in some measure, admired or even liked his mother, but her death at seventy-one had surprised nobody, and such grief as they felt for her had already been satisfied at the funeral. Dean Jevon Knapp, of St Nicholas', bustled up to Solly; he had left his cassock and surplice upstairs, and had put on the warm dry shoes which Mrs Knapp always took to funerals for him, in a special bag; he had his gaiters on, and was holding a large Scotch and soda.

'I have always thought this one of the loveliest rooms in Salterton,' said he.

But Solly was not allowed to answer. Miss Puss Pottinger, great friend and unappeased mourner of the deceased, popped up beside him.

'It is as dear Louisa would have wished it to be,' she said, in an aggressive but unsteady voice. 'Thursday was always her At Home day, you know, Mr Dean.'

'First Thursdays, I thought,' said the Dean; 'this is a third Thursday.'

'Be it what it may,' said Miss Puss, losing control of face and voice, 'I shall think of this as dear Louisa's – last – At Home.'

'I'm very sorry,' said the Dean. 'I had not meant to distress you. Will you accept a sip –?' He held out his glass.

Miss Pottinger wrestled with herself, and spoke in a whisper. 'No,' said she. 'Sherry. I think I could take a little sherry.'

The Dean bore her away, and she was shortly seen sipping a glass of dark brown sherry in which Cobbler, unseen, had put a generous dollop of brandy.

Solly was at once engaged in conversation by his Uncle George Hansen and Uncle George's wife. This lady was an American, and as she had lived in Canada a mere thirty-five years, still found the local customs curious, and never failed to say so.

'This seems to me more like England than at home,' she said now.

'Mother was very conservative,' said Solly.

'The whole of Salterton is very conservative,' said Uncle George; 'I just met old Puss Pottinger mumbling about At Homes; thought she was dead years ago. This must be one of the last places in the British Empire where anybody has an At Home day.'

'Mother was certainly one of the last in Salterton to have one,' said Solly.

'Aha? Well, this is a nice old house. You and your wife going to keep it up?'

'I haven't had time to think about that yet.'

'No, I suppose not. But of course you'll be pretty well fixed, now?'

'I really don't know, sir.'

'Sure to be. Your mother was a rich woman. You'll get everything. She certainly won't leave anything to *me*; I know that. Ha ha! She was a wonder with money, even as a girl. "Louie, you're tighter than the bark to a tree," I used to say to her. Did your father leave much?'

'He died very suddenly, you know, sir. His will was an old one, made before I was born. Everything went to mother, of course.'

'Aha? Well, it all comes to the same thing now, eh?'

'Solly, do you realize I'd never met your wife until this afternoon?' said Uncle George's wife. 'Louisa never breathed a word about your marriage until she wrote to us weeks afterward. The girl was a Catholic, wasn't she?'

'No, Aunt Gussie. Her mother was a Catholic, but Veronica was brought up a freethinker by her father. Mother and her father had never agreed, and I'm afraid my marriage was rather a shock to her. I'll get Veronica now.'

'Why do you keep calling her Veronica?' said Uncle George. 'Louie wrote that her name was Pearl.'

'It still is,' said Solly. 'But it is also Veronica, and that is what she likes me to call her. Her father is Professor Vambrace, you know.'

'Oh God, that old bastard,' said Uncle George, and was kicked on the ankle by his wife. 'Gussie, what are you kicking me for?'

At this moment a Hansen cousin, leaning on a stick, approached and interrupted.

'Let's see, George, now Louisa's gone you're the oldest Hansen stock, aren't you?'

'I'm sixty-nine,' said Uncle George; 'you're older than that, surely, Jim?'

'Sixty-eight,' said Jim, with a smirk.

'You look older,' said Uncle George, unpleasantly.

'You would, too, if you'd been where I was on the Somme,' said

Cousin Jim, with the conscious virtue of one who has earned the right to be nasty on the field of battle.

'You people certainly like it hot in Canada,' said Aunt Gussie. And she was justified, for the steam heat and three open fires had made the crowded rooms oppressive.

'I'll see what I can do,' said Solly and crept away. He ran upstairs and sought refuge in the one place he could think of which might be inviolable by his mother's relatives. As he entered his bathroom from his dressingroom his wife slipped furtively in from the bedroom. They locked both doors and sat down to rest on the edge of the tub.

'They're beginning to fight about who's the oldest stock,' said Solly.

'I've met rather too many people who've hinted that our marriage killed your mother,' said Veronica. 'I thought a breather would do me good.'

'Mother must have written fifty letters about that.'

'Don't worry about it now, Solly.'

'How is Humphrey doing?'

'I haven't heard any complaints. Do people always soak like this at funerals?'

'How should I know? I've never given a funeral tea before.'

[FIVE]

When Solly and his wife went downstairs again they found that most of the guests had turned their attention from drink to food, save for a half-dozen diehards who hung around the bar. The mourners were, in the main, elderly people who were unaccustomed to fresh air in the afternoon, and the visit to the cemetery had given them an appetite. The caterer directed operations from the kitchen, and his four waitresses hurried to and fro with laden platters. Ethel and Doris, ranking as mourners, pretended to be passing food, but were in reality engaged in long and regretful conversations with family friends, one or two of whom were unethically sounding them out about the chances of their changing employment, now that Mrs Bridgetower was gone. (After all, what would a young man with an able-bodied wife want with two servants?) Miss Puss had been expected to pour the tea, a position of special honour, but she gave it up after overfilling three cups in succession, and seemed to be utterly unnerved; little Mrs Knapp took on this demanding job, and was relieved after a hundred cups or so by Mrs Swithin Shillito. The fake beams of the dining-room ceiling seemed lower and more oppressive than ever as the mourners crowded themselves into the room, consuming ham, turkey, sandwiches, cheese, Christmas cake and tartlets with increasing gusto. Those who were wedged near the table obligingly passed plates of food over the heads of the crowd to others who could not get near the supplies. The respectful hush had completely vanished, laughter and even guffaws were heard, and if it had not been a funeral tea the party would have been called a rousing success.

The mourners had returned from the graveyard at four o'clock, and it was six before any of them thought of going home. It was the general stirring of the Montreal Hansens, who had a train to catch, which finally broke up the party.

'Good-bye, Solly, and a Merry Christmas!' roared Uncle George, who had returned to the bar immediately after finishing a hearty tea. His wife kicked him on the ankle again, and he straightened his face. 'Well, as merry as possible under the circumstances,' he added, and plunged into the scramble for rubbers which was going on in the hall. Cousin Jim was sitting on the stairs, while a small, patient wife struggled to put on and zip up his overshoes. 'Take care of my bad leg,' he said, in a testy voice, to anyone who came near. It was some time before all the Hansens had gone. Several of them trailed back into the drawing-room, in full outdoor kit, to wring Solly's hand, or to kiss him on the cheek. But at last they went, and the Saltertonians began to struggle for coats and overshoes.

Mr Matthew Snelgrove, solicitor and long-time friend of Mrs Bridgetower, approached Solly conspiratorially. He was a tall old man, stiff and crane-like, with beetling brows.

'Will tomorrow, at three o'clock, suit you?' he said.

'For what, Mr Snelgrove?'

'The will,' said Mr Snelgrove. 'We must read and discuss the will.'

'But is that necessary? I thought nobody read wills now. Can't we meet at your office some day next week and discuss it?'

'I think that your Mother would have wished her will to be read in the presence of all her executors.'

'All her executors? Are there others? I thought that probably you and myself –'

'There are two executors beside yourself, and it is not a simple will. Not simple at all. I think you should know its contents as soon as possible.'

'Well – if you say so.'

'I think it would be best. I shall inform the others. Here, then, at three?'

'As you please.'

Solly had no time to reflect on this arrangement, for several people were waiting to say good-bye. Dean Knapp and his wife approached last, each holding an arm of Miss Puss Pottinger, who wore the rumpled appearance of one who has been put into her outside clothes by hands other than her own. One foot was not completely down into her overshoe, and she lurched as she walked.

'We shall see Miss Pottinger home,' said the Dean, smiling but keeping a jailor's grip on Auntie Puss.

'Solly, dear boy,' cried that lady, and breaking free from the Dean she flung herself upon Solly's bosom, weeping and scrabbling at his coat. It became clear that she wanted to kiss him. He stooped and suffered this, damp and rheumy as it was; then, taking her by the shoulders, he passed her back to Mrs Knapp. With a loud hiccup Auntie Puss collapsed, and almost bore the Dean's wife to the floor. When she had been picked up, she was led away, sobbing and murmuring, 'Poor Louisa's last At Home – shall never forget –' They were the last to go.

'Well, well, well,' said Cobbler, strolling in from the hall, when he had helped the Dean to drag Auntie Puss down a rather icy walk, and boost her into a car; 'quite overcome with grief. Sad.'

'She was drunk,' said Solly. 'What on earth did you give her?'

'The poor old soul was badly in need of bracing,' said Cobbler. 'I gave her a sherry with a touch of brandy in it, and it did the trick. But would she let well alone? She would not. She kept coming back. Was I to refuse her? I tried her once without the brandy, but she passed back her glass and said, "This isn't the same." Well – she had seven. I couldn't put her on the Indian List; she'd have made a scene. Whatever she feels like tomorrow, I am pure as the driven snow. Never say No to a woman; my lifelong principle.'

He was helping Veronica to clear up the mess. Paper napkins were everywhere. Dirty plates covered the top of the piano. Cake had been ground into the carpet. The pillow of white roses in Mrs Bridgetower's chair had been pushed under it by the callous Cousin Jim, who wanted to sit down and had no feeling for symbolism.

'For heaven's sake leave that,' said Solly. 'Let Ethel and Doris cope with it.'

''Fraid the girls are a bit overcome,' said Cobbler. 'They told me they were good for nothing but bed. Odd phrase, considering everything.'

'Humphrey, what *did* you do?' said Veronica.

'Me? Not a thing. Just my duty, as I saw it. People kept asking for drinks and I obliged them. Really, Solly, those Hansen relatives of yours are something special. Hollow legs, every one of them.'

'Was there enough?'

'Just managed. Do you know that there were two hundred and forty-seven souls here, and not one of them was a teetotaller? I always count; it's automatic with me. I count the house at every Cathedral service; the Dean likes to know how he's pulling. I consider that the affair was a credit to your late Mum, but we nearly ran out of swipes. It was a close thing.'

He sat down at the grand piano, and sang with great expression, to the tune of the popular ballad *Homing* –

All things get drunk at eventide;
The birds go pickled to their snoozing;
Heaven's creatures share a mighty thirst –
Boozing – Bo-o-o-zing.

'Humphrey, stop it!' said Veronica. 'If you must do something, will you get me a drink? I'm completely done up.'

Cobbler got them all drinks, and while Solly and Veronica sat by the fire, trying to forget the trials and miseries of the past few days, he played Bach choral preludes on the old piano, to heal their wounded spirits.

[SIX]

Mr Snelgrove completed the reading of Mrs Bridgetower's will the following afternoon, just as the library clock struck four. He had enjoyed himself. Modern custom did not often require him to read a will and he felt that there was something splendidly professional and lawyer-like about doing so. When a testator is dead he is in the hands of God; certainly this was the belief of Mr Snelgrove who was, among other dignified things, chancellor of the diocese of which St Nicholas' was the Cathedral; but the testator's affairs on earth remain in the hands of his lawyer. There is drama in such a position, and Mr

Snelgrove greatly relished it. He blew his nose and removed his pince-nez in order to rub his old eyes.

The setting in which Mrs Bridgetower's will had been read was everything that the legal ham Mr Snelgrove could have wished. Outside the windows a light snow was falling from a leaden, darkening sky. Inside the library a wood fire burned, its light being reflected in the leaded glass of the old-fashioned book-jails which lined the walls. The room was comfortable, dark, stuffy and rather depressing. It was Christmas Eve.

His listeners looked suitably grave and impressed. Dean Knapp, sunk in a leather armchair, stroked his brow reflectively, like a man who cannot believe that he has heard aright. Miss Puss Pottinger sat bolt upright on an armless chair, refusing to yield to the splitting headache which seemed to possess her whole small being; from time to time her gorge rose sourly and searingly within her, but she was a soldier's daughter, and she forcibly gulped it down again. The fumes from Solly's pipe were a great trial to her. He was perched on the arm of a large chair in which Veronica was sitting. It was Solly who was first to speak.

'I think I've got the drift of the will, but I'm not quite sure,' said he. 'Could you let us have the meaning of it in simple language?'

Mr Snelgrove was happy to do so. Interpreting legal scripture to laymen was the part of his profession which he liked best.

'Shorn of technicality,' said he, 'the meaning of the will is this: all of your late mother's estate is left in trust to her executors – you, her son, Solomon Bridgetower – you, Laura Pottinger, spinster – you, Jevon Knapp, as Dean of St Nicholas' Cathedral. That estate, as outlined here, consists of this house and its contents and considerable holdings in investments. You, Solomon Bridgetower, are to continue to occupy the house, which has always been your home, but it is the property of the trust, and you may not dispose of it. But the income from the estate is to be devoted to the educational project which your late mother has outlined.'

'You mean, I don't get any money?' said Solly.

'You get a legacy of one hundred dollars,' said the lawyer.

'Yes, but I mean – the investments, and the money that brought in my Mother's own income, and all that – I don't quite follow –?'

'That money is all to be devoted to the education, or training, of some young woman resident in this city of Salterton, who is desirous of following a career in the arts. The young woman is to be chosen by you, the trustees. She must be not more than twenty-one at the time she is chosen, and you are to be responsible for her maintenance and training, in the best circumstances you can devise, until she reaches the age of twenty-five. She is to be maintained abroad in order, as your mother says, that she may bring back to Canada some of the intangible treasures of European tradition. That phrase, of course, rules out any possibility of her being trained in the States. And when she is twenty-five, you are to choose another beneficiary of the trust. And so on, unless the conditions under which the trust exists are terminated.'

'And I get nothing except a hundred dollars and the right to live in the house?'

'You get nothing, unless the condition is fulfilled which brings the trust to an end. If, and when, that condition is fulfilled and you are still living in this house, you receive a life interest in your mother's estate. Bequests are made to the two servants, Ethel Colman and Doris Black, which will be payable when the condition is fulfilled. Laura Pottinger receives a bequest of the testator's collection of Rockingham china. The Cathedral Church of St Nicholas will receive all of the testator's holdings in certain telephone and transportation stocks.

'There is a condition attaching to this latter bequest. Until the Cathedral gets the telephone stock, the Dean is to preach, every St Nicholas' Day, a special sermon on some matter relating to education, and these sermons are to be known as the Louisa Hansen Bridgetower Memorial Sermons. If there is any failure in this respect, the bequest is forfeit.'

Solly still looked puzzled. 'And all of this hangs –?'

'It all hangs on your having a son, Mr Bridgetower. When and if, you and your wife, Pearl Veronica, *née* Vambrace, produce male issue, who is duly christened Solomon Hansen Bridgetower, he becomes heir of all his grandmother's estate save for the bequests I have mentioned. But you are to have a life interest in the estate, so that he will not actually come into possession of his inheritance until after your death.'

'And if we have a child and it is a girl?'

'The trust will remain.'

'But it's fantastic.'

'Somewhat unusual, certainly.'

'When was this will made?'

'I read you the date. Your mother made this will less than three months ago.'

'It puts my wife and me in a pretty position, doesn't it?'

'It does not put anyone in an enviable position, Solomon,' said Mr Snelgrove. 'Did you not notice what it does to me? I am not an executor, though as an old and, I believed, valued friend of your Mother's, I might have expected that confidence; I am named solely as solicitor to the executors – a paid position. And the condition is made that if I have not settled all your Mother's affairs within one year from the day of her death, the estate is to be taken out of my hands and confided to Gordon Balmer – a solicitor for whom your Mother knew that I had a strong disapproval. You did not perhaps notice her comment that she thought that my "natural cupidity" would make me hurry the business through. "Natural cupidity" is a legal expression which she picked up from me and has turned against me. Your Mother has given us all a flick of her whip.'

'These memorial sermons,' said the Dean; 'they are to be preached until the Cathedral inherits? But what if the Cathedral never inherits? What if there is no son? I know many families – large families – which consist solely of daughters.'

'It will be many years before anything can be done to meet that situation, Mr Dean,' said Snelgrove. 'Meanwhile the sermons must be delivered, in hope and expectation. Any failure could cost the Cathedral a considerable sum.'

The Dean wrestled within himself for a moment before he spoke. 'Could you give me any idea how much?' he said at last.

'It would run between seven and ten thousand a year, I think,' said Snelgrove. All the executors opened their eyes at the mention of this sum.

'Then Mother was very rich?' asked Solly. 'I never knew, you know; she never spoke of such things. I had understood she was just getting by.'

'There are degrees in wealth,' said Mr Snelgrove. 'Your Mother would not seem wealthy in some circles. But she was comfortable – very comfortable. She inherited substantially from her own family, you know, and there was rather more in your father's estate than might have been expected from a professor of geology. He had very good mining contacts, at a time when mines were doing well. And your mother was a lifelong, shrewd investor.'

'She was?' said Solly. 'I never knew anything about it.'

'Oh yes,' said Snelgrove. 'I don't suppose there was anyone in Salterton who followed the Montreal and Toronto markets so closely, or so long, or so successfully, as your mother. A remarkable woman.'

'Remarkable indeed,' said the Dean. He was thinking about those sermons, and balancing another curate and new carpets against them.

Veronica had not spoken until now. 'Shall we have tea?' said she.

They had it from a remarkably beautiful Rockingham service. Miss Puss, who said nothing all afternoon, eyed it speculatively. Veronica noticed that she did so.

'Yours, Miss Puss,' said she, smiling.

'Mine,' said Puss Pottinger, softly and without a smile, 'if and when.'

[SEVEN]

'It was Christmas Day in the workhouse,' declaimed Humphrey Cobbler, pushing himself back from the late Mrs Bridgetower's dining-table. Christmas dinner with Solly and Veronica had made him expansive.

'Shut up, Humphrey,' said Molly, his wife. She was a large, beautiful, untidy woman, always calm and at ease. She threw a grape at her husband to silence him, but it missed his head and set an epergne jingling on the built-in sideboard.

'No offence meant,' said Cobbler, 'and none taken, I'm sure. I merely wished to convey to our young friends here, who have been studiedly avoiding the subject of Mum's Will all through this excellent dinner, that we are privy to their dread secret, and sympathize with them in their fallen state. I was about to do so through the agency of divine poesy, thereby showing a delicacy which I could hardly expect you, my thick-witted consort, to appreciate.'

Raising his glass, he declaimed again:

It was Christmas Day in the Workhouse;
The maddest, merriest day;
And all the paupers had gathered then
To make high holiday.

Then in strode the Workhouse Master
As they cringed by the grimy walls;
'I wish you a Merry Christmas,' said he;
The paupers answered –

'What have you been hearing?' said Solly. 'You aren't going to tell me that people are chattering about it already?'

'Not precisely chattering,' said Cobbler; 'more a kind of awed whispering. Rumours reached me this morning, just before we celebrated the birthday of the Prince of Peace with a first-rate choral service, that your Mum's Will was in the nature of a grisly practical joke, and that you are left without a nickel.'

'I thought it wouldn't take long to get around,' said Solly. 'Who was talking? There are only three people who know; they might have had the decency to keep quiet for a few days, at least. Who was it?'

'Calm yourself, my dear fellow,' said Cobbler. 'You are – let's see, what is it – twenty-seven. You really ought to have more worldly wisdom than to say that only three people know about your Mum's Will. You and Veronica know, and the Dean and unquestionably the Dean's wife; Puss Pottinger knows, and she is a mighty hinter; Snelgrove knows, and certainly his wife, and his partner Ronny Fitzalan, and probably at least two girls in his office who made copies of the will for the executors. Your excellent Ethel and Doris, who have hopes of legacies, have undoubtedly picked up a few things by listening at doors or hiding under your bed. That's twelve people already. What I know I was told this morning by one of my tenors whom you don't know, but who knows you. He heard it last night when he was carol-singing at the hospital. Your late Mum was notoriously a rich woman; everybody wants to know who gets the lolly.'

'I certainly didn't know she was a rich woman,' said Solly.

'That sounds silly, but I believe it,' said Cobbler. 'One never thinks of one's parents with any realism. She was always pretty tight with money when you wanted it; probably she told you she hadn't much, and you believed her, like a good boy. She came the penniless widow. You didn't use your eyes. You didn't look at this big house, full of hideous but expensive stuff; you didn't reflect that your Mum lived in considerable state, with two servants, in an age when most people have none; you didn't think that she had all this without doing any work for it. You didn't think that it costs a lot of money to continue the habits of the Edwardian era into the middle of the twentieth century. Nothing is so expensive as living in the past. No; you believed what you were told. You accepted all this as a normal, poverty-ridden hovel. But everybody else in Salterton knew that your Mum was a very warm proposition, and they were all crazy to know how she would cut up when she was gone.'

'What business was it of theirs?'

'Don't be stupid; people who mind their own business die of boredom at thirty. Don't you suppose the hospitals hoped for a chunk? Your father was a professor at Waverley University for years; do you think Waverley didn't have its hand out? The Cathedral wanted a slice, too. But nothing doing. And they say you don't get a red cent. Where is it all going? I don't mean to pry, you understand. I'm just aching to know.'

'All you have heard is that none of the places that expected a legacy got anything, and that I am not the heir?'

'Precisely. Are you going to give us the real story, or do you want Molly and me to feel that we aren't trusted, now that you are poor like us?'

'I suppose it'll all come out in a few days. You might as well know.'

And so Solly told the Cobblers the conditions of his mother's will. They opened their eyes very wide, and Cobbler gave a long whistle, but it was his wife who spoke.

'That's what you can really call laying the Dead Hand on the living, isn't it,' said Molly. 'I suppose it's something to be proud of, in a way; not many people have the guts to make a really revengeful will. They're too anxious to leave a fragrant memory, and few things are so fragrant as a million dollars. I suppose it's well over a million?'

'Haven't any idea,' said Solly. 'But I'm sure you're wrong about revenge. I mean, Mother was capricious, and very strong-minded, but revenge – it doesn't seem like her.'

'Seems very much like what I knew of her,' said Cobbler. 'You really must grow up, you know. Your Mum told you that she loved you, and you believed her. She made your life a hell of dependency, and you put up with it because she played the invalid, and tyrannized over you with her weak heart. She beat off any girls you liked, until you got up enough gumption to marry Veronica – or Veronica got enough gumption to marry you; I never quite knew which it was. That was only a bit more than a year ago. What peace have you known since? She made you come here and live with her, and like a couple of chumps you did it. She let it be known as widely as possible that your marriage grieved her.'

'Look here, you're talking about my Mother, who was buried the day before yesterday. I don't expect you to behave like other people, but you must show some decency. I know better than anybody how difficult she was, but she had very good reasons for everything she did. Of course they're not easily understandable, from an outsider's viewpoint. I've read and re-read her will today; it's very full, and very personal. She says that she has left the money away from me to prove me – to test what I can do absolutely on my own. She says she knows it will be hard, and advises me to take my father as an example. I know – it sounds very odd by modern notions of such things, but it is quite obvious that she meant it kindly.'

This was greeted with a studied silence by the others.

'Well, look at it from her point of view,' said Solly, when the silence had begun to wear on him. 'She always knew I was rather a feeble chap; it was her last try to put some backbone into me.'

'You're not a bit feeble,' said his wife, laying her hand on his.

'Yes, yes, I am. I don't pretend that this will isn't a shock, and I won't pretend to think it's really fair. But I see what she meant by it. And your suggestion that it was because of our marriage is sheer nasty spite, Humphrey. I won't say Mother liked Veronica, but I know she respected her. And certainly Ronny was as good as any daughter could have been to her during the past six months. You didn't marry me for money, did you?' said he, smiling at his wife.

'I don't think that is what Humphrey meant,' said Veronica.

'Well, what else is there?'

'Darling, if you haven't thought of it, I won't find it very easy to explain. Your mother leaves you her money – or the income from it, which is the same thing – if we have a son. Well? Must we set to work, cold-bloodedly, to beget a child, hoping it will be a son? If it is a daughter – try, try again. You know what people are. They'll be ready to make the worst of it, whatever happens. They'll have a splendid, prurient snigger at us for years. Don't you see?'

'Oh I'm sure Mother never meant anything like that,' said Solly.

'Then why did she make such a will?' said Molly. 'You've got to consider the generation your mother belonged to. She wasn't a big friend of sex, you know. She undoubtedly thought it would dry up the organs of increase in you both. Very pretty. Sweetly maternal.'

'I wish you people would get it into your heads that you are talking about my Mother,' said Solly, with some anger.

'Now look, Solly,' said Cobbler, 'talk sense. Ever since I first met you your main topic whenever you were depressed was what a hell of a time your mother was giving you. I've heard you talk about her in a way which surprised even me – and I specialize in speaking the unspeakable. You can't make a saint of her now simply because she is dead.'

'Shut up,' said his wife. 'Solly needs time to get used to the fact that his mother is dead. You know how you carried on when your mother died. Roared like a bull for days, though you rarely gave her a civil word the last few times you met.'

'Those were quarrels about music,' said Cobbler. 'We disagreed on artistic principles. Just showed how really compatible we were that we could talk about them at all. I bet Solly never talked to his mother about such things.'

'The terms of her will showed that she cared a great deal about artistic principles. Or about education, anyhow,' said Solly.

'I have not forgotten that she requested that *My Task* be sung at her funeral,' said Cobbler. 'The bill for that caper is outstanding, by the way. I only got a girl to do it at the last moment.'

'She sang it very nicely,' said Veronica.

'Good voice. A girl called Monica Gall. And it will be ten dollars.'

'Include it in the bill you send to Snelgrove,' said Solly, 'along with the charges for the choir, and yourself.'

'I played gratis.'

'Well, don't. Send Snelgrove a bill. I don't wish to think that my Mother was obliged to you for anything.'

'Oh, for God's sake don't turn nasty, just because I spoke my mind. If you want friends who echo everything you say and defer to all your pinhead notions, count me out.'

'Shut up, both of you,' said Molly. 'You're carrying on like a couple of children. But listen to me, Solly. You and Veronica may have some hard days ahead of you, and you've got to make up your minds now to stick together, or this idiotic will can make trouble between you. And the fact that you have no money will make it all the easier.'

'We have just as much money as we ever had,' said Solly. 'I still have my job, you know.'

'A junior lecturer, and quite good for your age. A miserable salary, considering that you are expected to live the life of a man of education and some position on it. Still, Humphrey and I are living very happily on less. But if I understand the conditions of the will, you have to live in this house, and keep it up, and keep Ethel and Doris on that money, and go on having children until you have a son. They say that clever men tend to have daughters, Solly, and I suppose you qualify as a clever man, in spite of the way you are behaving at present.' Molly's affectionate tone took the sting out of her words. 'But I think you should recognize that your mother has laid the Dead Hand on you and Veronica in the biggest possible way, and the sooner you see that the better you will be able to deal with it.'

'And you'd better not begin by holding a grudge against me,' said Cobbler. 'You are going to want all your friends, now that you have joined the ranks of the struggling poor. You are going to feel some very sharp pangs, you know, when you see all that lovely money, which might have been yours, going to support dear little Miss God-knows-who, while she studies flower arrangement in the Japanese Imperial Greenhouses, at the expense of your Mum's estate. So stop snapping me up on every word. I had nothing personal against your Mum. It is just that she symbolized all the forces that have been standing on my neck ever since I was old enough to have a mind of my own. And to prove my goodwill, I give you a toast to her memory.'

Amity was restored, and they drank the toast. Perhaps only Molly and Veronica heard Cobbler murmur, as he raised his glass, *'Toujours gai, le diable est mort.'*

[TWO]

Mrs Bridgetower's will would not, under ordinary circumstances, have become a matter of public interest until the probate was completed but, as Cobbler pointed out, there were institutions in Salterton which hoped for a legacy. Chief among these was Waverley University, and the rumour that it was to have nothing aroused some waspishness in the Bursar's office. Universities are, in a high-minded way, unceasingly avaricious. The thought that the wealthy widow of a former professor – a member of the family, so to speak – had not remembered the Alma Mater in her will (particularly when her son and presumed heir was also of the faculty) was unbearable. The rumour was that a trust had been set up, and moreover a trust with an educational purpose; if this were true, it was a slap in the face for Waverley. But was it true?

It is not a university's function to pry into private affairs. That is the job of a newspaper. Thus it was that, acting on a discreet tip from the Bursar's office, the Salterton *Evening Bellman* sought information from the three executors in turn. From Miss Puss it received the sharpest of rebuffs; the Dean temporized, and said that he was not free to speak until he had consulted the others; it was Solly who said that a trust was to be established, and that details should be sought from Mr Snelgrove. The lawyer, who loved secrecy, called the executors together to urge them to say nothing to anyone; nobody had any right to know anything about Mrs Bridgetower's estate until after probate. It was Solly who pointed out that this was impossible.

A detailed knowledge of law and ordinary common sense are not always found together, and it was Solly who had to explain the situation to Mr Snelgrove, as tactfully as possible. According to the will, the girl who was to benefit from Mrs Bridgetower's money must be chosen and launched on her course of study within a year of her benefactress' death: Mr Snelgrove was also to have the probate completed by that time, or else suffer the humiliation of seeing this juicy plum pass into the hands of another lawyer. Therefore, whether the trust was legally in existence before the probate or not; the girl must be chosen within a year, and that could not be done unless some knowledge of the impending trust were available to at least a few people. It took a surprisingly long time to get this through Mr Snelgrove's head, though he had drawn Mrs Bridgetower's will and ought to have foreseen it. His was the perplexity of the man who understands his situation intellectually but has not comprehended it emotionally, and he continued to say 'Yes' and 'I see' when it was amply clear that he did not see at all.

Though Solly was willing that something should be known of the trust, he was not willing that it should be publicly known that his mother had used him shabbily. His state of mind was by no means an uncommon one: his mother had been the bane of his life, but after her death he was determined that no one should think ill of her. So, after consultation with Veronica, he paid a visit to Mr Gloster Ridley, the editor of *The Bellman*, explained the situation to him, and asked for his help in putting the best face on the matter. This stroke of diplomacy, undertaken without the knowledge of the other executors or of Snelgrove, had excellent result. *The Bellman* published a reasonable amount of information about the trust and its purpose, made it clear that nothing would happen for some time, said kind things about the late Mrs Bridgetower's lifelong enthusiasm for the education of women, and gave no hint that the lady's son had been left a mere token bequest, or that there were any curious conditions attaching to the trust. Thus an agreeable version of the truth was made public, and the murmurs at Waverley were, for the moment, stilled.

Mr Snelgrove and Miss Puss were displeased, however. They both possessed that type of mind which gets deep satisfaction out of withholding information. If Miss Puss could have bought shoes without confiding her size to the salesman, she would have done it. So another meeting was called, and Solly was raked over the coals for talking to the press. Already he was learning useful lessons from his experience as an executor, and he let Snelgrove and Miss Puss talk until they were tired. Then he covered all his previous arguments once again, and pointed out that the effect of the newspaper article had been good, and that it had substituted a body of carefully chosen fact for spiteful rumour. He received unexpected support from Dean Knapp. It would be too much to say that Miss Puss and the lawyer were mollified, but they were temporarily subdued. Solly had a pleasant feeling that he was becoming the guiding spirit of the executors.

It was his idea, for instance, that the executors should always meet in the Bridgetower house. Snelgrove had read the will there, to satisfy his sense of drama; Solly contrived that the executors should meet there, arguing that, as the house was the property of the trust, the trustees should make use of it for their official deliberations. This gave him a certain advantage, for while it was true that the house was part of the trust, it was also his dwelling, and he played the role of host there. Miss Puss was first to recognize the implications of this, and she took her revenge at that second meeting, when she and Snelgrove were angry with Solly about the newspaper account of Mrs Bridgetower's will.

Veronica had met her at the door, and welcomed her. 'I think, dear, that it would be better if you were not present at the trustees' meetings,' said Miss Puss.

'Oh, I wouldn't dream of coming into the meeting,' said Veronica; 'I just wanted to help you with your coat.'

'I am sure you mean everything that is kind, dear,' said Miss Puss, 'but we must avoid any appearance of impropriety. I say this both as an executor and a friend. I am sure you hear everything in good time, as it is.' Veronica retired to another room with a red face, and a sense that she had been presumptuous in a house which was now, apparently, even less her home than when her mother-in-law had been alive.

Solly had overheard this exchange, and he was angry. He had not much spirit when it came to fighting for himself, but he was ready to fight anyone for Veronica. Therefore he took it out of Miss Puss rather more than was necessary, in a quiet way, and stored up a considerable quantity of resentment against her, to be worked off at his future convenience. If his mother had truly meant her will to make a man of him, it was working rapidly to make him a hard and bitter man. Laura Pottinger was his mother's oldest friend, and as such she had domineered over him from boyhood. But he was strongly conscious of the fact that as he had grown up, she had grown old, and he meant to put her in her place over and over again, if that should be necessary, until she learned what her place was.

It was clear to him also that Mr Matthew Snelgrove would have to be dealt with, for the lawyer took the line that the three executors needed guidance, and he was their obvious guide. When he had at last been made to realize that he could not in any way call in the information which *The Bellman* had given out, he warned the executors strictly against revealing any further terms of the will.

'I must tell you,' said Solly, 'that Veronica and I have already had a talk with Ethel Colman and Doris Black. They have both been with the family a long time, and had a right to expect legacies. You know that there are legacies for them – when I have a son. We thought it right that they should know.'

'But that is exceedingly irregular,' said Snelgrove. 'I am charged with the very difficult task of settling this large estate in a year; how am I to do so if my prerogatives are taken from me and information revealed and expectations raised before I have even had time to settle to the work?'

'The whole thing is irregular,' said Solly, 'and Veronica and I feel that Ethel and Doris deserve any consideration we can give them. They have a right to know where they stand. We can't possibly keep them both, or even one of them, on my salary. They must be free to take other jobs. And you might as well know that I offered to raise the money for their legacies myself, so that they could have them now. Otherwise we don't know how long they may have to wait.'

'But if you have told them the conditions of the will, they are certain to talk,' said Snelgrove. 'You know how things get around – even when nobody runs to the newspapers.'

'I know that you read my mother's will on Christmas Eve to the four of us and that on Christmas Day quite a few people knew that I had been cut out of it,' said Solly. To his astonishment, and triumph, the other three all blushed in their various ways. 'Certainly I didn't tell anyone in that time.'

'If irresponsible talk is permitted, your Mother's reputation may suffer,' said Miss Puss. 'That ought to mean a great deal to you.'

'And so it does,' said Solly, 'but I think that you will agree that my Mother has made it somewhat difficult to prevent hard things being said. People at Waverley have not stuck at saying she tricked them – led them to think they were to get a substantial sum, and then didn't come through with it. You ought to know, Auntie Puss, that she didn't care what anybody said, when she wanted things her own way.'

Miss Puss changed her tack. 'I suppose it is inevitable, but I wish that you did not involve Veronica so much in these affairs. I suppose she sympathized with the servants without any regard for the reflection on dear Louisa.'

'Veronica is my wife, Miss Puss,' said Solly. 'Mother often seemed to forget that, but there is no reason why anyone else should do so. She is in this as much as I am. I'll tell her whatever I think proper – and that is everything.'

A fight seemed imminent, and Snelgrove intervened, choosing his point of pressure badly. 'You have offered to pay Ethel and Doris legacies; what will you do for money? Have you insurance? Or savings?' He knew very well that Solly had neither.

'I have talked to my bank,' said Solly, with a smile. 'They are very friendly, and are ready to lend me money on my expectations.'

'Be careful of borrowing on that security,' said Snelgrove. 'You may involve yourself irretrievably. What if you never inherit?'

'You'll excuse me if I am more optimistic about that than an older man might be,' said Solly. 'I offered to get the banker a doctor's certificate that I am – in good health; he very decently said I needn't bother. I have a young and healthy wife. I assure you, Miss Puss and gentlemen, that I mean to inherit just as fast as I can.'

'Of course; of course,' said the Dean, and then blushed, realizing that his encouragement might be misinterpreted. He was extremely uncomfortable.

'My chief concern is that a proper regard be shown for dear Louisa's wishes,' said Miss Puss, who had an ill-understood but powerful feeling that Solly was outraging his mother's memory with indecent talk.

'Apparently she wished for a grandson,' said Solly, 'and I am going to do everything in my power to gratify her.'

It was in this uncomfortable strain that the executors' meetings continued. Solly called them whenever he thought it necessary. He summoned the Dean, Miss Puss and Snelgrove to tell them that Doris Black had decided to leave his employ, and that Ethel Colman meant to continue to live in the house as cook, on a reduced salary. She was already in receipt of the Old Age pension and meant to retire in another two or three years anyhow. She did not want to take another position at her time of life. Both the women had accepted his offer of a cash settlement of their legacies, and both were ready to sign a paper waiving any future claim on the estate. Snelgrove, groaning and protesting, was instructed to prepare such a paper and see it properly signed.

As he gained the commanding position among the executors, Solly developed quite a taste for meetings and schemes. He urged that they should lose no time in seeking out the beneficiary of Mrs Bridgetower's trust. He overrode the objections of Snelgrove and Miss Puss, pointing out that the choice might be a difficult and time-taking one. After one meeting, which filled three and a half rancorous hours, he insisted that a vote be taken, giving vast offence to Snelgrove, who had a tongue but no vote. The Dean voted with Solly, and within a week a discreet notice appeared in the *Bellman* explaining what the trust would be empowered to do, and asking those who were interested to make application in writing to Matthew Snelgrove, solicitor to the Bridgetower Trust.

It was a major victory, but it was not achieved quickly. Three months of the precious year of grace had elapsed, and it was the beginning of April when the advertisement appeared.

[TWO]

Considering the care which the executors took in wording their advertisement, it was misinterpreted in a remarkable number of ways. It was clearly stated that the recipient of Mrs Bridgetower's bounty must be female, not over twenty-one or under that age in December of the current year, and a resident of the city of Salterton. Nevertheless four young men proposed themselves; thirty-two applicants were over-age, one of them confessing to forty-six; they hailed from everywhere within the range of *The Bellman*'s circulation. It was made plain that the beneficiary must be a student of the fine arts, and these were defined as painting, sculpture, music, literature and architecture, and reasonable branches thereof. The applicants, who reached a total of eighty-seven, interpreted the word 'reasonable' in a large and generous sense.

There were potters who wanted to study in England, and weavers who wanted to study in Sweden. There was a jeweller who did not want to be a goldsmith or a silversmith, but said she was 'very hot on design'. The nearest thing to a sculptor was a young man who had done some interesting things in soap and saw no reason to go beyond this convenient medium. There were some genuine painters, and one real etcher. There were a few musicians, but all were over-age. The writers supplied depressing, ill-spelled and dirty manuscripts of their work, all of which seemed to be intended for poetry. There was one girl who wanted to be a recreation director and felt that a few years among the folk-schools of Europe would be good both for her and Europe. There were five girls who, representing themselves as writers, were in fact scholars who wanted to use the money for projects of research. There were dancers, one of them specializing in what she called 'modern ballroom and tap'. There was a girl who wanted to perfect herself in the use of the piano-accordion and the electric guitar. All expressed themselves in terms of inordinate ambition unfettered by modesty, and promised great achievement if they should be chosen.

It took the executors three weeks' work to reduce the applications to a short list. Solly could have done it in a night, but the others disapproved of his frivolous way of howling with delight or despair as he read the letters. They insisted that, in fairness to everybody and in keeping with the solemnity of their position, each letter should be read aloud and seriously discussed. This gave Miss Puss great opportunities to reflect on the quality of the young people of today, and to compare them, much to their disfavour, with the young people she had known at the turn of the century. Mr Snelgrove also felt it necessary to say his say on this congenial theme; although he complained tirelessly about the amount of time the proceeding took, he could not keep away from it. Solly explained to him that, as he was not an executor, it was not necessary for him to attend all of these sorting meetings, but the lawyer did not choose to understand the hint. It was clear that he loved it, for it fed his sense of importance. It began to appear, also, that he was proving to the ghost of Mrs Bridgetower that as she had chosen to oppress him, he could suffer with the best of them. He was also ticking up the legal expenses involved in settling her will.

When at last the short list was agreed upon, it was very short indeed. It contained only two names – Nicole John, who wanted to be an architect, and Birgitta Hetmansen, who was a painter.

Miss John exploded within a week. In reply to Snelgrove's letter, asking her to meet the executors for a preliminary talk, there came a reply from her father saying that his daughter's health would make the acceptance of any such benefaction entirely out of the question; he expressed huffy surprise that the executors had not thought of consulting him before entering into a plan to take his daughter from her home. Nothing further was seen or heard of Miss John.

Miss Hetmansen was a different matter. She appeared with a large portfolio of her work, and photographs of pictures which she had sold. She had some newspaper clippings in which her drawings and paintings were given favourable criticism. She had a very good letter from her teacher. She was a dark, personable, quiet girl and she pleased Miss Puss by comporting herself like a lady – not a lady of Miss Puss's own era, but the nearest thing that could be expected in these dark days.

She knew what she wanted. Her desire was to go to Paris, and she could name the teachers with whom she wanted to study, and knew where they were to be found. In all, the executors had three meetings with Miss Hetmansen, and at the last of these her teacher appeared, and spoke of her in high terms. The executors were delighted. It looked as though they had found their swan.

But one day Solly was called to the telephone to speak to Miss Puss. 'We must have a meeting at once,' said she; 'I have terrible news.' When the executors had gathered a few nights later, she brought out this news with a great show of reluctance. She had it on good authority that Miss Hetmansen was not a virgin.

'Does it matter?' said Solly.

'Let us never forget that the Louisa Hansen Bridgetower Trust is the creation and memorial of a woman who stood for everything that was finest in Canadian life,' said Miss Puss. 'We are certainly not going to spend one cent of her money on a hussy.'

'She's not a hussy,' said Solly. 'She's very nice. You said so yourself.'

'Any girl of whom it is possible to say what I have just said, when she is a mere twenty years old, is a hussy,' said Miss Puss. She then fixed the Dean with a bloodshot green eye, and continued, with menace. 'And if this is brought to a vote, don't suppose that you men can overrule me. I'll take it to the courts for a decision, if need be. Perhaps you care nothing for these things, but I knew Louisa's mind as none of you ever did.' She was ready for war. 'If you are afraid to tell this girl that she is not acceptable, and why, I am quite ready to take that duty on myself.'

But it was agreed that this would be unnecessary. Miss Hetmansen's letters and pictures were returned to her by mail, with a note saying that if she heard nothing further from the executors within seven days, it would mean that her application had been unsuccessful.

Miss Hetmansen was not a fool. She knew why she had been

refused. She had succumbed to the importunities of her teacher coolly, and almost absent-mindedly, with a vague feeling that an affair might do something for her colour sense. Apparently all it had done was to lose her a lot of money, and make her teacher untrustworthy as a critic of her work. She did not really care. She had great faith in her talent and she would get to Paris anyway. She was not the gossipy sort, but she remarked to a few people that the Bridgetower Trust, as it had now begun to be called, was primarily a good conduct prize, and strictly for amateurs.

And thus the trustees were left without a candidate, and it was June.

[THREE]

A superstitious belief persists in Canada that nothing of importance can be done in the summer. The sun, which exacts the uttermost from Nature, seems to have a numbing effect upon the works of man. Thus Matthew Snelgrove, while assuring Solly that he was going ahead at full speed in settling Mrs Bridgetower's estate, went to his office later in the morning, and left it earlier in the afternoon, and was quite unavailable at night. During the whole of August he went with his wife to visit her girlhood home in Nova Scotia, where he gave himself up to disapproving contemplation of the sadly unruly behaviour of the sea. Miss Puss Pottinger, according to her custom, went to Preston Springs for two weeks in June, to drink the waters and then, greatly refreshed, she went to a severely Anglican lakeside resort in Muskoka, and there hobnobbed with some Sisters of St John who had a mission nearby. Solly and Veronica went on a leisurely, cheap motor trip, hoping that a change of air might hasten the conception which had, so far, eluded them. They needed a holiday from the obtrusive benevolence of their cook Ethel, who had stayed with them at a reduced salary, and never allowed them for a moment to forget it; they were learning that a faithful family retainer is a two-edged sword. The Dean went to his summer cottage, removed his clerical collar and settled himself to fish by day and read detective stories by night. They were all glad to forget about the Bridgetower Trust.

But early in September Solly woke up one morning with a painful sense that only three months remained in which to make a choice. 'We must get to work at once,' said he to Veronica.

'Is there really such a hurry?' said she. Their holiday had greatly improved her health, and she looked dark, beautiful and serious as she lay by him in the large, old-fashioned bed. 'Would a few months make such a difference?'

'The will says, "Within a calendar year of the date of my death". Nobody would object if we stretched it a little, I suppose, but I am determined that it shall be carried out to the letter. Besides, I want to make old Snelgrove jump. He has a very poor opinion of me, and so has Puss. I'll show them. We'll send an accordion-player or a soap sculptor abroad to study, if need be, but we'll do it in the prescribed way and in the prescribed time.'

'You've become very determined.'

'I have indeed.'

[FOUR]

'If you're absolutely stuck for somebody to squander your Mum's money on, why don't you have a look at Monny Gall?' said Cobbler to Solly. It would be wrong to say that Solly had confided the growing embarrassment of the Trustees to his friend; Cobbler had been insatiably curious about everything connected with the Bridgetower Trust since he heard of it on Christmas Day, and he wormed information out of Solly and Veronica at every opportunity. It fascinated him, he explained, to think of so much lovely money looking for somebody to spend it.

'Who's Monny Gall?'

'If you ever listened to your local radio station you would know. She is the soprano of the Heart and Hope Gospel Quartet, who broadcast on behalf of the Thirteenth Apostle Tabernacle five mornings of the week, from nine-thirty to nine forty-five. I breakfast a bit later than you proletarians, and I never miss the H. & H.'

'Do you mean that it is good?'

'It is very good in its way. That's to say, it primes the pump of sweet self-pity, mingled with tremulous self-reproach and a strong sense of never having had a square deal from life, which passes for religion with a lot of people – housewives mostly. It is run by an unctuous gorilla who calls himself Pastor Sidney Beamis; he dishes out the Hope in a short, moderately disgusting prayer in which he tells God that we're all pretty awful but that the Thirteenth Apostles are having a bash at sainthood. The Heart is supplied by the Quartet, which is composed of his own family and Monny Gall. Pastor Beamis supplies a hollow, gutty bass; his son Wesley weighs in with a capon tenor – all headvoice and tremolo; Ma Beamis has a contralto tone like a cow mooing in a railway tunnel; and Monny Gall has a very nice soprano indeed – sweet, pure, and very naturally produced. You should hear them in *Eden Must Have Been Like Granny's Garden*, or *Ten Baby Fingers and Ten Baby Toes, That Was My Mother's Rosary*.'

'It sounds perfectly filthy.'

'It is. It fills me with perverse glee. But Monny is worth redeeming from this musical hell. She has positively the most promising voice I have ever heard in an untrained singer.'

'Then what is she doing with the H. & H.?'

'Why shouldn't she be with it? Her Ma, who is an extremely formidable old party, is a pillar of the Thirteenth Apostle Tabernacle. She tells Monny to sing for Beamis, and Monny sings. For nothing, what's more. For the greater glory of Beamis.'

'But if she's musical, why does she sing *Granny's Toes*, and so forth?'

'I didn't say she was musical; I said she had a lovely voice. You make the common error of assuming that singers are necessarily musicians. There are people, my dear Bridgetower, who sing because God has made them singers; very often they have no taste at all; they will sing anything, so long as they can open their mouths and give. That's Monny. Caught young, and taught well, I don't know what she mightn't rise to.'

'You appear to be greatly interested in her.'

'I am.'

'Is she pretty, as well as stupid?'

'Bridgetower, you wound me! She isn't pretty and she isn't plain; she's just a girl. But she has an unusual voice, which Beamis is wrecking. You ought to remember her; she's the girl who sang *My Task* at your Mum's funeral.'

'I don't remember anything about her.'

'I do,' said Veronica, who usually kept silent while Solly and Cobbler carried on their long, wandering, often quarrelsome conversations. 'I thought it was a lovely voice. Sweet and pure and rather remote.'

'Exactly. Monny can take a lot of the sting out of *My Task*. It's sheer gift; she hasn't any ideas about it. But something in her voice suggests beauty, and calm, and even reason, when what she is singing is unalloyed boloney.'

'She hasn't put in an application for the Trust.'

'Don't suppose the notion ever occurred to her. She's no climber. Her Ma keeps her down.'

'Are you suggesting that we should write her to consider it? Snelgrove would have a fit!'

'Yes, and if it were thought that I had brought her name up, old Puss would have a fit. She hates me with the one pure passion of her life; she's always trying to get my job away from me. I'm not her notion of a Cathedral organist. But I could get hold of Monny and ask her to put in a bid, if you like.'

'We've got to find somebody, and I don't give a damn who it is.'

'Oh come, Bridgetower; you are speaking of money; don't be bitter.'

'Why shouldn't I be bitter? I'm not greedy, God knows, but I'm human. The income on more than a million dollars, that might have been mine, is to be spent on a stranger. If my mother had left no money at all, I wouldn't have cared. If she had left the bulk of it to a charity, I wouldn't have cared. But she left it as she did to hurt me, and to register a final protest against my marriage. God, you'd think Veronica was a leper, and not just the daughter of a man she and Father quarrelled with twenty years ago. She has done everything that a will can do to humiliate and hurt me. I'm convinced she left me that hundred dollars simply to make the will hard to break. It would serve her right if her money did go to some wretched gospel-howler. If it outraged her cankered old soul in its smug Anglican heaven I'd be glad of it!'

'Oh Solly darling, you'll only make yourself ill,' said Veronica.

'Let him have it out,' said Cobbler. 'Choking back hatred and hurt feelings causes ulcers, high blood-pressure and arthritis. Fact. All the medical books say so. Better get it out in words. It's the inarticulate people, who can't rail against fate, who get nasty diseases. Have a good rage, Bridgetower. Would you care to hit somebody? You may hit me one moderate blow if it would really help. Pretend I'm your late Mum.'

'Don't joke about it,' said Solly. 'Don't you realize we've got to maintain this bloody great house on my cottage salary? That old Ethel hangs over us and pities us and bullies us because we're poor, and makes a favour of staying here when we'd a thousand times rather she went somewhere else. Just try to teach an extravagant old cook something about economy, if you want to break your heart!

And people keep writing to us for money; they think this damned Bridgetower Trust is a grab-bag for every kind of good cause. If we say the Trust can't give, they ask us for something personally. What have we got to give? The estate pays the taxes on this house, but apparently the estate has no obligation to pay its running expenses without a special meeting of trustees. So last week I had to beg the Dean and old Puss for enough money to get the downstairs drain unplugged, and it took an hour and a half of humming and hawing, and suggestions about trying Draino, to get it. I face a future of that kind of thing. A happy prospect, isn't it?'

'As Molly said, it's the Dead Hand,' said Cobbler.

'Dead Hand!' Solly thumped the table. 'It's the live hand, too. This house is part of a trust. During the summer Veronica put away some trinkets and odds and bobs that used to clutter up the mantelpieces. Last week old Puss came in, missed them at once, and insisted that they be put back. And when we boggled at it, she got Snelgrove to phone and say that, legally, we must maintain the house precisely as the Trust received it. Isn't that a sweet situation? She hinted that we ought to put away the Rockingham, but I'm going to use it every day, to spite her. I'll feed the cat off it; that's my right, and I'll do it.'

'Your late Mum was really a corker,' said Cobbler. 'Most people want to ensure that everything they leave will remain untouched, but she has actually found a way to do it. Of course she was singularly fortunate in having an old poison-pot like Puss for a best friend.'

'Well, you see how it is,' said Solly. 'I'm completely tied, and Veronica is put in a most humiliating position. What can we do? The only possible thing is to maintain what dignity we can, and insist that the terms of the will be kept as strictly for everyone else as they are for us. Therefore I insist that somebody be chosen and sent abroad by the Trust within the allotted time, and I do not give a damn who it is or what they are studying, or what rage, despair and misery comes of it. What Mother began, I shall finish, and nothing will come in my way.'

'All right,' said Cobbler; 'I'll talk to Monny Gall.'

[FIVE]

It was well into October before Monica Gall met the executors. She had, prompted by Cobbler, written a letter of application, in which she said simply that she liked singing, and wanted to learn more about it, and mentioned her connection with the Heart and Hope Quartet as evidence that she was serious, and had sung publicly. She gave the name of Pastor Sidney Beamis as a reference.

Miss Puss Pottinger was inclined to dismiss her application on the first reading. Miss Pottinger knew nothing of Pastor Beamis, and had never set foot in the Thirteenth Apostle Tabernacle, but she had a powerful contempt for what she called 'back-street religion'. This condemnation was superficially unjust, for the Tabernacle was in a disused shop on a business street. But it was to the back streets of the religious life that Miss Puss referred; in her Father's house were many mansions, but some of them were in better parts of the Holy City than others; the Thirteenth Apostle Tabernacle obviously belonged in the slums of the spirit.

The Very Reverend Jevon Knapp also disapproved of Monica's sponsorship, but he knew much more about it. He had an eighteenth-century distaste for Enthusiasm in religion, which he was prepared to defend on theological and philosophical grounds. He disliked the untidy beliefs of the Thirteeners, as they were often called. This sect had been founded in the USA by one Myron Coffey, an advertising salesman who found himself, in 1919, forty-five years old and not doing well in the world. It was in that same year that Mr Henry Ford, speaking in a witness box in Chicago, made his great declaration that 'History is bunk'. These apocalyptic words struck fire in Coffey. History was indeed bunk; the seeming division of history into years and eras was an illusion; the whole world of the senses was an illusion, obviously created by the Devil. All mankind of whom any record existed, were in fact coaevals in the realm of the spirit, which was the only real realm. Christ, Moses, Jeremiah – they were all right here, living and breathing beside us, if we could just 'make contact'. That could be done by prayer, searching the Scriptures, and leading a good life; Coffey explained the good life in terms of what he believed his mother's life to have been – unstinting service to others, simple piety, mistrust of pleasure, and no truck with thought or education beyond what was necessary to read the Good Book. All these wonders came to Coffey in a single week, culminating in a revelation that he was the Thirteenth Apostle, destined to spread the good news to mankind. And that news was that the New Jerusalem was right here, if only enough poor souls could 'make contact'. God was here: Christ was now. He fought down any last feeling that perhaps it was Mr Ford who was really the Thirteenth Apostle, and set to work. Thirty-odd years later, in two or three hundred cities in the USA and Canada, a few thousand Thirteeners continued his mission.

Dean Knapp knew all this, and thought poorly of it. He also had a poor opinion of the Thirteeners' local shepherd, Pastor Beamis. The Dean had met him, and thought him an ignoramus, and possibly a rogue, as well. He was professionally obliged to think as well of everybody as possible, but he confided to Mrs Knapp that Scripture came to his aid in the matter of Beamis; did not *Leviticus* xxi 18 expressly forbid the priesthood to 'he that hath a flat nose'? And had not Beamis the flat, bun-like, many times broken nose of the ex-pugilist? Mrs Knapp warned him not to speak such frivolities in the hearing of those who might not understand; the Dean's passion for Biblical jokes had put him in hot water many times. But she knew very well what her husband meant; there was about Beamis a hairiness, a clumsiness, a physically unseemly quality which sat ill upon a spiritual leader. The Jews of the Old Testament had done wisely to forbid the priesthood to grotesques.

It gave Solly much satisfaction to override Miss Puss and the Dean. Monica Gall should not be passed over because she belonged to a sect for which they felt a Pharisaical distaste, said he, and thereby gave offence to the Dean, who was not accustomed to be called a Pharisee by young men of twenty-seven. He had to swallow it, and after a good deal of haggling it was decided that Monica should be interviewed.

But should they not have some expert advice, asked the Dean. They had sought counsel outside their own group about Miss Hetmansen's work; could they judge a singer unaided? By a little juggling Solly was able to lead the Dean into proposing Humphrey Cobbler as adviser to the Trustees in matters of music; Miss Puss did not like it, but she did not oppose the Dean as she would have opposed Solly in such a suggestion. She contented herself with saying that Cobbler was probably a capable musician, though a detestable man.

Thus it was that on a Thursday night in mid-October the executors and their solicitor gathered in the drawing-room of the Bridgetower house, and there received Mr and Mrs Alfred Gall, their daughter, Monica, and Pastor Sidney Beamis.

Pastor Beamis had not been invited, but he was the first to stride into the room.

'Well, well, good evening Reverend Knapp,' he cried, seizing the Dean's hand in his clammy, pulpy paws; 'this is certainly a wonderful thing you fine folks are proposing to do for our little girl. Yes, and considering you're all Church of England people it shows a degree of inter-faith fellowship which is more than warming – more than warming. Now I know you weren't expecting me, and I'm not going to butt in, but because I have watched Monny grow, so to speak, from a gawky kid into a lovely girl, and because I think I may say that it has been my privilege, under God, to humbly have coaxed along her talent, I just couldn't stay away. I just had to be here.' He dropped his voice, and whispered to Knapp in a priest-to-priest tone – 'Family aren't much in the way of talkers; thought I might be able to steer 'em a little.' He gave the Dean an understanding leer, and patted him on the back. The Dean reclaimed his hand and wiped it on his handkerchief.

Pastor Beamis was so striking a figure that he temporarily obscured the Galls. He wore the full regimentals of a Thirteener shaman. His suit was of grey flannel, much in need of pressing; he had on a wing collar, and a clergyman's stock, which was of a shrill paddy green; the ensemble was completed by a pair of scuffed sports shoes in brown and white, above which could be seen socks in Argyll design. Inside these garments was a body which had won him the name of Chimp during his days in the ring; his face was large, baggy and bore blatant signals of hope, cheer and unremitting forgiveness.

The Galls, thought Solly, might have posed for a picture of Mr and Mrs Jack Sprat. Alfred Gall was thin to the point of being cadaverous, stooped, pale and insignificant. His wife was covered with that loose, liquid fat which seems to sway and slither beneath the skin, and she, because she wore too tight a corset, wheezed whenever she made the slightest effort. She had a look of nervous good-nature, and every few minutes she eased her false teeth, which seemed to pain her; indeed, as the evening wore on she began to suck air audibly, as though her dentures were hot.

Monica, as Cobbler had said, was neither pretty nor plain, though she was of a trim figure. She was plainly dressed, as became a Thirteener, and it was apparent to the X-ray eye of Miss Puss that the disqualification which had brought about the fall of Birgitta Hetmansen did not apply here.

Conversation proceeded uneasily. It was necessary, first of all, to make it clear to Pastor Beamis that Monica had not been summoned to receive a large sum of money. This task fell to Snelgrove, who found it congenial. It was then explained to the Galls how the Trust was expected to work.

'If your daughter should become the beneficiary, it would give her a most unusual opportunity to pursue her musical studies,' said the Dean.

'Yeah, I see,' said Mrs Gall, and fidgeted with the handle of her purse, sucking air painfully. 'It'd take her away from home, though.' She had chosen to sit on a low sofa, and appeared to be suffering discomfort from her corset, which had visibly ridden upward.

'Never had much of a chance m'self,' said Alfred Gall. 'Workin' since I was sixteen. Never known much else but work, I guess.' He laughed a short hollow laugh, like a man making light of an incurable disease.

Pastor Beamis was right; the Galls were not great talkers. Nor, it was soon clear, were they among those who eagerly embrace good fortune. They thought it might be nice if their daughter had a chance to study music abroad, but in the depths of their hearts it was a matter of indifference to them. The Pastor supplied all the enthusiasm. He talked a great deal about the opportunities a singer enjoyed to do the Lord's work, by uplifting people and turning their minds to the finer things of life; in his own work he had been able to observe the splendid harvest of souls which could be reaped through the Ministry of Music. He pleaded eloquently with the Galls not to deny their daughter the chance that was being offered to her to be a force for good in the world. It was at this point that Solly thought it necessary to correct the balance of power.

'We haven't made up our minds about Miss Gall, you know,' said he. 'We have considered her application carefully, and this interview is merely to find out more about her. None of us has heard her sing; she may not be the person we are looking for at all.'

'You haven't heard her on the Heart and Hope?' said Beamis. He was very merry about this. 'You folks must be late risers. Certainly is nice to be some people! Our little programme enjoys a very high rating locally, you know. And of course we tape it and broadcast it from seven other stations, beside the local one. It's by far the biggest religious independent in the province – barring metropolitan city broadcasts, of course. Monny's voice is known – and loved, as I can show letters to prove – by close to twenty thousand daily listeners.'

'What is she paid for that work?' asked Miss Puss.

'The Heart and Hope is not a paid quartet. We merely announce that we are unpaid on the air, and freewill offerings come in by every mail. Silver coins – O, it would touch your heart, some of them – and dollar bills and quite a few fives and tens. The law forbids us to ask for money on the air, but it comes, all the same. And every cent goes into the Tabernacle treasury.'

'You are the treasurer?' said the Dean, who could not resist it.

'I take care of the financial end, and of course the books are open to inspection by any of our members, any time they choose to see them.' Pastor Beamis fixed the Dean with a grimace in which brotherly love, transparent honesty and sorrow were mingled.

'You have some other work, then?' said Solly to Monica.

'She's a clerk at the plant where her Dad works,' said Beamis. 'In the Costing Department, Monny did very well in Commercial at High. But you're wrong when you say you haven't heard Monny; she sang at your dear Mother's funeral. A lovely little Classic – *My Task* – sweet thing. And did you realize that Monny had never seen or heard of it until eighteen hours before she went on the air – sorry, before the sad occasion? Mr Cobbler brought it to her the night before; she ran through it a coupla times with him; sang it perfectly at three the next afternoon. Monny's quite a little trouper. Get up anything at short notice and turn in a fine performance. Not many singers can do that. You've heard her, and you didn't even notice!' Pastor Beamis laughed chidingly.

'Our attention was elsewhere,' said Miss Puss, and the Pastor's rubber face immediately assumed an expression of understanding and condolence; but he was not abashed, which was what she had hoped for.

'I think we should hear Miss Gall now,' said Solly. 'I'll ask Mr Cobbler to come in.'

[SIX]

'Well?' said Solly to the executors, when at last Beamis had herded his charges out of the house and disappeared, still talking, down the walk. 'What did you think of her?'

'There is no question in my mind that she is a very nice girl,' said the Dean. 'It seemed to me that she handled herself modestly and with dignity in a difficult situation. But whether she is the girl we are looking for is very much an open question. I'm not impressed by her parents, or by that man, who seems to be a dominating influence in her life – if I may make such a remark without being accused of Phariseeism,' he added, cocking an eye at Solly.

'I suppose it's ability, rather than character, that we're looking for,' said Solly, avoiding the glance and looking at Snelgrove.

'Are they ever found apart?' said the lawyer.

'Very often, in the arts, I believe. Are we going to hold it against the girl that her parents are stupid and dominated by a quack evangelist? I thought she seemed intelligent and pleasant. If she can really profit by the kind of training we are able to give her – I should say, that we can pay for – isn't that the main thing?'

'Unless you believe that the girl is a genius, and so beyond the usual rules of probability, you must certainly take these other things into account,' said the Dean. 'You can educate her beyond her parents, and make her into something that they might not recognize, but you will not really raise her very far. You can polish and mount a pebble, but it remains a pebble. I do not blame the girl, of whom I know no more than the rest of you, but it is plain that she is being exploited by that creature Beamis; she sings in his quartet, which consists otherwise of his own family, and which I happen to know coins money. If she were a person of real character – more character than her parents, for instance – would she put up with that?'

'She's only twenty, Mr Dean,' said Solly, 'and, saving your reverence, it is not easy for a very young person to rebel against a clergyman who has full parental support. It seems to me that her voice is the real clue to the problem. What did you think of it?'

'I really can't say,' said the Dean. 'I was so embarrassed by the things she sang. I don't pretend to a deeply informed taste in music, but really –!'

'I can't quite agree,' said Miss Puss, who had sat in uncharacteristic silence since the Galls left. 'I was greatly moved by her singing of Tosti's *Good-Bye!* – a song I have not heard in many, many years. I suppose I am the only person here who recalls that it was the favourite ballad of Queen Victoria. Unfashionable now, possibly, but truly touching. Once, many years ago, I heard Melba sing it. And, do you know, this girl reminded me uncannily of Melba? Did you feel that?'

She had turned to Snelgrove. He had never heard Melba, but he knew she had been intensely patriotic during the First Great War, and was therefore an artist of the highest rank, so he frowned in a critical fashion and replied, 'Not quite Melba, perhaps, but I felt there was a smack of Clara Butt.'

This remark set Miss Puss and the lawyer off in a competition of recalling all the great singers they had heard, and as neither had wide experience this quickly became all the great singers they had heard of, whose names they brought up with apparent casualness; they did not say they had heard these queens of song, but they were not unwilling that others should think so; in charity it may be assumed that they had heard them on the gramophone. The names of Emma Eames, Amelita Galli-Curci, Geraldine Farrar, Louise Homer, Luisa Tetrazzini and Ernestine Schumann-Heink were used very freely, and startling comparisons drawn, without much regard for whether these ladies had been sopranos or contraltos. This cultivated pow-wow did much to raise the spirits of Miss Puss and Mr Snelgrove, and to give them, for the first time, a sense that they were patrons of art and fountains of culture. When the lawyer had scored heavily by dragging in 'our great Canadian diva, Madame Albani, whom I was once lucky enough to hear in Montreal' Solly thought that this had gone far enough.

'Perhaps we should return to the present day and hear what the one expert among us thinks of Monica Gall's voice,' said he. Cobbler, who had remained at the piano, dug vigorously into his hair with his fingers, until it stood on end like the wool of a Hottentot. Then he fixed the executors with his bright black eyes.

'Nice voice,' said he. 'Nice tone; well-placed, really, considering that she's had no training at all. But that's the trouble, you see: maybe we've heard all there is. Maybe nothing further would come, however much you trained it. Oh, that's not quite fair; it would be bound to develop a little bit, but who can say how much? Promising, probably. But how can you tell? We didn't really hear enough.'

'Then why did you not ask to hear more?' said Snelgrove. He liked an expert to behave like an expert, and not temporize.

'We could have listened to her for another hour without learning anything more than we did. Her music was terrible. I knew how things stood as soon as she opened her portfolio; it was jampacked with that awful cheap music printed on grey paper. All tripe. *Good-Bye!* was her star piece; I suppose Beamis thinks it's a classic. So it is, in the musical hell he and the Heart and Hope Quartet inhabit. To find out what her voice is really like, you'd have to work with her for a few months – increase her range, give her something to sing that would show what she could do, and generally explore the possibilities.'

'That's not very helpful,' said Miss Puss.

'I'm afraid it isn't. But it's honest. There's one thing to be said in the girl's favour. She's stood out against some very bad musical influences; her only teacher, I understand, is an aunt who plays the piano a little. And the Beamis association is abominable; couldn't imagine anything more calculated to wreck a voice and debauch a singer's taste. Yet, the fact is that the girl sings with a good deal of taste and a nice feeling for the words, considering the stuff she's singing. It must be native to her, though where she gets it I can't imagine. You're dead right, Miss Pottinger; she really did tear off old *Good-Bye!* with quite a sense of style, and it's not the easiest song in the world. There may be something there, if you want to dig for it.'

'We haven't any time for digging,' said Solly. 'We're desperate; the income on something like a million dollars has to be spent on somebody, beginning not later than next December 23. Can't we get some clearer opinion than what you've said?'

'Not from me,' said Cobbler. 'I can't square a flat Yes or No with my professional honesty; if I say she's no good I may be wronging you and the girl, and if I say she's a wonder the odds are just as strong that I am wrong. Certainly, if it were a question of some lessons with me, I'd say go ahead. I'd be happy to get such a pupil. But you are going to spend such a lot of money; you've got to show big results or look silly. If you want another opinion, I know where you can get one.'

'Yes?'

'Next month Sir Benedict Domdaniel is conducting two concerts in Toronto, on his way back from Australia and the States. He'll be there for ten days or so, rehearsing. If you like, I'll write to his agent and ask if he'll hear the girl, and give you his word on her.'

The effect of this was an even greater tonic to Miss Puss and Snelgrove than the mention of Melba had been. This was culture indeed – to enlist the opinion of one of the greatest conductors in the world who was also – this weighed heavily – a British knight! Why were they trifling with a cathedral organist when such distinction lay within their grasp? Condescendingly, as people used to hob-nobbing with gifted knights, they asked Cobbler to make the necessary arrangements, and of course to inquire, tactfully, what Sir Benedict's fee would be for such an interview.

It had not occurred to them to offer Cobbler any fee whatever.

[SEVEN]

The pattern upon which the Bridgetower Trust was to operate had already established itself before the Trust was officially in being – for

Snelgrove made it very clear that until the probate of Mrs Bridgetower's will the Trust had no funds, and a trust without funds was a mockery. The pattern was a simple one: nothing could be done without prolonged discussion, in which Miss Puss and Solly were certain to be opposed, with the Dean trying to keep peace and advocate common sense, and Snelgrove making all the trouble possible to an expert who has great influence but no vote. The seemingly simple matter of getting Monica Gall away to Toronto for an interview with Sir Benedict Domdaniel became, in their hands, an elaborate and vexatious manoeuvre.

The Dean thought that the Trust should pay her fare on the train, but need not necessarily pay for her meals while she was absent. Snelgrove said that as the Trust had no funds, it could not pay for anything. Solly pointed out that the Trust had already spent money, which Snelgrove's firm had advanced, on repairing drains in the Bridgetower house. Snelgrove countered by saying that he could justify such an expenditure before a court, but he could not justify spending any money on a candidate for the Trust's bounty who might prove, in the end, to be unsuccessful. Miss Puss felt that it was undesirable to encourage Monica to hope for success by paying her fare, but that the Trust ought to pay the fare of an older woman who would accompany her to Toronto, as a chaperone. The Trust would be in a very bad position, she pointed out, if any harm befell Monica while she was on a journey to a large city, undertaken at the request of the Trust. She was herself prepared to go with the girl, and to remain with her during her interview with the great man; Monica had shown herself to be a poor talker, and somebody who was not awed by greatness should certainly be on hand to see that her chances were not spoiled by sheer social ineptitude. Solly, out of spite, agreed, but said that if anybody went with Monica it should certainly be an accompanist, and recommended Cobbler for that task; his wife, Veronica, would be prepared to drive the two of them to Toronto in their car, and serve as moral watchdog; the Trust could defray the expenses of the motor trip and still be money ahead. It took an evening of wrangling to reach a deadlock on this question.

Another evening was consumed in haggling about Sir Benedict Domdaniel's fee. His agent had written to Cobbler saying that the great man could see Miss Gall, and would send a written opinion to the Trust, and that his charge for an audition would be two hundred and fifty dollars. Miss Puss was outraged, and spoke to Cobbler as though he himself had demanded this shocking sum; he replied, with spirit, that men like Domdaniel asked big fees for auditions simply in order that they should not be plagued by people who were not serious; he added some ill-considered words about amateurs, which gave deep offence. Snelgrove refused utterly to advance money for such a purpose. And so, after a very long and heated argument, it was decided that if Monica Gall herself could raise Domdaniel's fee, and her own journey-money, she could risk it on her chances. The Trust asked Cobbler to put this proposal to her, and he refused flatly to do it, adding with heat that if the Trust meant to be cheap, he was not going to be the goat for them. In the end, Snelgrove was instructed to offer her this unique opportunity to invest in her own future, by letter.

The Trust was somewhat astonished to receive a reply, by return of post, in which Monica said that she would be glad to pay her own expenses, and thanked them for the chance. It was a very good letter, typed and expressed in the dry language of business, and it made Solly and the Dean, at least, feel that Monica had not revealed the best side of herself at the earlier interview.

[EIGHT]

The date of Monica's meeting with Sir Benedict Domdaniel was set for November the first. On the fifth of the month Cobbler received the following letter, which he read aloud that evening to the assembled Trust.

Dear Humphrey Cobbler:

It was good to hear from you again. I recall with pleasure working with you during the Three Choirs Festival of 1937, and I hope that all goes well with you here.

Now, about your protégée, Miss Monica Gall. I had meant to give her an hour, at most, but as she has probably told you, we worked for nearly three. It took quite a time to get at her, for somebody – I believe she said one of the lady members of your Trust – had filled her full of nonsense about how to behave herself with me. She began by singing the two Handel songs you had hastily primed her with, but they told very little, as you can imagine. Then she sang Tosti's *Good-Bye!* which I had honestly never expected to hear sung seriously again on this earth, and did quite well with it. I asked her if she knew *The Lost Chord*, meaning to be facetious, and she shamed me by pulling a tattered copy out of her satchel and singing it quite seriously and nicely. Then she sang a lot of trash which is apparently in her wireless repertoire.

After this we had a talk, and I was strongly impressed by her sincerity, and absolute simplicity: She tells me she sings because she always has done so, and likes it, but it had never occurred to her to make a career of it. We were quite matey by this time, and she told me a good deal about her home, and her work, and then I took off my coat and she took off her shoes, which were much too tight, and we did some scales and exercises, and I found that with a bit of encouragement she has roughly twice the voice she has been using, with lots more to come.

What surprised me most was that she plays the piano well – facility and quite nice natural taste – but terrible stuff. It seems an aunt taught her. She played what she called *Dance, Micawber*, and instead of being a Dickensian medley by some lesser Percy Grainger it was Saint-Saens' *Danse Macabre*. When I mentioned Bach she looked prim, and I gather there is some queer religion behind her, for whom the classics of church music spell Popery or Pride. I think this is the clue to the girl; a real natural talent has been overlaid by a stultifying home atmosphere and cultural malnutrition.

In my opinion she is well worth any encouragement your Trust or whatever it is can give her. The voice is good – quite good enough to be worth proper training – though as you know it takes a year or eighteen months of work before the real nature of a voice emerges, and any serious predictions about a career can be made. But if this girl is not a singer of exceptional quality, she is certainly a musician; she has done a great deal under what appear to be extremely unfavourable conditions. I repeat, the great thing that seems to be wrong with her, considered as a possible artist, is that she has lived for twenty years in circumstances which are not discouraging to art – we see plenty of that – but in which art in any of its forms is not even guessed at. I discount, you understand, all this pseudo-religious twaddle she has been exposed to – music in the service of cant. She seems to have come through that so far without any irreparable harm. But she really doesn't know a damned thing.

If you can get her three or four years of training, or anything approaching it, do so by all means. If she is coming to England send her to me; I will be glad to give any advice or supervision I can.

You finally *did* marry that beautiful mezzo from Presteigne, did you not? Molly Ellis? I have the warmest recollections of her in *Gerontius*. Give her my best wishes.

Yours very sincerely,
BENEDICT DOMDANIEL

'Thank God,' said Solly when the letter was finished; 'that seems to settle that. We've found our phoenix.'

[THREE]

Monica put off inviting George Medwall to her farewell party until the day before it was to take place. In this, as in so many other things in life, she was trying to eat her cake and have it too. To eat it, by inviting the young man whom she liked best among those she knew: to have it, by pretending that she might, after all, not ask him, thus being fully loyal to Ma and the Thirteeners. No wonder, then, that the cake stuck in her throat and that when she came at last to invite him she did so in an off-hand and almost cold fashion.

George did not seem to mind. He was a realist, and he knew that a party dominated by Ma Gall and composed chiefly of young Thirteeners would have nothing to attract him but Monny herself. Monny attracted him powerfully. They were both employed by Consolidated Adhesives and Abrasives, the biggest industry in Salterton, and still called, by those who remembered its humble nineteenth-century beginnings, the Glue Works. George was a foreman with a department of his own, and Monica was a clerk in the costing department; they worked in separate buildings, a quarter of a mile apart, but he contrived to catch sight of her, if not actually to speak to her, every day. If Monica was to leave Salterton for several years, George meant to see her whenever he could, under whatever circumstances.

She approached him in the cafeteria, when they had both finished lunch.

'Sure I'll be there,' said George. 'We've still got fifteen minutes before one. Let's go for a walk.'

Bundled up against the sharp December weather, and under an iron sky, they walked up and down beside the blank wall of a large building in which the boiling-vats were housed. It was not precisely a lovers' lane, but they were together.

'I'm sorry to give you such short notice,' said Monica, who was ashamed of the way in which her invitation had been phrased.

'That's okay,' said George. 'I guess it wasn't very easy for you to ask me at all.'

'Well – you know how it is.'

'Sure. Don't think it worries me. But I'm certainly glad you're getting away from all that, Monny.'

'What do you mean by "all that"?'

'You know. Beamis, and the Heart and Hope. All that stuff.'

'They've been very good to me. I wouldn't have had this chance if I'd never been heard on that programme.'

'I know. But you're moving up into a bigger league, now. And about time. You've got a chance for some first-class training. It'll make a big difference.'

'It's not going to turn me against people who have been good to me, if that's what you mean.'

'Nothing would do that, Monny. You're not that kind. But you see what I mean, don't you? You'll be a long way off, and on your own. Not such a strong home influence; not so much religion. A bigger world altogether.'

'Oh, is that it? My home influence doesn't quite come up to your standards, is that it?'

'Now, Monny, don't take me up wrong. I never said a word against your home. But you know – it'll be different.'

'You'd better not say anything against my home.'

'No, no; I was just trying to be realistic about what's happened.'

'Oh, realistic! You always want to be realistic; it's your favourite word.'

'I guess so; I've tried to be realistic about my own life. It only makes sense.'

'I know. And it's made you the youngest foreman in the plant. But not the best liked, if you care to know.'

'I can't help that.'

'You could if you wanted to. But you hadn't been a foreman six weeks before you came down like a ton of bricks on senior men that were here long before anybody'd ever heard of you. Talked to them in a way they'll never forget or forgive. I suppose that was realistic.'

'As it so happens, it was. But let's forget that; I don't want to talk about those old dead-beats now.'

'They weren't dead-beats.'

'Now Monny; it was before you ever came to the plant. How do you know?'

'Some of them were Dad's friends. That's how I know.'

'Be reasonable. Can I run my department by letting fellows get away with murder, on the chance that they're friends of somebody in another department, who may have a daughter that I'll get to know some day? Why, I didn't even know your Dad then. And I won't pretend it would have made any difference, if I had.'

'Oh? My Dad's an old dead-beat, too, I suppose?'

'Say, what are we fighting about, anyway?'

'We're not fighting. But I just can't stand the way you brush aside everybody that hasn't got ahead as fast as you have. They're human, too, you know. I know them, and Dad's one of them. They haven't all had your chances. Dad's been working since he was sixteen; work's all he's ever known –'

'Sure. He's told me about it.'

'And just what do you mean by that?'

'That's your Dad's favourite routine. Work at sixteen. Work ever since. Never known anything but work. Excuses everything, I suppose.'

'Excuses what, may I ask?'

'Oh, nothing. Forget it.'

'No, I won't forget it. Come on, George. What does it excuse? You can't hint like that about my Dad and then just brush it off. – What are you laughing at?'

'I'm laughing at you, Monny. You know, you ought to make a fine singer. You've got the temperament.'

'Meaning what?'

'You're what's called a romantic. You see everything in full Technicolor all the time. Feelings before facts, that's you. But it's time somebody knocked some sense into your head.'

'Go on.'

'You swallow all that stuff about your Dad. Fine. Every kid believes what his father tells him, and so he should, but there's got to be a day when he makes his own judgement. Your Dad's okay, I guess; I don't know him very well. But the reason he's still pushing a broom here in the plant is simply because he can't do anything better. There's no disgrace in it. But let's not say it's because he's had a raw deal, eh? He's had the best deal he could get from life. Lots of fellows started even with him. One of them was Thurston, the plant manager –'

'Who climbed and clawed and lickspittled and backstabbed his way to the top. Your hero, I suppose. A realist.'

'Now Monny, don't go in for that stuff about everybody who's a success being a bastard. That's for failures of sixty; not for kids of twenty.'

'My Dad, George Medwall, is not a failure.'

'Monny, you're crazy. I wasn't talking about your Dad. But I will, as you seem to have him on the brain. If your Dad and your Mother are your ideals in life, don't take this money they're offering you to go away and study; stay right where you are. You've got all you want in life; stick with it.'

'You leave my family out of this! You talk like that awful old Miss Pottinger; you'd think she found me frozen to the bottom of a garbage can after a long winter. I'm proud of my family. Proud!'

'Sure; sure.'

'And don't treat me like a fool. Don't take that soothing tone. You make me sick, with your superior ways. What have you got to be superior about?'

'Monny, this doesn't make any sense.'

'Yes it does. Now let me tell you something, and don't ever forget it, George, because I mean every word. If there's one thing I hate in this world, it's ingratitude and disloyalty. And nothing, absolutely nothing, is going to make me disloyal and ungrateful. This sudden good luck isn't going to make a fool of me.'

'Nothing could make a fool of you, Monny. But don't call it luck. People only get chances if they're ready for them. It's not luck. It's character.'

'Loyalty's character, and so is decency. So don't talk realism to me if it just means being sniffy about my family and friends. I know them a lot better than you do. What makes you think you have a right to talk to me like this?'

Here was George's golden opening, but his realism did not extend far enough to reveal it to him. So he took it as a rebuke, and they walked the length of the boiler building in uneasy silence. George did not know what he should do, but he decided that it might help if he ate a small – a very small – portion of crow.

'I guess I've said too much. If you want to disinvite me to your party, Monny, go ahead.'

'If my family gives you such a pain, perhaps that would be best,' said Monica, hoping furiously that he would urge her to relent. But

George had a terrible trick of believing that people always meant what they said. And at this unlucky moment, the one o'clock whistle blew.

'I guess I'd better say good-bye, then,' said George; 'since I'm not to see you tomorrow night.'

'Good-bye, George,' said Monica, giving him her hand; 'and lots of luck.'

And thus she parted from the only man whom she had ever been disposed to consider as a suitor. Though George was grieved, he did his afternoon's work with his accustomed thoroughness, but Monica spoiled several important sheets of figures, and if she had not been leaving anyway her boss would have spoken sharply to her.

[TWO]

At supper that night, Mrs Gall asked Monica, 'bolt outright' as she herself would have described it, whether George Medwall was to be expected at the farewell party. When Monica said that he would not be there, and let it be thought that she had decided not to ask him, Ma Gall expressed great satisfaction.

'Glad you come to your senses at last about that fella,' said she. 'Now you're going away is a good time to break off with him. I never had any time for him myself, and your Dad'll back me up on that.'

'Foreman at twenty-eight,' said Mr Gall. 'Gone up like the rocket; he'll come down like the stick.'

They continued their discussion of George for some time, congratulating their daughter on her astuteness in having seen through him – a fellow who set himself up to give lip to men old enough to be his father, and one who, by accepting a foreman's job, had automatically removed himself from the jurisdiction of the union. Mr Gall was a great partisan of the union, which was a very quiet and conservative affair at the CA&A, but which he liked to think of as a bulwark against unimaginable tyrannies. George, being outside the union, was certainly not to be trusted; he had lined himself up with the bosses. Mr Gall knew all of these bosses personally, and was known by them, and on the human level, so to speak, he got on well with them and even liked them: but in another compartment of his mind they figured as faceless, bowelless, jackbooted tyrants, and he was pledged to thwart them in every possible way. George was on the wrong side of the fence.

For Mrs Gall, George summed up what she most feared in a young man who might become a son-in-law. He was not a Thirteener; he was not even a church-goer and felt no shame about saying so. He did not drink, he saved his money, and he was civil; she gave him all that. But there was in him a quality of ambition which disquieted her; it prevented him from being what she called likable. Furthermore, it had been clear during his two or three brief visits to the house that he thought of her only as Monica's mother, and Mrs Gall thought of herself very much as a Character, with a capital letter. It was as a Character that she liked to meet the world, and young people especially.

Monica had heard all that she could bear about George's shortcomings by the time supper was over, so she quickly washed the dishes – it was her night – and got out of the house, saying that she was going to Aunt Ellen's for a while. All the way there she reproached herself for having managed her talk with George so badly, and thought of clever defences of his character which she could have opposed to her parents' criticism – if she had dared. But it is never easy for children to defend their friends against disapproving parents.

Why had she flown out at George, turning everything he said to bitterness? It was not a lovers' quarrel, for she and George were certainly not lovers. He had never even kissed her, though once or twice it had been a near thing. If she had known it, George's realism was of the sort which says that a fellow does not kiss a girl unless he is serious about her; seriousness means an engagement, and he would not be engaged until he had enough money saved to marry; to kiss a girl to whom he could not offer marriage would be to trifle with her, not merely emotionally, but economically, and George's whole moral system was rooted in his conception of economics. But George and Monica worked upon each other as only lovers are supposed to do; she had more than once detected beneath his words a criticism of her family, and that she would not tolerate.

It was her old problem of wanting to have her cake and eat it. She felt, and despised herself for feeling, critical of her father and mother, of her older sister Alice, of Pastor and Mrs Beamis and their son, Wesley, of the whole Thirteener connection, for everything about them ran contrary to her great dream of life. While it had remained a dream, impossible of realization, she had been able to keep that criticism in its place. She had prayed for strength against it, and now and then her prayer seemed to be answered. But this Bridgetower

Trust business had upset her whole life. It had suddenly brought the dream out of the realm of the utterly impossible into the realm of the remotely possible. That afternoon with Sir Benedict Domdaniel had been at once the most elevating and releasing experience of her life, and at the same time ruinous to the balance which she had established between dream and reality. Since then criticism of her family and her circumstances had raged within her, and when George had hinted at what was so tumultuously present in her mind she had been unable to keep her head. It was as though he had read her intolerable, inadmissible thoughts, and dared to share them.

She would get advice from Aunt Ellen. After all, Aunt Ellen was responsible for much that was wrong with her.

Aunt Ellen was not at home, and she let herself into the little stucco cottage with the key which Aunt Ellen had given her years ago, when she was twelve. The tiny living-room was as neat as such a cluttered room could be. Monica switched on the lamp with the shade of pleated rose silk, and went at once to the bookshelves, from which she took a large, worn volume, and settled herself on the sofa with it.

Aunt Ellen's house, to anyone less accustomed to it than Monica, spoke all that could be known about Miss Ellen Gall. She was Mr Gall's older sister, and in her younger days had been considered a 'high-flyer' by many who knew her. She had been a milliner, during the last era in which such work was done in individual shops, at Ogilvie's, which in those remote days had been an important 'ladies' ready-to-wear' in Salterton. She still sold hats there, though she no longer made them; indeed, for many years she had been forelady of Ogilvie's hat department. From a pretty girl she had grown into a pretty woman, and latterly into a woman almost old, but still soft and pleasing, and very ready to smile. Her house, with all its odds and ends, was the house of a pretty woman.

But Ellen Gall had had a soul above hats, devoted to them as she was. She had played the piano with facility, and as the Galls had been Baptists before Mr Gall and his wife took up with the Thirteeners, Ellen had found herself organist and leader of the choir at the smallest and least important of Salterton's Baptist churches. She had never fully mastered the instrument, and she still used the pedals sparingly and tentatively, but she had played the organ, almost every Sunday, for more than twenty-five years. What she played was the piano music which she thought suitable to solemn occasions, and with an occasional gentle kick at the tonic or the dominant in the pedals she managed to the complete satisfaction of the church, which did not, by the way, pay her anything for this service. She had, at various times, given lessons in playing the piano, at fifty cents for a half-hour. But of late, when people had taken up the fad of Conservatory examinations and did not care for the sweetly pretty drawing-room music she liked, she had had no new pupils.

There are great musicians in the world who do not live in rooms which speak so decisively of a life given to music as the living-room of Miss Ellen Gall. There was no picture which was not musical in theme. Over the piano hung a collotype of an extremely artistic girl with a birdsnest of dark hair, playing the 'cello to a rapt old man with a white beard; it was called *Träumerei*. Over the bookcase was a picture of Beethoven, much handsomer than life, conducting the Rasumovsky quartet with great spirit. A little plaster bust with a broken nose, said to be Mendelssohn, sat on top of the rosewood upright piano. And everywhere on the walls were little pictures of opera singers, cut out of magazines and framed.

There was only one picture without musical significance in the room, and that was of a middle-aged man, somewhat bald, wearing rimless pince-nez. He had been Miss Ellen's fiancé, a high school teacher, and a man of great cultivation, for he had once had a poem printed in *Saturday Night*. They had been engaged for many years, waiting for his mother to die; it was agreed between them that their marriage would be too great a blow for the old lady to sustain, and they had considerately spared her. But when, at last, she did die, the high school teacher took a chill a few weeks later, and himself died of consumption the following spring. He had made Miss Ellen his heir, and she had moved his books and all his furniture into her house. But he had made her a legacy of something much greater; he had left her with the consciousness of having been loved deeply and gratefully (if not very adventurously), and this romance had sweetened Miss Ellen's life as many a marriage has failed to do. In her crowded, fusty little house she lived with her own kind of music, and with memories which made up even for the obvious decline of Ogilvie's.

The book which Monica took down was *The Victor Book of the Opera*, which the gramophone company had produced in 1917 to demonstrate the wonders of opera to a public which knew little of that art form – and also to let it be known what recordings of opera were available. Most of the singers whose pictures appeared in it, with elaborate coiffures, or richly whiskered, were dead; the costumes in which they were represented might appear, to a modern taste, to be funny and unbecoming. But to Monica, as to Aunt Ellen, it was still the bible of a great art with which they had no direct connection, and at which they dimly guessed. They listened to the Saturday afternoon broadcasts from the Metropolitan, of course, but in the theatre of their minds it was these dead ones of the past who appeared – Nordica, Emma Eames, Scotti, Caruso, and the brothers de Reske; from the fruity voice which served as guide to the broadcasts they heard of new singers, and new costumes and settings, but these never had the reality of the pictures in the book. This was the key to a great, glorious, foreign world; but it was a key which unlocked, not the door, but a spy-hole in it. And now, breathtakingly, the Bridgetower Trust seemed to have opened the door itself.

It was very like – well, rather like – another book in Aunt Ellen's library, which she and Monica had both read with deep enjoyment more than once. This was *The First Violin*, by Jessie Fothergill; in it, a humble English girl with a lovely voice was engaged as companion to a wealthy old lady who took her to Germany to study; and there she had learned to sing from the magnetic – but daemonic and sardonic – von Francius, and had engaged in a long and sweetly agonizing romance with one Courvoisier, who was first violin in the orchestra, a man of mystery, and, in the end (for this was an English novel and such a dénouement was inevitable) had proved to be a German nobleman, disguised as a musician for reasons highly creditable to himself and shaming to everybody else. It all took place in the real Germany, of course, the Germany before the end of the century, when Germans were terribly musical and cultured and even more romantic than the French. Domdaniel would do very well as von Francius, though he was rather too affable for a genuinely daemonic genius, and showed quite ordinary braces when he took off his coat. And who was to be the First Violin; who was to be Courvoisier?

It was awful to admit the thought, but how would it be possible to bring Courvoisier home to meet Ma? In the book he seemed to be a Catholic; wasn't there some mention of a chapel in his ancestral Schloss? No Protestant would want a church right in the house. Ma would simply fly right off the handle at the thought of a Catholic; she might even greet Courvoisier by singing one of those Orange songs she remembered from her childhood –

Up the long ladder
And down the short rope;
Hurrah for King Billy,
To Aitch with the Pope!

Ma always sang 'To Aitch', with an arch look, for a Thirteener would not use the word itself; but somehow that only made it worse. Ma and Pa were wonderful, of course. They had given her everything, except music. That had come entirely from Aunt Ellen. The Galls had never been able to afford a piano, though they had somehow afforded a succession of second-hand cars. But as Ellen had a piano, and obviously didn't need a car, what was the odds? If Monny wanted a piano, she could go to Ellen's. She owed everything to Ma and Pa, and if only the Bridgetower Trust had not suddenly disorganized her life she need never have faced the problem of confronting them with Courvoisier, and Courvoisier with them. But now this problem, and everything that went with it, possessed her, and made her quarrel with George, who was the only thing even remotely like Courvoisier on the horizon.

Girls in novels never seemed to have parents except when they were of some use in the plot, and then they were either picturesque or funny. The Galls were neither; they were oppressively real and many-faceted. The girl in *The First Violin* was a vicar's daughter, which was considered very humble by the other people in the book, but was not nearly so humble as being the daughter of one of the maintenance staff at the Glue Works. The only creature remotely like a vicar whom Monica had met was Dean Knapp, to whom she had taken an unreasonable dislike – not because of anything he had done or said, but because Miss Pottinger had hissed at her that she must address him as 'Mr Dean' and not, as she had supposed proper, as 'Reverend Knapp'. A vicar's daughter would have known that. And the vicar and his wife in the novel had had the good sense to keep out of the story.

Pondering on *The First Violin*, Monica hunted up the book, which she had not read for two or three years. What a *very* musical book it was! The chapters were headed, not with bits of poetry as in Francis Marion Crawford, many of whose works she had read in the set which had belonged to the dead high school teacher, but with quotations of music. She had played them all, but they were so short that they did not really mean much. One was called *Träumerei*, like the picture over the piano. She picked out the theme again, and it remained unrevealing as ever. She put the book aside and began to play. Turn to music when you are unhappy, dear; that was the frequent counsel of Aunt Ellen.

She played *Danse Macabre*, for it reminded her of Domdaniel, and was besides a nice gloomy piece, suiting with her mood of romantic turmoil. She brought out very strongly the motif which her aunt had assured her was the rattling of dead men's bones. It cheered her greatly, so she followed it with that sweet *Flower Song* by Gustave Lange, which was one of Aunt's favourites. As she played, Miss Gall returned.

It was always easy to talk to Aunt Ellen. She didn't have to have things explained to her so much as Ma always did, and when she disagreed she never jeered, which was Ma's way. Besides, Aunt Ellen was a specialist in romance and dreams, and she never seemed to think that anything was really impossible. When the wonderful news had come about the Bridgetower Trust, Aunt Ellen had not waited for Monica to suggest that this might be the pathway to the wonderful world of opera; she had been first to say it; she had led the way in marvellous speculation. There was no dream that had to be shielded from her, for fear that she might mock; she was eager for dreams, and provided cup after cup of the sweet, milky tea which she and Monica found so helpful in the dreaming game. But about family – well, even Aunt Ellen might not see what Monica was driving at there. And so Monica took what seemed to her to be a safe tack.

'That boy I've sometimes spoken about, Auntie, George Medwall, said something to me today which made me as mad as hops.' And she gave a version of George's few words which would have surprised him very much if he could have heard it. Monica had no intention of being untruthful; she merely told Aunt Ellen what George's words had conveyed to her at the time, with certain accretions which had developed since.

'Of course everything will be changed for you now, dear,' said Miss Gall, 'and I dare say you will get into quite a different sort of life. But you were very right not to hear a word against your family. The Fifth Commandment is sacred; honour thy father and mother. As we grow older we see it more that way. Your parents have been very good to you.' As she spoke, Miss Gall cast about in her mind for concrete instances of this goodness, but could find nothing sufficiently impressive to bring out. 'We never fully know what our parents have done for us,' she said, vaguely, and then added, finding safer ground, 'I know my father and mother were very, very good to me, and I don't suppose a day passes that I don't remember them and feel their love for me, and my love for them, all over again.' She smiled; she had turned a difficult corner very neatly.

'Yes, I know, Auntie, but they don't really seem to like the idea that I'm going away to study music. Music isn't real to them, the way it is to you and me. Ma never mentions it, except to make fun.'

'Oh, you mustn't mind your mother's fun,' said Miss Gall. 'She's always been like that. So gay when she was a girl, and it's grown with the years. That's really wonderful, you know, dear. So many people get gloomy as they grow older. We always supposed that was what drew Alfred to her.'

'Were they very much in love?' said Monica.

'Well, dear, I really couldn't say. I suppose they must have been. Alfred was very set on marrying her.'

'Was Dad very ambitious, as a young man?'

'Oh yes, I should certainly say he was. That was why he left school so young, you know. He wanted to be independent; he wanted to buy a car.'

'Didn't he have to leave school?'

'Gracious, no; Father pleaded with him to stay at school. There was no need for him to leave; Father was doing quite well, you know. But Alfred would have his way. And then he would have his way about marrying. And so it went, you see.'

'You mean his parents didn't want him to marry Ma?'

'They never discussed it with me, dear, but of course I couldn't help picking up a little of what was going on. It all seemed to be hasty, and there were quarrels, and your Mother's family –'

'Yes? Go on, Aunt, what about them?'

'Nothing dear, really. Just that they were rather strange people, and didn't want your mother to marry anyone.'

'They thought Dad wasn't good enough? Was that it?'

'No; if there was anything of that sort, it was on the Gall side. And of course my parents were disturbed that your Mother was quite a bit older than Alfred. But your Mother's family were – oh, I guess you've said it all when you say they were odd.'

'And Grandpa Gall didn't want him to marry into such an odd family?'

'Well, dear, parents often don't see things as young people do. And it's worked out very happily, so there's no good in talking any more about it, is there? No good ever comes of criticizing people, or guessing what might have happened if they'd done something they didn't do. We have to take care that we always do the right thing ourselves, don't we? And what a job it is!'

'But don't you think George Medwall was terrible? I mean, hinting that home influence would hold me back, and all that. I think that's a terrible thing to say to a person, don't you?'

'I suppose he doesn't really understand. Of course, there will be changes in your life, and probably in the way you look at a lot of things. But I'm sure there'll be nothing that your Father and Mother wouldn't approve of. You know, dear – we've talked about it over and over again – a life given to music is such a wonderful thing. Living for a great art, and meeting wonderful, cultured people, and being all the time in contact with lovely things – it's bound to change you. You'll soar far above us I dare say.'

'Oh, I won't,' said Monica. 'I'd hate to be like that. And I'd never feel I was above you, Aunt, never if I got to be the top soprano at the Metropolitan. It just wouldn't be possible for me. You've taught me all I know about music; how to read and play the piano, and harmony and theory, and accompany myself, and everything. If it hadn't been for you there just wouldn't have been any music for me. I owe my chance to you! This Bridgetower Trust is really yours; you must know that. I couldn't ever repay you, not if I lived to be a thousand and got to be the greatest singer in the world!'

'You can repay me by being a great artist, dear. And a great artist is always a lovely person, remember that. The really great ones were always simple and fine, and loved everything that was sweet in life. Keep yourself sweet, Monny, and remember that any gifts you have really belong to God. If you do that, you won't have to worry about me. I'll be so proud of you, I'll just be full of it all day and every day. And don't worry about your parents. They'll be proud, too. They're just too shy to say how proud they are of you. And I know you'll always be what they want you to be.'

Miss Gall was capable of talking in this strain at length, and so was Monica, so their conversation was long, repetitious and vastly comforting. When Monica went home at last she was persuaded that, when the time came, Courvoisier and Ma could be very happily reconciled to one another. It was just a job of keeping your aims clear and your ideals high.

[THREE]

For several days it had been clear to Monica and her sister Alice that the farewell party was going to be one of Ma's 'nights'. Mrs Gall was a woman whose normal lethargy and low spirits were relieved, from time to time, by brief bouts of extreme gaiety. For weeks she would declare that she couldn't be bothered with people – had no use for them at all, and didn't want the house cluttered up with them; at these times she was morose, untidy and rather dirty in her dress, never took her hair out of curlers, wore her teeth only at meals and – the girls knew this but did not speak of it even to each other – did not wash very often. Then, suddenly, the cloud would lift, the hair would be released, the teeth brought out of the sweater pocket where they had lain unseen but not always unheard, and Mrs Gall would 'doll up', to use her own expression, and ask the girls, jeeringly, why they never brought anybody into the house? Did they want to send her crazy for lack of company? Then the baking would begin, and in a few days there would be a party, consisting chiefly of a Gargantuan feed, with Mrs Gall the heart and soul of it. For a day or two afterward she would exult, breaking into sudden laughter as she recalled the rare old time she had had. Then, in an hour or two, she would fall into a pit of gloom from which even Pastor Beamis, toiling manfully, could not lift her.

She was conscious of this pattern in her life, and attributed it to her indifferent health. Everything she ate, she declared, ran to fat. She was a burden to herself; her breath was short, and she suspected the worst of her heart. From time to time she made attempts to get her fat down, picking at her food for a few days until she was so low in spirits that she would have a fit of weeping, and take a medicinal slice of pie. A doctor had once told her that sugar was a stimulant, and indeed it was to her; she resorted to it as a wealthier and more sophisticated invalid might have taken to a costly drug.

Perhaps the most extraordinary manifestation of her depression was that while it lasted she refused to go to the services and prayer-meetings of the Thirteeners. Her faith was as strong as ever, she protested, but she couldn't face the people; she simply wasn't up to it. She could endure no one but her family, and toward them she was morose, demanding – in Alice's word 'cussed'. Pastor Beamis paid more sick-visits to her than to any other member of his flock.

The quantity and elaboration of the baking that had gone on before the farewell party made it clear that Mrs Gall was going on the razzle as never before. It had been estimated that there would be, at the outside, twenty guests, and she had made ten large jellies, four layer-cakes, a fruit-cake, six dozen tarts and unnumbered cookies; in addition she had baked a ham and a turkey, made a mountain of potato salad, and had rifled her preserve cupboard to produce mustard pickles, chili sauce, pickled beetroot, pickled watermelon rind, pickled crabapples, pickled corn and pickled onions. A vast coffee urn had been borrowed from the Thirteeners' church, and in addition there was to be a punch, made of cold tea, grape juice and ginger ale, with extra sugar to make it fizz.

'I don't want nobody goin' home sayin' they didn't get their bellyful,' she said, as she surveyed these provisions on the afternoon before the great event. Out of the corner of her eye she saw Monica wince, and Ma Gall was gratified. Although she could never have formulated such a theory, she had a deep conviction that there was something salty, honest and salutary about bad grammar; it checked a tendency in the girls to get stuck-up notions. She could speak as fancy as anybody when she chose, but she didn't choose to indulge her daughters in this way. She deeply believed – though again this belief never jelled into anything so clear as a theory – that everybody, in their inmost thoughts, was ungrammatical, and that they translated those thoughts into fancy talk when they spoke, as a form of affectation. But they didn't impose on her. No siree, Bob!

'What are they going to do – besides eat themselves out of shape?' asked her daughter Alice.

'Oh, they'll find plenty to do. Somebody'll know some games, or somethin',' said Mrs Gall. 'Why don't you plan it, instead of leavin' the whole thing to me?'

'What can we do that anybody wants to do that Mrs Beamis won't pull a long face at?' said Alice.

'Alex and Kevin'll have lotsa things planned, you'll see,' said Mrs Gall. 'They're regular corkers, those two fellas. Laugh! – Say, will you ever forget the time they sneaked upstairs and got into a lot of your clothes and came down again like a couple of girls?' Mrs Gall laughed till she wheezed, turned a dirty red, and coughed deeply and ventriloquially, like a bull bellowing in a distant field.

'Yes, and they burst two of my dresses under the arms,' said Alice, sourly. 'Big sissies. It was a thrill for them to get into a girl's stuff and mess around with it.'

'Aw, they're a great coupla boys,' said Mrs Gall. 'They got some life in 'em, and that's what I like. Not always pilin' on the agony till they're so stiff-rumped they can't have any fun.' Again her eye wandered to Monica, who, as the supposed guest of honour, was showing little zeal for the party which lay ahead.

Night came, and with it the guests. Monica and Alice dressed in the small room which they had always shared, contriving somehow to make quite elaborate preparations in the two-foot gangway which was all the space left in the room between the double bed, the chest of drawers and the single chair. Alice depressed Monica by her unceasing gloomy predictions about the party. The elder of the two, Alice was the rebel; she was sick of the Thirteeners, and she was pretty sick of Ma. She was also sick of Monica, and the Bridgetower Trust had deepened her disgust with her sister's pretensions to culture. Alice was noisily anti-intellectual, though she had no clear notion of what it was that she was opposing. She was convinced that music and all that stuff was a lot of bull, and that was all there was to the matter. She worked in a bank, and had plans to better herself. The first step in these plans, Chuck Proby by name, was coming to the party. He worked in the bank, too.

'Chuck says all this religion is a lot of crap,' said Alice, putting as much colour on her mouth as she thought Ma would endure without noisy rebuke.

'If Ma heard you use a word like that she'd wash your mouth out with soap,' said Monica, who was rubbing Italian Balm into her hands.

'Ma's no one to talk about the words anybody else uses. Did you hear what she said when she finished laying the table tonight? "There; let 'em eat till they're pukin' sick", that's what she said. But the other day when I lost the heel off my shoe and said Damn she yelped about it for half an hour. No swearing – oh my, no! – but she'll talk as common as she likes. But anyhow, Chuck says all this religion is a lot of crap. He says he's a Probyite. He means by that he believes in himself. That's what makes me so crazy about him. He'll do something in the world. Not like Pa.'

'Pa's never had a real chance, Alice. He started to work at sixteen –' Monica's voice died away, for she was remembering what her aunt had told her, what George had said – all the disturbing things which gnawed at Pa's meagre personal legend. Alice was laughing.

'Crap,' said she, 'crapola!'

[FOUR]

By nine o'clock the party was beginning to warm up. It had started badly, for the earliest guests to arrive were twelve young Thirteeners, the others in the sept of thirteen with which Monica, at puberty, had been received into the Beamis flock. They were evenly divided as to sex, and there were three couples among them who were supposed to be romantically interested in each other. But vitality did not seem to be a characteristic of young Thirteeners, and they were quiet, almost furtive, in their approach to merry-making. They hung about the walls, and said 'Yes, thanks,' and 'No, thanks,' when addressed, and showed a distressing tendency to whisper among themselves. Miss Ellen Gall had come early, but she was not one to make a party 'go', and thus the whole burden fell on Mrs Gall. She pumped up gusto enough for everybody, pressing the sweet punch and cookies on them as soon as they arrived, toiling round and round the room, sucking air through her false teeth, and shouting 'Havin' a good time? That's right; enjoy yourselves!' in a way which made it clear that no lack of enjoyment would be tolerated. But the young Thirteeners were leavened after ten minutes by the arrival of Chuck Proby, who had a very worldly air, and then by Mrs Gall's favourites, Alex Graham and Kevin Boyle.

Alex and Kevin were close friends. They shared a boarding-house and, frequently, they shared a bed. They were happy together, giving each other advice about clothes, and helping each other in the demanding task of setting their hair in becoming waves. Mrs Gall, it need hardly be said, knew nothing of these intimacies and failed to understand Alice's broad hints; to her they were just a pair of vivacious boys who were always ready for fun, never spoke ill of anybody, and paid her flattering attentions. They were not Thirteeners, but they were pleasantly solemn about religion, and occasionally ventured philosophical reflections to the effect that there were a lot of things in the Universe that we didn't understand yet, and that it stood to reason that there was Something at the back of the wonderful world which we saw all around us. In the circle in which the Galls moved, the subdivision of humankind to which Alex and Kevin belonged was not understood – and indeed, if its existence were recognized at all it was thought to appear only among people whom wealth or an unwholesome preoccupation with the arts had corrupted; true, they seemed a little girlish, but in Mrs Gall's view there was nothing wrong with them that a couple of good wives couldn't put right, and she was always on the lookout for suitable girls for them; she would have been well pleased if her own two daughters had fallen in with this plan. They were great ones to 'josh' with her, and Mrs Gall could forgive anything in a josher. They made their entrance joshing.

'Madame,' said Alex, seizing her hand and kissing it amorously, 'the Count and I are too much honoured by the invitation to your soirée.'

Kevin produced a bouquet of paper flowers from behind his back and presented it to his hostess. 'Mine heart, she ees too full,' said he.

Mrs Gall laughed, wheezed, and roared in her chest. 'There you go!' she said, when she could speak; 'I knew you two would be up to somethin'. Come on and have somep'n t'eat, and cut it out, now! Remember my heart.'

'As if we could forget it,' said Kevin. 'Biggest heart in Salterton, and mine – all mine!' He feigned romantic ecstasy.

The young Thirteeners giggled nervously, anxious to show appreciation yet fearful of attracting attention lest they should be involved in the joshing, for which they knew they had no talent. Alex and Kevin greeted them all, still in their characters as foreign noblemen, but when they came to Monica they fell on their knees like Moslems, and bumped their heads on the floor.

'Proper deference toward a great talent,' they whispered. Then Mrs Gall led them off to be plied with sugar, in solid and liquid form.

Chuck Proby was alone in his failure to respond to this joke. He wore, without disguise, the look of a young man with a future who feels superior to his company.

The ascendency of Alex and Kevin was not to last long. Very soon after their arrival Pastor Beamis came in, accompanied by Mrs Beamis, who looked as though she had been carved out of teak (though not by pagans) and their son Wesley, who was small, thin, pimply and had a bad breath, but strove to offset these handicaps by great high spirits, within Thirteener limits. But the crown was put on the party by the great man whom they brought with them. It was none other than Gus Hoole, the radio announcer and director of the Heart and Hope programme.

The international world of entertainment had not heard of Gus Hoole, and might possibly never do so. But for a few thousand people in Salterton and its environs, he was emperor of a world of mirth, and at the centre of all the stirring, bustling things that came into their lives. He was head announcer at the local radio and television station, and there was no appeal for a good cause, no interview with a visiting celebrity, no civic function on a large scale, in which he did not have a part. He was a fountain of the newest repartee; he had a never-failing flow of heart-warming rhetoric; he had a sure instinct for making things go. He was, indeed, a truly kind and generous man who really liked to make people happy, and to assist crippled children, the aged, the blind, the tubercular, the cancerous, the amputees, the mentally retarded and all the other afflicted persons whom the streamlined benevolence of our day has taken to its great, departmentalized heart. But he had so exposed his good instincts to the air that they had become gross, ropy and inflamed. To have Gus Hoole do good to you was not unlike a very rough rape. He entered the crowded small house, and gave it precisely the same treatment as if it were a vast drill-hall, filled with people who must be persuaded to part with money in the name of charity or patriotism. Not that he roared; television does not need roarers; he merely boomed, in the heavy, pseudo-masculine, soggily sincere tones of a popular announcer.

'Wanted to come. Wouldn't be kept away,' he said, in response to Mrs Gall's flustered, overwhelmed greeting. 'Least I could do for our Monny, whom we are so soon to lose to the BBC. Can't stay long, I'm afraid. But wanted to come for as long as I could.'

Whereupon he took charge of the party. He was a man of professional tact, and he knew that the Thirteeners belonged in that category of religion which they themselves called 'the moderate-stricts'. Therefore dancing was out, and there must be no jokes mentioning drink or sex. Jokes about the excretory functions would be acceptable, however, and he made two, which were greeted with loud laughter topped by Mrs Gall. He led singing, for he was an adept in tongue-twister songs such as 'One warm worm wiggled up the walk, while another warm worm wiggled down'. He guided them through a song in which the boys had to match themselves vocally against the girls, singing in falsetto. He was rich in riddles and puns. He mustered enough hats for a game which involved the very rapid putting on and taking off of unsuitable hats, and in this Pastor Beamis showed himself to immense advantage. The party began to go swimmingly – so well, in fact that Gus Hoole felt it was safe to make a joke about drink, and did so. No one laughed so loudly as Pastor Beamis.

'That's a hot one,' said he, at last, wiping his eyes. 'Though it's not really a joking matter, of course. You can see right here, Gus, that when a bunch of fine kids get together for a good time, they don't need that stuff at all. They're just naturally drunk on their own high spirits.'

'But that doesn't mean you, Ma,' said Kevin, nudging Mrs Gall. 'Don't think I don't know about that jug you've got hidden under your bed.' She shrieked, and roared in her throat until it seemed almost that she might have a seizure. Kevin slapped her on the back and plied her with the sweet punch. 'You're drunk on sugar, Ma, that's what's the matter with you,' he said. She guffawed again, wildly, exaggeratedly, on a higher note, until Alice wondered if she might not actually throw up, right in the middle of the carpet.

There was no doubt about it, Gus Hoole made Monica's farewell party. Monica admitted it; she strove to enjoy it. Yet, somehow, real enjoyment would not come, coax it as she would with laughter. Aunt Ellen enjoyed it. She was not of the same world as Gus, but she was a simple woman, impressed by success, and she was quite prepared to admit that he was much her superior in matters of this kind. And there was no question but that Gus was giving his all.

He even had what he thought of, professionally, as a 'running gag', for the occasion. He had to be at Salterton's largest hotel at half-past ten, to supervise the drawing of the winning tickets in a charity raffle. That was why he was wearing his dinner jacket. (He had comically begged to be excused for appearing 'just in my working clothes'.) And so, from time to time, he looked at his wrist-watch, murmuring audibly, 'Mustn't be late; they pay me ten dollars a minute for this kind of thing downtown.' This show of comic avarice on the part of Gus, the widely-known, the professional Big Heart, was uproariously funny to the party. Even the young Thirteeners loosened up, and sniggered and neighed their delight. Then, with one of his famous lightning changes of mood, Gus became serious.

'Gotta go, folks,' said he, 'and when you gotta go, you gotta go.' (A whoop from Ma Gall, who found a lavatorial significance in this.) 'But seriously, I wish I could stay here with you lovely folks and emcee this affair right through till dawn. But the Mater Dee will be looking for me at the Paraplegics' Ball in just fifteen minutes, and it's time to say Good-bye. Before I go, Syd' – here he turned with an affecting boyishness to Pastor Beamis – 'would it be too much to ask to hear the Heart and Hope just once again?'

Pastor Beamis patted Gus on the shoulder like a man whose heart is too full for speech. Quickly he gathered Mrs Beamis and Wesley to him, and then beckoned to Monica, who found herself reddening as she joined them in the familiar formation.

'Doh,' whispered Beamis, and his wife emitted a low moó, upon which the others formed a chord. 'Granny' murmured the leader, and slowly, with immense expression, the quartet sang *Eden Must Have Been Like Granny's Garden*, much the most popular thing in the semi-sacred department of their repertoire.

It would be cynical to suggest that during this rendition there was any competition for the limelight, but if such a thing had been possible, Gus Hoole was certainly the winner. He stood motionless during the four verses, and as the motionless actor on the stage always draws the eyes of the audience, so did Gus. When the Quartet had finished, a few callow Thirteeners thought to applaud, but Gus stilled this unseemliness with a quick gesture. Stepping forward, he kissed Monica lightly on the cheek, exercising the licence which is allowed in the entertainment world, and then, in a carrying emotional whisper, he said, 'So long, kid; come back some day,' and went out, with head bent. It was a splendid exit.

Not everyone was sorry to see him go, strange as this may appear. Alex and Kevin resented his professional intrusion on their preserve as funnymen of the party. Mrs Gall, though honoured by his presence, was debarred by it from playing her role as the Earth-Goddess, the Many-Breasted Mother, dispensing food and drink. And so, as soon as Gus had left the house, she called everyone to supper by shouting 'Eats! Eats!' and bustling them into the back parlour, or dining room, where the table was laid. Mr Gall was set to work carving the turkey; Pastor Beamis hacked somewhat inexpertly at the ham. The young Thirteeners, considering their general lack of vitality, ate astonishingly. Indeed, two of the young men had a merry contest as to which could eat most, and made a great thing of it, egged on by the Thirteener girls. Ham, turkey, salad, pickles – the party chewed its way through these in short order, and then set to work on the sweet things. Because Christmas was not far away, there were crackers, and funny paper hats; the only person who did not wear a paper hat was Chuck Proby who, when urged to do so by Mrs Gall, said: 'Well, in the banking business we got to be careful,' and escaped with his dignity uncompromised.

When at last they had eaten – not everything, for that would have been impossible without some apparatus for forcible feeding, but as much as it seemed that flesh could bear – Mrs Gall disappeared to the kitchen, and returned almost at once, with the crown of the feast. This was a huge tray of small mince pies. The recipe called for a teaspoonful of brandy to be poured over each of these before it was eaten, but as Mrs Gall had no use for brandy she substituted – such is the genius of the born cook – the juice from two bottles of maraschino cherries.

'Come on, now,' she cried. 'Every one you eat means a happy month next year. Ain't that so, Pastor?'

And so the company, protesting that it could eat no more, ate a great deal more, and stowed away mincemeat soaked in maraschino cherry juice until the young men groaned and rubbed their stomachs histrionically, and the girls protested that they could touch their last swallow, that their back teeth were submerged in food, and all the other jolly things which people say to please so bounteous a hostess as Mrs Gall. Pastor Beamis won the prize for eating most mince pies (nine) and when he unwrapped it, it was a toy set of bagpipes. When he danced about the room playing his pipes, even Mr Gall laughed a little, and said that the Pastor was a card. Then they all settled down to 'top off' with shortbread and coffee.

It was at this time that Alex and Kevin crept away, to return in a few minutes wearing Derby hats, spats, and carrying canes; in their eyes they painfully gripped watch crystals, to simulate monocles. For the enjoyment of the sated guests – some of whom were already showing signs of that grim malady, a cake hangover – they acted out a little dialogue of their own composition, in which they declared that they were from jolly old London, by Jove, and that they were waiting impatiently for the arrival of Miss Monica Gall, the Salterton nightingale, don't y'know, who was coming over to Blighty to show them a thing or two about singing, eh what? Their English accents were not very well assumed, their English slang was derived from hearing people who had read Wodehouse talk about him, and their little masque did not seem to have a beginning or an end or much perceptible point, but it was received with enthusiasm, and Mrs Gall was in gales of mirth, just from looking at them being so funny.

'Yeah, that's the way she'll be talkin' when she gets back,' said she, jerking her head toward Monica. 'Just you be careful, my girl, not to pick up a lotta snottery when you're over there among all them dudes. You got to keep your feet on the ground, and not get so's we can't understand a word you say.'

'Monny'll be right up with the bigwigs when she's having lessons from Sir Thingumyjig,' said Wes Beamis.

'Well, for her sake I hope they're more open-handed in England than they've been here,' said Mrs Gall. 'The idea – invitin' us over there to talk about Monny's future, and never so much as offered us a cuppa coffee!'

'But Monny's getting the interest on a lotta money,' said Mr Gall. 'You have to remember that.'

'A cuppa coffee wouldn't have hurt,' said his wife. 'But no, they just sat around that room like so many Stoughton bottles and looked at us as if we was poison.'

'Let the boys go on, Ma,' said Monica.

The entertainment by Alex and Kevin did not so much come to an end, as it fell apart, and the evening took another sudden turn toward seriousness, as it had when Gus Hoole was taking his leave. Pastor Beamis spoke of the loss to the Thirteener Church which was caused by Monica's great good fortune. He referred feelingly to the blow that had been sustained by the Heart and Hope quartet. He and his wife and Wes wanted Monica to remember them, when she was far away, and to remember their repertoire, too, so that sometimes she might sing the Lord's songs in a strange land. And in order to keep them in her mind, he asked her to accept a gift.

Wesley Beamis produced it, from the entrance hall, and Monica unwrapped it as they all looked on. It was a dressing case, fitted with a mirror, brushes, bottles and hangers upon which clothes could be folded. Monica, who had a headache, was moved, and cried a little, but she pulled herself together and made a speech.

'I'll never be able to thank you enough,' said she; 'not just for this, though it's lovely, but for all the good times and all the kindness. Please don't talk as if I could ever forget you. I couldn't, and I wouldn't if I could. I'll always keep this with me, whatever happens, and no matter how long I'm away, or whatever happens to me –' She could say no more.

Pastor Beamis struck up *God Be With You Till We Meet Again*, and they all sang it, fervently and with a warmth which was, to Monica, agonizingly sweet and embracing. As she stood among them weeping, part of her feeling was of deepest shame that she could ever, for a moment, have felt stifled and cramped in this atmosphere, or have wished to get away from it. Miss Ellen Gall, in the back parlour among the ruins of the feast, wept too.

The guests went home, each with a kind word, and Wesley Beamis, made bold by the example of Gus Hoole, pressed a maraschino-tainted kiss upon her cheek at parting. He had had hopes of Monica, but now they were gone.

When the Galls were alone, Ma was seen to be slumped in a chair, beet-red in the face, and utterly exhausted. But she roused herself, thrust a piece of fruitcake into her mouth and rose.

'Come on,' said she; 'let's get these dishes done before we go to bed. I don't want any slopdolly housekeeping here.' She kicked off her shoes, removed her teeth, and went to the kitchen.

There she found that Alex and Kevin were well advanced on the first lap of the dish-washing. Good boys, thoughtful boys: make wonderful husbands.

[FOUR]

Christmas Eve. Unhappy and nauseated from the crown of her head to the soles of her feet, Monica lay in her berth aboard the *Duchess of Richmond*. Although she had several blankets and the steam heating hissed and muttered in the pipes, she was clammily cold. The boat – no, the doctor had said she must always call it the ship – toiled laboriously upward, seemingly determined to reach the sky, and hung poised for a few dreadful moments at the crest of the wave; the screws, lifted from the water, caused the whole vessel to shudder awesomely; then it plunged, writhing, into the depths again. Everything in the cabin jingled and shifted; the vomit-can, hooked ingeniously over the side of her berth, chattered metallically. Down the hallway, but clearly audible through the ventilation louvres in the door, somebody dropped a loaded tray.

The light in the middle of the cabin turned on with a snap, and Stewardess Rose Glebe was in the room, heavily rouged and bursting with well-being.

'Well, and how's the lonely girlie now?' she carolled. 'Still a weeny bit sicky-pussy? Never mind, dear, you're not the only one. Only six at First Class dinner tonight.'

Holding Monica firmly with one arm, Stewardess Glebe dealt the pillow several punishing blows. Monica retched powerfully but without result.

'Poor kiddie,' said the angel of light, laying her back again and straightening the blankets. 'Nothing to come, eh? That's no good; got to get something into your tummikins dear, or you'll wrench it loose with that there straining. Now look; I've brought you a lovely apple, all cut in pieces, and some ginger ale. You just get that down. No matter if you can't keep it. You've got to have something to raise, or you'll harm yourself. Doctor's orders. I'll come back before I go off duty, and help you down the hall, to the W, then I'll tidy your bed for the night. Now, now, you mustn't feel so sorry for yourself. Could be much worse, I tell you. Though it's a pity about Christmas Eve.'

'Can it be worse than this?' asked Monica, faintly.

'Much worse on the voyage over,' said Stewardess Glebe. 'That was a crossing, if you like. The old North Atlantic's no millpond in winter.'

With a smile of extreme cheer she vanished through the door.

Monica lay with her eyes closed for a few minutes, gathering courage. Then, with extreme caution, she took a sip of ginger ale and felt better at once. She nibbled a bit of apple, and became conscious that she was very hungry. Soon she was able to get up, bathe her face, and turn out the centre light; she switched on the reading-lamp in her berth and lay as quietly as the ship would allow, eating the apple lingeringly.

How noisy the ship was! All that creaking and groaning, night and day. And how empty! But then, as a fellow passenger had asked her, who would cross the North Atlantic in Christmas Week unless they had to? There were only twenty-two First Class passengers altogether, and of these seventeen were men – middle-aged, dull-looking men, obviously travelling on business. One of them, with whom she had had a brief conversation, was an apple man from British Columbia. Monica had anticipated the sea voyage as an exciting and perhaps even a romantic introduction to her new life. But when she found herself seated at a table in the dining saloon with a widow who was going to scatter her husband's ashes in his native Scotland, and a female Major in the Salvation Army, she had revised her opinion. Not that she had been allowed much time to explore the possibilities of the ship, for it had left St John in heavy weather, and Monica had been in her berth since the second day; this was the fourth day and the storm – not that the doctor or Stewardess Glebe would admit that it was a storm – seemed to be growing worse.

She had not lost heart, in spite of her illness. She had been elated at the thought of travelling First Class, and she did not know that this had been the cause of hot debate among the Bridgetower Trustees. Miss Pottinger and the Dean had thought Tourist Class much more suitable, but Solly had once more been indiscreet in talking to the newspaper, and the *Bellman* had announced its intention of providing Monica with a large bouquet of flowers, with which she was to be photographed, at the dock. It had been considered wrong that a protégée of the late Louisa Hansen Bridgetower should be photographed in anything less than First Class accommodation, and so, with much grumbling from Mr Snelgrove, that was what had been provided. The *Bellman*'s flowers, firmly held in a cage which the ship provided for them, rustled and waved in a corner of her cabin.

Getting away had been a strain. None of the Galls were travellers, and the belief had grown up among them, unspoken yet plainly understood, that once Monica had gone they need never expect to look upon her face again. People did travel about the world, it was true, and return to their families even after many years of absence, but the Galls could not believe that this would be so with one of their own. The sea voyage would almost certainly end in shipwreck; the more Mrs Gall thought of it, the surer she became. True, she did not say this to Monica in so many words, but she had a way of looking at her daughter, and melting into silent tears, which made speech unnecessary.

Mr Gall's solicitude expressed itself differently. Although he had been apparently indifferent to Monica's fate since her childhood, he now took great pains to find out what kind of toothpaste she liked, and what her preference was in cold cream, and bought her large stores of these things to take away. He was apparently convinced that the ordinary necessities of life could not be bought in England, and he repeatedly made her promise that, when these things were exhausted, she would let him know, so that he could send more. He seemed to be provisioning her for a voyage to the Isle of the Dead.

Monica had borne herself bravely through the partings, and had pooh-poohed the notion that there was any danger at sea, but during the days of her illness she had been troubled by a duality of mind. Certainly it had seemed to her that no vessel built with human hands could do what the *Duchess of Richmond* was doing and stay afloat. She had prayed, but the Thirteener faith had not armed her against such misery as this; she had tried to believe the ship's doctor, when he had assured her that nobody ever died of it (ha ha), and that her best plan was to stop thinking about herself and get up on deck; she had submitted to the shameful ordeal of a soapy-water enema given by Stewardess Glebe, who insisted that this treatment was sovran for sea-sickness; she had, in the worst of her trouble, fallen into a sleep which was more like a swoon, and troubled by horrible dreams. But, although one half of her mind told her that she was about to die, the other half had continued to dwell on hopeful visions of what she would do when, at last, the ship reached port. Refreshed by the apple and the ginger ale, she gave herself up to such speculation now.

England was sure to be fun. She had never thought much about that country, or made any special study of anything connected with it, but when she knew she was going there everything she had ever heard about England – and quite a few things she had never been conscious of hearing – collected and formed a pattern in her mind and she became, so far as her circle was concerned, an authority on the subject. England would be very quaint, and the people – though not so go-ahead and modern as the Canadians – would be exceedingly polite, honest and quaint as well. The Cockneys would be especially quaint, because they were so quick-witted, and so full of independence and courage. Cockneys might be expected to wear suits with hundreds of pearl buttons on them, on Sundays, just as they did in the photographs sent out by the British travel agencies; there would be splendidly uniformed soldiers, as seen in whisky advertisements; people in official positions were very likely to wear little wigs; there would be innumerable quaint customs – beating the boundaries, flinging the pancake, chewing the gammon, and the like, as described by the British Information Service; children might be expected to talk like grown-ups; it would rain most of the time, and this would be borne with immense good-humour; coffee would be awful but tea would be drunk in bucketsful; and there would be a lot of culture and gracious living and characteristic English understatement in evidence everywhere.

This was the country which was to transform her. She was determined that in most things she would be transformed. The simple clerk at the Glue Works (for she saw, more clearly every day, how simple she had been) would, after experiences which would deepen and ripen her emotional nature, change into the internationally-known diva. She would never forget her family, of course, and she would certainly never be a loose-liver, as some internationally-known divas had so reprehensibly been, but she would no longer be bound by the chains of the Thirteeners or the social habits of Salterton. Monica Gall, the internationally-known diva . . .

The name was not quite right. Indeed, the more often she repeated it, the less appropriate it sounded. Gall, in particular, would not do. An Irish name, Aunt Ellen had explained. Would it be better changed to Gallo, perhaps? Monique Gallo? Distinguished in appearance, with a spiritual beauty which seemed to shine from within, elegant yet simple in manner, living solely for her art and yet a familiar figure in the best society in Europe, Monique Gallo took shape in her mind. Monique Gallo, robed as Norma, acknowledging the applause of a vast audience before the curtains of a great opera house; Monique Gallo, in a black velvet gown relieved only by a few fine diamonds, graciously bowing at the end of a recital, while her accompanist wiped away his tears of pure artistic joy; Monique Gallo being drawn in torchlit triumph through the streets of Prague by a crowd of enthusiastic students, who had taken the horses out of her carriage . . . Why horses; why a carriage? Oh, probably a temporary gasoline shortage . . . Monique Gallo, who sang every kind of music with unmatchable understanding, concluding her recital with some simple, lovely ballad which left not a dry eye in the house. Monique Gallo telling stricken young men (not a bit like foremen at a Glue Works) that she must live for her art alone – an attitude which, while it broke their hearts, compelled them to love her all the more.

The apple and the ginger ale had been gone for perhaps half an hour before the picture began to darken. Not Monique Gallo now, but plain Monica Gall was musing on the plain words of Humphrey Cobbler when last she had seen him – 'chances are about a hundred to one that your voice is any better than scores of others; only work will tell the tale; this Bridgetower thing is really pretty much a fluke.' Well, it was a chance. She could always go back home and get a job.

The *Duchess of Richmond* climbed higher peaks, shivered more terribly, plunged in corkscrew fashion to even more abysmal depths. Monica turned very cold, broke into an icy sweat, and was noisily, searchingly sick into the rattling container . . . And again . . . And (Oh God, have mercy!) again.

[TWO]

'Miss Gall, from Canada? I'm from Jodrell and Stanhope. Here's my card – Frederick Boykin. I'll see to your luggage. Hope you had a pleasant voyage? Well, yes, I suppose it's bound to be a bit rough this time of year. Yes, it is a little foggy, but that's common in London, you know. Oh dear no, this isn't a *real* London fog; just a bit of a haze. Taxi! That's right, three cases and a trunk. Well, you can put two of the cases on the roof, can't you? You get inside Miss Gall, and I'll see to this . . . There; that's that. They hate trunks. Can't think why; they charge enough for 'em. Now, my instructions are to take you to

Marylebone Road – Three Arts Club – ladies' club, very respectable, and you'll see Mr Andrews tomorrow. Pity you can't see more out of the window. I suppose you saw a good deal of England coming down on the boat-train? Raining all the way? But you expected that, you say? Well I suppose it does seem queer to you, coming from all your snow, and so forth . . . The smell? I can't really say that I'd noticed any smell. Bit smoky, perhaps, but that's because of the haze – keeps the smoke down . . . Here we are; you go right ahead, I'll attend to everything. They're expecting you.'

Thus, within a quarter of an hour of her arrival in London, Monica found herself in a very small room, with nothing whatever to do. She had liked Mr Boykin, who was stout without being fat, and cheerful in what she supposed was the traditional Cockney way, and knew what he was doing. She had not so much liked the secretary of the Club, who was a very competent lady with a brand of genteel, impersonal hospitality which was new to Monica, and chilling. And what was she to do now?

She would read her book. Before leaving Canada she had laid in intellectual provision in the form of *War and Peace*, in a single large, heavy volume, complete with maps of Napoleon's Russian campaign, and an informative introduction by a celebrated critic. Under normal circumstances she would never have considered tackling such a cultural monster, but it seemed appropriate to the new life she was going to live. Aunt Ellen had advised it, for her dead fiancé had often spoken of *War and Peace* as the greatest of all novels. To read it would undoubtedly result in permanent mental enrichment. Seasickness had come between Monica and Tolstoy on the voyage, and she had read, in all, four confusing pages. She would get down to serious work on it now.

Many travellers have discovered that a book which seems strikingly appropriate in one country is insupportably tedious in another; the Lost Property offices of the world's airports are heavily stocked with volumes which have not travelled well. In less than ten minutes Monica had decided that Anna Pavlovna Sherer's party was not precisely what she needed at the moment (though unquestionably cultural); she was in the greatest city in the world, and she did not want to waste time sitting in a little room, with a bad light and a funny smell, reading about people who did not seem certain what their own names were. She would go for a walk.

The genteel secretary caught her in the hall, and cautioned her not to go far, not to get herself lost, and to appeal to a policeman if she did so. This was dampening to Monica's spirits, as was also the smell of Marylebone Road, which was just like that of her bedroom, only more intense and wet.

It was a sour, heavy smell; a wet smell, of course, in which the smoke of soft coal played a large part. But it was not a constant smell. Sometimes the soft coal was so powerful that Monica choked a little; and then, in a few yards, it would have changed to a smell like damp mattresses; once, Monica was reminded of the time when a wool warehouse had burned down in Salterton. It was not an actively unpleasant smell; indeed, it had a caressing friendliness about it – almost a familiarity, as though she had known this smell at some earlier time in her life, and were encountering it again. But in spite of this delusive familiarity the smell was the queerest thing Monica met in the Marylebone Road, which seemed to her, in other respects, not greatly unlike Toronto.

Baker Street. Had she, at some time, heard something about Baker Street? Nothing came to mind, and yet there seemed to be some familiarity in the address. The street names were pleasant; Nottingham, Devonshire, Harley – wasn't there something about Harley Street? It was odd; being in London was like being in a dream, or in a life you had lived before, in which things seemed to have meaning but wouldn't be pinned down.

But she had been warned not to go too far, and the haze seemed to be increasing as the light failed. She found her way back to the Club without difficulty, listening as she walked to the unfamiliar voices – some of them very hoarse and almost incomprehensible. The secretary shot a meaningless, professional smile at her as she passed the office door.

The smell inside the Club had deepened, and was a little warmer than it had been before, and there was a heavy premonition of food in it now. Monica lay on her bed until the gong sounded for dinner, and thought about Monique Gallo, to whom London and all the capitals of the world would seem like home.

[THREE]

The basement dining room of the Club was terrifying. It was not very large, but it was filled with alarmingly worldly girls who seemed to be perfectly at home. In the presence of these girls, with their loud, assured English voices – fully understandable and yet, for that very reason, so foreign and unaccustomed in tone and tune – Monica was, for the first time since she left home, afraid. But the efficient secretary came to her aid.

'Miss Stamper,' she said to a girl who was sitting alone at a table for two, 'this is Miss Gall from Canada. I'm sure you'll find a lot in common.'

Monica's first impression of Miss Stamper was that she was dirty. Her hair was dull. Her face seemed to have grime under the surface of the skin. Her stubby fingers were dark. But her round face was cheerful.

'I wonder why she thinks we'll find anything in common,' said she. 'Are you new here, too?'

By the time they had eaten the watery soup and moved on to the fatty mutton, they were on excellent terms. Peggy Stamper was from Norwich, and she had come to London to learn sculpture. She had been doing a lot of clay modelling, which explained and almost excused the grime. She was not yet nineteen, which gave Monica a certain advantage in age, but Peggy was English, and was thus better equipped to meet the strongly national atmosphere of the Club. It was, she said, intended for girls who were engaged in the arts, or studying them, in London, but what it really worked out to be was a cheap residential place for girls whose artistic inclinations had lapsed, or had always been secondary to some other sort of job. She was there because an aunt, who was partly paying for her training, thought it a safe place for her to be, but she meant to get out as soon as possible.

As they ate a pudding unknown to Monica, which seemed to be called Spotted Dog, she told Peggy about herself. But she noticed, with surprise, as though outside herself, that there were things she did not tell: Peggy heard a good deal about Monica, but she heard nothing of the Glue Works – only of an office job; nothing was said of Pastor Beamis and the Thirteeners – only of some broadcasting experience; the Bridgetower Trust emerged as the sponsor of a far-reaching contest in search of gifted young women, with Sir Benedict Domdaniel as its dominating figure. Not a word did she say with intent to deceive, but in that room, within earshot of those very English voices, facts presented themselves, somehow, in a rather different guise.

Indeed, as Monica went to bed, she was astonished to recall how the facts which she had given to Peggy, without being in the least distorted had been, by some instinct of caution deep within her, edited. Was it Peggy's fault? No, she had been very friendly, though in a way which was new to Monica – a way which suggested that she was glad to hear anything which she was told, but was not really seeking information and was not, perhaps, deeply interested. Was it something about England, which made real truth and real revelation impossible? Had that dreadful week on the Atlantic really drawn such a broad line between herself and her past? She was uneasy and puzzled until she went to sleep.

[FOUR]

Mr Miles Peter Andrews was the most elegant young gentleman that Monica had ever encountered in the flesh, yet he was not really what she would have called a snappy dresser – not as Alex and Kevin were, certainly. Cheerful Frederick Boykin had brought her from Marylebone Road by taxi to Fetter Lane, off which, in Plough Court, were the offices of Jodrell and Stanhope. She now sat in the private room of the junior partner, who looked at her in a weary, lawyer-like fashion, which made Monica feel that he could see right through her.

As a matter of fact, Mr Andrews knew next to nothing about her, and was trying to get his bearings. This was the girl from Canada, referred to his firm by – who was it – a Canadian firm called Snelgrove, Martin and Fitzalan, of some place called Salterton. It would have astonished the members of the Bridgetower Trust if they could have known how much in the dark Mr Andrews was about everything connected with their protégée. Mr Snelgrove, who had been entrusted with all the arrangements, had spoken importantly about 'our opposite number in London – fine old firm', as though Jodrell and Stanhope were in almost daily contact with his own office. It may even have been that Mr Snelgrove believed this to be – in a large, general way – the truth. But the fact was that on only one former occasion had Jodrell and Stanhope ever done any business in London for Snelgrove, Martin and Fitzalan of Salterton, and that had been many years ago, when Miles Peter Andrews was at Marlborough. He had been given Monica to look after because, as the junior, he got all the odds and ends, and perhaps also because his wife was musical in a well-bred, desultory way. Mr Andrews caressed his handsome moustache and blinked sorrowfully across his table at Monica.

'Your first visit to London, Miss – ah – Miss Gall?'

'Yes, sir. I came down from Liverpool yesterday afternoon.'

All things considered, it was unfortunate that Monica called him 'sir', though she did so from the best of motives; she thought she should be polite, and Mr Andrews was in roughly the same relationship to her as her former boss at the Glue Works – a man of power on the other side of a desk. But the word spoke volumes – volumes perhaps of untruth, but nevertheless, volumes – to Mr Andrews' English ear. He allowed his fine eyes to fall to the file which Mr Boykin had laid on his desk. There was not much in it, but a letter from somebody called Matthew Snelgrove made it clear that Miss Monica Gall was the beneficiary of a trust which was empowered to pay for her musical education. Mr Snelgrove, for all his assumption of familiarity with Jodrell and Stanhope, had not thought it necessary to tell them that the yearly income from about a million Canadian dollars might be spent on this project. So Mr Andrews drew his own conclusions from the fact that he had been called 'sir', and also from Monica's style of dress, which he knew to be neither smart nor expensive. When he spoke again his tone was distant, though kindly.

'Well, Miss Gall,' said he, 'we must make you as comfortable as possible, mustn't we. Our Chief Clerk, Mr Boykin, has arranged digs for you at a very good address – a Mrs Merry in Courtfield Gardens. She knows that you are a music student, and I believe she has made some special arrangement about noise. Now, as to money: we are empowered to pay all your fees for instruction, and any large bills; they can be rendered here, without reference to you. But you'll need money for ordinary expenses. What do you think you'll need? By the month, let's say?'

'I – oh, I wouldn't have any idea,' said Monica. 'I don't know anything about what it costs to live here. I'm not very good at English money yet. What would you think?'

'I don't suppose it will be very long before you know other students, and music students aren't very flush of money, as a usual thing. You wouldn't want to be above or below the average. Would five pounds a week do it? Say twenty-five pounds a month? That's three hundred a year, you know; very handsome, really, and all your big bills paid.'

Monica, who knew nothing about it, agreed that this was so, and Mr Andrews thought so, too, for a girl of the sort who called him 'sir'.

'Now as to teaching,' he continued, 'I see that is all to be in the hands of Sir Benedict Domdaniel. He will tell you what to do, and we shall pay the bills. I see here that Boykin is writing to Sir Benedict today, to say that you have come, and you will undoubtedly be hearing from him very shortly. So there really isn't anything more to discuss, is there? Except, of course, that if you need any help, or anything like that, get in touch with us. I'm away rather a lot, so you'd better ask for Boykin.'

Mr Andrews rose to his impressive height, and turned out the very faint gleam of geniality which had illumined his large blue eyes. Monica was shown out into Plough Court by Mr Boykin, who assured her that he would see that she was moved to Courtfield Gardens that very afternoon.

[FIVE]

'You'll be wanting a few sticks, won't you?' said Mr Boykin. He sat on Monica's trunk, which he and a disgruntled taxi-man had just dragged and boosted up three flights of stairs, getting his breath and surveying her new quarters.

'Semi-furnished was the wording of the advertisement,' said Mrs Merry. Her manner was not defensive, but there was a hint in her voice that, if hostility should arise, she was ready for it. 'I naturally expected that the young lady would want to have her own things about her. It was never mentioned to me that the young lady was from the Dominions.' Mrs Merry contrived, in this statement, to make it clear that in her view being from the Dominions was the sort of thing which a tenant would conceal for as long as possible.

Unquestionably Monica would be wanting a few sticks. There were no carpets on the floors and no curtains on the windows. The bedroom contained a single bed, a washstand upon which stood a very large jug in a basin, and a very small clothes-press in the Art Nouveau manner, with a bit of looking-glass let into the front of it. The sitting-room was furnished with one of those day-beds upon which it is uncomfortable to sit and even more uncomfortable to lie, a large discouraged pouffe covered with grubby cretonne, and a dirty, scarred little object which was probably once described as 'a handy smoker's chairside table'. There was nothing else.

The rooms were small and the distemper on the walls had been marked and scuffed by many tenants. Outside the windows, two feet from the glass, was the decorative balustrade which ran across the face of the house – a kind of fence with bulbous stone palings – so that it was easy to look out at the sky, but very hard to see down into the street.

'There are facilities for light housekeeping, as you see,' said Mrs Merry, opening the door of a small cupboard in which, indeed, there was a very old, scabby gas-ring and some shelving. She unveiled this wonder as though it clinched the desirability of her rooms.

'And when may we expect the piano?' said she.

'I'll have one sent round when Sir Benedict gives the word,' said Mr Boykin. Mrs Merry thawed a little at the mention of a title.

'I shall have to hold you responsible for any damage done in moving the instrument upstairs,' said she. Adding, to Monica, 'You'll be able to make as much noise as you like up here; there's nobody on this floor in the daytime, and rarely anyone downstairs.'

'That'll be great,' said Monica, who was thoroughly unnerved by Mrs Merry, and anxious to placate her. If Mrs Merry wanted noise, she would promise noise.

'I'll be getting along,' said Mr Boykin. 'Anything you want, give me a tinkle.'

'Well – what about the sticks?' said Monica. 'Shall I get them, and have the bill sent to you? Or what?'

Mr Boykin had not foreseen this; he had assumed that Monica would buy her own sticks.

'I'll have to speak to Mr Andrews about that,' he said. 'Don't do anything until you hear from me.'

'And what about Sir Benedict?'

'We'll be getting on to him; you wait till you hear from us.'

'Yes – and money? How do I get money to live?'

'Haven't you any on hand?'

'Very little.' As a matter of fact, Monica had twenty pounds in five-pound notes which she did not mean to touch. That was insurance against anything going wrong with the Bridgetower Trust. She was young, but she was no fool about money.

'Well, I haven't had any instructions yet. But don't worry. I'll get everything straightened away just as soon as I've had a talk with Mr Andrews. A Happy New Year, Miss Gall.'

Mr Boykin took his leave, reflecting that the law would be the most delightful profession in the world if only it didn't involve these odd little necessities to take care of people; they always wanted things which were, to the legal mind, superfluous and looked badly on itemized statements. Still, the girl had to have some furniture. And she was quite right not to buy it herself. That girl had her head screwed on right.

'What do I do about heat?' asked Monica when he had gone.

'The gas-fire and the hot-plate work from the meter above the door,' said Mrs Merry. 'You will be wise always to keep a stock of shillings on hand; it is useless to apply to me, for I simply cannot undertake to make change for my tenants. It is a rule which I have been compelled to make,' she said reproachfully, and left Monica alone in her splendour.

[SIX]

Splendour it was, to Monica, for she had never had a place of her own before, nor had she lived in such a grand house. Mrs Merry's establishment was in one of South Kensington's Italianate terraces, with an imposing entrance hall and a handsome, sweeping staircase. It was true that Monica's rooms were on the floor which had once sheltered the servants, and lacked the high ceilings and ornate plasterwork of the lower apartments: it was true, also, that the gas-fire was an inadequate, popping nuisance, and the inconveniently placed meter demanded shillings with tiresome frequency; and it was true that quite a long journey had to be made to the bathroom on the lower floor, for the large jug and basin were apparently not intended for use. But it was her own place, not to be shared with Alice or anyone, and she had high hopes of it. She settled down to wait for news from Mr Boykin.

During the first week of waiting she passed the time by exploring the part of London in which she found herself. She walked in Kensington Gardens and Hyde Park. The Albert Memorial, coming to her as a surprise, seemed a beautiful thing, and the Albert Hall, from the outside, splendid. She walked the Natural History Museum and the Victoria and Albert, and told herself that they were immensely educational. She found Cheyne Walk and the river. She became so well known in Harrods that the detectives began to watch her closely. While she was exploring it was not hard to keep her spirits up.

It was another matter when she was in her rooms in Courtfield Gardens. Mrs Merry was no cheerful Cockney; indeed, she was like nothing of which Monica had ever heard. She seemed to be rather grand, for she spoke in a refined manner, making a diphthong of every vowel, and she wore a look of suffering bravely borne which was, in Monica's eyes, distinguished. If Mrs Merry had given her any encouragement, Monica would have confided in her and sought her advice, but Mrs Merry kept her tenants in their place by an elaborate disdain, which she made particularly frosty for Monica's benefit. And so Monica spent her evenings alone, sitting on the day-bed as long as she could endure it, and going to bed when she could bear no more. During the first day or two she attempted to get on with *War and Peace*, but found it depressing, and as time wore on she suffered from that sense of unworthiness which attacks sensitive people who have been rebuffed by a classic. She read magazines and newspapers. There appeared to be an extraordinary amount of rape in London.

Meals were her greatest worry. Where could she eat? There were plenty of places which offered food, it was true, but she did not like any of them. There were horrible, dirty little holes-in-the-wall, which depended heavily on sausages and boiled cabbage for their bill of fare. And there were foreign restaurants which alarmed her because the food was all described in unknown tongues, and incomprehensible purple writing, and besides it was all too expensive to be enjoyed. In Chelsea she found coffee bars, but they seemed to be the exclusive property of oddly-dressed young men and women who made her feel awkward and unwelcome, and anyhow they did not offer much to eat. There were other Chelsea restaurants, kept by very refined ladies who, like Mrs Merry, gave out an atmosphere of highbred grievance; they provided extremely quaint and individual surroundings, stressing Toby jugs and warming-pans, but gave surprisingly little food for what they charged. And none of the food agreed with her. After a few days her largest meal had become a bready, cakey tea at a Kardomah in Brompton Road.

She could cook nothing in her room, for she had no pots – not even a kettle. It was a new and disagreeable experience to Monica to have to go to a public place and choose every bite that she ate, and she quickly came to dread it. She tried to reach Peggy Stamper at the Three Arts Club, but she had gone, leaving no address.

By the end of the second week she had a cold, and could barely repress panic about money. There had been no word from Mr Boykin. Every day, after the tenth day, she had told herself that she would call him on the telephone, or go to Plough Court to find him, but she did not do so, and knew, in her heart, that she was afraid. After all, what assurance had she that Jodrell and Stanhope would really do anything for her? Perhaps there had been some change in the situation in Canada; perhaps the Bridgetower Trust had collapsed, or changed its mind; perhaps, owing to one of those muddles about dollar and sterling currency, of which she had vaguely heard, it had proved impossible to get any money to England to support her; perhaps – this was when the cold had taken a turn for the worse – they had forgotten about her, or decided that she would not do, and would disclaim any knowledge of her if she went to see them.

Meanwhile she had made quite a hole in her reserve fund of twenty pounds. Eating was horribly expensive, and she tried to economize by bringing things to her rooms in bags, and eating them there. But this diet of apples and buns brought her no comfort. The cold – feverish and wretched, now, in spite of innumerable shillings pushed into the maw of the gas-meter – the raw damp of a London winter, and the peculiar London smell were wearing her down. She began to have spells of crying at night. And then, as the third week wore on, she dared not cry, because letting down the barriers of her courage in any way brought such horrible speculations, and tumbled her into such abysses of loneliness, that she could not sleep, but lay in her bed for hours, trembling and staring into the darkness. The charm of having her own establishment had utterly worn off, and her two bare rooms echoed hollowly.

She did not pray, for as *War and Peace* seemed to have lost its magic in crossing the ocean, so did the religion of the Thirteeners. That blatant, narrow faith could not be hitched to anything in her present situation; never, in this strange land, did she hear anyone speak in a voice which suggested the aggressive certainty of Pastor Beamis.

Yet she continued to write home, once a week, saying nothing of her misery and her fears. She was, she told her family, waiting to begin her studies; meanwhile she was seeing something of London.

What was the good of complaining to them? What could they do? And would they not be likely to say that it was just what they expected? Had they not, right up until the last minute, expressed doubt about the whole venture, which only the thought of the easy money kept from bursting into outright contempt? She was outside the range of her religion, and outside the range of her family. Whatever was to come, she must meet it alone.

If nothing had happened by the end of the coming week, she would get a job. Probably it would have to be dish-washing, or something of that sort; so much an outcast did she now feel that she could not conceive of getting the sort of clerical work she had done at home. In time – perhaps in two or three years – she would be able to scrape up enough money to go home, if the disgrace were not too great. Monica Gall, who was taken in by that crooked Bridgetower crowd – who had the nerve to think she could sing!

By this time her cold was much worse, and she had an ugly sore on her upper lip.

But on the Tuesday of the fourth week, Mrs Merry hooted refinedly up the stair-well that she was wanted on the telephone. It was Mr Boykin.

'Well, Miss Gall, how is it going?' said he. 'Hope you didn't think we'd forgotten all about you? Ha ha. Takes a little time to get an answer from Canada. But we now have the go-ahead on the extra furniture for you, and Mr Andrews suggests that I go with you to one of the second-hand shops in King's Road and see what we can do. Would this afternoon be convenient? Sure you've nothing else on? Very well; perhaps you'll make a sort of tentative list of what you'll be wanting. Oh, and Sir Benedict is now back from Manchester, and he says we may as well have the piano sent around at once, as you'll be wanting one. And he can see you next Friday at three-thirty, if you've nothing else to do at that time. His house is in Dean's Yard, Westminster. I'd be very punctual, if I were you; he's put off someone else in order to fit you in. 'Til this afternoon then.'

[SEVEN]

'Why do you want to be a singer?' said Sir Benedict.

Monica blushed, and held a handkerchief to the coldsore on her lip. 'I'm sorry to waste your time like this,' said she; 'it's just that I've such an awful cold I can hardly make a sound. I'm awfully sorry.'

'Oh, I didn't mean that. Of course you're terribly roopy; I just wanted to remind myself of what you sound like. But what I meant was, what's behind all this? Here you are, and these people in Canada are prepared to spend a great deal of money on your teaching. Is there something special about you? Why do you want to sing?'

'I want to be an artist.'

'Why?'

'Well – because it's a fine thing to be.'

'Why?'

'Because – because it makes you a fine person, and you can help people.'

'How?'

'You bring great music to them. You sort of – enrich their lives, and make them better.'

'Why do you want to do that?'

'It's what we're here for, isn't it?'

'I really don't know. Is it?'

'Well that's what art is for, isn't it? To make people better? I mean, you give people art, and it raises them up, and they see things differently, and it – it sort of –'

'I don't want to put words into your mouth, but perhaps you are trying to say that it *refines* them.'

'Well; yes, really.'

'Has it refined and enriched you?'

'I don't know.'

'You're not sure?'

'I'm not very good at it, yet.'

'But you think you'll be good at it if you have instruction?'

'Yes. I mean – well, yes.'

'Why?'

'I hope I have some talent.'

'Don't you know?'

'It's not a thing you can very well say about yourself.'

'Why?'

'Well – it sounds like blowing your own horn.'

'And why shouldn't you blow your own horn?'

'You're not supposed to.'

'You mean that you have travelled three thousand miles, at the expense of these people in your home town, to study singing under my guidance, and yet you think it indelicate to tell me, of all people, that you have talent.'

'It's really for you to decide that, isn't it?'

'Partly. But you ought to know yourself.'

'Well then, I think I have talent. And I want to sing more than anything else in the world.'

'That's better. But I wonder if you'll think that when you're fifty. It's a dog's life, you know, even if you do well at it. But there; you see you've got me talking silly now. Every old hand tells every novice that a life in music is a dog's life. It's not really true. If you're a musician that's all there is to it; there's no real life for you apart from it. Now listen: I haven't been bullying you like this just for fun: I've been trying to find out what you're up to. All I know at present is that you have a pretty fair little voice – good enough among several hundred others just as good. What training will do still remains to be seen. But unless you have some honest appraisal of yourself you haven't much chance. And all that appears now is that you think you have some talent, and are bashful about saying so: you want to sing, with some vague notion of benefiting mankind in general, and raising people a little above the mire of total depravity in which God has placed them. What do you want out of it for yourself?'

'I hadn't thought much about that.'

'Little liar! Now, answer me honestly: haven't you had day-dreams in which you see yourself as a great singer, sought after and courted, popular and rich – probably with handsome men breaking their necks to get into your bed?'

Monica blushed deeply, and was silent. None of her day-dreams had ever included bed.

'You see! I was right. In your heart of hearts you think of singing as a form of power: and you've got more common sense in your heart of hearts than you have on that smarmy little tongue of yours. You're right; singing is a form of power – power of different kinds. Singing as a form of sexual allurement – there's nothing wrong with that. Very natural, indeed: every real man responds to the woman with the golden, squalling, cat-like note, and every real woman longs to hurl herself at the cock-a-doodling tenor or the bellowing bass. Part of Nature's Great Plan. But sex-shouting's a trap, too. At fifty, your golden squall becomes a bad joke. What then? Teaching? If you're not born to it – and few of the sex-shouters are – it's a dog's life; pupils are fatheads, most of 'em. Are you trying for – well, when you're trained – a possible twenty-five years of that kind of glory? Because it is glory, you know – real glory.'

'I hadn't thought of it that way.'

'Not refined enough? Well, there's another kind of singing. The technique is the same, but the end is different. It depends on what you have in your head and your imagination; it means being a kind of bard, who reveals the life that lies in a great music and poetry. You use your voice to give delight. That's what music used to be for, you know – to capture the beauty and delight that people found in life. But then the Romantics came along and turned it all upside down; they made music a way of churning up emotions in people that they hadn't felt before. Music ceased to be a distilment of life and became, for a lot of people, a substitute for life – a substitute for a sea-voyage, or the ecstasies of sainthood, or being raped by a cannibal king, or even for an hour with a psychoanalyst or a good movement of the bowels. And a whole class of people arose who thought themselves music-lovers, but who were really sensation-lovers. Not that I'm a hundred per cent against the Romantics – just against the people who think that Romanticism is all there is of music. Well, there are the two kinds of singing. The sexual singer is, in pretty nearly all respects, the greater of the two, just as a mountain torrent is necessarily a greater force than the most beautiful of fountains: when she sings, she's a potent enchantress, and the music is merely the broomstick on which she flies. With the bardic singer, the music comes first, and self quite a long way second. Now: which sort of singing appeals to you?'

'Oh, the second, of course. The – bardic kind.'

'If you really mean that, I think the less of you for it. Far better to set out aiming as high as you can, and killing yourself to be one of the big, adored, sexy squallers. It argues more real vitality and gumption in you. Still, I don't trust you to know what you want. You're too full of a desire to please – not to please me, but to please your family, or your schoolteachers, or those people – the What's Its Name Trust – who are paying the shot for you. Those people never want you to have great ambitions or strong, consuming passions. They want you to be refined – which means predictable, stable, controlled, always choosing the smallest cake on the plate, never breaking wind audibly, being a good loser – in a word, dead. I admit that the world couldn't function properly without its legions of nice, refined, passionless living dead, but there is no room for them in the arts. So we'll see what you are after you've had a few months of work. At the moment you're just a nice girl with pots of money to spend on training. So let's get to work.'

'You'll let me study with you, then?'

'Not for a while. Not till we find out what your politics are.'

'Politics?'

'Haven't you any politics?'

'Well, Dad's a good union man, of course, so he always votes Conservative; he says the working man can get most out of them.'

'Sorry. Just a bad joke of mine. Let me give you a short talk on politics, and then you'll have to go. There are, the world over, only two important political parties – the people who are for life, and the people who are against it. Most people are born one or the other, though there are a few here and there who change their coats. You know about Eros and Thanatos? No, I didn't really suppose you did. Well, I'm an Eros man myself, and most people who are any good for anything, in the arts or wherever, belong to the Eros party. But there are Thanatossers everywhere – the Permanent Opposition. The very worst Thanatossers are those who pretend to be Eros men; you can sometimes spot them because they blather about the purpose of art being to lift people up out of the mire, and refine them and make them use lace hankies – to castrate them, in fact. You've obviously been in contact with a lot of these crypto-Thanatossers – probably educated by them, insofar as you have been educated at all. But there's a chance that you may be on the Eros side; there's something about you now and then which suggests it.'

Sir Benedict had risen, and was pushing papers into a briefcase. He rummaged on the top of his piano, and found a box containing some conductor's batons, and he put this in the case also.

'I'll get in touch with you from time to time to see how things are going and if your political colour has begun to show. Our first big problem is that you don't appear to know anything except how to read music and play the piano. I'll arrange some language lessons for you. And we must get your voice out from under wraps. You're all buttoned up, vocally and spiritually. I'm going to send you for a few months to the very best vocal coach in London – old Murtagh. He's a real artist, by the way, so take a good look at him. He'll unbutton you! He'll get a good healthy yell out of you if anybody can! Yes, I'll start you next Monday with Murtagh Molloy.'

[FIVE]

'You've the bar'l of a singer,' said Mr Molloy, giving Monica's waist a squeeze which was certainly intended to be professional, but which had a strong hint of larkiness about it, too. He had been feeling her diaphragm with his stubby, nicotine-stained fingers, blowing out sour clouds of cigarette smoke meanwhile. Suddenly he drew her arms about his waist. 'Feel this,' said he, and Monica felt his bulging, rubbery abdomen spring into embarrassing life under her hands. 'That's the way to do it,' said Murtagh Molloy, winking and lighting another cigarette.

This was going to take some getting used to, thought Monica. Sir Benedict had said that Molloy was the best singing coach in London, and she had expected someone comparable to himself; someone surprising, perhaps, but distinguished. Had not Domdaniel described him as an artist, an Eros-man? But here, on the second floor of a house in Coram Square, was a stumpy Irishman, bald and fifty if he was a day, who bade her feel his stomach, and talked about singing as if it were wrestling. Murtagh Molloy was a long way from the daemonic von Francius in *The First Violin*.

'Ben wants me to do what I can for you,' said Mr Molloy, 'and I'll do't because he's an old friend. But I'll be frank; if you don't come across with the goods – out you'll go. I won't waste time on duds, and it's not everyone I can teach anyhow. You've got to be *simpatico* – d'you know *simpatico*? Means we've got to get along. I worked with a dozen teachers when I was young. I even had a few lessons with ffrangcon-Davies in his last years. You wouldn't know anything about him; a great, great artist. Why, I even worked for a while with William Shakespeare – ah, I thought that'd make your eyes bug – not the poet, of course, but the singing teacher – died, oh, it must be more than twenty years ago. But the greatest of them all was Harry Plunket Greene. You've heard of him? No? He was in Canada often. Worked with him off and on for years. Well, the point is, I was *simpatico* with 'em all, and that's why they could teach me, and that's why I could learn from them. If you're *simpatico* you can get down to business without a lot of palaver; hard words don't hurt, and praise doesn't puff y'up – makes you humble. Now, let's hear you sing something. What've you there?'

'I've got a terrible cold,' said Monica, apologetically.

'You don't have to tell me that. But Plunket Greene used to say that all a singer needed was two teeth and a sigh. D'you get that? Something t'articulate with, and a wisp o'breath. What's that? Old Tosti's *Good-Bye!* That'll do fine.'

Monica fought down her fears as well as she could, and sang. To her surprise, she sang rather well. Molloy accompanied her with a delicacy and helpfulness which she had not expected from the blunt, punching manner of his speech. But a greater surprise was to follow.

'Would you believe I once heard old Tosti play for Melba when she sang that?' said Molloy. 'Long, long ago, but I recall it very well. I'll give you an idea.'

He sang the song himself. It was unlike any singing Monica had ever heard, for although his voice was unremarkable in tone, and he sang without a hint of exaggeration or histrionics, it became as he sang the most compelling and revealing of sounds. The song invaded and possessed her as it had never done in all the time she had known it. Her own rendition, moulded by Aunt Ellen, was carefully phrased and built up emotionally until, she flattered herself, the final repetitions of 'Good-bye' provided a fine and satisfying climax. But as Molloy sang the song there seemed to be no calculation of this kind, and the phrasing was hardly apparent. Yet the whole song was sung with a poignancy of regret which was the most powerful emotion that Monica had ever heard expressed in music. 'It's unbearably sad when you really understand it,' Aunt Ellen had said, thinking of her dead lover, and Monica had striven to re-create that sadness herself; sometimes she had succeeded, until the sob mounting in her throat brought on a prickling of the eyes, and then a fullness in the nose which ruined the singing. But that was real feeling, wasn't it? And that was what made great music, surely? Yet here was Murtagh Molloy, apparently as cool as a cucumber, giving rise to a sadness in her which swept far beyond anything she could associate with Aunt Ellen and the dead schoolteacher. This was the sadness of all the world's parting lovers, of all the autumns since the beginning of time, of death and the sweetness of death. Monica was moved, not to tears, but to a deep and solemn joy. This, then, was the bardic singing of which Domdaniel had spoken.

'I surprised you, did I?' Molloy was looking intently at her. He winked, and picked up what was left of his cigarette from the end of the keyboard. 'When you came in here you thought I couldn't sing because I didn't look like it. Well, it's a long study, girl, and while I was at it me beauty went on me. Now, how do you think my performance compared with yours?

– 'Ah, now, don't blush; I shouldn't have asked you. But you see the difference, don't you? You were dipping your bucket into a shallow well and I was dipping mine into a deep one. No, no, not experience; I've had no more experience than most men. But I know what to do with mine, and I know how to get at it. Your song was all careful little effects. Well, good enough. But mine had one powerful effect. It had the proper muhd.'

Monica was now sufficiently accustomed to Molloy's way of speaking to recognize that this was his way of saying 'mood'.

'The muhd's everything. Get it, and you'll get the rest. If you don't get it, all the *fiorituri* and exercises in agility and *legato* in the world'll be powerless to make a good singer of you. The muhd's at the root of all. And that's what I teach my beginners, and my advanced pupils, and some who've gone out into the world and made big names, but who come back now and again for a brush-up or some help with special problems. And mostly it all boils down to the muhd.

'That's what I'll teach you. You'd better come five days a week for a while. Ben says money's no object in your case, praise God! I think we'll get on – *simpatico*. And the muhd'll do wonders for you. Actually makes physical changes, in a lot o' people. Funny thing, I've known it to clear up terrible cases o' halitosis almost overnight. Not that that's your trouble. But you're stiff as a new boot and you've an awful Canadian accent as I suppose you know. It banishes regional accents completely.'

As Monica ran down the stairs and out into Coram Square it did not occur to her to wonder why the muhd had not banished Molloy's very marked Irish accent. And in justice to him, it must be said that it was greatly diminished when he sang. She knew only that she was where she wanted to be, in the hands of a great teacher. She would master the secrets of the muhd. She would be a bardic singer like Murtagh

Molloy. And if it involved having her waist hugged, and hugging his stomach in return – let it be so.

[TWO]

In the months of hard work which followed, Monica's enthusiasm never failed. Even during the preliminary six weeks when Molloy would not allow her to sing at all, in any sense which she understood, she was obedient. For an hour a day, five days a week, she stood before him, striving as best she might to follow his instructions.

'Feet a little apart. Let your neck go back as far as it will – no, don't move it, *think* it and let it go back itself. Now, *think* your head forward and up *without* losing the idea of your neck going back. Now you're poised. Get the muhd, now – this time it'll be joy. Think o' joy, and *feel* joy. Open your lungs and let joy pour in – no, don't suck breath, just let it go in by itself. Now, with your muhd chosen, say 'Ah', and let me hear joy. – Christmas! D'you call *that* joy! Maybe that's the joy of an orphan mouse on a rainy Monday, but I want the real, living joy of a young girl with her health and strength. Again – Ah, your jaw's tense. Get your neck *free*; think it free, and your head forward and up, and your jaw *can't* tense. Come on, now, try it again.'

It was a technique for learning to command emotion – or, as Molloy preferred to call it, muhd. It became apparent to Monica that her range of emotion was small, and her ability to manifest it in sound, infinitesimal. This was dismaying, because she had been used to thinking of herself as a girl with plenty of emotional range; she could *feel* so much. But Molloy had his own way of extending the range of feeling and expression in his pupils.

'Your emotional muscles are weak, and what y'have are stiff. D'you go to the theatre? Well, you should. In fact, you must. Go to the Old Vic; go to any Shakespeare – any big stuff at all. Watch the actors. Working like dogs, when they're any good. Muhd, muhd, muhd, all the time; lightning changes, and subtleties like shot silk, winking and showing up new colours every second. Without a command o' muhd the work'd kill 'em. But it doesn't; they thrive on it. Never sick, and live to massive ages. And why? Because muhd's life, that's why. D'you know the Seven Ages o' Man, in *As You Like It*? Well, here, take this book and get it by rote for tomorra.'

Work on the Seven Ages of Man became, under Molloy's enthusiastic direction, a riot of muhd.

'We start off calmly – the philosophic vein.' Molloy's face was suffused with an appearance of weighty thought, and his stumpy frame took on the characteristic pose of those statues of nineteenth-century statesmen, to be seen in municipal parks – one foot advanced, and a hand outstretched as though quelling the applause of an audience.

All th' world's a stage,
And all the men and women merely players.
They have their exits and their entrances,
And one man in his time plays many parts,
His acts being seven ages.

Here Molloy underwent a startling metamorphosis; with knees bent, swaying gently from side to side, he hugged an imaginary baby to his ashy waistcoat.

At first the infant,
Mewling and puking in the nurse's arms.

'Ah, the wee soul!' said he, then like lightning banished the infant, and put on an expression which suggested a sick chimpanzee.

Then the whining schoolboy, with his satchel
And shining morning face, creeping like snail
Unwillingly to school.

The chimpanzee gave place to something very airy, with hands clasped over its heart.

And then the lover,
Sighing like furnace, with a woeful ballad
Made to his mistress' eyebrow.

Working on these lines, Molloy breathed the muhd of the soldier, the justice, and the Pantaloon – this last such a picture of trembling, piping eld as even the Comédie Française has never attempted. And his final portrait of dissolution –

Sans eyes, sans teeth, sans taste – sans everything –

seemed to couple senility with the last ravages of paresis in a manner truly frightening.

It was not ham acting. It was something more alarming than that. Into each of these shopworn clichés of pantomime Molloy injected a charge of vitality which gave it a shocking truth. Vocally his performance was powerful, if in bad taste; physically it was rowdy and grotesque; but his meaning was palpable. To Monica it was a revelation; she had never seen anyone carry on like that before. She admired, and loyally fought down the embarrassment which rose in her. She was quite sure, however, that she could never do it herself.

Such resistance was like catnip to Molloy. Part of his profession was to prove to people that they could do what they believed to be outside their powers. Monica was put to work, exhorted, bullied and cajoled until, in a week or two she could cradle the baby, whine, sigh, roar, dogmatize (stroking an imaginary beard), shake like the Pantaloon, and at last, with eyes closed and hands hanging limp like the paws of a poisoned dog, await the stroke of death. Compared with Molloy's Protean performance hers was the merest shadow, but it was far beyond anything that she had ever dreamed she might achieve.

'Now we're beginning to get somewhere,' said Molloy on the day when, at the third time of repetition, Monica had excelled herself. 'Y'know, between ourselves, the stage people are always after me. A lot o' them come for lessons, y'see, and they say, "Murty, you're a born director, and there's a dearth of 'em; how about it?" But I say, "Boys, if it was only a question of speech, I'd do it like a shot, but I've no talent for the tableau side o' the thing. I've th'ear, but I lack th'eye".'

This was the process of vocal and spiritual unbuttoning which Sir Benedict Domdaniel had said would be accomplished by Murtagh Molloy. From the Seven Ages of Man they progressed to the First Chorus from *Henry V*, and at the beginning of each lesson Molloy would say – 'Right; now let's have it – *O for a Muse afar!*' Obediently Monica would set her feet apart, poise her head on her neck, breathe a muhd commensurate with England's martial glory and declaim –

O, for a Muse of fire –

and so to the end of the speech, with horses, monarchs, and apologies for the inadequacy of the Elizabethan theatre, all complete. She was becoming quite pleased with herself, torn between her pride in being able to satisfy Molloy, and a sense of shame in the amount of noise and strutting which that involved.

In these declamatory exercises she was not permitted to speak the words in her accustomed way, and at first she used her true ear to copy Molloy's own accent. But when she did this he astonished her by declaring that she was speaking with a pronounced Canadian twang, and compelled her to adopt a tune and colour of speech which certainly was not English as she heard it spoken by Mrs Merry, or by any of the people she met in chance contacts, but which she learned to identify in the theatre, at the performances of classical plays to which she was constantly being urged by Molloy. It was not the 'English accent' mocked by Kevin and Alex, and forbidden by her mother, but it was not Canadian either; it was a speech that Garrick would not have found very strange, and of which Goldsmith would have approved.

Going to the theatre was, at first, a lonely business, and she did not like it. She had studied one or two of the plays of Shakespeare in school, but she had never associated them with any idea of entertainment. Nor was her first visit to the Old Vic a happy one, for the play was *The Comedy of Errors*, very cleverly transformed by a young director with his name to make into a mid-Victorian farce, in which the two Antipholuses, in chimney-pot hats and Dundreary whiskers, and the two Dromios, in identical liveries, rushed up and downstairs on a twirly scaffolding which was called Ephesus, until at last they were united with an Aemilia and a Luciana in crinolines and ringlets. Several critics had said that this treatment illuminated the play astonishingly, but for Monica it remained a depressing mystery. She was happier when, in a few weeks, it gave place to *Romeo and Juliet*. Peggy Stamper, dirtier than before, had hunted her up, and they went together. Afterward they discussed the play in detail at a Corner House and Monica expressed strong disapproval of the conduct of Friar Lawrence; if he had not tried to be so clever, everything might very well have been straightened out, and the lovers made happy. But then, said Peggy, where would the tragedy have been? And was it not better that Romeo and Juliet should have been unhappy, and tremendous, than happy, and just like everybody else? Monica would not have this; common sense, said she, was surely to be expected of everybody. But if you fill the world with common sense, countered Peggy, there'll be precious little art left. Art begins where common sense leaves off. And, perhaps as a result of Molloy's unbuttoning process, Monica had to agree that this was so.

Without becoming intimate with Peggy, Monica saw a good deal of her, and they did much of their theatre-going together. She met some of Peggy's friends, who were all art students and not particularly articulate or interesting, inclining to shop-talk, dirt, corduroys, beer and fried foods. But in their company she visited some of the galleries (for Molloy had urged her to study gesture and bodily posture in paintings and sculpture, as visible evidences of muhd) and learned enough from them to realize that she had no taste, and was unlikely ever to develop any. Peggy kindly attributed this to her musical interests, and Monica reconciled herself to possessing, like Molloy, th'ear but not th'eye.

These casual acquaintanceships were not enough to keep Monica from being very lonely and often in low spirits. Except for her visits to Molloy most of her days were long and dull. True, she went every morning to Madame Heber for a lesson in French, which she shared with two dry young men who were preparing for the Civil Service, and every afternoon at five o'clock she had a lesson in German from Dr Rudolph Schlesinger, in the company of a spotty girl who was mastering that language so that she might read Freud in the original. Language study, and the exercises which Molloy ordered, filled up much of the time she spent in her rooms in Courtfield Gardens. But she still had plenty of time in which to be lonely. The few sticks which she and Mr Boykin had purchased had made her rooms convenient, though far from luxurious, and she had learned how to feed herself economically and fairly well. She was even able to keep almost warm, though the gas-meter was remorseless in its demand for shillings. And, as winter wore away and spring came she began to see some of the strange, irregular beauty of London. But loneliness would not be banished, and Sundays were an endless weariness. Against all Thirteener custom, she began to go to Sunday movies.

Her cold resisted treatment, and became a sullen catarrh. Molloy refused to recognize its existence. 'It's nothing at all,' said he one day when she apologized for a coughing fit; 'it's the dust in the air. You'd probably never get rid of it unless you took a long sea-voyage – maybe not then. Lots o' people have a congestion like that all their lives. Now me, for instance: I'd spit y'up a cupful o'phlegm any morning in the week. But I don't let it bother me.' And so Monica decided that she would not let it bother her, either. But it did bother her, and particularly at night.

Her work with Molloy was the only life-giving element in her existence. Little by little he satisfied himself that she had some rudimentary notion of what muhd was, and could summon a small amount of it at will. It was true that Monica found it difficult to make love to a chair, which he regarded as an important test.

'Garrick could do't,' said he; 'time and again he'd astonish his friends that way. And it's all a question of muhd. To th'artist, with his imagination at command, and his experience of life to draw on, making love to a chair is just as possible – not as easy, maybe, or as pleasant – but just as possible as making love to a pretty girl. Now watch me: I'm going to make love to you.'

The somewhat severe and admonishing expression which Molloy usually wore when he was teaching gave way to an alarming leer, and he approached Monica with youthful step. Seizing her hand he dropped on one knee and pressed it to his lips. 'My darling,' said he and, rising, pressed her to him with many variations on this simple endearment, which appeared to be the only one he could think of. When it seemed that he must inevitably kiss her he suddenly broke away, and looked sternly into her eye.

'Y'see? That's the way it is with the living subject. Now – what d'you say to this?'

And with a sudden turn he addressed himself to an armchair, caressed its dingy upholstery, knelt to it, entreated it to be his, praised its hair and complexion, called it his jewel, and swore that he could not live if it spurned him. Monica could not laugh, for unquestionably Molloy had the muhd, and however ridiculous his behaviour might be, the power in his voice might not be denied.

Nor could she rid herself of a feeling that Molloy liked showing her how to make love. He never missed a chance to feel her diaphragm, or gauge the expansion of her ribs at the back. And now, in these exercises with the chair it was always hard to know what he might do next. Obedient and teachable, Monica would do her best to pour out adoration for Molloy's unappetizing armchair.

'It's feeble,' he would say. 'Now you're not going to tell me that a girl like yourself doesn't know what love-making is. Eh? Don't blush; if you expect to be an artist you must get your feelings at command. Work on it at home, and show me what you can do next day.'

Part of Monica's inability to enter whole-heartedly into these scenes of passion with the chair sprang from a feeling that other eyes than Molloy's were upon her. There were two doors in his teaching-room, one of which led to the landing, and the other, which had a glass transom over it, presumably to his private apartments; it was from this latter door that occasional rustlings and soft thumpings were heard while lessons were in progress. And one day, as Monica was leaving, she met a short, grey-haired woman on the landing, who gave her a gimlet look through a pair of steel-rimmed spectacles – a look which, from a stranger, was surprising indeed. As soon as the woman had disappeared into Molloy's apartment a sound of voices raised in high and unamiable converse broke out, and was audible until Monica had gone down the stairs and into the street.

[THREE]

It was late in her first spring in London that Monica visited Lorne and Meg McCorkill in South Wimbledon. She never fully understood how they came to know of her existence, although they explained it at length; but as they both talked at once, the chain which led from a friend of theirs in Salterton, who knew a Thirteener who had obtained her address from Pastor Beamis, and who had (the Salterton friend, that is to say) mentioned it in a letter to – no, no, not the McCorkills, but to another Saltertonian, now resident in London – who had passed it on to them: she had never fully understood it. But it was a beautiful spring day, when she had been wishing that George Medwall wrote better letters, less concerned with the inner politics of the Glue Works, that a letter arrived for her, written in an unknown hand, which addressed her thus –

Dear Monica,

You don't know us, but mutual friends in Canada have told us about *you*, so Hi and all that stuff. Lorne and I have been over here in the Great Frost for over two years now, and we know just how tough it can be for a lonely Canuck. So why don't you come out and have a real Canadian meal with us some night next week, Friday maybe? We are always home, so if Friday is no good, pick your own night. You can just get on the Underground at Earl's Court and come right to the end of the line. Anybody will direct you from there. Better let us know by mail when you are coming because Gawd only knows what will happen if you try to phone in this country.

Be seeing you –
MEG McCORKILL

Beaver Lodge
Hubbard Road
Wimbledon, SW 20

Thus it was that a little after six on the following Friday evening Monica walked down Hubbard Road looking for Beaver Lodge. It was not hard to find, for on the gate was painted the name in rustic lettering which simulated sticks of wood, and at one of these a painted animal, not too hard to identify as a beaver, was gnawing. The woodwork of the semi-detached villa was bright with new paint, and a man on a ladder was dabbing delicately at a second-floor casement. He spied Monica as she came in the gate, and with a shout of 'Hi!' he climbed down and hurried forward to greet her.

'Good to see you,' he roared; 'certainly good to see you. Can't shake hands – all over paint; just grab me by the wrist. Hey Meggsie! – I'm Lorne McCorkill; just call me Lorne. This is Meg. And where's Diane? Hey, Diane!'

'She's playing with that Pamela, and I suppose we'll have to get an earful of what Pamela's Mothaw's been saying,' said Meg McCorkill, who had appeared in a very gay and brilliantly clean apron. 'Hello dear, it's certainly great to see you. Come on in.'

They bustled Monica into Beaver Lodge, which was a beautifully clean and bright little house – so clean and bright, indeed, that Monica was startled, for her eyes had become accustomed to the dinginess of Mrs Merry's, the comfortable but seedy furnishings of Molloy's teachingroom, and the downright squalor of the Heber and Schlesinger quarters.

'Isn't this lovely,' said Monica; 'it's like being at home!'

'Aw, you poor kiddie!' said Meg McCorkill. 'Did you hear that, Lorne? Oh he's gone to change out of his paint-clothes.' She raised her voice to a piercing shriek. 'Lorne, didja hear what Monica just said? The minute she set foot in the door she said this was like home. How's that, eh?'

Lorne returned; he was wearing moccasin slippers, and was struggling into a sweatshirt which had the name of a western Canadian university printed across its chest. 'That's swell,' he said; 'just swell. That makes up for all the trouble it was to get this paint here. Because let me tell you kid,' said he, very emphatically, 'every wall and piece of woodwork in this house is covered with real Canadian rubber-base paint. None of this English oil-base stuff for me. We brought it over, and fought it through Customs, and now it's on, and at least we know it isn't all going to shale off in wet weather. And that's something you can certainly count on here, boy – wet weather. Now how's about a real drink. Do you have yours straight, or on the rocks, or with water?'

Monica had been brought up in strict abhorrence of alcohol in all forms, but mixing with Peggy Stamper's friends had taught her to drink beer, in very small quantities. Meg saw her hesitation.

'Make us a Canadian Lyric, Lornie,' said she. 'Monica's too young for straight hard liquor.'

They were in the kitchen, a gleaming room with a Canadian electric stove and a Canadian refrigerator in it; in a corner a Canadian washing-machine, with a round window in its middle, spied on them with this Cyclops eye. While Lorne worked with ice and bottles, Meg explained that they had imported these kitchen articles into England, because they could not possibly make do with the inferior local products. And what a trouble it had been! Everything electric had to be altered to accord with English notions of electrical current. And as for repairs – it was lucky that Lorne was able to turn his hand to pretty nearly anything – a real Canuck in that respect. God! cried Meg (who was very free with strong language, but did not seem to mean anything much by it) English women certainly put up with murder in their kitchens. Frankly, in their place, she'd just tell some of these English husbands where they got off at. But then, the poor mutts never knew anything better, so what was the use of telling them? They just seemed to be born sloppy. Their clothes! Had Monica ever seen anything like some of the comic Valentines you met just walking around the streets? In Medicine Hat – she and Lorne were both Westerners – they'd be taken in charge by the police.

By this time Lorne, with much shaking and measuring, had composed the Canadian Lyric, a cocktail made of equal parts of lemon juice and maple syrup, added to a double portion of rye whisky, and shaken up with cracked ice.

'The trouble we had getting real maple surrp!' said Lorne. 'But I ran it down, finally, in a dump in Soho – a grocery that gets all kinds of outlandish stuff – and here it is, with that real old Canuck flavour! Boys-o-Boys! Just pour that over your tonsils and think of home! Say, where is Diane, anyway?'

Perhaps it was lucky for Diane that she made her appearance at this moment. She was a pretty little girl of about ten, with a fresh complexion.

'Sorry to be late, Mummy,' said she; 'I was playing with Pam, and I forgot.'

'Hear that?' said Meg to Monica, as though expecting her to notice some serious symptom of disease in her child. 'That's what we're up against, all the time. Of course, she hears it in school, and it's sure tough to fight school. Now, Little Pal,' she said, directing her attention to Diane, 'how often does Mom have to tell you to call her Mom, or even Mommie, but not that awful *Mummy*? Jeez, you make me sound like something in a museum.'

'Sorry, Mom,' said the child.

'I just can't bear that awful mush-mouthed way they have of talking,' said Meg to Monica again. 'If she takes that home, she'll be a laughing-stock.'

Monica, not knowing what else to do, agreed.

As the evening progressed, she found herself agreeing to many other things, for in Beaver Lodge not to agree in any criticism of England was to be a traitor to Canada. Monica had never given much thought to Canada, as an entity, before; she was a Canadian, and if she had been challenged on the point she would have said that she was proud of it, but if the challenger had probed further, and asked her upon what foundations her pride rested, she would have been confused. But at Beaver Lodge there were no uncertainties: England was a compost-heap of follies, iniquities and ineptitudes. A great country – well, at one time, perhaps – but its greatness was passing. How could a country, where fish was offered for sale on marble slabs, perfectly open to dust and dirt, expect to hold a position of supremacy? The dirtiness of the English, in the eyes of Lorne and Meg, was their greatest crime.

Such conversation was apparently intended to lend savour to the meal, which consisted of tomato juice out of a can (they had their juices sent to them from Canada, every month) and real Western Canadian beef.

'You couldn't touch the beef here,' said Lorne, as he carved. 'It'd be criminal to feed it to Diane. This country, I tell you – their herds are riddled with TB.'

'What's TB, Daddy?' asked Diane.

'It's an awful disease you get from dirt, honey,' said Lorne. 'You know how Daddy tells you to always hold your breath when you're passing a drain in the road, and it's steaming? The cows breathe dirt, and they get TB.'

Having eaten the safe beef, they had a banana-cream pie which was, in part, a traitor, for although the lard in the pastry was from Canada (as was the flour too, of course) the bananas were purchased in England, and were from the Canaries, and thus not the large plantains to which Canada is accustomed. The meal concluded with coffee, made in what Meg declared was 'the real, old-fashioned

Canadian way' in an electric percolator; it was very good coffee, and Monica was grateful for it.

She ventured to ask how it was that the McCorkills were able to get so much of their food from home?

'Lorne's work makes it possible,' said Meg. 'And if it didn't I don't know where we'd turn. He's with the marketing board, you know, and we can make arrangements which probably wouldn't work otherwise. And, frankly, if we couldn't get most of our stuff from home, I'd kick right over the traces; I wouldn't risk feeding Diane the stuff they have here. I've warned her not to accept food in the houses of any of the kiddies she plays with. It's not an easy rule to enforce, but if a kiddy knows just what germs she may be taking into her system, she uses her head.'

It was when Diane had gone to bed that Meg confided one of her chief worries. 'She was less than eight when we left home,' said she, jerking her head upward to indicate the child, 'and more than two years is a long time for a kiddy. In spite of all we can do she's just getting to talk like all the kids around here, and the other day she said, "Mommy, when are we going back to America?" *America!* Get it! Well, I just dropped everything, and I must have talked to her for fifteen minutes about home, and how she must always make it clear to the people here that there's all the difference in the world between Canada and the US. But where do you suppose she picked up an expression like that? From her teacher, of course! Gosh, they don't seem to be able to distinguish – I mean, you'd think they'd realize we were part of the Commonwealth, wouldn't you? I mean, when we're the granary of the world, and all through the war we were the Arsenal of Democracy, and everything?' Meg became almost tearful as she thought of this instance of British indifference to Canadian individuality.

'Diane's young,' said Monica, trying to think of words of comfort for these exiles. 'You won't have to worry about her; she's so pretty; I don't know when I've seen such a pretty complexion. There's something good that England has given her; all the children here have a lovely high colour.'

'Yeah, and they've got broken veins in their cheeks by the time they're thirty,' said Meg, who was so plainly resolved not to take comfort in anything that Monica decided not to try again.

After the conversation had passed through an embittered discussion of the scandalous price of fruit in England – 'Didja ever try to buy a peach in Fortnum and Mason's? Half-a-crown each, and taste like wet kleenex! We bring everything in from home' – the McCorkills turned their attention to what Monica was doing in this desperate land. To her surprise, they did not assert that she could have learned to sing just as well in Canada; when she told them about Sir Benedict Domdaniel, and about Murtagh Molloy and his insistence that she should be able to call up the memory of any emotion at will (she did not tell them about making love to a chair) they were impressed, and said what luck it was that she should have a chance to study with such people. In the realm of the unknown they were quite happy to acknowledge English, or European, supremacy: it was in the things which touched their daily life that they were impossible to please. It came to Monica suddenly, in the midst of a tirade about the utter impossibility of eating English bread – they baked their own, though it was a nuisance – that the McCorkills' vast disrelish for England meant no more than that they were uprooted, afraid, and desperately homesick. It was not a very remarkable flash of insight, but she was only twenty-one, not at all accustomed to knowing things about people which they had not fully recognized themselves, and it did much to soothe her self-esteem, which had been badly bruised during her five months in London.

Monica was not, in fact, accustomed to thinking anything which was contrary to the opinion of any older person with whom she was talking, and it was the McCorkills who first made this adult luxury possible to her. Thus it was that, when Lorne had walked her back to the Underground Station – 'You should never walk around in this city by yourself at night. Do you ever look at the Sunday papers? God, the things that go on! And even ministers in awful cases! Wouldn't it just rot your socks, though?' – she was in high spirits and very well pleased with herself. She had enjoyed the accustomed food, and the cleanliness, and the genuine kindness and warmth of heart which Lorne and Meg had shown her, but she did not feel in the least committed, on that account, to acceptance of their opinions. A Thirteener upbringing had until now denied her the delights of social hypocrisy, and these came with a special sweetness. She had even let the McCorkills think that she would join them at some future meeting of a Canadian Club of which they were members – 'Hard to keep it going, though; so many people seem to lose interest, or they get mixed up with people who live here, and don't seem to want to get together with their own folks' – though she was determined in her heart that she was not going to spend another evening talking about English dirt and wondering why the English could never learn to make coffee. This new freedom to say one thing and think another came to Monica all the more sweetly for coming late, and she liked the McCorkills all the better for not feeling it necessary to agree with them in her heart.

During her long ride back to Earl's Court on the Underground she felt happier than at any time since leaving home. The warmth of the late spring night and the beauty of the city were hidden from her as she sped through the earth in the rattling tube, but she felt them in her heart. If it was to be a fight between England and Canada for the love of Monica Gall, she knew that England would win. Some of the folk songs that she had latterly been studying with Molloy were so powerfully present in her mind that she had to sing them under her breath, unheard by the other passengers because of the noise of the train.

William Taylor was a brisk young sailor,
He was courting a lady fair –

William Taylor had probably eaten a lot of fish that had been exposed to the air on marble slabs, too, but it had not apparently diminished his joy in life.

As I went out one May morning,
One May morning betime,
I met a maid, from home had strayed,
Just as the sun did shine.

This maid unquestionably had one of those superb strawberries-and-cream complexions which degenerated into broken veins after she was thirty, but at the time dealt with in the song she was breathing a wonderful, fresh muhd, and that was what really mattered.

From the Underground Station Monica walked slowly to Courtfield Gardens, happy in the moonlight and without a thought for the clerical rapists who might lurk in every areaway.

How gloriously the sun doth shine,
How pleasant is the air,
I'd rather rest on a true love's breast
Than any other where.

Thus sang Monica, and when two men returning from a pub called 'very nice' from the other side of the street, she waved her hand to them, feeling neither shy nor frightened. It was the first time, since coming to England, that she had sung simply because she was happy. She was not thinking of George Medwall. He came into her mind once, but she dismissed him. He would not do here. He was not a McCorkill, but he did not fit into the new world which she had decided to make her own.

[FOUR]

At the end of June a report was forwarded to the Trustees of the Bridgetower estate by Jodrell and Stanhope, as follows:

In re the Bridgetower Beneficiary

Dear Sirs and Madam:

As reported to you in our communication of January 3 the beneficiary of the Bridgetower Trust, Miss Monica Gall, is comfortably lodged at 23 Courtfield Gardens, SW5. In reply to the specific inquiry of Miss Laura Pottinger, Miss Gall is visited on the first business day of each month by our Mr Boykin, who reports that the landlady, Mrs Merry, says that Miss Gall has at no time entertained a visitor in her quarters other than a Miss Margaret Stamper, a student at the Slade School of Art. If it is thought necessary to appoint a moral guardian for Miss Gall, we cannot undertake such duties, though we will approach Sir Benedict Domdaniel in this matter if so instructed by you.

Attached is a report on Miss Gall's musical studies from Sir Benedict Domdaniel (Encl. 1) and also a statement of disbursements made by us on your behalf (Encl. 2). Assuring you of our advice and service at all times,

Yours truly,
Miles Peter Andrews
(For Jodrell and Stanhope
Plough Court
Fetter Lane
London EC4)

The first enclosure may be given in full:

To the Bridgetower Trustees
Salterton, Ontario,
Canada.

Sirs:

Since your protégée, Monica Gall, came to England to work with me, I have seen her twice. On the first occasion I heard her sing, and was frankly not as impressed with her possibilities as I was when I heard her in Toronto. The voice was very muffled and somewhat lifeless. Therefore I sent her to a first-rate coach, Mr Murtagh Molloy, who has been working with her several days a week since then, and who has been able to do a good deal with her. I heard her again about a week ago, and her voice is at last beginning to declare itself.

It is a good soprano – promises to be really good – but is somewhat 'veiled' or 'covered' – Humphrey Cobbler can explain these terms to you – for a little more than an octave in the lower part. But the range is a fine one, from b below middle C to g'''.

However, as you are well aware, there is more to singing than the possession of a pleasant tone and a big range. The voice must be interesting, and this is a matter of brains, or temperament, or both, and so far Miss Gall, though a nice girl, has not shown anything out of the ordinary in either of these departments. Perhaps her biggest handicap, as I believe I said to you before, is that she has virtually no general cultivation, and though she seems to have some imagination, she has had nothing with which to nourish it.

With a view to remedying this difficulty I am packing her off to Miss Amy Neilson, who lives in St Cloud – an American lady who takes two or three girls into her house for coaching in history and literature, and shows them a good time in Paris – sights, shopping and whatnot. I have known Miss Neilson for many years and can vouch for her. Three months there should make a great difference to Monica; I have written to Amy, asking her to give special attention to the girl's musical background, and have had a copy of Grove's *Dictionary of Music and Musicians* sent there for that purpose. When she returns in the autumn we shall see what we shall see.

Murtagh Molloy, on whose judgement I place great reliance, says that Monica is young for her age and needs waking up. We shall see what can be done.

Yours sincerely,
BENEDICT DOMDANIEL

Dean's Yard
Westminster SW1

It was Enclosure 2 which startled the members of the Bridgetower Trust, assembled one hot July night to consider these communications.

'I must say they're very cool about our money,' said Solly, who had been having trouble meeting some bills, and was sore on the subject.

'We may rely on Jodrell and Stanhope,' said Mr Snelgrove, sticking up for the profession.

'Perhaps we may, but what about Domdaniel?' said Solly. 'He's "packing her off" for three months in France without so much as by-your-leave. Have we given him an absolutely free hand?'

'Yes, and look at this,' said Miss Puss, who had secured the itemized account as soon as Snelgrove had laid it down. 'Grove's *Dictionary of Music and Musicians*, forwarded from Bumpus to France – nine volumes, twenty-seven guineas – one hundred and fifty dollars! For books, of all things! Can't she learn from anything less than that?'

'Not a hundred and fifty dollars, Miss Pottinger,' said Snelgrove; 'you are forgetting the rate of exchange.'

'So far as I am concerned, a five-dollar bill and a pound note are the same thing,' said Miss Puss. 'If there is any drop in the value of the pound, I am sure it is merely temporary.'

'And look what Domdaniel is paying himself,' said Solly. 'He's seen her twice, and he's soaking us ten guineas a time. And this fellow Molloy – five lessons a week at three guineas each! Svengali would have been glad of such fees. We'll have to protest. This is ridiculous.'

'We're making a beggar on horseback of this girl,' said Miss Puss, 'and she'll ride to the Dee. Mark my words.'

It was Dean Knapp who undertook the ungrateful task of being the Voice of Reason.

'We must bear in mind that we are simply appointed to carry out the terms of the Trust,' said he, 'and the income from your mother's estate, Solomon, is very large. Indeed, if what is spent to maintain and instruct the girl during the next six months is no more than we shall have to pay to settle this statement, it will not disperse one-quarter of the total in a year. Have we any right to accumulate money?'

'We have no right to accumulate funds at all, except what might be dictated by common prudence,' said Mr Snelgrove. 'Certainly we cannot withhold money. When Mrs Bridgetower made this will I tried to reason with her, but I am sure you all know how effective that would be. She was determined that her beneficiary should not be stinted.'

'Not stinted!' said Solly. 'And here I am pushed to the very edge of my bank account to settle a bill for a hundred and thirty-two dollars for repairs to Mother's old car, when I've already had to sell my own to get ready money! It's intolerable!'

'It is the law,' said Mr Snelgrove. 'We are not empowered to build up any large surplus. I fear that we shall have to tell Jodrell and

Stanhope to spend more – and get Sir Benedict to spend more. Discreetly, of course. The girl need not actually know.'

'As I understand it, we have to spend the income on roughly a million dollars, which is invested in three and four per cents, and with taxes deductible,' said the Dean, and when Mr Snelgrove nodded, he looked for a time at the ceiling, and then spoke what was in all their minds. 'More than any of us is ever likely to have for himself.'

'That is one of the difficulties of being a trustee,' said Mr Snelgrove; 'that is why trustees often behave so strangely.'

That night Miss Puss was very severe with her old housekeeper, who had left a light burning needlessly, and Solly went to bed drunk, to Veronica's great distress. Though the difficulties of their marriage had been many since they came under the Dead Hand of Mrs Bridgetower, this was something new.

[SIX]

'There you have it,' said Sir Benedict. 'Orders from headquarters: we must spend more money. I must spend more on having you trained. You must spend more, presumably, on your way of living. The lawyers here are doubling your personal allowance.'

'O dear,' said Monica. 'I wish they wouldn't do that.'

'Why? Didn't you learn anything about spending money in Paris? I particularly asked Amy to give you a few pointers about that.'

'She did. She was wonderful to me, and told me a lot about clothes and make-up and hair-dos and things. But, please, Sir Benedict, I don't want to get involved in all that kind of thing. It's not what I'm here for.'

'But apparently it is what you're here for. These Bridgetower people want their money spent, and it's your job to spend it. Most girls would jump at your chance.'

'No, no. I'm here to be trained as a singer – a musician, I hope –'

'Why the distinction?'

'Amy took three of us to a party in Paris that some musical people were giving, and a string quartet played, and afterward I was talking to them, and said I was training to be a musician, and when they found out I was a singer, they laughed. One of them said, "Music is a very nice hobby for a singer; it gives him a complete change from his profession".'

'I know; musicians are full of jokes about singers. Justified, most of them. But we'll try to make a musician of you, as well. What's that to do with all this extra money which must be got rid of?'

'Well, I can't escape a feeling that it will make it harder for me to do what I want to do. I mean – it seems to cushion life, somehow. It cuts you off from people, and experiences, and that's just what I need. I found that out in Paris. Those girls at Amy's; they were awfully nice, and I had a fine time, but they weren't serious. They're just dabblers –

in the nicest possible way – but still dabblers. I'm serious. I want to be a professional. If possible I want to be an artist.'

'And you're afraid having plenty of cash will cut you off from that?'

'Yes. Don't you agree?'

'Look around you, I'm far from rich, but I'm pretty comfortable, and I take care to keep my fees high. But I'm rather widely regarded as an artist.'

'Of course. But you've made your way. You didn't begin with all this.'

'My family were well-off; I was born with a very good weight of silver spoon in my mouth. In my student days I never missed a meal or wore a shabby suit, and I worked just as hard and agonized just as much as the fellows who hadn't sixpence. All money can do for a musician is keep him from discomfort and worry about bills – and that's a very good thing.'

'Those girls in Paris were all ambitious, until it meant real work. But they all knew they didn't actually have to work, and that made all the difference.'

'Had they any talent?'

'I don't know. But how do I know that I've any talent myself?'

'You don't, but you're industrious. Murtagh says you work like a black. But that has nothing to do with money. You really must shake off these fat-headed nineteenth-century notions you have about musicians being romantic characters who starve in garrets, doing immense moral good to the world through the medium of their art. Now look here: money alone can't hurt you. If you're a fool, or if you haven't any talent, or not enough, it will influence the special way in which you go to the devil. Money is a thing you have to control; it must play the part in your life that you allot to it, and it must never become the star turn. But take it from me, too much money is less harmful than too little. Wealth tends to numb feeling and nibble at talent, but poverty coarsens feeling and chokes talent, and feeling and talent are the important things in your job and mine.'

'Yes, but – I don't know whether I have any talent, and neither you nor Mr Molloy will say anything one way or the other. And I do know that I haven't much feeling. Mr Molloy says so, too. He's always at me to express more, but I haven't much to express.'

'What would you have to express – at twenty-one?'

'Surely if I have any feeling, any insight into music, it ought to show itself by now?'

'Not necessarily. Some people are born with huge, gusty typhoons of feeling, all ready to be unleashed. Others have to learn to feel. And when they're both forty, you'd have a hard time telling one from the other. But when they're fifty the typhoons will be getting weaker, and the feeling which has been carefully nurtured and schooled may well be growing still. I don't suppose anybody ever told you that.'

'Never.'

'Look at your physical type. Medium blonde, northern-looking, good solid bones, strong as a horse, I'll bet, and with an excellent, good big head. You're not one of those little southern passion-pots, with a rose in her teeth and a stiletto tucked into her garter. *She's* got feeling; *you've* got intelligence. She's a sprinter, you're a miler. You'll have to learn, painstakingly, things that she seems to have known from her cradle. But because she's never had to learn them, they may desert her quickly – after an illness, or when her lover runs off with another girl, or something. Whereas you, once you've learned a thing, will cling to it like a bulldog, or like a snapping-turtle which is supposed never to relax its hold till sundown.'

'I see,' said Monica, who was overjoyed to be compared to a bulldog or a snapping-turtle under these circumstances.

'So get on with the job. Stop fretting because you're not worldly-wise and chock-full of Beethovenian *Sturm und Drang* at twenty. That's not your type at all. Stop fussing that comfort is going to knock the props from under your genius. Develop what you've got: make it possible for your emotions to grow. Get on with the job. Work, work, work. How are the languages?'

'Not too bad, Amy said.'

'Well, work harder and make them damned good. And do what Murtagh tells you; if anybody can make a singer of you, he will. And you may take it from me that you'll get all the experience you want, soon enough. Most people reach a point where they're wishing experience would stop crowding them. Anyhow, it isn't what happens to you that really counts: it's what you are able to do with it. The streets are crammed with people who have had the most extraordinary experiences – been shipwrecked, chased out of Caliph's harems, blown sky-high by bombs – and it hasn't meant a thing to them, because they couldn't distill it. Art's distillation; experience is wine, and art is the brandy we distill from it. – Now, you'll have to go. I've a man coming about some music for a contemporary composers' series. And don't worry; we'll think of some ways to spend the Bridgetower money. – By the way, did you ever know this Mrs Bridgetower?'

'Oh no; she was an invalid for years, I think. Anyway – I wouldn't have known her.'

'She sounds like a loony. This Trust of hers is silly. Still, if the money has to be spent, we'll spend it.'

[TWO]

Experience – well, Paris had been experience. Amy Neilson had taught her a lot about eating, for instance. It had been a surprise to Monica to find that her very best manners weren't the thing at all, according to Amy, and she had had to modify them, not in the direction of more gentility, but less. And the gay little laugh with which she had been accustomed to pass off any social difficulty – Amy had quickly rooted out that little laugh. There had been, well, dozens of things that Amy had discouraged, always in the kindest possible way, and Monica had been a quick learner. Her clothes had been reformed in the direction of plainness; some rings and earrings, which were certainly not expensive, but which she had once thought very pretty, had been discarded; a tendency toward cuteness in dress and manner had withered under Amy's hint that to be cute was not the whole end of woman.

Yes, that was all experience. But shallow, surely? Not the raw material for one of Molloy's muhds. What else? That party to which Amy had taken her in that wonderful apartment on the Rue Scheffer – just like the movies, with a view which included the Eiffel Tower – that had been experience. For it was a very musical party, to introduce the work of a promising young composer, and Monica had gone to it in a reverential spirit. And what had happened? The assembled musicians, and patrons and critics and concert agents had listened far less intently and politely than the audience of the Community Concerts in Salterton would have done; some of them, sitting on a stair which led to a gallery above the salon, had actually *talked*, in loud whispers, and not about the music, either! That was experience, surely – to discover that in Paris, of all places, real music-lovers could be so rude as to talk while music was being played? She had mentioned this to Amy, and Amy had laughed. 'You don't have to be serious about it all the time,' she had said. But surely you did have to be serious about it all the time? Wasn't that what Sir Benedict had just been telling her?

But Sir Benedict wasn't very serious. He just shot off a lot of talk which seemed to be serious, and turned suddenly into jokes – the silly kind of jokes the English seemed to like so much. Still, a visit to him always made Monica feel that music was something even better than being serious – it was exciting. And what a marvellous person! So tall, and with a wonderful figure, even though he was fifty-three (she had checked him in *Grove*) and it didn't matter a bit that he was so bald and had really an uncommonly big nose. Her attitude toward him was worshipful, but she did wish he would explain himself a little more fully. His remark that she was intelligent, for instance. Why couldn't he have expanded that? If she was intelligent, why couldn't she summon up more muhd for Molloy?

What had he meant when he said that some people had to learn to feel? Surely that was a contradiction? And all that about distilling experience from the wine of life. What experience had come her way that could be distilled? Did he mean that everything was experience?

As Monica pondered, a large, middle-aged nun, with a school-girl in her charge, entered the bus and sat down beside her. The nun composed her vast skirts, and fished a rosary of workmanlike appearance from their depths. 'Come along now, Norah,' she said in a loud, cheerful voice to the girl at her side, 'never waste a minute; let's say a rosary for the conversion of the people on the bus.'

Was that experience? Could it be made into anything? Did it add anything to her?

Distilling thus, Monica went back to Courtfield Gardens, buying some special cakes for her tea on the way, to celebrate having spent half an hour with the exciting Sir Benedict.

[THREE]

October passed in more work with Molloy. A splendid combination gramophone and radio had arrived one day at Courtfield Gardens for Monica, with a note from Sir Benedict urging her to make good use of it, and to buy as many records as she wished. It was unfortunate that on the very day of the arrival of this glossy monster, Peggy Stamper and one of her dirty young men in corduroys dropped in.

'Coo!' said Peggy, surveying it in wonder; 'have you bought that?'

'I suppose so,' said Monica; 'it's to be part of my training.'

Peggy and the young man commented freely, and not without envy, on the kind of training which demanded so costly an object, and it was plain to Monica that the radiogram put her, so far as these two were concerned, in a different world from themselves. They were poor on principle; it was part of their creed that nobody who was serious about art ever had a bean, and those of their group who had allowances from home took good care not to offend against this tenet. When they left, Monica knew, without anything having been said about it, that her position on the fringe of Peggy's group had become even more remote. They had nothing against her, but obviously she was rich, and that was that.

Without being aware that she was doing so, she salved her wound in a manner common to the rich; she bought a lot of expensive albums of recordings, some swansdown cushions for her divan, and some luxurious things to eat; these expenditures numbed, but did not remove, her sense of loss. So she increased the dose of her anodyne; she bought some new clothes – really good ones, of the kind that Amy approved for the well brought up young girl, and a quiet but expensive winter coat. If she had lost her place in the corduroy group, she might as well be thoroughly out of it. The clothes and the pleasure of listening to the machine insulated her against loneliness for almost a fortnight. But she knew, every night, and as she prepared her breakfast each morning, that another bout of that terrible destructive despair which had seized her on her first arrival in London was imminent, waiting for an opportunity to descend. It would not be quite the same, for her circumstances had changed, but it would be of the same essence.

Sometimes she had to fight hard against panic. Should she confide in Meg McCorkill? Yes, but confide what? That she was afraid that money was cutting her off from serious work and the people who might be her friends? How silly it seemed when put into words! That the English winter, which was now beginning, filled her with dread? That pegging away at French and German made her feel like a schoolgirl, without a schoolgirl's resilience against the boredom of study? Meg would have a ready and immediate remedy for both those ills – frequent visits to Beaver Lodge. But three months in Paris, and the English spring, had put a barrier between her and the raw simplicities of Beaver Lodge which seemed to her to be insurmountable.

Of course she had Molloy's unfailing method of summoning and controlling emotion. She had only to breathe a happy and confident muhd, and serenity and confidence would certainly follow. But it didn't work. She determinedly set about it on two occasions, and both ended in crying fits. Real heaviness of heart could not be budged by such imaginative effort.

[FOUR]

Relief came suddenly. One day, at the end of a lesson in which Molloy was particularly exacting, he said: 'Sir Ben wants to hear you tomorrow, and he's coming here. So be on your best behaviour and do me credit.'

Half an hour of the next day's lesson had passed before Sir Benedict Domdaniel appeared; in Monica's eyes he seemed more elegant than ever against the background of Molloy's shabby teaching-room, and beside the stubby figure of the Irishman. He heard her sing some of her folksongs, and declined Molloy's earnest request that she be allowed to recite some passages of Shakespeare for him.

'Done much about scales, Murtagh?'

'Not yet, Ben, but I'm goin' to get at them right away. She's ready for a good grind on exercises. But you know my way; the exercises must be linked with some real music, or you'll get nothing but a technical voice. But now the voice is warmed up, I can see where we're goin'.'

'You've done a good job. Better voice than I thought it might be.' He smiled at Monica. 'Are you pleased with yourself?'

'I can't say,' said she. 'You must be the judge.'

'Yes, but you know that you sing better than when you came here, don't you?'

'It feels better; I didn't know I had such a big range.'

'Your voice is beginning to declare itself. Some technical work will make it very useful. But at present you haven't much to say with it, have you? And that's really what I've come about; it's time you went to another coach.'

'Leave Mr Molloy!'

'Oh no, not at all. He'll continue the work on your voice, make it agile and strong and give you a sound technical equipment. But I think you ought to go to another man to learn something about music generally, broaden your musical experience. You don't want to be just a singer; well – you must learn something more than singing.'

'Aw, now, Ben, I'll give her all o' that she can take,' said Molloy; 'I've started her already on some Shakespeare, and if you'd only let her show you what she can do, you'd get the surprise of your life. Come on, give him the Seven Ages –'

'Murtagh, I don't want to hear the Seven Ages or anything else. I know exactly what I want her to do, and if you'll listen –'

'Ben, some day you'll insult me once too often. Are you suggesting that I'm not capable of giving this girl a good cultural training? Is that what you mean? Because if so –'

'You're the best voice-builder in London. I tell you that, and don't forget I got my training with old Garcia, and I know what I'm saying. Isn't that enough for you?'

'You want to snatch a promising pupil away from me and give her to God knows what charlatan –'

'She's not your pupil; she's my pupil, and I'm responsible to the What's-Its-Name Foundation for her. I'm doing the best I can for her. That's why I sent her to you in the first place, Murtagh, and if you weren't so damned stubborn you'd know it. And I'm not taking her from you; I just want to send her to Revelstoke for some coaching in things you probably haven't time for.'

'What in the name o' God are you sending her to Revelstoke for?'

'Excellent reasons, my dear Murtagh; excellent reasons. Let's say that it's to broaden her musical experience, and leave it there.'

'It'll do that. That fellow's worthless, Ben, and you know it.'

'On the contrary. I have been working on some of his things for my series of contemporary music broadcasts, and he has been most helpful. And I'll tell you more: he's one of the best of our younger composers.'

'Ha! Quite the little genius.'

'Yes, quite the little genius.'

'But an impossible fellow to get on with.'

'Exactly what he says about you, so it's a draw. Now you mustn't take away the character of Monica's new teacher before she's even seen him, Murtagh, so shut up. And it's no good shouting any more, because I've settled everything. Monica, tomorrow at four o'clock you are to call on Mr Giles Revelstoke; he lives at 32 Tite Street – on the top floor. He'll be expecting you, and he'll undertake some general musical training for you. And that's what you need.'

After a little further pacification of Molloy, Sir Benedict carried Monica off in his car, and went some distance out of his way to leave her at Courtfield Gardens. As they were parting, he said: 'By the way, I made rather a bloomer last time we were talking; I re-read the letter from the lawyers afterward, and I don't think I should have told you that we had to spend more money on you. Apparently you're not supposed to know, though I don't really see how it's to be kept from you. I'm a terrible chatterer – my little vice. Anyhow, it's not my business to fall in with lawyers' schemes like that. It's a fact; more money must be spent. That's why I feel we can afford Revelstoke now. You'll like him. Delightful chap.'

[FIVE]

Thirty-two Tite Street was a gloomy house across the road from a large Infirmary, from whose windows came an unceasing sound which Monica at first thought was the weeping of baby chicks, but which she later learned was the crying of infants in the nurseries. A rack of cards in the hall told her that Giles Revelstoke was on the top floor, and she was about to press the bell beneath his name when she heard someone coming down the stairs very rapidly and noisily, shouting 'Sorree, sorree' in a loud voice. It was a very tall young man with tousled hair, who arrived beside her as her finger was poised to push.

'You want Giles?' said the young man. 'Don't ring; don't dream of ringing; you'll cut him to the heart if you ring. Go right up, and right in without knocking, and if you don't see him about give a cooee. Most informal fellow in the world. Hurry up, old girl; up you go.'

Monica had dressed herself elegantly for this first meeting with her new teacher, and had worked up a sense of the dignity of the occasion. She did not want to burst upon him without all the proper formalities. But the tall young man was not to be gainsaid, so she went up two flights of long dark stairs, and found a door at the top which opened into what was plainly a studio, an extremely crowded and untidy room furnished with a large work table and an upright piano, and beyond that nothing recognizable as furniture, but with heaps of books, papers and music piled on the floor and all the other flat surfaces. The only pleasing thing about the room, apart from a large black cat asleep on the piano top, was a dormer window set in the sloping roof which gave a view, through chimneypots, toward the Thames.

Should she sit down? But where? She stood for a few minutes, then picked her way through the debris on the floor to the window and looked out of it for a while. But she was disturbed by the sense that she was in somebody else's room. She must not make free. But where was Mr Revelstoke? Had he forgotten that she was to come at four? The tousled young man had said that he was at home. This was quite unlike a visit to Molloy, who was as punctual as the clock, or to Sir Benedict, whose valet was always at hand to take her at once to the great man. What had Molloy called Revelstoke? 'Quite the little genius'. This looked like a genius's room. But how to inform the genius of her presence?

She coughed. Nothing happened. She coughed again, and walked about heavily, making a noise with her feet and feeling a fool. Should she go downstairs again, and ring the bell?

No; she would play the piano. She seated herself and played what came first into her head, which was her one-time favourite, *Danse Macabre*. The cat roused itself, yawned at her, and slept again.

She had played for perhaps three minutes, when a voice said very loudly behind her, 'Stop that bloody row!' She turned, and standing in the doorway was a man. He was utterly naked.

Nothing in Monica's previous experience had prepared her for such a spectacle, and it was the most shocking sight, within the bounds of nature, that could have confronted her. The Thirteeners, and everybody else with whom she had ever been intimately acquainted, thought very poorly of nakedness. Courtships, even when carried to lengths which resulted in hasty and muted weddings, were always conducted fully dressed. The intimacies of married life were negotiated in the dark, under blankets. Shame about nakedness was immensely valued, as a guarantee of high character. It is true that, when in Paris, Monica had been taken to the Louvre several times by Amy Neilson, and she had learned to look at naked statuary – even the Hermaphrodite – without betraying the discomfort she felt in the presence of those stony, bare monsters; but that was art and idealized form – no preparation for what she now saw – a naked man, not especially graced with beauty, coloured in shades which ranged between pink and whitey-drab, patchily hairy, and obviously very much alive.

He was smiling, which made it all worse. He seemed quite at his ease; it was she – she who was in the right, she the clothed, she the outraged one, who was overset. Monica had never fainted in her life, but she felt a lightness in her head now, an inability to get her breath, which might well rob her of consciousness.

'You're the Canadian Nightingale, I suppose,' said he. 'I forgot you were coming. Hold on a jiffy, while I get some clothes. But don't play that trash any more.'

And a jiffy it was, for he was back again almost at once, wearing flannel trousers, and with his bare feet thrust into worn slippers, buttoning his shirt; he went behind the piano, picked up a bundle of woman's garments and threw them through the door into the next room, shouting, 'Come on, Persis, you lazy cow, get up and make us some tea.' The reply, which came through the door in a rich and well-bred contralto, was brief, and couched in words which Monica had never heard spoken in a woman's voice before. 'Shut up,' replied Revelstoke, 'can't you behave yourself when we have company – a distinguished guest from the Premier Dominion, our mighty ally in peace and war? Be a good girl and get some tea, and we shall have music to restore our souls.'

He took the cat in his arms and stroked it, as he turned again to Monica. 'You mustn't mind a degree of informality here which you haven't met in the elegant environs of Sir Benedict Domdaniel. Brummagem Benny, as we sometimes call him in the musical world – without a hint of malice, mind you – likes to do himself very well. And properly so. He must keep up a position commensurate with his great and well-deserved reputation. But I, you see, am a very different sort of creature. You are now in the editorial offices of *Lantern*, undoubtedly the most advanced and unpopular critical journal being published in English today. The significance of the name will not escape you. *Lantern* – it is the lantern of Diogenes, searching for the honest, the true and the good, and it is similarly the lantern, or lamp-post, referred to in the good old Revolutionary cry 'A la lanterne!' – because from this *Lantern* we suspend the hacked corpses of those whom we are compelled to judge harshly; you will not miss, either, the allusion to that Lantern Land which Master Francis Rabelais describes in his *Pantagruel* (with which I presume that you are amply acquainted) and which was the habitation of pedants and cheats in all branches of the arts; we allude to it slyly in our title by a species of gnomic homophony which will at once be apparent to you. This is a workroom, and workrooms are apt to be untidy. This will soon be your workroom, too, if we get on as well as I hope we shall. You had better meet my friend, Pyewacket, a delightful but musically uncritical cat.'

He was interrupted by the entry, from the bedroom, of a tall girl of twenty-three or four, wearing a not very fresh slip and nothing else; her long dark hair was hanging down her back and she had the tumbled look of one who has risen from bed.

'Match,' said she to Revelstoke. He found one on the table and gave it to her.

'Allow me to introduce Miss Persis Kinwellmarshe, daughter of Admiral Sir Percy Kinwellmarshe, retired, now of Tunbridge Wells. Miss Kinwellmarshe is one of my principal editorial assistants. We have been engaged in a type of editorial conference known as scrouperizing. You do know Rabelais? No? Pity!'

Monica disliked Miss Kinwellmarshe on sight. She had Bad Girl written all over her, and in addition she was extremely handsome, with a finely formed nose, through the crimson-shadowed nostrils of which she now seemed to be looking at Monica.

'It's a pleasure to meet any acquaintance of Mr Revelstoke's,' said she.

Monica knew when she was being mocked, but Amy's prime injunction – 'You can never go wrong by being simple, dear' – came to her rescue. So she bowed her head slightly toward Miss Kinwellmarshe, and said 'How do you do?'

Miss Kinwellmarshe, taking the match, turned and went to the kitchen. *She's got a butt-end on her like a bumble-bee*, said the voice of Ma Gall, very clearly, inside Monica's head, – so clearly that Monica started.

'Now, let's do some work,' said Revelstoke, who appeared to have enjoyed this encounter. 'You've been with the ineffable Molloy for a while, Sir Benny tells me. An admirable coach, with a splendid, policeman-like attitude toward the art of song. Sing me a few of the things he's taught you.'

Unlike Molloy, he made no move to accompany her, so Monica sat at the piano and sang half-a-dozen English folksongs. She could not have explained why it was so, but the knowledge that Miss Kinwellmarshe was within earshot had a tonic effect on her, and she sang them well.

'The accompaniments are charming, aren't they?' said Revelstoke. 'Cecil Sharp had a delightful small talent for such work. But of course folksongs are not meant to be accompanied. Just sing me *Searching for Lambs* without all that agreeable atmospheric deedle-deedle.'

So Monica sang the song again. If he thinks I've never sung this without accompaniment he certainly doesn't know Murtagh Molloy, she thought.

'Not bad. You have a true ear, and a nice sense of rhythm. – Ah, here is dear Miss Kinwellmarshe with the tea. I won't ask you to take a cup, Miss – I forget for the moment – yes, of course, Miss Gall, but you shall have one when you've finished singing. Now, Brum Benny tells me you have a special line in Victorian drawing-room ballads – such a novelty, and so original of you to have worked it up in a time when that kind of music is so undeservedly neglected. I understand that Tosti's *Good-Bye!* is one of your specialties. I can hardly wait. Will you sing it now, please. You won't mind if we have tea as you do so? The perfect accompaniment for the song, don't you think?'

Miss Kinwellmarshe had laid herself out voluptuously on the work table, pillowing her head on a pile of manuscript and permitting her long and beautifully wavy hair to hang over the edge; the splendour of her figure in this position was somewhat marred by the dirtiness of the soles of her feet, but it was clear that she aimed at large effects, and scorned trifles.

'I haven't sung that song for several months,' said Monica. Indeed, she had learned to be thoroughly ashamed of Tosti under the rough but kindly guidance of Molloy. How could Sir Benedict have mentioned it! These English! Sly, sneaky, mocking! You never knew when you had them.

'But after we have put a favourite work aside for a time, we often find that we have unconsciously arrived at a new understanding of it,' said Revelstoke, and he was smiling like a demon.

'I'd really rather not,' said Monica.

'But I wish it. And I dislike having to remind you that if I am to teach you anything, you must do as I wish.' His smile was now from the teeth only.

He just wants to roast me in front of that grubby bitch, thought Monica. I'll walk out. I'll tell Sir Benedict I won't bear it. I'll go home.

But she met Revelstoke's eyes, and she sang. She was angrier than she had ever been in her life. She hated this man who dared to show himself naked, and whose talk was one smooth, sneering incivility after another; she hated that nearly naked tart lolling on the table. She hated Sir Benedict, who had been making fun of her behind her back. She was so full of passionate hatred that her head seemed ready to burst. But she had not spent six months with Murtagh Molloy for nothing. She took possession of herself, she breathed the muhd, and she sang.

She finished, and the seven bars of *diminuendo* regret on the piano were completed. There was silence. The first to break it was Miss Kinwellmarshe, and her comment was a derisive, dismissive, derogatory monosyllable.

'Not at all,' said Revelstoke; 'and let me remind you, Persis, that I am the critic here, and any comment will come from me, not you. Take yourself off, you saucy puss, and do some typing, or wash up, or something.' Rising, he hauled Miss Kinwellmarshe off the table and pushed her toward the kitchen, giving her a resounding slap on her splendid buttocks. She repeated her previous comment with hauteur, but she went.

'Now,' said he, 'let's get down to business. What's that song all about?'

Monica had occasionally been questioned in this way by Molloy, and she always hated it. A song was a song, and it was about what it said; it was almost bad luck to probe it and pull it to pieces, for it might never regain its shape. But Revelstoke had made her sing against her will, and she knew that he could make her speak. Might as well give in at once and get it over.

'It's about people saying good-bye.'

'People?'

'Lovers, I suppose.'

'Why are they saying good-bye?'

'I don't know; the song doesn't say.'

'Doesn't it? Who wrote it?'

'Tosti.'

'The music, yes. When did he live?'

'Oh, quite recently; Mr Molloy once saw him.'

'Who wrote the words?'

'I – I don't know.'

'Oh, then I assume that you consider the words of small importance in comparison with the music. Do you think it is good music?'

'No, not really.'

'How would you describe it?'

'A sort of drawing-room piece, I suppose.'

'Yes, yes; but technically?'

'A ballad?'

'No, not a ballad. It is hardly a tune at all – certainly not a hummable sort of tune like a ballad. It's what's called an *aria parlante*. Know what that means?'

'A sort of speaking song?'

'A declamatory song. So there must be something to declaim. The words were written by a Scottish Victorian novelist and poet called George John Whyte-Melville. I see that your copy of the song gives his initials as "G.T." and robs him of his hyphen; just shows what the firm of Ricordi thought about him. Ever heard of him?'

'Never.'

'An interesting man. Quite successful, but always underestimated his own work and was apt to run himself down, in a gentlemanly sort of way. Wrote a lot about fox-hunting, but there is always a melancholy strain in his work which conflicts oddly with the subjects. His biographer thought it was because his married life was most unhappy. Does that seem to you to throw any light on that song?'

'It's very unhappy. You mean that perhaps it wasn't lovers, but himself and his wife he was writing about?'

'I am charmed by your implied opinion of the married state. Married people are sometimes lovers, and lovers are not always happy. Why are they unhappy, do you suppose?'

'Well, usually because they can't get married. Or because one of them may be married already.'

'There can be other reasons. Read me the first verse.'

In a constricted tone, and without expression, Monica read:

Falling leaf, and fading tree,
Lines of white in a sullen sea,
Shadows rising on you and me;
The swallows are making them ready to fly
Wheeling out on a windy sky –
Good-bye, Summer,
Good-bye.

'You see? A succession of pictures – the fall of the leaf, the birds going south, a rising storm, and darkness falling. And it all adds up to – what?'

This is worse than Eng. Lit. at school, thought Monica. But she answered, 'Autumn, I suppose.'

'Autumn, you suppose. Now let me read you the second verse, with a little more understanding than you choose to give to your own reading –

Hush, a voice from the far away!
'Listen and learn', it seems to say,
'All the tomorrows shall be as today.
The cord is frayed, the cruse is dry
The link must break and the lamp must die.
Good-bye to Hope,
Good-bye.'

What do you make of that?'

'Still Autumn?'

'An Autumn that continues forever? Examine the symbols – lamp gone out, chain broken, jug empty, cord ready to break, and all the tomorrows being like today – what's that suggest? What is the warning voice? Think!'

Monica thought. 'Death, perhaps?'

'Quite correct. Death – perhaps: but not quite Death as it is ordinarily conceived. The answer is in the last verse –

What are we waiting for?
Oh, my heart!
Kiss me straight on the brows!
And part – again – my heart!
What are we waiting for, you and I?
A pleading look, a stifled cry –
Good-bye forever,
Good-bye!

There it is! Plain as the nose on your face! What is it all about? What are they saying Good-bye to? Come on! Think!'

His repeated insistence that she think made Monica confused and mulish. She sat and stared at him for perhaps two minutes, and then he spoke.

'It is Death, right enough, but not the Death of the body; it is the Death of Love. Listen to the passion in the last verse – passion which Tosti has quite effectively partnered in the music. Haste – the sense of constraint around the heart – the pleading for a climax and the disappointment of that climax – What is it? In human experience, what is it?'

Monica had no idea what it was.

'Well, Miss Lumpish Innocence, it is the Autumn of love; it is the failure of physical love; it is impotence. It is a physical inadequacy which brings in its train a terrible and crushing sense of spiritual inadequacy. It is the sadness of increasing age. It is the price which life exacts for maturity. It is the foreknowledge of Death itself. It is the inspiration of some of the world's great art, and it is also at the root of an enormous amount of bad theatre, and Hollywood movies, and the boo-hoo-hoo of popular music. It is one of the principal springs of that delicious and somewhat bogus emotion – Renunciation. And Whyte-Melville and old Tosti have crammed it into twenty lines of verse and a hundred or so bars of music, and while the result may not be great, by God it's true and real, and that is why that song still has a kick like a mule, for all its old-fashionedness. Follow me?'

Monica sat for a time, pondering. What Revelstoke had said struck forcibly on her mind, and she felt that it would have opened new doors to her if she had fully understood it. And she wanted to understand. So, after a pause, she looked him in the eye.

'What's impotence?'

Revelstoke looked at her fixedly. Ribald comment rose at once to his tongue, but Monica's seriousness asked for something better than that. He answered her seriously.

'It is when you want to perform the act of love, and can't,' he said. 'The difficulty is peculiar to men in that particular form, but it is equally distressing to both partners. The symbolism of the poem is very well chosen.'

There was silence for perhaps three minutes, while Monica pondered. 'I don't see the good of it,' she said at last. 'You take an old song that hundreds of people must have sung and you drag it down so it just means a nasty trouble that men get. Is that supposed to make it easier for me to sing it? Or are you making fun of me?'

'I am not making fun of you, and I have not done what you said. I have related quite a good poem to a desperate human experience which, in my opinion, is the source from which it springs. If you think of a poem as a pretty trifle that silly men make up while smelling flowers, my interpretation is no good to you. But if you think of a poem as a flash of insight, a fragment of truth, a break in the cloud of human nonsense and pretence, my interpretation is valid. When you sing, you call from the depth of your own experience to the depth of experience in your hearer. And depth of experience has its physical counterpart, believe me; we aren't disembodied spirits, you know, nor are we beautiful, clear souls cumbered with ugly indecent bodies. This song isn't about "a nasty trouble that men get" – to use your own depressingly middle-class words; it is about the death of love, and the foreknowledge of death; it is an intimation of mortality. As you say, hundreds of people have sung it without necessarily looking very deeply into it, and thousands of listeners have been moved without knowing why. Poetry and music can speak directly to depths of experience in us which we possess without being conscious of them, in language which we understand only imperfectly. But there must be some of us who understand better than others, and who give the best of ourselves to that understanding. If you are to be one of them, you must be ready to make a painful exploration of yourself. When I came in here just now, you were playing a rather silly piece in a very silly way. You sang your folksongs like a cheap Marie Antoinette pretending to be a shepherdess. Domdaniel wants you to be better than that, and so he has sent you to me.'

'Do you think Sir Benedict thinks about songs and poetry the way you do?'

'Sir Benedict dearly loves to play the role of the exquisitely dressed, debonair, frivolous man of the world. But he's no fool. And he thinks you are no fool, too. He told me so. Here's your cup of tea that I promised you.'

It was very nasty tea. Monica drank it reflectively. After a time, during which Revelstoke had stared intently at her, he said –

'What are you thinking about?'

'I was thinking that you're not really *simpatico*.'

'I've no time for charm. Many people think me extremely unpleasant, and I cultivate that, because it keeps fools at a distance.'

'Mr Molloy says you're quite the genius.'

'Mr Molloy, in his limited way, is quite right. – Well, are you coming to me for lessons?'

'Yes.'

'All right. Give me thirty shillings now, for your subscription to *Lantern*. Here's a copy of the latest number. And next time you come here, have the politeness to ring the bell. It'll spare your blushes.'

[SIX]

If Monica had been in danger from loneliness and boredom before, she would now have found herself in danger of being exhausted, had it not been that, as Sir Benedict had said, she was as strong as a horse. She thoroughly enjoyed the excitement. Molloy continued to take her association with Revelstoke as an intentional affront offered to his own powers as a teacher by Domdaniel, and he worked her very hard on exercises designed to develop those two characteristics of the voice which he called, in his old-fashioned nomenclature, 'the florid and the pathetic', and which Sir Benedict preferred to call 'agility and legato'. He imparted his infallible method to her in a sort of pedagogic fury, nagged ceaselessly about the importance of breath and posture in the control of nervousness, and inquired searchingly about what she ate, and how much. In a veiled manner, he inquired about the regularity of her bowels. The poise of her head and the relaxation of her jaw become obsessions with him, and sometimes she woke in the night, startled to hear his voice shouting 'Head forward and up – not backward and down – lead with your head!'

Revelstoke said very little to her about the production of her voice, and it did not take her long to discover that he knew little about it. 'Let the ineffable Murtagh teach you the mechanics,' said he, 'and I'll take care of your style.' But he led her on to tell him what Molloy did and said at lessons, and she, finding that imitations of the Irishman amused him, could not resist the temptation to oblige, now and then, though she felt rather cheap afterward. Molloy was so truly kind, so unstinting in his efforts on her behalf, and yet – it was not easy to resist a young and clever man who wanted her to make sport of the older, exuberant one. She salved her conscience by telling it that she meant no real unkindness, and that everybody, including Sir Benedict, laughed at him.

With Revelstoke she toiled through a great amount of the literature of song, not studying it for the purpose of singing but, in his phrase, 'getting the hang of it.' Nevertheless, this process was hard work, and involved excursions into poetry in English, German and French which taxed and expanded her knowledge of those languages.

She knew no Italian, and Revelstoke urged Sir Benedict to find a teacher for her. This added to her day's work considerably, for Signor Sacchi was a zealot, yearning to get her into Dante at the first possible moment.

It was with English, however, that she had most trouble. Molloy, as good as his word, had moderated her Ontario accent to a point where she had occasional misgivings that her mother would consider her present speech 'a lotta snottery'. But it would not do for Revelstoke. He condemned much in her new manner of speech as 'suburban', and insisted on a standard of purity of his own. Her former models, the actors at the Old Vic, he dismissed out of hand; their speech reeked, he said, of South London tennis clubs.

'English is not a language of quantities, like Latin,' he said, over and over again, 'but a language of strong and weak stresses. A faulty stress destroys the meaning and flavour of a word, and distorts the quality of a line of verse. Without a just appreciation of the stresses in a line of verse, you cannot sing it – for singing is first, last and all the time a form of human eloquence, speech raised to the highest degree.'

His manner of teaching was confusing to Monica's straightforward intelligence, for she never knew when he was joking. She had been accustomed in her schooldays to teachers whose jokes were infrequent, and clearly labelled. But after a few weeks she learned to identify certain tones of voice which signified irony, and even to enjoy it, though hers was by no means an ironical cast of mind. It was the variety and apparent depth of his knowledge which principally amazed her, and she never became accustomed to his ability to quote from the Bible, though it was obvious that one who lived so evil a life (Miss Kinwellmarshe's garments were forever turning up in unforeseen places) must be an unbeliever.

One day, after he had talked to her for half an hour about Schubert's settings of poems by Müller, and of the ability of a poet of very modest achievement to inspire a musical genius of the first order, she ventured to thank him, and to say that it was wonderfully educational. He understood that the clumsiness and seeming patronage of the phrase concealed a genuine humility of feeling, but he uttered a warning which lodged itself in her mind.

'I know what you mean,' said he, 'but I wish you wouldn't use words like "educational", which have grown sour from being so much in the wrong people's mouths. What we are doing isn't really educational. It's enlightening, I suppose, and its purpose is to nurture the spirit. If formal education has any bearing on the arts at all, its purpose is to make critics, not artists. Its usual effect is to cage the spirit in other people's ideas – the ideas of poets and philosophers, which were once splendid insights into the nature of life, but which people who have no insights of their own have hardened into dogmas. It is the spirit we must work with, and not the mind as such. For "the spirit searcheth all things, yea, the deep things of God".'

Thus, rather quickly, all things considered, Revelstoke persuaded Monica to give up her determination to learn like a parrot, and to imitate her masters without really understanding what they did, and brought her to a point where she could feel a little, and understand, respect and cherish her own feeling.

[SEVEN]

'Old Giles is one of the best; it's a treat to know him – but it's his bloody menagerie that kills.' Thus spoke Bun Eccles to Monica a few weeks after her lessons with Revelstoke began, as they were having a drink in the saloon bar of The Willing Horse. Monica agreed heartily.

In fairness she had to admit in her own mind that Eccles himself was a prominent and disturbing element in Revelstoke's menagerie. John Macarthur Eccles was the young man whom she had met coming down Revelstoke's stairs the first day she visited him; he was an Australian painter, always called Bun, which was an abbreviation of Bunyip. Very early in their acquaintance Monica asked him indignantly why he had urged her to go up without warning, knowing what he knew. His answer was characteristic: 'Well, kid, I'd just dropped in on 'em and they were as mad as snakes, and I wanted to find out what you'd all do.'

Bun was grandiloquently called the Art Editor of *Lantern*. He did woodcuts and ornamental spots for the magazine, and was supposed to take care of its typography, but as he understood little of this craft, and rarely knew what day of the week it was, the work was usually done by the printer. *Lantern* was printed by a very good firm, Raikes Brothers, because a nephew of the senior Mr Raikes was interested in it, and sometimes had his satirical verses printed in it. Raikes Brothers also looked after the mailing of copies to subscribers, because nobody else connected with the magazine had a complete list of those fortunate creatures, though there was a shoe box somewhere with index cards in it, upon which Miss Kinwellmarshe had written the names and addresses of some of them. *Lantern* was without a business manager, although it had an impressive list of editors and contributors. It also lacked any facilities for dealing with possible advertisers, though two or three extremely persistent publishers and musical firms had sought out some responsible person at Raikes Brothers, and positively insisted on buying advertising space.

It was *Lantern* which accounted for Revelstoke's menagerie. The copy which he gave to Monica on her first visit mystified her completely; it resisted her most earnest attempts to find out what it was all about. It was handsomely printed, and contained several articles which were manifestly very angry and scornful on a high level, and some photographs and caricatures. But everything in it seemed to presuppose a special body of knowledge in the reader, and to allude to this private preserve of indignation and disgust in a way which shut out the uninitiated. It was not for some time that she learned that *Lantern* really was a very special publication. It was devoted in a large part to criticism of critics – of literary critics, theatre critics, critics of painting, and music critics. These critics were, it appeared, without exception men of mean capacities and superficial knowledge; it was the task of *Lantern* to show them up. Of course, if you did not read the popular critics in the first place, *Lantern* meant nothing to you.

Revelstoke wrote about music himself, and was one-half of the editor-in-chief; the other half was a frail, gentle creature called Phanuel Tuke, who looked after the literary side. Tuke was not particularly indignant; his long suit was critical sensibility, and he was always discovering masterpieces which coarser critics had overlooked, or finding beauties in books which the rough fellows in the Sunday papers and middlebrow weeklies had condemned as tripe. It was widely believed in his circle that stupendous integrity was lodged in Tuke's meagre frame, and that he was unquestionably the foremost wit of his day in London. His wit was of the sort which is called dry; indeed, it was so very dry that Monica could not detect any flavour in it at all, smack her lips as she might over some of his most valued remarks and apt rejoinders. But she was sure the fault was hers. Apart from the elusive quality of his wit, she liked Tuke, who was a decent little man and needed mothering, even by young virgins.

Tuke's constant companion and defender was a plain, square Irish girl in her early thirties, called Bridget Tooley; she was always on the lookout for a chance to fight somebody for Tuke. She wrote, in some sense that was never clearly defined, and apparently her stuff was too good to be published very often. When Tuke was late with his material for *Lantern* it was always Miss Tooley who stumped up the stairs and broke the news. For no very good reason Revelstoke's flat was the headquarters of the publication, to the great alarm of his landlady, Mrs Klein. She had come to England as a refugee, and had never accustomed herself to English law as it relates to lodgings and apartments; in consequence she was perpetually in dread that the police might descend upon her and charge her with permitting a business to be conducted on her premises, without having an appropriate licence. Poor soul, she could not comprehend how little like a business *Lantern* was, and so she appeared from time to time, like the wicked fairy in a ballet, and made pitiful scenes.

Nobody was particularly rude to Mrs Klein except Odo Odingsels, the photographer. He was a very tall, loose-jointed man of some northern European stock which was never identified; he had beautiful, liquid brown eyes, but his appearance was spoiled by his unusual dirtiness, and by a form of spotty baldness from which he suffered, and which made his head look as though it had been nibbled by rats. It was his unpleasant way to shout loudly at Mrs Klein in German, which made her cry. This was embarrassing, but it was widely admitted that Odingsels was a genius with a camera, and must be allowed his little ways.

These were the principal visitors to the flat in Tite Street – if the term visitor may be applied to someone who may come at any hour of day or night, and stay for anything up to ten hours at a stretch. It was not uncommon for Monica to have a lesson with Revelstoke while Tuke and Tooley whispered over a manuscript in a corner, and Odingsels ate fish out of the tin almost under her elbow. Pyewacket contended with her at every lesson for the master's attention. But Revelstoke's concentration was complete, and she learned to disregard external distractions while they were working. All external distractions, that is to say, except Miss Persis Kinwellmarshe.

'You got the wrong ideas about Old Perse,' Bun Eccles told her. 'She's just supplying something Old Giles needs; sheilas are his hobby. Never without a girl; can't leave 'em alone. Now me, for instance, I like a squeeze and a squirt now and then, same as the next chap, just to make sure everything's still attached to the main, but beer's my real hobby. But Old Giles – he's never had enough. And it's the same with Perse; she likes it. But apart from that all there is between 'em is a sort of intellectual companionship, you might call it. Old Giles is a genius, you see, and that's what Perse really wants. Her home, you see – well, her Dad's an ex-admiral, wears a monocle, still wishes the *Morning Post*'d never folded up – and she's in revolt against all that. Doesn't want to be a lady in Tunbridge bloody Wells. Maybe she's overdone it, but she's a decent old cow, is Perse.'

'She doesn't need to be so dirty about her appearance,' said Monica, thinking this was safe ground for criticism.

'Aw, now kid, she does; it's revolt, see? And she's one of the lucky ones that looks just as good dirty as clean. She's a real stunner. I know. Anatomy. All that stuff. Perse is damn near perfect, but not poison perfect, you know, like those bloody great stone Greek sheilas in the Louvre. Have you looked seriously at her knees? Cor stone the crows, kid, that's perfection!'

'Knees! I'm surprised that's all you've seen.'

'Aw now, stow that, Monny. That's small-town stuff. Sure I've seen all there is to see of Perse; she's posed a bit, as well as her hobby. But good knees are very, very rare. And when you get past all that pommy lah-di-dah she's a real nice girl.'

'I'll bet!' said Monica. It was not irony on the level of *Lantern*, but it was heartfelt. 'Next thing you'll be telling me she has a heart of gold.'

'Well, so she has.'

'Bun, that girl's a tramp, and you know it.'

'Aw now, Monny, that's not like you. Perse is a wagtail, nobody denies it, but what's that to you? You don't have to be like her, if you don't choose. But don't come the Mrs Grundy around the *Lantern*; it's the wrong place for it. I'll get you another half-pint, to sweeten you up.'

Monica had taken to going to The Willing Horse every day with Bun Eccles, but she could never rid herself of a feeling of guilt. There she was in a pub – what would have been called a 'beverage room' at home – drinking beer. By the standards of her upbringing she was on the highroad to harlotry, but no harm ever befell her, and Eccles seemed to look on her as a friend, and to ply her with half-pints for no reason other than that he liked her. She even reached the point of paying for drinks herself, as it seemed to be quite all right for girls to do so in *Lantern* circles. Amy had told her, 'You don't have to drink, dear, but never make a fuss about not drinking.' And here she was, drinking like a fish, by her reckoning – often two and three pints of beer in a day – and the admonitions of Ma Gall and the adjurations of Pastor Beamis grew fainter in memory.

It was interesting, however, that some of her mother's saltier remarks kept intruding themselves into her mind, spoken in her mother's own tones, especially in connection with Miss Kinwell-marshe. Monica had not realized that there was so much of her mother in her. The feeling which often plagued her that she was drifting away from her family in speech and outlook was complemented by the realization that some of the mental judgements she passed on the people around her were unquestionably her mother's, and couched in her mother's roughest idiom. It was frightening;

sometimes it seemed like a form of possession. For what she wanted most was experience, that experience which is supposed to broaden and enrich the soul of the artist, and what could Mrs Gall conceivably have to do with that?

To her surprise, she quickly gained a place in the *Lantern* group, for she possessed accomplishments alien to them. She could work a typewriter, and produce fair copy even on the senile portable Corona which was all the magazine owned. None of the others could use more than two fingers, and Miss Tooley and Miss Kinwellmarshe always fought bitterly about which should undertake this degrading work. Tuke wrote illegibly in pencil; Revelstoke wrote an elegant Italian hand, but so small that it was a penance to read much of it. Monica's professional speed seemed like magic to them. She could also keep books in an elementary fashion, and though *Lantern* had only one misleading petty cash book, she could come nearer to making it balance than anyone else. This was power, and Monica, who badly wanted to be indispensable to this glittering array of talent, was not slow to recognize it. She became more and more irregular in her visits to Madame Heber and Dr Schlesinger, for Tuke was happy to talk to her in French, and Odingsels and Mrs Klein provided her with plenty of practice in German. She could not elude Signor Sacchi, for she was a beginner in Italian, and she did not want to miss any of her lessons at Coram Square, where Molloy was working so hard to show himself the superior of Revelstoke. But there were days when Monica spent six and eight hours at a stretch in the flat in Tite Street typing, talking, accounting and learning. She became as familiar as Miss Kinwellmarshe with the small and disorderly kitchen; she lost her shame about going downstairs to the WC on the second floor landing (for Revelstoke's bathroom consisted of tub and basin only and was, as a usual thing, full of imperfectly laundered and extremely wet garments belonging to himself and Persis Kinwellmarshe). She was useful, she was wanted, and if she had been able to banish her hot gusts of disapproval of Persis, she would have been completely happy.

[EIGHT]

The Bridgetower Trustees had little, in these days, to draw them together, and their meetings were infrequent. After the June meeting in which they received the melancholy news that they would have to spend more on Monica, they did not meet again until the 21st of December, the second anniversary of the death of Louisa Hansen Bridgetower. There was not much for them to do except to hear Mr Snelgrove read two letters, of which the first was from the London solicitors, presenting their account of disbursements and expressing the hope, in a joyless, legal kind of way, that they were spending enough money. The other, and as usual the more interesting, letter was from Sir Benedict, and read thus:

Your protégée has been faring much better since her return from Paris where, as I expected, Miss Amy Neilson was able to do a great deal for her. She learns readily and is sensitive to atmosphere, and she now comports herself in a way which will smooth her path in the secondary, but important, social side of a singer's career.

In addition to her work with Mr Molloy, and her languages (to which Italian has been added) I am sending her to Giles Revelstoke for coaching in the literature of song, and some of the general musical culture which she so badly needs. You may be familiar with some of his work; he is, in my opinion, one of the most promising composers to appear in England for many a decade, and is especially gifted as a song-writer in a period when the real lyric gift is extremely rare. He speaks well of her progress.

You will be interested to know that I have taken upon myself to bring Monica to the attention of Lady Phoebe Elphinstone, who does a great deal of admirable work in introducing Commonwealth and American students to English families with whom they spend holiday periods which might otherwise find them at a loose end. Lady Phoebe has arranged that Monica shall spend the Christmas vacation period with a Mr and Mrs Griffith Hopkin-Griffiths of Neuadd Goch, Llanavon, Montgomeryshire. They are delightful people (Lady Phoebe assures me) and a taste of country-house life will be a pleasant experience for Monica, with whose character and talents I am increasingly impressed, and quite in line with the desires expressed for her by her late patroness, Mrs L. H. Bridgetower.

'Well!' said Miss Pottinger. 'Country-house life! I only hope she has the gumption to take an appropriate house-gift. Should we cable her about it, I wonder?'

'I had gained the impression that there was no country-house life left,' said Dean Knapp; 'but then, in Wales probably things are on a much humbler scale.'

'That is really all we have to consider,' said Mr Snelgrove, 'except expenditure. In spite of what Jodrell and Stanhope have been able to do, the money keeps piling up at the bank. It is unlikely that there will be any official questioning of our handling of funds, at least for some time, but we must bear in mind that we can be called upon for an accounting by the Public Trustee at his discretion.'

When the meeting was over, Veronica served the Trustees with coffee and Christmas cake, using the fine Rockingham service which Auntie Puss regarded as her own.

'And how have you been keeping, Veronica?' said that lady, eyeing her speculatively.

'Very well, thank you, Miss Pottinger,' said Veronica, but she wore a look of strain which was becoming habitual. Nearly two years had passed since the reading of Mrs Bridgetower's will, and so far there was no sign that she might have a child, and retrieve the Bridgetower money for her husband.

[NINE]

It was on the 21st of December that Monica set out from Paddington, travelled to Shrewsbury, changed her train and crossed the border of Wales to Trallwm, and there took a local to Llanavon. She had in her luggage a suitable house-gift (a large and expensive – but not embarrassing – box of candied fruits of appropriately Christmas-like appearance) so Miss Pottinger need not have feared for her on that score. But she carried in her heart misgivings about country-house life which were all that Miss Pottinger could possibly have desired. Everything that she had ever read, or seen in the movies, or heard, about the county gentry of Great Britain came back to her: would she have to hunt foxes? would she be despised because she could not ride a horse? what about the inevitable awesome butler? what about the equally inevitable heiress of broad acres, a picture of British hauteur and beauty (Miss Kinwellmarshe was cast mentally for this role) who would make her feel like a crumb, while being exquisitely but coldly polite all the time? Lady Phoebe Elphinstone had been perfectly wonderful and not a bit awesome, on the one occasion when Monica had met her, and Lady Phoebe's secretary, Miss Catriona Eigg of Uist, had been helpful and kind in every possible way, even to suggesting the box of fruits, but neither of these benign presences was on the train with her as she moved, at the deliberate pace of Welsh trains, from Shrewsbury to Trallwm.

There was, however, a man in the same carriage whom she had seen get on the train at Oxford, and who had, like herself, changed at Shrewsbury. A young man, apparently English from his clothes and his easy way with porters; a shortish, plumpish young man with a high colour (incipient broken veins in the cheeks?) and short dark hair very neatly brushed. As well as a large valise he carried a briefcase crammed with books, which he kept close to him on the seat as though its presence were a comfort. In his hand he had an orange-bound pamphlet, which he read with great concentration, moving his lips as he did so, and occasionally making phlegmy noises, apparently clearing his throat. But the farther they travelled from Shrewsbury the greater his excitement became, and the less he worked over his book; at times he hung right out of the window, and gaped at the landscape. As a castle became fleetingly visible, nesting among trees, she thought he muttered 'Peacock'. When the train drew up at a tiny station labelled Buttington he threw open the door and said in an awed voice, under his breath 'The Battle of Buttingtune, 893', and stared in all directions at small holdings and distant hills until the guard locked him in again. He sank back on the seat, and stared at Monica with unseeing eyes. 'An old and haughty nation, proud in arms,' he whispered, and then repeated it, with greater emphasis. When the train drew up at Trallwm he hastily consulted his yellow pamphlet, leaned well out of the window, and fixed a porter with his eye.

'Arrgh!' he cried, in accents of despair. 'Arrgh!' – but no further utterance came.

'Yessir? What can I do for you, sir?' said the porter, and the young man fell back upon the seat, deflated.

Monica, with the inflexible determination of women travelling, snatched the porter for herself, and had her luggage transferred to the local for the coast which would take her to Llanavon. She took good care to get into a carriage far from the afflicted young man.

But when, half an hour later, she dismounted at Llanavon station, he did so too, and when a girl of about Monica's own age approached them and said 'For Neuadd Goch?' it was he who said, 'Yes, thanks, I'm John Scott Ripon.'

Monica had never heard the name of her destination pronounced by a Welsh tongue. Lady Phoebe and Miss Eigg of Uist had tended to hurry over it and avoid it.

'Miss Gall?' said the girl. 'I'm Ceinwen Griffiths; you're going to my uncle's, aren't you? I've brought the trap, because it's a fairly clear day, and I thought you might like to ride that way. Mr Lloyd'll take care of your luggage, and somebody'll bring it up in an hour or so.'

She led the way to a pretty governess-cart, drawn by a pony. Monica had never seen such a thing before, and Ripon was delighted with it. He couldn't, he said, have possibly hoped for anything better.

Introductions left Monica somewhat flattened. John Scott Ripon, it appeared, was not English, but an American Rhodes scholar, and he seemed to get on very easy terms with Miss Ceinwen Griffiths in a matter of minutes. She was a girl who, without being pretty, was uncommonly attractive, for she had a soft and winning air, beautiful legs, and quite the loveliest speaking voice that Monica had ever heard; everything that she said was so beautifully articulated, and so charmingly stressed, that it was a kind of music. This was not the habitual downhill tune of English speech, or the tangle of stressed and unstressed syllables upon which Revelstoke insisted, but a form of speech-play – a delight in sound and words for their own sake. It was fascinating, and it struck Monica mute. But not Ripon.

'I made a terrible boob of myself on the train,' said he, as they set off in the pony-trap. 'I was trying to speak Welsh to the porter at Trallwm. I'd been studying this book, you see – *Welsh in a Week* – and I wanted to say "A wnewch chwi edrych ar ol fy nheithglud?" – thought I'd surprise him. But it all died in my throat. Of course I knew he'd speak English, but I thought I'd try it. I always like to try everything. Much Welsh spoken around here, Miss Griffiths?'

'No, hardly at all. A little on market days, when the people come in from the hills. And they wouldn't have spoken to you, except in English; it makes Welsh people shy, hearing it spoken by English-speaking people.'

'Do you speak it at all?'

> *'Annhebig i'r mis dig du.*
> *A gerydd i bawb garu;*
> *A bair tristlaw a byrddydd*
> *A gwynt i ysbeiliaw gwydd;*

– do you follow?'

'No, but it sounds great.'

'That's a comment on today's weather by one of our old poets; you won't find it in *Welsh in a Week*. But I'm not a fair example. My father's quite a well-known Celtic scholar.'

'Oh, that's wonderful! Then it'll be an even greater pleasure to meet him.'

'You won't meet him. I'm staying with Uncle Griff and Aunt

Dolly; they're dears, too, but not the least bit Celtic scholars. You'll see.'

'But it was an understandable mistake. You see, I've looked your uncle up in *Burke's Landed Gentry*. Terrific ancestry, so I thought he might be very hot on Welsh history, and customs and whatnot.'

'You've been doing your homework, haven't you? Uncle Griff will talk to you about genealogy all night, but any Welshman will do that. No, Uncle Griff's not a scholar, but he's a landed gent.'

'Unbroken tenancy of the Neuadd Goch estate since 1488, the book said.'

'Oh, how beautifully you say Neuadd Goch!'

'No kidding?'

'Well – not very much kidding.'

Miss Ceinwen Griffiths, it appeared, was not only very attractive but an accomplished flirt. Monica began to feel reservations about her.

They had mounted a steep hill, and were now driving along a ridge. Because the pony cart was high, they could see over the hedges on both sides of the road, toward England on the right, and toward the mountains of Wales on the left. It was such country as Monica had never seen before, rolling, gentle, quiet in its winter sleep, yet with an air of mystery which could not be explained. Perhaps it was the quality of the light, which varied so greatly within the range of her vision. Where they were it was not quite so fine a day as Miss Griffiths had said; as the pony trotted through the lanes the air was wet and chilly on their faces. But a mile or two away on the English side of the ridge the sun shone in golden patches, moving slowly across the side of another hill. On the Welsh side it seemed to be raining in the middle distance, for there the land was purplish, as though it had been bruised, but near these darkened patches were stretches of grey obscurity, which occasionally stirred and heaved, for it was mist. But beyond the purple, and the mist, and a few pools of tearful sunlight, rose mountains which caught a little wintry glory from an unseen setting sun, and were otherwise deepest blue-black. Their heads were in cloud.

'On a good day you can see the two peaks of Cadeir Idris from here,' said Ceinwen, 'but not often in winter.'

'Marvellous!' said Ripon. 'Just the country for *Morte d'Arthur*.'

'We like it very well,' said Ceinwen.

'Oh, come on, Miss Griffiths, that won't do! It's absolutely terrific, and you know it. Leave understatement to the English. I'm an enthusiast; they say all Americans are, but it's not true. But I am. I enjoy things while I've got 'em. I'm a romantic. Don't discourage me.'

'I won't. Wales always seems very beautiful to people when they first come to it. Perhaps we try to restrain our own feelings so as not to seem to be boasting. Now we leave the Cefn, and drop into this little wooded place. It's called Cwm Bau.'

'Cwm, a valley, and bau – let's see, wait till I get out *Welsh in a Week* – or will you tell us?'

'In English it means the Dirty Dingle – though why nobody knows, because it's very pretty, as you see. And then we go up the hill on the other side to Neuadd Goch. You haven't said anything, Miss Gall; I hope you don't find your first sight of Wales disappointing?'

'I'm an enthusiast, too,' said Monica; 'but I'm not very good at words. I think it's the loveliest landscape I've ever seen.'

'I truly hope that it will be kind to you.'

[TEN]

Life at Neuadd Goch was kind indeed. Monica knew nothing of country life; in Canada she had had the usual experiences of cottage life at lakesides with the joys of insects, privies, boiled water and the thunder of rain on the roof, but an ordered and comfortable existence in the midst of natural beauty was utterly new to her. In this house there was no window which did not look out upon a view of the beautiful valley on one lift of which it stood, and the variations of light changed these views from hour to hour, and sometimes from minute to minute. The farms and cottages in the landscape, thatched and built of white plaster and blackened oak beam, were so picturesquely pretty that she could not believe that they were real farms at all, for her only experience had been of the plain-faced farmsteads of her own part of Ontario. She fell immediately and deeply in love with North Wales, and in this affair she was rivalled by John Scott Ripon. As for the family at Neuadd Goch, they were everything that was kind and charming. No awesome butler, but two maids so obliging that Monica suspected them briefly of hypocrisy, managed affairs. She liked Ceinwen better than any girl she had met since leaving home, and desperately wanted her as a 'best girl friend' – but Ceinwen was not aware of this North American relationship, and was quite as flirtatious in her behaviour toward Monica as she was toward

Ripon. And Mr and Mrs Hopkin-Griffiths were very old hands at entertaining house guests, and knew that the art lies in leaving them to themselves a great part of the time. Monica and Ripon arrived on the afternoon of the twenty-first of December; by tea time the day following they felt as though they had been at Neuadd Goch for a glorious year, and on the morning of the twenty-third they were such seasoned country folk that they went for a walk after breakfast, wonderfully happy. Ripon was bursting with talk.

'I've got it straightened out now,' said he. 'Ceinwen is the daughter of Professor Morgan Griffiths, who is only a half-brother of our host, who is Hopkin-Griffiths, and very big stuff in this part of Wales, and a timber man in a large way. That's where the money comes from. He doesn't seem to work, but that's his craftiness. Dolly was a widow when she married him; she's English and has a son – that's the son she's always talking about who may come for Christmas. The Squire seems very fond of the boy, but I think I detect a note of worry in his voice when he talks about him. It makes it interesting, I think, everybody being halves and steps. Now in my family we're all fully related, and I can't say it makes either for interest or good feeling. What about your family?'

'Oh my family hasn't got any specially interesting relationships. It seems to make them interesting, being Welsh. When I was a child I sometimes used to wish we had a romantic foreign strain of some sort, to cheer things up.'

'That's what I don't understand. Ceinwen seems to make a lot of being Welsh, but the Squire, who is the real thing, and can trace his ancestry back to Bleddyn ap Cynfyn, takes it very lightly. You heard what happened last night when I asked him about it at dinner; he just laughed and said he supposed it was true, but that it had never made much difference one way or another. He likes me calling him "Squire" though, especially when I explained about my fondness for *Gryll Grange* and Squire Gryll. I was astonished he'd never heard of it. D'you know, Monica, I don't think these people understand or value what they have. I don't suppose it's twenty-five miles from here to the Mary Webb country, but would you believe that when I asked Mrs Hopkin-Griffiths about it, she had never heard of Mary Webb? And they've lived all their lives close to Shropshire, but they don't seem to know anything about Housman. George Herbert? Unknown! Of course I don't mean that they ought to develop those things as we do in the States. God forbid! But you'd think they'd know about them, wouldn't you? I mean, what do you suppose gives shape and focus to their lives?'

'Do books give shape and focus to your life?'

'Why certainly. Don't they yours?'

'No. You must be a very literary sort of person.'

'I wouldn't say that. But you have to see and feel life in terms of something. Think; what makes you tick? What shapes your life?'

'Music, I suppose.'

'Well, there you are.'

'But not quite the way you mean. I hear music all the time. I've always done so, even though I've tried very hard not to.'

'Why did you do that?'

'When I was very small I once told my mother about it, and she said I must break myself of the habit, or it would drive me crazy. So I tried, but I didn't succeed. The music is always at the back of my mind. It's not particularly original, but on the other hand it isn't anybody else's. It's just that I feel in terms of music. And when I can be quiet enough to get at what's going on in my mind, the music is what gives me a clue.'

'Have you ever tried to write it down?'

'Oh no. And I don't want to try. I'm not a composer. It's just that music is a part of my way of feeling things. I only realized that a few months ago. And do you know that when I finally discovered that my mind worked that way, it set me free from that fear of going mad. And until I was free of the fear, I hadn't really admitted to myself that it was there. But for years I had been listening to my inner music guiltily. It was like – oh, like being let out of a jail! You're the only person I've ever told about that.'

'I'm glad you told me, and I'll keep it to myself. Look at that view! Now I'm appreciating it in literary terms, and you're interpreting it in some kind of inner music which is incomprehensible to me. So I ask you again: what does it mean to the people who live here? By what means do they interpret it to themselves?'

'Do you know, I've just had the most extraordinary experience? Look at these hedges; do you know what they are?'

'Of course I do; they're holly.'

'Yes, but – I've never seen holly before. Oh, I've seen a few sprigs, imported to Canada for decoration, and I've seen imitation holly. But this is the real thing – miles and miles of it – just growing beside the roads as a hedge. All my life I've associated holly with Christmas, but

I never really knew till this minute why. I never understood that it was something real. I've seen it on paper wrapping, and in pictures, and I never knew why it went with Christmas, except that it was pretty. But here it is, in December, green leaves and red berries and all! It's like suddenly getting a mysterious piece of a jigsaw puzzle to fit into place.'

Ripon solemnly removed his hat. 'This is a sacred moment,' said he. 'Sacred to me, anyhow, as a student of literature. You have just made the great discovery that behind every symbol there is a reality. For years you have accepted holly as a symbol of Christmas, unquestioningly, like a true Anglo-Saxon believer. And now, in a flash, you know why it is so. It is because, in this land which gave you your Christmas, holly is at its finest at this time of year. Perhaps we should cause a carved stone to be erected on this spot, to identify forever the place at which, for one human being out of the whole confused race, a symbol became a reality.'

They were standing in the lane which traversed Cwm Bau, and at this moment Ceinwen rounded the corner, leading an aged donkey, across whose back two large willow-work panniers were fixed.

'We've been admiring the holly, as only North Americans can,' said Ripon.

'Good,' said Ceinwen; 'then you can come with me and gather a lot of it. I thought I might catch you, so I brought plenty of gloves and two broom-hooks. I know where we can get mistletoe, too.'

It was idyllic to gather holly and mistletoe with Ceinwen, to take it back to Neuadd Goch and hang it in festoons on the staircase, to put sprigs of mistletoe in places where, Griffith Hopkin-Griffiths assured them, mistletoe had been hung for as long as anyone could remember.

Neuadd Goch was not an uncommonly old house, though it stood where two very old houses had preceded it. The older, which had been built before the Welsh Tudors had sought their fortune in England, had been supplanted by a Jacobean house which, after a fire in the first decade of the nineteenth century, had been replaced by the present building. It was not the sort of house which attracts the attention of connoisseurs, for it had no special architectural distinction; but it was wonderfully pleasing and comfortable. Its park and its gardens were pretty, but not remarkable. It was not large enough to be a mansion, but it was quite large enough to hold its owners, their servants, and ten or twelve guests without crowding. It was fully and admirably what its name said – it was the Red Hall at Llanavon, modestly appropriate.

Whether it took its character from its owners, or whether they became like it, nobody could say. Mr Hopkin-Griffiths certainly was as red as his own house. His face was brick red, round, and wore a look of surprise allied to firmness; his hair was of a red which had faded from its original foxy shade to a browner tone. His hands were red and covered at the joints with red hair. As with so many of his race, a few red hairs grew capriciously out of the tip of his nose. He gave an impression of bluntness in his speech and manner, but those who knew him were not deceived; he came of a family which had foreseen the time for getting out of goats and going into sheep, in the fifteenth century; had dropped sheep for cattle in the eighteenth; and had added timber to cattle in the nineteenth. His neighbours respected Mr Griffith Hopkin-Griffiths as a smooth man.

Dolly, his wife, was a charming, walking monument to her own beauty as it had been thirty years ago; she had not changed her way of dressing her hair, and though she had yielded a little in matters of clothing she still looked more like the 'twenties than the 'fifties. She even made up according to the methods she had perfected in her youth, and it was a credit to the good qualities of her face that the effect was not grotesque. Seen at a distance, by a short-sighted man, she was a pretty, frivolous ghost from the period immediately following the First World War; seen closer, there was about her the pathos of the woman who has not quite grown as old as her years, either in body or mind.

She came upon them as they were hanging the last of the Christmas greens.

'Mistletoe!' she cried. 'Oh, what fun! You'll be absolutely worn out with gallantry, Mr Ripon. Oh, I do so hope Gilly can come. Don't you, Ceinwen? Yes, I'm sure you do! It'll be no sort of Christmas without at least two young men.'

Monica and Ripon were by now very familiar with this hope that Gilly, her son, would be able to get away from his work in London to join them at Christmas. By many broad hints Mrs Hopkin-Griffiths implied that Ceinwen must be especially anxious for his presence; Monica and Ripon were happy enough to fall in with this notion on the part of their hostess. The young are usually, out of sheer good nature, ready to indulge the sometimes clumsy romantic ideas of their elders.

If it was idyllic to hang the Christmas greens, it was Dickensian to drive the twelve miles to Trallwm and buy Christmas gifts. The rule at Neuadd Goch was that gifts exchanged among guests and family must not cost more than a shilling. It was on Christmas Eve that they made the journey, Monica, Ripon and Ceinwen in the Squire's serviceable Humber.

'The sheer bliss of this robs me of speech,' said Ripon. 'Here we go, on Christmas Eve – get that, Christmas *Eve* – to buy Christmas presents. If I were at home, I would have finished my Christmas shopping a full two weeks ago; I would have wrapped everything in elaborate paper, and tied it with expensive plastic twine. I would approach the great festal day prepared for everything but a good time. But here I go, prepared to squander ten shillings at the utmost on the very eve of the day of giving; for the first time in my life I have got Christmas into focus. Tomorrow I shall worship, I shall feast and – quite incidentally, I shall give and receive. And that's how it ought to be. It's Dickensian. It's Washington Irving-like. It's the way Christmas ought to be.'

They spent all day making their purchases, for the shilling rule had been made in a time when a shilling bought a bigger variety of possible gifts than it does now. But Ripon persuaded a bookseller and stationer to let him rummage among some old stock, and produced a wonderful variety of paper transfers, Victorian post-cards, and works of edification which had once been sold as Sabbath School prizes. And in an outfitter's he got a dicky for ninepence, and an almost forgotten oddity – a washable 'leather' collar – which he said would be just the thing for Mr Hopkin-Griffiths. Monica, who did not want to be outdone, turned up some cards of pretty old-fashioned buttons in a woolshop and, after much pondering, bought another copy of *Welsh in a Week* to give to Ripon, who had been mercilessly teased by their hosts and Ceinwen about his earlier adventures with that work. At mid-day Ripon took the two girls to lunch at The Bear, where they ate fat mutton with two veg. following it with prunes doused with a custard of chemical composition, and some surly cheese. But even this did not crush their spirits.

Driving back to Llanavon, Monica and Ripon agreed that it had been one of the happiest days they had ever known. Their protestations of pleasure made Ceinwen shy at first, then effusive, and the drive ended in an atmosphere which a cruel observer might have described as maudlin, but which was in truth full of genuine, warm, though possibly facile feeling.

They rushed into the house in time for tea, hungry from the asperities of The Bear, and hungry too as only emotion can make one. Mrs Hopkin-Griffiths scampered out of the drawing-room to meet them.

'Oh darlings, it's too, too wonderful. He's been able to come! I never quite dared to hope but he's here. Gilly's come! It's going to be a perfect Christmas!'

Swept forward by her excitement they burst into the room. There, before the fire, stood Giles Revelstoke.

[ELEVEN]

That night, having made herself ready for bed, Monica went to the bathroom to clean her teeth, a maiden; in slightly less than fifteen minutes she returned to her room, her teeth clean, and a maiden no more.

There was only one bathroom at Neuadd Goch. It had formerly been a bedroom, and was a chamber of considerable size, in a corner of which was a very large and deep bath, encased in mahogany and standing on a dais; there was also a large and ornate marble basin, a full-length cheval-glass with candle-brackets, an armchair and a side chair, and a set of scales upon which it was possible to weigh oneself by sitting on a large, padded seat. There was a couch of the type familiar in the best-known picture of Madame Récamier, with one arm and a partial back. The two large windows were richly curtained to the floor. This splendid chamber was for ablutions only; the water closet was housed in mahogany splendour in a smaller room nearby: it had a bowl in the agreeable Willow pattern.

If Monica had not been a North American her fate might have been very different; in each bedroom was a washstand, with ewer and basin, and night and morning a copper pitcher of boiling water. But she had been accustomed all her life to clean her teeth in running water, and so she went to the bathroom in her dressing-gown, her toothbrush and a tube of paste in her hand. She would only be a minute, thought she, so she pushed the door around, but did not bolt it. It was not quite closed, and less than a minute later Giles Revelstoke, towel in hand and in his dressing-gown, pushed it open.

'Oh, I'm sorry,' said he.

And then, because Monica looked so attractive with her hair brushed out, and her mouth foaming slightly with pink dentifrice, and because the lamplight in the bathroom was so charming, and because the couch was so conveniently at hand, and probably also because it was Christmas – because of so many elements so subtly combined, Monica returned to her bedroom in just under a quarter of an hour, much astonished and even more delighted.

As always when something important had happened, she wanted a time of quiet in which to think about it. But that was not to be hers just yet. As she was opening her door, a figure hastened to her side out of the darkness of the stairs. It was Ripon.

'Want to talk to you for a minute,' said he, and hurried into the room after her.

Monica's bedroom was large, and as the electricity at Neuadd Goch – a private system – operated only on the ground floor, it was lit with a large oil lamp by the bed. She and Ripon were in a rich gloom, but it was plain that he was excited.

'You get into bed and keep warm,' he said. 'I'll sit here. Listen; Ripon the sleuth has done it again! I just got the lowdown on this whole situation from Ceinwen; she's a bit put out that this chap Revelstoke has turned up – she was hoping against hope that he wouldn't, and Mrs H.-G. was aching that he should. We've been misled by Mrs H.-G.; Ceinwen does *not* look on this Giles as Prince Charming. And do you know why? It's a fantastic deal among the older generation. Ceinwen is to marry Revelstoke; Mrs H.-G. wants it because she is keen for him to settle down, live a quiet life in the country, and be a good boy. It appears that he isn't a very good boy in London. She's got quite a bit of money, you see, left her by her first husband, who was a stock-broker, of all things. And the Squire wants the marriage because he will then leave this house and estate to Ceinwen, on condition that they change their name from Revelstoke to Hopkin-Griffiths, thus continuing the name at Neuadd Goch. And Ceinwen's father, Professor Griffiths, wants it because he wants her to have Neuadd Goch, which he thinks ought to be in his part of the family anyhow, and the marriage will make him retroactively county gentry, instead of just a well-known scholar. Did you ever hear anything like it?'

'No,' said Monica. 'But surely it all depends on what Ceinwen and Giles want?' It was fortunate that it was dark in the room for it was the first time she had ever called him Giles, and she blushed deeply.

'Ah, that's what you'd think, and what I'd think, but it's not what these people think. And that's what makes it fascinating. It's like finding oneself in a Victorian novel. I've got to re-adjust all my thinking about the set-up here. You see, I had it all worked out on the Hamlet-theme; I asked myself why Mrs H.-G. was so wild to have her son come home, when there seemed to be so much doubt about it. I mean, nobody ever said he couldn't come; they just said he mightn't. Well – it was plain as a pike-staff. Revelstoke was a Hamlet-figure, unconsciously jealous of the Squire, identifying himself strongly with the late Revelstoke, and bitter against his Ma. It sees itself, doesn't it? I was crazy for him to come home, because I've never had a chance to observe a man in the Hamlet-situation at close quarters. But how wrong I was!'

'You certainly do see life in terms of literature, Johnny.'

'Well – just look at the fun I have! But now, you see, I'm bang in the middle of one of those terrific novels about Who Gets the Dibs; the next thing to be decided is – are we in a Jane Austen situation, or a Trollope situation?'

'Does it have to be one or the other?'

'But you can't call it a modern situation?'

'Well, it's happening now, isn't it?'

'Only in a very limited sense. There are whole climates of thought and feeling which aren't really modern; I can't see a situation where two people are being pushed toward marriage in order to save family name, and family pride, as modern.'

'Go on; I bet it happens all the time.'

'You're just being feminine and perverse. Anyhow, you said you felt in terms of music; I feel in terms of literature.'

'All right, then; where do we fit into the plot?'

'Frankly, I don't see that you come into it at all, except as a fringe figure – Nice Girl for Christmas Purposes. But for myself – well, I don't mind telling you that I go for Ceinwen in quite a big way.'

'So soon?'

'Don't be naive. I have the feelings of a poet. There's a remarkable quality about her, don't you think? Sort of figure in a poem by Yeats? Or really more like one of those wonderful women in the poems of Dafydd ap Gwylim. You know that Welsh verse she recited to us the first day, when we were in Cwm Bau? That was Dafydd ap Gwylim. I asked her, and then I read up on him in the encyclopaedia. Wonderful, warm, infinitely fascinating women, full of passion yet teasingly chaste.'

'Johnny, you've got a really bad case.'

'It's not anything that can be described as a case. Here she is, being sacrificed to ideas which don't really come into her climate of thought and feeling at all; she's in the wrong book. The thing is, can I get her into the right book?'

'Johnny, I want to go to sleep. And if anybody hears you talking at the top of your voice in my room, you won't get Ceinwen into any book at all. You go to bed now.'

Monica leapt out of bed and fetched a small parcel from her chest of drawers.

'Just so you won't think I'm unsympathetic, here's your Christmas present now. Don't open it until morning. It's something that will be useful to you in getting Ceinwen back into the right book.'

She pushed him out of the door, bearing her gift, which was, of course, another copy of *Welsh in a Week*.

Rid of Ripon, she was able to attend to her own affairs, and her first act was to fetch the lamp, and set it on the floor beside the full-length mirror which formed part of the front of the large wardrobe. Then, chilly as it was, she took off her nightdress and studied herself in the mirror with satisfaction.

By the laws of literature which meant so much to Ripon, her first experience of sex should have been painful, dispiriting and frightening. But it had been none of these things. She had been too confused and surprised to take great heed of the physical side of the encounter; it had all been so strange – the nearness, the intimacy of the posture, the inevitable and natural quality of the act itself; though new to her, it did not seem utterly unaccustomed, but rather like something dimly but pleasurably remembered from the past – and this in itself was strange. What had moved her more than these things were the endearments which Revelstoke had whispered, and the kindness and gentleness with which he had carried out his purpose. Nobody had ever spoken to her in such a fashion before. She had been kissed once or twice in a very tentative way, but that was nothing; this had touched the tender places of her spirit, caressed and stirred them, bringing her a fresh consciousness of life. And again this was not utterly strange, but like the resumption of something once cherished, and lost for a time.

She should feel evil, depraved – she knew it. But, miraculously, at this moment when she should have stood in awe of her mother, and Pastor Beamis and the whole moral code of the Thirteeners, she felt, on the contrary, free of them, above and beyond them as though reunited with something which they sought to deny her. She knew something which they could never have known, or they would not have talked as they did. If Ripon had known about it, he would have said that she had moved into a new climate of feeling.

Gazing at her naked body in the mirror she stretched, and preened, and looked at herself with an intent and burning gaze. She was, by the standards of her upbringing, a ruined girl, and she had never looked better or felt happier in her life.

She slipped again into the nightdress, blew out the lamp and jumped into bed. Almost at once she was asleep. But not before a new and warming Christmas satisfaction rose from the deeps of her mind: What a smack in the eye for Persis Kinwellmarshe!

[TWELVE]

Did the morrow bring remorse? It did not. When Monica ran into the dining-room the squire told her that she looked fit as a fiddle, and gave her a smacking Christmas kiss. Ripon followed his example; he was a literary kisser and presumably his salute had some inner significance which was not to be apprehended by the unlettered. When Ceinwen entered a moment later, and was kissed by her uncle, Ripon did not have quite the courage to go on, and shook her warmly by the hand. But Monica had still to be kissed by Revelstoke, and he saluted her in a friendly fashion which could not have aroused suspicion in the most observant mother; it was precisely the sort of kiss, which, a moment later, he gave Ceinwen. Monica was inwardly amused; nobody knew what she knew!

'Gilly, there's the most awful thing happened,' said Mrs Hopkin-Griffiths to her son. 'Mr Mathias has sent up a message that Mr Gwatkin is too ill to play at the service this morning. Rheumatism, poor old thing – real arthritis; he hasn't really been able to do anything with the pedals for years, and now it's in his hands so badly he simply can't manage. Will you be a dear and play for Morning Prayer?'

'But mother, I'm not an organist.'

'But dear, you'll be quite good enough. Everybody knows you can play anything. Why, when you were just a lad, I remember how you did wonders with a coach-horn after only an hour or two. It's a very small organ.'

'I know, and it's a very out-of-tune organ too, I'm sure. I'd rather not.'

'Now dear, don't be disappointing. Mr Mathias is counting on you.'

'But I don't know what music he wants, or anything.'

'We always have very simple services. You're sure to be able to manage. And think what a thrill it will be for everybody! They all know your things have been broadcast; they'll think it wonderful, whatever you do.'

'I know, that's what's so embarrassing. I don't want to impose on their ignorance; it's immoral.'

'Oh Gilly, what nonsense! Very well then, don't play. I've promised Mr Mathias you will, but I suppose I must just swallow my pride and go to him before service and say you won't. It's humiliating, but of course I wouldn't ask you to put yourself out.'

The upshot was that under this maternal blackmail Revelstoke played, and did things with the organ of St Iestyn's Church which would not have been approved by a Fellow of the Royal College of Organists but which sufficiently astonished and delighted his hearers, who had not heard the pedals of the parish instrument for some years past; Revelstoke even essayed pedal chords from time to time, and contrived a few impressive roars at moments of climax, and was altogether satisfactory. Mr Mathias beamed from the vicar's stall, and threw in an extra hymn, just to make the best of the occasion. But the triumph of the morning was after the service when, as an organ postlude, he improvised a medley of Welsh airs; the difficulty was that, so long as he continued to play, the congregation would not leave the church, so in the end he had to stop and indicate with a wave of his hand that there would be no more.

His mother was delighted. She stood happily at the door of the Church, beside Mr Mathias, ostensibly to wish everyone a Merry Christmas, but in reality to garner compliments on the brilliance of her son. The Neuadd Goch party walked home bright with reflected glory. Even Ripon recovered from having been given three copies of *Welsh in a Week* (Monica's, and one from the squire, and one – unkindest cut – from Ceinwen) and said that he had loved every minute of the service, and felt much nearer to Washington Irving than ever before, but wasn't the singing a little under par for a Welsh congregation?

'It's a lie that all the Welsh can sing,' said Mr Hopkin-Griffiths; 'the truth is that some can sing but they can all yell. And they were quiet this morning because they were listening to our Canadian visitor; I never was told that you could sing like that, my dear. We'll want to hear more from you this afternoon.'

'I'm a pupil of Giles', which should explain it,' said Monica, and once again Mrs Hopkin-Griffiths launched into an account of the fine things that had been said, and how well he had played, and how, perhaps, after all, there might be some sense in his treating music as a profession.

'Mind you, Griff and I couldn't be more sympathetic about Gilly's music,' she said to Monica and Ripon, who were walking with her. 'We've always said it was a wonderful gift, ever since he became so serious about it at school. There was a master there in his time who was wonderfully gifted – quite professional, really. And Gilly has made friends among musicians – one of them is this Sir Benedict Domdaniel, and I've heard he's charming, though of course a Jew – but Jews are wonderfully gifted, aren't they, and we must always remember it and particularly at Christmas. And some of his things have been broadcast, which is awfully good, too. And of course he's so deep in this magazine – *Lantern*, isn't it – and we thought that might lead to a job with a publisher, or something like that. And even a pupil! You know dear, you could have knocked me down with a feather, as the people say around here, when you came in yesterday, and knew Gilly, and he was your teacher. When Lady Phoebe gave us your name, it meant nothing to us – just that you were a Canadian studying in London, and of course I thought from the London School of Economics, because that's where the Canadians all seem to go, and the dear knows why, because it seems to make them so gloomy and farsighted about nasty things. Gilly was thunderstruck. Thought I'd asked for you on purpose. He so resents any interference from me in his London life you know. But it was sheer chance; though Lady Phoebe always seems to think we're musical, though I don't know why. But music as a profession – well, nobody we know has ever done it, and one hears about the risks, and everything. What do you think, dear? Of course it's different for you; you're wonderfully gifted – oh, don't say you aren't, because I can tell just by looking at you. And also I expect you've your way to make. But Gilly could have such a different life, if he chose, and one does so want one's son to make the right choice. Tell me what you really think.'

Monica could not conceive of anyone who had it in him to be a composer being anything else, nor was she interested in promoting a marriage between Revelstoke and Ceinwen. Her reply was a model of modesty and tact; she was not a proper judge, she said, but she knew that Sir Benedict had a very high opinion of Giles' work, and especially his songs. She could have spared her breath, for Mrs Hopkin-Griffiths was not really listening; she had her eyes on Revelstoke and Ceinwen, who were ahead of her, and who seemed to have nothing to say to one another.

After luncheon the squire and Mrs Hopkin-Griffiths retired to their rooms, he for a frank sleep, and she for what was more delicately called 'my usual rest'; Ripon was doing his best to find the way into Ceinwen's climate of feeling, and Monica was too full of happiness to want to disturb them, for her adventure of Christmas Eve had made her generous and charitable; she had some hopes of a talk with Revelstoke, but he too vanished, so she went for a walk by herself, up the hill behind the house, and over a moor which was wild and romantic enough to satisfy the most eager heart. She wandered there for almost two hours, thinking over and over again that she was now a woman, and that she had a lover, and that life was sweeter than she had ever known it to be. Not a thought had she for the Galls in Salterton, who would at this time be sitting amid the ruins of Mrs Gall's calorifically murderous Christmas dinner, fighting, in the name of Christian charity, a losing fight against their mounting ennui and repletion. She returned to Neuadd Goch just in time for tea, and found herself the only member of the party who was in a really good temper.

After tea the squire asked her to sing. 'Music at Christmas, always,' said he; 'I will remember as a boy, in this room, my pater always sang at Christmas – just one song, Gounod's *Nazareth*. Wonder if anybody sings it now? And my Aunt Isobel sang *The Mistletoe Bough*. Can't have Christmas without music.'

Somewhat to Monica's surprise Revelstoke moved to the piano to play for her, which was not his custom at lessons. She sang *The Cherry Tree Carol*, which she had learned from Molloy, and he improvised an accompaniment of considerable beauty, using the simple tune as a point of departure for harmonies remote from any that might have been expected by a conventional ear, but evocative of an atmosphere wonderfully congruous with the simple legend of the song. To Monica it was a delight, and she sang well, but the listeners received it with apathy. She sang *Blow, Blow Thou Winter Wind*, and this time Revelstoke confined himself to a piano part which respected the intentions of Dr Thomas Augustine Arne. But Monica wanted to return to the adventure of improvisation, so she sang *Jésu Christ en Pauvre*, trying to interest the Hopkin-Griffiths by saying that it was a folksong of her native land.

'Really, dear?' said her hostess, 'and I suppose it reminds you of home and familiar things. How sweet.'

'Yes, it does,' said Monica. It was the first in a series of lies which she was to tell during the next few days, all calculated to throw her Canadian past into a pleasing and romantic light. For she had never heard *Jésu Christ en Pauvre* until she learned it from Molloy, and certainly the singing of wistful French-Canadian folksongs had never been a Christmas pursuit of the Gall family, or anyone they knew. But pretence is wonderfully stimulating to the artistic mind, which is why some people lie for fun, rather than from necessity. The tender feeling and insight with which Revelstoke had illumined *The Cherry Tree Carol* he brought in greater measure to the naive, spare little legend of Christ disguised as a poor man, and when the song was done he and Monica were well content with it.

'Good, good,' said the squire, in a voice which made it plain that he had felt and understood nothing. 'Now, Ceinwen, tune your pipes. Let's have a Welsh song. Always like a Welsh song at Christmas.'

'Where are those Welsh songs I sent you last year, Uncle Griff,' said Ceinwen; 'I'll sing you one of those.'

A brief search discovered them in the music bench. 'I wanted you to have them because I helped edit these two collections,' said she. 'My name is in the introduction – "Our thanks are also due to" – me, along with a few others. So you see you're not the only one to get your name on a bit of music, Gilly.'

This was plainly meant to be a pleasantry, but Giles was not willing to take it so. 'More weeping little modal tunes; I can't bear the way the Welsh folksong people arrange their stuff,' said he.

'We heard what you like done with Welsh tunes this morning,' said Ceinwen, without good humour.

She sang *Y Gelynen*, explaining that it was in praise of the holly bush; her voice was small, pure and sweet, and prettily suited to the rippling, trilling refrain of the song. She did not sing in any way as well as Monica, but there was an individual quality and a justness of musical feeling about her singing which gave it charm. From Revelstoke's expression as he played it was plain that he did not like the accompaniment, and by the fourth verse he had begun to guy it, so slightly that only Monica noticed.

Next Ceinwen sang a Christmas carol, *Ar Gyfer Heddiw Bore*, and this time he treated the accompaniment to please himself. Ceinwen was put off by his improvisation; she was a good singer, but she was not up to that. And it was clear to Monica that Revelstoke's treatment of the theme was clever but unsympathetic; he was not helping the singer, he was showing off. The colour had left Ceinwen's cheeks, and her green eyes seemed to darken.

The squire beat time to the Welsh songs with his hand, and nodded from time to time to show that, while he might not understand the words, he was sure they were full of Welsh Christmas cheer.

'The last song I'll sing is a particularly fine one,' said Ceinwen; 'it is called *Hiraeth*.'

'Aren't you going to tell us about it?' asked Ripon. 'Please do. This is wonderful, really it is. I'm living in a novel by Peacock,' he said, beaming at the squire, who accepted the remark with a smile, having learned by now that it was a compliment.

'It is about the longing for what is unattainable, which is called "hiraeth" in Welsh. The singer is someone very old, who begs the wise and learned men of the earth to say where hiraeth comes from; all the treasures of the earth perish, gold, silver, rich fabrics and all the delights of life, but hiraeth is undying; there is no escape from it even in sleep; who weaves this web of hiraeth?'

'Splendid,' said Ripon; 'real Celtic magic.'

'Oh I don't know,' said Revelstoke. 'The Welsh make a fuss about their hiraeth as if they'd invented it; it's common to all small, disappointed, frustrated nations. The Jews have used it as their principal artistic stock-in-trade for two thousand years. It's the old hankering to get back to the womb, where everything was snug. Whimpering stuff.'

'Now that you've made it seem so delightful, I'll sing it,' said Ceinwen.

The accompaniment was a simple but effective succession of chords, played in harp-like style, against which the tune appeared almost as declamation. Revelstoke played it thus for the first verse, and then he began to experiment; his arpeggios whined, they groaned, they shivered piteously. It was cruel caricature of the deep feeling of the words and the simple beauty of the air, and it made Monica's flesh creep with embarrassment. Ripon, though no musician, could understand the import of this right enough, and even the Hopkin-Griffiths knew that all was not well.

What will she do, thought Monica. He'll break her down. There'll be tears in a minute, and what had I better do?

Ceinwen was not the weeping sort. She finished the song, and, as Revelstoke was bringing his accompaniment to a close in a series of sour chromatic progressions she whipped off her left shoe and hit him over the head with it. Then she struck at his hands again and again, bringing from the old Broadwood yelps and twanglings which mingled with his extravagant and astonishing curses.

There was an alarming scene, in which everybody accused and nobody apologized. There was a general withdrawal to bedrooms, and some slamming of doors. But to the amazement of Monica and Ripon everyone turned up at dinner apparently in excellent spirits, and Ceinwen and Giles pulled a cracker together with that extra, clean-hearted goodwill which is seen in people who have had a thoroughly satisfactory quarrel.

After dinner they rolled up the rug in the drawingroom, the maids and outside men came in, and there was dancing to the gramophone.

'The Welsh are rather a hot-tempered race,' said Revelstoke to Monica, as they danced.

And that was all that was ever said about it.

[THIRTEEN]

The week which followed was passed in walks, visits to neighbouring country-houses, and motor jaunts to special places of beauty, including a day of great glory when the young people drove through Gwalia Deserta and explored the gorge at Devil's Bridge; Monica sat in the front seat of the car with Revelstoke all that day. She met several Welsh people, and was astonished by the vivacity and genial spite which they brought to social conversation, and which was unlike anything she had experienced among the people of England. But Monica was more astonished by herself than by anything external. She began to talk about her family; she was often alarmed by what she said, for she found that she was weaving a legend around the Galls.

The Welsh had a national character, or at least they were strongly under that impression. Very well; if they chose to play the Celt, she would play the Canadian. She spoke of Canadian Christmasses, finding in them pleasing and picturesque qualities which would surely have astonished her mother, or even those nationalist zealots, the McCorkills. She deepened the snow, intensified the cold, and enthused retrospectively about winter sports in which she had never taken part. Driving in cutters on the frozen waters of the harbour at Salterton, for instance; she had never done it, but neither did she claim to have done so; she simply described it as if at first-hand. And ice-boating – there was excitement! When she talked of these things her tongue ran away with her, and though she spoke no clear untruths, she implied a whole world which had no counterpart in her past. She did not suppress the Glue Works or the Thirteeners; she simply did not feel a necessity to mention them.

'What a liar you are!' she said one night to her image in the mirror. But the next day her resolve to guard her tongue vanished; she wanted to be as interesting as Ceinwen, whom she liked but whose rapid alternations of temperament began to excite her jealousy. The girl was playing the Celt all over the place, muttering in Welsh to please Ripon, and teaching him Welsh objurgations, as one might teach a parrot to swear. That affair was going swimmingly, but Revelstoke had not said an intimate word to her since Christmas Eve.

It was what she did to her family which most alarmed Monica in her soberer moments. Ma Gall began to appear as a wonderfully salty character, a lady, of course, but with the strength of pioneer ancestry behind her. Ma Gall was, she told Mrs Hopkin-Griffiths, a natural gourmet, delighting in food and bringing to it family secrets which produced dishes of incomparable savour, unknown in the British Islands. This tower of mendacity was erected on the trifling foundation of a rather dull Indian Pudding which Mrs Gall had learned to make from her mother.

Of course, those who embark on such a game as this must be trapped into lies at last.

Monica's entrapment, and her punishment, came almost at the end of her stay at Neuadd Goch. It was at dinner, on New Year's Eve, the night of the County Ball, a festivity which was to be the crown of the entertainment provided by the Hopkin-Griffiths for their guests. Ripon, who was filled with true gratitude toward his hosts, had made them a graceful speech before dinner, saying that their kindness would never be forgotten while he lived, and that he hoped that at some future time he might pass it on, in the same spirit, to visitors to his own land. He did it well, and keeping away from talk of climates of feeling, created an atmosphere of open-hearted friendliness which inevitably led to talk of the bonds which united the English-speaking world. Monica could not contain herself.

She spoke of her admiration for and debt to the British people, and did it in such a way that there was nothing pompous or unseemly about it. But she could not leave it there. This feeling, she said, was not only her own, but had long been that of her family. The Galls, she asserted, were of United Empire Loyalist stock.

This fell rather flat, for nobody present seemed to know what United Empire Loyalists were. So she explained that they were those loyal subjects of King George III, who at the time of the American Revolution, deserted their worldly goods and migrated to Canada, in order that they might keep the inestimable privilege of living under the British flag. Though she did not say so, it could be understood from her words that the descendants of these people formed a vigorous, splendid, but unassuming core of leadership – a kind of democratic aristocracy – in Canada.

In the high and charged atmosphere of the moment – the climate of feeling – this would have been acceptable enough, but Revelstoke fixed her with a sardonic eye.

'What's so remarkable about that?' said he. 'Why should they do otherwise than leave the country if they didn't like the Revolution? Are you asking us to admire them simply because they were loyal? Surely that's the least Britain could have expected of them. Honouring people for being loyal is like honouring them for being honest; it's a confession of an essentially base and cynical attitude toward mankind. It's either that or it's just sentimental silliness.'

Perhaps Monica should have hit him on the head with her shoe. But she was, beneath the superficial part of her mind which was boasting and prattling, so conscious of the untruth of what she was saying, that she felt disproportionately rebuked. She felt that everybody at the table was disgusted with her, and ashamed for her, as a foolish little braggart. She felt that she had been sharply and contemptuously put in her place. Of course there was no such general feeling. Mrs Hopkin-Griffiths was thinking how distinguished Giles looked when he was nicely washed and had on his dress suit, and hardly heard what was said. The squire thought the boy was much too rough on the little Canadian; loyalty ought to be encouraged, or where would we all be? Ceinwen thought: well, there's her reward for laying herself out to charm Master Giles, the dirty English pig (though as she thought this in Welsh the last term was not quite so stinging as it seems in translation). Only Ripon guessed at the truth.

The County Ball was held in Trallwm, in the Assembly Rooms, which was a grand term given to a largish public-hall-of-all-work; and the corridors and anterooms surrounding it, in the Town Hall. It was prettily hung with holly and Christmas decorations, and had been furnished for the occasion by a local dealer with some really handsome antiques, and so it was a pleasant setting for an occasion when most of the guests brought a genuine spirit of gaiety with them.

It was a mixed assemblage of county gentry, well-to-do farmers and townspeople, and it was ostensibly in aid of the hospital. The squire could well remember – and never ceased reminding everyone he met of the fact – the days when a velvet rope divided the dancing floor, and the county danced on one side, and the lesser folk on the other. But those days were gone, and everybody said, with varying degrees of sincerity, that they were glad of it. The Neuadd Goch party were disposed to enjoy themselves, except Giles, who hated the music but had not quite enough determination to stay at home.

Balancing the ballroom, at the other end of the main corridor of the Town Hall, was the Court Room, which had been arranged as a sitting-out room; it was splendidly suited to such a purpose, for it was a maze of fenced-in compartments, wells and cubby-holes which allowed sitting-out couples quite enough privacy, if they wanted it. It was here that the kindly Ripon led Monica, and as they could not, in the gloom, find anywhere else that was not taken by a seriously whispering couple, they climbed into the prisoner's dock, which was high and surrounded by a fence of spikes – presumably to keep felons from leaping into court and menacing the learned counsel. They sat on the little bench inside it.

'Don't take it so hard,' said Ripon, after a few moments of silence.

'Eh?'

'What Revelstoke said at dinner. You've been dragging your wings ever since. He's a bastard; he likes to take it out of women. Look what he did to Ceinwen at Christmas.'

'But, Johnny, this was different.'

'Yes, I know it was.'

Monica began to weep. Ripon gave her his handkerchief, held her round the shoulders, said soothing and not very coherent things, and after a time restored her to some sort of order.

'It's not the end of the world. You've just got to see it as it was. You'd been boasting, and he slapped you down. It was nasty of him, but that's all it was.'

'I'd been making a perfect fool of myself. I've been doing it ever since I came here. You must all despise me.'

'No, no. I'll be frank; you've been giving us quite a line about Canada and your people and all that, but anybody with half an ear could tell that you were only asking to be patted. It wasn't even boasting. It was just putting a best foot forward. Nothing to be ashamed of. These people invite it, you know.'

'Welsh people, you mean..'

'All the people in these islands. They're so self-satisfied. You have to hate them, or you have to try to pull yourself up even with them. I know all about it. When I'm at home I'm not terrifically American, but over here I have to act a part, or disappear. You were just trying not to disappear; and because you're such a hell of a good singer it would easily have passed as the rather charming egotism of the artist, if dear Gilly hadn't stuck his knife into you. You were just the tiniest bit silly; but he was intentionally brutal.'

'Do you mean that, Johnny, about having to act a part, and the people here being so strong in themselves, and that?'

'Of course I mean it.'

'It's not just something you got out of a book?'

'What would be wrong with it if I did get it out of a book? As a matter of fact, it's in lots of books. Have you read any Henry James?'

'No; did he write about that?'

'Sometimes. We've been living in a kind of Henry James climate for the past few days. The American getting the works from Europeans was some of his favourite themes. "This arrogant old Europe which so little befriends us", he called it. But your mistake was that you didn't act a part; you were trying to make yourself believe it, and that never works. That's bad art.'

'Well, what should I do?'

'Why don't you try passing as white? You know about the light-skinned Negroes in the States, who move North and live among whites as one of themselves? The only way to get on in peace with the people over here is to conceal as well as you can that you're not one of themselves – pass as white. Minimize the differences; don't call attention to them. This country's full of Canadians, Australians, New Zealanders, yes and Americans, all passing as white, because if they let it be known what they are, the natives will patronize the living bejesus out of them. They don't really mean to be unkind; they just have this wonderful sense of being God's noblest work. – Now it's getting near the New Year. We must go back to the ballroom. Pretty soon all these Welshmen and Englishmen will be singing one of the most pedestrian verses of Robert Burns, and kissing each other. I wouldn't miss it for worlds, and if you won't be offended, I'll hunt up Ceinwen. Happy New Year, Monica darling!'

[SEVEN]

Phanuel Tuke switched off Monica's radio-gramophone.

'Well,' said he, 'if fate is unkind to my verse, I shall at least be known to posterity as the man who provided Giles Revelstoke with the words for his first work of undoubted genius.'

Revelstoke's menagerie was assembled in Monica's living-room because she had the best wireless set among them. They had been listening to a broadcast on the Third Programme of his *cantata da camera*, called *The Discoverie of Witchcraft*. Tuke had not written the words, but had selected them; the libretto was made up of recitative passages chosen from Reginald Scot's *Discoverie*, verses from Ben Jonson's *Masque of Queens*, and a witch-trial or 'process' adapted from *Malleus Malleficarum*. Monica knew the words well; she had typed them many times, for the singers to study, and for the seemingly endless needs of the broadcasting people.

'I still think Brum Benny should have let Giles conduct,' said Persis Kinwellmarshe. She was not sufficiently musical to venture any opinion on the composition itself, but she had found plenty of matter for vehement partisanship in the politics surrounding the broadcast.

'Now Perse, give that a rest,' said Bun Eccles. 'Giles himself admits he's no hand at conducting. Why risk a good chance like this just to wave the stick? He can't manage an orchestra and even you know it.'

'He'd be perfectly all right if Benny didn't hang over him all the time and offer advice and fuss him.'

'Benny's responsible to the BBC, you know that. He got them to do *Discoverie*; he has to deliver the goods. Giles said so himself.'

'Giles may have said so to you, Bun dear, but I know damn well what he thinks. It's the old story: young man of genius under the wing of old man of talent – and the old man will bloody well see that he stays under his wing. Tonight will settle all that, though. It ought to put Giles right on the top of the heap.'

'Does anyone know what he will get for this broadcast?' said Odo Odingsels. He had tucked his lean length into a corner and all through the music had been eating the food which Monica provided.

'There won't be much left of his fee when all the costs are paid,' said Bridget Tooley. 'The expense of copying the scores will eat up most of it. But of course he'll have them for subsequent performances, and over the years the rentals might amount to a good deal.'

'Can't count on that,' said Odingsels. 'This isn't going to be a popular work. No use pretending.'

Odingsels was the only one of the group who knew much about music. Giles had friends, but no intimates, among musicians. Odingsels knew what he was talking about, and ordinarily the others deferred to him. But Persis would not do so now.

'Why not?' said she. 'You've heard it. Isn't it the most exciting thing in this contemporary music series?'

'I don't know,' said Odingsels; 'I haven't listened to any of the others. Have you?'

Miss Kinwellmarshe had not.

'It's good, mind you,' said Odingsels. 'In parts it's wonderfully good. I didn't mean that it wasn't. But it's hard to perform. The music is difficult; it sounds simple, quite a lot of the time, but just you look at the score. It's an inconvenient size. It isn't a song cycle, that any singer and his accompanist can carry round the world in a music-case. And it isn't a big work that an amateur choral society can chew on for two or three months. It calls for soprano and bass-baritone soloists, a double quartet of better than average choral singers, and an orchestra consisting of string quartet and double-bass, with piano, oboe and French horn. Just the size to be neglected.'

'I suppose a good deal will depend on what the critics say,' said Tuke.

'A little. Not much.' Odingsels seemed determined to be discouraging. 'Critics of any importance aren't likely to commit themselves heavily on a new score that they haven't examined by a composer they don't know. Giles won't find himself made over-night. It's only in the more trivial arts like literature, and theatre and ballet that critics wield that sort of power.' He grinned irritatingly.

'Giles will be ready for them,' said Persis. 'He's been walloping them in *Lantern* for three good years. I don't suppose that will make them like him, but it will let them know that he will have a reply for anything they want to say. I don't expect for a minute that he'll get his due from them, but they'll have to be civil.'

'Why?' said Odingsels.

'I've told you. Because of *Lantern*.'

'How many critics do you think read *Lantern*? Who do you suppose takes it very seriously except ourselves? How many well-known or influential names are on the subscription list? Sometimes I think we are deceiving ourselves about *Lantern*. In my really sane moments I know it. How lucky that none of us has to live by it.'

'Odo, why are you being so bloody-minded tonight? Is it because Giles has had a wonderful work performed? I know you hate anybody else's success, but is it necessary for you to be so completely poisonous?'

'Persis, my pretty darling, I am a realist. Giles has had a very good piece of music performed. A lot of people will have heard it. Some will have liked it, others will have hated it, and some others – perhaps the biggest number – will not have paid any particular attention. Of those who have liked it, perhaps half will remember Giles' name. It is slow work, becoming known as a composer. What has Giles done? He's written perhaps fifty songs and a couple of suites for small orchestra; he's had a few things done publicly, and I believe four years ago he gave a small recital of his own stuff to which not one critic of the first rank turned up. This is his real beginning – tonight. In ten years, if he works hard, he may be quite well known as a rising young composer.'

'Oh, come; sooner than that, surely,' said Tuke.

'Giles is a slow worker. This piece has been on the stocks for a good eighteen months, to my knowledge. He spends so much time on other things.' Odingsels cast a leer at Persis.

'Too true,' said she. 'He has far more than his share to do on *Lantern* and of course he has to waste his energies teaching, and doing musical odd jobs, to keep the pot boiling.'

'He isn't the only one on *Lantern* who has personal work to attend to,' said Miss Tooley. 'If you are insinuating that Fanny and I don't pull our weight, I'd like to say that you should be the last person to criticize; you do nothing at all, except provide occasional cups of indifferent tea. And of course keep your eye peeled for cracks in the ceiling.'

'Now girls, stow that,' said Bun Eccles. 'We all know what Odo meant; he meant Giles spends a lot of time playing bunny-in-the-hay with you, Perse, but maybe that's why he writes good music. Why don't you look at it that way, and be happy?' He raised his glass of beer toward Persis, and drank to her.

'If he doesn't want to teach, I don't suppose he has to,' said Monica. 'And if I take up his time being taught, I certainly save it getting the *Lantern* accounts out of tangles.'

'Oh, we know you're quite the little woman of business,' said Persis. 'But unfortunately he can't give up teaching; he has to have the money. If that tight-fisted old mother of his would give him whatever you pay him for lessons, he wouldn't need to bother.'

'Doesn't he have family money?' said Tuke.

'He's got a tiny income from some money his father left him directly. Otherwise not a bean. His mother's terribly rich; she could easily let him have a very good allowance. She lives someplace in Wales, in a tremendous house, with every luxury, and now and then she sends him a few quid, for birthdays, or something. It's a shame people like that can't die, and let their money do some good. But no, she thinks not having anything will make him get a steady job. I suppose she sees him leading the municipal orchestra at Torquay, or someplace. Mothers! I think the most disgusting and immoral relationship is between mothers and sons – no, on second thoughts, between fathers and daughters. The old ones just want to eat the young ones up.'

Persis knit her dark brows and looked very beautiful, brooding on the psychological horror of Mrs Hopkin-Griffiths and Admiral Sir Percy Kinwellmarshe.

'It is of course utterly unrealistic to suppose that reputations in literature are made overnight,' said Tuke, who had been brooding on Odingsels' hard words. 'One despises egotism, of course, but one instances oneself; one can give Giles a few years, and one is perhaps more *engagé*, but one has certainly not been overwhelmed with recognition. As for music being, *au fond*, more serious than letters, well – one feels perhaps that those who are committed to an art are the best judges of its limits.'

'Better judges than technicians, however capable,' said Miss Tooley, bridling. Everybody knew that when Tuke began to refer to himself as 'one' Bridget would do battle for him. 'Particularly when their own stuff appears so seldom.'

'My best work is for connoisseurs of really imaginative photography,' said Odingsels, grinning. 'I don't have to publish to get recognition.'

The menagerie was working up for one of its periodical ugly fights, but at this point Monica brought in another plate of sandwiches, and Bun Eccles went the rounds with more beer. The greedy could say no more while this lasted, and Tuke, who had a gift for talking and eating without missing a chew or a syllable, gained a great advantage. He proceeded to contrast the powers of music and poetry, being scrupulously fair, but, as he knew very little about music, not especially enlightening, though extremely strong on sensibility.

Monica went back to her bedroom, where she made the sandwiches, to be sure that the supply should not fail; she knew that when Revelstoke was not present, the menagerie could only be controlled by heavy sedation with food and alcohol. They quarrelled astonishingly, and about things which she rarely understood in detail, though she knew by her native good sense that jealousy lay at the root of it. Every time an issue of *Lantern* appeared there was one of these pow-wows, and the pattern was fixed; Tuke was offended by Odingsels, and Miss Tooley and Odingsels fought bitterly; Eccles, who was thoroughly a painter, and bored by men of words, lost patience with them all, and got drunk; Persis Kinwellmarshe asserted that there would be no *Lantern* without Revelstoke, and was called whore for her pains by Bridget; Revelstoke laughed and cursed at them all. At last Mrs Klein would appear and complain that her other lodgers were discommoded by the noise, and Odingsels would make her cry. On one occasion Monica could bear it no more, and took Mrs Klein's part; to her astonishment her display of temper put them all in great good humour, and improved her position in the group. After one of these brawls, which she found tiresome and exhausting, but which they seemed to enjoy, Revelstoke would marshal the *Lantern* forces again and work would proceed once more in its ill-organized, imperfectly understood fashion.

But Revelstoke was not at hand now, to keep all their bad-tempered egotism in check. And Monica was afraid that Mrs Merry would not take the attitude of Mrs Klein, who always managed to say, at some point in her complaints – 'I'm full of sympasy for ze artist; I am grateful to have ze artist under my roof' – a protestation invariably greeted by Odingsels with a shout of 'Halt die Schnauze!' Mrs Merry was not full of sympathy for anyone, except perhaps herself, and would certainly complain of any noise to Mr Boykin on his monthly visit with the rent. Monica wished heartily that she had not asked them to listen to Giles' broadcast on her receiving-set.

Yet it had seemed such a chance to get in with them, to strengthen her position. She was not so simple as to think that she had no place in the *Lantern* group; the finances of the magazine, such as they were, were understood by her alone, and Raikes Brothers had of late shown a tendency to call her when they wanted a decision about anything. She had been in the happy position of having two pounds ten to lend to Tuke on an occasion when he needed that sum very badly, and Revelstoke himself had been her champion a few weeks later, and had compelled the poet to pay back the ten shillings, which was all he could afford. She had a place, but it was the bottom place. And here it was six weeks after that encounter in the bathroom at Neuadd Goch, since when he had not so much as kissed her!

Why? Why could he not see that she loved him? She was not a ninny; she did not sigh and lallygag like Juliet; she put herself heart and soul into the business of *Lantern*, and although it could not be said that its position was any better than before, it was certainly clearer. She managed to get his attention for fifteen minutes one day and explained the whole financial situation to him. He had been bored, and had told her in a huff that if people hadn't enough wit to appreciate *Lantern*, he could do nothing about it. He wrote for the bloody magazine, didn't he? What more did she expect him to do? Hawk it on street-corners? But Monica would not believe that this expressed his true feeling; if he was really committed to the publication – and he was – he must desire its financial success; it was axiomatic. So she troubled him no more about it, and plunged into even more discouraging talks with Raikes Brothers, who were beginning to want something on account.

Not that she expected to win him by a flashing display of business method; she was not so foolish as that. But what better approach had she, what more effective way of showing that anything she had in the way of skills or talents was at his command? Her heart was full of love, but externally she remained neat, silent, and perhaps a little too quick at producing pencils and pieces of paper; once or twice she sensed that it is convenient, but perhaps not wholly romantic, to be the person to whom everyone turns for a clean bit of india-rubber. She could not hope to be useful to him musically; was she not his pupil? How, then, could she serve except with the typewriter and the account-book, in the use of which she was more expert than anyone else in the group? She wanted desperately to be one of the menagerie. She tried to swear, but it was a failure. She could not use filthy words, as Persis did; a Thirteener upbringing and, she felt, a native fastidiousness, prevented her; she had also a grudging recognition that what suited the opulent sluttishness of Persis did not appear so well in her. However, she sought to liven up her conversation with a few bloodies until one day she caught Odingsels' ironic eye on her, felt deeply foolish, and tried no more.

They never thought of her as one of themselves. She thought of them as Bohemians, though they would have hooted at so romantic and unfashionable a word, taking it as further evidence that she was an outsider. But under their Bohemianism they were very English. No, ridiculous! Odingsels – nobody knew quite what he was, but he was certainly not English. Bridget Tooley's father was a lawyer in Cork; she was Irish as – Ma Gall's expression came pat to memory – as Paddy's pig. Bun Eccles was an Australian, and abused the English as Pommies. Revelstoke himself was English, of the Eton and Oxford variety, and of course the hateful Persis –

Ah, Persis was the one! There was a creature who managed to have the best of two or three worlds! To be the draggle-tailed gypsy, with all the advantages of great and apparently indestructible beauty, and at the same time to be able to come the well-bred English lady – that was having it with jam and syrup at once. She was the one who created the atmosphere which excluded Monica. She was the one who did not have her speech corrected by Revelstoke. She was the one who did not have to know that 'glory' was a trochee, instead of a spondee, which was what both Monica and Eccles made of it. She was the one who did not have to do anything about *Lantern*, though she was always in the way when the work was most pressing. And why? Because she was Revelstoke's mistress, his recreation, his hobby, his –

Monica, who was cutting bread, sawed savagely at the loaf. Filthy abuse that was pure Ma Gall rushed up into her throat, her head hurt and her eyes seemed to fill with blood. She had to sit down on the bed to recover herself.

Oh, it was so unfair! Why couldn't she be to him what Persis was, and at the same time a helper and a constructive influence in his life? She was better than Persis. She was; she was! Why couldn't he see it? How could he stand that creature, who took baths now and then for fun, but not to get clean, and who kept tufts of long hair in her oxters because she said real men liked it? Monica was clean (though Amy had taught her not to talk about 'personal daintiness') and cleanliness ought to count. She would do anything for Revelstoke, be anything he wanted. And he had turned to her once. He must have some feeling for her. It could not be otherwise.

Meanwhile the noise from the other room was increasing. Two or three guests had made journeys to the watercloset down the stairs, shouting their contributions to the discussion as they went up and down. There had been some rapping on the ceiling by the lodger below, to which Eccles had replied with a few hearty stamps. Persis was developing the theme of parental stinginess in her extremely carrying voice. Monica knew that she would have to go in and shut them up. She held a cool bottle of beer to her forehead for a couple of minutes, and went back to the living-room.

She entered just as Mrs Merry came in from the hall. The landlady wore a look of aggrieved hauteur, and when she spoke her accent was more refined and wholly diphthongal than usual.

'Miss Gall, I am really compelled to ask your guests to leave,' she began, but got no further, for behind her appeared Revelstoke, and with him Sir Benedict Domdaniel. The menagerie greeted them with a roar.

The appearance of the great conductor created a difficult situation for everyone. Mrs Merry was in a particularly ticklish spot, for she had to reconcile her landlady's indignation with her elation at having a celebrity (and a titled one, too) under her roof – and there were the promises she had made to the lodger downstairs to drive the rowdies out into the street. Persis, who had been making very free with Brum Benny's name, was revealed as one who had never met him personally, and had not quite the brass to be insulting when she was introduced. Monica, who had been thinking passionately of Revelstoke as a lover, had now to greet him timidly as a guest, feeling the very least of his menagerie; she was uneasy, also, about Domdaniel, who had not encountered the menagerie before, to her knowledge and who, at this moment, contrasted strangely with them, like a royal personage photographed among the survivors of some disaster. But Domdaniel managed the whole thing very well.

'We seem to have come at the peak of the party,' said he, smiling affably at Mrs Merry, and bending so low over her hand that she thought, for one golden but panic-stricken moment, that he was about to kiss it. 'A very great occasion, and I'm sure you'll understand; our friend has been covering himself with glory.' It was this easy, glossily splendid manner, which had won him the name of

Brummagen Benny among the envious; unable themselves to rise to such heights, they took revenge by recalling his plebian origin. And a severe critic might have said that his manner was not thoroughly well-bred; it was too accomplished, too much a work of art, for mere 'good form'. He presented Revelstoke, who greeted Mrs Merry with proprietary charm, as though she were his guest. At the same moment Odingsels bowed his piebald poll toward Mrs Merry's startled face, and put a glass of beer into her hand.

'The last thing of which I am desirous –' she began, with immense graciousness, but was unable to sustain this fine beginning, and went on – 'It would ill become me to – it is certainly not my desire to intrude a note of solemnity into such an occasion as this, but you will understand my position *vis-à-vis* Mrs Porteous who occupies the flatette below, and whose advanced years and habit of life –' She floundered.

'Mind your manners,' said Revelstoke to the menagerie, and they obeyed, to the point of congratulating him in stagey whispers.

'Oh, please, please!' cried Mrs Merry, laughing throatily, and gesturing with her glass of beer, like some marchioness in an old-fashioned musical comedy, 'don't feel that you must whisper. That I could not bear! Please, Sir Benedict, beg them not to whisper.' She bent upon Sir Benedict a look of arch agony. With him at her side, looking so gallantly into her eyes, Mrs Merry would have incited the party to dance clog-dances upon the head of Mrs Porteous.

'I have a proposal which I think will settle everything,' said he. 'Suppose we all go to my house, and continue the party there. I've lots to drink, but if you've any food, Monica, perhaps you'll bring it along. And as we have inconvenienced you, dear lady, I hope that you will forgive us and make one of the party.'

Smiling his most winning smile, he gazed deep into Mrs Merry's eyes, mentally signalling to her – Say no; say no; you can't leave the lodgers; say no. But Mrs Merry was not susceptible to telepathy; she was borne aloft on a cloud of social glory; this was as it had been when that worthy solicitor, Maybrick Merry, was alive, and they had invited three couples to dinner every second Thursday, and once an MP had come. 'Yes, yes,' she carrolled; 'I'll run and get my wrap.'

It was quite ten minutes before Mrs Merry had changed her clothes, put on all her rings, and run a darkening stick through the grey patches in her hair. Monica had plenty of time to line her rubbish pail with *The Times* and put the food in it, and Bun Eccles providently carried the beer downstairs, in case Sir Benedict should have overestimated his supplies. Sir Benedict had gone down to wait in his car, and Revelstoke admonished the others to come quietly. And, upon the whole, they did so, except that Odingsels insisted on carrying Persis downstairs pick-a-back, and tickled her legs as he did so, making her squeal. And it was unfortunate that Eccles, who insisted on carrying both the food and the drink, caught his heel in a worn bit of stair carpet, and – determined to save the drink – allowed the rubbish-pail to go crashing down to the landing.

A door opened and somebody – almost certainly Mrs Porteous – poked a parrot-like head, adorned with an obvious wig, into the hall. 'Well,' she gobbled, 'this is the first time that anything like this has ever happened here, and if it is what comes of giving shelter to Commonwealth students –'

Odingsels, with Persis on his back, lurched toward her.

'Shh!' said he. 'We are taking this lady to a nursing-home for an abortion, and I must ask you please not to make so much noise.' Down the lower flight he went at a gallop, with Persis shrieking and fizzing like a soda-syphon on his back. Bun retrieved the food, and, acting on sudden inspiration, pushed a sandwich into Mrs Porteous' hand, then crammed the remainder into the pail, and raced after him. It was Monica who heard the last of Mrs Porteous' unflattering comments and prophecies.

On the pavement there was a slight resurgence of ill-feeling, for everyone wanted to crowd into Sir Benedict's handsome car, which was manifestly impossible. Odingsels would not be parted from Persis, and Mrs Merry, with the superior cunning of middle age, got the front seat next to the great man for herself; at last Revelstoke and Tuke were crammed into the back seat, and Monica and Bun were left to follow in a taxi with a disgruntled Miss Tooley.

'Fanny can't resist luxury,' she said, 'and as soon as he smelled that real leather upholstery he was done for. Not a terribly nice characteristic, really.'

The house in Dean's Yard was empty, for the servant did not sleep in, but Domdaniel quickly found glasses, and in five minutes the party had been resumed. Odingsels and Persis had changed from quarrelling to silent, intimate pawing, and they needed a sofa to themselves. Miss Tooley was being distant toward Phanuel Tuke, which involved standing quite close but with her back turned partly toward him. Sir Benedict moved about, making them at home, but he soon found how needless this was; the menagerie was at home wherever it was assembled. But Mrs Merry had a highly developed, indeed a swollen, social sense; unquestionably she thought of herself as 'the senior married woman present' and she set to work to establish a high tone of behaviour. She pursued her host, she complimented him on the taste in which his house was furnished; she confided that she could judge people instantly by the glassware they used; she sincerely hoped that they were to be favoured with a little music later on, as it would be such a treat; she let it be known that when her husband was living they had several times met Madame Gertrude Belcher-Chalke, whose renditions of Scottish songs were such a delight, and who must certainly be known to Sir Benedict; and, well, yes, she would be glad of the teeniest drop of Scotch – no more than a drop, mind – and plain water.

Monica, who had had no opportunity to recover from her nerve-storm, soon found the kitchen, took the hacked loaf – fetish for the hateful Persis – from the rubbish-pail, and began once more to make sandwiches. The capacity of the menagerie for food was boundless and she, true daughter of Ma Gall, had bought in ample viands. It soothed her to make sandwiches, and it kept her away from the others.

But she had not been long alone before Sir Benedict slipped quickly through the door.

'I'll have a quiet drink out here with you,' said he. 'I can't convince your landlady that I don't play the piano at parties.'

'I'm terribly sorry,' said Monica; 'it was wonderful of you to rescue us, and terribly kind to ask her. She's having a marvellous time.'

'I told her to persuade Revelstoke to improvise something,' said he. 'A dirty trick, but self-preservation, and so forth. Have a drink. You look as if you needed one. What's the matter?'

'Nothing. We heard the broadcast.'

'What did you think?'

'I thought it was wonderful. But you know what my opinion is worth.'

'Don't hedge. Did you like the work?'

'I don't know. It's awfully strange. Not as strange as lots of modern music; not so sort of repellent. It doesn't fight the listener. But mystifying. I wish you'd tell me about it.'

'I've done so; I conducted it. It's quite a solid piece of work, though I wish he'd study with a really first-rate man on composition for a while. He can't completely say what he means, yet, in orchestral terms. Most of the instrumental writing is brilliant, but there are a few passages of awful muddle that I couldn't persuade him to change. What he does best, of course, is write for the voice, and that lifts him above all but a few today. This isn't an age when many composers seem to care about the voice; they want to use it in all sorts of queer ways, and often they do marvellous things, but it's not really singing, you know. It's abuse of the voice. But his stuff is wonderfully grateful to sing and that, combined with a modern musical idiom, gives it great individuality.'

'I suppose a lot depends on what the critics say?'

'A bit. Not too much, really. Far more depends on what chaps like me say.'

'Anyhow, he'll be able to deal with the critics in *Lantern*.'

'That's precisely what I'm afraid of. He wastes too much time on that nonsense.'

'Nonsense?'

'Yes. What's the good of fighting critics? Mind you, some of them are very able, particularly when judging performances. But only a few can form any opinion of a new work. Most of them are simply on the lookout for novelty. They hear too much, and they hear it the wrong way. They get like children who are peevish from having too many toys; they are always tugging at the skirts of music, whining "Amuse me; give me something new." Giles hasn't shown them anything particularly new. He's not an innovator. But he has an extraordinary melodic gift. Now you just watch the critics and see how many of them are able to spot that.'

'You don't think much of *Lantern*?'

'My dear girl, these little reviews and magazines of protest and coterie criticism come and go, and they don't amount to a damn. They're all right for what's-his-name – Tuke and that formidable female bodyguard of his – but Revelstoke is a serious man; he ought to be at work on music. You've rather involved yourself with this *Lantern* thing, haven't you?'

'I help a bit with the accounts.'

'Good enough. You're what – twenty-two? It's all right for you. Gives you a taste of that sort of thing, and we're all the better for a taste. But Revelstoke is thirty-three. Time he was over all that, and down to serious work.'

'Do you think teaching is a waste of his time?'

'Not if it brings in money he needs. But this *Lantern* is just an expense of spirit in a waste of shame.'

'Shakespeare. Sonnet something-or-other.'

'Bright child. He's making you do some reading.'

'Yes. – And *Lantern*'s not the only waste.'

'You mean that gang in there? They're no more a waste than any other pack of friends, I should say. Many fine things are written about friendship, and there's a general superstition that everybody is capable of friendship, and gets it, like love. But lots of people never know love, except quite mildly; and most of them never know friendship, except in quite a superficial way. Terribly demanding thing, friendship. Most of us have to put up with acquaintanceship.'

It was flattering to Monica to be enjoying, for the first time, a conversation with Sir Benedict which was not about music, and which was not crowded by the press of his engagements. She fell into a trap; she tried to be impressive; she tried to be his age.

'But don't you think people like that, who live such irregular lives, are terribly exhausting? I mean, they must drain away a lot of his vitality, which should be saved for music. I don't want to gossip, but it's common knowledge that he's terribly taken up with that girl in there – the dark one – and I don't know when he finds time to do any work. Do you think he ought to get off into the country, somewhere, and really slave at his music?'

'No; I don't. When I was your age I might have thought so, but I know better now; you can't write music just by getting away from people. Slavery is for the technicians, like you and me; we thrive under the lash. But creators must simply do what seems best to them. Some like solitude: some like a crowd. As for the girl, why not? When I was a student in Vienna my teacher told me how often he had seen old Brahms, when he was all sorts of ages, strolling meditatively home from the house of a certain lady who lived in the Weiden. Couldn't matter less. Nothing, nothing whatever really stands in the way of a creative artist except lack of talent.'

'You don't think a disorderly life matters?'

'Wouldn't suit me. I couldn't answer for anyone else.'

'Then you don't think that Shakespeare was right – about the expense of spirit in a waste of shame?'

'It's only shame when you feel it so. And he obviously doesn't feel it. You are the one who feels it, and there can be only two explanations of that: either you're more of a missionary than a musician, or else you're jealous of that girl with the black hair and blue eyes.'

Monica turned back to her bread-cutting. She had never been much of a blusher, but she knew that her appearance had changed in many tell-tale ways.

'Am I right?' said Sir Benedict, taking a pull at his drink. 'Well, falling in love with one's master is recognized practice in the musical world. Even in his eighties I can remember old Garcia having to fight 'em off, to protect his afternoon nap. Well, go ahead by all means. Anything to broaden your range of feeling.'

Monica turned toward him, and her expression was so angry, her eyes so brilliant, and the bread-knife in her hand so menacing, that Sir Benedict skipped backward.

'I hate you damned superior Englishmen!' said she. 'Murtagh Molloy tells me I have no emotion; Giles Revelstoke treats me like the village idiot because I haven't read everything that's ever been written, and you tell me to fall in love because it will extend my range of feeling! To hell with you all! If I haven't got your easy, splattering feelings I'm proud of it. I'll throw this all up and go home. I won't stay here and be treated like a parrot, and learn to say "Polly wants a cracker" in just the right accent and with just the right shade of feeling! I hate the whole pack of you, and I hate your rotten little Ye Olde Antique Shoppe of a country. I'd rather go home and be a typist in the Glue Works than take your dirt for another day.'

Sir Benedict looked thoughtfully at her for a full minute, then he said: 'You're perfectly right, my dear, and I apologize.' Monica made a dreadful face, snorted painfully, and burst into tears. She had never been a pretty weeper.

Sir Benedict had for many years made it a habit to carry two handkerchiefs, one for his own nose and one for other people's; he produced the second now, shook out its folds and gave it to Monica just in time to hide a very messy face. Then he sat her down on the kitchen table and sat beside her, holding her tenderly.

'You mustn't mind us,' said he; 'it's just a way of going on that we have carried over from the nineteenth century, when we really ruled the waves. Molloy would be terribly hurt if he knew you had called him an Englishman. As for me, I'm English, right enough, but not really out of the top drawer; there is a large grandpaternal pop-shop in Birmingham which it would be ungrateful of me to deny. Revelstoke is English, too, and I don't mind telling you that I worked it that you should go to his mother for Christmas. Not that she, or Giles, knew, of course; I cooked it up with Miss Eigg, who is an old friend of mine; I thought it might be more friendly for you. Weren't they nice people? Surely Giles must have relaxed a little, in his own home? Of course he plays the great man with these silly hangers-on of his, but it's only mannerism.

'I didn't realize you had any really strong feeling for him. But what I said was quite sincere, and not meant to be hurtful. A love-affair, if it is anything more than a tennis-club flirtation, does enlarge one's range of feeling. Of course that isn't why one does it, but you must understand that I was speaking as your teacher and adviser, looking at the thing from outside. And of course what looks unique and glorious to you, at your age – and is so, too, of course – has a rather more accustomed look from my age and my point of view. The terrible truth is that feeling really *does* have to be learned. It comes spontaneously when one is in love, or when somebody important dies; but people like you and me – interpretative artists – have to learn also to recapture those feelings, and transform them into something which we can offer to the world in our performances. You know what Heine says – and if you don't I won't scold you: "Out of my great sorrows I make my little songs." Well – we all do that. And what we make out of the feelings life brings us is something a little different, something not quite so shattering but very much more polished and perhaps also more poignant, than the feelings themselves. Your jealousy – it hurts now, but if you are as good an artist as I begin to think you are, you'll never have to guess at what jealousy means again, when you meet with it in music. And love – don't ask me what it is, because I can't tell you anything more than that it is an intense and complex tangle of emotions – you'll have to feel that, too. Everybody claims to have been in love, but to love so that you can afterward distill something from it which makes other people know what love is or reminds them forcibly – that takes an artist. Do you feel a little better now?'

'Gluh.'

'Good. And you won't go back to the Glue Works tomorrow?'

A shake of the head.

'Then perhaps we should return to the others, or they will think that I am up to no good with you, and although that would be flattering to me, in a way, I don't think it really desirable.'

But at this moment Mrs Merry came into the kitchen. She wore a splendid, elevated look, more like a martyr than Monica had ever seen her; her teeth were bared in a smile which suggested that the first flames of the pyre were licking at her toes.

'Sir Benedict, I must leave you now,' said she. 'It is quite time – indeed it has been made obvious to me that it is far past time – that I quitted the gathering.' She gave a slight, refined hiccup, and burst into tears.

For the first time in his life Sir Benedict had no clean handkerchief to offer. But Mrs Merry, a lady even in grief and liquor, fished one out of her bosom, and held its lacy inadequacy to her lips.

'My dear lady, has anyone ill-used you?' said he. In perfect fairness he should have sat Mrs Merry on the table and held her, but he did not.

'My fault,' she quavered. 'Intruded. Went too far. Artist – high strung. Should have remembered.'

Sir Benedict took the glass from Mrs Merry's hand and hunted in a cupboard where the cooking things were. He found a bottle of cherry brandy, and poured a generous slug. 'Drink this, and tell us all about it,' said he.

'Mr Revelstoke – a genius, of course. And fresh from a great success. – Well, if you insist. Oh dear, I shall never be able to drink such a lot! – Well, I ought to have known. Madame Gertrude Belcher-Chalke was just the same after a concert – *élevée*, indeed one might say utterly *ballonnée* – and hardly civil for hours. I meant no harm. Asked him to play. Well, I mean – a musician? Surely he *plays*? He said no. I pressed. I mean, they *expect* to be pressed. Nono. Press again. Nonono. I entreat the others to support my request. That man with the nasty picked-looking head shouts something in German. Then Mr Revelstoke rushes to the piano and says – "For you, for you alone, you lovely creature!" And plays.' Here Mrs Merry's bosom heaved as no bosom has heaved since the heyday of the silent films. She drained the cherry brandy to the dregs. 'He played *Chopsticks*!' she cried and hurled her glass dramatically into the sink.

Sir Benedict proved amply that a conductor of the first rank is not only a notable interpretative musician, but also a diplomat and an organizer of uncommon ability. He soothed Mrs Merry. He shooed Monica upstairs to his own bedroom to wash and restore her face. He enlisted Eccles to help him bring champagne up from the cellar. He brought the party to some semblance of unity and enjoyment. And, finally, he went to the piano.

'Giles and I want to play something for Mrs Merry,' said he. 'It is called *Paraphrases*, and it is what all musicians play when they are happy.'

Drawing Revelstoke down at the piano by his side, Domdaniel compelled him to join in a duet; with great verve and gusto they played the twenty-four variations on *Chopsticks* which were written by Liszt, Borodin, Cui and Rimsky-Korsakov. Mrs Merry, very much at the mercy of her feelings and with her remaining self-possession disappearing beneath the champagne, managed to get to the piano, against which she posed, smiling soulfully at Sir Benedict until, suddenly, all meaning disappeared from her face and she fell heavily to the floor.

Eccles, expert in such affairs, lifted her head and fanned her. Mrs Merry opened her eyes, and she smiled blissfully. 'Put me to bed and don't bend me,' said she. And thus the party ended.

[TWO]

On stage and screen the business of getting a drunken person to bed is always represented as uproariously funny. Monica, Revelstoke and Eccles found it merely laborious. Mrs Merry was a Junoesque woman in her late fifties; as a deadweight, she was not easily budged. It seemed that they had no sooner stuffed her untidily into a taxi at Dean's Yard, than they had to haul her out of it at Courtfield Gardens. The men held her upright while Monica paid the taxi, and while they hoisted her up the steps, Monica retrieved her shoes, which fell off in that process. When they got her inside, there was the problem of the stairs. It was not that she was so heavy (though she was substantial) as that she offered no handholds. They made a Boy Scout chair with their hands, but in her satin gown she slipped twice to the floor before the first step was mounted. At last they were compelled to take Mrs Merry up her own staircase as if she were a piano; Eccles crawled up the steps on his hands and knees, with Mrs Merry on his back, steadied, and to some extent borne, by Revelstoke and Monica. It was slow, noisy and toilsome. When they reached the landlady's room they tumbled her into bed with everything on but her shoes, and climbed on to Monica's quarters, greatly exhausted.

'Good thing I liberated this,' said Bun, pulling a bottle of Sir Benedict's champagne out of one of the large poacher's pockets in his jacket. 'Don't suppose you've such a thing as a bottle of brandy, Monny?'

Monica had not. Eccles was philosophic. He removed the wire from the bottle and then, seizing the bulbous part of the cork in his teeth, he gave a tremendous wrench; when the champagne spurted he checked it dextrously with his thumb. 'Here,' he said, passing it to her, 'stab yourself and pass the dagger.'

Monica had had only one glass of champagne at the party, and Revelstoke, who never drank much, had taken little more. They were both glad of a refreshing pull at the champagne, but did not want more than a gulp or two. He was still in high spirits, which he could support on excitement alone; he had enjoyed the party, springing as it did from his personal success; the only annoyance he felt was with Persis, who had vanished with Odingsels. Monica was too much elated at having him in her living-room, almost to herself, to want other stimulant. But Eccles was a hardened and persistent drinker. When his turn at the bottle came he did not take it from his lips until it was empty. Then – 'I want a bath,' said he; 'humping the old trout upstairs has brought me out in a lather.' He rose, belched cavernously, waved a casual farewell and went. They heard him go down the stairs; the bathroom door was slammed and its noisy bolt pressed home; water ran, and the whole house hummed with the rumble of pipes.

'I hope he doesn't come to any harm,' said Monica.

'Not Bun,' said Revelstoke, 'but he may have a doze in the tub.'

What now? Girls in books and plays always seemed to know what to do when left alone with the men they loved; Monica hadn't an idea in her head.

'Would you like something to eat?' she said.

He wanted nothing to eat.

Silence that went on for minutes.

'It was wonderful of you and Sir Benedict to rescue me. I was afraid Mrs Merry was going to throw us out.'

'Would have served them right. They have no manners.'

'It would have been a shame, though, just as you came. We wanted to celebrate the broadcast.'

'You saw how they celebrated.'

'They all said you were a genius.'

'I wish I had their certainty.'

'I thought it was magnificent.'

'Did you really?'

'Of course I don't know much about it. You know that. But if you won't laugh, I'd like to say that I think you have an extraordinary melodic gift.'

'Oh? How do you mean?'

'Well, of course you know that I'm no judge of modern music, or any music, really, but I think I have a feeling for it, and it seems to me that so many modern composers write for the voice without having any real understanding of it, or love for it. And all the vocal part of *Discoverie* seemed to me to be so wonderfully singable. The idiom was modern, of course, but the feeling was – you know, the feeling you get with Handel, the feeling that you are in expert hands. The singers could settle into their parts, without having to be getting ready all the time for the next bit of acrobatics. A certainty of touch, I suppose you would call it.'

'That's very shrewd of you. The others don't really know anything about music, and what they say doesn't matter. Odingsels knows a good deal, but he's terribly jealous of anyone who makes a mark, you know. That's why he's pinched Persis for tonight; wants to take me down a peg.'

Monica had heard all her life that Opportunity knocks but once. But when Opportunity knocks, the sound can bring your heart into your mouth. No use dithering. She plunged.

'Do you think she'd have behaved like that if she really loved you?'

'I've never thought for an instant that she loved me.'

Opportunity had a foot in the door and was thundering on the knocker. Now was the moment. She felt awkward and plain; her head was light and seemed to be thumping. But, beneath these discomforts, she was elated. She was alive as never before.

'If I had Persis' chance to show that I loved you I could do things for you that she can't. You're a genius. I know it and she doesn't. I care about it and she doesn't. I'm ignorant and silly, and I made a fool of myself, at your mother's house at Christmas, boasting and pretending. You must have despised me. But I wanted to impress you. I suppose I ought to have known better, but I didn't. And you had shown that you had some feeling for me. And there it is.'

As she finished this speech, sitting bolt upright on the uncomfortable day-bed, looking at the carpet, Monica's mind was almost entirely filled with a sense of having taken an irrevocable step, of having gone beyond the bounds of modesty which had been established for her in twenty-two years, of having burned her bridges: but there was room also for a sense of wonder, and indeed of admiration, for herself, and a pleased recognition that she had spoken plainly and well. She was ashamed of these latter sensations, and tried to banish them, but they would not go. Very far at the back of her mind a triumphant Monica was exulting, *I've done it, I've done it, I've brought it to the point!*

Revelstoke looked at her for a time, smiling, and twisting the ring which he wore on his left hand. He looked as he had looked when first she saw him, when he interrupted her playing of *Danse Macabre*.

'If you love me, prove it,' said he.

He means going to bed with him, she thought. Well, I knew that. I'm ready.

'I know that sounds hatefully egotistical,' he went on, 'but I have always wondered what people meant when they talked about love. My mother has always told me that she loves me, but it's astonishing how little she will do to show it; the love between us always seems to mean great concessions on my part, and very little ones on hers. And there have been girls – quite a few girls – who were sure they loved me, and whom I thought I loved, but it never seemed to go beyond what was pleasant and flattering to themselves. Once they had me, as they thought, under their thumb, they wanted great changes in me. I do not propose to change to anybody's pattern. That is the charm of Persis; she doesn't expect changes in me, and she certainly doesn't mean to make any in herself. She knows that I am no Darby, and certainly she is no Joan. Now, I have a suspicion – and I know it is caddish of me to mention it at such a tender moment as this – that you want to reform me, and make me better. Am I right?'

'No.'

'Don't you want to make a quiet haven for me, in which I shall write immortal music, while you keep bad influences from the door, and do wonders with our tiny income?'

'No. You must do whatever seems best to you.'

'You have no notions about marriage?'

'I hadn't thought about it.'

'Swear?'

'I swear.'

'Then let me tell you a thing or two. Our meeting at Neuadd Goch was a shock to me, and when I thought you had planned it, I hated you and determined to do you a very bad turn for it. But when I found out from my mother that it was all quite unplanned, I was delighted to find you there, and our encounter in the bathroom was proof of it.

You were silly, bragging about your family; I don't know anything about them, but every word you said was palpably false. And what were you trying to do? You wanted to impress *my* family. Why? Did you think them so marvellous that you couldn't live without their admiration?'

'They were kind to me; I don't know any other people like that. I wanted to be a little bit like them, I suppose.'

'You think you are devoted heart and soul to music, but you will waste so much effort and stoop so far to impress the first examples of our declining county gentry you meet? Well, never mind. Now listen: I don't love you. Is that understood? But if ever I do love you, I'll tell you. I'll be absolutely honest with you. But because I fall short of loving you, that doesn't mean that I don't want you, and that I am not sometimes extremely fond of you. Meanwhile, you think you love me. Shall we act on that assumption?'

He led her into the bedroom, and there the atmosphere which had so enraptured Monica at Neuadd Goch was created again. Giles would not say that he loved her, but that was only a form of words; could he treat her so if he did not? She would not believe it.

He undressed her, and an incident occurred which she was to remember always. She stood in her slip, shy and unaccustomed, and as he began to remove his own clothes, she turned to get into the bed. But he caught her by the arm, and, removing the slip, stepped backward and looked long at her nakedness.

'You must get used to being looked at,' said he. 'It is beautifying to be seen naked by those we love, and the body grows ugly if it is always huddled under clothes. Nakedness is always honesty, and sometimes it is beauty: but even the finest clothes have a hint of vulgarity. Never make love with your clothes on; only very common people – really common people – do it.'

It was a long night of love, and when at last Revelstoke slept, Monica lay beside him feeling triumphant and re-born. He was hers. Though he had spoken coldly to her, and bargained, and said flatly that he did not love her, she was confident. She would win him at last. He should be brought to say it. He would love her, and tell her so.

[THREE]

What the critics said was a matter of concern to all of the menagerie, and it was during the week that their opinions appeared, and were chewed over at Thirty-two Tite Street, that Monica's new relationship with Giles became apparent to the inner circle of *Lantern*.

It was Persis who was first to learn of it. The day after the party in Dean's Yard she strolled round to Tite Street at about four o'clock in the afternoon, expecting a brief quarrel and a reconciliation. But when she climbed the stair to Giles' apartment she found the outer door closed.

This was something unknown to her. Giles never closed that door except as a signal that he was working, and was not to be disturbed under any circumstances. Since she had known him, he had never closed it except when she was in the flat, and very rarely then. She could not conceive that it was meant to exclude her, so she tried the handle. The door was locked. This certainly did not mean that Giles was from home, for he seldom troubled to lock his flat. She knocked, peremptorily. There was a stirring inside, so she gave the door a hearty kick. It opened, and Monica appeared in the crack, dressed in slacks and with a scarf tied around her head; in her hand was a mop.

'Shhh!' said Monica, laying a finger to her smiling lips.

'What d'you mean, "Shh!"'

'I mean Giles is sleeping, and you'll disturb him.'

'Sleeping! And what are you doing, may I ask?'

'Cleaning the kitchen,' said Monica; 'somebody's left it in an awful mess. If you like to come back later this evening, I'm sure he'll be pleased to see you.'

The door closed. If Persis had been the swooning kind, she would have swooned with rage. As it was, she gave the door a few more kicks, and stamped down the stairs.

The encounter gave a new dimension to Monica's happiness. She had driven Giles from Courtfield Gardens that morning before seven o'clock, for she did not want him to be found there by Mrs Merry, and she had no idea how long the landlady would sleep. Shortly after the shops opened she had followed him to Tite Street in a taxi, bearing with her brooms, soaps and cleansers, as well as the necessaries for a splendid breakfast. She served him his food on a tray, kissed him, and told him to go back to sleep, as she meant to be busy for several hours. He was too astonished to resist.

'My God, I have fallen into the hands of a Good Woman,' he said, as she left the room, but she merely smiled as she closed his door.

Then began such a ridding-out as the flat had never known since

Giles had lived there. All Ma Gall's hatred of slopdolly housekeeping, transfigured by love, was unleashed in Monica; she shook things, beat them, scrubbed and scoured them, rubbed, polished and dusted them; wearing rubber gloves, and using lye and a knife, she scraped the rancid and inveterate grease out of the stove; she washed every dish; she got rid of a large, reeking jam-pail, which had been the flat's principal ash-tray for some months and had never been emptied. She washed Pyewacket's dish, to the cat's astonishment and displeasure. She raised an extraordinary dust, and worked miracles. When she was finished, after six hours' toil, the flat was only moderately dirty – which was cleaner than it had been since she had known it. It smelled better. It looked better. But except for the dirt, nothing in it was altered.

Monica was too wise to move things about, or attempt to impose order on Giles' chaos. She was content to clean up the chaos, but not to alter it. Music and books still heaped the top of the piano, but they no longer blackened the hands. The large trestle table which was covered with *Lantern* papers was still heaped high, but the heaps were neater around the edges. The bathroom was gleaming, and some underthings of Persis', which customarily hung on a piece of twine from corner to corner, had been removed, and were awaiting removal in a bag in the kitchen. And the kitchen – its stench no longer caught at the throat, the dirty linoleum and the foul grey mess beneath it had been removed from the drying board; two tins of cleanser had gone into the waste-pipe so that when it belched (as it did whenever water went down it) it belched a harsh, carbolic smell, and not a breath from the charnel-house. All the things for which Giles cared nothing had been cleaned and put straight; all things for which he cared had been cleaned and left in familiar disorder.

And to cap it all, Persis had come and been repulsed. Monica was happy as any bride in her dream house. She drew a bath in the clean bathroom, lay down in it, and sang a few snatches recollected from *The Discoverie of Witchcraft*.

'I have been gathering Wolves' hairs
The mad Dog's foam, and the Adder's ears;
The spurgings of a dead man's Eyes,
And all since the Evening Star did rise.'

It was not ideal as an outpouring of the joy of love (though it was not without some reference to her house-cleaning work) and she did not sing it in the hope of catching Giles' ear. It was a simple burst of delight. But Giles put his head around the door.

'Didn't know you could sing any of that,' said he.

Remembering his words of the night before, she did not make a show of concealment, but lay still in the water.

'I can sing all the soprano part. Do you want tea? I'll be out in a minute.'

She could not bring herself to use the unpleasant towel, nor yet the shower curtain, so she had to dry herself on her head-scarf and her handkerchief, and remain damp where these would not suffice. She did not care. She sang as she mopped, patted and fanned herself dry:

'A Murderer, yonder, was hung in Chains,
The Sun and the Wind had shrunk his Veins;
I bit off a Sinew; I clipp'd his Hair,
I brought off his Rags, that danc'd i' th' Air.'

'You've been busy,' said Giles, when she took tea into the work-room.

Monica made no reply. She had made several resolutions as she worked, and one of them was that she would never draw attention to anything she did for him, or seem to seek praise. Patient Griselda was only one of the parts she meant to play in the life of Giles Revelstoke and it was certainly not the principal one. Nor did she mean to camp in that flat. So when she had fed him the sort of tea he liked – large chunks of thickly buttered bread smeared with jam, strong tea and soggy plumcake – she said that she would have to go, as she had work to do for Molloy.

'There'll probably be people looking in during the evening,' said she. 'Shall I get the papers and see if there is anything about the broadcast? Persis was here earlier, and I gathered that she will be back again.'

'Very likely,' said Giles. But as soon as she had gone, he burst into loud laughter. He was thinking of Persis.

[FOUR]

When Monica returned at nine o'clock, the menagerie was assembled, and it was characteristic of them that they all said they wanted to see the papers, but none of them had bought any. When she appeared with all the principal ones, fresh and clean, they fell upon them eagerly, and rumpled them, and read pieces aloud derisively, to show how superior they were to the events of the day. But of the lot, only two papers had brief references to the broadcast.

By the following Sunday, when all the papers which might be expected to say anything about *The Discoverie* had made their appearance, there was a creditable total of seven notices. They ranged from two brief, cautious comments on the quality of performance through four others, which were complimentary in a pleasant but unimportant fashion about the work itself, assuring the public that Giles was 'promising' and 'original' and that his score was 'musicianly'. But the longest, and most impressive, in the most influential of the Sunday journals, was the one by Stanhope Aspinwall.

It would have delighted most composers. It treated *The Discoverie of Witchcraft* seriously, complimented Giles on the fine sense of form which it revealed, praised the splendid melodic gift which Domdaniel had mentioned, and also called attention to the inferiority of the purely instrumental passages, though it said that they were interestingly laid out for the small group of instruments used. But it was the two final paragraphs which made Giles angry. They read:

'In spite of the high quality of the work as a whole, and the brilliance of many pages, the hearer who hopes for great things from Mr Revelstoke may be disturbed by a quality in *The Discoverie of Witchcraft* which can only be called "literary". The choice of theme is strongly romantic, and none the worse for that – but it is a literary form of romance. The portions of the text which are not by Ben Jonson are drawn from two seventeenth-century books on witchcraft which have no particular grace of style but which have, from time to time, roused the enthusiasm of amateurs of literary *curiosa*. Even the skill of the musical treatment of this matter cannot persuade us to take the theme – witchcraft – seriously. In another composer this would cause no concern; we should be sure that he would grow out of it. But Mr Revelstoke is known – indeed, principally known, at present – to the musical world as a musical journalist. Though musical gifts and literary skill have often gone hand in hand there comes a time when one or the other must take the lead. Mr Revelstoke will forgive me if I point out that, as Schumann, Berlioz and Debussy in their time had to give up their avocation as writers to embrace their fate as composers, that time has also come to him. In brief, he must give up what he does well and devote himself to what he does best.

'What he does best is to match fine poetry with eloquent, graceful and seemingly inevitable melody. The cantata form of the composition under review is commandingly used, and it is this sense of drama, even more than the lyric passages, which make *Discoverie* an important new work; there is a foreshadowing here of that rare creature, a real composer of opera. But Mr Revelstoke must find his way toward opera not through his present literary enthusiasms, but by clearing the literary rubbish from the springs of his musical inspiration.'

'But it's a rave, old man,' said Bun Eccles when he had read it. 'You said he'd given you a rocket, but it's a rave! He says you're marvellous, and all you've got to do to be twice as marvellous is to get down to work. Cor stone the bleedin' rooks, you don't know what a bad notice is! Why, I've seen chaps – painters – really chewed up in the papers; told to go and find some honest, obscure work, and trouble the world no more – that kind of thing. I don't understand what's eating you.'

'I will not be school-mastered, and lectured, and ticked off by Mr Bloody Aspinwall,' said Revelstoke. 'I will not be told to stop writing criticism of critics by a critic. I will not be known-best-about by a man who knows nothing of me except what he reads in *Lantern*.'

'He just wants to shut you up,' said Persis. 'You've probably exposed him so often as an incompetent that he's taken this way of revenging himself. You're dead right, Giles; you'd be a fool to pay any attention.'

This was the opinion of Tuke and Tooley, as well. They did not want Giles to lose his enthusiasm for *Lantern*. They knew that if he withdrew from the magazine it could not survive another issue, for not only did he supply the workroom and most of the enthusiasm, but he also supplied Monica, whose secretarial work had made the production of the magazine much easier.

'Of course you have it all your own way,' said Tuke; 'you have only to reply to this in *Lantern*, and that will be the end of Mr Aspinwall. It will be one of the few times when a creative artist has been able to answer a critic quickly and finally.'

Monica's could understand nothing of this. She thought Aspinwall's notice wonderful. And when she found opportunity, she looked through the back numbers of *Lantern*, and found no attack upon that critic whatever from Giles' hand. What she did find, in an early copy, was a suggestion in one of Giles' articles that he admired Aspinwall's judgement alone among the London critics of the day. It made no sense to her. Giles' ravings against Aspinwall seemed sheer perversity.

But she did not say so. A week, during which their intimacy had grown every day, had taught her that contradiction was not the way to reach Revelstoke's heart, or his head. He could not bear to be crossed in anything. He could only be reasoned with about matters which were of no importance to him. And so she kept silent about what she thought until she had either ceased to think it, or had banished her disagreement to the depths of her mind, as disloyalty. She did not join very readily in the general condemnation of Aspinwall; she did not, as the witty Persis did, refer to him always by an obscenity which somewhat resembled his name; she did not speak as though he were an enemy of everything that the *Lantern* group stood for. She had resolved that she would not try to make Giles anything other than what he was. And her compliance was showing results.

'Quite plainly there is a new *maîtresse en titre,*' said Tuke to Tooley one day as they climbed the stairs. And Bridget Tooley, who had already changed her attitude toward Persis, marvelled once again at how long it took even Phanuel Tuke to see what a woman saw at once.

[FIVE]

The word 'mistress', insofar as she had thought of it at all, had always held a dark splendour for Monica. Because of her beauty, even Persis had not spoiled this notion that women who lived with men out of wedlock breathed a special, exciting and romantic air. But now she was a mistress herself, and although it had its excitements and rare, deep satisfactions it was by no means what she had, dimly, foreseen. It was very agreeable to be deferred to by Tuke and Tooley, and to see the baleful glint in Persis' fine eyes, but there was a lot of hard work about it.

Giles liked comfort, though he had no intention of supplying it for himself, and once the flat was running in a reasonably orderly manner, he wanted it to continue that way. And *Lantern*, now that she had a bigger say in its production, took more of her time. Giles made a pretext to ask Domdaniel to cancel her German and Italian lessons, so that this time would be provided. And he began to work her mercilessly at her singing lessons. The success of *Discoverie* had raised his ambition as a composer to a new pitch. He hunted out and revised his songs – which were far more numerous than Odingsels' estimate of fifty – and it was her task to copy the new versions neatly; under his tuition she became a quick, deft and pleasantly ornamental copyist. But he also began to write new songs, and as she was at hand, he arranged the *tessitura* of these new works to suit her voice, making them inconveniently high for the majority of singers. His choice of lyrics tended toward poets not widely popular and usually dead; his settings of modern verse were few. His sensitivity to poetry, and to the rhythms of English, was reflected in all his songs, but in the new works it expressed itself in complications of time, and in prolongations of phrase, which made them very hard to study, though wonderfully easy to hear. It was Monica's delight, and also her despair, to slave at these songs through countless revisions, while the composer visited upon her all the irritation and dissatisfaction which he felt with himself. Giles never praised her. When a song had reached its final form, and she had sung it precisely as he wanted it, he would sometimes say, 'Got it now, I think.' But it was of himself that he was speaking.

The flat ceased to be the hang-out of the menagerie, for Giles was too busy to be bothered with them, except when *Lantern* work was to be done, or when he wanted conversation and a party. Of course they blamed Monica for coming between him and his old friends. And of course they wondered what on earth he saw in her.

Sometimes she joined in this wonder herself, for as a lover Giles was fully as demanding as he was when he was teaching her to sing what he had written. Indeed, the two kinds of experience were uncomfortably similar. He could be tender, but he could not be patient. He was experimental and ingenious, demanding for himself aspects of pleasure which she could not comprehend, and therefore could provide only by happy accident. If luck was not with her he might scold; worse, he might laugh at her. Once, after what had seemed to her a wonderful, ecstatic afternoon in the pokey little bedroom of the flat, she had turned to him, certain that the moment had come, whispering, 'Do you love me?' He had replied, 'What if I say no?' The sardonic glint in his eye warned her not to press the matter. She could not conceal her hurt, so she rose, dressed herself, and made him the stodgy, jammy tea-meal which he liked. She knew better than to ask that question again.

She did not spend the nights at Tite Street. She did not dare, for fear that Mrs Merry would tell Mr Boykin, who would tell Mr Andrew, who would tell the Bridgetower Trust – who would tell her mother. But except for her lessons with Murtagh Molloy she spent almost all of her waking hours there. Her first decision to preserve some aloofness from Giles had quickly weakened; the harder he worked her, the more he nagged her about the most minute details of her singing, the more tyrannous his demands as a lover, the less was she able to keep away from him.

Bun Eccles alone of the menagerie seemed to have any true estimate of her relationship to Giles.

'You've certainly got it bad, kid,' said he to her one day as they sat in The Willing Horse.

'Worse than bad,' she replied. 'It's abject.'

'Well, cheer up. You'll get over it.'

'Only when I'm dead.'

'Bad as that?'

'Yes; bad as that.'

It was Bun who sent her to a physician.

'You got trouble enough, Monny, without getting landed with a baby. You can't expect Giles to do anything about it. He belongs in the great nineteenth-century tradition, when geniuses littered the earth with stupider-than-average kids. So you just cut along and see my friend Doc Barwick; I'll tell him you're coming, and why, and he'll put you wise. Self-preservation is the first law of fallen women and a couple o' quids' worth of prevention is better than fifty guineas' worth of dangerous cure.'

And thus a new and unwelcome complication was introduced into her love for Giles. Monica had been brought up with a Fundamentalist's horror of this particular interference with Nature, and with an ill-defined but strong notion that if the consequences of sin were avoided now, some triply-compounded exaction would be made at last. She faithfully did as Eccles' friend bade her, for she feared open disgrace, but she added immeasurably to her sense of guilt by doing so.

By the irrational account-keeping of unhappy love, the humiliations and labours which she underwent for Giles made her love him the more; and the more she loved him, the more inevitable it seemed to her that some day he must recognize the burdens which she had incurred on his account, and love her for it. He could not know the truth, and still withhold his love from her. Such indifference could not be reconciled with her estimate of his character.

Easter fell late, and it was the beginning of March when Molloy said to her, one morning – 'Got a message for you from His Nibs; wants you to study the *St Matthew Passion* thoroughly and in a hurry – which can't be done, as he well knows. But he's conducting the Oxford Bach

Choir in a performance on the first Sunday in April, and he wants you to be one of his London soloists. Oh, nothing tremendous, so don't think it! You'll be the soprano False Witness – seven glorious bars in your part. But he thinks it's time you got a smell of public performance, and here's your chance. You're to bone up on the whole job, sit in the choir, sing your bit, and get your expenses paid. Know any Bach?'

'I've been through the *Anna Magdalena Notebook* with Revelstoke.'

'Ever look at the *Passion*? Ever hear it?'

'Never.'

'We've a month; we'll scratch the surface.'

It seemed to Monica that they did much more than scratch the surface; she slaved at it, and Molloy even made her study the full score, so that she might have some acquaintance with classical orchestration. He forbade her jealously to seek help from Giles. 'What would a fellow like that know about this sort of music?' he demanded, unreasonably. It was not Giles' musical competence he doubted, but his moral worth. Molloy had a cult for the *Passion* which astonished Monica, for she had not supposed him to be a deeply religious man. 'If the Bible was divinely inspired, so was the *Matthew Passion*,' said he; 'you've not only to know it note for note and rest for rest – you've to feel it in the furthest depths of your soul.' It was in this spirit that they worked.

The effect on Monica was deeply unsettling. As the great music took possession of her, it became a monumental rebuke to the life she was living. Without having done so consciously, she had moved far from the Thirteener faith; the altered conditions of her life shoved it into the background, and when she thought of it at all, it was the crudities of its doctrine, the sweaty strenuosities of Pastor Beamis, and the trashiness of its music which recurred to her. Not that she condemned it in such clear terms, for to have done so would have been to condemn her family, and her own former self. Loyalty was as strong in Monica as it had been when she declared to George Medwall that nothing would make her untrue or ungrateful to her home. Fifteen months was not long enough to shake that resolve, though it was long enough to give quite another colour to the situation. The Thirteener faith was like a shoddy and unbecoming dress which she had ceased to wear, but had not yet thrown out.

The bigotries of Ma Gall, and the palaverings of Beamis were not the whole of Monica's religious experience, however. Christian myth and Christian morality were part of the fabric of her life, dimly apprehended and taken for granted behind the externals of belief. And it is what is taken for granted in our homes, rather than what we are painstakingly taught, which supplies the bones of our faith. Monica believed, as literal truth, that her Lord had died on the cross to redeem her, Monica Gall, from the Primal Sin of Adam; a life of devotion of His will was her duty and her glory; strict adherence to the Ten Commandments was the whole moral law; her sins were fresh wounds in the body of her wounded Lord. Because of the special nature of the Thirteener faith – the notion that historic time was an illusion, and that it was possible to 'make contact' with Christ by living a godly life – Christ seemed at times to be awesomely and reproachfully present and palpable, grieved because she could not break through the prison of her own imperfection and exist fully with Him. She had not been much troubled by this sense of His imminence since she was sixteen, when she had been somewhat worried by sexual fantasy, but it returned to her now, with new strength, as she worked over the pages of the *Passion*.

The noble utterance of Bach wakened in her a degree of religious sensibility of which she had never previously been conscious. She had outgrown the Thirteeners and in one or two daring moments had thought of herself as finished with religion; but in the presence of this majestic faith she was an unworthy pygmy. She was overwhelmed, frightened and repentant. It seemed to her that there was something ominous and accusatory in the fact that Domdaniel had chosen her to appear as a False Witness.

'But why?' she asked Molloy. 'It says in the score that the part is to be sung by an Alto, and it's plain enough that I'm no alto. Has there been a mistake? Should we tell him?'

'No mistake at all,' Molloy replied. 'You can sing the notes all right, and the other Witness is a very light tenor, so the balance will be better than if he was paired with some girl with a big, bosomy note. Ben knows what he's doing; it's that covered, *chalumeau* effect of your lower register that he wants – hints at something a bit spooky.'

Revelstoke was quick to see the change in her, and it was characteristic of him that as Monica's reluctance to yield increased, so did his demands as a lover.

'I like you much better in this Lenten mood,' he said one afternoon, as she lay beside him, very near to tears. 'For a while I had begun to doubt if you could make love in anything but the key of C Major, but this is a far, far better thing. Mr Revelstoke is pleased to report to the Bridgetower Trust that the pupil is making steady progress.'

Wretched and guilty as Monica had felt, these words filled her with a piercing delight. If this were sin, how sweet it was!

[SIX]

In the front row of the Oxford Bach Choir sat Monica, soberly dressed and self-possessed, a professional in the midst of amateurs. Behind her rose the ranks of undergraduates, dons male and female, dons' wives and daughters, which comprised the Choir; before her was the orchestra, part local and part brought down from London, and ranging in demeanour from the splendid calm of the concert-master and the aloof grandeur of the harpsichordist to the fussy eccentricity of the player of the *viol da gamba*. High above them, and inconveniently placed for the conductor, was the organ-loft, into which the ripieno choir of boys had been packed. The Sheldonian Theatre was crowded with a university audience, so much odder and frowsier than a London audience, so young in the main, so long of hair, so fortified with scores of the *Passion*. Monica was conscious that many eyes had found her, and that she was looking very well. And why not? Had she not been made free of the room in the Divinity School where the London artists made ready for the performance? Had not Miss Evelyn Burnaby, the great soprano, spoken to her in the pleasantest terms, when Domdaniel had introduced them, and asked for help with a difficult zipper on the back of her gown? Monica felt every inch a professional, and concealed her surprise that the Sheldonian Theatre was not a theatre at all, as she understood the word, but a kind of arena which looked as though it might be used for some sort of solemn, academic circus. The ceiling was beautifully painted, and she had to check herself from gaping upward at it; everywhere in the building there were odd little balconies, pulpits and thrones; part of the audience was very high up, almost under the roof. Altogether a wonderful place in which to make one's first, real professional appearance as a singer. Nothing at all to do with the Heart and Hope Quartet.

It was five minutes past eleven, and by that curious instinct which audiences have, silence fell suddenly and Sir Benedict Domdaniel, elegant in morning dress, walked to his place, raised his baton, and the introduction to the *Passion*, rising majestically from its first deep pedal-point, began. Monica's knowledge of this music was intimate but remote, for she had heard it only as it sounded on Molloy's piano and her own. She had rehearsed once with Domdaniel in London, again with a piano, but she had no conception of how it would sound with the heavy forces of organ, double orchestra and continuo, and the double choir. The mighty, ordered grandeur came from everywhere about her, and she seemed to shake and vibrate with it. It was a glorious and alarming experience. In her capacity as a very minor soloist she rose and sat with the choir, and sang with the sopranos, keeping her voice well down, both that she might not make mistakes through lack of rehearsal, and that its superior quality should not singularize it among the amateur choristers. Standing in the midst of these voices and instruments, she was conscious as never before of the power of music to impose order and form upon the vastest and most intractable elements in human experience.

She was conscious also, and for the first time, of why Domdaniel was regarded as a great man in the world of music. He conducted admirably, of course, marshalling the singers and players, succouring the weak and subduing the too-strong, but all that was to be expected. It was in his capacity to demand more of his musicians than might have been thought prudent, or even possible – to insist that people eased themselves, and to help them to do it – that his greatness appeared. With a certainty that was itself modest (for there was nothing of 'spurring on the ranks' about it) he took upon himself the task of making this undistinguished choir give a performance of the *Passion* which was worthy of a great university. It was not technically of the first order, but the spirit was right. He had been a great man to Monica, for he could open new windows for her, letting splendid light into her life: but now she saw that he could do so for all these clever people, who thought themselves lucky to be allowed to hang on the end of his stick. Without being in the least a showy or self-absorbed conductor he was an imperious, irresistible and masterful one.

At one o'clock the performance halted, to be resumed again at half-past two. As soon as she left her place in the choir Monica was claimed by John Scott Ripon who bore her off to the George restaurant for lunch.

'Poached salmon and hock,' said he. 'Fish is the only possible thing during the *Passion*, don't you agree? And hock, to keep your pipes clear for your solo bit – just a single glass, because we don't want you to be not only false but drunk. Now tell me all your news. How's the ineffable Giles? Still the same old Satanic genius?'

'He's well. Why do you inquire about him in that sneering way?'

'Well, Monny, you're surely the last person to ask that, considering how he behaved toward you at Christmas. I've been doing a bit of research on him. Reading *Lantern*. Dreadful muck, most of it. Who's this twit Tuke? I mean, how second-rate can you get? But Giles' stuff is very good – very good, that's to say, considering how old hat all that sort of thing is now.'

'Old hat? You think it's old-fashioned?'

'Monny, it's not as good as old-fashioned. It's just plain out-of-date. All that preciosity belongs to the 'twenties. The modern line for little mags and reviews is frightful dyspeptic anger and working-class indignation and despair and shameless gut-flopping self-pity – real Badly Behaved Child stuff. *Lantern* belongs to a much earlier, more romantic time, the Wicked 'Twenties, when every Englishman of the intelligentsia was ashamed of himself because he wasn't a Frenchman; it belongs to the era when chaps boozed on absinthe, when they could get it, and wished they had the guts to take drugs. No, *Lantern*'s an oddity; I suppose there's a public for it among chronic harkers-back and hankerers-after, but it is not going to attract anything really first-rate. Except for Giles. He can really write. Of course outsmarting the critics is always good fun, and popular, too. Nobody likes critics, and I seriously doubt if there is an artist of any kind worth his salt anywhere who wouldn't poison every critic if he could. I mean, why not? You create something – it's your baby. Then along comes some chap, quite uninvited, and points out to the world what a puny, rickety little shrimp it is. Of course you want to kill him. Critic-baiting is very good fun, and they're easy game. But Giles does it in a rather old-fashioned style, all the same. He's a man of the 'twenties. A Satanic genius, as I said.'

'You mean he poses?'

'Certainly. Don't we all? He just does it a bit more obviously and consistently than most.'

'You're quite wrong, Johnny. His music isn't a pose. It's very fine. And that's not just my own opinion.'

'Oh, quite. I don't deny it for an instant. You saw what Aspinwall said about his broadcast piece? When Aspinwall takes him seriously, it's important. Aspinwall is one critic that Giles can't make a fool of. But that's what's so silly about Giles; he's obviously a real genius –

whether first, second or third-rate I don't know, but certainly more than just a competent chap. But he has to act the genius, as well. And the way he plays the role isn't the modern way. And maybe he isn't play-acting. Ceinwen says that all that bad temper and sardonic laughter and nonsense is quite natural to him. It would be hard luck to look like a fake when you were simply being yourself, wouldn't it?'

'You've been seeing Ceinwen?'

'Not seeing. Writing. But I am going to see her in the Easter vacation. Her father has asked me to stay for a bit.'

'Is it serious, Johnny?'

'Yes, it is, really. But I don't know – I can't imagine her in Louisiana, standing with her back against the wall of the family shoe factory.'

Monica found herself in the role of confidante, and being young she had little patience with it, unless she were given an opportunity to confide in return. It was over the coffee that she told Ripon about herself and Giles, and said a little about the religious scruple which was troubling her. His reply had that clarity, objectivity and reasonableness which is possible only to advisers who have completely missed the point.

'If it makes you unhappy, break it off. You're a charmer, you know, Monny, in your quiet way; it's a quality you have of looking as if you could say a devil of a lot if you chose, but had decided not to – a kind of controlled awareness; so you don't have to behave as if Giles was the only pebble on the beach. You'll have dozens of chaps after you. What if he is a genius? Being a genius doesn't excuse being a bastard. Not that we should be too hard on him. I mean, how would you like to be the son of Dolly Hopkin-Griffiths, who doesn't know one note from another, and wants you to settle down to honest work? And I'm sure he hates old Griff, though Ceinwen says not. But it's a Hamlet situation, as I told you at Christmas. And what he's taking out on you is his resentment against Dolly, for being unfaithful to Daddy.

'But the religious business – I'd pay it no mind, if I were you. You're an artist, Monny. You'll have to shake off that Fundamentalist stuff. If you are of a religious temperament, be religious like old Bach, not like a grocer with a hundred thousand recollections of short-weight chewing at his vestigial conscience. No, no; live in the large, Monny; dare greatly; sin nobly.' Johnny had finished the bottle of hock, and was shouting a little.

No, Johnny simply did not understand. Be religious like old Bach! As the afternoon session of the *Passion* got under way the religion of old Bach seemed more than Monica could bear. The pathos of the Prologue to the Second Part worked searchingly within her, as the voice of the contralto soloist (Miss Emmie Heinkl, herself, if the truth were known, the mistress of a director of the Midland Bank) repeated –

Ah, how shall I find an answer
To assure my anxious soul?
Ah! where is my Saviour gone?

Quickly followed the recitative in the Court of Caiaphas, then the chorale begging for defence against evil, and then – Christ's Silence Before Caiaphas, and the False Witnesses! She could not stand; she could not sing; she was unworthy, and what might be forgiven in others could never be forgiven in her! Terror seized her. She must not sing; she was unworthy!

But when the moment came she stood, she sang – and sang well – and sat again. For the remainder of the *Passion* her head throbbed, she was in misery, and she feared that she might burst into tears.

She was surprised when, after the performance, Sir Benedict offered her a seat in his car for the drive back to London; she was still more surprised to find that no one else was to drive with them.

'You were very nervous,' said he, as they sped toward Abingdon.

'I didn't think I could utter.'

'But you did. That's Molloy's training. That's being a pro.'

'I was afraid of the music.'

'Well you might be. So was I.'

'Oh no!'

'Oh yes. Not of the choir or the orchestra, or anything like that, of course. But I never conduct the *Passion* or the *B Minor* without a sensation that the old Cantor is listening. It's not the kind of thing I readily admit to, because if publicity people got hold of it, the result could be very sticky. But I'm telling it to you, because this was your first public performance of any consequence, and I think it may be helpful to you. Don't make sloppy nonsense of it, but remember, sometimes, when you sing, that if the composer were listening you'd want him to be satisfied with you. Don't presume to guess what his answer might be. Don't conjure up silly visions of him nodding his peruke and saying "Well done!" But use it as an exercise in humility. That's what all of us who perform in public must pray for at dawn, at high noon, and at sunset – humility.'

'It was humility that nearly finished me today. Sir Benedict, may I ask you a very personal question? I don't mean to be impertinent, but I truly want to know.'

'Yes?'

'With the *Passion*, does it make a very great difference to you – not being a Christian?'

'Ah, I gather that the widespread notion that I am a Jew has reached you. As a matter of fact, I'm the second generation of my family to be baptized and safe in the respectable bosom of the Church of England – just like that eminently respectable fellow Mendelssohn. But to speak honestly, I'm nothing very much at all, which is reprehensible on all counts. Theologians and philosophers are terribly down on people who are nothing at all. But I find it's the only thing that fits my work. I tackle the *Passion* like a Christian – quite sincerely; but I don't carry it over into my fortunately rare assaults on *Also sprach Zarathustra*. One's personal beliefs are peripheral, really, if one is an interpreter of other men's work; Bach was devout, but it is far more important for me to understand the quality of his devotion than to share it.'

'Mr Molloy says you must feel the *Passion* in the very depths of your soul.'

'Quite true, but don't interpret Murtagh simple-mindedly. He knows perfectly well that you can feel *Hamlet* without believing in ghosts.'

'I see. At least, I think I see.'

'But what about you – for I assume that this inquiry about me is leading up to something about yourself. What about you and the *Passion*? You've been brought up something tremendously devout and Bibliolatrous, if I recollect aright. You mentioned humility nearly wrecking your performance today. Of course it couldn't have been humility. What was the trouble?'

'I'm in a muddle about my personal life.'

'Still in love with Revelstoke?'

'Yes, I am.'

'Is it serious?'

'As serious as it can be.'

'And I take it from your manner that he doesn't reciprocate?'

'He doesn't feel as I do.'

'How does he feel? Now please don't cry. And what has this got to do with humility?'

'The music – I'm afraid I'm living a very wrong sort of life – and the music made me feel despicable.'

'I'm driving, and I simply can't do anything about it if you're going to cry. However, you will find a handkerchief in my left-hand topcoat pocket, and there are others in my portmanteau. But I most earnestly beg you not to cry, but to listen very carefully to me. First, despising yourself isn't humility; it's just self-dramatizing. If you're living in what is pompously called sin with Revelstoke, you'd better be sure you are enjoying it, or you will soon find that you have neither your cake nor your penny. I've seen a great deal of sin, one way and another, and the biggest mug in the world is the sinner who isn't getting any pleasure from it. I'm not taking your situation lightly, though you may think so. I'm talking sense, but I'm too old to get any pleasure out of playing the sage, and making heavy weather with my trifle of worldly experience. My best advice to you is: clarify your thinking about your situation, and act as good sense dictates. Don't torture yourself with vulgar notions about what the neighbours will think, but get this maxim into your head and reflect on it: chastity is having the body in the soul's keeping – just that and nothing more.'

They talked all the way to London in this strain. Monica explained, and Sir Benedict advised, but nothing new was said. When at last he stopped at Courtfield Gardens he summed up:

'Remember: you must clarify your thinking. I know it's the last thing you want to do, but you must do it. If necessary, take a couple of weeks off and go to Paris. Get away from him, and see things in perspective. And when you've made up your mind, stick to your decision. And finally, don't suppose that I'm going to allow this to wreck your work, because I won't.'

Within an hour, Monica had gone to Tite Street, and discovered Giles in bed with Persis Kinwellmarshe. There was a quarrel of proportions and ferocity of which Monica had never dreamed. It ended with Giles telling her that her chief trouble was that she had no sense of humour.

Two days later she flew to Paris.

[SEVEN]

Paris in Spring is not an easy place in which to nurse a grudge against oneself. Monica arrived with a long face and a heart full of what she conceived to be self-hatred, but her spirits began to rise almost as soon as she was in Amy Neilson's pretty house in St Cloud, and before the first evening was over she had confided her trouble to that wise and capable woman. She had not meant to confide; she had fully meant to grapple with the problem alone. She was humiliated by her readiness to spill her story to anyone who might be sympathetic; it seemed so weak. But Amy was an American and a woman, and might understand better than Ripon, who was a man, or Domdaniel, who was English. A little to her surprise, Amy came down flatly on the side of conventional morality.

'These affairs don't do,' said she. 'Particularly not with girls of your temperament. Their tendency is always to harden you, and what would you be like if you were hardened? You'd be very much like your mother, my dear. Oh, different in externals, I'm sure, but very much like her. And in spite of all the nice loyal things you've said to me about her from time to time, I don't think that will answer. What was it you said he told you – that you had no sense of humour? Lucky for him. A woman with a sense of humour would never have taken up with him in the first place. He sounds an impossible person. Oh, a genius, perhaps. Benedict is always discovering geniuses; it's a craze with him; he's terribly humble about not being a composer himself, and he's always exaggerating the talent of young men who show promise. But suppose Giles Revelstoke is a genius? Geniuses are not people to make a woman happy. The best he could do for you would be to marry you and make a drudge of you. No, you've done the right thing. Get over him as fast as you can.'

'But perhaps that's what I'm for – to drudge for somebody far above me. I'm nothing very much, and I know it.'

'Benedict says you can become a very good singer. That's something. Let me be very frank, dear. You're not what I call a big person. It's not just being young, it's a matter of quality. You've got a fair amount of toughness, but essentially you're delicate and sensitive. You must preserve that. It's true you have no sense of humour, but very few women have. You should be glad of it. It's not nearly such a nice or important quality as silly people make out. Wit and high spirits and a sense of fun – yes, they're wonderful things. But a sense of humour – a real one – is a rarity and can be utter hell. Because it's immoral, you know, in the real sense of the word: I mean, it makes its own laws; and it possesses the person who has it like a demon. Fools talk about it as though it were the same thing as a sense of balance, but believe me, it's not. It's a sense of anarchy, and a sense of chaos. Thank God it's rare.'

'Maybe what Giles has is a sense of humour.'

'You may be right. He sounds like it. But my advice to you, dear, is to get yourself out of this before you're hurt worse than you are – which isn't nearly as badly as you think, I dare say. It isn't sleeping with a man that makes you a tramp; that's probably healthy, like tennis or yoghourt. But it's having your feelings hurt until they scar over that makes you coarse and ugly. You're not the temperament to survive that sort of thing.'

And thus the pattern of Monica's Easter in Paris was set. She was getting over Revelstoke. Amy did not refer to the matter again, but she kept Monica busy with French conversation, French literature, shopping, and visits to plays and sights. And Monica, who was beginning to recognize the chameleon strain in her nature, seemed most of the time to fit very well into the stimulating, pleasant, sensible atmosphere which Amy created.

But in her inmost heart she was hurt and puzzled by the failure of all her advisers to comprehend anything of her feelings. They seemed to know what was expedient, and self-preservative, and what would lead to happiness when she was fifty, but they appeared to have no comprehension at all of what it was like to be Monica Gall in love with Giles Revelstoke. Even Ripon, who was not more than a year or so older than herself, could marshal all the facts and make a judgement about them, but not even Domdaniel could grasp the irrationalities of the situation. Must one live always by balancing fact against fact? Had the irrational side of life no right to be lived? The answer did not have to be formed; the irrational things rose overwhelmingly from their deeps whenever she was not strenuously bending her mind to some matter of immediate concern.

Did she want to be a singer? She had been assured so often that it lay within her power to be one, but not since she left Canada had anyone thought of asking if that were truly her desire. What was it, after all, to be a public performer of any kind? One morning, when Amy was busy elsewhere, Monica strayed into the museum of the Opéra to pass the time. She had been there before, but under Amy's firmly enthusiastic guidance; she had been told to marvel, and she had obediently marvelled. But now, alone, she looked about her. How dreary it was! So many pompous busts of Gounod; Gounod's real immortality was through the wall, on the great stage. But here was the monocle of someone called Diaghilev; Amy had said something about him, but who was he, and what had he done? Where was his immortality? And these pianos of the great – how small they seemed; they bore about them a suggestion that they must have been played by very small men. And these worn-out ballet shoes to which names, presumably great, were attached – was this trash all that the darlings of the public left behind them? There were things here which had belonged to great singers, bits of costume and pitiful, dingy stage jewellery. This was what remained of people who had breathed the muhd as she could hardly hope to breathe it; was this worth the struggle? Would it not be better to be Revelstoke's drudge and his trull, contributing thereby to something which might live when they both were dead?

She brought herself near to tears with these gloomy broodings. She looked out of a window across the Rue Auber, where a sign caught her eye; it said 'Canada Furs', and suddenly she was sick with longing for the cold, clean, remorseless land of her birth. Why had she ever come away, to get herself into this mess?

Luncheon raised her spirits, and she was a little surprised to discern that what she had really been thinking about, and longing for, was immortality – and a vain, earthly immortality at that, the very kind of thing which the Thirteeners (who were in no great danger of attaining it) condemned so strongly.

Ah, the Thirteeners! After that shaking hour in the Sheldonian, when she had sung her seven bars, and felt herself sealed of the seal of Bach, she could no longer be one of them. But what, then, was she? A whirligig, like Domdaniel, who confessed that he took the colour of whatever work he was engaged on at the moment? But that was unjust to a man whom the world called great, and who was certainly the greatest man in every way that she had ever met. It was, indeed, a moral judgement. And what was it that Domdaniel had said to her, on that drive from Oxford, concerning her own harsh judgement on herself? – 'Moral judgements belong to God, and it is part of God's mercy that we do not have to undertake that heavy part of His work, even when the judgement concerns ourselves.' But wasn't that just gas? If you didn't make moral judgements, what were you? Well, of course Domdaniel said that you were an adult human being, and as such ought to have some clear notion of what you were doing with your life. Clarity, always clarity. The more she puzzled, the less clear anything became.

Reflection, even on these somewhat elementary lines, was hard work for Monica, and it made her very hungry. After her lunch, she continued her wandering through familiar tourist sights, putting in time until she should meet Amy again, and return to St Cloud. Her wanderings took her to the Panthéon.

A vivid imagination is not of great use in the Panthéon, unless one knows much of the earthly history of the great ones who lie buried there, and can summon splendid visions of them to warm the grey, courteous unfriendliness of its barren stones. In spite of Amy's cramming, Voltaire was not a living name to Monica, nor was Balzac, or any of the others who gave the place meaning, and everywhere the bleak, naked horror of enthroned Reason was ghastly palpable. Within five minutes she had left the place, and wandered on a few paces into the church of St Étienne du Mont.

All she knew of this church was that it possessed a remarkable rood-screen which Amy, stuffing her charges with culture like Strasbourg geese, had insisted that she see and admire. And there it was, its two lovely staircases twining upward toward a balcony surrounding the High Altar; Monica, as upon her first visit, longed to climb one of them and look down into the church; she yearned, for no reason that she could define, to see that balcony filled with singing, trumpeting, viol-playing angels. She sat down in a corner, and stared, trying to see what existed only in her imagination.

She saw no musical angels, but she became conscious of the windows, so strong and jewel-like in colour. She was warmed and soothed by the dark splendour, and some of the pain in her head – the fullness and muddle – began to go away. She hated thinking, and was ashamed of hating it. But thought was like the Panthéon. Here was feeling, and feeling was reality. If only life could be lived in terms of those windows, of that aspiring, but not frightening, screen! If only things and feelings existed, and thoughts and judgements did not have to trouble and torture!

She was conscious of movement and sound nearby, but it was not for some time that she looked to see what it was. Quite close was a canopy, not very high, of stone, under which was a tomb, not particularly impressive. A grille surrounded it, but an old woman was reaching through this fence, as she knelt, and as she prayed she rubbed the stone gently with her arthritic hand. Tears stood in her eyes, but did not fall. A Negro came near, knelt until he was almost prostrate, prayed briefly, and left.

What could it be? Monica found a sacristan, and soon had her answer. It was the tomb of St Geneviève, the patroness of the city of Paris.

'Formerly in the Panthéon,' said the man, 'but it was taken from there and publicly burned when the church was re-dedicated to Reason; the ashes and relics were brought here when all that foolishness was over.'

Then, in the darkness beneath the canopy, there was something of a saint? A saint who had found a haven here after the persecutions of Reason? She had never considered saints before. But, with a sense of awe and wonder that she had never known, Monica went to the tomb and, when no one was near, knelt and stretched her hand through the grille.

'Help me,' she prayed, touching the smooth stone, 'I can't think; I can't clarify; I don't know what I want. Help me to do what is right – *no!* Help me – help me –.' She could not put any ending on her supplication, for none would express what she wanted, because she did not know what she wanted.

Nevertheless, when she met Amy at the end of the afternoon, she seemed in splendid spirits, and Amy was convinced that she was forgetting Giles Revelstoke, and that the whole thing had been one of those fusses about very little, which were so common among girls who matured late.

[EIGHT]

Within three hours of her return to London, Monica was at the flat in Tite Street; her excuse was that it was hopeless to try to reach Revelstoke by telephone, and she must make her own arrangement about future lessons, or else give an embarrassing explanation to Domdaniel. Giles greeted her more warmly than he had ever done.

'I've something that I think you'll like,' said he, handing her a bundle of music paper. It was a *solo cantata* for a soprano voice with piano accompaniment. She looked quickly through it; the manner was very much his own – the old *solo cantata* form, recitatives alternating with melodic passages, but in a modern idiom; she saw immediately that the *tessitura* of the lyric passages was unusually high and that the recitatives lay in a lower register. Yet it was for one voice.

'You haven't looked at the title,' he said.

It read:

KUBLA KHAN
a setting of Coleridge's poem, by
GILES REVELSTOKE
for MONICA GALL

'A present,' said he. 'We'll work on it, and you'll sing it the first time it's heard which, if my plans don't fall through, will be quite early next autumn – Third Programme again.'

She did not dare to ask if this were an amends for the quarrel before Easter. And what did it matter? She did not dare to ask if this meant that he loved her; even that did not seem to matter, now. The great fact was that he was in better spirits than she had ever known, and that they were to work together again. *On something written specially for me* – it was that voice which she had heard within herself before, that voice of which she was afraid, because it spoke so selfishly and so powerfully.

But – Oh, Saint Geneviève, was this your doing?

'There's another thing,' said Giles. 'I've been approached – only approached, mind you – by the Association for English Opera; they wanted to know if I had anything in their line. It was *Discoverie* that interested them; they were very complimentary.'

'Giles!'

'Yes, I know. I can't tell you what it was like, talking about it to people who really knew, and could understand what was implicit in it, as well as what was staring out of the score. The upshot of it was, they want something. Now don't go off the deep end, because it's all very tentative. I haven't anything – not on paper – but I've been tinkering with a notion for years. So I'm to make a sketch, and rough out some of the scenes, and they'll hear it. Wait, wait – don't exult too much; there's a sticker even if they like it. They're broke. They can't commission a new work, but they can do one if it's up to standard. Production here; perhaps production in Venice. But I don't see how it's to be done.'

'But it must be done! It's unthinkable that it shouldn't. Why can't you do it? Would it take too long? How long does it take to write an opera?'

'Well, Rossini used to knock one off in three weeks, when he was in form. It can also take any number of years. The one sure thing is that you have to live and eat while you're doing it. If I'm to do this, I must give up all teaching – not that it brings in much – I'd have to give up everything else – bits of film work, editing, the lot. I'm a fairly rapid worker, but an opera is a back-breaker – worse than a symphony in lots of ways. And the costs can be staggering; copying the parts can eat up a packet. The Association is long on prestige, short on cash. I can't expect help from them.'

'Would your mother help?'

'I've asked her, and she has sent me fifty pounds and a lecture, saying that there will be no more, and couldn't I find a professorship in a conservatoire, or something. The worst of it is, Raikes are getting rough about the *Lantern* bill and I had to give them the fifty to keep them quiet.'

'Giles, with this on hand, you'll have to give up *Lantern*.'

'That is what I positively refuse to do. Nothing would please Aspinwall better. He wants to kill *Lantern*, and I am not going to oblige him.'

'Giles, listen to me. Do you really think *Lantern* is so good? Why must you sacrifice to it? Because it is a sacrifice. People I know say it's – only one of a lot of small magazines, and not the best, except for your things; everyone agrees they're wonderful. Why can't you give it up?'

'Because it is a personal mouthpiece which I value. I know that a lot of the stuff in it is tripe; do you suppose I really thrill to the off-key twanglings of Bridget Tooley's lyre? Or even to Tuke's tosh? You can't tell me anything about *Lantern* that I don't know. But I have said my say in it for four long years and I want to go on. I might have dropped it if Aspinwall had not so clearly revealed that he wants me to do so, but I shall keep it on to spite him, even if the opera goes up the flue in the process. No, if I write *The Golden Asse*, it must be done with *Lantern* still in existence.'

'*The Golden Asse*? Is that what it's called? You have a story?'

'I have one of the oldest and best stories in the world; it is *The Golden Asse*, by Lucius Apuleius. I have been haunted by it since boyhood, and any operatic jottings I have done, have been done with it in mind.'

They talked long and eagerly, for Giles was off his guard as Monica had never known him to be. He was enthusiastic; he forgot to play the genius; he was – she was ashamed of herself for admitting the phrase, even mentally – almost human. But talk as they might, the ground never changed. He wanted to write his opera: he must somehow get money to live while doing so, and to pay the heavy costs involved: he would not give up *Lantern* because he was convinced that somewhere in London a malignant demon named Stanhope Aspinwall was consumed with the desire that he should do so.

'But it's lunatic,' cried Monica, in exasperation; 'I don't suppose Aspinwall really gives a damn.'

'I know what I'm talking about,' said Revelstoke, and as he seemed about to close himself up in his unapproachable character again, she let that matter drop.

Of course this conversation led at last to the pokey bedroom, where Monica, for the first time in her life, really enjoyed what passed – enjoyed it not because it gave pleasure to Giles, or because it was a sign that she held some place in his life, or because it was a proof of her freedom, but because it gave pleasure to herself, and because it was herself, and not Persis, to whom he had confided his great news. It was plain enough that Giles needed her.

He should need her more. Monica conceived a great plan. She would find the money which should make possible the writing of *The Golden Asse*.

[NINE]

Her first proposal was that she should go to Sir Benedict, and ask him to lend Giles enough money to keep him going for a year. Giles vetoed this plan at once; his attitude toward Domdaniel was an unpredictable mingling of admiration for his great gifts as a conductor, and contempt for his success. 'I'm not going to give it to him to say that he made it possible for me to write anything,' said he; 'if I'm to have a patron it won't be Brummagem Benny.' And from this position he would not budge. It was pride, and Monica admired him for it, though she could not have analysed it.

Nevertheless, if she could not go to Domdaniel, Monica's list of possible patrons was at an end. She knew no moneyed people. She confided her trouble to Bun Eccles, as they sat in The Willing Horse.

'Why don't you finance it yourself?' he asked.

'Me?' said Monica, incredulous.

'Well, Monny, you know your own affairs best, but you look to me like a pretty flush type.'

'Oh, Bun, I'm a church mouse. I've always been poor. I mean, Dad had to leave school at sixteen, and we've always just managed, you know. All I've got now is this scholarship thing.'

'It seems to amount to a good deal. You've got some pretty

expensive clothes, Monny, and all kinds of costly junk in that flat at Ma Merry's. Are you sure you're really poor, or are you just one of those people who assume that they're poor? Have you ever gone without a meal? Ever had less than two pair of shoes? I have, often, but I don't consider myself poor. I mean, I'm not telling you what you should do. I'm just asking. But the menagerie thinks you're rolling.'

It took Monica a full two days to comprehend this, but in the end she was forced to admit to herself that she was not really poor – was, indeed, very well situated. She had all her bills paid; she could buy things on tick; she got five hundred a year, now, as pin-money. The idea was breath-taking; she did not want to be well-of – that was something one said of people against whom one felt an honest working man's grudge. People who had more than enough money (with a few splendid exceptions like Domdaniel) were for that very reason morally suspect. But at last she accepted the reality of her situation.

Once again she sought Eccles' advice, and then began such a complication of chicanery as Monica had never dreamed possible. Eccles had a genius for the finance of desperation, and assuming that she wanted as much money as possible, he gave himself a free hand. Within a week he had sold her expensive radiogramophone and her collection of records. ('They are going to Mr Revelstoke's for a time,' she explained to Mrs Merry, and the landlady was impressed.) He sold some of her personal luggage, including the fitted case which she had been given by the Thirteeners; it was gone before she realized what was happening. He persuaded her to dispose of quite a large part of her wardrobe. He even got ninepence for *War and Peace*, which had been unopened for fifteen months. All this was done in an ecstasy of haggling and what he called 'flogging'.

'This clothes caper is absolutely endless, Monny,' he explained. 'We can go on and on. You buy a few smart things every month, charge 'em, wear 'em once and turn 'em over to me. I flog 'em. Good for eight or ten quid. These lawyers aren't going to snoop through your cupboard. Go right ahead till they squawk.'

Well, thought Monica, Sir Benedict said they wanted me to spend more money.

She had a few pounds in hand, left from the money she had received for her visit to Paris. Eccles pounced on it.

'You can save a lot on food,' said he, 'and you'd better let me have a look at your gas-meter. Those things eat shillings. There's a little jigger inside that controls how much you get for a bob; I'll just bring over a tool I have, and put yours right. I don't doubt Ma Merry's been swindling you; the only fair thing is to make an adjustment right now. Pity you don't have your own electric light meter; I've a sweet little trick with a magnet that does wonders with one of those. Still, can't be helped. Oh, you'd be amazed what money you can raise when you know how!'

Monica was indeed amazed, and the uneasiness she felt was shouted down by her pleasure in being able to put a substantial sum of money – nearly two hundred pounds – in Giles Revelstoke's hand. He was delighted.

'You're keeping me!' he shouted.

'No, no; it's a loan, or an investment, or something like that. You mustn't mind.'

'But I don't mind. I love it. I've never been kept by a woman before.'

The situation seemed to gratify something perverse to him. He knew how Monica came by the money, and he delighted in calling it 'her immoral earnings'. But she very soon discovered that it had been a mistake to give him the money, for he had no idea of how to keep it, or use it sparingly. He did not want things for himself, particularly, but he gave Raikes Bros. another fifty pounds on the *Lantern* account, and he gave a party for the menagerie, to whom he confided, as the best joke in the world, that he was now Monica's kept man. Monica was so torn between shame and exultation that, for the first time in her life, her digestion troubled her. All the better, said Bun Eccles; she'd want less to eat.

The menagerie thought it all wonderful, and Tuke and Tooley courted Monica embarrassingly, seeing in her the saviour of *Lantern*. It was true that Miss Tooley, who kept Tuke (but in a sublimated, disciple-like way), made a few veiled references to the iniquity of diverting trust funds: and it was also true that Tuke, who was deeply hurt because he was not to make the libretto of *The Golden Asse* (which Giles was adapting himself) was a little bitter about artists who sold themselves for money. Persis was jealous, because she could not afford to keep Giles; it would have been such a sell for her straight-laced parents if they had discovered that she kept a man. But she shut up when Eccles suggested to her that she might try her luck on Piccadilly, and put her earnings into the general fund. Though there were under-currents, it was accepted among them that Monica was a heroine.

Eccles had no money, but he gave his talent to the acquirement and husbanding of anything that Monica could lay her hands on. There was only one source of income which he ruled out.

Odingsels approached Monica one evening, and sitting beside her, so that his unpleasant head was very close to hers, said: 'If you really want money, I can always pay you for work – though I can't afford to contribute anything for nothing. But I do figure studies – the nude, you know – oh, nothing unpleasant and very well thought of by judges; the right models are always a problem, and it so happens that you have an excellent figure, of just the sort I require. You know me, Monica, and I am sure you have no silly ideas about such things. I could run to ten guineas a sitting, and I could make use of you quite often.'

Monica was willing; after all, if Persis could take off her clothes for Odingsels, so could she. But Eccles was firm.

'No you don't,' said he.

'But he says it's not dirty pictures. And it's ten guineas a time. I don't mind. Why, Bun, you know you employ models yourself. What's the fuss?'

'Monny, some day that fellow is going to be in very bad trouble. And when he is, you don't even want to know about him, see? Now don't argue. You're not going to do it.'

And although Monica was rebellious, she obeyed.

The fact was that the small engagements and sources of income which Giles gave up to work on his opera – some examination of manuscripts for a music publisher, some arranging of music for the BBC, scores for documentary films, and some occasional critical writing outside *Lantern* – might have brought him twenty pounds or so a month. Monica was providing him with about twice that sum, but it all vanished without anybody seeming to be better off. The same hand-to-mouth methods of finance continued; for Monica, who understood the management of money best, was not asked to take charge of it. Nor did it ever seriously occur to her that it should be so.

Monica never thought of herself as keeping Giles; she thought of it as financing the creation of *The Golden Asse*, which went swimmingly. Giles worked very hard, and during the time when he should have been teaching her (and he was still sending his bills to Domdaniel for her lessons) she kept up her work for *Lantern*, and provided him with food, comfort and companionship in bed. But other people thought of the situation quite differently, as she discovered within a few weeks.

Ripon had written to her soon after their meeting in Oxford, to ask her to go with him to the Vic-Wells Ball; he had been asked to go with a party, and wanted a partner. She grudged the money for the costume-hire, but when Ripon called for her, not very happily disguised as a toreador, she was ready in an outfit which included a large panniered skirt and a tricorne hat, which the costumier called a Venetian Domino.

The ball was held in the Albert Hall, not very far from Courtfield Gardens, and when they arrived the floor was well filled with those characters inseparable from such occasions. There were soldiers and sailors of all sorts, whole tribes of gypsies, Harlequins and Columbines in all shades, and platoons of Pierrots; there were fifteen or twenty head of Mephistopheleses, and quite as many Gretchens; Cavaliers and Roundheads abounded. These were the staples, the bread-and-butter, of disguise. In addition there were the lazy people who had come as monks, or simply as robed figures, and the over-zealous people who had come in costumes so ingenious and original that they could neither sit down nor dance, but wandered the floor smirking self-consciously, and hoping to be admired. The saddest of these was a gentleman whose costume consisted of a clever arrangement of Old Vic and Sadler's Wells programmes; people kept stopping him to read the fine print, and to debate about what it said, quite as if he were not inside it. There were homosexuals in pairs and singly, their eyes – they hoped – speaking volumes to understanding hearts. A few Lesbians swaggered menacingly in very masculine costumes, smacking their riding-boots with whips. A pitiful little man, dressed with loving care to resemble Nijinsky in *L'Après Midi d'un Faune*, crept about in a contorted posture, meant to remind the beholder of the best-known picture of the great dancer in that part; but it was pathetically apparent that he had a crooked spine. Like all costume balls, it was a fascinating study in self-doubt, self-assurance, thwarted ambition, self-misprision, well-meaning ineptitude and, very occasionally, imagination or beauty.

Monica found it dull. A year ago she would have exulted in such an affair, but tonight she thought it rather silly, and was annoyed that Ripon had to wear his spectacles with his costume if he were not to trip over things and tumble on the stairs.

When he had gone to fetch drinks, she stood in one of the upper corridors, wondering how soon it would be before she could decently ask to be taken home. She was conscious that the door of a box near her had been opening and shutting indecisively, but she was taken unawares when a stumpy Mephistopheles burst from it, seized her arm, and dragged her inside. They were at the back of the box, which was otherwise unoccupied, and at a little distance, over the railing, the full rampaging splendour of The Veleta was to be seen. The Mephistopheles snorted within his mask for a moment, then seized Monica and kissed her.

She was too surprised to resist, conscious chiefly of the hot-buckram-and-glue smell of the mask, and when the Mephistopheles clutched at her again, she stumbled backward into a chair, bearing him down with her.

'It's about time,' snorted the figure, in a Cork accent which could only belong to one person known to Monica.

'Mr Molloy!' she cried.

'You'd better call me Murtagh,' said the Mephistopheles, tearing off his mask, and showing a very red face. 'We've some business together, my girl, that's waited long enough.' He made another dart forward and thrust his hand deep into the bosom of the Venetian Domino. It was an inexpert move, too vigorous; the hooks on the back of her gown burst, and his hand stopped not far from Monica's stomach. She seized his arm and removed it.

'Whatever is wrong,' said she. 'Are you ill?'

'B'God I'm not ill, but I'm fed up,' said Molloy. 'Seein' you day after day, growin' lovelier and lovelier and – oh hell! Monica, you've got to be good to me; that fella'll ruin you, and never think the toss of a button about it. I could love you – I could teach you – God, there's nothing I'd not do for you! You'll say I'm old, but it's not the truth. I could be young for you, my darlin', I could! Be kind to me; I'm begging you!'

He looked almost ill, as he squirmed on his knees on the floor in front of her, and he seemed to be in a torment of passion that was partly physical desire, for at one point he seized Monica's right leg beneath her skirt and kneaded it painfully. He smelled of drink, but it was not drink that ailed him.

'Mr Molloy, what can I do for you? You mustn't go on like that. Tell me what's the matter. No! Stop that, or I'll have to go away.'

He raised a terrible, tear-swollen face to her, and groaned. 'I want you,' he said. 'I love you.'

'But – you mustn't; it won't do.'

'Oh, it won't do, won't it? Well, if you don't want to be decent, b'God we'll be indecent! And no surprise to you, either. It won't be the first time for you, nor the tenth, nor the hundredth, so shut up and keep still!'

So this is rape, thought Monica, strangely cool, as she was dragged down upon the fusty carpet of the box. The Venetian Domino outfit included a large lace fan, mounted on heavy sticks, a formidable bludgeon; she cracked Molloy smartly over the skull with it, as he snuffled and puffed above her. His face grew small with pain; all its features seemed to draw together; she gave him a shove and he rolled over on the floor, still too hurt to utter.

'You shouldn't have done that,' said Monica, in what she felt to be a schoolmistressy way. But what was there to say? 'What ever made you do such a beastly thing?'

But Molloy could not answer. She wriggled over the floor, impeded by her large panniered skirt, to a point where she could hold his head in her lap and nurse it. After a time he was able to open his eyes. And again she asked him: 'What made you do such a thing?'

'I love you,' he sobbed, with tears of pain and despair running down his cheeks. 'Oh God, you can't know what I've been through, with the thought of you and that fella. – And now they say you're keepin' him; your fancy-man. – Shouldn't I have known what was goin' on, the way your lower octave kept gettin' stronger and richer? – If you're meat for him, why the hell aren't you meat for me? I could do miracles for you. I could make you famous. I wouldn't drag you down and ruin you. – But I'm just an old fella to you – an old fool. Aw God, that's the hell of it.'

He wept, and Monica wept with him, but it cannot be pretended that they understood each other. Two puritanisms were in conflict, and could not meet. But under that, in a realm below the morality which was bred in the bone, they wept for the sadness of all unrequited love, all ill-matched passion, and the prancing rhythm of The Veleta mounted to them like the indifference of a world where all loves were happy.

The door of the box opened a crack, and someone peeped in; then it opened fully, and admitted a short figure in a purple domino and a mask. Outside the mask it wore a gleaming pair of steel-rimmed spectacles.

'Get up outa that, Murt, and come on home,' said the figure.

Molloy started. 'Norah!' said he.

'Myself,' said the purple domino. 'Did you think you'd given me the slip, my fine wee fella? Come on now, and don't trouble Miss Gall any more.'

Molloy got unsteadily to his feet, helped by Monica. The purple domino, hands on hips, offered no assistance. He was a sorry figure, for one side of his moustache was gone, and the paint on his eyebrows had run down his face in streaks. Without a word to Monica he went through the door.

'You'd better not come for any more lessons till you hear from me,' said the purple domino. 'He won't be himself for a few days. Och, these artists! You'd better be married to a barometer; up and down, up and down all the time.'

'Are you Mrs Molloy?'

'I am. And I've no word of blame for you, my girl, though I advise you to watch your step in future with himself. He can't resist a good pupil; wants to run away with 'em all. But I've always kept him respectable, and please God I always will. Which isn't light work, in the line we're all in. But it's lose that, and lose all.'

And such is the power of anything which is said with a sufficient show of certainty that Monica, who was robbing her benefactors to maintain her lover, nodded solemnly in agreement as the door of the box closed behind the purple domino.

[EIGHT]

'I am entirely agreed that Miss Gall should come home if this family crisis demands it,' said Miss Pottinger, 'but you have not yet fully convinced me that it is the duty of the Bridgetower Trust to pay her expenses.'

The other trustees groaned in spirit. During the three years of the Trust's existence Miss Puss, contentious by nature, had grown even more insupportable. She fancied herself in the role of a keen woman of business, husbanding money which these foolish men would have squandered; she demanded elaborate and repetitive explanations of the obvious; she made notes in a little book while the others were speaking, thereby missing much of the point of what was said; she pawed through all the bills and lawyer's statements, demanding explanations and comparing costs with some standard of expenditure adopted by herself in her youth, and now invalid. Although she was believed to be nearly eighty, she had an appetite for committee-work which exhausted Solly, the Dean and Mr Snelgrove. They all, in their various ways, hated her.

It was half-past ten, and the Bridgetower house, now so meagrely heated by Solly, was growing colder; since half-past eight they had been chewing away at a single decision. Mr Snelgrove decided to allow himself the luxury of a calculated loss of temper.

'Let me repeat once more that I fully realize that I am merely the solicitor and legal adviser of this Trust,' said he, 'but I urge you with all the force at my command to seize this opportunity of spending some of the Trust money. If it is not done willingly, you may find yourselves compelled to do it unwillingly. I have told you repeatedly that the Public Trustee is disturbed by the way in which your funds are accumulating. Unless you want an investigation, and all the disagreeable circumstances which will come with it, you had better snatch at this chance to spend two or three thousand dollars. Miss

Gall's mother is reported to be seriously ill; she fears that she may die, and she wants to see her daughter. If she dies, and it comes out that you have denied her daughter the means of visiting her, you will not like what people will say. You will not like it at all.'

'Has Miss Gall no funds in hand?' demanded Miss Puss. 'She has received a very substantial allowance, and of late her expenditures have been remarkably heavy – far heavier than can be justified by a student life. I have said that she may come home for a time, so far as I am concerned. But we are empowered under the will of the late Louisa Hansen Bridgetower – whose memory seems to be growing very misty in your minds – only to spend money on her artistic education. Can this jaunt be justified on those grounds? That is what I want to know.'

'Personally I do not care the toss of a button whether the journey is educational or not,' said Snelgrove. 'But you had better understand this: Mrs Bridgetower left, when all charges were paid, rather more than a million dollars to this Trust. As invested, that brings in roughly $31,000 a year to be spent on this wretched girl, after all taxes on income and property are paid; spend as she will, and reckoning my own expenses and those of my London colleagues, and the money for travel abroad, and the fees of the teachers, there is still about $45,000 of unspent money in our funds, to which we have no right. The Public Trustee wants to know when we are going to spend it, and he wants it spent as soon as possible.'

'Whose money is it?' asked Solly, a light in his eye.

'It is Monica Gall's money,' said Snelgrove, 'and the sooner we get it off our hands the better I shall like it.'

'You are surely not suggesting that we give it to her in a lump sum,' said Miss Pottinger. 'We are instructed to educate the girl, not to debauch her.'

'Must we suppose that she would use the money foolishly?' said Dean Knapp. 'I have seen little of her, but what I saw, and the reports from Sir Benedict, certainly do not suggest that she is an imprudent girl. With some guidance by us such a sum might be put aside by her for future expenses incidental to her career. Everyone knows of cases in which a little money in hand has tided people over difficult times, and greatly smoothed their way.'

'It is not a little money,' said Miss Puss. 'It is a great deal of money. Certainly it would never occur to me to call it a small sum. Of course, I have always had to manage rather carefully.'

This was a hint at the $3,500 a year which the Dean's wife received from her father's estate, a sum which, added to the Dean's stipend, was supposed to make the Knapps unbecomingly worldly. Miss Pottinger, who had lived on inherited money all her life, was a positive socialist about the inherited money of other people.

'Big or little, I wish I had it,' said Solly. He looked shabby and sharp; his hair wanted cutting, and his grey flannel trousers wanted pressing. He could have afforded to make himself tidy, but tidiness did not accord with the character of Wronged Son which he now played regularly at the meetings of the Trustees. 'Still, I agree that it is quite a lump to throw into her lap all at once. Surely this could have been foreseen? Why haven't we made it over to her, or banked it for her, every quarter? Isn't this rather late in the day to tell us about it?'

Mr Snelgrove looked at Solly for a little time before he spoke, choosing his words.

'The delay was my fault, Solomon,' said he. 'I had some hopes, as you had yourself, that this Trust would not be of long duration. When we all heard the good news that you and Veronica were expecting a child, I said nothing about the matter, because I thought it might all be adjusted more agreeably when that child was born, and the Trust perhaps ended by that event. I accept any blame there may be. My intention was of the best.'

The Dean, always tactful, struck in.

'I suggest that we wire Miss Gall to come home at once, to relieve her mother's mind. When she is here we can talk to her and make some arrangement which will satisfy the Public Trustee. And of course the Trust should bear all expenses.'

Thus it was decided, for even Miss Puss quaked at the bogy of the Public Trustee.

[TWO]

Through the long night which divided Canada from England, Monica was carried fifteen thousand feet above the ocean in the humming Limbo of a luxury aircraft. Mr Boykin had brought the word to Courtfield Gardens: 'Your mother is seriously ill, and the Bridgetower Trustees think you had better go home for a time. I've made all arrangements, and everything is in this envelope. Can you be at the terminus tonight at six-thirty? Good. Now, you really mustn't distress yourself.' Mrs Merry, whom Mr Boykin had fearfully enlisted as his ally in delivering this news, also urged Monica not to distress herself. As they seemed to expect it, she did her best to be somewhat distressed, and the thought of leaving Revelstoke gave her the necessary fuel for a show of concern. But she had no feeling of reality concerning the news about her mother. None of the Galls ever thought seriously about sickness or health, and death was a theological, rather than a physical, fact to them. Ma was ill. Well, Ma was always up and down but the strength of her spirit, in elation or depression, remained constant. She would find Ma depressed, no doubt, and in bed, but she would persuade Ma to feel better again, as she had done so often before. What might seem to be serious illness to outsiders was a different thing when you knew Ma.

But to return to Canada! As the plane sped on through the darkness it was as though a limb, long numbed, regained its feeling. She had had so much to do since Revelstoke began his work on *The Golden Asse* that even her perfunctory letter-writing had fallen far behind. She had so little time to write, she told herself; in her more honest moments she recognized that she had so little to write that would have made any sense to her readers at home. That had always been the trouble about letters – finding things that her family would be interested in, and of which they could approve. She was no writer. How could she make what she was doing real to her parents? How much could she reveal without bringing, in return, their mockery or a scolding?

The visit to Neuadd Goch, for instance, which was now more than a year behind her. She had told Ma something of it – a very little, really – about the beauty of the countryside, the charm of the house, and the kindness of the Hopkin-Griffiths. Ma's reply had been sharp enough about 'your swell new friends' and strongly disapproving of the news that Monica had been to a Christmas service as offered by the Church of England – 'Does this mean you are changing your religion? What do you expect to get from that?' On the whole, it had been politic not to mention her small part in the *Matthew Passion*, or the perplexities and anguish which it had brought. That was the trouble; you couldn't tell Ma anything really important without running a risk of hurting her. And it went without saying that her sharpness arose from hurt feelings; question that, and you might find yourself thinking that it sprang from ignorance, jealousy and meanness, which was inadmissible; loyalty could not permit such thoughts.

Loyalty! Monica had not forgotten her protestation of loyalty when

George Medwall hinted that she might want to abandon some of the beliefs and attitudes of her family. She had meant it then, and she still meant it. But she had not realized how costly such loyalty might be. She had not foreseen that it could mean keeping two sets of mental and moral books – one for inspection in the light of home, and another to contain her life with Revelstoke, and all the new loyalties and attitudes which had come with Molloy, and particularly with Domdaniel. To close either set of books forever would be a kind of suicide, and yet to keep them both was hypocrisy. As Monica pondered her problem she felt that she was perplexed and tormented unendurably; but anyone looking at her on the plane might well have thought that she looked uncommonly animated and happy.

Letters were no good as a means of communication. She had written as faithfully and as fully as she could, but there were things which did not belong in letters, and which she would now have a chance to tell her mother face to face. And if her letters were poor and thin, what about the ones she received? Ma's letters were a record of small facts . . . 'thought I'd go to church this morning but did not feel I could tackle the stairs . . . your Dad is patching the linoleum in the upstairs hall, but it don't hold the tacks like it used & guess will have to think of new . . . Donny is growing like a weed & is cute as a fox & says Ganny plain as plain.' And food, always food! Mrs Gall was a Sunday afternoon letter-writer, and every week contained a description of the Sunday menu . . . 'Guess you don't get eats like that over there Eh Monny?'

More informative were the letters of her sister Alice, now Mrs Charles Proby. Chuck Proby was getting on faster in the service of his bank than he had expected, and he had taken Alice to wife, and abandoned his idea that religion was a lot of crap at the same time. Religion had an important place in a young man's progress. The Probys, however, had taken a long upward step in the religious world, for they had left the Thirteener fold and associated themselves with the United Church, where a vastly superior group of people were to be met. Their union had been blessed with a son, Donald, and snapshots and detailed accounts of the progress of this wondrous child made up the bulk of Alice's letters. There was still room, however, for a general, nagging discontent to assert itself. Alice had Chuck and Donny; Chuck had a safe job and prospects; but life did not move quickly enough for Alice, who felt the need for a bigger house and a more important husband and an apparently endless list of labour-saving household devices. She frankly envied Monica, whose luck had been so good, and who had no problems, and nobody to consider but herself.

George Medwall wrote now and then, but less frequently as the months went by. He was getting on. He was saving money. He was sick of boarding-houses. He hoped she was keeping well. He had seen her father, who looked okay. Far, far better were the very rare epistles which Kevin and Alex wrote together, and illustrated with funny pictures. But they were tactful, and urged her not to think it necessary to write in return, though she did so.

Worst of all, when it came to answering them, were the letters from Aunt Ellen, so long, so kind, so loaded with a tremulous curiosity about the richly musical world in which Monica was now living. Aunt Ellen was dying to know all about it and to share it as far as possible. But everything she said made it so plain that Aunt Ellen had hold of the wrong end of the stick, and that the musical world she imagined was that intense, genteely romantic world of *The First Violin*. And she wanted Monica's life to be cast in that mould, wanted it so badly that it would have been inexcusable cruelty to disillusion her. There was the danger, too, that nothing must be told to Aunt Ellen which had not also been told to Ma, for Ma was sure to find out, and make trouble. Thus Monica was forced to deny Aunt Ellen the romantic crumbs which she might otherwise have afforded her. If Aunt Ellen knew that Monica was in daily association with a man who was writing an opera, she would be transported; it would give her a real and abiding joy. But if Ma knew, Ma would simply want to know why she saw him every day, and if he slept at the same place that he worked. It was bitter hard work writing to Aunt Ellen.

As Canada drew nearer, however, all of these considerations gave way to excitement and anticipation. Coming down at Gander – wonderful! The coffee was not what the McCorkills would have called 'real Canadian coffee', being that characterless grey drink common to lunch counters in all countries; the Quebec carved figures, and the factory-made beaded moccasins, spoke of no Canada which Monica had ever known; but the genuine uncivil Canadian fat woman behind the counter, and the excellent quality of toilet paper in the Ladies were home-like indeed. And the air, the cool, clear air, which had not been breathed and re-breathed by everybody since the time of Alfred the Great – that was best of all.

On to Montreal and Dorval airport. On to Montreal's Windsor

Station, that massive witness to the love-affair between Canada and its railways. Thence to a train which would carry her to Salterton – a real Canadian train, smelling of carpets and stale cigar-smoke, which toiled and rumbled through the country-side whistling, and ringing its bell, and puffing defiance at anyone who might dare to suggest that it was not really going very fast. Monica rode in the parlour-car, gazing rapturously at the snowy landscape, even while eating her luncheon of leathery omelet and cardboard pie. Yet to her it was the food of the gods, for this was an omelet of Canadian leatheriness, a pie of real Canadian cardboard!

Salterton! But nobody at the station to greet her. Well, of course telegrams which you sent to announce your arrival did have a way of appearing, with every show of smart efficiency, after you had well and truly arrived. She took a taxi to her home.

Dad answered her ring at the bell. He looked older, thinner and very weary.

'Oh God, Monny, it's good to have you here,' he said. And then, breaking into the tears which he had so long held back – 'It looks like we're goin' to lose your Ma!'

[THREE]

If it were still the fashion to see ghosts (and it may be asked if such revelations are not a matter of fashion or, if a more pretentious phrase is demanded, of intellectual climate) Veronica Bridgetower would very often have seen the ghost of her mother-in-law, Louisa Hansen Bridgetower. While she had lived, Mrs Bridgetower had worn her large, ugly house close about her, like a cloak. Her spirit was in every room; her will in some way influenced every thought and action on her premises. In his bachelor days Solly had tried to escape her by making an eyrie for himself in the attic; there his bedroom and his workroom and a little washroom had provided him with a complete kingdom; he had but to close the door at the foot of the stair and his mother could not pursue him; her ailing heart had prevented her from mounting those stairs for ten years before she died. But she was there, none the less, and he had always known that every creak of a bedspring and every scrape of a chair was heard and considered by her sharp ears. When he had married, he had brought Veronica to this house. Mrs Bridgetower had pleaded, with the sweet self-abasement possible only to those who are completely sure of their power, that her son and his wife should make their home with her – for if they were to leave her, might she not be frightened in that large house, alone except for her two old servants?

Alone; yes, she would have been alone in the sense that one is alone in a familiar, comfortable garment. She, frightened, there? She had Solly and Veronica in her pocket, and well she knew it. They had lived with her. How, they asked each other, could they refuse?

I have never had a home of my own, thought Veronica, as she lay beside the sleeping Solly. The January wind roared around the house, making the storm-window outside the bedroom rattle fiercely, as though to rebuke this rebellion against Fate. Though of course I've been terribly lucky, she added, hastily placating whatever, or whoever, might be listening to her thoughts.

Lucky? Oh, yes, for was she not the daughter of Professor Walter Vambrace, who had written a book on the Enneads of Plotinus? And was it not a privilege to grow up in the atmosphere of strenuous thought which that austere scholar created? And to realize that Father was a cousin of the Marquis of Mourne and Derry, and if eight people had died young and childless Father would have had the title? It was true that Father and Mother never quite got on together, chiefly because he was such an aggressive free-thinker, whereas Mother was a devout Catholic. But Mother had always been so sweet, so abstracted, so truly kind. It was sad that since her marriage she saw her parents so seldom, though they lived not much more than a mile away.

But then, her marriage with Solly had been so beset with difficulties on both sides. And although the Vambraces and Mrs Bridgetower had made the best of it when it was plain that it could not be prevented, there had been clear indications that they were doing precisely that – making the best of it. Solly had tried to keep it secret from her that his Mother thought their marriage a great mistake. How like him it was to try to spare her! But of course she knew. How could anyone who lived with Mrs Bridgetower help knowing? Her mother-in-law's opinions were as palpable in that house as was the smell of heavy upholstery.

It could not be pretended that she had been made at home in Mrs Bridgetower's house. She had learned all the rules – what chairs not to sit in, what doors to close and which to leave open, what books and papers might be read, and when, and her mother-in-law's long rosary of pills, which had to be worked through every day – but she had never learned the spirit of the house, because it was Mrs Bridgetower's spirit. She had tried with uttermost patience and submission to be a good daughter-in-law. She had even dressed Mrs Bridgetower's body for burial, arranged her hair and painted her face – Ah, there it was again, the thought that would not down! Years ago, at a children's party, Veronica had been blindfolded and asked to identify a group of objects on a tray; one of these was a kid glove which had been stuffed with paper, and thoroughly soaked; she had dropped the chill, damp object with a shudder, and only the self-control which her father had instilled in her had kept her from weeping with fright. Painting the face of her dead mother-in-law had revived and hideously prolonged that sensation, and she had not wept on that occasion, either. She had done her best to be a good daughter-in-law because it was part of being a good wife, part of her love for Solly. Why, then, would his mother not leave her alone, even after death?

Mrs Bridgetower was everywhere in this house. Across the hall was the room in which she had died. Below, in the drawing-room, was her chair. Everywhere, all was as she had left it, and her watch-dog, Miss Laura Pottinger, took care to see that nothing was changed. This was not Veronica's house, and her husband's; it was the property of the Bridgetower Trust, and they lived in it simply as caretakers – caretakers who paid the big coal bills and tried to keep it clean.

Why could they not go elsewhere? But she had never even asked Solly why, and she would never do so now. For it was Veronica's terrible secret that Mrs Bridgetower owned her husband, as well as everything else in the house. He, who had been high-spirited and amusing in his ironic, undergraduate way before their marriage, had become more and more like his Mother since his Mother's death. A severity, a watchfulness had grown on him, and all the more quickly since the birth of the child.

She had never seen the child, but the nurse had told her, against doctor's orders, that it had been a fine boy. It was the boy which might have broken the Trust, might have given them Mrs Bridgetower's fortune, might have enabled them to sell this hateful, haunted house, might have delivered them from this bondage. But the boy had been born with his navel-cord tight around his neck, strangling as he moved toward the light.

Had that been Mrs Bridgetower's work, also? If she had drawn the spiteful will, if she still possessed this house, might she not also be capable of that?

Solly had wept with her, had taken her away for as long a holiday as they could afford, and then – had promised that there would be more children. He had meant to be kind and courageous, but Veronica feared the thought of more children. The doctor said that there was not the slightest reason for fear. But the doctor was not Mrs Bridgetower's daughter-in-law; she could not tell him that she feared the vengeance of a dead woman whose son she had stolen.

Solly had become grimmer, and they had grown poorer, trying to keep up the house, and old Ethel, on his modest university lecturer's salary. It was not that they seriously lacked money; it was, rather, that all the appurtenances of an income far greater than their own, and all the habits which went with money and a large house, hung around them, and they were both poor managers. Their poverty was illusory, but it was perhaps the more destructive and humiliating for that. And here she lay, fearing the future – fearing, more than she dared admit to herself, the man whom she so much loved, who was passing more and more into the possession of the woman who had so much hated her.

Still, was this not better than that year which had followed Mrs Bridgetower's death – the year when Solly had hoped that they might have a son, and halt the whole business of forming the Trust? She had borne patiently with his first flogging of himself to beget a child; they had pretended to each other that it was a joke – but they knew in their hearts that it was no joke. And as time passed, and nothing happened, Solly grew frightened and suddenly could make love no longer. He sought medical advice; the doctor said that there was nothing wrong with him, and suggested in the easy way of doctors that he must relax. Yes, relax. Rest would work a cure.

That rest-cure had been a troubled time. If a man is trying to recover from impotence, when is he to assume that he has refrained long enough? The deceptions and mockeries of Solly's body distressed them both, for Veronica longed for him, and could not always dissemble her longing. Both felt the Dead Hand of Mrs Bridgetower; its chill had frozen the very fountain of their passion, brought winter to the garden of their love.

Then, as the doctor had said he would, Solly recovered, and with a new determination and greater caution they sought an heir – no, a son. And, after the months of pregnancy, with the chances that it would be a daughter at least evenly weighed against them, the stillborn son had come to mock their hopes. Veronica had endured it all, and could endure anything the future and – if it were indeed a fact – the posthumous malignancy of her mother-in-law might bring, if only she did not lose Solly. But so often now it seemed that he was possessed by the spirit of his mother at least as much as by the nature which she so much loved, and it was this that brought her, in such nights as this, a terror which was desolating and bleak.

More children! Sometimes, when Solly made love to her, she could have wept, could have shrieked with misery. For in the very climax of love he might have been struggling with the spirit of his Mother, so oblivious did he seem of Veronica. And did he want a child, or was it rather vengeance on his tormentor, and the recovery of her money, which he sought to plant in his wife's body?

Who could say that Louisa Hansen Bridgetower was dead? Freed from the cumbrous, ailing body, freed from any obligation to counterfeit the ordinary goodwill of mortal life, her spirit walked abroad, working out its ends and asserting its mastery through a love which was hate, a hatred which was love.

– Suddenly Solly started up in the bed, his eyes staring, muttering hoarsely. He often had bad dreams now. Quickly she woke him. He smiled, looked very young, kissed her and laughed at himself.

'Let's go and get something to eat,' he said.

In the large kitchen, in expiation of her gloomy and almost disloyal thoughts, Veronica made toast and scrambled eggs. They liked to eat in the middle of the night, childishly defying old Ethel and the solemn spirit of the house.

'The Gall girl's been home almost a week now,' said Solly, as they ate.

'What do you hear about her mother?'

'Improving, apparently. Knapp has been keeping in touch. He's very kind about such things.'

'What ailed her?'

'Gall, appropriately enough. A really bad go of gallstones. She's more frightened than hurt, I gather. They'll operate and she'll be all right in a few weeks. People are extraordinary; apparently they were all convinced that she would never pull through; she's never been seriously ill before. Getting Monica home has brought her round.'

'Good. It'll be a load off Monica's mind.'

'Yes. Old Puss is beginning to hound her about giving a recital here before she goes back. To show what's been done with our money, presumably. Well, it'd better be good.'

[FOUR]

Dr James Cobbett was widely considered in Salterton to be a promising young man, but he was still at that delicate stage of his career when people called him '*young* Dr Cobbett'; however, this meant that when he wanted advice he could readily turn to his father, '*old* Dr Cobbett'. He did so in the case of Mrs Gall.

'She ought to be in hospital, but they're all scared to death of hospitals,' said he: 'fantastic to run into such prejudice nowadays. She ought to have a cholecystotomy as soon as possible, but they won't hear of it. The family have no regular doctor, though this woman has been having what she calls bilious attacks for at least a couple of years; I'm sorry they got hold of me. They seem to think if I can "tide her over" as they call it, she'll be able to manage. She's sworn she'll diet, live on slops – anything. The old man even asked me if there wasn't some way of melting gall-stones by taking medicine. They're just scared of the knife.'

'What are you doing?'

'Usual thing. Got two nurses on. The daughters and the husband sit with her at night. Morphia – though I can't do too much with that, because I suspect fatty degeneration of the heart – she's probably twice her optimum weight. She's in the static stage now, but it can't last long. They're kidding themselves that she's getting better, but of course she isn't.'

'No, no; of course not.'

'Well, what do I do?'

'I don't see that there is anything more that you can do. What do you think is the real trouble? Have they some kind of religious scruple about surgery?'

'No. They're Thirteeners, whatever that means. But the preacher was at the house the other day when I called – a fellow named Beamis – and when I explained the situation to him he was perfectly reasonable. Tried to persuade her to go to hospital. Did everything he could, really. But the old girl kept sobbing and moaning "Don't let 'em take me; please don't let 'em take me". I felt like a fool.'

'There's no need for you to feel like that, Jimmy. You've given the best advice – the only advice, really. If they don't take it, you can throw up the case, but I wouldn't, if I were you. If people are determined to commit suicide by the long and painful course of going against medical opinion, it's hard to watch, but I don't think you want to be known as the kind of doctor who throws up cases.'

'I had a little hope until this week. The younger daughter is home, now. You've heard of her; she's the girl that's being educated with old Mrs Bridgetower's money. They insisted on putting off a final decision till she came. She's far above the rest of them, and she's certainly not scared. I've talked to her very frankly; she knows exactly what'll happen. I got her to the point of saying that her mother should go to hospital. "I'll tell her myself", she said, and we went into the room together. But the old lady must be a mind-reader. She snatched the girl's hand, and began to scream. "Monny, don't let 'em take me; Monny, don't let 'em get me in that place", she shrieked, over and over again. The girl looked dreadful; I was really sorry for her. Her mother made her swear, then and there, with a Bible in her hand, that she should not be taken to hospital. "You see how it is", she said to me, and I suppose I do, in a way. But she said a funny thing to me, as I was leaving. "You realize that your decision may be bringing about your mother's death?" I said –'

'Now Jimmy, that was a mistake.'

'Yes, I know it was, but I was mad. It's all so senseless! But she looked me straight in the eye and said: "My decision *may* do so, Dr Cobbett, but your decision would do so beyond any doubt. My mother lives by the spirit as well as by the flesh; if I kill the spirit by delivering her, frightened and forsaken, into your hands, what makes you think that you can save the flesh?" Now what do you make of that? A layman ever dare talk to you in that way?'

'Speaking after more than thirty years of practice, I think the girl is right. Under stress, you know, Jimmy, people sometimes speak wiser than they know. I suppose if the girl had said yes, you could have doped the mother enough to get her to hospital and operate on her. But it would have been a serious risk. And – I don't know – if the whole cast of her mind, and her level of intelligence, and everything about her is against having her life saved by science, I question if we've any cast-iron moral right to save it.'

'The job of the profession is to preserve life, under all possible circumstances.'

'Oh, I know. I was taught that, too. And as long as you never learn anything but medicine, you'll probably continue to think so.'

'I'm sorry you take it like that, Father.'

'Don't be hurt, Jimmy. I'm sorry you've got such a miserable case. But they do turn up, from time to time. Hang on; it's your duty, and it can't last long.'

[FIVE]

Mrs Gall's illness had already lasted for two weeks and two days when Monica came home. The first violent onset had utterly demoralized Mr Gall, who fully believed his wife's agonized protests that she was dying. He had no experience of illness, except for occasional coughs and colds, and the Galls had no physician, now that old Doctor Wander, who had attended to the children, had died. He had called Alice, and Alice had called young Dr Cobbett. But she did not call him until morning, heeding the widespread complaint of doctors about night calls, and had been scolded by Dr Cobbett when he arrived, for not calling him sooner. By that time Mrs Gall had discovered that if she lay very still, with her knees up, and breathed as shallowly and as slowly as possible, her pain was less. But she was deeply frightened.

She was only a little less frightened when the doctor disposed of her fear that she had cancer. This was her secret dread, which she had hugged to herself for years. But if it were not cancer, what was it? Dr Cobbett talked in big, unfamiliar words, but it emerged that he did not know what it was, either. Myocardial infarction; what could that be? Acute pancreatitis; an obstructive neoplasm; volvulus of the small intestine? Young Dr Cobbett was kindly and able, but he was not above astonishing the simple. When Mrs Gall, feebly supported by her husband, showed strong resistance to going to the hospital, he astonished them even more, in the hope of breaking down their determination. But it was useless, and as he could not put Mrs Gall in hospital by force, he had to leave her at home, and get Nurses Gourlay and Heffernan to take care of her. The nurses were as much affronted as he by the Galls' refusal to accommodate themselves to the needs of medical science, and they let their displeasure be felt. Nurse Gourlay, indeed, made no secret of the fact that if she had her way, there would be a law to compel people to do what the doctor said was best for them.

Mrs Gall was down, but she was not out. Pain and fright lent her courage, and she gave Nurse Gourlay a piece of her mind; for Nurse

Heffernan, a softer sort of woman altogether, she reserved her fears that she might die, and her dread that her ailment might yet turn out to be cancer. Nurse Heffernan seized the chance to say that if only Mrs Gall would go to hospital, like a good girl, they'd have her leppin' like a goat in a couple of weeks. But Mrs Gall was firm: no hospital.

Her resolution was strengthened by morphia, which Dr Cobbett ordered in doses sufficient to control her pain. But in her morphia dreams there detached itself from some submerged mass of fear and floated upward into Mrs Gall's consciousness a notion that she was being held against her will in a bawdy-house, which was also a hospital, and where the wildest indecencies were demanded of her. She had too much cunning to confide these dreams to Nurse Heffernan, who would certainly have derided them, because of her professional stake in hospitals; she told them instead to her daughter Alice, during the eight hours of the night when neither nurse was on duty.

It was Alice who insisted that Monica should be sent for. She was not a bad or unkind daughter, but she took her duties as Charles Proby's wife heavily, and she was impatient of what she considered 'nonsense'. Not to go to the hospital was nonsense. To have delusions of being in a bawdy-house was nonsense. There were times when Alice was very close to thinking that being ill, which involved claims upon the time and charity of busy, ambitious young matrons, was nonsense. Nonsense had to be stopped. And why should she carry the weight of all this nonsense when Monica was living abroad, free of all care, thinking of nobody but herself?

'Every tub must stand on its own bottom,' said Alice, and went to see Mr Snelgrove. It was on the sixteenth day of Mrs Gall's illness that Monica arrived home, and was greeted by her father with his pathetic cry of fear that Mrs Gall might die.

Dr Cobbett and the nurses seized upon Monica as a new ally. By this time Dr Cobbett was virtually certain that Mrs Gall had acute cholecystitis and might die even if she were now moved to the hospital. But it was his task to do everything in his power to save her, and he would have risked an operation at an even later date: it must also be admitted that he loved to have his own way, and wanted to beat down this insurrection against the righteous forces of Hygeia.

Monica would not be bustled. She was a strange figure now in the stuffy little house. Her manner of speech, her clothes, her demeanour were all at odds with it. Nurse Gourlay did not dare to bully her;

Nurse Heffernan, who had a feudal streak in her, accepted Monica as the mistress, to be heeded right or wrong. Monica took on the night nursing.

'Monny, are you there?'

'Yes, Ma, right here.'

'Monny, you won't let 'em take me to that place?'

'No, Ma; don't worry.'

'I've been there. I was there this afternoon. But I run away. I run away in my night-gown. A couple o' fellas in the hall seen me, and they tried to grab me. Was it bad? – Monny, was it bad?'

'Was what bad, Ma?'

'Was it bad they seen me in only my night-gown?'

'No, no; not bad. It was only a dream.'

'It wasn't a dream. I was there. Monny, when they get you in there they make you do awful things. It's a bad-house. There was girls there I used to know. Kate Dempster was there, flirtin' her tail just like she used when we was girls. Kate's a bad girl. Am I a bad girl, Monny?'

'No, Ma, you're a good girl.'

'Are you a good girl, Monny?'

'Yes, Ma, I'm a good girl.'

'Then why do you talk so funny? You're talkin' all the time waw-waw-waw so I can't make you out. You ain't Monny!'

'Yes, yes dear, I'm Monny. You mustn't upset yourself. I'm Monny and I'm right here.'

'No you ain't. Monny don't talk like that. You've sent Monny away! And I'm a bad girl, and they'll put me in the bad-house!'

'Quiet, dear. Let me give you a sip of this. Just a sip.'

'I'm a bad girl. – Monny, will I die?'

'No, dear, of course not. You had a very good day today.'

But it was not a good day. It was what Dr Cobbett called 'a remission'.

The period of remission lasted for seven days. To the nurses the vomiting, the bloating, the wasting away of flesh, the groaning and the recurrence of pain were the accustomed circumstances of serious illness. To Alfred Gall, who had never seen his wife in such straits, it was an agony for which he could find no expression. Morning and night he would go to the door of her room, look at the inert form in the bed and listen to its heavy breathing, after which he would creep away, his face marked with fear and loss. Only his sister Ellen had power to raise any hope in him. Alice was impatient of his spiritlessness; it was her temperament to talk about troubles, and to find relief in talk; she had no understanding of her father's stricken silence. Monica was gentle with him, but her energies were saved for the long vigils at her mother's bed-side.

Not all of their talks in the night were coloured by Mrs Gall's semi-delirium. True, most of what was said was in the pattern of fear and delusion, countered by love and reassurance. But for Monica her mother's rational spells were more exhausting than her wanderings, for in them it was emphasized and re-emphasized that to her mother she was now in part a stranger. Her manner of speech had changed, and Mrs Gall could not be comforted easily in the new, clear, warm speech which Monica had been at such pains to learn; but she could not undo it, could not go back to the speech of her home, for the new speech had become the instrument of the best that was in her mind, and heart. It seemed to her cruel and shameful that it should be so, but she was forced to admit the fact; it was so. To speak as Ma wanted her to speak was not only difficult, but it was a betrayal of Revelstoke, of Domdaniel, of Molloy and all the poets and musicians who stood behind them in time. Did she love these things more than her own mother? She put the question to herself, in those words, many times, but never dared to give either of the possible answers. Loyalty demanded that she give love, and she gave it as fully as she was able.

Loyalty demanded truth. But Mrs Gall, fearing death, returned again and again to incidents in her own life, at which she could only bring herself to hint, though in delirium their nature was revealed a little more clearly. She was convinced that she had sinned unforgivably, and that her sins were sexual in their nature. She named no names, spoke of no incidents; perhaps there had been none. But during her lifetime the only morality to which she had ever given a moment of serious thought, or to which she had ever paid solemn tribute, was a morality of sexual prohibition; she felt now that she had not been true to it, yet she could not confess her transgression or give clear expression to her remorse. Instead, she accused herself vaguely, and suffered in the tormented images of her morphia dreams.

She was specific in her demands and exhortations to Monica, however. Was Monica a good girl? The question came again and again when she was partly conscious, and thus phrased, from Mrs Gall, it could have only one meaning. Monica had no intention of saying that, in her mother's terms, she was not a good girl. But she had to meet the question in her own mind. Was she? To say yes was disloyal to home, to the woman who was in such distress at her side. But there were seven of these weary nights, and before the last Monica was sure of her answer. She was a good girl. Chastity is to have the body in the soul's keeping; Domdaniel had said it, and everything in her own experience supported it. And this decision, more than anything else, divided Monica from her mother when her mother most needed her. Her mother's idea of good and bad would not do for her.

If these ideas were invalid for her, what else that was valid had her mother to give her? Nothing, thought Monica; not with any sense of freedom, of breaking a lifelong bondage, but sadly and with pity for her mother and herself. But on the sixth night, after a brief period of sleep, Mrs Gall opened her eyes, and looked at her daughter more clearly than she had done since her homecoming.

'I been asleep.'

'Yes, Ma. Do you feel a little rested?'

'Was I talkin' foolish a while ago?'

'The hypodermics make you dream, dear.'

'And I guess I go on pretty wild, eh?'

Monica was about to deny it, but she looked into her mother's eye, and saw a twinkle there. Mrs Gall laughed, feebly but unmistakably.

'Yes, you were pretty wild, Ma.'

'You bet I was. I've got quite an imagination. That's where you're like me, Monny. Always remember that. You got that from me.'

Tears came into Monica's eyes; they were tears of happiness, for at last she shared something with her mother. She wept, and laughed a little, as she said –

'Yes Ma, I got that from you. We're very alike, aren't we?'

'Yes, I guess we are.'

The period of remission ended, unmistakably, a few hours later, on the morning of the seventh day, and Dr Cobbett said that peritonitis, which would certainly be fatal, had come, as he had expected it would under the circumstances. The family last saw Mrs Gall, leaden grey, with eyes partly closed and seemingly already dead, though the doctor called it 'shock'. She died at four o'clock the following morning. Only Monica was with her then.

[SIX]

'I think it is my duty to emphasize once again that this need not have happened,' said young Dr Cobbett as he prepared to fill out the certificate of death.

'My mother was always used to having her own way,' said Monica, 'and there is no point in discussing that now. The decision was mine, made according to her wishes, and if you feel that this matter should be carried any further, I shall be ready to answer any official questions.'

Dr Cobbett did not want to pursue the matter. All he wanted was an admission that he had been in the right, and he saw that he was not going to get it. So he continued.

'How old was your mother?'

Monica did not know. It had always been understood that it was 'bold' to want to know the ages of one's parents; it was like uncovering their nakedness, in the Bible. When Aunt Ellen was consulted, Monica was surprised to learn that her mother was fifty-six. Then when Monica was born, Mrs Gall had been thirty-three – ten years older than her own age, attained last December. Mrs Gall, fat and toothless, her hair streaked with grey, had somehow seemed to be without age – a mother.

'I guess living with Dad wasn't much incentive to her to keep herself up,' said Alice.

After her first outburst of grief, Alice was unpleasantly practical. Mr Gall could not be sent off to work on such a day, but neither could he be endured in the house, which must be made ready for the funeral. It was Alice who packed him off to her house, with complicated instructions about what he was to do for little Donald. Aunt Ellen, too, stayed away from her work, and it was Alice who put her at the job of calling and telegraphing the necessary relatives, from her own home. This, Alice explained to Monica, was more convenient and meant also that Aunt Ellen would pay for the telegrams; it could be her share of the funeral expenses.

At nine o'clock on the morning of their mother's death, Alice prepared coffee for herself and Monica, and sat down to make plans.

'The funeral can be from Queen Street United,' she said; 'I'll get Reverend Calder on the phone right away.'

'But why?' said Monica. 'Why not from the Tabernacle? Mother never had anything to do with Queen Street United.'

'Monny, let's face it. Do we want Ma's funeral to be a Thirteener circus, with Beamis spreading himself all over the place? You remember old Mrs Delahaye's funeral? – Well?'

'But that was her church, Alice. That's what she'd want.'

'What makes you so sure? I've heard her say things about Beamis that certainly didn't sound as if she had much use for him.'

'But wouldn't it seem odd?'

'Not half as odd as a Thirteener funeral. Chuck and I go to Queen Street United. We could arrange it.'

'I don't see it that way, Alice.'

'What's it matter to you? You're independent. You'll be away out of this as soon as you can get. But I've got to live here. Listen Monny – Chuck's boss will probably be attending this funeral. I don't want him coming to the Thirteener Tabernacle, and getting the idea that those are the people we associate with.'

'Alice, you're a snob!'

'Who's talking? Lady Haw-haw-haw; even when she was out of her head Ma used to make fun of you, right up till the last. Snob? Listen, I've got my own way to make. I'm not being carried by anybody else's money. And I'll tell you another thing, just while we're speaking our minds: I think Ma ought to have been put in the hospital, so there.'

'Then why didn't you put her in yourself, before I came home?'

'Because Dad insisted on waiting for you. You've always been the Big Mucky-Muck around here, and now you've got this Trust behind you, Dad and Ma were scared of you. It had to be Monny's decision. Well, you decided, and a fine mess you made of it. If you'd used common sense Ma would be well and strong now, and not dead upstairs. If you want my straight opinion, you killed Ma.'

'Alice, you're over-excited. I did what I did out of kindness; I swear it.'

'I never said you didn't. But Ma won't be the first one that's been killed by kindness.'

But the final arrangement was for a funeral at the Thirteener Tabernacle. It was not a complete victory for Monica. Pastor Beamis, who knew nothing of Alice's desire to displace him as spiritual adviser to the family, took his position for granted, and began to plan a service; he wanted Monica to sing a solo, and preferably two; he wanted to get the Heart and Hope Quartet together again, to make a special re-appearance at the graveside; it would draw a record crowd, he said, and what a comfort that would be to Brother Gall. Monica did not refuse without consideration; she fought with herself for the greater part of a day, but in the end she refused. Her reason was that she did not feel that she could control her voice well enough to sing upon such an occasion. But the inner voice, increasingly powerful in her thoughts, said: *Don't be a hypocrite; you're ashamed of them.*

The inner voice was cruel. So often it put the worst construction on everything, and in that respect it was like a conscience. But it spoke no morality which Monica could associate with a conscience – unless, somewhere, she were developing a new conscience, suited to her new needs. But if that were the case, why was the voice so often cruel? Sometimes it spoke with the unmistakable tones of her Mother, but in this instance it used the voice of Giles Revelstoke.

The three days before the funeral were tiring, after the long trial of Mrs Gall's illness. Ineffectual as he was, decency demanded that Mr Gall be consulted about the more important arrangements, and it was his wish that the funeral be held partly at the house and partly at the Tabernacle. Alice wanted it to be at the undertaker's chapel which, she pointed out, was so undenominational that you could imagine yourself anywhere. But in this last bid for social advancement she was defeated.

She and Monica bickered all the time, and quarrelled at least once a day. Their worst encounter was at the undertaker's, when they were choosing a coffin.

'Can you show us anything in oak?' said Alice.

The undertaker could show them something in oak; he mentioned the price.

'I don't think we want anything as expensive as that,' said Monica.

'Who's we?' said Alice; 'I think it's very nice.'

'It's too expensive. Dad shouldn't be burdened with that on top of everything else.'

'Who said Dad's going to be burdened? Who do you think is paying for this?'

'We all are, I suppose; we'll have to arrange some system of shares.'

'Listen, Monny, we're all paying according to what we have. Aunt Ellen has done telegrams. Chuck and I are looking after flowers at the house and the church. Dad'll have all he can manage settling up for the doctor and nurses, even with his insurance. That means that this is your share. See?'

'You mean I'm paying for the funeral?'

'None of the rest of us have got a sugar-daddy.'

'But Alice – the Trust money isn't for private expenses. Mr Snelgrove would never allow it. I had no idea you were thinking like this!'

'If you don't know how to get money without saying what it's for by this time, you'd better learn. Chuck'll tell you, if you want; he's a banker and he knows how these things are done. Now get this through your head; you're not going to bury Ma on the cheap. You're the rich one; well, you can just spend some of it on Ma. It'll be the last thing you can do for her and you'd better just make up your mind to do it right. It'll be sure to get around if you don't: you can depend on that.'

Monica protested, but she could not do so with much vigour. If she could rob the Trust for Revelstoke, why not for Ma? There was no answer to that question – not even such an answer as the uncomfortable inner voice could give. But it was a bitter blow to her to discover, as she did very soon, that not only Alice, but Dad and Aunt Ellen, were looking to her to pay all the heavier costs of this occasion. It was not wholly that they wanted money; it was that her supposed possession of money made her, in their eyes, the head of the family. Not moral authority, or age, but hard cash was what decided the matter. She could never again be a child in her father's house, because she had more money than he.

The funeral came, and passed. Eleven relatives from out of town arrived, and were fed; seven of them were given overnight lodging at the Gall house and at Aunt Ellen's. They were all Gunleys, relatives of Mrs Gall, and like her they tended to be fat and sardonic. The night before the funeral they assembled for a family pow-pow, and Mr Gall and Alice, between them, gave a dramatic account of Mrs Gall's last illness. Alice tried to weight the story a little by emphasizing the doctor's assertion that Mrs Gall need not have died, and that Monica's decision that she should not go to the hospital was the deciding factor. But she got nowhere with the Gunleys.

'Ada always liked her own way,' said Aunt Bessie Gunley; 'stubborn as they come.'

'Yep; independent as a hog on ice,' agreed Noble Gunley, a second cousin in the hardware business.

They appeared to glory in Mrs Gall's defiance of the entrenched powers of the medical world; she had died as she lived, a Gunley through and through.

Pastor Beamis did not extend himself at the funeral as much as he could have wished, but he respected the desire, put to him strongly by Alice and Monica in their different ways, for conservatism. He was conservative, by his lights. He prayed for the family, in turn and by name, and managed to give Almighty God an excellent capsule account of Monica's high associations abroad. He spoke eloquently of the late Mrs Gall, informing a somewhat surprised group of listeners that she had been open-handed, devout, courageous, a lifelong lover of all that was beautiful (this tied in neatly with his prayerful reference to Monica) and a constant source of inspiration to himself in his pastoral work. Accompanied by Mrs Beamis on the piano, and his son Wesley on the vibraphone, he sang *Swinging Through the Gates of the New Jerusalem*. But by comparison with some of his more unbuttoned efforts, it was conservative.

Chuck Proby's boss did not come, after all. He sent the head accountant, as the most suitable person to represent the august entity of The Bank at the funeral of the mother-in-law of a promising, but still junior, employee. The Bridgetower Trust was represented by Dean Knapp, who declined Pastor Beamis' pressing invitation to sit on the platform, but who behaved himself beautifully, even when his sensibilities were most outraged, and spoke with real Christian kindness to the Gall family afterward.

Not that Alfred Gall noticed who spoke to him. The light which, however it may have appeared to the outside world, had been sufficient to fill his life, had gone out, and he was in darkness. All through the funeral he sat like a man carved in wood.

Alice wept copiously. She had a valuable talent for allowing her grief free play when it was most wanted, and suppressing it at need. But, certainly in her own estimation, at least, she wept in the same spirit as Dean Knapp prayed at her mother's funeral – sincerely, but not as a Thirteener.

Monica lacked Alice's ability to present her feelings suitably. She had wept for her mother at the time of her death. At the funeral she found herself lifted up by a wave of emotion which she knew to be optimistic, and which at first she thought was relief that the long ordeal was over at last. But as Beamis prayed, she heard the inner voice, speaking this time not as her mother or as Giles, but in a voice which might have been her own, and it said: *You are free. You did your best for her, and now you are free. You will never have to worry about what you can tell her, or what would hurt her, again.*

[SEVEN]

The day after the funeral Monica found herself in a disordered and neglected house which she was apparently expected to put in order, and keep indefinitely for her widowed father. It was plain that Alice meant to do nothing, and Aunt Ellen had her job. She made a beginning, and quickly tired of it. Doing domestic work for Revelstoke was one thing; this was a very different matter. Should she call in a cleaning-woman? No, that would be unwise on several counts. It would encourage the family to think that she had cash in hand, and in reality she was very short; she had left all she could spare with Revelstoke. It would also defer the time when some permanent arrangement was made for Mr Gall, and that was pressing; she wanted to get back to London as soon as she could. She must be diplomatic.

Her new position in the family, that of the moneyed daughter, made diplomacy easier than she had foreseen. It was so easy, indeed, to persuade her father to fall in with her suggestions that she was a little ashamed of herself, and of him. At a family council she made it clear that she must return to London; much depended on it, she said. She meant *The Golden Asse*, but did not say so. The family, assuming as people without money are wont to do, that all the affairs of moneyed people concern money, agreed. How was Dad going to manage? To everyone's surprise, Dad himself had a plan; Alice and Chuck and little Donald should move in with him. Alice was quick to quash that proposal.

'Three generations in one house never works,' said she. 'You see it everywhere. I think it'll be far better if every tub stands on its own bottom.'

After much beating about the bush it was finally agreed that Miss Gall should give up her pretty little house, and move in with her brother. That was what Monica wanted; that was, indeed, what she had decided to arrange. But it hurt her, nevertheless, that Miss Gall had to be the sacrifice. Aunt Ellen was the only one of them who was not toadying to her because of her supposed riches; that good woman was simply and extravagantly proud of Monica because she was gaining a place in the world as a singer, and she would have laid her head on the executioner's block without complaint, if thereby she could have advanced her niece's career.

Still, now that Ma was dead, it was possible to confide more fully in Aunt Ellen, and Monica spent many nights in the pretty, crowded sitting-room of her aunt's house, where she had learned her first lessons in music. She sang for Miss Gall; she sang Revelstoke's songs to her, which Aunt Ellen did not really like, but which filled her with pride none the less. She sang the folk-songs and the songs in an older musical idiom which she had learned from Molloy, and these delighted the little woman. She said, quite truly, that she had never heard anything so fine before. And when Monica asked Aunt Ellen's advice about her programme for the Bridgetower Recital, her cup was full and brimming over. This, at last, was the real musical life!

For there was to be a Bridgetower Recital. The members of the Trust had advanced the idea very delicately, fearing that Monica might be too prostrated with grief at the death of her mother to sing for some months. They were surprised, but gratified, by the resilience of her spirits. Yes, she said, she would be happy to sing for any audience they chose to assemble. Yes, she thought that Fallon Hall, at Waverley University, would be an excellent place for a recital. No, she was not in the least dubious about filling it with her voice; she had sung in the Sheldonian Theatre, and at Wigmore Hall, and size did not alarm her. Certainly, she would plan a programme in the course of a few days. The question of mourning? Well, would it not be possible to include in her programme a short group of songs of a devotional nature? She would like to do so, as a form of memorial to her mother. The Trust thought this most suitable and proper, and were delighted with her for thinking of it.

Miss Puss was particularly pleased by the whole notion of the recital. Indeed, she revealed a romantic strain in her character which the others had not suspected, but which came out clearly at a meeting held, with Monica present, to discuss all the details of the great affair.

'There is a point which I wish to raise,' said Miss Puss, positively blushing, 'which may seem – I hardly know how to phrase it – fanciful to you gentlemen, and which may at first seem strange to our protégée, Miss Gall. It has long been the custom of singers, when embarking upon their careers, to choose a name for professional use – a *nom de guerre*. The instances of Melba and Nordica arise at once to mind; Melba was Helen Mitchell – an honourable but scarcely inspiring title – and Nordica was Lillian Norton. Nor must we forget our own dear Marie Lajeunesse, which we shall certainly not do if we think of her as Madame Albani. They chose names, you see, which were remarkable for euphony, and ease of recollection. Mind you, I do not say that a name with a certain, well, asperity about it is a barrier to success. Who has forgotten Minnie Hauk? Well – I put it to you, Minnie Hauk! But the exception in this case strengthens the rule. Consider the great Yendik – born Kidney! Well, you will have gathered by now what I am driving at. Our dear Monica – (Monica's eyes opened to their uttermost to learn that she was dear to Miss Puss, but she was becoming inured to surprises) – has a lovely Christian name. But Gall? A name honoured in Ireland, certainly, but is it quite the thing for the concert platform? Can one imagine it on posters, programmes? Can we be of assistance in finding something more suitable – more euphonious and easily memorable? I confess that I have pondered over this matter a good deal during the past few days, and what I want to suggest' – and here Miss Puss positively glowed – 'is that the forthcoming recital would be a most suitable place for the assumption of a new name. And the name I propose – a name compounded of parts of Monica and Gall, a sort of anagram – is Gallica.'

Up from the depths of Monica's memory floated the name of Monique Gallo; how long ago that was – more than two years! How she had changed.

'It is wonderfully kind of you, and I can't tell you how much I appreciate your thoughtfulness,' said she, 'but I think, all things considered, I had better keep my own name. You see, I have sung twice for the BBC as Monica Gall, and I have sung at Wigmore Hall in a recital of new work by Giles Revelstoke, which attracted a good deal of attention. I have sung for Sir Benedict under my own name, as well; so perhaps it would be a mistake to change it now, just when it is beginning to be known.'

How oily I am getting, she thought. That sounded just like Giles imitating somebody he despised.

Aunt Puss was quick to swallow her words.

'I had no desire to seem arbitrary or intrusive,' said she; 'I only wished to draw attention to a recognized professional custom.'

'I think it is a custom which is falling into disuse,' said Solly.

'That may not be entirely a good thing,' said the Dean. 'A career in art must often mean great changes in personality – much abandoned in the past, and much learned. I've sometimes thought we might all be the better for taking new names when we discover our vocations.' He looked kindly at Miss Puss, who was flustered and cast down. One of the few flashes of romance in her life had been quenched.

Poor old chook, thought Monica. She wants to make something;

she wants to create, and Gallica would be in some measure her creation. She would be particularly nice to Miss Puss when the meeting was over, to salve the wound.

It was at this meeting that Monica was told of the substantial sum of money which the Trust had on hand, and which was legally hers. It was Mr Snelgrove who explained it to her, and when he reached the point where he had to say that she could have it and do as she pleased with it he could hardly bring the words to his lips. As a lawyer he knew what the position was, and in that capacity he had been urging the Trust to get the money off its hands; but Mr Snelgrove was also a man – a dry, conservative, stuffily prudent, snobbish old man – and the thought of turning over so much money to a girl of very common background, who might commit the Lord only knew what follies with it, deeply shocked him. Nor was he without heart; the sight of young Solomon Bridgetower sitting in what ought to be his own house, looking as though he had bitten a lemon, while this strange girl was given money which might have been his, hurt Mr Snelgrove's sense of justice – which a life devoted to the practice of the law had not wholly eroded away. But at last Mr Snelgrove was done with his humming and hawing, and his meaning was clear.

'Of course I am very much surprised,' said Monica, 'and more than ever grateful to the late Mrs Bridgetower. You need have no fear that the money will be wasted, or frittered away in trivial spending. Indeed, I can tell you now that I should not dream of using it for purely personal benefit. With your approval, I should like to use a small part of it – a few hundred dollars – to settle my mother's funeral expenses. I shall pay it back as soon as I am able, out of my own earnings. The remainder will be used exclusively for musical purposes of which I shall give you a full account when the time comes.'

She spoke soberly, but her heart was singing. From the minute she understood the drift of Mr Snelgrove's harangue, she knew precisely what she was going to do with that money. It would be more than enough to close the gap between what the Association for English Opera could afford to spend in producing *The Golden Asse*, and what was necessary to do the job properly, and with a decent margin for unexpected needs. She would now be able to make it possible for Giles to take a giant step in his career, and she could do it decently, without robbery, padding of expenses, and selling second-hand clothes. Like many people when they suddenly get their own way, she saw the hand of God in it. But she was not so lost to discretion as to talk of her plan to the Trust, until she actually had the money.

The Trustees were somewhat surprised, and the Dean at least was relieved, that she did not take the news of her windfall in a frivolous or greedy spirit. They badly wanted to know what she was going to do, but pride forbade them to ask. So they passed on to a discussion of the invitations to the Bridgetower Recital. For of course it was to be an invitation affair, and they meant to get the utmost possible glory out of it for themselves. Glory was all that they stood to get from the Bridgetower Trust, and having parted, though vicariously, with $45,000 they badly felt the need of something in return.

[EIGHT]

The period during which Monica was preparing herself for the recital was enlivened for the whole British Commonwealth, and several millions of interested people in the USA, by what was known as the Odingsels Obscenity Scandal. Odo Odingsels, described to Monica's astonishment and private amusement as 'a fashionable Mayfair photographer', was arrested on charges of selling, at very high prices and to a small but constant clientele, indecent photographs of men and women highly placed in society and politics. The nature of these photographs, the newspapers said, was of an obscenity to astonish the most hardened libertine, for not merely were they filthy in themselves but they brought into disrepute people for whom the whole world had the utmost respect and affection. The man Odingsels was plainly a criminal lunatic of horrifying depravity; employing models sufficiently like his subjects (though as a usual thing younger and more pleasingly formed) he put the heads of the victims on them by brilliant photographic trickery, employing photographs purchased from news agencies and portrait photographers. The newspapers dwelt with well-simulated horror on the lifelike and astonishing effects which this perverse combination of artistry and technique produced. The Old Bailey had been cleared while the jury examined the monster's work, and the Judge had admonished them to secrecy. Nevertheless, it was said on sufficient authority that European Royalty, British Royalty, the White House – nay, the very Vatican itself – were spattered.

Ransacking its recollection for some yardstick of enormity to apply, the press came up, not very appositely, with the Oscar Wilde case, and a bright young journalist, remembering that Wilde had once lived in Tite Street, made great play with the fact that Odingsels frequently 'resorted' there, to the editorial offices of a publication called *Lantern*, run by a Chelsea group which was made out to be as unsavoury as the laws of libel would permit. Another point of similarity with the Wilde affair was that Odingsels showed no proper dismay in the dock, but grinned and sometimes laughed outright when evidence was given that he had received as much as one hundred guineas for a single exclusive print.

Odo's counsel, a celebrated silk, attempted to defend him on the ground that many of his ingenious photographs, representing celebrated figures in world affairs, were essentially political in subject, and satiric in intent. They were, he said, the modern counterparts of the vigorous, sometimes savage, and often suggestive political caricatures of Rowlandson and Gilray. He created a sensation in court when he produced a list of Odingsels' clients and began to read it; extraordinary as it seemed, some of the photographer's victims were themselves purchasers of obscene portraits of other eminent people. The Judge did not permit the reading of the list to go far, but read it himself, declared it to be, for the present, irrelevant, and no more was heard of it. But the eminent silk had read enough to set the newspapers buzzing; it was, Fleet Street agreed, the liveliest thing since the great hue and cry after homosexuals a few months before. Leaders appeared under such headings as 'Curiosa In High Places'. Much was made of the fact that the learned Judge, after looking through a portfolio of Odingsels' work, said, 'These things would make a vulture gag.' He also said that the models who lent themselves to the production of such filth should be discovered and dealt with appropriately.

'Thank God for Bun Eccles,' said Monica, drinking this in with her breakfast coffee, 'or I might have to stay here for a few months. I wonder if they'll get Perse? A girl with as many moles as she has oughtn't to be hard to identify – but the slops can't strip every tart in London, matching up shapes.' – From which it may be seen that Monica did not phrase her private thoughts as elegantly as she did her speeches to the Bridgetower Trustees. – 'I wonder who I would have been the body of, if I'd gone to him? I always knew he was no good. I just hope Giles has enough sense not to try to go to his rescue by appearing as a character witness, or something.'

For five days the wonder raged, and at last a shuddering smudge appeared in the newspapers which was described as a radio-photograph of Odo Odingsels being escorted from the Central Criminal Court by twelve police, while a crowd of five hundred angry women tried to slaughter him with umbrellas and rotten vegetables. His offence was such a strange one, and the law relating to it so various and confused, that the best the Judge was able to do for him was to send him to prison for five years, three of which were to be spent in hard labour.

Much was made during the trial of the unsavouriness of Odingsels' appearance; the Judge and the newspapers were at one in agreeing that his outward form was the true mirror of his soul. Monica and everyone else learned that the type of mange from which he suffered was called *alopecia areata*, and everywhere harmless, afflicted citizens wrote to the papers protesting that this ailment was not a mark of turpitude. But the Odingsels Obscenity Scandal vanished as suddenly as it came.

There were two days when the name of *Lantern* was prominent in the news, and when people who had never seen a copy were writing of it as a scabrous and scruffy publication, when she had to be very firm with herself, to keep from sending a cable of warning advice to Giles. But she knew how furiously he would resent such interference; three or four weeks in Canada, domineering over her relatives, had awakened her considerable talent for bossiness, but she must not use it on Giles. Of late his touchiness had reached new heights; hard work on *The Golden Asse* raised his spirits, but drove him to new excesses of freakishness. And so much of it was directed against Stanhope Aspinwall! The critic had been favourable but pernickety in his judgement of *Kubla Khan* when it was broadcast; Monica was inclined to think well of him because he had written of her singing in terms of warm praise . . . 'an artist still somewhat tentative in her approach but plainly possessed of uncommon abilities . . . combines vocal qualities usually considered to be mutually exclusive – extreme agility and brilliance in the upper register with a warm and expressive tone . . . a purity of English pronunciation and delicate interpretation of poetic nuance which recalls the late Kathleen Ferrier'. Monica had suggested to Giles that, as he had taught her all she knew, this praise was for him, but he would not hear of it. 'All these old critics go ga-ga about a new girl if she isn't a positive gargoyle,' he had said, and had raged on about Aspinwall's criticism of the piano part of the cantata as unduly elaborated. And when, a few weeks later, Giles had given a recital of his work at Wigmore Hall, and Aspinwall had once again praised her warmly, and found some faults in the music, Giles became quite impossible.

He had procured a picture of Aspinwall (through Odingsels, it was now unpleasant to remember), had framed it and hung it in the water-closet which was one flight downstairs from his own apartment. He made a point of using the paper for which Aspinwall wrote in order to wrap his garbage; he bought several copies every week, cut out Aspinwall's signed articles, and hung them in the water-closet, as a substitute for the toilet roll, though Mrs Klein and the other lodgers objected strongly. On one embarrassing occasion he took Monica to a concert and, finding that they were sitting behind Aspinwall (which he swore he had not arranged) he badgered the critic by tapping on the back of his seat, and making insulting remarks, just loud enough to be heard, in the intervals. He even began to write obscenely abusive letters to Aspinwall, but Monica and Bun Eccles intercepted them, and so far as they could judge, none had escaped their watch.

'Pay no attention,' Bun had said when she confided her worry to him; 'old Giles is a genius, and when he's working at full steam he gets ratty. Some of the things he does are a bit crook, Monny, but he's sound as the bank – too right he is. Wait'll he gets the opera done, then you'll see.'

Well, she thought, the first thing is to get the opera done, and hope Aspinwall likes it. So she cabled Giles that the money difficulty was settled, explained it in detail in a letter, and worked even harder for the Bridgetower Recital.

[NINE]

When the day came Monica's nervousness, as always, took the form of depression, a sense of unworthiness, and a fear not of failure but of a spiritless mediocrity. By now she had some experience of this state, and recent reflection had convinced her that it was part of her heritage from Ma; her imagination, and her ups and downs of feeling, were Ma's. Well, she must not let them dominate her life, as they had dominated the life of Mrs Gall.

But it is one thing to reason with depression, and another to lift it. All day she was gloomy. She had procured invitations for her own friends. Would Kevin and Alex draw attention to themselves in some unsuitable way? Would George Medwall, with whom she had had two or three brief, uneasy conversations, come at all, and would it bother her if she could not see him in the audience? The Canadian Broadcasting Corporation had asked to make a tape-recording of part of the concert; was that going to mean a microphone to fix her with its disapproving, steely face, somewhere directly in her view? Why, she wondered, did anyone want to be a singer?

Did she indeed want to be a singer? What singer whom she knew did she admire? In her present mood she could think of none. Singers! The creatures of a physical talent, constantly fussing about draughts in spite of their horse-like health – conscious that their voices might drop a tone if the room were too hot. Evelyn Burnaby, with whom she now had some acquaintance, and whom she admired as an artist – did she really want to be like Evelyn? So dull, except when she sang.

And Ludwiga Kressel – a genuine *diva*, that one, to whom Domdaniel had introduced her after a performance at Covent Garden. Ludwiga had dominated the party, a powerful, brass-haired woman, with a sense of humour as heavy as her own tread. She had compelled them all to silence while she told them of her experiences with the stage director at the Metropolitan. She had been unable to continue, convulsed by her own fun, yet protesting through her big-throated laughter, 'However funny I am I cannot be so funny as Graf.' She had got to the Metropolitan because she had previously secured an engagement in Vienna. 'Byng is impressed by Vienna, but Vienna is nothing, nothing at all.' Did she want to think like Ludwiga, who talked endlessly of 'concertizing' and 'recitalizing'? Did she want to live like Ludwiga, whose ferocious schedule of plane travel made it possible for her to cram the greatest possible number of appearances – operatic and concert – into a single season? No, no; not like Ludwiga.

By six o'clock she was in the depths, and wanted a drink more than anything else. No – obviously not more than anything else, for a drink was easily within her reach; Kevin and Alex had been discreetly keeping her modest needs supplied. But a drink before a concert might disturb her voice, so it was out of the question for her to have one. She knew very well, as she denied herself, that she was by that abnegation settling her shoulders to the singer's yoke.

The recital was to be at half-past eight, and well before eight she was entering the artist's door of Fallon Hall. The artist's door, in this case, simply meant the entrance to a poky little room, piled half-full with folded wooden chairs and ferociously over-heated by steam coils, at one side of the stage. But this was what an 'artist's door' meant in her native land – not the mysterious and somewhat furtive side-doors which led to stages in England, nor the glorious, lamplit courtyard which led to the stage entrance of the Paris Opera; she entered Fallon Hall itself by just the same door as the public used; for after all, what had an artist to conceal, or what marked him off from the general public? Nothing, of course; nothing but a world of dedication.

Having failed to open a window, or find a janitor to do it for her, Monica was fearful that she might take cold even before her concert. The air was hot and dry, so she went into the corridor, and at last found another room, dark and not so hot, where faculty meetings were held, and here she concealed herself until five minutes before the concert was to begin.

Her accompanist, Humphrey Cobbler, had not yet arrived, and Monica worried furiously. But with a minute to spare he appeared, much rumpled and utterly unpressed, but in evening clothes and plainly in very good spirits. During rehearsals she had learned to know and like Humphrey very much, and so now she was able to speak sharply to him about his lateness.

'But I'm not late,' said he, smiling indulgently. 'You don't suppose they'll get going before eight forty-five? My dear, the nobility and gentry, the beauty and chivalry, not to mention the money and the stretched credit, of Salterton are assembling to hear you. You can smell the moth-balls and the bunny coats away back here if you sniff. And it's all for you. Don't fuss; glory in it.'

'I can't glory. I think I'm going to be sick. Oh, Humphrey, this scares me far worse than the BBC, or anything I've ever done.'

'But why?'

'Because it's my home town, that's why. You couldn't understand. You're an Englishman; you haven't got Salterton in your bones; you didn't grow up with those people out there meaning the larger world to you. So far as they know me at all, they know me as a stenographer at the Glue Works. And right now that's exactly what I feel like.'

'Listen, poppet, it's very charming of you to love your home town, but now is the time to put that love in its proper place – which is right outside Fallon Hall, in a snowbank. Salterton can't be your measure of success or failure; what you think are its standards are just the standards of childhood and provincialism. You've been away long enough to recognize that your home town is not only the Rome and the Athens of your early life, but also in many important ways a remote, God-forsaken dump. Those people out there are just provincial professors, and bankers, and wholesale druggists who want to be proud of you if you give them half a chance, but who will just as readily take any opportunity you give them to keep you down. Now: don't try to dominate them; you're not a lion-tamer. Go out on the platform and do what your teachers have told you, and what you know to be right and best, and pay no heed to them at all, except when courtesy – the high courtesy of the artist – demands it. We'll walk up and down this corridor, you and I, taking deep but not hysterical breaths, until the head usher tells us that all the bunny coats are in their seats. Come on, Monica: head forward and up, back long and easy, and – what does Molloy say? – breathe the muhd.'

[TEN]

The first part of the Recital was over, and Cobbler returned Monica to the Faculty Room, shut the door and guarded it from outside. It had gone well. That is, she knew that she had sung well, and the audience, after a rather watchful beginning, was prepared to like her.

It was true, as Cobbler had said when she first discussed her programme with him, that she was giving them something tough to chew. But – 'It's a fine programme,' he had said, 'and I'm delighted you're getting away from that fathead notion that music must always be performed in the chronological order of its composition. The audience here has had a thorough Community Concerts training; they'll be expecting you to start off with a Classical Group, putting your voice through its hardest paces while it's still cold and before you've really got the feel of the hall or the audience, and then a group of Lieder, to show that you know German, and a French group, to show that you know French, and then a Contemporary Group, consisting entirely of second-rank Americans, and topping off with a Popular Group, in which you really let your hair down and show how vulgar and folksy you can be. But this makes sense.'

The programme was prepared on a principle which she had learned from Giles; not the chronology of composers, but a line of poetic meaning, was the cord on which the beads were strung. And so she had begun with Schubert's *An die Musik*, and after that noble apostrophe she plunged straight into Giles' own *Kubla Khan* which was certainly tough chewing for a Salterton audience, as it took fifteen minutes to perform and without being in the mode of what Cobbler called 'wrong-note modernism' was written in an idiom both contemporary and individual to the composer. Then, as relief, she had sung a group of folksongs of the British Isles as she had learned them from Molloy. The folksongs had stirred the audience to its first real enthusiasm, for they all felt themselves competent judges of such seeming simplicity.

Now an interval, and then a group of three songs which the audience was asked, in a note on the programme, not to applaud. These were the songs which Monica intended as her memorial to her mother. The oak coffin, the five black Buicks at the funeral, and the red granite tombstone, like a chunk of petrified potted meat, which Dad and Alice wanted, were trash. But in these songs she would take her farewell of Ada Gall.

First would be Thomas Campion's *Never weather-beaten Saile*. She would follow it with Brahms' *Auf dem Kirchhofe*, and if anyone thought it gloomy – well, let them think. And last, Purcell's *Evening Hymn*, noble and serene setting of William Fuller's words. Would any who had known Ma – Dad, for instance, or Aunt Ellen – find the reflection of her spirit which Monica believed to lie in these songs? During the night-watches at her bedside, Monica had thought much about Ma, and about herself. They were, as Ma had said in her last fully rational utterances, much alike. For in Ma, when she told tall stories, when she rasped her family with rough, sardonic jokes, when she rebelled against the circumstances of her life in coarse abuse, and when she cut through the fog of nonsense with the beam of her insight, was an artist – a spoiled artist, one who had never made anything, who was unaware of the nature or genesis of her own discontent, but who nevertheless possessed the artist's temperament; in her that temperament, misunderstood, denied and gone sour, had become a poison which had turned against the very sources of life itself. Nevertheless, she was like Ma, and she must not go astray as Ma – not wholly through her own fault – had gone. In these songs she would sing of the spirit which might have been her mother's if circumstances had been otherwise. Alice had not hesitated to say that she had killed their mother by giving in to her wilfulness. Well, it was not true; what was best in her mother should live on, and find expression, in her.

Monica had often heard of singers losing awareness of themselves while facing an audience – of losing the audience, and existing for that time only in their music. She had never quite believed it. But that was her own experience while she sang the three songs which she had, in her own mind, set aside as a memorial to her mother. She was back in the Faculty Room before she emerged from that inner calm. Humphrey Cobbler kissed her on the cheek and – sure sign in him of strong feeling – said not a word, but left her to herself.

Her tribute offered and her final peace made with the spirit, not departed but strongly present, Monica found the remainder of her recital pleasant and, all things considered, easy. She sang a group of settings of poems by John Clare, Thomas Lovell Beddoes and Walter de la Mare which Giles had written for her, and their sombre beauty led the hearers out of the memorial atmosphere which had been created, and left them ready for Berlioz' *Nuits d'été*, and the final group of songs, which was four Shakespeare lyrics, in settings by Purcell and Thomas Augustine Arne, which Giles had arranged from the gnomic and scanty original accompaniments. The audience had made up its mind after the memorial songs that it liked Monica – liked her very much and was proud of her – and the applause as she left the stage was warm, and mounting. There were even a few greatly daring, un-Canadian cries of 'Bravo!' which Monica attributed, rightly, to Kevin and Alex.

'Sticking to plan?' said Cobbler.

'Yes; go back on the crest of the applause, and one good encore,' said Monica. This was a piece of practical wisdom from Domdaniel; Giles hated encores because they disturbed the shape of his programmes; Molloy believed in singing as long as one delighted listener remained in the hall; the balance lay with Sir Benedict.

So, as the applause mounted for fifty seconds, until there was actually some stamping – stamping in Fallon Hall, and from a stiff-shirt audience at that! – Monica remained out of sight, judging the sound. And when it seemed to her that it would go no higher, she returned to the stage, amid a really gratifying uproar. Ushers moved forward with flowers; a large and uncompromising bunch from the Bridgetower Trustees, a very handsome bunch from Kevin and Alex, a bouquet containing a card which read, 'With Love and Pride from the Old Heart and Hope Quartet' (which made Monica blush momentarily, for she had havered a little about inviting the Beamises) and two or three others. Cobbler, greatly enjoying the fun, for such recitals did not often come his way, helped her to pile them all on top of the piano, and she sang her single encore.

'Never sing below your weight in an encore; try to do something you haven't done earlier in the evening; and try to sing something they'll like but probably haven't heard before.' These were the words of Domdaniel, talking to her about public appearances several months before. So Monica had determined to sing Thomas Augustine Arne's *Water Parted*.

It was a song which she deeply loved, though Giles laughed at her for it. '"May this be my poison if my bear ever dances but to the very genteelest of tunes – *Water Parted*, or the minuet in *Ariadne*",' he would say, to her mystification, until one night when he had taken her to the Old Vic to see *She Stoops to Conquer*, and had nudged her sharply when the line was spoken. But he had prepared an accompaniment for it, for her special use, and had set it in a key which made the best use of what he called her 'chalumeau register', as well as the brilliance of her upper voice.

Water parted from the sea
May increase the river's tide –
To the bubbling fount may flee,
Or thro' fertile valleys glide.

Tho' in search of lost repose
Thro' the land 'tis free to roam,
Still it murmurs as it flows
Panting for its native home.

She sang it very well, though this was the first time she had ever sung it in public. She sang it as well, perhaps, as she ever sang it in her life, though in later years her name was to be much associated with it, and audiences were to demand it in and out of season. She performed that feat, given to gifted singers, of making the song seem better than it was, of bringing to it a personal significance which was not inherent in it. But Monica always protested that the song was great in itself, and that she merely revealed in it what had gone unnoticed by others, too hasty to make a personal appraisal of a song by a composer usually dismissed as not really first-rate. She was already, under Revelstoke's guidance, developing a faculty of finding worth where others had missed it, and this was to give her repertoire a quality which was the despair of her rivals.

But there, in Fallon Hall, she sang *Water Parted* for the first time, and lifted her audience to an even greater pitch of enthusiasm.

'I think we may call it a triumph,' whispered Humphrey Cobbler, as they bowed again and again.

[ELEVEN]

'An undoubted triumph!' cried Miss Puss Pottinger, as Monica was led by Cobbler into the Bridgetower home. The house was full of people – more people than had been in it since Mrs Bridgetower's funeral – and they all appeared to be in that state of excitement which follows a really satisfactory artistic achievement. Their excitement varied, of course. There were those who talked of the concert, and there were those who talked of politics and the stock market; but all their talk was a little more vivacious, or vehement, or pontifical because of what they had experienced; music had performed its ever-new magical trick of strengthening and displaying whatever happened to be the dominant trait in them.

But Cobbler knew his work too well to allow Monica to be snatched from him. With the technique of a professional bodyguard he guided her to the stairway, rushed her up it, and into the little second-floor sitting-room where Solly and Veronica were waiting with food and drink.

Singers must eat, and there have been those among them who have eaten too much. As amorousness is the pastime of players of stringed instruments, and horse-racing the relaxation of the brass section of the orchestra, so eating is the pleasure, and sometimes the vice, of singers. After a performance, a singer must be fed before he or she can be turned loose among their admirers, or else somebody may be insulted, or even bitten. Cobbler had told Veronica that Monica would need something substantial, and preferably hot. So, in the upstairs sitting-room, a dish of chops and green peas, a salad, a plate of fruit and a half-bottle of Beaune were in readiness.

As Monica devoured them gratefully – for she had eaten nothing since mid-day, and had taken only a glass of milk at five o'clock – a close observer might have thought that even more than a meal had been prepared. When Solly had given Cobbler a drink, he said that they really must go and talk to their guests, and led the accompanist away, leaving Monica and Veronica alone.

Veronica was a poor diplomat, and she had small relish for the task before her; but she had undertaken it on behalf of her husband, and she decided that the best thing was to jump in with both feet, and get it over.

'Monica – I hope you don't mind me calling you Monica – Solly and I want to ask a favour of you. A large favour, and it isn't easy to ask.

But – we're terribly hard up. And we wondered if you could possibly lend us some money.'

Monica looked up, not appearing to best advantage with her mouth full. This was one development she had not foreseen.

'I know it must seem strange to you, but I suppose you have heard about the conditions of my mother-in-law's will?'

Monica shook her head. 'Not a whisper,' said she.

'You must be one of the few people who hasn't heard something. But of course you've been out of the country. Still, I thought your – some of your relatives might have written to you about it. It seems to us – to Solly and me – that everyone knows about it. Well, it's complicated, but it comes to this; the Trust which supports you has all Mrs Bridgetower's money for its funds. When she died, my husband was left one hundred dollars, and that was all. It was a blow; I know you'll understand that. But it wasn't as though he was free. The money may come to him; it will come to him if we have a male child. Had you not heard anything of that?'

'Nothing,' said Monica, and felt suddenly cold in the warm little room.

'Yes. If we have a male child, the Trust automatically ends. But till that time all the money goes to you. We had a child, you know – you didn't? – well, we had a son, but he was born dead. It was a sore disappointment. Not wholly, or even mostly, because of the money but – you do understand, don't you? We don't hold ill-will against you. After all, it might have been somebody else – anybody with talent. But we're chained to this house, which costs a terrible lot to keep up, even when the Trust undertakes to keep it in repair. And my husband is still only a lecturer, and even with Summer School fees, and what he can get by writing now and then for the radio, and so forth, we can't keep our heads above water. We're not merely broke; we're terribly in debt. Now, of course Solly knows that the Trust has just made over $45,000 of surplus funds to you. – I hate saying this, but under other circumstances that would have been our money. I'm asking if you could let us have ten thousand, to tide us over?'

Monica looked, but could not speak.

'You see, we have hopes. We hope for another child. But suppose it isn't a boy? Suppose there is never another boy? I don't want to let myself talk about my mother-in-law, but it's so cruel! If we could get free of the house, we might snap our fingers at the whole thing, but we can't – at least we haven't quite gone so far as to sacrifice all hopes in order to get out of this net. And meanwhile – you understand, don't you, that I'm talking to you as a friend, and I'm not trying to wring your heart, really I'm not – I only want you to know how things are – our marriage is being twisted out of shape. Solly is a drudge, and I'm a baby-factory, bound to go on and on, until we have a son. It's a horrible vengeance – because she hated me – because I took her son –'

Veronica was not a weeping woman, but her mute distress was more terrible to another woman than tears could be.

Oh God, thought Monica, if only I had enough sense not to always tell everything I know! I've told Giles I've got $45,000, or close to it, when the funeral's paid for, and that's what he'll be counting on. If I go back with less – I couldn't explain it to him, ever. These people wouldn't be real to him. Nothing's real to him except the opera, and I'm real because I've been able to support him while he wrote it, and can help to pay to get it on.

But what can I tell Veronica? Tell her that an artistic venture demands every cent of this money, when she and her husband think of it as theirs? What could a plan like that mean to people who are in this sort of mess? Tell her my lover must have every penny I can get, like a tart giving her earnings to her pimp, for fear of a black eye? How real would Giles seem to them? What can I say?

The silence between them was more than either woman could bear, and it was Veronica who broke it.

'It would be a loan, of course, a matter of business – we wouldn't dream of asking more than that. I mean, we'd have to arrange a rate of interest; we wouldn't expect you to lose by it.'

Monica was frozen with discomfiture and pity, but she could not find anything to say. Veronica could not be silent, now; anything was better than silence. She continued:

'I know, of course, that what I'm asking you to do is quite illegal. Solly has tried to get loans out of the funds from Mr Snelgrove, and it can't be done. If you let us have some money, we might all end in jail, I suppose. Or at best it would look terrible if anyone found out.'

Monica had to speak.

'I wouldn't care how illegal it was, if I could help you,' said she. 'I just can't. There's a very good reason – I swear to you that it's a good reason – why I can't, but at present I'm unable to explain it. I will explain as soon as I can, and as fully as possible. But you must believe that it isn't greed, or stinginess, or because I don't admire you and your husband very much, and want you to think well of me. But I can't do it.'

'I thought that would be your answer,' said Veronica, without rancour; 'Solly said you had spoken of a plan of some sort to the Trustees. But you see that I had to try, don't you?'

The noise of the party mounted to them, and Solly came to fetch his wife and Monica. A quick glance told him what he most wanted to know, and he did not allow his obligatory high spirits, as host, to flag. To lose all hope is, in a way, to be free, and it often brings with it a lightening of mood. Downstairs they went, into a sea of compliments, of enthusiasm, of success.

Much later, as Monica lay in her bed, she thought of the party with satisfaction, and yet somewhat remotely. It had been the occasion for an outlet of the enthusiasm which her recital had evoked, and which had not expended itself in the applause at Fallon Hall. She had done her duty. She had tried at first to bring Dad into the circle of enthusiasm; he had appreciated her solicitude, but it was doubtful if he really knew any more about the affair than that Monny had, in some mysterious way, made a hit with these big-bugs. It was not that he was stupid; he was dim, remote and, since the death of his wife, only partly alive. Aunt Ellen was quite different; it was not at all hard to find people for her to talk to; Cobbler had been very good to her. Alex and Kevin, astonishingly assured and competent at a party far above their accustomed welkin, had been kind about looking after Dad.

For Monica had not been able to do so. Everybody wanted to talk to her. One or two had liked *Kubla Khan*, and said so; some had spoken very kindly about the songs sung in memory of Mrs Gall. But *Water Parted* seemed to have impressed everybody.

Yet what strange things they found in it! 'I wish I knew what was in your mind when you sang that!' Over and over again she heard that comment, differently phrased. Many, as soon as they had said it, gave her their notion of what the song had meant to her. A surprising number took it as a song of nostalgia for Canada, cherished by her during her exile abroad – an idea which had never entered her head. Some were convinced that it was a love-song.

What did it mean to her? It meant what *Hiraeth* meant to Ceinwen Griffiths – a longing for what was perhaps unattainable in this world, a longing for a fulfilment which was of the spirit and not of the flesh, but which was not specifically religious in its yearning. It meant her surge of feeling at the tomb of St Geneviève. It meant the aspiration toward that from which she drew her strength, and to which she returned when the concerns of daily life were set aside. It was the condition of being which lay beyond the Monica Gall who bossed Dad and Aunt Ellen into living together, who quarrelled and lost her dignity with her sister Alice, who spoke in honeyed words to the Bridgetower Trustees, who denied poor Veronica Bridgetower the money which might deliver her from a hateful bondage, who cheated and scraped for Giles Revelstoke, and endured all his whims in return for his absent-minded and occasional affection. It lay through, but beyond, the world of music to which she was now committed – the singer's bondage which tonight had so plainly shown to be hers. It was the yearning which had been buried in the heart of her mother, denied and thwarted but there, forever alive and demanding. It was a yearning toward all the vast, inexplicable, irrational treasury from which her life drew whatever meaning and worth it possessed. It was the yearning for –? As Ceinwen's song had said, not all the wise men in the world could ever tell her, but it would last until the end.

[TWELVE]

'I trust that you will not think that I have acted unwisely, but that is what has been done with the large sum of money which you made over to me in February. I hope that the enclosed reports will persuade you that it has been well spent.' Thus ran part of Monica's letter to the Bridgetower Trustees, which Mr Snelgrove read to them at a meeting held in the following May.

'I'm sure Mother would have been greatly surprised to know that she had partly financed the production of a new opera,' said Solly, and the others could only agree.

And such an opera! The criticisms which Monica had enclosed were all agreed that it was an extraordinary work, containing flashes of genius, but freakish in the extreme. That the principal tenor should have been transmuted into an ass, by sorcery, was part of the story. But that he should bray – musically, of course, but still undoubtedly braying – for the whole of the middle act, was certainly hard to swallow. Part of the audience had refused to take it seriously as a musical work, and had been tempted to boo. But Stanhope Aspinwall, in two long articles which he wrote about the new opera, rebuked them sharply. Here, he said, was the most original musical talent to emerge for many years, asserting itself – pulling the public's leg, perhaps, but that was the privilege of genius. His analysis of the work contained many criticisms which, he said, he had been obliged to bring against Giles Revelstoke's work on several occasions – lyricism at the expense of dramatic movement, conventional passages of orchestration which seemed to have been thrown together in a hurry and never revised, a sacrifice of musical to literary values in some sections – but judged as a whole, a work of splendid qualities.

All of the critics agreed that in Monica Gall, the Canadian soprano who played the small but important role of Fotis, the serving-maid turned sorceress, the world of chamber opera had gained the most gifted singer of many years. She could not act particularly well, but that could be mended. It was good news indeed that the British Opera Association had chosen this work to perform in Venice, in September, at the Festival. There was even a kindly mention of the fact that some of the money for the excellently-mounted production had been supplied by a Canadian trust fund, founded for the furtherance of the arts; thus, the British critics agreed, the dominions were returning some of the loving care and cultural dower which had been lavished upon them in their early days by the Motherland. It was to be hoped that more might follow.

'Without knowing it, we seem to have covered ourselves with glory,' said the Dean, laughing. But Miss Pottinger and Mr Snelgrove agreed in all seriousness. 'Certainly we made no mistake when we chose Monica Gall for the first beneficiary. I wonder if we shall have to choose another. May I say that I hope not?'

They all looked at Solly. They knew that since late April, Veronica had been pregnant.

'You cannot possibly hope that as fervently as I do, Mr Dean,' said Solly, with a laugh which took some of the bite out of the remark.

It was at about that same time that Chuck Proby (as Mr Gall could not be persuaded to do it) went to the cemetery vault, where the body of Mrs Gall was identified by him, and buried in the grave which the now soft ground permitted to be dug. The law demanded it, and someone has to do these things.

[NINE]

Monica had been five full days in Venice, and so far she had seen no more of it than could be glimpsed in flittings from her hotel to the theatre, and thence to Giles' favourite restaurant. True, she had been several times in a gondola, which might have been romantic if she had not always been accompanied by her portable typewriter, or the very heavy suitcase which contained the orchestra parts for *The Golden Asse*, or Giles himself in his anti-Venetian mood. The city was a tourist-trap, he told her, and its romance was spurious; the Venetians were all scoundrels; had they not launched income tax, the science of statistics, and state censorship of books upon the world? He laughed away her meek proposals that, when the long days of work were done, they might see some of the sights; he had seen the sights, years ago, and they were not worth having. They had not come to Venice to be tourists, but to work.

Monica, who had not seen the sights, would not in the least have minded being a tourist. Giles laughed still more, and said that she was provincial. Apparently this was a very dreadful thing to be, and she timidly asked Domdaniel about it.

'Giles is playing the man of the world,' said he. 'You mustn't mind. Everybody's provincial if you put 'em in the right spot to show it, and nobody more so than the man who won't be impressed, on principle. When we get this mess straightened out I'll show you the town; I know some very pleasant people here.'

The mess to which he referred was *The Golden Asse*, which had been undergoing revision ever since its appearance in London in May. The work had revealed weaknesses in performance, and when Revelstoke had been convinced that the weaknesses were real, and had tried to correct them, the opera had seemed to collapse; its individual parts were still good, but they could not be made to stick together satisfactorily. Domdaniel had been reassuring; the commonest thing in the world, said he; always happened when a big work wanted revision; all that was needed was patience. But patience had worn thin, for *The Golden Asse* was to appear as part of the current Music Festival in Venice, and revisions had gone on, minutely but tiresomely, until yesterday. Most of the tinkering had been done on the orchestral interludes which linked the many scenes of the opera; Monica had copied, and re-copied, and copied again, principally because it was convenient for her to do so, being so close at hand, but also to save the money of the Association for English Opera – money which she had herself provided in substantial but insufficient amount. There is no such thing as enough money for opera, she had discovered.

The pattern of work was surprisingly regular. Domdaniel would find fault with a passage, and suggest how it might be re-cast: Revelstoke, after argument, would re-write the passage in his own way: Domdaniel, having first said that the new version would do splendidly, was likely to find in a few hours that it was – well, not quite right, and suggest further revision, usually along the lines he had originally proposed. Revelstoke would again re-write, producing something manifestly inferior to what he had done before. Domdaniel would then suggest that the earlier revision be used – with a few changes which he could easily make himself, to spare Giles trouble. But Giles did not want to be spared trouble; he wanted the music as he had written it in the beginning. There were shocking rows.

The parts which would shortly be distributed to the music desks in the orchestra were a muddle even for musicians, who are used to muddled parts. Over the neat script of the professional copyist were gummed countless bits of paper upon which were corrections in Monica's script, almost as neat. But over these might be further corrections, in Giles' beautiful but minute script, or in the bold hand of Domdaniel. Further revision appeared, in Domdaniel's hand, in red pencil. Yet, somehow, at orchestra rehearsals the players made sense of it all. Philosophical and usually patient men, they interpreted the muddle under their eyes, and brought forth beauty.

That was what made it all worth while. *The Golden Asse* was a thing of beauty. Giles' libretto followed faithfully the second-century story of the unfortunate Lucius, whose meddling in magic caused him to be transformed into an ass, from which unhappy metamorphosis he was delivered only after he had achieved new wisdom. But the character of the music emphasized the tale as allegory – humorous, poignant, humane allegory – disclosing the metamorphosis of life itself, in which man moves from confident inexperience through the bitterness of experience, toward the rueful wisdom of self-knowledge. Where the music came from, not even Giles' most intimate associates – and this now meant Monica and Domdaniel – could guess, for as the work had progressed he had grown increasingly freakish, his moods alternating between one of morose incivility and another of noisy hilarity. There was nothing of the serene wisdom of his music to be discerned in himself.

The journey to Venice had been, for Monica, a misery. She had travelled with Giles and the stage director, Richard Jago. Giles had insisted that *wagon-lits* were an extravagance, so they had slept in their seats; nor would he hear of meals in the restaurant-car – they must picnic, it would be so much cheaper and jollier. So they had eaten innumerable hard rolls into which lumps of bitter chocolate were stuffed, fruit-cake, and cheese, with occasional swigs at a flask of brandy. Monica had not liked this stodgy diet, and had bought a few pears for herself; they had made her ill, as Giles, who had an English mistrust of fruit, had predicted, and after their arrival in Venice Domdaniel had had to dose her for a couple of days with Fernet Branca.

But it was not the physical discomforts of the journey which had made it so exhausting. Giles was in one of his hilarious moods, and insisted that she and Jago sing lewd rounds with him, for hours at a time. Giles was entranced by rounds and catches, especially those of the seventeenth and eighteenth centuries in which, as they were sung, simple-minded obscenities were revealed. And so, to the astonishment of their fellow-travellers (when they had any) they sped across Europe to the strains of –

Adam catch'd Eve by the furbelow,
And that's the oldest catch I know;
Oho, did he so!

Jago, who was a mild and withdrawn young man, could never quite master the time of that one, and Giles abused him whenever they sang it. They had better luck with –

I lay with an old man all the night;
I turned to him, and he to me;
He could not do so well as he might
He tried and he tried, but it would not be.

But Giles' favourite was the most musically intricate and poetically inane of his large repertoire. It was a true 'catch', and the words ran –

I want to dress; pray call my maid,
And let my things be quickly laid.
What does your Ladyship please to wear?
Your bombazine? 'Tis ready here.
See here, see here, this monstrous tear,
Oh, fie! It is not fit to wear.

But when the 'catch' made itself heard, he would enjoy it as heartily as any port-soaked member of an eighteenth-century catch-club, and smack Monica resoundingly on her bottom as he sang 'And let your bum be seen?' – as though there were some possibility that the point might be missed.

'For God's sake, Giles, will you stop acting the Beloved Vagabond for just half an hour? My head aches,' Jago would protest.

'You have no zest for life,' Revelstoke would reply. Or he might sulk for a time, or doze. But soon he would be at it again, insisting that they try once more to master Purcell's –

I gave her cakes, and I gave her ale –

which they never succeeded in doing, for Jago was not up to it. Monica was heartily glad, dulled though her senses were by the nausea which the bad pears had caused her, when the train crept through some dirty suburbs and Giles announced that they were at last sniffing the undeniable stench of the Queen of the Adriatic.

Still, that was all past now. The first Venetian performance of *The Golden Asse* in its revised version was to take place tonight, and Monica, at half-past four, was already in her dressing-room, arranging and re-arranging her make-up materials, or lying on a sofa looking out at Venetian rooftops, so quiet under the September sunshine.

To be here, in a dressing-room all her own, in the celebrated Teatro della Fenice – was that not romance enough, without common, touristy sight-seeing? Yes, certainly it was. One must grow up some time, and would she not herself be, in a few hours, one of the sights of Venice? Yes, of course, that was the idea. And anyhow, after the first night was out of the way, Sir Benedict would take her sight-seeing.

At twenty-three, resting can be hard work. Monica was thoroughly tired of it. She ran down the broad, empty passages until she came to the large, gold-framed mirror which was fastened to the wall in the long gallery which gave the artists access to the stage and passed through the door from daylight into the darkness of the huge stage itself. Above her was the soaring, dusty mystery of the flies, hung thickly with drop-scenes; somewhere, high in the lantern above the stage, a sunbeam penetrated the murk, touching the cobweb of fly-lines in a dozen places before it came to rest at last on one of the huge canvases. Once again Monica experienced the unfamiliar feel of a raked stage, so subtle in its enticement toward the footlights, so unexpectedly resistant in its retreat toward the back-cloth – for the single basic setting which served for *The Golden Asse* was already in place. One setting for an opera with eighteen scenes – it still seemed strange to her, nurtured on the elaborate naturalism in *The Victor Book of the Opera*; yet it was wonderful how well this unit-setting worked. She yielded to the slope, and stood directly in front of the prompter's box, looking across the orchestra pit toward the ornate music desk from which, in a few hours, she must follow Domdaniel's nuances of direction.

Then she raised her eyes, and became conscious that in the dimness of the beautiful theatre something was happening – some work was in progress. As she became accustomed to the gloom she saw that a work-party of those little old women who seem to be inseparable from European opera houses were busy hanging garlands of fresh flowers across the front of the first tier of boxes.

For an instant she felt, stronger than ever before, the mixture of elation and dread which she was learning to recognize as part of her professional life, part of her fate. It was exquisitely delicious and terrifying.

Then, suddenly, from the wings there came a slight draught, and hastily clutching a scarf about her throat she scampered back to the protective warmth of her dressing-room.

[TWO]

When next she stood upon that stage and felt the gentle urging of the rake toward the footlights, she resisted it, not only because she must go nowhere that Richard Jago had not told her to go, but also because she knew by now that crowding the footlights is not the best way for a singer to make herself heard; Domdaniel had given her the valuable tip that stage centre, fifteen or twenty feet from the footlights, is the preferred place on most good operatic stages, and Monica had learned all the polite ways of getting herself to that precise area. For the Association for English Opera was a very polite organization; no shrewishness, no temperament, no bluster marred its rehearsals as sometimes happens among the operatic stars of lesser breeds without the law; nevertheless, there were well-tried English ways of establishing that what was best for the individual singer was also best for the work, for the production, for the balance of the ensemble, and when the position of advantage was Monica's by right, she had no trouble in getting it. She shared it now with Amyas Palfreyman, the tenor who sang the part of Lucius; Mr Palfreyman was a contradiction of everything that Ludwiga Kressel had said about tenors – that they were all fat, short, the possessors of too-small noses and an excess of female hormones; he was tall, lean, beaky of nose and, if not aggressively masculine, certainly not effeminate; furthermore, he liked Monica and gave her all the help he could without compromising his own role. Monica was very lucky to be making an important early appearance with Mr Palfreyman, and she knew it. Lucky, too, to be under the direction of the great Sir Benedict Domdaniel who, from his place in the pit, kept everything under his control, blending the ensemble of voices and orchestra with immense skill, so that the singers rested upon his conducting as gently and as confidently as gods in a Renaissance picture, resting upon a cloud. Ordinarily the Association for English Opera could not have afforded the services of Sir Benedict; he appeared in Venice, as he had done in London when the opera was first heard, at something like half his ordinary fee, because he wanted to advance the music of Giles Revelstoke.

Oh yes, Monica was very lucky, and she knew it, but during the performance she had no time or inclination to glory in her luck; she was too busy showing fortune that she was worthy of its favours. She had slaved to learn the craft of the opera singer; make-up, classes in posture, hours of toil with the demanding Molloy – she had spared herself nothing. Not only was she able, now, to sound right; she could also look right. She had learned from Giles to be naked before him and to be neither ashamed nor brazen; it was not so very different to appear before a great audience with the same candour. Not that she was naked, though the costume which the designer thought fit for the entrancing servant-enchantress Fotis was a revealing one. 'Not every day you get an opera singer who peels well,' the designer had said, 'so we may as well make the most of you.' And that was what he had done. The mirror in the long gallery beyond the stage told Monica a pleasing tale. It was amazing, she thought, how well a rather sturdy girl ('strong as a horse', Sir Benedict had said) could be made to look. Oh, it was good to be as strong as a horse and yet, on a large stage, to look pleasantly fragile!

Domdaniel in the pit was not the only good angel who was watching over her. She moved about the stage in the pattern taught her by Richard Jago. She maintained the mental discipline – the dual consciousness of the actress, which enabled her to give herself to her part, and at the same time to stand a little aside, criticizing, prompting and controlling – which had been so carefully imparted to her by Molloy. And as well as the feat of balance which enabled her to keep all these elements in control she still found a place in her mind for the humility of the interpreter toward the creator, of which Domdaniel had spoken as they drove from Oxford. It was not to the spirit of Bach, long-dead, but to Giles, very much alive and somewhere in the theatre, that she made her offering: would he be pleased?

He certainly should have been pleased, for the opera was very well received. It provided a kind of delight particularly pleasing to an Italian audience, for it gave almost unbroken opportunities for beautiful singing; modern enough in idiom, it was not modern in asperity and rejection of sheer vocal charm; but neither was it sentimental, a succession of musical bon-bons. It was, some of the critics who had descended upon Venice for the Festival said in their dispatches to Germany, to Rome and to Paris, a comic masterpiece – goldenly, sunnily comic, splendid in its acceptance of the ambiguity of man's aspirations toward both wisdom and joy. Musically it was somewhat novel to Italian ears, for virtually all of its music was either for the ensemble or for the orchestra; but, as the Italian critics pointed out, firmly but kindly, this suited the English voices, which were fine instruments, governed by keen musical intelligence, but not of the highest operatic order. Amyas Palfreyman was generously praised, particularly for his musical braying in Act Two, when he was transformed into an ass; and Monica Gall was mentioned in all the notices as a new singer of great promise, freshness, and uncommon agility and sweetness of voice combined with a lower register which was striking in the scene where she figured as an enchantress.

But these sweets were to be enjoyed later, after the critiques had been collected. The immediate reward was the cheering at the end of the performance, when the cast appeared again and again in front of the curtains; when Sir Benedict appeared with them, and called the orchestra to its feet; when Sir Benedict led Giles Revelstoke forward for the kind of ovation which an audience chiefly Italian gives to a composer who has delighted it.

It was a great evening, marred a little by Giles' behaviour afterward when Sir Benedict, who liked to keep up certain princely customs, invited the company to have supper with him at the Royal Danieli. The applause had affected Giles adversely, and he was in his morose mood; he would not go, and he took it ill that Monica did want to go. He thought she should have been pleased enough to return with him to their very modest hotel near the Fenice. She felt some concern for him, as he stood apart, scowling at the party as it embarked in gondolas. But when, half an hour later, she was sitting at Sir Benedict's left hand on the terrace which overlooks the Grand Canal (the place of highest honour, on his right hand, was understandably reserved for Lalage Render, the British *première danseuse étoile* who danced the role of Psyche in the ballet of Cupid and Psyche which was one of the high points of the opera) she was not troubled about Giles, or about anything. She was perfectly happy, for she knew that she had done well, and (true Canadian that she was) she could enjoy her treat because she had earned it.

But the best was still to come. Sir Benedict took her back to her hotel by gondola, and although he may have found it slightly chilly, and though Monica was perpetually readjusting the scarf around her throat, it was romantic and moonlit enough. When he helped her ashore he thanked her for a delightful evening and kissed her hand. Monica started a little, and drew it away more quickly than was polite.

'What's the matter?' said Sir Benedict.

'Nothing; nothing at all. Only – this seems all wrong. I mean, I feel very much your pupil and – I don't know, I suppose I feel I ought to be thanking you – or something.'

'You make me feel fully a hundred and ten,' said Domdaniel, his bald head gleaming nacreously in the moonlight. 'Still – good of you. I hope you'll be my pupil for a long time. But after tonight I'm very happy to think of you as a fellow artist, as well.' And he kissed her hand again.

Monica was not at all sure how she found her way to bed.

[THREE]

The opera was scheduled for only eight performances in Venice, and when the first of these was successfully over, Monica was free to see something of the city, which she did in the company of Domdaniel. He was an ideal sightseer, for he knew when to stop, had friends in the city, was acquainted with the best restaurants and thoroughly understood the first principle of aesthetic appreciation, which is that it can usually be doubled by sitting down. Monica, flattered by her new status as fellow-artist, had never enjoyed herself so much. Surely such attention from the great man meant that she had finally made the grade, and was counted among the Eros-men rather than the Thanatossers? Indeed, she began to wonder if she might not be something of a sex-squaller as well, for as she travelled about the city with Domdaniel she observed young men eyeing her and pulling furiously at their ear-lobes; a few of the more daring flung out their hands, with the index-finger leading, as she passed, and Sir Benedict explained that these were gestures of admiration, comparable to the wolf-whistles which she had heard (always for other girls) at home.

Giles remained sullen, and she saw little of him. On the fourth day Domdaniel said, as they were at lunch together –

'Giles has got his way at last. He's going to conduct tonight.'

'Oh? Will we have to rehearse with him?'

'No, no; but keep your eye on him very closely. He's anxious to make a good job of it.'

'Of course. But I didn't know he was scheduled to take any performances here. He never mentioned conducting to me. Are you going away?'

'No I'm not, and he isn't. But he wants to conduct very much, and he's persuaded me to persuade Petri that it will be all right – and I only hope it is.'

'Are you worried?'

'Well, it's a difficult situation. You see, with my reputation, I'm rather a draw, and quite a bit of the preliminary seat-sale was based on that. People know that I do a good job with opera, and with a company which doesn't contain any other names of international reputation – except for Render, and she's not a singer – that's important. But I can't very well stuff that down Giles' throat. After all, he's the composer, and he's extremely touchy. But he really isn't a conductor.'

'He's a marvellous accompanist.'

'My dear girl, quite a different thing. Conducting opera is a first-class juggling trick, and Giles is no juggler. He fidgets and flogs his people. He radiates dissatisfaction. You know how singers are about atmosphere. Once a sense of strain has been created the whole thing can go to bits. Still, I had to put it to Petri, when Giles was so insistent on it, and Petri wasn't a bit easy to persuade. The trouble is, if I refuse to do this for him, he thinks I'm trying to keep him down.'

'How awful! What a tangle!'

'Oh, not really. You should see what an opera company can create in the way of hell when it tries. Still, I feel responsible to Petri, who expected me to be on the job every night.'

'Will you be there tonight?'

'Oh, I'll probably drop in.'

Sir Benedict was there before the overture, in the back of a box, supposedly out of sight, though the singers were all aware of his presence. Signor Petri was very much in evidence, huge and imperial in evening dress, dropping into the dressing-rooms before curtain time to make trivial conversation in careful English, with very much the air of a man who is not saying what is on his mind. And Giles, taut and abrupt, visited every singer before the half-hour call, charging them to watch his beat, as there would be passages which he would take somewhat differently from Domdaniel.

And so he did, but for the first twenty minutes or so *The Golden Asse* went as well as usual. There was a different quality of tension on the stage, for singers were loyally determined to support their composer; but they could not rest confidently upon his conducting as they did upon that of the masterly Domdaniel. His beat was clear, and if his manner was peremptory and his face sometimes showed irritation (with what? with himself, the orchestra, or the singer? how can a tenor with his body working in one vast integrated effort to produce the best tone, allied with the suitable gesture, possibly be expected to know?) they had their own professional experience, and their own musicianship, to sustain them. But when the first of the important orchestral interludes came, it was clear that something was very wrong.

Of the fourteen hundred-odd people in the theatre, perhaps a hundred and fifty really knew what the trouble was; another five or six hundred sensed that something was amiss but could not have identified it; the remainder knew only that the music which had been so melodious before, had taken on a queer turn which was probably attributable to some unfamiliarity of idiom. But for several bars a section of the orchestra would be at cross-purposes with the rest; or a vigorous entry would come a beat too soon, or too late; or sounds which no system of musical logic could account for would assert themselves, only to be subdued by the furious, quenching gesture of the composer's left hand.

As the performance progressed, it became nervous agony for the people on the stage, deeper mystery for the listeners. The singers, upon the whole, fared well, for nothing completely disorganizing happened to their part of the score, though portions of accompaniment, faintly familiar, yet unaccustomed, rose to their ears. Yet, because they were the most exposed part of the musical forces, they suffered, and their occupational sensitivity to atmosphere worked strongly against them. The philosophy of the orchestra manifested itself in shrugs, which could be seen from the boxes and galleries. But the only outright fiasco of the evening was the ballet of Cupid and Psyche; the six dancers engaged in it were exposed, for the eight minutes of its duration, as men and women who seemed not to know what they were doing. Even Lalage Render, who was admired wherever ballet was understood for her classic perfection, seemed suddenly to be hopping arbitrarily and rather foolishly about the stage, at odds with the music.

The frequent variation of time signature, which was one of the chief characteristics of Giles' score, and which gave his music the variety and subtlety of nuance which was its chief beauty, seemed to be at the root of the trouble; the opera was not precisely as the company had learned it.

When, at last, the curtain descended, there was applause. For was not *The Golden Asse* the chief success of the Music Festival that year? And were there not many good people present who, having been assured that they were to hear a masterwork, were humbly ready to accept whatever they heard as belonging in that category? But it was not the kind of applause which had greeted the earlier performances. When Giles did not come at once from the pit to the stage, Amyas Palfreyman tried to find him, to appear before the curtain with the company. But the applause did not last long enough to make a thorough search possible. The company dispersed to their dressing-rooms greatly disturbed; they had taken a few calls, but they could not forget that at the end of the ballet of Cupid and Psyche there had been several hisses and some murmuring from the gallery.

When Monica went into her dressing-room, Giles was there, sitting on the sofa. His expression was furious, but she was not deceived; there was a forlorn look about him which she had never seen before, and it filled her with pity. She ran to him and tried to put her arms about him, but he pushed her away.

'Well – a fine bloody mess that was,' said he.

'Giles, what was wrong?'

'That damned orchestra. Wouldn't follow the score, wouldn't follow my beat – absolute chaos! I explained the whole thing to them beforehand, and they said they understood – anyhow the first fiddle did – but they had no idea what they were doing. I could cheerfully have killed the lot of them!'

'Poor Giles.'

'Don't "Poor Giles" me. I saw you, shuddering and making faces, like Palfreyman and all the rest of them, whenever we got into trouble.'

'We didn't. It was only that –'

'You did. You were all mugging like lunatics. Do you think I can't see? You were throwing the show away with both hands. I don't particularly blame you. You're nothing but a bloody little colonial greenhorn who doesn't know anything about professional conduct, but Palfreyman was flat for the last two acts, and he was glaring at me with his eyes sticking out like doorknobs. I could have thrown my stick at him!'

'I'm sure he was just trying to follow your beat, Giles. We all were, honestly. What was the trouble?'

'I've told you the trouble. I was trying to give *my* opera, instead of Brum Benny's, and everybody behaved as if I were demanding some obscene impossibility. I'm almost ready to believe you were all in cahoots to do it.'

'Oh, Giles!'

'Yes, you're all hypnotized by the great Sir Benedict. What the composer wants is nothing; it's what Sir Benedict wants that counts. He's bought the whole lot of you with blarney and champagne suppers, and I'm just a stooge.'

'No, it isn't like that a bit –'

'What's the good of saying that? D'you think I can't see? What do you suppose I've been doing since I came here? Fighting for my own music. And it appears I've lost the fight.'

And so on; much more to the same effect, until there was a soft knock on the door, and Sir Benedict came in.

'Well, we ran into a spot of bother,' said he, smiling.

'"We" didn't run into anything. I ran into something. I ran right smack into the fact that my music seems to mean less in this theatre than your ideas about it.'

'But my dear fellow, why did you do it?'

'Is it so extraordinary that I should want a chance to conduct my own opera?'

'No. You know what I mean. Why did you try to revise the score at the last minute?'

'I did not revise it; I simply restored it to what I originally meant it to be. I've heard your version, with all the neat, conventional little bridges and re-writes and revises you've stuck into it, to make it the kind of Leipzig Conservatory stuff you'd write if you could write anything at all. I've heard it and it's just so much Zopf!'

'Giles, Giles, nothing went into your score that was mine. You approved every change and every cut; many of the revisions were in your own hand. Now let's be reasonable –'

'Revisions I made with a pistol at my head! I never wanted to revise; I damned well knew when the opera was finished. You were the one who wanted to tinker.'

'All right, let's forget that for the moment. But really, my dear man, if you peel off sometimes as many as seven revisions from a score you must expect trouble. The concert-master tells me that the conductor's room was knee-deep in gummed paper –'

'I knew he'd be clearing himself to you! They all run to you! Did he tell you he said he understood the revisions?'

'He told me he argued with you, and finally said they'd do their best. Be sensible, Giles. He doesn't speak English particularly well and I expect you bullied him. The orchestra are first-rate men, but they can't do miracles; you should have realized that when you'd pulled off all the revisions there were bound to be difficulties, because quite a few of them weren't gummed to the parts – they were written in by hand. Still, it's done now, and we'd better say no more about it at present. It's not the end of the world.'

Giles would no doubt have retorted that it was the end of the world, simply from necessity to dissent from Domdaniel, but it was at this moment that Signor Petri, the manager, came in. A huge man, of immense dignity, and at this moment deeply solemn.

'Mr Revelstoke, this was very, very wrong of you,' he said.

'I don't see that. If your orchestra can't follow a score, why is it my fault?'

'Mr Revelstoke, I have been with Gnecchi, and he showed me the orchestra parts and they were incomprehensible in many places. There is a place in Act Three, in the ballet, where there are discrepancies of as much as six bars in some of the parts. Signora Render is very distressed and who wonders? The theatre doctor is with her now. You made her look a fool. You should not have – what is the word I seek – monkeyed with that score.'

'I did not monkey with the score. I restored it to what I wrote, and it was as clear as day.'

'To you, perhaps. To no one else.'

'Damn it, Petri, my score had been revised and patted and pulled and buggered about and I wanted it to be played as I wrote it. Has a composer no rights in this theatre?'

'Every right, Mr Revelstoke. Every respect. La Fenice has presented new scores by Verdi, do not forget it, and by many very great men. But not even Verdi has a right to insult my audience, and make my artists appear to be analphabets in public, and that is what you have done. Now hear what I have to say –'

'Jesus Christ, Petri, come off it; and stop talking at me like a musical Mussolini, you fat –'

'Now Giles, now Giles,' said Domdaniel, 'let's not have a scene.'

'No, no, no; by no means; no, no, no,' said Signor Petri with the calm of a thunderstorm restraining itself.

Giles howled with laughter. 'It only needed that!' he cried; 'the ultimate touch of farce! No, no, let's not have a scene. The Jew is cool as a cucumber; the Wop is a monument of marble calm. Only the Englishman has lost his phlegm. Why not have a scene? Give me one good reason. I'm the one who's been wronged, and I'd bloody well like to have a bloody great scene.'

Signor Petri lifted the hand of a Roman consul. 'You forget, Mr Revelstoke, the presence of the Signora Gowl,' said he. 'Now listen to me: you will not conduct this opera again in this theatre, and by tomorrow night the orchestra parts must be restored to their proper condition, or my men will refuse to play. Perhaps you do not realize it, but tonight's reception would have been disastrous if we had not been pulled through by our efficient claque. That is all I have to say. An apology to the company, to Gnecchi on behalf of the orchestra, to the Signora Render and a generous recognition to the leader of the claque – these things I leave to your own discretion. Signora. Sir Benedict.' With a splendid mingling of courtesy, and scorn for Giles, Signor Petri made his departure.

Giles was laughing again. His laughter seemed a little forced, but it did not stop until Sir Benedict spoke very firmly to him.

'Cut out that nonsense,' said he, 'and stop playing the fool. Face the fact, Giles, you've made a mess of this business. The best thing you can do is take Petri's advice and go around now and make your peace with everybody. Then we can all forget this fiasco and get ready for the job of putting those parts right tomorrow. It'll take several hours, but if we all get down to it early, it can be done in plenty of time.'

'I've no intention of being the goat for you and Petri. Everybody seems to think themselves wronged in this matter. What's the trouble with you? Surely you've gained face? The great Sir Benny can pull the company through anything; you don't catch him messing about with scores. He's even independent of the claque. Hurray for Benny!'

'I've lost face with Petri because I begged him to let you conduct. I personally guaranteed you. But that's no matter. You're perfectly right. You are the one who matters. And that's why you had better start on a round of the dressing-rooms right now, smoothing things over.'

'Is that an order, Sir Benedict? Because if so you can relish the unusual experience of having one of your orders disobeyed. I'll do no apologizing and no smoothing. Not even with the Signora Gowl. So you can get into your street clothes just as fast as you like, Monica, because I discern that the Big Boss is going to take you out for another of those charming little suppers at the Danieli, and you can both have a lovely time telling one another what a naughty boy I've been.'

'Now Giles, no use taking it out on Monica.'

'Oh no, let's leave Monica out of it, of course. I've written an opera, and you've put the finishing touches on it. And I've made a singer, and you are in the process of putting the finishing touches on her. She's been my mistress for nearly two years, but you always work best on somebody else's material.'

'Giles, don't talk like that,' said Monica.

'Why not? Why are we all so mealy-mouthed this evening? Go with

Brum Benny if that's what you want. He can do a great deal for you. Much more than I.'

'You're being unreasonable and silly, and saying things you don't mean,' said Monica. 'I'm not going anywhere with anybody; I'm here for you. But I'm not here to encourage you to make a fool of yourself. Sir Benedict is right; this isn't the end of the world. All you have to do is admit you tried something that didn't work, and it'll all be forgotten within a week.'

'Nobody is going to hold this against you,' said Sir Benedict; 'not even Aspinwall.'

'What about Aspinwall?'

'He was here tonight. I didn't mean to tell you. He had of course heard about the revisions – I mean the big re-writes, not the trivial things that you dispensed with tonight – and came to hear the work in its new form. A pity he came tonight. But I was talking with him, and he's coming tomorrow night, so –'

'So he'll hear *The Golden Asse* as it ought to be heard, under the baton of the great conductor and with all his personal ideas worked into it! This was all that was needed! You've been canoodling with Aspinwall!'

And Giles broke into a flow of obscene abuse against the critic which was remarkable even for him. His face, so white before, became blotched with red, and there were moments when it seemed that he must choke.

'Christ, this is the end,' he said, at last. 'This has been a great night for me. You've grabbed my opera, you've grabbed my girl, and now you've been apologizing for me to the man I hate and despise most in the world. All right: take the lot!'

He made for the door, but Monica caught him before he could go.

'Wait just a minute,' she said. 'I'll come with you.'

'I don't want you with me.'

'But I want to be with you.'

'Oh, you think I need you? The conceit of women! When a man is angry or down on his luck, he must need one of them. Get away from me. You've been insufferable ever since you came back from Canada with that potty little bit of money. Do you think I haven't seen you playing the suffering saint all over the place, sacrificing yourself right and left, and thinking you were getting immortality in return? Because you gouged a tuppenny-halfpenny Canadian trust, you crooked little bitch? Not a penny of it came out of your hide. Because you used your money to buy a good part in my opera, do you think I'm eternally sold to you? Oh, really, Monica, you're even stupider than I'd supposed! Of course it was your money that got you into *The Golden Asse*; what else? Not your talent, I can assure you. Not your slatepencil squeal on a high D. Get out of my sight; your vapid mug makes me spew! I've made a passable singer of you, and taught you the elements of your other principal use. And I'm heartily sick of you.'

This time he went.

[FOUR]

Next morning at half-past nine (which is bright and early for people who have finished their previous working day at midnight) Sir Benedict and Monica were hard at it in Petri's office, restoring the orchestral parts to their original form; Domdaniel dictated, Monica transcribed (those who have taken music from dictation know what fidgetty work it is) and Gnecchi gummed the freshly-written slips into their proper places on the music. By half-past four the job was done, and that evening the opera was performed, after a few early moments of nerves, better than ever before. It was not until Monica was back at her hotel that she had the time and the calm of mind to consider the scene of the night before.

Giles had disappeared. He had left no forwarding address, but had gone very early in the morning, presumably to catch a train. But what train no one could say, for at Padua he could have gone southward, or from Milan he could have made his way back to England. Sir Benedict had taken this news calmly.

'He'll cool in the same skin he got hot in,' said he.

'You don't think I ought to try to find him?'

'It will be easier for all of us, if we don't meet for a few weeks. Do you particularly want to see him soon?'

'Yes; I'm worried about him.'

'What a forgiving nature you have.'

'No; he didn't mean what he said. You know how terribly he exaggerates everything.'

'And so you're willing to hunt him up, and let him make a doormat of you.'

'No, no; but I'd like to be sure that he's all right.'

'Well, I never give advice in love affairs, but I've been in love myself, and it's always useful to preserve your self-respect.'

'I'm sure you're right, Sir Benedict.'

Of course he was right. She knew that Giles' hard words about her buying herself into his opera were just the froth of his anger. Still, when all the anger had been discounted, might there not be some drop of truth left? Was that the way he really thought about her? Had he really endured her simply because she could bring him the money – little enough, in terms of the sums involved in staging even so modest a production as *The Golden Asse* – that he needed? No, that was unthinkable. If money was all he wanted, he need not have slept with her, and though he had never told her that he loved her, he had never concealed his pleasure in their physical union. Much more than a physical union it had become, and well she knew it; not only could Giles not conceal his need for her and his dependence on her tenderness and unquestioning adoration (for that was what it was, and she could not pretend otherwise) but the spite of Persis was strong corroborative evidence. Nevertheless, Monica had not the self-confidence or the detachment to trust her judgement in this matter. Who has, that is deeply in love? The love which is strong as steel under one assault, may crumble like ash under the breath of another. Giles had touched Monica on her weakest point, which was her belief in her own worth as a woman, a lover; she was deeply convinced that she was, like Fotis in the opera, only a clumsy pretence-enchantress.

She pondered for another day on the subject, turning it over and over, until at last self-doubt, masquerading as self-respect, made her write a letter.

Dearest Giles,

After thinking for a long time about what you said on Thursday night, I am sure we had better break off, and not see each other again – at least not for a long time. Of course I didn't take what you said at its face value, because I knew how angry and hurt you were. But you hurt me very much. Just the fact that you knew so well how to hurt me makes me think that you had been turning some of those things over in your mind, and when you were angry, they came out.

What I have felt about you has been plain, I think. I could have said some of it, if you had wanted that, but I tried to show it in other ways. You once told me that when you loved me you would say so, and as you have never said it I know that you don't, and Thursday night – even with all the anger left out, makes me fear that you could very easily despise me. So I won't come for any more lessons, and perhaps after a while when I don't feel about you as I do now, we will be able to meet again, quite ordinarily.

Please understand what I am trying to say. I could give everything for you, even self-respect and wanting to be a really good singer and all that, if you wanted me to. But you don't, and I won't go on forcing it on you. But as I can't stay with you and be a doormat, I have decided to leave you and do the best I can on my own. I love you, and I always shall, but you don't want love. So God bless you (though I know how you hate people to say that) and I will ask Bun to pick up my things from Tite Street.

MONICA

It was not in the least like any of the letters she wanted to write – the splendidly haughty one, the moving unaffected one, the poetic one fit for an anthology of great love-letters – but she had neither the heart nor the talent for literary flights. She sent it off to the Tite Street flat, and concluded her engagement in Venice in deep distress of mind. Even the great reception which *The Golden Asse* was given at its last performance, and the good notices she had from all the critics, and the flowers from some unknown music-lover, and the eloquent farewell of Signor Petri, had no power to ease her inward hurt. She changed her plans for a holiday in Italy, and a visit to Amy Neilson, and returned to London as fast as the airways could take her.

[FIVE]

Monica had not long been in her flat in Courtfield Gardens before Mrs Merry appeared.

'I've brought you a few letters which came during the past two or three days,' said she. They were dull; one with a Canadian stamp, addressed in George Medwall's careful hand, was on top.

'There were no messages,' said Mrs Merry. 'Mr Revelstoke telephoned yesterday to know when you would be home, and as I had had your telegram I said you'd be back this evening.'

Was Giles anxious to see her, then? He had been too sure of her devotion to show any concern about her goings and comings before. Did he feel that he should unsay the cruel things he had said in Venice? But cruel things cannot be unsaid; they may be forgiven, and Monica was ready to forgive, but she was certain that she would not forget. She unpacked because it gave her something to do – something which would keep her in her flat. But all the time she wanted to go to Tite Street. She must not do so, for her letter had been plain; she had broken with Giles. Apparently he had received her letter, and he wanted her; otherwise why that unaccustomed inquiry? Did he think he knew her so well that he could be sure she would run to him as soon as she came back to London? Then he did not know her at all. Desperately as she loved him, she had some pride; she must preserve her self-respect, as Sir Benedict said.

But suppose he were lonely and hurt? The bad performance of *The Golden Asse* had ravaged him as only she knew. It was all very well for Sir Benedict and Petri to say that it had not been disastrously bad; they meant only that the audience had not hissed – or had only hissed once. To Giles anything below the high mark of achievement which he set for himself was disaster. What had Ripon called him, in mockery? A Satanic genius? True, for he was proud as Lucifer. But he had not Lucifer's self-sufficiency. She knew that, better than anyone else in the world. For although he would not tell her how much he needed her tenderness and understanding, she could feel it. And feeling his need, could she withhold herself from him? Was she not, in this realm, more knowledgeable than he? Was she not one of the Eros-men, and had not Domdaniel called her a fellow-artist? Should she not have a spirit above personal hurts? Should she not be ashamed to withhold her presence and her comfort from Giles as a means of revenge?

Yes, what she was doing was revenge – a tortured, unworthy passion which fouled her love. What she was doing was all those things he hated, and rightly. It was provincial. It was common. It was probably colonial and Saltertonian and Non-conformist and typically American and lower-middle-class and non-U and all the other things he taunted her with being, in his impatient desire that she should be, like himself, a true artist who looked at the world with level and open eyes.

It had been a little after nine o'clock when she reached Courtfield Gardens from the air terminal. It was half-past eleven when she climbed the stairs in Tite Street.

[SIX]

The house had a Sunday night stillness, and the tiny globes which Mrs Klein used to light the stairs exaggerated the chapel-like gloom of its Ruskin Gothic. On the second flight, which led to Giles' top floor, the cat Pyewacket was sitting; he miaouled when Monica stooped to stroke him, and ran upward ahead of her. The door at the top of the stair was closed.

She remembered that earlier time when she had returned from a journey to find Giles in bed with Persis; the door had not been closed then. Did this show some greater degree of caution? But suppose Persis were again with him? Did it really make any difference to the consuming fact that she loved him, and could not live apart from him, and must therefore endure anything from him? If Persis were there, she would have to accept it, and drudge for Persis as she drudged for Giles. The abjection of her love was complete.

The door was locked. She had a key – the only key other than Giles' own, and he had given it to her not in order that she might have free access to the flat, but because he was always losing his own key, and wanted another in safe keeping in case he should at some time find himself locked out. She unlocked the door and pushed it open. It moved heavily, for a blanket lay on the floor against it.

She had meant to call 'Giles' – but the gas stifled the name in her throat and she retreated down the stairs, choking and gasping. Pyewacket, who had rushed through the door ahead of her, dashed out of the flat and down the stairs, spitting and snarling.

Get help? No; go in. She crumpled her scarf over her mouth and nose, and ran through the living room to the windows, which were closed but not fastened, and opened easily. Was it safe to turn on a light? She knew nothing of gas. Would it ignite? Would there be an explosion? Where was Giles?

Giles lay on the floor, in pyjamas and dressing-gown. In a score of films which Monica had seen, the discoverer of someone in such a position ran to them at once, felt the pulse, listened to the heart, stared into the face. But she was so frightened that she shrank against the windows, to get air and to be as far as possible from him. It was some time before she found courage to creep forward (why? did she fear to waken him?) and look at his face in the very little light which came through the windows. His skin was dark; it seemed to her that it was black. His lips were parted, and he did not breathe. She should take his pulse. But she dared not touch him. He was dead, and she was afraid of his body.

It did not occur to her until this minute to turn off the gas-fire which hissed a foot or two from his head. Now she did so, walking around the body in a wide circle because she dared not reach across it to the gas-tap. And as she knelt by the grate she saw that in each of his hands was a piece of paper. In one of these she recognized her letter.

Was it her first thought that she had driven him to take his life? It was not. Her first thought was that if that letter were found, she would be accused of having done so.

Danger dispersed her panic. She must behave sensibly now, or God knew what would happen to her. She retreated to the window again, and made her plan.

Thank Heaven she was wearing gloves! Monica was not a great reader of detective fiction, but she knew that dreadful retributive magic could be worked with fingerprints. With luck, nobody need know that she had ever been in the flat. Less fearful than before (but still fearing that he might wake and blast her with some sarcasm, as he had done at times when he woke from sleep to find her looking into his beloved face) she went to the body, and gently drew the letter from the right-hand fingers. It was not difficult. With it safely in the pocket of her coat, she looked quickly through the flat. A few of Persis' undergarments were, as usual, hanging wetly above the bath. Leave them? Yes. Let Perse look out for herself. Then she crept back into the living-room and closed the windows as they had been before.

The other paper? Without a light she could not tell what it was, but it was a long clipping from a newspaper. Well, there could be no harm to her in that. Without a farewell glance at the black face Monica turned on the gas once again, tip-toed to the door, closed and locked it, and went as quietly as she could down the stairs. The blanket could not be pulled back into place, but that could not be helped. Pyewacket was at the street door, and she and the cat went out together into Tite Street. The squalling of babies in the hospital over the way was audible almost until she reached the Embankment. It was now twenty-five minutes to twelve.

She did not stay there long. Mist was rising from the river, and the Embankment was cold and inhospitable. Nevertheless, there were people there: lovers soddenly embracing, hands groping beneath their mackintoshes; a man and woman in middle age, talking passionately in some unknown language; one of London's inassimilable poor, filthily bearded and rustling from the newspapers which were stuffed in the legs of his trousers. Monica walked slowly, trying to think, but repeating: Giles is dead; he wanted them to think I drove him to it; he wanted to get me into trouble; he loved me; he didn't love me; he wanted to spite me; he did it from despair; he did it for revenge; he hated me. It led nowhere.

A policeman passed and re-passed her. 'Anything wrong, miss?' said he.

'No; nothing thanks.'

'Waiting for anyone?'

'No.'

'Well, if I may suggest it, miss, if you've seen all you want to see of the river, it might be a good idea to go home. Would you like me to get you a cab?'

'Thank you; that would be very kind.'

Why a cab? She was well-dressed, and wearing gloves. Amy always said that a lady should never appear on the street without gloves. How providential it was, sometimes, to know the ropes of ladyhood.

[SEVEN]

The coroner was that fortunate creature, a man really happy in his work. He delivered his summing-up to the jury with a professional flourish and a sense of style which, without being in any way unseemly, showed a degree of satisfaction.

They had heard the evidence, said the Coroner, and he hoped that they had heeded his two or three adjurations to mark it well, for it was of a complexity not common in such investigations. The body of Giles Adrian Revelstoke had been identified by Mr Griffith Hopkin-Griffiths of Neuadd Goch, Llanavon, his step-father; who had also testified that his stepson was thirty-four years old and so far as he knew had been in good health. The body had been discovered at half-past nine on the morning of September 29 by his landlady, Mrs Maria Augusta Klein, and his pupil, Miss Monica Gall. Miss Gall, who acted as a secretary and amanuensis to Mr Revelstoke, had arrived to do some work on the magazine *Lantern*, of which Mr Revelstoke was one of the editors, and had found the door of his flat locked – an unusual circumstance. She had called Mrs Klein, who assured her that Mr Revelstoke was at home, and accompanied her to the door of his flat. After repeated loud knocking, Miss Gall had opened the door at Mrs Klein's suggestion, using a key which, as a member of the *Lantern* staff, she had with her. They found Mr Revelstoke dead on the floor, with some evidences of a paroxysm, and had called the police.

The evidence of the police was that there was a strong smell of coal gas in the room, that the windows were closed, and that a blanket had apparently been used to block the crack under the main doorway. The police pathologist had testified, however, that death was not caused by gas, but by suffocation. Although the tap of the gas-fire was turned on when the police arrived, no gas was coming through and examination of the meter – one of the familiar shilling-in-the-slot meters – showed that it had run out at a time which could not be determined. It appeared, therefore, that Mr Revelstoke had been overcome with gas, and that when the gas in the room began to disperse – for the windows did not give a tight seal to the room – he had partly recovered. Nausea from the gas had caused him to regurgitate a considerable quantity of vomitus into his mouth and in his partly-conscious state he had been unable to free himself from it; the heavy, snoring breathing characteristic of certain stages of gas poisoning had caused him to draw a quantity of vomitus into his lungs, which had brought about death by suffocation. The opinion of the pathologist was that this had happened six or seven hours before he was discovered, which was to say at some time between two and three in the morning.

A verdict of suicide would certainly occur to the jury, but they must weigh the following considerations very heavily against it. The evidence of Miss Persis Kinwellmarshe (present in the court with her father, Rear-Admiral Sir Percy Kinwellmarshe) and another associate in the *Lantern* work was that she had seen the dead man after his return from Venice, and that he had appeared to be in his usual spirits, sardonic but cheerful. She had prepared a picnic supper which they had shared on the night of Sunday, September 28. Mr Revelstoke had spoken then in his usual amusingly unrestrained fashion of a critique of his opera *The Golden Asse*, written by Stanhope Aspinwall of the Sunday *Argus*, which she had brought to him. This was the newspaper clipping which had been found in the dead man's hand; she had received it from Mr Phanuel Tuke, a co-editor of *Lantern*, who had thought that Mr Revelstoke would like to have it. The dead man had laughed at Mr Aspinwall's critical pretensions.

Mr Stanhope Aspinwall, the respected music critic, had given evidence that he had never known Mr Revelstoke personally, though he had once sat in front of him at a concert, and had received two or three very abusively-worded letters from him. Therefore there could be no question of enmity between these men. The critique found with the body referred to the revised version of the composer's opera which Mr Aspinwall had travelled to Venice to see within the past fortnight; he had seen it twice, and some part of his review had been devoted to a comparison between the opera as conducted by the composer, and by Sir Benedict Domdaniel. He had said that Mr Revelstoke was a thoroughly incompetent conductor, and in that capacity was the worst enemy of his own genius as a composer. The intention of the review was favourable, and certainly it must be considered so by an unprejudiced reader.

There was the evidence, however, of John Macarthur Eccles, the other friend who had visited him on Sunday night, that Mr Revelstoke was extremely sensitive to criticism, although he pretended to hardihood respecting it. There was the evidence, also, of Sir Benedict Domdaniel, the dead man's musical and literary executor, that Mr Revelstoke had been under unusual strain during the revision of *The Golden Asse*, which had brought on exaggerated alternations of melancholy and defiant high spirits, and that Mr Revelstoke had left Venice abruptly after being told by Sir Benedict and the manager of the Fenice opera house that he could not conduct his opera there again.

There was the evidence also of Mr Phanuel Tuke that the magazine *Lantern* was in financial straits.

Taken with a romantic predisposition this added up to a story of a gifted young man who felt that the world had scorned him and who had taken his own life in a period of depression. But on the other hand, there had been equally strong evidence that Giles Revelstoke had loyal friends, that his latest and most ambitious work had been received with acclaim on the continent, and by Britain's foremost musical journalist had been mentioned as 'of the same great family as Mozart's *Magic Flute*, one of the serenely wise creations which form the crown of beauty in music'. A conductor of world fame – Sir Benedict Domdaniel again – had said that Giles Revelstoke was a composer of unquestionable genius who was just beginning to come into his mature productive period. Therefore, before they blotted the close of such a life with the stain of a suicide verdict, let the jury reflect that while it may have been possible, and indeed seemed probable, that Giles Revelstoke meant to take his life, he had not in fact done so; the gas supply had failed, and had it not been for the unlucky fact that he had suffocated before fully waking he would not have died. Under the circumstances the Coroner recommended a verdict of death by misadventure.

The jury were not of a romantic turn of mind. They were, with two or three exceptions, elderly, poor men who hung about in Horseferry

Road with the hope of being called for duty on coroner's juries, counting the few shillings they received as a pleasant windfall to add to their pensions. After a brief drag at their pipes in the retiring-room they shuffled back into court, and gave the Coroner the verdict for which he had asked.

And so it was pronounced. The Coroner, who did not get a distinguished audience every day, and who liked to give a cultured twist to his duties when he could, had passed the time while the jury were conferring, scraping in the ashes of his mind for a live coal. And, from some long-ago popular article about Schubert, he produced one which flamed quite brightly for the moment.

'By the death of Giles Adrian Revelstoke,' said he, 'music loses a rich treasure, but even fairer hopes.'

Good, kindly man, he almost wished that he had not said it, for so many of his hearers wept.

[EIGHT]

Ideally, important things should happen late, as the climax of the day, but the inquest took place in the morning, and from its close until bedtime all was slow, torturing diminution for Monica.

There was luncheon with Stanhope Aspinwall, who sought her out when the court adjourned, asked the favour of her company and bore her off to the ladies' annex of his distinguished club. He was a short, bald man, one of the dwindling army of pince-nez wearers, precise in speech, and clearly burdened with guilt.

'If I had for one instant supposed,' he said as they took coffee, 'that my comments on his conducting – fully justified, I firmly insist – might have put such a dreadful thought in his head nothing could have induced me to publish them in that form. For there was asperity; I admit to asperity. He had pestered me with letters – such letters as nothing would induce me to show to anyone, though I have kept them – and my personal feeling toward him was cool, though certainly not hostile. But for his talent – let us be honest, and say genius – I had nothing but admiration. I say this to you because you have become associated with his work in the mind of the public, and I expect that you will be even more so in future. Of course it is foolish for me to link myself even in my own mind with this tragedy, but I do so. How can I do otherwise, foolish or not? Those letters – who would not have resented them? I admit to you freely that this will be a dreadful lesson to me. Asperity: asperity is the bosom-sin of the critic.'

The afternoon papers had not, all things considered, much to say about the inquest. The worst comment was headed –

ADMIRAL'S DAUGHTER IN LOVE-NEST
'My Knickers': Lush Model

Another one dug up the fact that Giles had been a regular visitor to the prison where Odingsels was serving his time, and spoke sternly of highbrow filth and *Lantern*. But Revelstoke was not likely to be known to most of their readers and they had rottener fish to fry.

Mrs Merry insisted on a long heart-to-heart with Monica, wearing an exaggerated version of her usual expression of anguished distinction. 'Her haemorrhoidal rictus', Giles had called it, and the phrase recurred to Monica again and again, spoken in Giles' voice, as the landlady talked.

'I shall never forget the night that he and Sir Benedict played for me,' said Mrs Merry; 'a moment to be cherished in memory, now alas, in sorrow. It was his kindness which won one.' She talked for a satisfactory hour, revising her memory of the past in the light of the present.

Monica found that she had to give Bun Eccles a scratch dinner in her flat. He clung to her, and he would talk of nothing but Giles. He had brought a bottle of whisky, of which he drank all but one tot, and it was only by showing great firmness that she kept him from passing out.

'What stonkers me, Monny, is that it was gas.' This was the burden of his cry. 'Poor old Giles, to go by the gas route. Because I'd hocussed his meter, you see, Monny. Made it give more than it wanted to for a bob. And if I hadn't done that, there mightn't have been enough to do for him, see? Maybe if it had conked as little as five minutes sooner – Jesus God, drowning in his own puke like that, poor old chap! I killed him, Monny. No, it's no use saying I didn't. Maybe I didn't in law, but I did in fact, and I'll always have to live with that. God knows what it'll do to me. It's not so tough for you, Monny – no, no, I don't mean you're not hurt like us all, and worse than anybody. But you've nothing to reproach yourself with. You were always wonderful to him. Yes, yes, you were the only one. Old Perse was bellowing like a heifer in court today, because her old Dad had been giving her the gears. She gave Giles that piece of old Aspinwall's; shouldn't have done it, of course, but who was to know? Now she's saying she killed the only man she loved, or who really loved her. Aw, but – Perse was just a recreation to Giles; he knew what she was. Anybody could butter Perse's bun, and he knew it. But you were true to him, so you haven't anything to regret. And you're game, Monny. Game as Ned Kelly, and you'll get on your feet again. Wish I thought I'd do the same. You brought him life, Monny, and me, with my meddling, I greased the skids for him. How am I going to face that, every morning of my life? Poor old Giles. The best of chaps.'

At last she got rid of Bun, and when he was gone she wished him back. For what was she to do now? She had not opened her letters for several days, and she turned to them to avoid the horror of thought.

Only three were other than bills and circulars. The McCorkills, in the kindest terms, offered her the refuge of Beaver Lodge, if she wanted it; if she wanted to be alone, said Meg McCorkill, that was how it would be; they hadn't seen anything of her for a long time, but if she needed them, she had only to say the word.

The second letter was from Humphrey Cobbler. Had anybody troubled to tell her, he asked, that Veronica Bridgetower was pregnant? The child was expected late in December or early in January. He was sure she did not know, and it was none of his business, but if the Bridgetower Trust did not see fit to warn her that, in a few months, she might be displaced as beneficiary of that money, he thought it pretty shabby. And where could he get copies of some of Giles Revelstoke's songs? Was there a chance that he could get his hands on a score of *The Discoverie of Witchcraft*? He had been asked, out of the blue, to do something for a special programme of the Canadian Broadcasting Corporation, and he wanted to make their eyes pop. Or ears pop. Or whatever popped when you got a musical surprise. Any use writing direct to Revelstoke himself? He wished her well in Venice and was hers with love.

The third letter was the one from George Medwall which had been waiting for her when she returned from Venice. It read:

Dear Monica;

This is not an easy letter to write, because I am not sure there was ever anything definite between us. Still and all, I had definite ideas that I wanted to marry you, and maybe you got some idea of that kind from something I said. But we have not had a chance to talk for a long time what with your mother's death when you were last home and being very busy with the concert. The fact is if there was ever anything like an engagement between us or even a firm understanding I am asking you now to release me from it as if you do I am going to ask another girl as I am in a position to do so now. You know her. She is Teresa Rook whom you will remember as Mr Holterman's secretary and a crackerjack in her job. It is plain now and has been for quite a while that our paths have separated, but there is no reason why we can not be friends. I am not saying a word to Tessie till I hear from you which I hope will be as soon as convenient.

Your sincere friend
GEORGE MEDWALL

Her first feeling was one of surprise that George should ever have thought it possible that she might marry him. This gave way at once to shame at such snobbery, and a recollection that she had once had fuzzy, but real, designs on George. But it did seem queer now, and there was no use pretending. Had not George said to her many times, during the period of their intimacy, 'Get wise to yourself, Monny; you have to get wise to yourself, or you're everybody's stooge.' Since those days she had been trying to get wise to herself.

Of course she remembered Tessie Rook; she was just made for George; together they would go far, and George would probably end up as president of the CAA, a towering figure in the allied worlds of sandpaper and glue. She sat down to write a generous reply at once, and tears which she had not been able to weep in the coroner's court poured out now, pretending to be tears of happiness, as she thought of good old George and that sweet Tessie.

But in the end this diversion was at an end, and Monica was left with no course but to face the fact that Giles Revelstoke had not been dead when she took her letter from his hand, and that if she had thought more of him and less of herself he need not have died at all. By her selfishness and littleness of spirit she had killed him.

[NINE]

In describing Domdaniel as Giles Revelstoke's musical and literary executor the Coroner was premature; but it was Sir Benedict's desire to act in that capacity, and he lost no time in showing his fitness for it. Giles left no will. When Griffith Hopkin-Griffiths arrived at the Tite Street flat, late on the day that the body was discovered, it was to find Sir Benedict virtually in charge; with great tact he undertook to have Giles' belongings packed and sent to Wales; from that it was no great step to secure permission to take care of his manuscripts until their fate was decided. It was not many days until a great music publishing house showed interest in acquiring at least some of them.

In the period immediately following Giles' death it might have appeared that Sir Benedict used Monica without proper regard for her feelings. He insisted that she pack all the dead man's clothing and books and arrange for their removal; she found that she had to sell the furniture, which was of small value, to a dealer in the King's Road; she had to arrange for the removal of all the rubbish which comprised the files and business apparatus of *Lantern*. Mrs Klein needed her flat, and it had to be cleared. Tuke and Tooley had nowhere to house the wreckage of the magazine; Raikes Brothers certainly did not want it. As Monica could not bring herself to get rid of it, she put it in storage, in her own name.

Thus she was in and out of the flat a dozen times a day, arranging for the sale of things which had grown dear to her, including the very bed in which she had so often lain with him. But nothing was worse than the making of a rough catalogue of his music, which she prepared under Domdaniel's direction. Thin, pale and silent, she did as she was bidden.

When the great house of Bachofen began to show interest in the music, it took Mrs Hopkin-Griffiths surprisingly little time to arrange for Sir Benedict to have full power to deal with them. The daily papers had taken small interest in Giles' death, but the important Sunday papers carried long articles and many letters about him, and within three weeks England was given to understand that she had lost a man of consequence. The first person to see the possibility of this situation was Phanuel Tuke, who arranged with a publisher to bring out a collection of Giles' *Lantern* articles, prefaced with an appreciative essay by himself; for this purpose he wanted the *Lantern* files, and was greatly vexed with Monica because they were already in storage, and Miss Tooley was put to the trouble of doing her master's drudgery in the British Museum.

It was a shrewd move on the part of the music publishers to put themselves behind the promotion of a Commemorative Concert of Giles' work; it would serve as a test of his possible popularity. Sir Benedict was holding out against their offer to buy some of the publication rights; he wanted them to buy all. They were willing to bide their time. Meanwhile they were ready to spend something to see how much Giles was potentially worth.

The announcement of the concert, to take place in late November, was productive of more interest than the publishers had thought possible in their most sanguine dreams. Among musical people there was a sudden vogue for Giles Revelstoke, much of it attributable to Stanhope Aspinwall, whose two commemorative articles, published on successive Sundays in the *Argus*, set off the enthusiasm of lesser men. Not that Aspinwall was wholly commendatory; the faults which he had found in Giles' work while he was alive were still censured – but his virtues were praised much more generously. The change in emphasis, though carefully engineered, was noteworthy and effective.

'Believe me, Monny, if you want to attract real, serious attention to your work, you can't beat being dead,' said Bun Eccles. He had several sketches of Giles and reproduction rights were selling well. 'I've half a mind to try it myself, one of these days. Let 'em think they drove me to it by neglect. Trouble is, how are you going to cash in when you're dead?'

Sir Benedict was organizing the concert, and the first artist he secured for it was Monica. Speaking for the publishers, he was able to propose the highest fee she had ever been offered in her brief career.

'But am I the right person?' she asked. 'My name won't draw anybody into the hall. Why not Evelyn Burnaby?'

'She'll be there, as well,' said Domdaniel. 'A good deal of Giles' latest and best stuff was written for you, and that's very good publicity, discreetly used.'

Monica did not like that suggestion, and said so.

'We'll have lots of time for fine feelings afterward,' said he. 'Our job right now is to get the best and showiest hearing possible for Giles' work. He taught you some of the things you'll sing; they're built into your voice, precisely as he wanted them. Don't fuss.'

'I hate to have my personal relationship with him exploited.'

'It's your artistic relationship with him that's being exploited – if that's what you want to call it. Years after Trafalgar, Lady Hamilton used to go to concerts where Braham was billed to sing *The Death of Nelson*, and at a telling moment in the song she would faint noisily and have to be carried out. I'm not asking you to do anything like that. I'm asking you to make known the authentic voice of Giles Revelstoke – because that's what you are – and to begin the establishment of an unquestioned tradition about the performance of some of his best work. You ought to be damned thankful you're in a position to do it.

The fact that you were his mistress is trivial. If that's what's troubling you, for God's sake go back to Pumpkin Centre or wherever it is you came from, and set up shop as a teacher. Now, make up your mind, and don't waste my time.'

Monica had never known Sir Benedict in this mood, and it did not take her long to decide that she would do as she was told. Amy Neilson had been right; she was not a big person; she must be obedient to her betters.

Still, the idea was hateful to her, and when she told Sir Benedict of her decision he knew it, and softened a little.

'There's a necessary element of showmanship in every performing artist, however great or however sensitive,' said he, 'and without it they're not worth a damn. As long as you have it under control, it's quite all right. Don't fuss; I'll see you through.'

Don't fuss. But it wasn't fussing; it was terror barely kept under control. Terror that, while cataloguing Giles' music, she might throw herself on the floor and howl like a dog. Terror that, when she haggled with a secondhand dealer about Giles' bed-clothes, she might wrap the counterpane about her and rush shrieking into the King's Road, like widowed Hecuba. Terror that, when she saw a policeman, she might cry, 'I killed him,' and put out her wrists for the handcuffs.

She knew very well that she would not do any of these things. They were not things she *would* do but rather things which, from time to time she *wanted* to do. She was astonished at her own capacity to suffer inwardly, to give way to excesses of grief and panic, and at the same time to present a stoical front to the world. Three times she dreamed that Giles came to her, his eyes ablaze, his mouth distorted with rage, and menaced her with a bloody knife. But although this dream paralysed her with terror, its after-effect was life-enhancing, and she woke moist, panting and stirred to the depths of her being. Her mirror told her the strange news that such dreams were becoming. 'Get wise to yourself, Monny,' said George Medwall; she felt that she had never been farther from self-knowledge in her life, though self-possession never deserted her.

Nevertheless, her nervous exhaustion could not be wholly concealed. Molloy was well aware of it, for she worked with him every day, in preparation for the concert, and he was unsparing. Since the incident of the Vic-Wells ball his attitude toward her had changed; he was less eager to impress, he was more diffident and yet more intimate; he demanded more and hectored less. She had quite lost her fear of him, and they were good friends.

'You're riding for a fall,' said he, one October day after a particularly rigorous hour. 'You want a vacation the worst way. Mind, you'll be all right for the concert; I guarantee't. But after that, I wouldn't want to be answerable. Get away t'hell out o' this for a while. Go back to Canada, why don't you? Then come back and start afresh. You're on the quicks of your nerves now, and that can't last. Sit down for a while and I'll get Norah to give us all some tea.'

A few days later it was Sir Benedict who suggested a holiday. 'I'd thought about Canada for Christmas,' she said. 'Some friends of mine are having a crisis in their lives, and I'd like to be there.' And then, greatly to his astonishment, she told him about Solly and Veronica Bridgetower, and the curious condition which governed the existence of the Bridgetower Trust. 'So you see how it is,' she concluded; 'if they have a son – and I truly hope they will – it will be the end of all this for me. My good luck has depended on their bad luck, and ever since I found out about it, I've felt like the most horrible kind of gold-digger. If it hadn't been for *The Golden Asse* I couldn't have gone on. I'm glad I did, but that's all over now, and I want to behave decently, if there's any way of doing so.'

Thus it was that, with Sir Benedict's permission, and some arrangements with Boykin, she found herself in Cockspur Street a few days later, booking a steamship passage for the last week in November. As she filled out applications, her gaze travelled upward to a poster which urged settlers to come to Canada at once. Radiating health and goodwill like a red-hot stove, a young man in shirt-sleeves stood in a field of wheat, his bronzed face split with a dazzling grin. I suppose he represents my country, thought Monica, though I've never met anybody like that in my life. Odd that he should be so young, and that I feel so old.

Before the week of the concert, there was a duty which could not be shirked; she must go to Neuadd Goch, and present an account of what she had been doing to Giles' mother. She longed to get out of it. She would have done anything to avoid it. But Domdaniel could not go, and there was no one else. So, in a dreary wet week she went, and found herself once again in the familiar house though not, she thanked Heaven, in the bedroom she had occupied before.

Mrs Hopkin-Griffiths was more business-like than Monica had expected. She understood everything; she accepted the few pounds which had been realized by the sale of Giles' odds and ends without shame; she signed the papers which needed signing. It took about an hour.

'Thank you, my dear,' she said when it was all done. 'I'm sure you know how grateful Griff and I are for all of this. I'm sure it must have been hateful – all the selling and arranging and ridding-out. I couldn't have faced it, and Griff hates London so much. You and Sir Benedict have been perfectly wonderful. Funny – I've always been the kind of person that people do things for. I wonder why? I wish there were something we could do for you. Of course, it was always so extraordinary about you being Giles' pupil; he never had any others, you know; and turning up like that at Christmas. It seemed a sort of fated thing – but I suppose that's silly, really.'

'You will be coming to London for the concert, won't you?'

'Dear, will you think me utterly dreadful if I say that I won't be? I honestly don't think I could face it. No, I shall stay right here. The funeral was too awful. I don't know how I got through it.'

'Certainly for those who knew him, a concert of his music, at this time, may be very moving.'

'Do you think so? Perhaps. I couldn't say. You see, I don't really know anything about Giles' music. I really knew nothing of that side of him. Was his opera really terribly good?'

'Stanhope Aspinwall keeps relating it to *The Magic Flute*.'

'Really? Is that very good? Griff and I never saw it, you know. Is it likely to be done again, ever? When it was on in London Griff was seedy and we simply didn't feel up to the journey at that time. And then when it was done in Venice, we had already been to Baden, where we've gone for years – really I don't think I could face the winter without it – and what with the extra expense, and the time it was done, and everything, we simply didn't make it. Of course I reproach myself now. But what's done's done, eh? – Would you like to see his grave?'

Monica had determined that she would not go back to London without visiting Giles' grave, but she did not want to do so with Dolly Hopkin-Griffiths. But there was nothing for it but to do as she was asked, and so they set off on foot.

The churchyard at Llanavon was a pretty one in summer, but in the early days of November it was dank and cold, and the dripping yews were at their gloomiest. The mound beneath which Giles lay had been sodded, but had not subsided to the level of the ground and as yet there was no marker; but he lay in the influence, so to speak, of a large Celtic cross which was dedicated to the memory of the Hopkin-Griffiths family. It was an early Victorian cross, ugly but strong, and the sight of it raised Monica's spirits; it was so solid, it must surely last forever. She was glad that Giles lay there among all those red-faced Welsh squires, with open countryside beyond the churchyard walls; it stilled a deep feeling which had troubled her that he was somewhere, agonized, confined and alone. This was, she well knew, a pagan concept of death, but she had not until this time been able to subdue it.

Mrs Hopkin-Griffiths prayed briefly, and wept a little, but she had no power to remain silent for long. 'I come every day, unless the weather is simply dreadful,' said she. 'Guilt, I suppose. You see, my dear, I have a terrible feeling that I failed Giles. Can it have been about marrying Griff? But Griff was as good to Giles as Giles would let him be – and I felt I had a right to happiness, you know. But children judge so harshly. I loved him very much, and he surely knew that. But I've always been such a selfish woman, and silly, too – yes, don't deny it, dear, out of politeness. I don't know why it all went wrong. I've argued with myself about it so much, and Griff has been quite wonderful about reassuring me. But all the same, I come back to the feeling that if I hadn't failed him – whenever or however it was – Giles wouldn't be here now. Griff won't let me say it, but I'll say it to you, dear: I sometimes feel I killed Giles.'

Monica, who was utterly convinced that she had killed Giles herself, did what she could to dispel his mother's unhappiness.

'You're very kind, dear,' said Dolly; 'although we haven't really known you long, Griff and I both think of you as a very special friend. Indeed – I said we wanted to do something for you, and I don't see why everything has to be so secret – you know those musical manuscripts of Giles'? Would you like one of them? Sir Benedict suggested it, really. He said that one of them was dedicated to you. Perhaps you'd like to have it. I don't know whether it's a proper gift or simply a piece of scrap. But I'm sure Giles must have been fond of you. I wish he'd been fonder of you, or somebody like you. We had hoped it would be Ceinwen, but she's been engaged for months to a dentist in Rhyll; Griff likes him, because he's descended from Brochwell Yscythrog, but I do wish he were a proper doctor, and not a dentist; but there it is; you can't have everything. It would have made me very happy to see him settled, with somebody to look after him.'

That night, when they were going to bed, Dolly brought up the matter of the manuscript of *Kubla Khan* again. 'I'll write to Sir Benedict, and say you're to have it,' said she. 'And my dear, perhaps you'd like to have this as well.' She pressed something into Monica's hand; when she reached her bedroom she looked, dreading that it might not, after all, be the thing she hoped it was. But she need not have feared. It was Giles' ring.

In the mid-eighteenth century James Tassie made a great many beautiful copies of Greek gems; Giles's ring was one of these – a green stone in which was engraved a figure of Orpheus bearing his lyre. The naked god was incised, and could be transferred to wax, as a seal. Giles had always worn it on the little finger of his left hand, but Monica slipped it on her fourth.

She left for London the following day, and although she desired it passionately, she could not arrange to make another visit to the churchyard without revealing the purpose of her walk to Dolly, and thereby getting her unwanted company. However, the train passed within sight of the church and the yews around it, and as it did so Monica was at the window of her carriage, the ring at her lips.

[TEN]

The night of the Commemorative Concert found Monica more nervous than ever before. She had been wretched all day, and Molloy, coming into the artists' room very early himself, found her there before him, white and tense.

'Now see here, it's time you learned proper concert behaviour, because you won't always have me around to nursemaid you,' said he. 'B'God you look like a picture o' "Found Drowned". You've been worse than cryin' – you've been holdin' in! We're goin' to do some work right this minute, m'lady.'

After ten minutes of bullying and cajolery he had restored her poise.

'Now you can breathe,' said he. 'You'd breath enough before, but not usable; you were all puffed up with grief – chest locked, throat tight, all blown out like a frog. What's got into you? Is it Giles?'

Of course she did not say that it was Giles; it took Molloy a few minutes to persuade her to admit it.

'Well, you can just forget about Giles till tonight's work's over. Yes, I said forget about him. It's his memorial – I know that as well as yourself. If you're going to do him proud you must think about yourself, not about him. Yes, yes; a public performer's first duty is to himself, and unless he remembers that he can't do his duty to the public. You must understand it rightly: cherish the art in yourself, not yourself in art, as the Russian fella says. That's the pitfall; so many singers just have a lifelong love-affair with Number One, and they've no rivals, I can tell you! Cherishing the art in yourself is a very different class of thing.'

'But I'm so anxious to do well tonight, for Giles' memory, I've let myself get into a state. I couldn't help it. I'm sure you understand really, Murtagh. You're only pretending to be cross.'

'Listen, girl, I know what you mean, and don't think I'm not sympathetic. But I'll tell you something about Giles; he was always an amachoor, as far as public performance went. Oh, a fine composer, I grant you. Some o' that stuff'll live, you mark my words. But as a performer, he was an amachoor, and I don't just mean inexperienced; I mean he was the prey of all kinds o' silly ideas; he couldn't concentrate on the job – not in the right way. Genius – yes: discipline – not an idea of it. Now you're a professional. You've got standards he didn't know about and I've given you training he never had. So keep hold of yourself; you and the music are the important things for the next couple of hours.'

Thus enjoined, Monica comported herself very creditably. She sang *Kubla Khan*; she sang the soprano part in *The Discoverie of Witchcraft*; she sang with Amyas Palfreyman in the Potion and Metamorphosis Scenes from *The Golden Asse*. And, at the close of the concert, she joined Evelyn Burnaby and Palfreyman in Giles' three-voice setting of the Dirge from *Cymbeline*. So great was the professional calm of concentration with which Molloy had pervaded her that she never faltered, and afterward, at the party in Domdaniel's house she was praised by everybody. Molloy did not praise her, but when their eyes met, he winked a wink that was like the slamming of a door and that, so far as Monica was concerned, was praise indeed.

When the last guests were going, Domdaniel asked her to stay for a moment. 'I'll take you home,' said he, 'but there are one or two things I want to talk about first. You're away to Canada tomorrow night, aren't you?'

It proved to be a long moment. When all but Monica had said goodnight, he kicked off his pumps, removed his evening coat and lay down on a sofa; she began to collect glasses and plates to take them to the kitchen.

'Leave that alone,' said Domdaniel; 'Fred'll take care of it in the morning.'

'I'll empty these ash-trays; if they're left, they'll make the room smell.'

'Let it smell. Sit down. Or would you like to lie down? Take your shoes off.'

Monica was conscious now that she was very tired. So she did take her shoes off, and as she walked toward a couch across the room from him, Domdaniel laughed.

'Dance Micawber,' said he. 'The first time I saw you I told you to take your shoes off, and you played Dance Micawber for me.'

Monica blushed; it was not pleasant to be reminded of her earlier simplicity.

'Rather a Dance Micawber we've been through tonight,' he continued. 'Thank God it's out of the way; we've all done our duty for a while, and it's a relief.'

'Did you think it went well?'

'Very well.'

'Were the people from Bachofen's pleased? Will they go ahead with publication now?'

'Yes. They've known what they were going to do for a couple of weeks; the ticket-sale for tonight convinced them. They'll bring out the whole of Giles' stuff, taking eighteen months or a couple of years, probably, but making a good job of it.'

'Mrs Hopkin-Griffiths will be pleased. Do the royalties go to her?'

'Oh, certainly. For a woman who professes to know nothing of business or music, she's remarkably astute. Well, good luck to her.'

'I suppose the royalties will amount to quite a big thing?'

'Impossible to say. We've done everything possible – filled Wigmore Hall for a concert of contemporary music, by a young composer, recently dead under circumstances which some people think romantic. That's only six hundred people, but an important six hundred. It'll keep the music from sinking out of sight and having to be painfully revived.'

'But the music itself – Mr Aspinwall has called the opera great. Do you think so?'

'I suspect Aspinwall of having a bad conscience about Giles. I don't like to talk of greatness, because I'm never entirely sure what it means; Giles' music is individual, melodious and I admire it very much. Haven't I shown that?'

'Yes; I didn't mean to be prying. It's just that Mr Aspinwall has been so lavish with his praise – for him. He even says Giles' libretto for *The Golden Asse* is marvellous, and he was always complaining about Giles being literary at the expense of music. But he says now that it's philosophical.'

'Yes, very funny, that, because nobody was less philosophical than Giles. Extraordinary how people sometimes create so much better than they live. The metamorphosis of physical man into spiritual man: a great theme. But though he could do it in art he couldn't do it in life. Ah, well; the future of his music lies now with Bachofen and the gods. I've done my part for the present and I'm glad it's over.'

'You've been marvellous about it all. I know Giles would be terribly grateful.'

'It would be for the first time, then.'

Monica said nothing.

'Have I shocked you? *De mortuis nil nisi bunkum* – is that the line? Well, I'm sorry. I don't want to be bitter, but I knew Giles, and gratitude wasn't one of his characteristics.'

'I knew him, too.'

'Yes. You loved him. And tonight I'm in just a sufficiently nasty mood to ask you this: did he ever show any understanding or appreciation of your love?'

Again Monica said nothing.

'You slaved over his music. Did he ever say anything about that? Did he ever thank you for the way you sang his stuff?'

'Why should he? I was lucky to have the chance. And I must say, Sir Benedict, that I haven't been trained to expect thanks or praise for the way I sing. Neither you nor Mr Molloy has ever told me I sing well. Not directly, anyhow. There have been times when a good word would have been very helpful, but I learned not to look for it. I assumed it was the custom between teacher and pupil. If I have any opinion of my own voice, or the way I sing, I've learned it from the critics, not from my teachers. Giles was like you and Murtagh in that.'

'Twaddle! We were demanding, as was entirely proper; but I've seen him treat you like dirt. Perhaps humiliating you in public was his way of showing affection. Maybe you're the kind of woman who gets her satisfaction from being kicked. I never saw Giles treat you other than badly.'

I should never have spoken to him like that, thought Monica. No wonder he's cross with me. And didn't he call me a fellow-artist? How could I be so forgetful, so ungrateful? And Murtagh was so good to me tonight. Am I becoming one of those people who never get enough praise?

Apparently Domdaniel regretted what he had said, for he continued: 'Don't suppose I wasn't fond of Giles myself. I was. Too fond of him, I've often thought. I did all that I could to bring him forward. I never grudged anything that I could do to advance him, or help him. I even sent you to him for teaching when I knew he was desperately hard up. I've regretted that often enough, if you want to know. I'm a perfect fool about people; I thought somebody like you might humanize Giles; that's why I went through all that cloak-and-dagger business to get you to his family for Christmas, a couple of years ago. I meddled in Giles' affairs, and in yours. And don't suppose I don't realize now that I meddled disastrously.'

Monica spoke now. 'No, I don't think that. Not disastrously.'

'Yes, disastrously. I committed one of the great follies. I tried to mould somebody else's fate. And you've seen how it ended. Don't think I don't know that I killed Giles.'

Sir Benedict had expected this to produce an effect, and he was ready for incredulity, for tears, for hysteria, for anger. But when Monica burst into peals of laughter he sat bolt upright on his sofa, glaring.

'What's the trouble? Are you all right? Would you like a drink? Some water? For God's sake stop that laughing! What ails you?'

'It's just that you are the fourth person who has insisted to me that he killed Giles Revelstoke.' And she told him about Bun Eccles, about Stanhope Aspinwall, about Mrs Hopkin-Griffiths.

'But that's rubbish,' said Sir Benedict, angrily. 'Fiddling with a gas-meter: half London does it. Aspinwall's article – he flatters himself; ever since somebody suggested that cruel criticism killed John Keats every lint-picker hopes to get his man. I simply don't believe it about his mother; the world is full of perfectly healthy men who had silly, selfish mothers. I'm talking about something quite different – something serious. Giles was jealous of me, of my reputation, in spite of the twenty years between us. Incredibly stupid of him, because he was something I wasn't – a composer, and I cherished and loved that part of him. But I was a conductor, very much in the limelight, and he wanted to be that, as well as what he was.

Utterly senseless. But it was an obsession. This suicide – I can only think that it was a way of getting back at me. When I made it plain at La Fenice – and got Petri to back it up – that he was no conductor and probably never would be, it killed him. But this is the terrible thing: I was so angry with him, so resentful of his nonsense, that I genuinely wanted to do him down. I got a mean pleasure from it. Of course he committed suicide, but that's by the way; he died of mortification and thwarted ambition, and I suppose I'm responsible. Morally, I killed him.'

Should she speak? Yes – whatever might come of it – yes!

'Morally, you may have had something to do with it. But in cold fact *I* killed him; first I broke his heart, and then I deserted him when he was dying.' And Monica told him her story at length.

For some time Sir Benedict said nothing. Then he rose and prepared himself a large brandy-and-soda. Returning to his sofa he sat, in shirt-sleeves and stocking feet, leaning forward toward her.

'You're convinced you killed him?'

'Yes, I am.'

'Feel dreadful about it?'

'Every morning I wonder how I'll live till night without telling somebody. And now I've done it.'

'You mustn't tell anyone else. Understand? I'm not talking idly. What you did would probably be considered – not murder, most certainly not that – but manslaughter, or criminal neglect, or something of that order. Because, after all, you did turn the gas back on. Nothing can change that. And it's vital that you should clarify your thought on this matter. Whatever deception you may have to practise on other people, you must not, under any circumstances, deceive yourself. Now swear to me that you will never tell anyone. Come along. This is very serious.'

'What should I say?'

'Oh – let's not bother with operatic oaths. But I command you never to tell anyone. Will you obey?'

'Yes. I promise.'

'Right. I'm your sin-eater. Now, quite apart from legal nonsense, let's consider this matter. You found him, and thought he was dead.'

'Yes, and my first thought was to save my own skin.'

'Because he held your letter in his hand – your letter in one hand and Aspinwall's hard words about his conducting in the other.'

'Yes.'

'He laid himself down to die with those two papers, in order to make it plain to the world what had killed him.'

'I suppose so.'

'He knew you were coming back to London that night. Do you think he counted on you going to the flat?'

'He may have done.'

'He knew you. He was much cleverer than you. He knew there was a good chance that you would find him. Indeed, you had the only key.'

'I've thought of all that.'

'Well, what shall we call it? A self-pitying act, or the act of a scoundrel? Or was he out of his mind?'

'Considering the way I behaved myself, I have no right to make a judgement.'

'Not on him. You are perfectly right. But you must – you absolutely must – make a judgement on your own behaviour. Suppose that letter had been found? Do you think anyone would have seriously believed that you drove him to suicide? Nobody thought Aspinwall had done so – except himself, and it may teach him to mind his Ps and Qs in future – because his notice was about ten lines of blame, and nearly a column of high praise. This letter of yours was a love-letter, wasn't it?'

'I told you. It was breaking off with him forever. It was a cruel letter, and –' She could not finish.

'Have you it still? Could I see it?'

She had it with her always, for she could not destroy it, and yet she dared not leave it where it might be found. She gave it to him from her evening bag.

Sir Benedict read and re-read it. 'That's what you call breaking off forever, is it?' said he. But Monica, who was weeping as she had not wept since Giles' death, said nothing. He threw the letter into the fire, and in an instant it had gone forever.

'I believe that makes me what is called an accessory,' he said.

[ELEVEN]

Sea-sickness has never been recommended for its tonic effect on the spirits, yet as Monica made her return voyage across the North Atlantic her distress of body was paralleled by a marked improvement in her state of mind. She could not account for it, and it was not like her to try. Confession to Domdaniel had been very helpful. She had wanted to tell someone of her guilt, and the only other possible person was Eccles, who would never have done. Not only was he convinced that he had killed Giles himself – though with the best of intentions – but he had gone on the booze, and could not be trusted to keep her secret. Still, he was a dear friend. He had given her the best of his sketches of Giles. It was the one which had appeared on the cover of the programme at the Commemorative Concert; Tuke had wanted it for his book, but Bun was determined that Tuke should not get it. This, and the fact that Aspinwall rather than himself had been asked to write the appreciation of Giles which appeared in that same programme, had made Tuke very waspish, and he had threatened to sue Monica for seizing the physical assets (a cardboard box of subscribers' cards, five muddled files of dog-eared correspondence, a complete run of the magazine, and three cartons of assorted trash) of *Lantern*. But nothing would come of that. Nobody cared about *Lantern* any longer, save Raikes Brothers, who were trying to collect their bill from Mrs Hopkin-Griffiths. All that was behind her. And, to her surprise and shame, Giles seemed to be behind her, too. She grieved for him, but her guilt was retreating from her; he no longer appeared in her dreams. The numbness of her spirit was vanishing, and to her astonishment it left regret and bereavement, but little pain, behind it. When she stepped off the boat in Canada it was with the sensations of a widow, but not of a murderess. She was still sure that she had killed Giles, and that it was through grievous faults in her character that she had done so. But, somehow, she had accepted the fact. To that extent, at least, she had clarified her thinking.

Salterton, this first few days of December, was looking its grey worst. And her home, now that Ma was gone, was unwelcoming – not because of anything that was said or done, but because it was empty of spirit. Of course, there was the physical difficulty about beds. There were only two bedrooms; Dad had one, and Aunt Ellen the other. Monica declined the offer of a place in her aunt's bed; sleeping alone or with a man had unfitted her for a tucking up with an elderly maiden lady who had two regular, resounding coughing-fits every night. Neither Dad nor Aunt Ellen was at home between half-past eight and half-past five, and what was Monica to do? She visited Alice once or twice, but that did not serve her turn, for when she was with her elder sister all London, all Paris, all self-possession and hard-won self-knowledge seemed to slip from her, and they quarrelled as bitterly as when they had shared the tiny bedroom at home. As bitterly? Far worse, now, for both had gained substance of personality. Alice was aggrieved that Monica had money; that it was money which had 'fallen into her lap'; that her own ambition scorched mercilessly upon the need for a new and bigger house, whereas Monica had no such vital problem; that Monica had acquired high and mighty ways which (Ah, shade of Ma Gall!) could not possibly be real because she had not been born to them, and was therefore guilty of 'sticking it on'. It was inconceivable to Alice that what had been learned, and thoroughly digested, could become more truly one's nature than the attitudes and customs of the family into which one had been born. She was herself in flight from her family, but the ball and chain was always on her leg. She grudged Monica her freedom from this servitude, and believed that it had been easily won. A couple of visits to Alice were quite enough.

One obligatory evening, spent at the movies with George Medwall and Teresa Rook, and a silent friend of George's, exhausted that source of companionship. She liked Kevin and Alex still, but could not conceal from herself the fact that they were a little afraid of her.

So there she was, sleeping on the sofa in the living-room of her father's house, without even a place where she could stand her picture of Giles. She had to keep it in her music-case, and get it out like a miser his treasure, when nobody was at home.

It was foolish, and she knew it was foolish, but Monica caught herself thinking that it was somehow inconsiderate of everyone she knew to be working when she herself was on holiday: she was so much a Londoner now in her own estimation that she supposed that people in smaller places must necessarily be less busy than herself. What a fool I am, she thought, when she surprised herself in this mood; I need a metamorphosis, like Lucius in Giles' opera. I'm in great danger of a love-affair with Number One.

But if the welcome of her family was feeble, that of the Bridgetowers was unexpectedly warm. Diffidently, Monica had telephoned to Veronica to inquire after her health, and had at once been asked to dinner. So friendly was the atmosphere that she was able to say how much she hoped that the child Veronica was carrying would be a boy, and so plain was her sincerity that Solly and Veronica believed this, at first appearance, improbable statement.

'It's extremely good of you,' said Solly. 'Of course, we have hopes. You know that things haven't been easy. But we aren't pinning everything on it. If it's a boy – wonderful! If it isn't, it's not the end of the world. I think one of the secrets of life is that one must give up caring too much about anything. I know that sounds terrible, but for a lot of people it's the only possible philosophy. You blunt the edge of fate by being stoical. My Mother cared too much about having her own way; result – a remarkable artist gets her start – well, that's what they say about you, Monica, so don't protest – an extraordinary opera gets its first production. Neither of them things Mother would have foreseen or desired, to be truthful. She just wanted to let us feel the weight of her hand. Well, let's not talk about it any more, or I shall be saying things like "It makes you think, don't it".'

Not only from the Bridgetowers, but from the Cobblers, Monica received a flattering and heart-warming welcome. And though she had not meant to do any work for a time, she began to do some daily practice with Cobbler, to get her out of the unfriendly little box that she called her home. There was no piano there, for Aunt Ellen had been compelled to part with hers; her new home had no room for it.

It was Cobbler who persuaded Monica to sing on the occasion of the fourth Bridgetower Memorial Sermon. 'Come on,' he said; 'you sang at the old girl's funeral. Since then you've become the great interpreter of Revelstoke's songs, among other things. This may be the last of these memorial capers – I'm betting on a boy – and we want to do it up right. The choir is going to do *Lo, Star-Led Chiefs* – top-notch Christmas rouser – because the Dean wants to preach about the Wise Men of the East. Now, why don't you sing Cornelius' *Three Kings* from his *Weihnachtslieder* and top the thing off in style? We'll shove it up a couple of tones, and show what you can do. Come on, be a sport! This may be your last year on the Bridgetower gravy-train; why not show you've no hard feelings.'

But Monica would not consent, until one day Dean Knapp telephoned and asked her so pleasantly to assist at the service that she could not refuse without seeming churlish. She still resented the Dean, because of Auntie Puss Pottinger's rebuke, when she had spoken of him as 'Reverend Knapp'. Well, it was high time to get over such nonsense.

High time indeed. On the morning of December the sixth, which is St Nicholas' Day, and the day also of the Bridgetower Sermon, she went to Cobbler's to rehearse, and found Humphrey and Molly in a great state of triumph and excitement.

'I was right,' shouted Cobbler, dancing in the middle of his chaotic living-room. 'It's a boy!'

'What's a boy?'

'Baby Bridgetower! Who else? Here safe and sound, everything screwed on tight, fingers and toes complete – even hair, I'm told by those in the know. You see what a prophet I am; I'm going to go into the business. Slip happy couples my card at weddings – "Five Months hence, Consult Cobbler; Put your Sexpectations on a Scientific Basis; Strictest Confidence Observed". There's a fortune in it!'

'But I thought it wasn't due for another month or more?'

'Sit down, and have some coffee,' said Molly Cobbler. 'And shut up, Humphrey, you're being silly. As a matter of fact, it was a rather nasty business. Veronica has been awfully well during her pregnancy, you know. Not a bit like last time. So they weren't worrying about a thing. But last night, somewhere around three in the morning, Veronica woke up and thought she heard a storm window rattling in another room. Now shut up, Humphrey – I'm telling this and I want to tell it my own way. The room in which she heard the sound was old Mrs Bridgetower's room, which was queer, because nobody ever opens the windows in there; it's kept just as the old lady left it, and Puss Pottinger sees that nothing is moved. But Veronica must have been confused by sleep – Humphrey, shut up! – and went in there. Solly woke when he heard a terrible scream, missed Veronica, and started to look for her. But he didn't think of looking in his mother's room until he had searched in several other places, and when he finally found her, she was on the floor in a terrible way – very badly frightened, a bit irrational and quite a way on in labour. Anyhow, they got the doctor, and he popped her right into old Mrs Bridgetower's bed, and that's where young Solomon was born at half-past five this morning.'

'And serve Ma Bridgetower damn well right,' said Humphrey. 'She got the first child, but Veronica was too many for her this time. Now Molly, nobody's going to convince me that Veronica didn't have some kind of wrestle with that old woman in the middle of the night, so shut up! That's love. That's devotion, and I call your attention to it,' said he, shaking his head at his wife like a solemn golliwog. 'Why don't we whip over there right now and drink a toast to the infant trust-breaker? Better take our own bottle; the Bridgetowers aren't always prepared for toasts. But there's a better day coming on, if I may say so without giving Monny the fiscal creeps.'

So it was that about a quarter of an hour later Monica was in what must still be called Mrs Bridgetower's drawing-room (for it never lost that character) drinking a toast to Mrs Bridgetower's grandson. In spite of Cobbler's efforts the feeling in the room was restrained, and Monica knew very well why it was so: the Bridgetowers, for all their goodwill and kind words, felt that they were taking from her money upon which she counted for another year, and were wondering how much she resented it.

Well, thought Monica, it's up to me. I'm the one who has been trained to communicate emotion readily, and gracefully, and with an artist's control. Unless this gathering is to be a wretched frost, I must supply the warmth. We've all got to grow up some time, so here goes.

'Is there any chance that I could see Veronica and the baby, just for a moment?' she said to Solly.

'As far as I'm concerned, certainly,' he replied. 'The doctor did a lot of fussing earlier – apparently it's unsanitary, or illegal, or inconvenient for the profession, or something, for a baby to be born at home; he insists on referring to the child as "a preem"; I think I've persuaded him that the worst is over and Veronica can stay here. Come on up.'

Old Mrs Bridgetower's bedroom was not a pretty room, but it had much frowsty comfort about it, and old Ethel had made a fire in the grate; it was not needed, but it was very cheerful and a touch of childbed luxury. Already there were flowers from the Knapps and – marvellous in the telling – some from Miss Puss. Veronica was lying back on a heap of pillows, eating bacon and eggs.

'I know it's unromantic for a gasping, new-delivered mother to be so hungry,' she said, 'but I've had a long sleep, and I'm famished. Look at him. Isn't he a pet?'

The pet lay in a small clothes-basket on a low table by the bed. Monica, who had never seen so new a baby, found it rather repulsive. But that was not what she had come to say.

'He's adorable, and I wish him long life and every happiness,' said she, breathing a fairy-godmother muhd and bending over the basket. *After all*, said a voice, startlingly loud and familiar in her head, *you're giving this goblin upwards of a million dollars – not that it was ever yours.* She started slightly, for it was the voice of Giles Revelstoke. Was he, like Ma, going to be one of the voices which complicated her life, and at the same time kept her romanticism from running away with her?

These thoughts did not interrupt her as she turned from the basket to the bed. She leaned over it and kissed Veronica gently; but

Veronica was chewing at her late breakfast, and as she did not halt in time, Monica kissed an undulant, chewing cheek. They both began to laugh: Veronica because she was happier than she had been in her life; Monica because the inner critic had made her prima donna-like performance seem ridiculous. *Stop behaving like Ludwiga Kressel*, said Giles' voice. And as they laughed, Solly and the Cobblers began to laugh, though they could not have said why, and Mrs Bridgetower's bedroom rang with happy laughter. The embarrassment had quite gone, and Monica knew that nobody there was wary of her any longer.

'Let's have another nip,' said Cobbler; 'Veronica too. But we mustn't get stewed. There's the Memorial Sermon at four-thirty.'

'You must all come back here afterward,' said Solly. 'We'll have a party – small but select. But – oh, hell, I suppose we must ask The Trust. Well, it'll be for the last time. Tea for them, Ronny, from Old Puss's Rockingham service.'

[TWELVE]

At twenty-five minutes past four that afternoon Monica was sitting on a small chair beside the organ console in St Nicholas' cathedral; it was a position of vantage, for she could see all of the nave by peeping between two large pillars, but she was not likely to be seen. She felt silly in a purple cassock and a ruff, and she did not think that the veil on her head was becoming; still, it was what Cobbler wanted her to wear, and she would not be a complainer, as Anglicans seemed to attach so much importance to ritual dress. But if she had to wear costume, she wished it could have been a better fit, and did not smell so pungently of choir-boy. She was not to walk with the choir in procession: no women – apparently it was another Anglican caprice. 'You're to be clearly heard but not clearly seen,' Cobbler had said, and she was well enough content to slip into her place unnoticed.

Cobbler himself now joined her. 'Let's have a look,' said he, leaning over her shoulder to peep between the pillars. 'Quite a good house; nearly a hundred; not bad for a weekday and a business day; old Nicholas, Bishop and Confessor, ought to be pleased; the late Louisa Hansen Bridgetower would have expected a bigger crowd for her memorial sermon, but she had no humility. There's Solly . . . old Snelgrove . . . Auntie Puss; the Bridgetower Trust in force. You know, the cathedral will soon have its Bridgetower bequest? Wonder if I could get any of it to rebuild the organ? Well, here goes.' He played a brief flourish and then was silent, as the choir was heard in the distance, beginning the processional hymn.

The Dean read the lesson for the day, and Monica paid little attention after the words . . . *thy voice shall be, as one that hath a familiar spirit* . . . reached her ears. Like me, she thought; only I have two; Ma speaks to me sometimes, in her very own voice, so that I'm sure I'm not talking to myself, and today Giles has spoken to me twice, as though he were right behind me. Yet I don't think I'm out of my head, and I'm certainly not a spiritualist. Will it always be so? Will I acquire other voices as I go through life? It isn't frightening – not a bit – but it's certainly odd. Is it perhaps my substitute for thinking – orders and hints and even jokes from deep down, through the voice and personality of someone I've loved – yes, and feared? I ought to make up my mind. Certainly before I decide what I've got to decide. But I've never been much good at making up my mind, and I'm rotten at deciding things, especially since I went away to study and got into such deep water.

Musing thus, she heard nothing of the Dean's prayer in which he petitioned that God might make all assembled there mindful of the goodness and example of St Nicholas, bishop and confessor and (extraordinary juxtaposition, which the Dean deeply relished) of Louisa Hansen Bridgetower, and all others our benefactors. But she came out of her musing when Cobbler and the choir burst into the 'top-notch Christmas rouser' in which Dr William Crotch of Oxford so melodiously bodied forth the eighteenth-century piety, the formal fervour, of Bishop Reginald Heber –

Lo! star-led chiefs Assyrian odours bring,
And bending Magi seek their infant King!

Here was splendour which glorified the dank December twilight and made the modest cathedral, for its duration, a true dwelling-place of one of the many circumscribed, but not therefore ignoble, concepts of God.

Solly, too, heard nothing of the prayer after the mention of his Mother's name. If ever there were a time to make peace with his Mother's troubled spirit, it was now – now that the son was born who would deliver him from the hard humiliating conditions of her will. Yet – did that spirit desire a reconciliation? What had called Veronica from sleep so early this morning? With what had Veronica struggled in Mrs Bridgetower's bedroom, so that he had found her unconscious amid overturned tables and chairs? He was neither mad nor fanciful: he had no doubt who, or what it was that had sought to prevent the live birth of his son. He knew what it was, also, that was at last defeated.

It was a time for forgiveness. Against the strict prohibition of his faith, Solly prayed for his Mother's soul.

The anthem over, the lights were dimmed and, somewhat carelessly marshalled by the verger, the Dean went into the pulpit, turned to the East, and said: 'In the name of the Father, and of the Son, and of the Holy Ghost, Amen.

'Dearly Beloved: We have gathered here as part of the celebration of the festal day of our patron, St Nicholas of Smyrna, but particularly in obedience to the wish of the latest of our benefactors, Louisa Hansen Bridgetower, who desired that for a fixed period a sermon should be given on this day, relating to the subject of education.'

Monica was scarcely conscious of withdrawing her attention. As a child she had never listened to sermons, and now that she was a grown woman she had never re-considered her position; she was one of the many who feel that it is quite enough to be present while a sermon is being preached. If the Dean had been conscious of her state of mind, he would have recognized it sadly and without condemnation. He had never concurred in the opinion held by many of his brother clergy that learning and eloquence are forms of worldly indulgence to be eschewed; he tried to preach as well as he could. But he had not risen to a deanery without knowing how many people resent being asked to use their heads in church.

What should I tell him, thought Monica? He'll let me have all the time I want, I know, but it isn't fair to him to dawdle, as though I were the only person concerned. She began to run over Domdaniel's letter in her head; it had come three days ago, and she had read and re-read it until she had it by heart:

I can't think of any way of putting this gradually [it had begun] so I'll say it at once, and not make two bites of the cherry: will you marry me?

Your immediate decision, I am certain, will be to say no. I understand how you felt about Giles, and I am not such a fool as to think that I would ever command love of that sort from you or anyone. Certainly this is the wrong time to write to you in this vein, but I have been quite unable to help it. Because I love you.

He wouldn't say that unless he really meant it, thought Monica. He's always terribly direct. The people who call him Brum Benny only see his formal, courteous manner, and they mistake it for palaver. But he's never said a thing to me he didn't mean. If he says he loves me, he does.

As she pondered this unaccustomed sensation of being loved, the Dean was getting into his sermon. –

Education is learning; and learning is apprehension – in the old sense of sympathetic perception. We cannot all perceive the facts of our experience in the same way. As we draw near to the sacred season of Christmas we may fitly turn our attention to the ways in which the birth of Our Lord was perceived by those who first knew of it. Much has been made of the splendour of the vision of the shepherds, as told by St Luke. But so far as I know, little has been said of the fact that it needed an angel and a multitude of the heavenly host to call it to the attention of these good men that something out of the ordinary had happened. Nothing short of a convulsion of nature (if I may so call it without irreverence) could impress them, and the Gospel tells us that they praised God 'for all the things that they had heard and seen'. There are many now, as then and always, who learn – who apprehend – only by what they can hear and see, and the range of what they can hear and see is not extensive. And, alas, instructive interruptions of the natural order are as few today as they were two thousand years ago . . .

Nevertheless, no girl thinks very much about marrying a man seriously older than herself, and one whom she has respected as a being far above her, and a figure of world renown in his particular form of art. How had he written of that? –

I am old enough to be your father; nevertheless you must take my word for it that I am still young enough to be a lover. But I will not deceive you; at my age love is not, and never can be, the whole significance of life. I have known enough of love in my own experience, and seen enough of it in the lives of other people, to have some fear of it, as well as the awe and delight which it inspires. I cannot say, I will be young for you, because that would be folly; let me say that I will be the best that is in me for you. I do not ask you to love me as you might a young man, but to love me, if you can, for what I am.

If you say that this cannot be, I shall understand very well why; but do not suppose that I shall not be downcast. It would be dishonest to say, as a younger man might have every excuse for doing, that my love for you is the whole of my life. At my age, my work is bound to be the mainspring of my existence. But if you were with me, my work would have a sweeter savour. Because it is your work, too, I know that you will understand this, and not think that I am being either cool or pompous. You are the custodian of an important musical tradition – you know how Giles wanted his songs to be sung. I do not seek to intrude on that, but I think I could be helpful with it.

Your work, too! like being called a fellow-artist! Still, he was fifty-four – or was it fifty-five, now? And there was Giles' voice, hatefully bawdy, as she had last heard it on the train to Venice –

I lay with an old man all the night –

How dare Giles! But what would people say? That she had done it to be Lady Domdaniel. What would Alice make of that? Oh, Alice! Family always knew where to dig the knife in! But Giles, Giles was not someone who could be put aside. Particularly not when she had failed him so disastrously.

But could she not admit, now, that when she found him seemingly dead on the floor, beneath her revulsion from his blackened face, her stunning loss, her self-accusation, there had been – perceptible for an instant and then banished as a blasphemy against her love – a pang of relief, of release? Should she not clarify her thought? No! Let others talk of clarity. It is a cautery too terrible to be applied to one's own most secret wounds. Perhaps, working for a worthy perpetuation of his work, there might be atonement. And, after atonement, a recognition of what she had felt in that instant of naked truth.

Meanwhile the Dean was continuing with his sermon:

If the shepherds needed a prodigy to stir them, the Wise Men needed no more than a hint, a new star amid the host of heaven. In art, and especially the Christmas card art which will so soon be with us, that star is usually represented as a monstrous illumination which a mole might see. That is so that the shepherds among us may understand without a painful sense of insufficiency the legend of the Kings. For legend it is; the Gospel tells us but little of these men, but legend has set their number at three, and has given them melodious names. The legend calls them Kings, and Kings they were indeed in the realm of apprehension, of perception, for they were able to read a great message in a small portent. We dismiss great legends at our peril, for they are the riddling voices by means of which great truths buried deep in the spirit of man offer themselves to the world. Gaspar, Melchior and Balthazar stand as models of those – few, but powerful at any time – who have prepared themselves by learning and dedication to know great mysteries when the time is ripe for them to be apprehended by man . . .

Of course a girl really wanted a lover who was hers alone, who had never loved anyone else – or at least not seriously – and who promised to give everything to love. That was what all the magazines which were dismissed as 'cheap' said, and the cheap magazines were right; that was why cheap magazines sold in hundreds of thousands, instead of in tens, like *Lantern*. But even at twenty-four, one could see that sometimes these knights, when they appeared, had a way of dwindling into something like Chuck Proby, who was probably living for love if you gave him the benefit of every doubt, but who never mentioned it, and seemed to be making a hard struggle of it. Or a sobersides like George Medwall, who was so proud of the fact that Teresa would not have to work after their marriage, but who saw life in terms of accretion – get some money, get a wife, get a house, get some children, get a bigger house, get more money – all for love, but the world hopelessly lost somewhere along the line. Domdaniel made no pretence:

> Kind friends have probably told you that I have been married before. [They hadn't, and this had surprised her.] It is true that when I was a young man I married and if you have ever been curious enough to look me up in *Who's Who* the 'mar. dis.' there will tell you what happened. She was a singer, like you – though in the cold light of recollection I can say that she was never as good a singer as you – and it didn't work. Nobody's fault entirely. Now I know that marriage between artists of any kind needs a little more understanding than matches where there is no relentless, fascinating rival perpetually working to seduce both parties. I wanted you to know this.
>
> I want to go on, but I have said everything that is to the point, and I know that pleading and begging and entreaties, though they might work on your gentle heart, aren't fair in a case like this. I would cut a ridiculous figure as a whimpering suitor. So I shall say only that I love you, and if you are ready, even in the most tentative fashion, to consider marrying me, will you let me have some word?
>
> BENEDICT DOMDANIEL

One must be logical. If Giles had never been, or if she had never known him, what would she say to this? But what was the good of thinking like that? Giles couldn't be wished away. And she would never be free of him. By his suicide he had put his mark on her forever. Moving the green Orpheus slowly back and forth on her finger, Monica gave herself to tender thoughts of Giles.

The Dean, having dealt with the Magi to his satisfaction, had moved on. –

> A third figure, who perceived Our Lord in his own fashion, is particularly sympathetic, and presents in one of the most touching stories of the childhood

of Christ another sort of apprehension, and that the rarest. He is the aged Simeon, who knew Our Lord intuitively (as we should say now) when He was brought to the Temple on the eighth day for His Circumcision. Not the forcible instruction of a band of angels, nor the hard-won knowledge of the scholars, but the readiness of one who was open to the promptings of the Holy Ghost was the grace which made Simeon peculiarly blessed. We see him still as one of those rare beings, not so much acting as acted upon, not so much living life as being lived by it, outwardly passive but inwardly illumined by active grace, through whom much that is noblest and of most worth has been vouchsafed to the world . . . Oh, trusting, patient Simeon, the first to know, of his own knowledge, the Holy Face of God!

It's a muddle, thought Monica. A muddle and I can't get it straight. I wish I knew what I should do. I wish I even knew what I want to do. I want to wipe out the terrible thing I did to Giles. I want to go on in the life that has somehow or other found me and claimed me. And I want so terribly to be happy. Oh God, don't let me slip under the surface of all the heavy-hearted dullness that seems to claim so many people, even when they struggle and strive to keep their heads above the waves! Help me! Help me!

'Psst! He's winding up. You next.' It was Cobbler's voice.

Monica sang, giving her full attention to what she was doing; sang well and happily, all her perplexities banished as she balanced the delicate vocal meditation above the great chorale in *Three Kings from Persian lands*. And when she was finished, she found that her mind was cleared, and she knew what she should do.

Benediction, and a rustle as the congregation rose from its knees. 'Wait for me in the vestry,' said Cobbler, 'and we'll get back to Bridgetower's for the party. But meantime, I simply can't resist this. Keep your eye peeled to see if any of the Bridgetower Trust get the Joe Miller of it.' And triumphally he burst into *For unto us a child is born, Unto us a son is given* on the great organ.

But Monica did not wait. Before the party she must go to the cable office to send Benedict his answer.

Also by Robertson Davies

THE REBEL ANGELS

The University of St John and the Holy Ghost (Spook) is jolted out of its crabbed and scholarly pursuits by the return to its Gothic walls of the evil, brilliant Brother Parlabane and by the miraculous discovery of an unpublished manuscript by Rabelais. Coincidentally, beautiful, sexy Maria Magdalena Theotoky is doing postgraduate work on Rabelais (provoking a not entirely academic response in the breasts of her colleagues . . .) and when the manuscript disappears all the unbridled furies of sex, vanity and violence are let loose.

'You won't forget *The Rebel Angels* in a hurry' – Alan Sillitoe

THE DEPTFORD TRILOGY

Who killed boy Staunton? Around this central mystery is woven a glittering, fantastical, cunningly contrived trilogy of novels. Seamlessly woven into each other, yet entirely separate, they lure the reader down labyrinthine tunnels of myth, history and magic – exhilerating anti-dotes to a world where 'the fear and dread and splendour of wonder have been banished'.

and

WHAT'S BRED IN THE BONE

KING PENGUIN

Bedbugs Clive Sinclair

'Wildly erotic and weirdly plotted, the subconscious erupting violently into everyday life . . . It is not for the squeamish or the lazy. His stories work you hard; tease and torment and shock you' – *Financial Times*

The Awakening of George Darroch Robin Jenkins

An eloquent and powerful story of personal and political upheaval, the one inextricably linked with the other, written by one of Scotland's finest novelists.

In Custody Anita Desai

Deven, a lecturer in a small town in Northern India, is resigned to a life of mediocrity and empty dreams. When asked to interview the greatest poet of Delhi, Deven discovers a new kind of dignity, both for himself and his dreams.

Collected Poems Geoffrey Hill

'Among our finest poets, Geoffrey Hill is at present the most European – in his Latinity, in his dramatization of the Christian condition, in his political intensity . . . The commanding note is unmistakable' – George Steiner in the *Sunday Times*

Parallel Lives Phyllis Rose

In this study of five famous Victorian marriages, including that of John Ruskin and Effie Gray, Phyllis Rose probes our inherited myths and assumptions to make us look again at what we expect from our marriages.

Lamb Bernard MacLaverty

In the Borstal run by Brother Benedict, boys are taught a little of God and a lot of fear. Michael Lamb, one of the brothers, runs away and takes a small boy with him. As the outside world closes in around them, Michael is forced to an uncompromising solution.

A CHOICE OF PENGUIN FICTION

Monsignor Quixote Graham Greene

Now filmed for television, Graham Greene's novel, like Cervantes' seventeenth-century classic, is a brilliant fable for its times. 'A deliciously funny novel' – *The Times*

The Dearest and the Best Leslie Thomas

In the spring of 1940 the spectre of war turned into grim reality – and for all the inhabitants of the historic villages of the New Forest it was the beginning of the most bizarre, funny and tragic episode of their lives. 'Excellent' – *Sunday Times*

Earthly Powers Anthony Burgess

Anthony Burgess's magnificent masterpiece, an enthralling, epic narrative spanning six decades and spotlighting some of the most vivid events and characters of our times. 'Enormous imagination and vitality . . . a huge book in every way' – Bernard Levin in the *Sunday Times*

The Penitent Isaac Bashevis Singer

From the Nobel Prize-winning author comes a powerful story of a man who has material wealth but feels spiritually impoverished. 'Singer . . . restates with dignity the spiritual aspirations and the cultural complexities of a lifetime, and it must be said that in doing so he gives the Evil One no quarter and precious little advantage' – Anita Brookner in the *Sunday Times*

Paradise Postponed John Mortimer

'Hats off to John Mortimer. He's done it again' – *Spectator*. A rumbustious, hilarious new novel from the creator of Rumpole, *Paradise Postponed* is now a major Thames Television series.

Animal Farm George Orwell

The classic political fable of the twentieth century.

A CHOICE OF PENGUIN FICTION

Maia Richard Adams

The heroic romance of love and war in an ancient empire from one of our greatest storytellers. 'Enormous and powerful' – *Financial Times*

The Warning Bell Lynne Reid Banks

A wonderfully involving, truthful novel about the choices a woman must make in her life – and the price she must pay for ignoring the counsel of her own heart. 'Lynne Reid Banks knows how to get to her reader: this novel grips like Super Glue' – *Observer*

Doctor Slaughter Paul Theroux

Provocative and menacing – a brilliant dissection of lust, ambition and betrayal in 'civilized' London. 'Witty, chilly, exuberant, graphic' – *The Times Literary Supplement*

July's People Nadine Gordimer

Set in South Africa, this novel gives us an unforgettable look at the terrifying, tacit understanding and misunderstandings between blacks and whites. 'This is the best novel that Miss Gordimer has ever written' – Alan Paton in the *Saturday Review*

Wise Virgin A. N. Wilson

Giles Fox's work on the Pottle manuscript, a little-known thirteenth-century tract on virginity, leads him to some innovative research on the subject that takes even his breath away. 'A most elegant and chilling comedy' – *Observer* Books of the Year

Last Resorts Clare Boylan

Harriet loved Joe Fischer for his ordinariness – for his ordinary suits and hats, his ordinary money and his ordinary mind, even for his ordinary wife. 'An unmitigated delight' – *Time Out*